Contents

Plan Your Trip

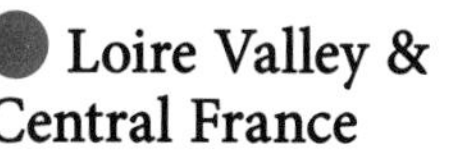

Discover France

Contents

Discover France

In Focus

Survival Guide

This Is France

Snooty, sexy, superior, chic, infuriating, arrogant, officious and inspired, France never fails to stir up passionate opinion. Even if you've never set foot on French soil, it's a place that already seems immediately familiar: every time you've gazed at an impressionist painting, watched a new-wave film or sipped on a glass of sparkling Champagne, you've been letting a little bit of Gallic flair seep into your soul.

France is all about art and seduction, Roman to Renaissance and beyond. Stroll the lily-clad gardens Monet painted and sip *un café* in a Parisian cafe where Sartre and Simone de Beauvoir met to philosophise. Imagine the glorious life of French kings at bourgeois Versailles or view tomorrow's art stars at new headline-grabbing museums up north. Ride magnificent mechanical elephants in an old Nantes shipyard. Listen to Marseille rap and Parisian jazz. Sense the subtle infusion of language, music and mythology in Brittany, brought by 5th-century Celtic invaders. Yes, French culture fills any stay in France with never-ending possibilities.

The country's feast of fine food and wine woos every traveller. But gastronomic France goes far deeper than Parisian bistro dining, long lunches outside, shopping for fruit and veg at the market and wolfing down croissants hot from the *boulangerie* (bakery). Taste wine with world-class sommeliers in Bordeaux; visit an Atlantic Coast oyster farm; drink sparkling Champagne in ancient cellars in Reims; tour a Provençal melon farm; harvest olives, peaches and cherries in the hot south; and realise that food is as much an *art de vivre* (art of living) for the French as an essential to survive.

Then there is the *terroir* (land) and its wonderful variety. Its rich and fabulous journey starts in northern France with chalky cliffs and sand dunes, continues south through to pea-green vineyards, and onwards to the bright blue sea of the French Riviera.

“Sense the subtle infusion of language, music and mythology”

Hall of Mirrors at Château de Versailles (p103)

France

France
0 100 km
0 50 miles
ELEVATION
2500m
2000m
1500m
1000m
700m
500m
200m
100m
0
NORTH SEA
English Channel (La Manche)
ATLANTIC OCEAN
ENGLAND
LONDON
Dover
Plymouth
BELGIUM
BRUSSELS
LUXEMBOURG
GERMANY
SWITZERLAND
Cologne
Dunkirk
Calais
Boulogne-sur-Mer
Lille
Lens
Arras
Amiens
St-Quentin
Dieppe
SOMME
Étretat
Honfleur
Rouen
Beauvais
Chantilly
Cherbourg
Bayeux
Caen
Vernon
Giverny
PARIS
Versailles
Chartres
Reims
Épernay
CHAMPAGNE
Verdun
Metz
Nancy
LORRAINE
ALSACE
Strasbourg
Obernai
Sélestat
Baccarat
Colmar
Belfort
Basel
Troyes
Chaumont
NORMANDY
Alençon
Roscoff
Paimpol
Île d'Ouessant
Brest
Morlaix
Cancale
St-Malo
Dinard
Dinan
Mont St-Michel
Presqu'île de Crozon
Carhaix-Plouguer
BRITTANY
Quimper
Concarneau
Josselin
Rennes
Vannes
Carnac
Belle Île
Le Mans
LOIRE VALLEY
Orléans
BURGUNDY
Auxerre
Châtillon-sur-Seine
Blois
Chambord
Cheverny
Angers
Tours
Amboise
LA SOLOGNE
Villandry
Saumur
Azay-le-Rideau
Chenonceaux
Nantes
Vézelay
CÔTE D'OR
Dijon
Besançon
Beaune
Autun
JURA
Lausanne
Évian-les-Bains
Les Portes du Soleil
Poitiers
La Rochelle
Cognac
Limoges
LIMOUSIN
Guéret
Cluny
Mâcon
Vichy
Roanne
Clermont-Ferrand
Thiers
Puy de Dôme (1465m)
Lyon
Annecy
Aix-les-Bains
Megève
Chamonix
Mont Blanc (4810m)
Chambéry
A1
A4
A5
A6
A10
A11
A13
A20
A28
A31
A71
A72
A83
A84
A86
N137
52°N
50°N
49°N
47°N
46°N

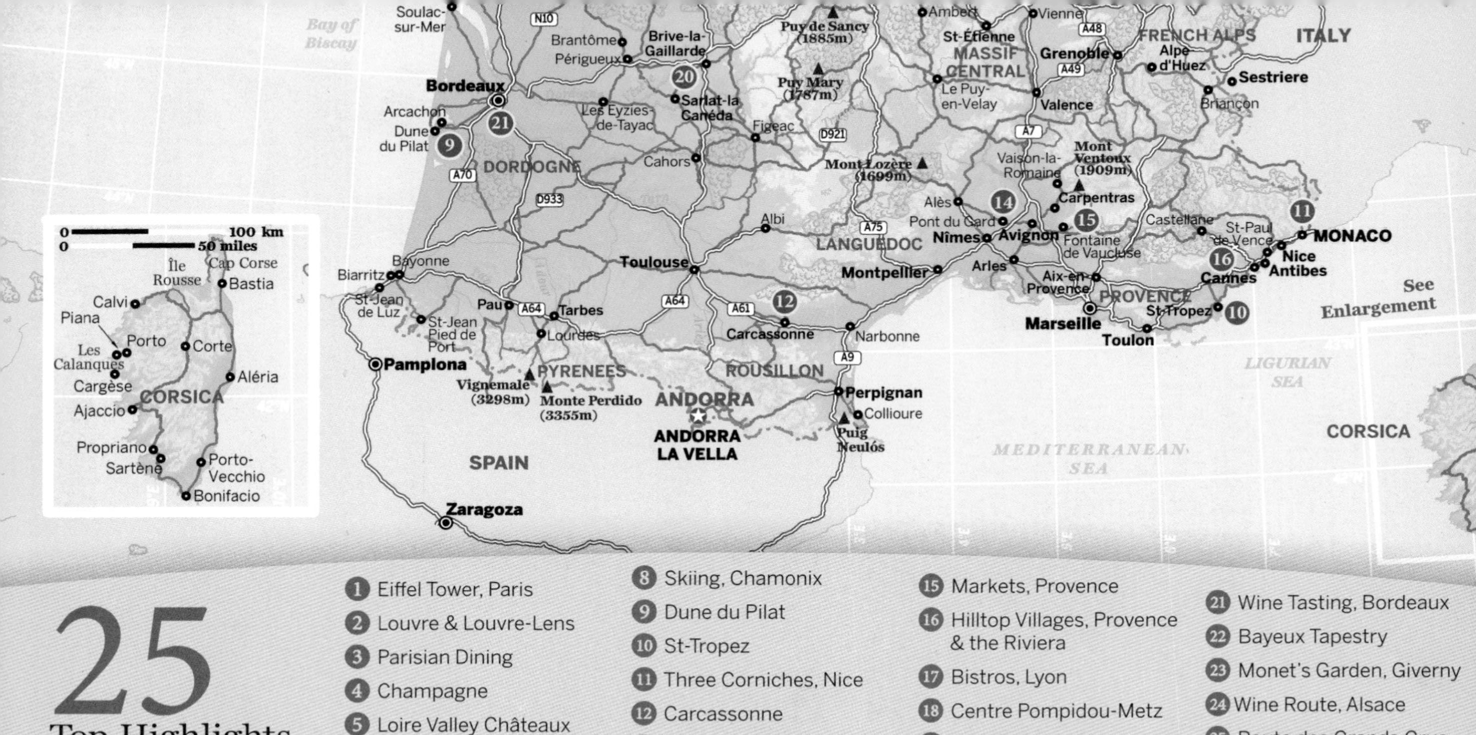

25 Top Highlights

1. Eiffel Tower, Paris
2. Louvre & Louvre-Lens
3. Parisian Dining
4. Champagne
5. Loire Valley Châteaux
6. Ste-Chapelle & Chartres
7. Mont St-Michel
8. Skiing, Chamonix
9. Dune du Pilat
10. St-Tropez
11. Three Corniches, Nice
12. Carcassonne
13. D-Day Beaches, Normandy
14. Pont du Gard
15. Markets, Provence
16. Hilltop Villages, Provence & the Riviera
17. Bistros, Lyon
18. Centre Pompidou-Metz
19. Carnac Megaliths
20. Grotte de Lascaux
21. Wine Tasting, Bordeaux
22. Bayeux Tapestry
23. Monet's Garden, Giverny
24. Wine Route, Alsace
25. Route des Grands Crus, Burgundy

25 France's Top Highlights

Eiffel Tower

Seven million people visit the Eiffel Tower (p62) annually but few disagree each visit is unique. From an evening ascent amid twinkling lights to lunch up the tower in the company of a staggering city panorama, there are 101 ways to 'do' it. Pedal beneath it, skip the lift and hike up, buy a crêpe from a stand here or a key ring from a street vendor, snap yourself in front of it, visit it at night or – our favourite – on the odd special occasion when all 324m of the tower glows a different colour.

1

2

Louvre & Louvre-Lens

Art aficionados have never had it so good. Linger over the lush collection of 35,000-odd pieces – think paintings, sculptures, artefacts, royal crown jewels, Sèvres porcelain and so forth – in Paris' palatial Musée du Louvre (p68). Then catch a TGV to Lens, a once-forgotten mining town 200km north of the capital that everyone suddenly knows about thanks to the opening of the equally magnificent Louvre-Lens (p172). Above: Musée du Louvre (p68), Paris

Parisian Dining

Be it old-fashioned bistro, new millennium neo-bistro, Michelin-starred gastronomic meal or street-stall crêpe, dining in the City of Light is irresistible. And with innovative places hitting the scene, restless tastebuds have never been better served: try gourmet burgers at Blend (p87), the Parisian take on tapas at Le 6 Paul Bert (p90) or the crazy culinary wonders cooked up in the kitchen of superstar chef David Toutain (p85). Parisian dining is an essential part of the capital experience.

3

The Best... Boutique Sleeps

HIDDEN HOTEL
Packed with Parisian style, and tucked away just off the Champs-Élysées. (p80)

COUR DES LOGES
Four period townhouses in old Lyon; one superb boutique hotel. (p235)

L'HÔTEL PARTICULIER
Top spot in Arles, housed inside an 18th-century private mansion. (p263)

LA COLOMBE D'OR
Indulge in this former hang-out of Chagall, Matisse and Picasso. (p331)

The Best... Châteaux

VERSAILLES

France's grandest, busiest and most glorious château, just a quick skip from Paris. (p103)

CHAMBORD

François I's modest country retreat features a staircase rumoured to have been designed by Leonardo da Vinci. (p198)

CHENONCEAU

This château is the work of several aristocratic ladies, hence its nickname: the Château des Dames (Ladies' Château). (p197)

CHEVERNY

Impossibly elegant and still owned by its founding family. (p193)

BLOIS

No single castle better illustrates architectural history. (p192)

IMAGES ETC LTD/GETTY IMAGES ©

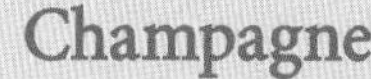

4 Champagne

Name-brand Champagne houses, such as Mumm (p157), Mercier (p162) and Moët & Chandon (p161) in the main towns of Reims and Épernay, are known the world over. But much of Champagne's best liquid gold is made by almost 5000 small-scale vignerons (winegrowers) in 320-odd villages. Dozens of Champagne *maisons* (houses) welcome visitors for a taste and shopping at producer prices, rendering the region's scenic driving routes the best way to taste fine bubbly amid rolling vineyards and gorgeous villages. Left: Épernay at sunset

LIONEL LOURDEL/GETTY IMAGES ©

5 Loire Valley Châteaux

If it's aristocratic pomp and architectural splendour you're after, this regal valley is the place to linger. The Loire is one of France's last *fleuves sauvages* (wild rivers) and its banks provide a 1000-year snapshot of French high society with its profusion of beautiful châteaux. If you're a romantic seeking the perfect fairy-tale castle, head for moat-ringed Azay-le-Rideau (p196) and Villandry (p209) with its dreamy gardens. Left: Château de Villandry (p209)

Ste-Chapelle & Chartres

6

This is a top experience reserved strictly for sunny days. Be stunned and inspired by the stained glass in Paris' Ste-Chapelle (p65), one of Christendom's most beautiful places of worship. Then head out of town to Chartres, where you can't get bluer blue than the awesome stained-glass windows of Cathédrale Notre Dame de Chartres (p107). Right: Ste-Chapelle (p65), Paris

7

Mont St-Michel

The dramatic play of tides on this abbey-island in Normandy is magical, mysterious and full of folklore. Said by Celtic mythology to be a sea tomb to which souls of the dead were sent, Mont St-Michel (p129) is rich in legend and history, keenly felt as you make your way barefoot across rippled sand to the stunning architectural ensemble. Hook up with a guide in nearby Genêts for a dramatic day hike across the bay.

Adrenalin Kick, Chamonix

Sure, 007 did it, but so can you: skiing the Vallée Blanche (p241) is a once-in-a-lifetime experience. You won't regret the €75-odd it costs to do the 20km off-piste descent from the spike of the Aiguille du Midi to mountaineering mecca Chamonix – every minute of the five hours it takes to get down will pump more adrenalin in your body than anything else you've ever done. Craving more? Hurl yourself down Europe's longest black run, La Sarenne, at Alpe d'Huez.

Below: Skiier, Chamonix

8

The Best... Cathedrals

CATHÉDRALE NOTRE DAME, PARIS
The cathedral to end all cathedrals; sadly, no hunchbacks in sight when we visited. (p77)

CATHÉDRALE NOTRE DAME, CHARTRES
If stained glass is your thing, you won't find any finer than in the luminous windows of Chartres' cathedral. (p107)

CATHÉDRALE NOTRE DAME, REIMS
Climb the cathedral tower for a bird's-eye view of this Champagne city. (p160)

CATHÉDRALE NOTRE DAME, AMIENS
Marvel at the largest Gothic cathedral in France. (p173)

CATHÉDRALE ST-ÉTIENNE, METZ
This lacy beauty is famous for its intricate spire. (p171)

The Best... Iconic Beaches

PLAGE DE L'ÉCLUSE
Old-fashioned bathing tents bring an air of the belle époque to this exclusive Breton beach in Dinard. (p136)

PROMENADE DES ANGLAIS
Join the sun-worshippers on Nice's pebbly beach. (p320)

BD DE LA CROISETTE
Private beaches full of rich and famous guests characterise Cannes' cinematic seafront. (p332)

PLAGE DE PAMPELONNE
Pout like Bardot in the classic Riviera resort at St-Tropez. (p337)

GRANDE PLAGE & PLAGE MIRAMAR
Biarritz's beaches have been in vogue since the Second Empire. (p274)

Dune du Pilat

The Dune du Pilat (p266) is a 'mountain' that just has to be climbed. Not only is the coastal panorama from the top of Europe's largest sand dune a stunner – it takes in the Banc d'Arguin bird reserve and Cap Ferret across the bay – but the nearby beaches have some of the Atlantic Coast's best surf. Cycle here from Arcachon and top off the heady trip with a dozen oysters, shucked before your very eyes and accompanied by *crepinettes* (local sausages).

9

10 St-Tropez

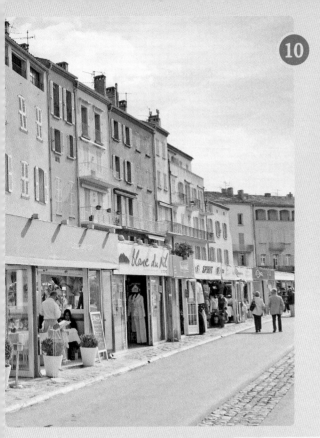

No seaside town in France is more fabled than the old fishing port of St-Tropez, where millionaire yachts jostle for space at the Vieux Port with peddling street artists and tourists by the million. Arrive early to catch the best of St-Tropez' atmospheric Place des Lices (p336) market, breakfast at La Tarte Tropézienne (p338), gorge on fine art at the Musée de l'Annonciade (p336), frolic away the afternoon over lunch and hobnobbing, or flop on the sand at achingly hip Plage de Pampelonne (p337). Brigitte Bardot, eat your heart out.

11 Three Corniches, Nice

It's impossible to drive this dramatic trio of coastal roads (p340), each one higher and with more hairpin bends than the next, without conjuring up cinematic images of Grace Kelly, Hitchcock, the glitz of Monaco high life, and the glamour of the royal family – all while absorbing big view after big view of sweeping blue sea fringing Europe's most mythical coastline. To make a perfect day out of it, shop for a picnic at the cours Saleya (p326) morning market before leaving Nice. Right: A coastal road near Èze (p341)

GU/GETTY IMAGES ©

12 Carcassonne at Dusk

That first glimpse of La Cité's sturdy, stone, witch's-hat turrets above Carcassonne (p317) in the Languedoc is enough to make your hair stand on end. To properly savour this fairy-tale walled city, linger at dusk after the crowds have left, when the old town belongs to its 100 or so inhabitants and the few visitors staying at the handful of lovely hotels within its ramparts. Don't forget to look back when you leave to view the old city, beautifully illuminated, glowing in the warm night.

JUSTIN OUELLETTE/GETTY IMAGES ©

13 D-Day Beaches, Normandy

The broad stretches of sand are quiet now, but on 6 June 1944 the beaches of northern Normandy (p123) were a cacophony of gunfire and explosions, the bodies of Allied soldiers lying in the sand as their comrades charged inland. Just up the hill from Omaha Beach, rows of gravestones at the Normandy American Cemetery & Memorial (p126) bear testimony to the price paid for France's liberation from Nazi tyranny. Left: Normandy American Cemetery & Memorial (p126)

Pont du Gard

This Unesco World Heritage Site (p315) near Nîmes in southern France is gargantuan: 35 arches straddle the Roman aqueduct's 275m-long upper tier, containing a watercourse that was designed to carry 20,000 cu metres of water per day. View it from afloat a canoe on the River Gard or pay extra to jig across its top tier. Oh, and don't forget your swimming gear for a spot of post-Pont daredevil diving and high jumping from the rocks nearby – a plunge that will entice the most reluctant of young historians.

14

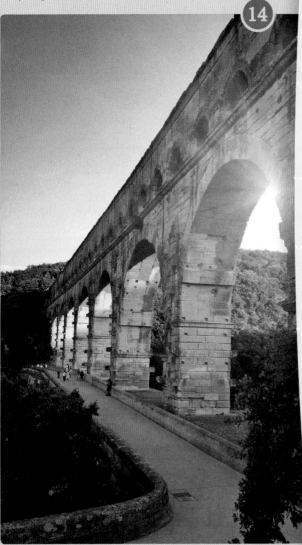

The Best... Medieval Villages

SARLAT-LA-CANEDA
Golden and gorgeous, the Dordogne's gem boasts some of France's most beautiful medieval architecture. (p213)

CARCASSONNE
Be bewitched by the witch's-hat turrets of this Languedoc beauty. (p317)

ST ÉMILION
Combine wine tasting with medieval enchantment in this Unesco-listed village. (p268)

ST-PAUL DE VENCE
Art history sits alongside historic architecture in this hilltop village on the French Riviera. (p329)

DINAN
Wander the cobbled streets and sturdy ramparts of one of Brittany's oldest villages. (p143)

The Best... Foodie Cities

PARIS

Bursting with buzzy bars, iconic bistros, historic cafes and Michelin-starred marvels. (p85)

LYON

Famous for its pig-centric cuisine, and often touted as France's top foodie town. (p236)

MARSEILLE

Tuck into authentic bouillabaisse (fish stew) in Marseille's atmospheric old port (p300).

STRASBOURG

Savour sauerkraut, sausages and lots of beer in an Alsatian *winstub* (wine room). (p164)

DIJON

Dijon mustard and some serious Burgundy reds for wine lovers. (p204)

Provençal Markets

No region is more of a market-must than this one. Be it fresh fish by the port in seafaring Marseille (p298), early summer's strings of pink garlic, melons from Cavaillon all summer long or wintertime's earthy 'black diamond' truffles, Provence (p292) thrives on a bounty of fresh produce – grown locally and piled high each morning at the market. While you're here, stock up on dried herbs, green and black olives marinated a dozen different ways, courgette flowers and oils. Above: Sea urchins for sale; Left: Cours Saleya market (p326), Provence

Hilltop Villages, Provence & the Riviera

16

Impossibly perched on a rocky peak above the Mediterranean, gloriously lost in back country, fortified or château-topped… southern France's portfolio of *villages perchés* (p330) is vast and impressive, and calls for go-slow touring – on foot, by bicycle or car. Most villages are medieval, built from golden stone with cobbled lanes, flower-filled alleys and hidden squares silent but for the glug of a fountain.

Right: View of Cote d'Azur (French Riviera) from Èze (p341)

JEAN-PIERRE LESCOURRET/GETTY IMAGES ©

Lyonnais Bouchons

17

The checked tablecloths and decades-old bistro decor could be anywhere in France. It's the local cuisine that makes *bouchons* (small bistros) in Lyon (p236) unique, plus the culinary customs, such as totting up the bill on the paper tablecloth, or serving wine in a glass bottle wrapped with an elastic band to stop drips. Various piggy parts drive Lyonnais cuisine, but have faith – this city is said to be the gastronomic capital of France. Dine and decide.

Centre Pompidou-Metz

Bright white by day, all aglow after dark, this is the star of the northern France art scene (p170). A provincial cousin to the well-known Centre Pompidou in Paris, this modern art museum was designed by a world-class, Japanese-French duo of architects and is as much an architectural gem as an exhibition powerhouse, easily on par with Bilbao's Guggenheim and London's Tate. Part of the experience is a designer lunch, aka edible art on a plate, at the museum's La Voile Blanche. Below: Centre Pompidou-Metz, designed by Shigeru Ban & Jean de Gastines

18

The Best... Viewpoints

EIFFEL TOWER
The capital's 'metal asparagus' needs no introduction – it's just a must-visit.(p62)

BASILIQUE DU SACRÉ-CŒUR, PARIS
This Montmartre landmark gives a different perspective on the capital. (p59)

AIGUILLE DU MIDI, CHAMONIX
If you can handle the height (3842m), unforgettable summit views of the French, Swiss and Italian Alps await. (p222)

FOURVIÈRE, LYON
The essential viewpoint for admiring Lyon's architecture. (p233)

PIC DU JER, LOURDES
Panoramic views of Lourdes and the central Pyrenees. (p281)

Carnac Megaliths 19

Pedalling past fields dotted with the world's greatest concentration of megaliths (p141) gives a poignant reminder of Brittany's ancient human inhabitants. No one knows for sure what inspired these gigantic menhirs, dolmens, cromlechs, tumuli and cairns to be built. A sun god? A phallic fertility cult? It's a mystery worth acquainting yourself with during a visit to northern France. One kilometre north of Carnac, the Alignements du Ménec, touting a mind-boggling 1099 stones, is the area's largest menhir field.

The Best... Nature Parks

PARC NATIONAL DE LA LUBÉRON Forests, gorges and traditional villages add to the appeal of this great bird-watching spot. (p313)

PARC NATIONAL DES ÉCRINS Miles of high-altitude trails make this a hiker's paradise. (p248)

PARC NATIONAL DE LA VANOISE France's oldest national park is as close as you'll get to untouched wilderness. (p248)

PARC NATIONAL DES CALANQUES Clifftop paths wind through France's newest national park. (p304)

PALEOLITHIC/GETTY IMAGES ©

20 Grotte de Lascaux

Europe's oldest prehistoric paintings are hidden deep in the limestone caves of the Vézère Valley. None are more breathtaking than those inside the Grotte de Lascaux (p214), decorated with the most sophisticated cave art ever discovered (in 1940 by four lads out looking for their dog!), including a mural of a bull measuring over 5.5m. The original cave is closed to prevent irreparable damage to the priceless paintings, but key sections have been recreated – to astonishing effect – in another cave nearby.

21 Bordeaux Wine Tasting

The Bordeaux region's wine is famous worldwide; a visit to its vineyards is a must for wine lovers. Quintessential wine town St-Émilion tickles palates with robust reds, while the Médoc is packed with grand names, such as Mouton Rothschild, Latour and Lafite Rothschild. Complete your wine-tasting tour with a course at École du Vin (p267) and an unforgettable meal with some AOC Bordeaux at La Tupina (p263).

HOLGER LEUE/GETTY IMAGES ©

DEA PICTURE LIBRARY/GETTY IMAGES ©

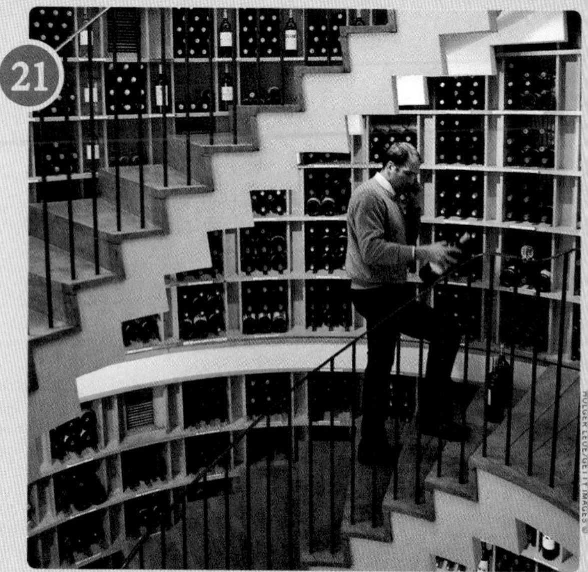

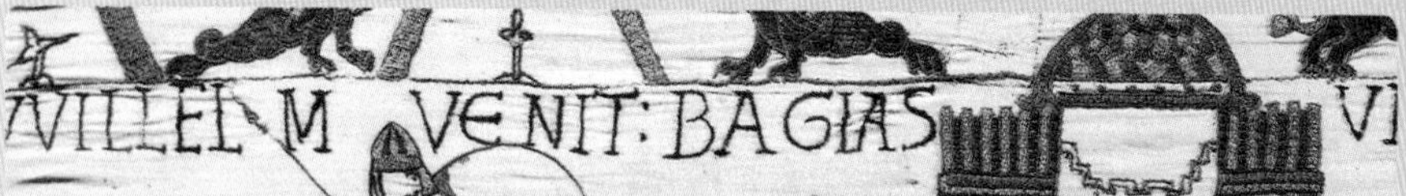

22 Bayeux Tapestry

Stretching for a mind-boggling 68.3m, the world's most celebrated tapestry (p122) is among France's most treasured historical artefacts. The work of art illustrates William the Conqueror's invasion of England in 1066. It was thought to have been commissioned in England by the Bishop Odo of Bayeux, William's half-brother, for the opening of Bayeux cathedral in 1077, although some argue it was produced in France.

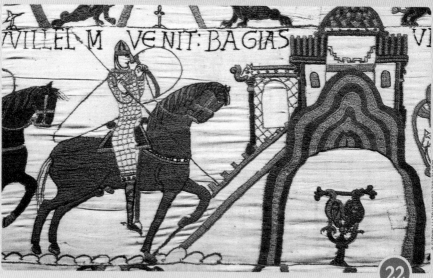

Monet's Garden, Giverny

Claude Monet purchased this idyllic Norman country house (p125) in 1883 and spent the next 30-odd years redesigning its gardens and grounds, adding trees, greenhouses, ornamental ponds and – most famously – a graceful Japanese bridge that any art lover will feel they have seen before. They have – on canvas. Giverny's grounds provided the inspiration for some of Monet's most famous works, most notably his iconic *Nymphéas* (Water Lily) series. No prizes for guessing where the lily-coated pond can be found.

23

The Best... Island Escapes

ÎLE DE LA CITÉ
This little island in the heart of Paris is a refuge from the modern metropolis. (p64)

BELLE ÎLE
Brittany's largest island is as beautiful as its name suggests. (p136)

ÎLES DE LÉRINS
These tiny islands provide the perfect getaway from Cannes' summer bustle. (p336)

ÎLES D'HYÈRES
A trio of Mediterranean islands fringed by sand, coastal paths and crystal-clear sea. (p339)

ÎLE D'OUESSANT
Explore shipwrecks on this wild, windswept island 32km off the Breton coastline. (p136)

Alsatian Wine Route

This is one of France's most popular drives – and for good reason. Motoring in this far northeast corner of France (p171) takes you through a kaleidoscope of lush green vines, castles and mist-covered mountains. The only pit stops en route are half-timbered villages and roadside wine cellars, where fruity Alsace vintages can be swirled, tasted and bought. To be truly wooed, drive the Route des Vins d'Alsace in autumn, when vines are heavy with grapes waiting to be harvested and colours are at their vibrant best. Below: Vineyards in Alsace

24

The Best... Shopping

PARIS
From flea markets to haute couture, Paris' shops have it all. (p95)

CHAMPAGNE
Épernay (p161) and Reims (p156) are stocked with cellars; pick up bottles of bubbly direct from the source.

NICE
Don't miss the Riviera's largest outdoor market, on the cours Saleya. (p326)

QUIMPER
Buy colourful *faïence* (earthenware) in Finistère's half-timbered capital. (p139)

BORDEAUX
Tour the vineyards and take home some top vintages. (p260)

STRASBOURG
Pick up handmade chocolates and gingerbread in this stately northern city. (p164)

25

Route des Grands Crus, Burgundy

No route is more sublime to saunter along at a snail's pace than this famous Burgundy wine trail. Narrow lanes wend their way from main towns Beaune (p209) and Dijon (p204) to countryside villages safeguarded by steeple-topped churches and château turrets peeping down between trees. Vines cascade down the slopes to picture-postcard hamlets where generations of vintners open their century-old cellars to those keen to taste and buy. Lovers of fine wine and the slow-paced good life: this is your heaven. Above: Vineyards in Burgundy

France's Top Itineraries

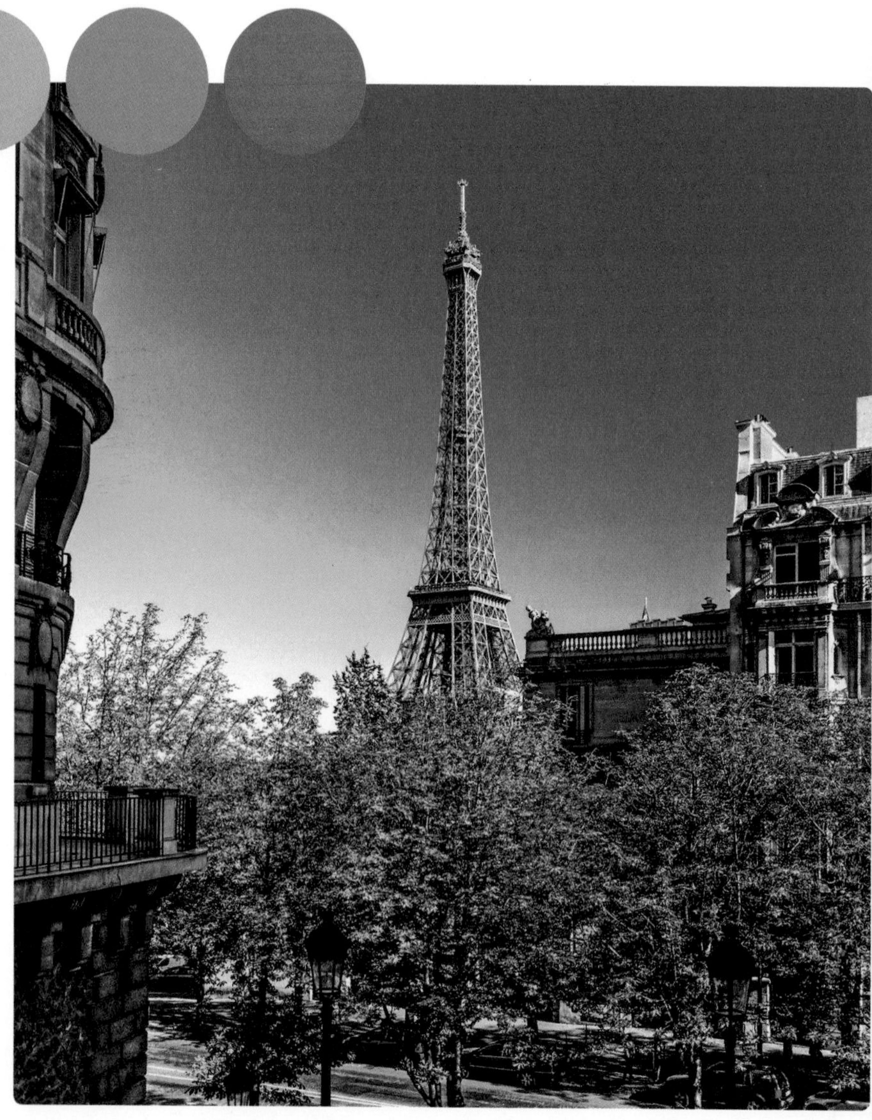

Paris to Chartres Capital Trips

5 DAYS

Five days should be just enough time to delve into the delights of the City of Lights and add on a few days' sightseeing beyond the capital, including visits to Versailles, Monet's gardens at Giverny and the medieval city of Chartres.

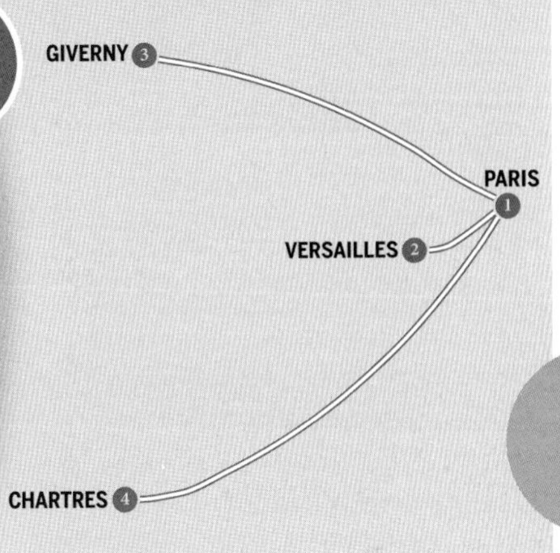

1 Paris (p51)

Every French adventure has to begin in Paris. With a couple of days you can squeeze in the **Eiffel Tower**, **Notre Dame** and the **Louvre**, plus a **river cruise** along the Seine and a stroll around **Montmartre**. Base yourself on the Left Bank to be near the main sights or the Marais on the Right Bank to be near hip dining and nightlife.

PARIS ➔ VERSAILLES

30 minutes From Pont de Sèvres in the 15e.

30 minutes From Paris' Left Bank stations on the RER Line C5.

2 Versailles (p102)

Day three takes you to Louis XIV's country retreat at **Versailles**, claimed as the grandest château of them all. Guided tours take in the château's main rooms, including the **royal apartments** and the **Hall of Mirrors**.

PARIS ➔ GIVERNY

50 minutes From Paris St-Lazare, followed by a quick shuttle-bus trip. **One hour** Along A13 and N13; follow signs to Vernon.

3 Giverny (p125)

On day four, catch the train from Paris to **Claude Monet's house and gardens** in Giverny. It's where the artist painted some of his most famous canvases. Don't miss the photo opp on the **Japanese bridge**. At the nearby **Musée des Impressionismes**, the work of other impressionists takes centre stage.

PARIS ➔ CHARTRES

One to 1¼ hours From Paris Montparnasse.

1¼ hours Along A10 and A11 motorways.

4 Chartres (p107)

On the last day, bid farewell to Paris and head to medieval Chartres. The city's ancient streets and squares are riddled with charm, but it is the **Cathédrale Notre Dame** – France's best-preserved medieval basilica – that takes your breath away. The cathedral's 172 stained-glass windows, almost all dating to the 13th century, are world-renowned.

Eiffel Tower, Paris (p62)

Blois to Tours
Architectural Elegance

France is synonymous with fabulous châteaux, and they don't get more French-fabulous than those lacing the Loire Valley. This trip from Blois follows the course of the Loire River via the elegant, history-rich city of Tours.

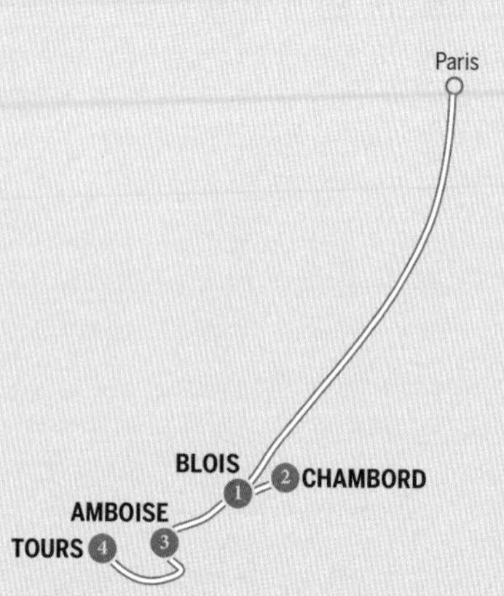

1 Blois (p191)

An easy two-hour train trip from Paris' Gare d'Austerlitz or Montparnasse (or two hours along the A10 motorway) brings you to Blois, a deeply historic town looming large on a rocky escarpment on the northern bank of the majestic Loire River. Once the seat of power for the French monarchy, the town's **château** is a glorious romp through French architectural history. Built as a showpiece rather than a defensive fortress, it showcases four different periods of architecture – from Gothic to classical – and its lavish main hall featured in Luc Besson's 1999 biopic of Joan of Arc. Don't miss a post-château meander around the warren of an old town wrapped around Blois' 17th-century cathedral, followed by a gastronomic feast – alfresco in summer – at **L'Orangerie**.

BLOIS ➔ CHAMBORD

40 minutes. **20 minutes** Along the D33.

2 Chambord (p198)

Devote day two to the Loire's most magnificent **castle**, Chambord. It was built by François I as a country retreat, but he hardly ever stayed there. A famous double-helix staircase spirals up to the rooftop, which gives wonderful views over the château's landscaped park. True château fiends absolutely must squeeze in a detour to **Cheverny**, famed above all else for its late-afternoon **Soupe de Chiens** (feeding of the hunting dogs). An easy drive links the twinset and both are included in organised minibus trips from Blois.

BLOIS ➔ AMBOISE

20 minutes. **30 minutes** Along the N152.

3 Amboise (p200)

From Blois, head west to Amboise, another enchanting royal town where you can visit another impressive **royal château** and unexpected treat, **Clos Lucé**. It's the retirement pad where Leonardo da Vinci beavered away on wacky creations during his later years; the house museum is packed with life-size prototypes of da Vinci's inventions, and many are dotted about the particularly handsome grounds.

AMBOISE ➔ TOURS

35 minutes. **30 minutes** Along the N152 or quieter D751.

4 Tours (p195)

The final day takes you via the lovely **Château de Chenonceau** – an absolutely unmissable and appropriately swoonworthy address more photographed than any other château – en route to Tours, the Loire Valley's main city. Its twin-towered Gothic **cathedral** dominates the skyline, but you can also visit several museums, including the elegant, art-filled **Musée des Beaux-Arts**.

Château de Chambord (p198)

Mont St-Michel to Avignon
Unesco Treasures

This trip takes in France's biggest, finest, oldest and loveliest; every stop is a Unesco World Heritage Site, making the trip a must for culture vultures and history buffs. From otherworldly abbeys to iconic cathedrals and Roman ruins, this adventure has it all.

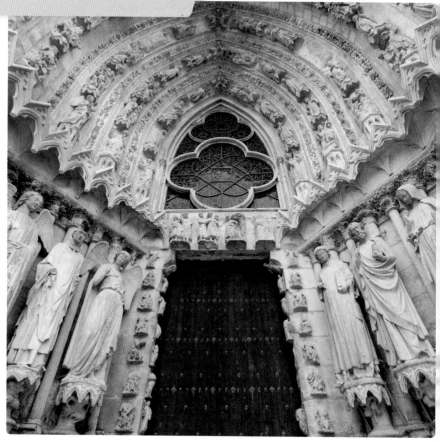

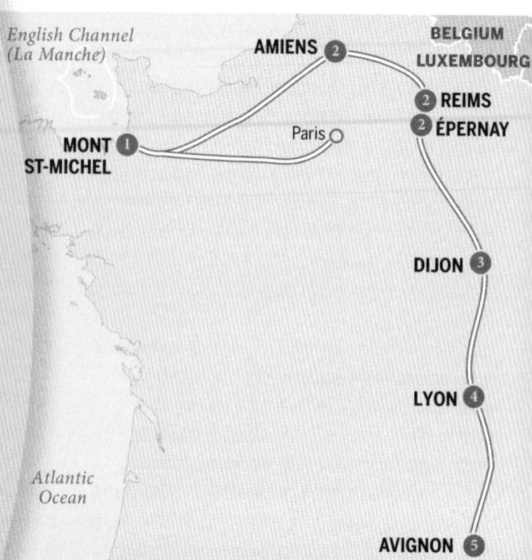

1 Mont St-Michel (p129)

France's iconic island abbey, Mont St-Michel, is a three-hour car trip from Paris (along the N13 and A84) or 3½ hours by train (TGV from Paris to Rennes, then a regional train to Pontorson and bus 6 to Mont St-Michel). Mont St-Michel is best seen at dawn, dusk or after dark when it's lit up like a Roman candle. Walk around the mount before delving in or hook up with a guide in nearby **Genêts** for a bare-footed walk across the sands. Break the journey to Champagne with a stop in **Bayeux** to admire the world's most celebrated embroidery, which vividly recounts the story of the Norman conquest of England in 1066.

MONT ST-MICHEL ➜ AMIENS

Three hours Along the A84, A132, A29 and A16 motorways. **Three hours** From Pontorson via Rennes to Paris Montparnasse, then Paris Gare du Nord to Amiens.

2 Champagne (p156)

Is there possibly any more sparkling region in France to stop in transit than Champagne in northeastern France? Tasting the bubbly tipple in name-brand Champagne houses in **Reims** and **Épernay** aside, there is also the remarkable Gothic Unesco World Heritage twinset of **Reims** and **Amiens'** cathedrals. Awe-inspiring is an understatement.

AMIENS ➜ DIJON

Five hours Along the A29, A26, A4, A5 and A31. **3-¾ hours** From Amiens to Paris Gare de Nord, then from Paris Gare de Lyon to Dijon.

Cathédrale Notre Dame, Reims (p160)

3 Dijon (p204)

Burgundy has two wonderful World Heritage Sites around an hour's drive from **Dijon:** the hilltop basilica of **Vézelay** and the Cistercian abbey of **Fontenay**. The monks are long gone, but both continue to inspire quiet contemplation.

DIJON ➜ LYON

2¼ hours Along the A31 and A6. **Two hours**.

4 Lyon (p228)

Lyon's architectural heritage encompasses everything from Roman ruins to Renaissance town houses, and most of the city has been designated a World Heritage Site. The monuments and museums are a major draw, while the city's culinary reputation ensures its busy *bouchons* (small bistros) buzz round the clock.

LYON ➜ AVIGNON

2¼ hours Along the A7. **One hour** Via the TGV.

5 Avignon (p308)

The beautiful walled city of Avignon safeguards an impressive **papal palace** and a **medieval bridge**. Further afield, Provence is littered with Gallo-Roman monuments including **Pont du Gard**, the world's largest and best-preserved Roman aqueduct, easily reached by car from Avignon.

Nice to Biarritz
Coast to Coast

This tour begins on the big blue Mediterranean before crossing the Pyrenees to the Atlantic Coast. En route you'll encounter ritzy cities, quaint villages and lofty mountains – not to mention a wealth of unforgettable views.

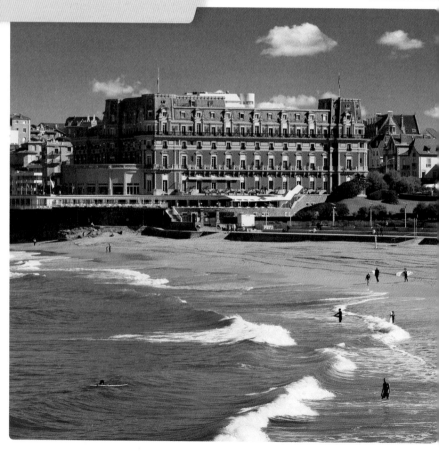

1 Nice (p320)

Start the trip in the Côte d'Azur's classic beach town, Nice. Kick back along the **Promenade des Anglais**, shop at the **cours Saleya market** and explore the backstreets of **Vieux Nice**. With an extra day, you could visit the city's **art museums**, motor out of town along a trio of jaw-dropping coastal **corniches**, or ride a train along the coast to moneyed **Monaco**.

NICE ➔ CANNES

30 minutes. **45 minutes** Along the coastal N98.

2 Cannes (p332)

After Nice, head west to star-spangled **Cannes**. Spot famous faces along **bd de la Croisette**, cruise out to the idyllic **Îles de Lérins**, then spin along the Mediterranean coastline for a day in chi-chi **St-Tropez**.

CANNES ➔ MARSEILLE

Two hours Along the A8 motorway, longer along the coastal N98. **Two hours**.

3 Marseille (p292)

Rough-and-ready Marseille encapsulates the fiery spirit of the French south. Sample **bouillabaisse** by the harbour, climb to the **basilica** and cruise to the island fortress of the **Château d'If**. An optional and oh-so-elegant detour might take in **Aix-en-Provence**, where Cézanne painted his most famous canvases.

MARSEILLE ➔ CARCASSONNE

3½ hours Along the coastal N98. **Three hours**.

4 Carcassonne (p317)

A three-hour cruise along the Mediterranean takes you to Carcassonne, one of the Languedoc's most beautiful medieval towns. The oldest part is the crenellated fortress known as La Cité, a maze of winding lanes and alleyways overlooked by witches hat towers. Don't miss the stunning view from the battlements.

CARCASSONNE ➔ LOURDES

You'll need your own wheels to explore the Pyrenees.

5 Lourdes (p280)

West of Carcassonne, the snowcapped peaks of the **Pyrenees** zig-zag along the Franco-Spanish border. Less visited than the Alps, these wild mountains offer fantastic walking and wildlife-spotting, and plunge people into the heart of one of the world's most visited pilgrimage sites, the holy city of **Lourdes**.

LOURDES ➔ BIARRITZ

2¾ hours **1¾ hours** From Lourdes along the A68, D1 and D810.

6 Biarritz (p274)

Switch the saw-tooth peaks of the Pyrenees for glitzy beach-babe Biarritz. With its belle époque architecture and gorgeous bays, this coastal city is ideal for further forays into **French Basque Country**: the ancient pilgrims' village of **St-Jean Pied de Port** and the riverside town of **Bayonne** are on your doorstep.

Biarritz (p274)

Paris to Paris
The Grand Tour

This is the big one: a whistle-stop circular adventure around France, taking in as many must-see sights as possible. It's doable in two weeks if you pack things in, but we've suggested optional side-trips for each area if your timetable allows a bit more flexibility.

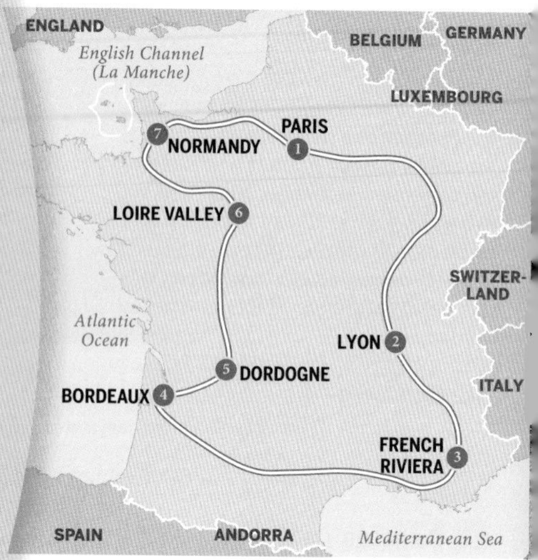

Paris (p51)

Kick off with at least two days in the French capital, ticking off as many sights, museums and restaurants as you can. Add in another couple of days for day trips to either **Château de Versailles**, the cathedral city of **Chartres**, or Champagne capital **Reims**.

PARIS ➔ LYON

Two hours From Paris Gare de Lyon aboard a TGV. **About five hours** Along the A6 motorway.

Lyon (p228)

From Paris, it's a speedy TGV trip to the lovely Roman city of Lyon. Spend a day exploring the sights, monuments and museums of this elegant cultural hub, followed by an evening meal in a traditional Lyonnais *bouchon*. Ideally, you should allow some time to explore the French Alps – base yourself in the shade of Mont Blanc in **Chamonix**, or lakeside in **Annecy** – but if you're pushed for time, skip the mountains and head directly to the French Riviera.

LYON ➔ NICE

Four to five hours On the TGV. **Less than one hour**.

French Riviera (p319)

You could soak up weeks lounging along the Côte d'Azur, but for this trip we've allowed two days: one for the lively city of **Nice**, and another for the playground principality of **Monaco**. En route you'll have the chance to experience France's most dazzling drive, along the coastal **corniches**. Big blue views aside, keep your eyes firmly on the (steep, hairpin-laced) road.

NICE ➔ BORDEAUX

Two hours. **Eight hours** Via direct TGV, longer if changes are required.

Bordeaux (p260)

Mark the start of week two with a cross-country flight to the capital of French winemaking, **Bordeaux**. It's a beautiful city in its own right, but for most people it's Bordeaux's viticultural heritage that's

Chamonix (p240)
ZYLBERYNG DIDIER/HEMIS.FR/GETTY IMAGES ©

the main draw. Tailored minibus trips are ideal if you're short on time: try to choose one that includes visits to the vineyards of the **Médoc** and the hilltop village of **St-Émilion**.

BORDEAUX ➔ SARLAT-LA-CANÉDA

2¾ hours. **2¼ hours** Along regional roads.

5 The Dordogne (p213)

Meander inland through the rolling countryside of the **Dordogne** en route to one of France's loveliest medieval towns, **Sarlat-la-Canéda** (the Saturday market here is a real biggie). Devote at least a day to visiting the amazing prehistoric artworks of the world-renowned **Grotte de Lascaux** and the other caves of the **Vézère Valley**.

SARLAT-LA-CANÉDA ➔ TOURS

Four hours. **Six hours** Usually with changes at Souillac and Limoges.

6 The Loire Valley (p188)

From Bordeaux, it's on to the Loire Valley and its fairytale **châteaux**. Base yourself in the cafe-busy city of **Tours**, and visit da Vinci's house in **Amboise**, the graceful palace of **Chenonceau** and François I's lavish hunting lodge, **Chambord**.

TOURS ➔ BAYEUX

3¼ hours. **5 hours** Change at Caen

7 Normandy (p118)

From the Loire, travel north via the abbey of **Mont St-Michel** en route to Bayeux, which makes an ideal base for tracing the story of two landmark invasions. William the Conqueror's raid on England in 1066 is dramatically recounted in the **Bayeux Tapestry**, while **Normandy's beaches** will be forever linked with the historic events of 6 June 1944 – known to the French as Jour-J, and to the rest of the world as D-Day. From Bayeux, it's a short hop back to the journey's end in **Paris**.

France Month by Month

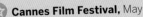

Top Events

- **Festival d'Avignon,** July
- **Fête du Citron,** February
- **Fête des Lumières,** December
- **Cannes Film Festival,** May
- **Monaco Grand Prix,** May

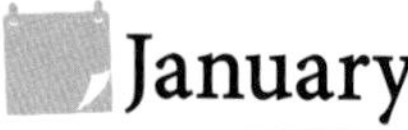

January

Vive le Ski!

Grab your skis, hit the slopes. Resorts in the Alps, Pyrenees and Jura open mid- to late December, but January is the start of the French ski season in earnest. Whether a purpose-built station or lost Alpine village, there's a resort to match every mood and moment.

Hunting Black Diamonds

No culinary product is more aromatic or decadent than black truffles. Hunt them in the Dordogne and Provence – the season runs late December to March, but January is the prime month.

February

Nice Carnival

Nice makes the most of its mild climate with this crazy Lenten carnival (www.nicecarnaval.com). As well as parade and costume shenanigans, merrymakers pelt each other with blooms during the legendary flower battles. Dunkirk in northern France is another French city to celebrate Mardi Gras with gusto.

Citrus Celebrations

It's no surprise that Menton on the French Riviera was once Europe's biggest lemon producer, given its exotic Fête du Citron (Lemon Festival, www.feteducitron.com). These days it has to ship in a zillion lemons from Spain to sculpt into gargantuan carnival characters.

Left: French flags

March

Féria Pascale

No fest sets passions in France's hot south blazing more than Féria de Pâques (www.feriaarles.com), held at Easter in Arles to open the bullfighting season. Four days of street dancing, music, concerts alfresco and bullfighting is what this exuberant event is all about. Not all bulls die.

April

Counting Sheep

During the Fête de la Transhumance, an ancient festival in late April or May, shepherds walk their flocks of sheep up to lush green summer pastures; St-Rémy de Provence's fest is among the best known. Or head to villages in the Pyrenees and Massif Central to witness this transit.

May

May Day

No one works on 1 May, a national holiday that incites summer buzz with its *muguets* (lilies of the valley) sold at roadside stalls and given to friends for good luck. In Arles, Camargue cowboys show off their bull-herding and equestrian skills at the Fête des Gardians.

Pèlerinage des Gitans

Roma flock to the Camargue on 24 and 25 May and again in October for a flamboyant fiesta of street music, dancing and dipping their toes in the sea (www.gitans.fr).

Starring at Cannes

In mid-May, film stars and celebrities walk the red carpet at Cannes, Europe's biggest cinema extravaganza (www.festival-cannes.com).

Monaco Grand Prix

How fitting that Formula One's most glamorous people rip around the streets of one of the world's most glam countries at the Monaco Grand Prix (www.grand-prix-monaco.com).

June

Fête de la Musique

Orchestras, crooners, buskers and bands fill streets with free music during France's vibrant nationwide celebration of music on 21 June (www.fetedelamusique.culture.fr).

Paris Jazz Festival

No festival better evokes the brilliance of Paris' interwar jazz age than this annual fest in the Parc de Floral (http://parisjazzfestival.paris.fr).

July

Tour de France

The world's most prestigious cycling race ends on av des Champs-Élysées in Paris on the third or fourth Sunday of July, but you can catch it for three weeks before all over France – the route changes each year but the French Alps are a hot spot (www.letour.fr).

Bastille Day

Join the French in celebrating the storming of the Bastille on 14 July 1789 – countrywide there are firework displays, balls, processions, parades and lots of hoo-ha all round.

Festival d'Avignon

Rouse your inner thespian with Avignon's legendary performing-arts festival (www.festival-avignon.com). Street acts in its fringe fest are as inspired as those on official stages.

 **Jazz à Juan**
Jive to jazz cats in Juan-les-Pins at this mythical Riviera music fest, which has been around for 50-odd years. Jazz à Juan (www.jazzajuan.fr) commands tickets, but the fringe 'Off' part of the music festival does not.

Festival de Cornouaille
Traditional Celtic music takes over the Breton town of Quimper during this inspiring summer festival in late July (www.festival-cornouaille.com).

August

Celts Unite!
Celtic culture is the focus of the Festival Interceltique de Lorient (www.festival-interceltique.com), when hundreds of thousands of Celts from Brittany and abroad flock to Lorient to celebrate just that.

 **Proud to be Breton**
The Fêtes d'Arvor is a passionate celebration of Breton culture. Think street parades, concerts and dozens of authentic *festoù-noz* (night festivals) spilling across the half-timbered, cobbled Vannes (www.fetes-arvor.org, in French).

September

The Rutting Season
Nothing beats getting up at dawn to watch mating stags, boar and red deer at play. Observatory towers are hidden in woods around Château de Chambord (p198), but when a valley like the Loire is so choc-a-bloc with Renaissance hunting pads, who cares which one?

 **Braderie de Lille**
The mountains of empty mussel shells engulfing the streets after three days of mussel-munching have to be seen to be believed. Then there's the real reason for visiting Lille on the first weekend in September – its huge flea market is Europe's largest.

October

 **Nuit Blanche**
In one last-ditch attempt to stretch out what's left of summer, Paris museums, monuments, cultural spaces, bars, clubs and so on rock around the clock during Paris' so-called 'White Night' (www.paris.fr), aka one fabulous long all-nighter!

November

Beaujolais Nouveau

At the stroke of midnight on the third Thursday in November the first bottles of cherry-red Beaujolais *nouveau* wine are cracked open – and what a party it can be in Beaujolais, Lyon and other places nearby!

December

Alsatian Christmas Markets

Visitors meander between fairy-light-covered craft stalls, mug of *vin chaud* (warm mulled wine) in gloved hand, at Alsace's traditional pre-Christmas markets.

Fête des Lumières

France's biggest and best light show, on and around 8 December, transforms the streets and squares of Lyon into an open stage (www.lumieres.lyon.fr).

Far left: Christmas market, Alsace
Left: Tour de France

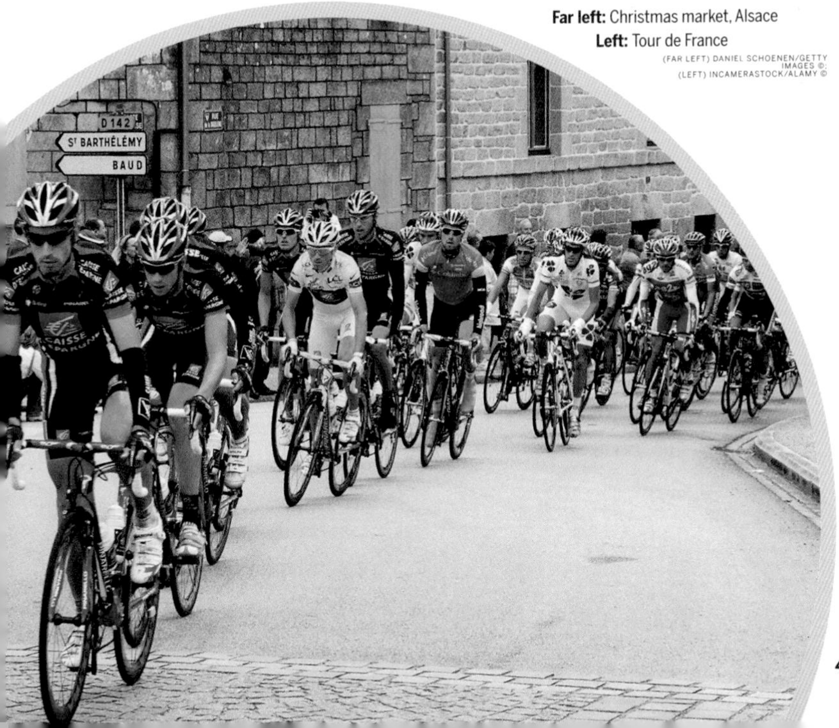

What's New

For this new edition of Discover France, our authors hunted down the fresh, the transformed, the hot and the happening. Here are a few of our favourites. For up-to-the-minute recommendations, see lonelyplanet.com/France.

1 **EIFFEL TOWER FACE-LIFT**
On the 1st floor of Paris' emblematic tower, two glitzy new glass pavilions house interactive history exhibits; outside them, visitors can peer d-o-w-n through vertigo-inducing glass flooring to the ground 57m below. (p62)

2 **CAPITAL ART EXCITEMENT**
No two Paris museum openings have been more eagerly awaited than the Musée Picasso (p327) and Frank Gehry's extraordinary Fondation Louis Vuitton (p75). Both museums finally opened to the public in October 2014.

3 **LE CAMINO, LE PUY-EN-VELAY**
Few journeys across France are as spiritual as the Chemin de St-Jacques pilgrimage route across the Masif Central, through the Lot Valley and French Basque country, to Santiago de Compostela in Spain. This new museum tells the story. (Musée de St-Jacques de Compostelle; www.lecamino.org; 2 rue de la Manécanterie; adult/child €3/1.50; 2-6pm mid-Apr–Jun & Sep–mid-Oct, 12.30-8pm Jul & Aug)

4 **THE CONFLUENCE, LYON**
The renaissance of Lyon's industrial wasteland, where the Rhône and Saône rivers meet, continues: its crowning glory, the Musée des Confluences, opened in December 2014 glittering in steel-and-glass crystal. (p232)

5 **LA TYROLIENNE, VAL THORENS**
The French Alps is not all about winter snow sports. Enter the world's highest zip line. Dare you! (www.la-tyrolienne.com; rides €50)

6 **MUSÉE RENOIR, CAGNES-SUR-MER**
Renoir's Riviera home and studio, secreted away in citrus and olive groves, has reopened and is more engaging than ever – admire *Les Grandes Baigneuses* (The Women Bathers; 1892) and unknown sculptures by the impressionists. (p339)

7 **MUCEM, MARSEILLE**
No single building better reflects the miraculous makeover of this mythical Mediterranean port than MuCEM, snug in a 17th-century fortress and breathtaking latticed shoe-box linked by a sky-high footbridge. (p292)

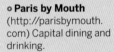

Get Inspired

Books

- **A Year in the Merde** (Stephen Clarke) Expat Brit's rant on dog poo, bureaucracy and more.
- **More France Please, We're British** (Helena Frith Powell) Life in rural France.
- **Everybody Was So Young** (Amanda Vaill) The French Riviera in the roaring twenties.
- **Me Talk Pretty One Day** (David Sedaris) Caustic take on moving to France, and learning the lingo.
- **Paris in Color** (Nichole Robertson) No photographic title better captures the colours of the capital.

Films

- **Cyrano de Bergerac** (1990) Glossy version of the classic, with Gérard Depardieu.
- **La Môme** (La Vie en Rose; 2007) Biopic of French singer Édith Piaf.
- **Bienvenue Chez Les Ch'tis** (2008) Comedy satirising France's north–south divide.
- **Midnight in Paris** (2011) Woody Allen tale about a family in Paris, with dream scenes set in the 1920s.
- **The Artist** (2011) Most awarded French film in history; romantic comedy with charismatic actor Jean Dujardin.

Music

- **Eternelle** (Édith Piaf; 2002) Excellent intro to the sparrow chanteuse.
- **Histoire de Melody Nelson** (Serge Gainsbourg; 1971) France's most-loved crooner.
- **L'Absente** (Yann Tiersen; 2001) Raw, emotional music from a multitalented Breton.
- **Château Rouge** (Abd al Malik; 2010) Rap music by Franco-Congolese rapper and slam-poet.
- **Voilà Voilà, the Best Of** (Rachid Taha; 2011) Cross-cultural sounds from Franco-Algerian DJ and singer.

Websites

- **Météo France** (www.meteo.fr) Weather forecasts.
- **SNCF** (www.sncf.com) French national railways.

- **Paris by Mouth** (http://parisbymouth.com) Capital dining and drinking.
- **Wine Travel Guides** (www.winetravelguides.com) Practical guides to France's wine regions.
- **France 24** (www.france24.com/en/france) French news in English.

Short on time?

This list will give you an instant insight into the country.

Read *Stuff Parisians Like* (Olivier Magny) has brilliant vignettes on Parisians and the French by a Parisian sommelier.

Watch *Amélie* (2001) is a film about a gal who sets out to make her Montmartre neighbourhood a happier place.

Listen *Le Voyage dans la Lune* (2012) offers electronica from French duo AIR ('Amour, Imagination, Rêve').

Log on www.franceguide.com is a French government tourist-office website.

Montmartre (p58), Paris
KRISTIN PILJAY/GETTY IMAGES ©

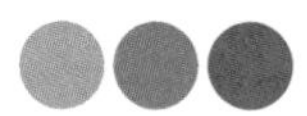

Need to Know

Currency
Euro (€)

Language
French

ATMs
At airports, train stations and city street corners.

Credit Cards
Visa and MasterCard widely accepted.

Visas
Generally not required for stays of up to 90 days (or at all for EU nationals); some nationalities need a Schengen visa.

Mobile Phones
European and Australian phones work. Only American cells with 900 and 1800 MHz networks are compatible.

Wi-Fi
Free in many hotels, train stations and airports.

Internet Access
Most towns have at least one internet cafe. Costs €3 to €6 per hour.

Driving
Steering wheel is on the left, drive on the right. Be aware of the 'priority to the right' rule.

Tipping
At least 10% for good service. *Service compris* means service is included.

When to Go

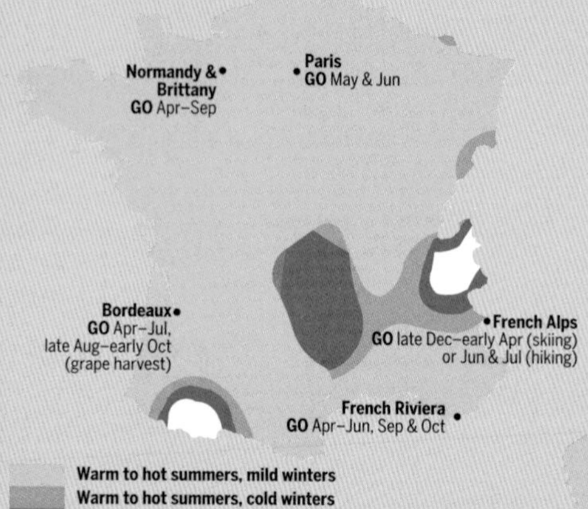

High Season (Jul & Aug)
- Queues at big sights and on the road, especially August when the French holiday
- Christmas, New Year and Easter equally busy
- Late December to March is high season in French Alpine ski resorts

Shoulder (Apr–June & Sep)
- Accommodation rates drop in southern France and other hot spots
- Spring brings warm weather and plentiful local produce
- Visit in autumn for the *vendange* (grape harvest)

Low Season (Oct–Mar)
- Prices up to 50% less than high season
- Sights, attractions and restaurants open fewer days and shorter hours

Advance Planning
- **Three months before** Book flights and accommodation; book tickets for popular festivals and sporting events, such as the Festival d'Avignon and Nice Jazz Festival.
- **One month before** Book train tickets via the SNCF website (www.sncf.com) to get the cheapest fares. Arrange car hire. Reserve dinner at top tables in Paris, Nice and elsewhere.
- **Two weeks before** Choose which guided walks and tours you want to do, and book if necessary. Order euros, or charge up your pre-paid card.

Your Daily Budget

Budget less than €100

- Dorm bed: €15–35
- Double room in budget hotel €60–80
- Free admission to many attractions first Sunday of month
- Set lunches: €12–18

Midrange €90–190

- Double room in a midrange hotel: €80–180
- Lunch *menus* (set meals) in gourmet restaurants: €20–40

Top End more than €190

- Double room in a top-end hotel: €180–200
- Lower weekend rates in business hotels
- Top restaurant dinner: *menu* €50, à la carte €100–150

Exchange Rates

Australia	A$1	€0.70
Canada	C$1	€0.70
Japan	¥100	€0.72
NZ	NZ$1	€0.62
UK	UK£1	€1.26
US	US$1	€0.79

For current exchange rates see www.xe.com.

What to Bring

- **Sunglasses, sunscreen and mosquito repellent** Vital for southern France.
- **Plug adaptors** France uses two-pin European plugs; UK, US and others need adaptors.
- **A corkscrew** Essential for impromptu picnics; few bottles of French wine are screwtop.
- **French phrasebook** Choose one with a good food section.
- **Travel insurance** Check the policy for coverage on snow sports, luggage loss and health care.
- **EHIC Card** Covers health care for EU citizens.
- **ID and passport** Don't forget visas if required.
- **Driving licence** Your standard home licence should be sufficient.

Arriving in France

- **Paris Charles de Gaulle**

Trains, buses and RER (*Réseau Express Régional*); to Paris centre every 15 to 30 minutes, 5am to 11pm.

Night buses; hourly, 12.30am to 5.30am.

Taxis; €50–60; 30 minutes to Paris centre.

- **Paris Orly**

Orlyval rail, RER and buses; at least every 15 minutes, 5am to 11pm.

Taxis; €40–55; 25 minutes to Paris centre.

Getting Around

- **Train** France's railway is fast, extensive and efficient. Regular trains travel to practically every town and city.
- **Car** Having a car buys freedom and flexibility, but driving in big cities can be a nightmare.
- **Bicycle** A hip way of navigating Paris, Lyon and other big cities.

Accommodation

- **Hotels** Wide range of budget, midrange and top-end hotels.
- **Chambres d'hôte** Staying in a B&B is particularly popular in rural France.
- **Châteaux** Some châteaux have been converted into luxurious hotels or B&Bs.

Be Forewarned

- **Shops** Nearly everywhere shuts on Sunday and public holidays. Shops usually close for lunch from noon to 2pm.
- **Restaurants** Few serve all day; orders are generally taken between noon and 2pm, and 7pm to 10.30pm, six days a week. Sunday evening and all day Monday are popular times to close.
- **Driving in France** Tolls are charged on motorways *(autoroutes)*. Automatic cars are very unusual in France.
- **Crowds** Many sights are at their busiest in July and August, but this can be a good time to visit Paris, as it's when most French people go on holiday.

gan

Paris & Around

Paris has all but exhausted the superlatives that can reasonably be applied to any city. Notre Dame, the Eiffel Tower, the Seine – at sunrise, sunset, at night – and Left Bank–Right Bank differences have been described countless times. But what writers haven't quite captured is the grandness and magic of simply strolling the city's broad avenues past impressive public buildings and exceptional museums to parks, gardens and esplanades.

With more famous landmarks than any other city, the French capital evokes all sorts of expectations: of grand vistas, of intellectuals discussing weighty matters in cafes, of Seine-side romance, of naughty nightclub revues. Look hard enough and you'll find them all. Or set aside those preconceptions of Paris and explore the city's avenues and backstreets as though the tip of the Eiffel Tower or the spire of Notre Dame weren't about to pop into view at any moment.

Arc de Triomphe (p60)
NEIL EMMERSON/CORBIS ©

Paris & Around
CLICHY
Cimetière Sud
Bd Bessières
Porte de Clichy
17E
See Central Paris – North Map (p72)
Av Bineau
Péreire-Lavallois
R de Rome
Neuilly-Porte Maillot
Gare St-Lazare
Av Foch
Charles de Gaulle–Étoile
8E
Auber
TRIANGLE D'OR
Seine
Lac Inférieur
Jardins du Trocadéro
Jardin des Tuileries
Musée d'Orsay
4
Jardin du Ranelagh
16E
Champ de Mars-Tour Eiffel
3
Bois de Boulogne
Lac Supérieur
Boulain-Villiers
7E
Avenue du Président Kennedy
LEFT BANK
Av Mozart
Av de Saxe
Porte d'Auteuil
Sq Henry Paté
6E
Javel
Av Émile Zola
Ste-Périne
Parc André Citroën
R Lecourbe
Gare Montparnasse
Boulevard Victor
R de la Convention
R de la Croix Nivert
Cimetière du Montparnasse
5 (11km)
15E
R de Vouillé
Bd Victor
Denfert Rochereau
Nouveau Cimetière
Parc Georges Brassens
Bd Lefebvre
Issy–Val de Seine
Île St-Germain
Jacques Henri Lartigue
Sq de la Porte de la Plaine
R d'Alésia
14E
Sq Jean Moulin
Bd Périphérique
Issy Ville
VANVES
Parc Rodin
MALAKOFF
MONTROUGE
0 2 km
0 1 mile
Cimetière Parisien de Bagneux
ARCUEIL

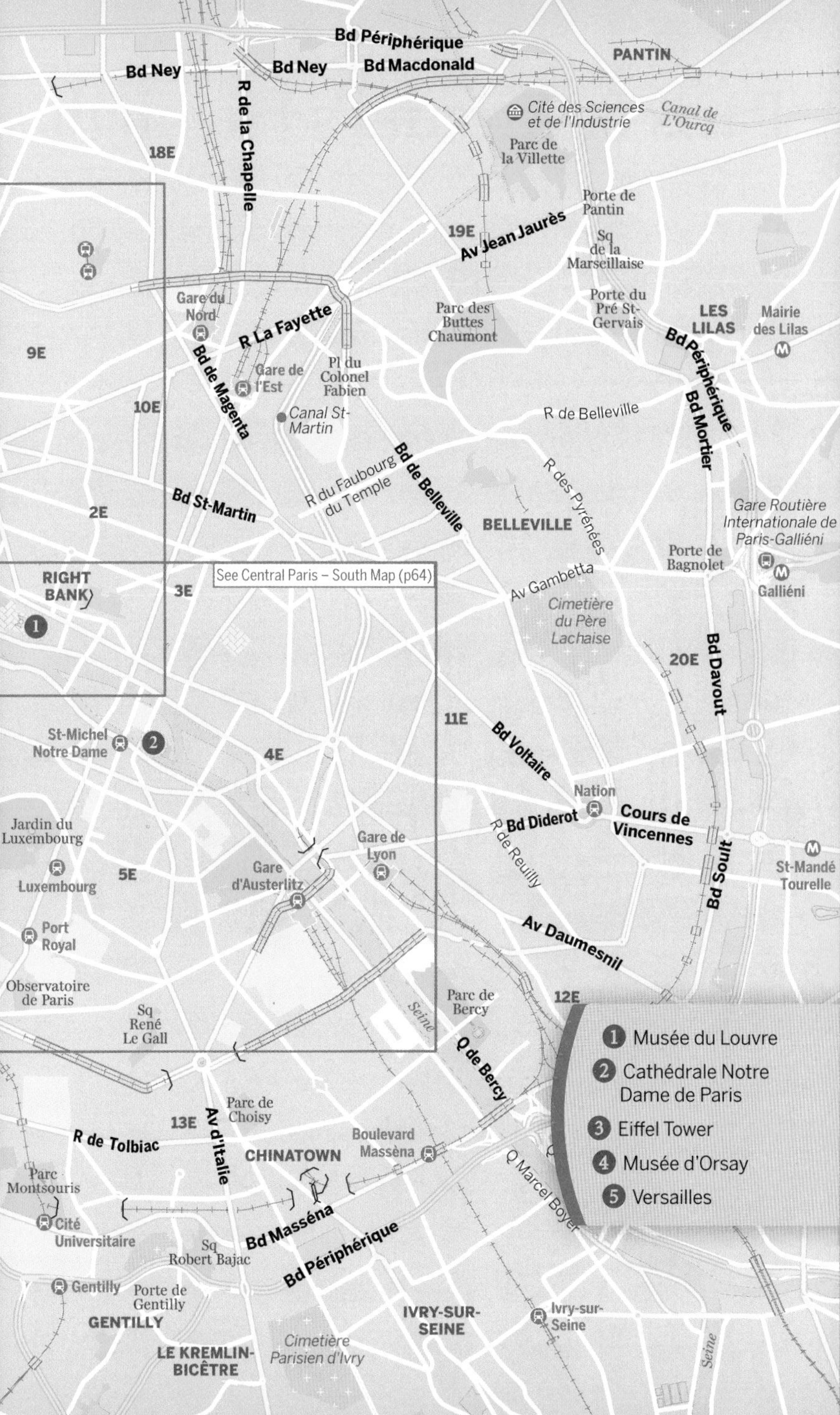
Bd Périphérique
PANTIN
Bd Ney
Bd Ney
Bd Macdonald
R de la Chapelle
Cité des Sciences et de l'Industrie
Canal de L'Ourcq
Parc de la Villette
18E
Porte de Pantin
19E
Av Jean Jaurès
Sq de la Marseillaise
Porte du Pré St-Gervais
Gare du Nord
R La Fayette
Parc des Buttes Chaumont
LES LILAS
Mairie des Lilas
9E
Bd de Magenta
Gare de l'Est
Pl du Colonel Fabien
Bd Périphérique
10E
Canal St-Martin
R de Belleville
Bd Mortier
Bd de Belleville
R des Pyrénées
R du Faubourg du Temple
Bd St-Martin
2E
BELLEVILLE
Gare Routière Internationale de Paris-Galliéni
RIGHT BANK
See Central Paris – South Map (p64)
3E
Porte de Bagnolet
Av Gambetta
Gallieni
Cimetière du Père Lachaise
20E
Bd Davout
11E
St-Michel Notre Dame
4E
Bd Voltaire
Nation
Jardin du Luxembourg
Bd Diderot
Cours de Vincennes
R de Reuilly
Gare de Lyon
St-Mandé Tourelle
Luxembourg
5E
Gare d'Austerlitz
Bd Soult
Port Royal
Av Daumesnil
Observatoire de Paris
Parc de Bercy
12E
Seine
Sq René Le Gall
Q de Bercy
Parc de Choisy
13E
Av d'Italie
R de Tolbiac
Boulevard Massèna
CHINATOWN
Q Marcel Boyer
Parc Montsouris
Cité Universitaire
Bd Masséna
Sq Robert Bajac
Bd Périphérique
Gentilly
Porte de Gentilly
GENTILLY
IVRY-SUR-SEINE
Ivry-sur-Seine
Cimetière Parisien d'Ivry
LE KREMLIN-BICÊTRE
Seine
1 Musée du Louvre
2 Cathédrale Notre Dame de Paris
3 Eiffel Tower
4 Musée d'Orsay
5 Versailles

Paris & Around's Highlights

The Louvre

France's most famous museum and gallery (p68) is also one of the world's finest. From artistic masterpieces such as the *Mona Lisa* to ancient antiques like the *Venus de Milo*, there's enough here to fill an entire lifetime of visits.

1

2 Cathédrale Notre Dame de Paris

France has its share of stunning cathedrals, but none can match the might and majesty of Notre Dame Cathedral (p77), Paris' most-visited monument. Idyllically situated on an island in the middle of the Seine, the cathedral is renowned for its stained glass and soaring Gothic architecture, not to mention an unmissable panorama over the rooftops of Paris.

PAWEL LIBERA/GETTY IMAGES ©

Eiffel Tower

3

No Parisian visit would be complete without a trip up the Tour Eiffel (p62). But the 'metal asparagus' was very nearly torn down in the early 20th century (it only survived because it made an ideal radio-antenna platform). Today around seven million visitors a year venture to the top. Try to time your visit for dusk when it's less crowded and the city lights begin to twinkle.

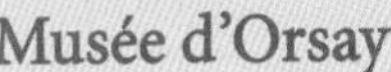

4

Musée d'Orsay

It might not be as monumental as the Louvre, but for many people this fine-arts museum (p73) offers a more-rewarding experience. Housed in a turn-of-the-century train station overlooking the Seine, the museum contains France's national collection of art from the 1840s to 1914, including key works by Renoir, Degas, Monet, Cézanne and Vincent van Gogh. Absolutely not to be missed.

5

Château de Versailles

Versailles (p102), the former residence of the kings of France, is the best place to appreciate the astonishing might and majesty of the French monarchy. With its lavish gardens, priceless antiques, glittering decor and impossibly over-the-top architecture, it also explains why the Revolutionaries were so desperate to bring the aristocracy's excesses to an end.

Paris & Around's Best...

City Views

- **Eiffel Tower** Need we say more? (p62)
- **Cathédrale Notre Dame de Paris** Gargoyles, flying buttresses and unforgettable views. (p77)
- **Centre Pompidou** Head to the rooftop – it's high! (p63)
- **Basilique du Sacré-Cœur** Look out from the dome of Montmartre's basilica. (p59)
- **Galeries Lafayette** Staggering – and free – views from the top floor of this grand department store. (p96)

Romantic Spots

- **Musée Rodin** Swoon over Rodin's garden-framed *The Kiss*. (p63)
- **Eiffel Tower** At the top, there are three marriage proposals every hour! (p62)
- **Jardin du Palais Royal** No urban garden is so elegant. (p61)
- **Canal St-Martin** Stroll hand-in-hand along towpaths. (p76)
- **Le Coupe-Chou** Dine by candlelight in a vine-clad, 17th-century townhouse. (p92)

Places to Eat

- **Septime** Beacon of modern cuisine near Bastille. (p91)
- **Restaurant David Toutain** Mystery tasting courses dreamt up by one of the capital's most creative chefs. (p85)
- **Derrière** Cheeky apartment-style dining with sophisticated home-cookin' feel. (p91)
- **Bouillon Racine** Art Nouveau 'soup kitchen' from 1906. (p92)
- **Frenchie** A modern take on a traditional back-street bistro. (p88)

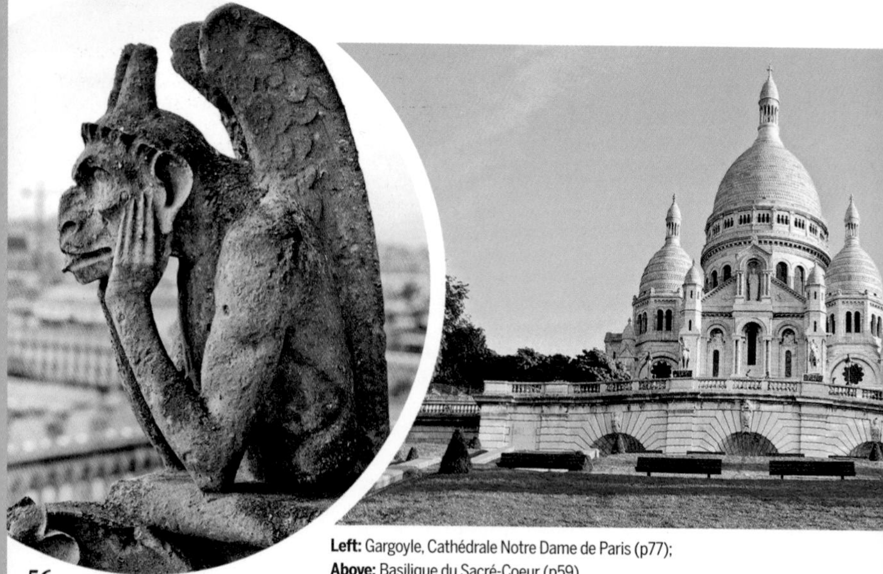

Left: Gargoyle, Cathédrale Notre Dame de Paris (p77); **Above:** Basilique du Sacré-Coeur (p59)

Quintessential Cafes

- **Les Deux Magots** Too famous for its own good, but a Left Bank must. (p94)
- **Le Pure Café** Sink an espresso in the cafe where *Before Sunset* was filmed. (p94)
- **Café La Palette** Fashionable, fin de siècle cafe; erstwhile stomping ground of Cézanne and Braque. (p94)
- **Claus** Only in Paris: an 'haute couture' breakfast cafe. (p87)

Need to Know

ADVANCE PLANNING

- **As early as possible** Book accommodation and make restaurant reservations.
- **One week before** Dodge the queues by buying tickets online for Versailles, the Louvre, Grand Palais exhibitions and Centre Pompidou.
- **Tickets** Pick up concert, musical and theatre tickets from Fnac and Virgin Megastore.

RESOURCES

- **Paris Convention & Visitors Bureau** (www.parisinfo.com) The city's central tourist office.
- **Go Go** (www.gogoparis.com) 'Fashion, food, arts, gigs, gossip'.
- **Paris.fr** (www.paris.fr) Comprehensive city information.
- **My Little Paris** (www.mylittleparis.com) Insider secrets from Parisian writers.
- **Paris by Mouth** (www.parisbymouth.com) Latest local tips.

GETTING AROUND

- **Metro & RER** Paris' subway system runs between 5.30am and midnight; tickets are also valid on buses.
- **Bicycle** The capital's bike-rental scheme, Vélib', has over 1500 stations dotted across the city.
- **Boats** Scenic cruise boats run regularly along the Seine.

BE FOREWARNED

- **Arrondissements** Paris addresses are split into 20 *arrondissements* (districts); 1er for *premier* (1st), 2e for *deuxième* (2nd), 3e for *troisième* (3rd) etc.
- **Museums** Most museums close on Mondays but some, including the Louvre and Centre Pompidou, close on Tuesdays instead.
- **Bars & Cafes** A drink costs more sitting at a table than standing, and more on a fancy square than on a backstreet.
- **Metro stations** Avoid late at night: Châtelet-Les Halles, Château Rouge (Montmartre), Gare du Nord, Strasbourg-St-Denis, Réaumur-Sébastopol and Montparnasse-Bienvenüe.

Montmartre Walking Tour

Pretty squares, cobbled streets and city views – plus famous cabarets and artistic connections – make Montmartre the quintessential Parisian neighbourhood. It's ideal for exploring on foot, as long as you can handle the hills.

WALK FACTS

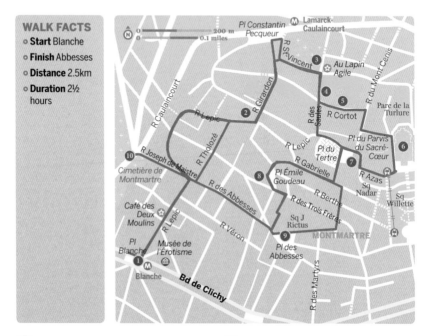

- **Start** Blanche
- **Finish** Abbesses
- **Distance** 2.5km
- **Duration** 2½ hours

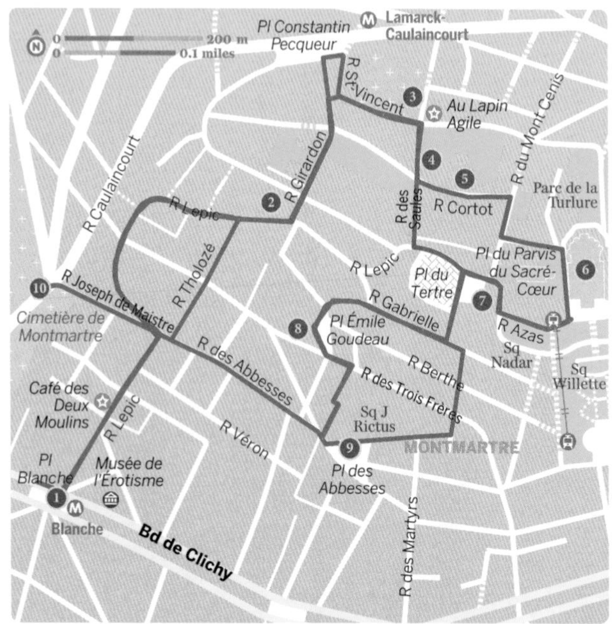

1 Place Blanche

Begin outside Blanche metro station. To the northwest is the legendary **Moulin Rouge** beneath its red windmill. To the right is the saucy **Musée de l'Érotisme** (www.musee-erotisme.com; 72 bd de Clichy, 18e; admission €10; 10am-2am; M Blanche). Halfway along rue Lepic is **Café des Deux Moulins**, where Audrey Tautou worked in the film *Amélie*.

2 Montmartre Windmills

Further along rue Lepic are Montmartre's twin windmills: the **Moulin de la Galette**, immortalised in an 1876 painting by Renoir, and the **Moulin Radet**, now a restaurant.

3 Cimetière St-Vincent

This cemetery on rue St-Vincent is the final resting place of Maurice Utrillo (1883–1955), the 'painter of Montmartre'. Just east is the notorious cabaret Au Lapin Agile, named after a mural by caricaturist André Gill, which still features on the west wall.

4 Clos Montmartre

South along rue des Saules is Clos Montmartre, a tiny vineyard that produces around 800 bottles of wine a year, which are auctioned for charity in October.

5 Musée de Montmartre

This **museum** (www.museedemontmartre.fr; 12 rue Cortot, 18e; adult/child €9/5; 10am-6pm; M Lamarck–Caulaincourt) is housed in Montmartre's oldest building, a 17th-century house once occupied by Renoir, Utrillo and Raoul Dufy.

6 Basilique du Sacré-Cœur

Inside this iconic landmark (www.sacre-coeur-montmartre.com; place du Parvis du Sacré-Coeur; dome adult/child €6/4, cash only; 6am-10.30pm, dome 9am-7pm Apr-Sep,to 5.30pm Oct-Mar; M Anvers), 234 steps spiral up to the dome and one of Paris's most spectacular panoramas.

7 Place du Tertre

It would be hard to miss this square, one of the most touristy and vibrant spots in Paris, packed with buskers and portrait artists.

8 Bateau Lavoir

The Bateau Lavoir is where the artists Modigliani, Picasso, Kees Van Dongen and Max Jacob lived in an old piano factory (later a laundry). The original building was at No 13; it burned down in 1970 and was rebuilt two doors away in 1978.

9 Abbesses Metro Station

Take the steps from place Émile Goudeau and walk to place des Abbesses to see the famous art-nouveau entrance to the Abbesses metro station, designed in 1912 by Hector Guimard.

10 Cimetière de Montmartre

At the western end of rue des Abbesses is Montmartre's largest **cemetery** (8am-5.30pm Mon-Fri, from 8.30am Sat, from 9am Sun; M Place de Clichy), where you'll find the graves of Émile Zola, Alexandre Dumas and Edgar Degas, among others. The entrance is on rue Caulaincourt.

Paris In ...

TWO DAYS

Kick off with a morning cruise or tour, then concentrate on the most Parisian of sights and attractions: **Notre Dame**, the **Louvre**, the **Eiffel Tower** and the **Arc de Triomphe**. In the late afternoon have a coffee or glass of wine on **av des Champs-Élysées** before making your way to **Montmartre** for dinner. The following day take in such sights as the **Musée d'Orsay**, **Ste-Chapelle**, **Conciergerie**, **Musée National du Moyen Âge** or **Musée Rodin**. Dine in the hip area of **Le Marais**.

FOUR DAYS

With another two days spare, follow our walking tour of Montmartre, take a cruise along the **Seine** or **Canal St-Martin**, meander further afield to **Cimetière du Père Lachaise** or the Bois de Boulogne, or squeeze in a side trip to **Versailles**. You might also visit the **Musée du Quai Branly** or do a spot of shopping along the **Champs-Élysées**. By night choose from the many restaurants and bars in **Bastille**, **Opéra** and **Montparnasse**.

Cimetière du Père Lachaise (p81)

Discover Paris & Around

At a Glance

- **Louvre & Les Halles** (p61) Right Bank of the Seine, dominated by Paris' monumental art museum.
- **Le Marais & Bastille** (p62) Hip dining, drinking 'hoods.
- **Étoile & Champs-Élysées** (p60) Paris' famous (shop-laced) boulevards.
- **Montmartre** (p58) Touristed artistic quarter.
- **St-Germain & Les Invalides** (p71) Left Bank café life & Paris' grandest park.
- **Latin Quarter** (p67) Historic university district, Sorbonne as centrepiece.

PARIS

POP 2.2 MILLION

Sights

EIFFEL TOWER AREA

Musée du Quai Branly Museum

(Map p72; www.quaibranly.fr; 37 quai Branly, 7e; adult/child €8.50/free; 11am-7pm Tue, Wed & Sun, 11am-9pm Thu-Sat; M Alma Marceau or RER Pont de l'Alma) No other museum in Paris so inspires travellers, armchair anthropologists and those who simply appreciate the beauty of traditional craftsmanship. A tribute to the diversity of human culture, Musée du Quai Branly presents an overview of indigenous and folk art. Its four main sections focus on Oceania, Asia, Africa and the Americas.

An impressive array of masks, carvings, weapons, jewellery and more make up the body of the rich collection, displayed in a refreshingly unique interior without rooms or high walls.

ÉTOILE & CHAMPS-ÉLYSÉES

Arc de Triomphe Landmark

(Map p72; www.monuments-nationaux.fr; place Charles de Gaulle, 8e; adult/child €9.50/free; 10am-11pm Apr-Sep, to 10.30pm Oct-Mar; M Charles de Gaulle–Étoile) If anything rivals the Eiffel Tower as the symbol of Paris, it's this magnificent 1836 monument to Napoleon's 1805 victory at Austerlitz, which he commissioned the following year. The intricately sculpted triumphal arch stands sentinel in the centre of the

Place de la Concorde (p61)

Étoile (star) roundabout. From the viewing platform on top of the arch (50m up via 284 steps and well worth the climb) you can see the dozen avenues.

Place de la Concorde Square
(Map p72; 8e; M Concorde) Paris spreads around you, with views of the Eiffel Tower, the Seine and along the Champs-Élysées, when you stand in the city's largest square. Its 3300-year-old pink granite obelisk was a gift from Egypt in 1831. The square was first laid out in 1755 and originally named after King Louis XV, but its royal associations meant that it took centre stage during the Revolution – Louis XVI was the first to be guillotined here in 1793.

LOUVRE & LES HALLES

Jardin des Tuileries Gardens
(Map p64; ⏲7am-11pm Jun-Aug, shorter hours rest of year; M Tuileries or Concorde) Filled with fountains, ponds and sculptures, the formal, 28-hectare Tuileries Garden, which begins just west of the Jardin du Carrousel, was laid out in its present form, more or less, in 1664 by André Le Nôtre, who also created the gardens at Vaux-le-Vicomte and Versailles. The Tuileries soon became the most fashionable spot in Paris for parading about in one's finery. It now forms part of the Banks of the Seine World Heritage Site listed by Unesco in 1991.

Jardin du Palais Royal Gardens
(Map p72; 2 place Colette, 1er; ⏲7am-10.15pm Apr & May, to 11pm Jun-Aug, shorter hours rest of year; M Palais Royal–Musée du Louvre) FREE The Jardin du Palais Royal is a perfect spot to sit, contemplate, and picnic between boxed hedges or shop in the trio of arcades that frame the garden so beautifully: the Galerie de Valois (east), Galerie de Montpensier (west) and Galerie Beaujolais. However, it's the southern end of the complex, polka-dotted with sculptor Daniel Buren's 260 black-and-white striped columns, that has become the garden's signature feature.

This elegant urban space is fronted by the neoclassical **Palais Royal** (closed to the public), constructed in 1633 by Cardinal Richelieu but mostly dating to the late 18th century. Louis XIV hung out here in the 1640s; today it is home to the **Conseil d'État** (State Council; Map p64).

The **Galerie de Valois** is the most upmarket arcade with designer boutiques like Stella McCartney, Pierre Hardy, Didier Ludot (p96) and coat-of-arms engraver Guillaumot, at work at Nos 151 to 154 since 1785. Across the garden, in the **Galerie de Montpensier**, the Revolution broke out on a warm mid-July day just three years after the galleries opened in the Café du Foy. The third arcade, tiny **Galerie Beaujolais**, is crossed by **Passage du Perron**, a passageway above which the writer Colette (1873–1954) lived out the last dozen years of her life.

Paris Museum Pass

If you think you'll be visiting more than two or three museums and monuments while in Paris, buy a **Paris Museum Pass (http://en.parismuseumpass.com; 2/4/6 days €42/56/69).** The pass is valid for entry to some 38 venues in the city – including the Louvre, Centre Pompidou, Musée d'Orsay and the Musée Rodin (but not the Eiffel Tower). It will get you into another 22 places outside the city, including the châteaux at Versailles and Fontainebleau and the Basilique de St-Denis.

One of the best features of the pass is that you can bypass the long ticket queues at major attractions (but not always the security queues).

The Paris Museum Pass is available online and at participating museums, tourist desks at the airports, branches of the Paris Convention & Visitors Bureau, Fnac outlets (www.fnactickets.com) and major metro stations.

PAWEL LIBERA/GETTY IMAGES ©

Don't Miss Eiffel Tower

No one could imagine Paris today without it. But Gustave Eiffel only constructed this elegant, 320m-tall signature spire as a temporary exhibit for the 1889 World Fair. Luckily, the art nouveau tower's popularity assured its survival. Prebook tickets online to avoid long ticket queues.

Lifts ascend to the tower's three levels; change lifts on the 2nd level for the final ascent to the top. Energetic visitors can walk as far as the 2nd level using the south pillar's 704-step stairs.

Refreshment options in the tower include the 1st-floor 58 Tour Eiffel, the sublime 2nd-floor Le Jules Verne, and, at the top, a champagne bar.

NEED TO KNOW

Map p72; 08 92 70 12 39; www.tour-eiffel.fr; Champ de Mars, 5 av Anatole France, 7e; lift to top adult/child €15/10.50, lift to 2nd fl €9/4.50, stairs to 2nd fl €5/3, lift 2nd fl to top €6; lifts & stairs 9am-midnight mid-Jun–Aug, lifts 9.30am-11pm, stairs 9.30am-6.30pm Sep–mid-Jun; M Bir Hakeim or RER Champ de Mars-Tour Eiffel

Église St-Eustache Church

(Map p64; www.st-eustache.org; 2 impasse St-Eustache, 1er; 9.30am-7pm Mon-Fri, 9am-7pm Sat & Sun; M Les Halles) Just north of the gardens snuggling up to the city's old marketplace, now the bustling Forum des Halles, is one of the most beautiful churches in Paris. Majestic, architecturally magnificent and musically outstanding, St-Eustache has made spirits soar for centuries.

LE MARAIS & BASTILLE

Paris' *marais* (marsh) was converted to farmland in the 12th century. In the early 17th century, Henri IV built the place

Royale (today's place des Vosges), turning the area into Paris' most fashionable residential district and attracting wealthy aristocrats who then erected their own luxurious *hôtels particulier* (private mansions).

Centre Pompidou Museum

(Map p64; ☎01 44 78 12 33; www.centrepompidou.fr; place Georges Pompidou, 4e; museum, exhibitions & panorama adult/child €13/free; ⌚11am-9pm Wed-Mon; 📶; Ⓜ Rambuteau) The Pompidou Centre has amazed and delighted visitors ever since it opened in 1977, not just for its outstanding collection of modern art – the largest in Europe – but also for its radical architectural statement. The dynamic and vibrant arts centre delights with its irresistible cocktail of galleries and cutting-edge exhibitions, hands-on workshops, dance performances, cinemas and other entertainment venues. The exterior, with its street performers and fanciful fountains (place Igor Stravinsky), is a fun place to linger.

Musée Picasso Art Museum

(Map p64; ☎01 42 71 25 21; www.museepicassoparis.fr; 5 rue de Thorigny, 3e; admission €11; ⌚11.30am-6pm Tue-Sun, to 9pm 3rd Sat of month; Ⓜ St-Paul or Chemin Vert) One of Paris' most beloved art collections reopened its doors after a massive renovation and much controversy in late 2014. Housed in the stunning, mid-17th-century Hôtel Salé, the Musée Picasso woos art lovers with 5000 drawings, engravings, paintings, ceramic works and sculptures by the *grand maître* (great master) Pablo Picasso (1881–1973). The extraordinary collection was donated to the French government by the artist's heirs in lieu of paying inheritance tax.

Place des Vosges Square

(Map p64; place des Vosges, 4e; Ⓜ St-Paul or Bastille) Inaugurated in 1612 as place Royale and thus Paris' oldest square, place des Vosges is a strikingly elegant ensemble of 36 symmetrical houses with ground-floor arcades, steep slate roofs and large dormer windows arranged around a leafy square with four symmetrical fountains and an 1829 copy of a mounted statue of Louis XIII. The square received its present name in 1800 to honour the Vosges *département* (administrative division) for being the first in France to pay its taxes.

If You Like... Art Museums

If the Louvre and Musée d'Orsay sent you into a wild state of ecstasy, you risk pure unadulterated delirium with this smart selection of lesser-known but equally impressive art addresses.

1 **MUSÉE RODIN**

(Map p64; www.musee-rodin.fr; 79 rue de Varenne, 7e; adult/child museum incl garden €6/free, garden only €2/free; ⌚10am-5.45pm Tue & Thu-Sun, to 8.45pm Wed; Ⓜ Varenne) Auguste Rodin's former studio and garden is one of the most peaceful places in central Paris, and a wonderful spot to contemplate his famous work *The Thinker*.

2 **MUSÉE DE L'ORANGERIE**

(Map p64; www.musee-orangerie.fr; Jardin des Tuileries, 1e; adult/child €9/6.50; ⌚9am-6pm Wed-Mon; Ⓜ Concorde) Located in the Jardin des Tuileries, this museum exhibits important impressionist works, including a series of Monet's *Decorations des Nymphéas* (Water Lilies), plus works by Cézanne, Matisse, Picasso, Renoir, Sisley, Soutine and Utrillo.

3 **DALÍ ESPACE MONTMARTRE**

(Map p72; www.daliparis.com; 11 rue Poulbot, 18e; adult/8-25yr €11.50/6.50; ⌚10am-6pm, to 8pm Jul & Aug; Ⓜ Abbesses) Just west of place du Tertre, this madcap museum houses more than 300 surrealist works by Salvador Dalí (1904–89), including the famous Mae West lips sofa.

4 **LA PINACOTHÈQUE**

(Map p72; www.pinacotheque.com; 28 place de la Madeleine, 8e; adult/child from €12.30/10.80; ⌚10.30am-6pm Sat-Tue & Thu, to 9pm Wed & Fri; Ⓜ Madeleine) This private museum takes a nonlinear approach to art history, with exhibits that range from Mayan masks to artist retrospectives.

Central Paris – South

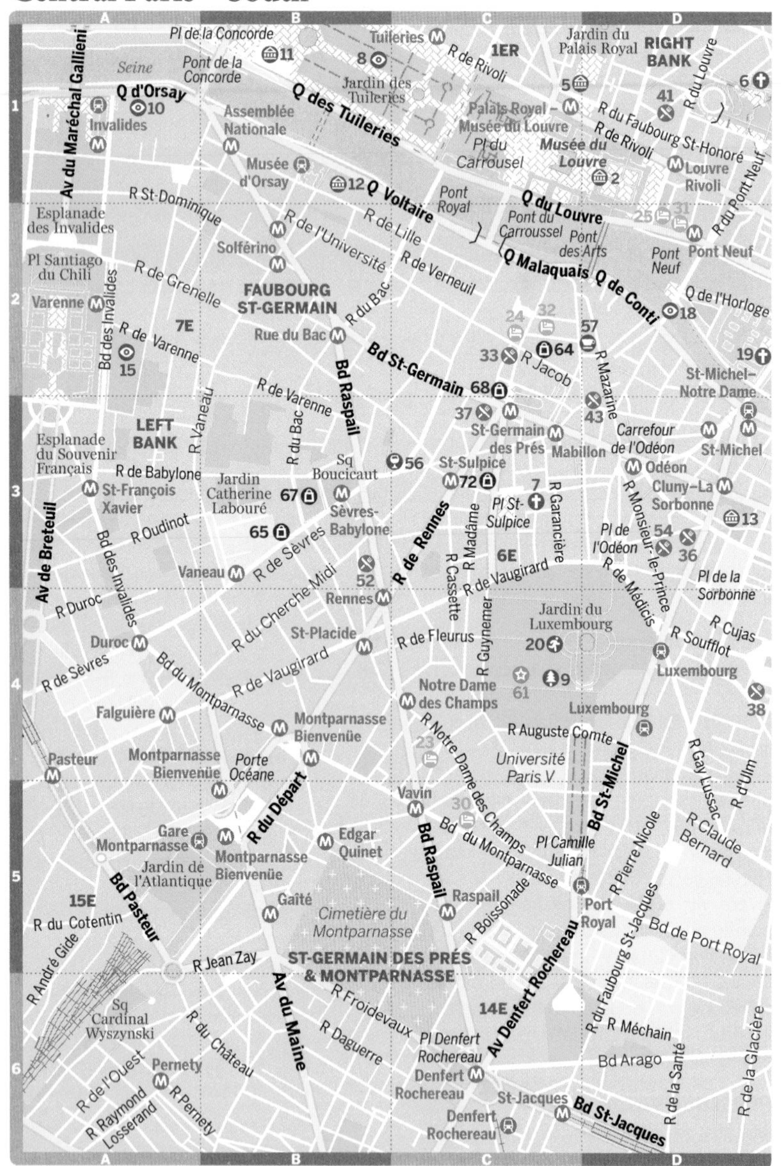

THE ISLANDS

Paris' two inner-city islands could not be more different. The bigger Île de la Cité is full of sights, including Notre Dame, while little Île St-Louis is residential and much quieter, with a scattering of boutiques and restaurants – and legendary ice-cream maker Berthillon.

Sainte-Chapelle Chapel

(Map p64; ☎01 53 40 60 80, concerts 01 42 77 65 65; http://sainte-chapelle.monuments-nationaux.fr; 8 bd du Palais, 1er; adult/child €8.50/free, joint ticket with Conciergerie €12.50; ⏰9.30am-6pm daily, to 9.30pm Wed mid-May–mid-Sep, 9am-5pm daily Nov-Feb; MCité) Try to save Sainte-Chapelle for a sunny day, when Paris' oldest, finest stained glass is at its dazzling best. Enshrined within

Central Paris – South

Don't Miss Sights
1 Cathédrale Notre Dame de Paris E3
2 Musée du Louvre D1

Sights
3 Centre Pompidou E1
4 Conciergerie E2
5 Conseil d'État C1
6 Église St-Eustache D1
7 Église St-Sulpice C3
8 Jardin des Tuileries B1
9 Jardin du Luxembourg C4
10 Ministère des Affaires Étrangères A1
11 Musée de l'Orangerie B1
12 Musée d'Orsay B1
13 Musée National du Moyen Âge D3
14 Musée Picasso F2
15 Musée Rodin A2
16 Panthéon E4
17 Place des Vosges G2
18 Pont Neuf D2
19 Sainte-Chapelle D2

Activities, Courses & Tours
20 Shetland Ponies for Hire C4

Sleeping
21 Five Hotel E5
22 Hôtel Caron de Beaumarchais F2
23 Hôtel Danemark C4
24 Hôtel d'Angleterre C2
25 Hôtel de la Place du Louvre D2
26 Hôtel Emile F2
27 Hôtel Jeanne d'Arc F2
28 Hôtel Minerve E4
29 Hôtel Tiquetonne E1
30 L'Apostrophe C5
31 Le Relais du Louvre D2
32 L'Hôtel C2

Eating
33 Au Pied de Fouet C2
34 Berthillon F3
35 Bofinger G3
36 Bouillon Racine D3
37 Brasserie Lipp C3
38 Café de la Nouvelle Mairie D4
39 Café Saint Régis E3
40 Candelaria G1
41 Claus D1
42 Derrière E1
43 JSFP Traiteur D3
44 L'AOC F3
45 Le Clown Bar G1
46 Le Coupe-Chou E4
47 Le Petit Marché G2
48 Les Pipos E4
49 Marché aux Enfants Rouges F1
50 Marché Bastille G2
51 Marché d'Aligre H3
52 Marché Raspail B3
53 Pirouette E1
54 Polidor D3
55 Sola E3

Drinking & Nightlife
56 Au Sauvignon C3
57 Café La Palette D2
58 Le Baron Rouge H3
Les Deux Magots .... (see 68)

Entertainment
59 Opéra Bastille G3
60 Opéra Bastille Box Office G3
61 Théâtre du Luxembourg C4

Shopping
62 38 Saint Louis F3
63 Chez Hélène G2
64 Gab & Jo C2
65 La Grande Épicerie de Paris B3
66 La Manufacture de Chocolat H2
67 Le Bon Marché B3
68 Le Chocolat Alain Ducasse C2
69 Marché Mouffetard E5
70 Merci G1
71 Paris Rendez-Vous E2
72 Pierre Hermé C3
73 Shakespeare & Company E3

the **Palais de Justice** (Law Courts), this gemlike Holy Chapel is Paris' most exquisite Gothic monument. Ste-Chapelle was built in just six years (compared with nearly 200 years for Notre Dame) and consecrated in 1248.

The chapel was conceived by Louis IX to house his personal collection of holy relics, including the famous Holy Crown (now in Notre Dame).

Conciergerie Monument

(Map p64; www.monuments-nationaux.fr; 2 bd du Palais, 1er; adult/child €8.50/free, joint ticket with Sainte-Chapelle €12.50; 9.30am-6pm; M Cité) A royal palace in the 14th century, the Conciergerie later became a prison. During the Reign of Terror (1793–94) alleged enemies of the Revolution were incarcerated here before being brought before the Revolutionary Tribunal next door in the **Palais de Justice**. Top-billing exhibitions take place in the beautiful, Rayonnant Gothic **Salle des Gens**

d'Armes, Europe's largest surviving medieval hall.

Pont Neuf — Bridge

(Map p64; M Pont Neuf) Paris' oldest bridge has linked the western end of Île de la Cité with both river banks since 1607, when the king inaugurated it by crossing the bridge on a white stallion. The occasion is commemorated by an equestrian **statue of Henry IV**, known to his subjects as the Vert Galant ('jolly rogue' or 'dirty old man', perspective depending).

View the bridge's seven arches, decorated with humorous and grotesque figures of barbers, dentists, pickpockets, loiterers etc, from a spot along the river or afloat.

LATIN QUARTER

The centre of Parisian higher education since the Middle Ages, the Latin Quarter is so called because conversation between students and professors until the Revolution was in Latin. It still has a large population of students and academics affiliated with institutions that include the world-famous Sorbonne university. To the southeast is the city's beautiful botanic gardens, the **Jardin des Plantes.**

Musée National du Moyen Âge — Museum

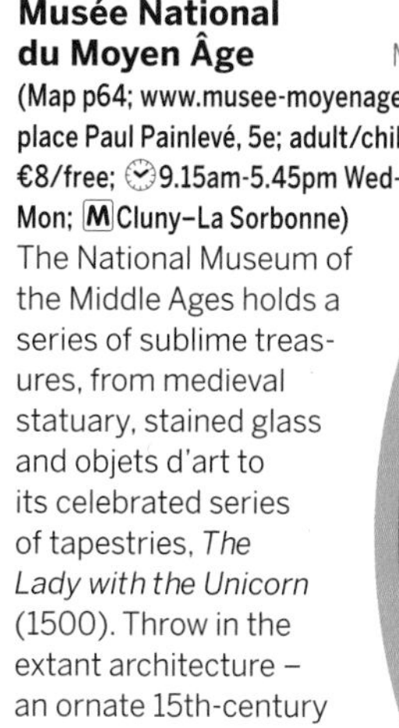

(Map p64; www.musee-moyenage.fr; 6 place Paul Painlevé, 5e; adult/child €8/free; 9.15am-5.45pm Wed-Mon; M Cluny–La Sorbonne) The National Museum of the Middle Ages holds a series of sublime treasures, from medieval statuary, stained glass and objets d'art to its celebrated series of tapestries, *The Lady with the Unicorn* (1500). Throw in the extant architecture – an ornate 15th-century mansion (the Hôtel de Cluny), and the much older *frigidarium* (cold room) of an enormous Roman-era bathhouse – and you have one of Paris' top small museums. Outside, four medieval gardens grace the northeastern corner; more bathhouse remains are to the west.

Panthéon — Mausoleum

(Map p64; www.monum.fr; place du Panthéon, 5e; adult/child €7.50/free; 10am-6.30pm Apr-Sep, to 6pm Oct-Mar; M Maubert-Mutualité, Cardinal Lemoine or RER Luxembourg) Overlooking the city from its Left Bank perch, the Panthéon's stately neoclassical dome stands out as one of the most recognizable icons in the Parisian skyline. Originally a church and now a mausoleum, it has served since 1791 as the resting place of some of France's greatest thinkers, including Voltaire, Rousseau, Braille and Hugo. An architectural masterpiece, the interior is impressively vast (if slightly soulless) and certainly worth a wander. The dome is closed for renovations through 2015 (other structural work will continue through 2022).

Panthéon

BRUNO DE HOGUES/GETTY IMAGES ©

Don't Miss

Musée du Louvre

Few art galleries are as prized or daunting as the Musée du Louvre, Paris' pièce de résistance. This is one of the world's largest and most diverse museums, home to more than 35,000 works of art – from ancient antiquities to priceless masterpieces by da Vinci, Michelangelo, Rembrandt and many more.

Map p64

☎ 01 40 20 53 17

www.louvre.fr

rue de Rivoli & quai des Tuileries, 1er

adult/child €12/free

⏲ 9am-6pm Mon, Thu, Sat & Sun, to 9.45pm Wed & Fri

Ⓜ Palais Royal–Musée du Louvre

Key Exhibits

The vast Palais du Louvre originally served as a fortress built by Philippe-Auguste in the 12th century. It was rebuilt in the mid-16th century as a royal residence, and the Revolutionary Convention turned it into a national museum in 1793.

Tickets are valid for the whole day, so you can come and go as you please.

For many, the star attraction is Leonardo da Vinci's *La Joconde*, better known as *Mona Lisa* (Room 6, 1st floor, Denon). This entire section of the 1st floor of the Denon Wing is hung with masterpieces – rooms 75 and 77 have enormous French paintings from Ingres, Delacroix *(Liberty Leading the People)* and Géricault *(The Raft of the Medusa)*, while rooms 1, 3, 5 and 8 contain transcendent pieces by Raphael, Titian, Botticini and Botticcelli.

Also of note are the gilded-to-the-max Napoleon III Apartments (1st floor, Richelieu), Dutch masters Vermeer (Room 38, 2nd floor, Richelieu) and Rembrandt (Room 31, 2nd floor, Richelieu), and 18th- and 19th-century French painting collection (2nd floor, Sully).

Guided Tours

The Louvre is huge, so consider taking one of the self-guided thematic trails (1½ to three hours; download trail brochures in advance from the website) ranging from a Louvre masterpieces trail to the art of eating, plus several for kids. Even better are the Louvre's self-paced multimedia guides (€5). More-formal, English-language guided tours depart from the Hall Napoléon, which has free English-language maps.

La Grande Pyramide

The main entrance is through the 21m-high Grande Pyramide, a glass pyramid designed by the architect IM Pei. If you don't have a Museum Pass (which gives you priority), avoid the longest queues (for security) outside the pyramid by entering the Louvre complex via the underground shopping centre Carrousel du Louvre.

Local Knowledge

Musée du Louvre

BY NIKO SALVATORE MELISSANO, MUSÉE DU LOUVRE

1 WINGED VICTORY OF SAMOTHRACE

It's impossible to reduce the collections of the Louvre to a hit parade... A definite highlight is the *Winged Victory of Samothrace* atop the Daru Staircase (1st floor, Denon Wing). I adore her wings. I just cannot stop contemplating her from all angles. She is, moreover, very photogenic.

2 THE SEATED SCRIBE & MONA LISA

I could admire this statuette (Room 22, 1st floor, Sully Wing) from the ancient Egyptian empire for hours: the face of the scribe (probably that of Saqqara), like his posture (a little 'yoga') and his deep stare, say several things to me: serenity, strength of character, eternal wisdom. Then there is *La Joconde* (*Mona Lisa*; Room 6, 1st floor, Salle de la Joconde, Denon Wing) and that amazing fascination of why and how she intrigues spirits with her mysteries.

3 COUR KHORSABAD

With its enormous human-headed winged bulls, this courtyard on the ground floor of the Richelieu Wing is a jump in time into the cradle of one of the oldest cultures in the world: Mesopotamia. During the region of King Sargon II in the 8th century, these bulls, carved from alabaster, guarded the Assyrian city and palace of Khorsabad (northern Iraq). Their bearded faces with bull ears and a heavy tiara of horns wore a benevolent smile. A mix of force and serenity, perfectly balanced despite their colossal size, these protective monsters with four or five paws were a measure of the power of the Assyrian Empire in its heyday.

4 GRANDE GALERIE

It's a real highlight, this gallery (1st floor, Denon Wing), with masterpieces from the great masters of the Italian Renaissance: Leonardo de Vinci, Raphael, Arcimboldo, Andrea Mantegna...

The Louvre

A HALF-DAY TOUR

Successfully visiting the Louvre is a fine art. Its complex labyrinth of galleries and staircases spiralling three wings and four floors renders discovery a snakes-and-ladders experience. Initiate yourself with this three-hour itinerary – a playful mix of Mona Lisa obvious and up-to-the-minute unexpected.

Arriving by the stunning main entrance, pick up colour-coded floor plans at the lower-ground-floor **information desk** ❶ beneath IM Pei's glass pyramid, ride the escalator up to the Sully Wing and swap passport for multimedia guide (there are limited descriptions in the galleries) at the wing entrance.

The Louvre is as much about spectacular architecture as masterly art. To appreciate this zip up and down Sully's Escalier Henri II to admire **Venus de Milo** ❷, then up parallel Escalier Henri IV to the palatial displays in **Cour Khorsabad** ❸. Cross room 1 to find the escalator up to the 1st floor and staircase-as-art **L'Esprit d'Escalier** ❹. Next traverse 25 consecutive galleries (thank you, floor plan!) to flip conventional contemplation on its head with Cy Twombly's **The Ceiling** ❺, and the hypnotic **Winged Victory of Samothrace sculpture** ❻ – just two rooms away – which brazenly insists on being admired from all angles. End with the impossibly famous **The Raft of Medusa** ❼, **Mona Lisa** ❽ and **Virgin & Child** ❾.

TOP TIPS

➡ **Floor Plans** Don't even consider entering the Louvre's maze of galleries without a Plan/Information Louvre brochure, free from the information desk in the Hall Napoléon

➡ **Crowd dodgers** The Denon Wing is always packed; visit on late nights Wednesday or Friday or trade Denon in for the notably quieter Richelieu Wing

➡ **2nd floor** Not for first-timers: save its more specialist works for subsequent visits

MISSION MONA LISA

If you just want to venerate the Louvre's most famous lady, use the Porte des Lions entrance (closed Tuesday and Friday), from where it's a five-minute walk. Go up one flight of stairs and through rooms 26, 14 and 13 to the Grande Galerie and adjoining room 6.

L'Esprit d'Escalier
Escalier Lefuel, Richelieu
Discover the 'Spirit of the Staircase' through François Morellet's contemporary stained glass, which casts new light on old stone. **DETOUR»** Napoleon III's gorgeous gilt apartments.

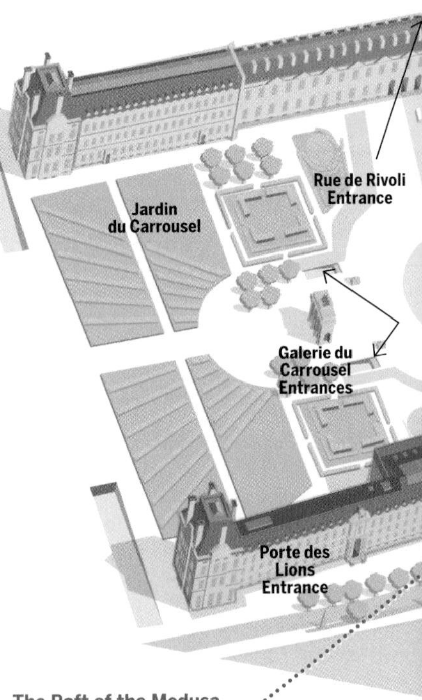

The Raft of the Medusa
Room 77, 1st Floor, Denon
Decipher the politics behind French romanticism in Théodore Géricault's *Raft of the Medusa.*

DEA/G.DAGLI ORTI/GETTY IMAGES ©

CY TWOMBLY FOUNDATION/GETTY IMAGES ©

Cour Khorsabad

Ground Floor, Richelieu

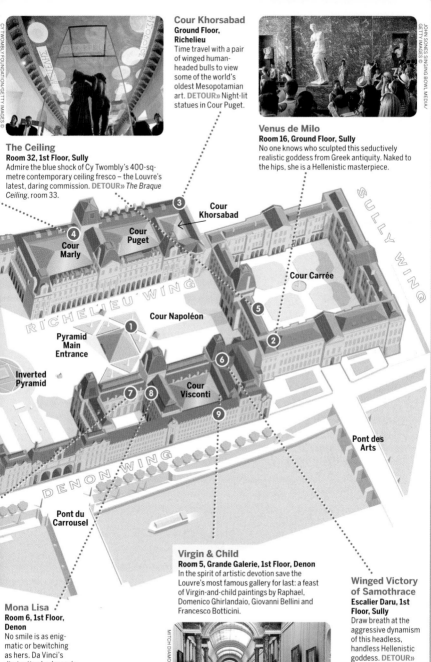

Time travel with a pair of winged human-headed bulls to view some of the world's oldest Mesopotamian art. **DETOUR»** Night-lit statues in Cour Puget.

JOHN SONES SINGING BOWL MEDIA/GETTY IMAGES ©

Venus de Milo

Room 16, Ground Floor, Sully

No one knows who sculpted this seductively realistic goddess from Greek antiquity. Naked to the hips, she is a Hellenistic masterpiece.

The Ceiling

Room 32, 1st Floor, Sully

Admire the blue shock of Cy Twombly's 400-sq-metre contemporary ceiling fresco – the Louvre's latest, daring commission. **DETOUR»** *The Braque Ceiling*, room 33.

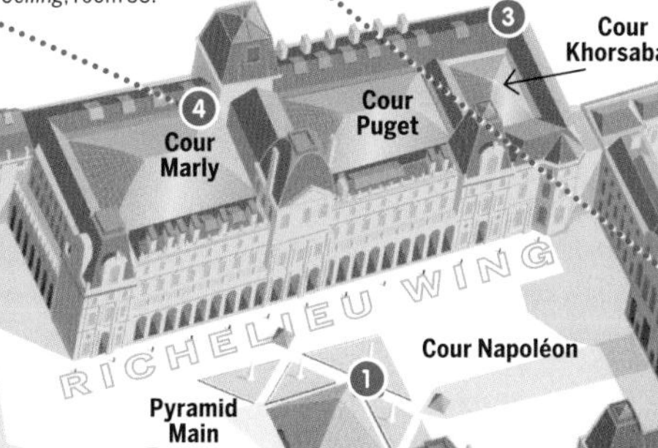

Virgin & Child

Room 5, Grande Galerie, 1st Floor, Denon

In the spirit of artistic devotion save the Louvre's most famous gallery for last: a feast of Virgin-and-child paintings by Raphael, Domenico Ghirlandaio, Giovanni Bellini and Francesco Botticini.

Mona Lisa

Room 6, 1st Floor, Denon

No smile is as enigmatic or bewitching as hers. Da Vinci's diminutive *La Joconde* hangs opposite the largest painting in the Louvre – sumptuous, fellow Italian Renaissance artwork *The Wedding at Cana*.

MITCH DIAMOND/GETTY IMAGES ©

Winged Victory of Samothrace

Escalier Daru, 1st Floor, Sully

Draw breath at the aggressive dynamism of this headless, handless Hellenistic goddess. **DETOUR»** The razzle-dazzle of the Apollo Gallery's crown jewels.

Central Paris – North

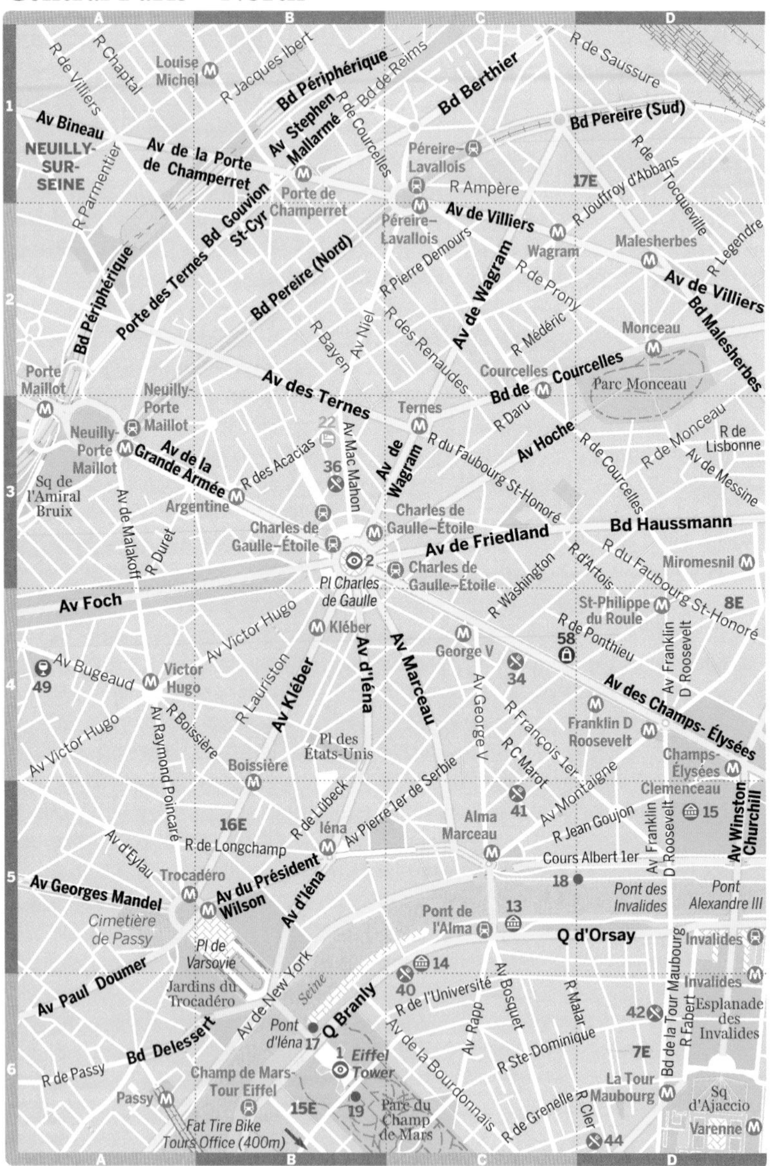

ST-GERMAIN & LES INVALIDES

Despite gentrification since its early 20th century bohemian days, there remains a startling cinematic quality to this soulful part of the Left Bank, where artists, writers, actors and musicians cross paths and *la vie germanopratine* (St-Germain life) is *belle*.

Musée d'Orsay Museum

(Map p64; www.musee-orsay.fr; 62 rue de Lille, 7e; adult/child €11/free; 9.30am-6pm Tue, Wed & Fri-Sun, to 9.45pm Thu; M Assemblée Nationale or RER Musée d'Orsay) Recently renovated to incorporate richly coloured walls and increased exhibition space, the home of France's national collection from the impressionist, postimpressionist and art nouveau movements spanning the

Central Paris – North

Don't Miss Sights
1 Eiffel Tower ... B6

Sights
2 Arc de Triomphe ... B3
3 Basilique du Sacré-Cœur ... H1
4 Cimetière de Montmartre ... F1
5 Cimetière de Montmartre Entrance & Conservation Office ... F1
6 Clos Montmartre ... G1
7 Dalí Espace Montmartre ... G1
8 Galerie des Galeries ... F3
9 Jardin du Palais Royal ... G5
10 La Pinacothèque ... F4
11 Musée de l'Érotisme ... G2
12 Musée de Montmartre ... G1
13 Musée des Égouts de Paris ... C5
14 Musée du Quai Branly ... C5
15 Palais de la Découverte ... D5
16 Place de la Concorde ... E5

Activities, Courses & Tours
17 Bateaux Parisiens ... B6
18 Bateaux-Mouches ... D5
19 Fat Tire Bike Tours ... B6
20 L'Open Tour ... F4

Sleeping
21 Edgar ... H4
22 Hidden Hotel ... B3
23 Hôtel Amour ... G2
24 Hôtel des Arts ... G1
25 Hôtel France Albion ... G3
26 Hôtel Langlois ... G3
27 Hôtel Vivienne ... G4
28 Loft ... F2

Eating
29 Blend ... H5
30 Chez Plume ... G3
31 Cul de Poule ... G2
32 Floquifil ... H4
33 Frenchie ... H4
Frenchie To Go ... (see 33)
34 Ladurée ... C4
35 L'Ardoise ... F5
36 Le Hide ... B3
37 Le Miroir ... G2
38 Le Pantruche ... G2
39 Le Petit Trianon ... H2
40 Les Ombres ... C6
L'Office ... (see 43)
41 Philippe & Jean-Pierre ... C5
42 Restaurant David Toutain ... D6
43 Richer ... H3
44 Rue Cler ... D6
45 Verjus ... G5
Verjus Bar à Vins ... (see 45)

Drinking & Nightlife
46 Angelina ... F5
47 Experimental Cocktail Club ... H5
48 Harry's New York Bar ... F4
49 St James Paris ... A4

Entertainment
50 Au Lapin Agile ... G1
51 Moulin Rouge ... F2
52 Palais Garnier ... F4
53 Palais Garnier Box Office ... F4

Shopping
54 Didier Ludot ... G5
55 Galeries Lafayette ... F3
56 Galeries Lafayette - Home Design ... F3
57 Galeries Lafayette - Men's Store ... F3
58 Guerlain ... C4
59 La Petite Robe Noire ... G5

1840s and 1914 is the glorious former Gare d'Orsay railway station – itself an art nouveau showpiece – where a roll-call of masters and their world-famous works are on display.

At the top of every visitor's must-see list is the museum's painting collections, centred on the world's largest collection of impressionist and post-impressionist art.

Église St-Sulpice — Church

(Map p64; http://pss75.fr/saint-sulpice-paris; place St-Sulpice, 6e; ⏲7.30am-7.30pm; Ⓜ St-Sulpice) In 1646 work started on the twin-towered Church of St Sulpicius, lined inside with 21 side chapels, and it took six architects 150 years to finish. What draws most visitors isn't its striking Italianate facade with two rows of superimposed columns, its Counter-Reformation-influenced neoclassical decor or even its frescoes by Eugène Delecroix, but its setting for a murderous scene in Dan Brown's *The Da Vinci Code*.

You can hear the monumental, 1781-built organ during 10.30am Mass on Sunday or the occasional Sunday-afternoon concert.

Jardin du Luxembourg Park

(Map p64; numerous entrances; ⏲hours vary; Ⓜ St-Sulpice, Rennes, Notre Dame des Champs or RER Luxembourg) This inner-city oasis of formal terraces, chestnut groves and lush lawns has a special place in Parisians' hearts. Napoléon dedicated the 23 hectares of the Luxembourg Gardens to the children of Paris, and many residents spent their childhood prodding 1920s wooden **sailboats (per 30min €3; ⏲Apr-Oct)** with long sticks on the octagonal **Grand Bassin** pond, watching puppets perform Punch & Judy–type shows at the **Théâtre du Luxembourg (Map p64; www.marionnettesduluxembourg.fr; tickets €4.80; ⏲usually 3.30pm Wed, 11am & 3.30pm Sat & Sun, daily during school holidays; Ⓜ Notre Dame des Champs)**, and riding the *carrousel* (merry-go-round) or **ponies (Map p64)**.

BOIS DE BOULOGNE

The 845-hectare **Bois de Boulogne (bd Maillot; Ⓜ Porte Maillot)** owes its informal layout to Baron Haussmann, who, inspired by London's Hyde Park, planted 400,000 trees here in the 19th century. Along with various gardens and other sights, the park has 15km of cycle paths and 28km of bridle paths through 125 hectares of forested land.

It's also home to one of the capital's most high-profile new contemporary art galleries – the **Fondation Louis Vuitton (www.fondationlouisvuitton.fr; av du Mahatma Gandhi, 16e; Ⓜ Les Sablons)**, designed by Frank Gehry, with 12 curvaceous giant 'sails' crafted from 3600 glass panels.

Be warned that the area becomes a distinctly adult playground after dark, especially along the Allée de Longchamp running northeast from the Étang des Réservoirs (Reservoirs Pond), where all kinds of prostitutes cruise for clients.

The Bois de Boulogne is served by metro lines 1 (Porte Maillot, Les Sablons), 2 (Porte Dauphine), 9 (Michel-Ange-Auteuil) and 10 (Michel-Ange-Auteuil, Porte d'Auteuil), and the RER C (Avenue Foch, Avenue Henri Martin). Vélib' stations are found near most of the park entrances, but not within the park itself.

If You Like... Family Travel

If you're in town with the kids, you're gonna love these dependable family outings. For the lowdown on current exhibitions and events with kids in mind see *Pariscope* and *L'Officiel des Spectacles*.

1 **CITÉ DES SCIENCES**
(☎01 56 43 20 20; www.cite-sciences.fr; Parc de la Villette, 19e; adult/under 26yr €9/6; ⏲10am-6pm Tue-Sat, to 7pm Sun; Ⓜ Porte de la Villette) This is the city's top museum for kids, with three floors of hands-on exhibits for children aged two and up, plus two special-effects cinemas, a planetarium and a retired submarine. The only drawback is that each exhibit has a separate admission fee (though some combined tickets do exist), so you'll have to do some pretrip research in order to figure out what's most appropriate.

2 **PALAIS DE LA DÉCOUVERTE**
(Map p72; www.palais-decouverte.fr; av Franklin D Roosevelt, 8e; adult/child €9/6; ⏲9.30am-6pm Tue-Sat, 10am-7pm Sun; Ⓜ Champs-Élysées–Clemenceau) Attached to the Grand Palais, this children's science museum has excellent temporary exhibits (eg moving lifelike dinosaurs) as well as a hands-on, interactive permanent collection focusing on astronomy, biology, physics and the like. Some of the older exhibits have French-only explanations, but overall this is a dependable family outing.

3 **MUSÉE DES ÉGOUTS DE PARIS**
(Map p72; place de la Résistance, 7e; adult/child €4.40/3.60; ⏲11am-5pm Sat-Wed May-Sep, 11am-4pm Sat-Wed Oct-Dec & Feb-Apr; Ⓜ Alma Marceau or RER Pont de l'Alma) Raw sewage flows beneath your feet as you walk through 480m of odoriferous tunnels in this working sewer museum. Exhibitions cover the development of Paris' waste water–disposal system, including its resident rats (there's an estimated one sewer rat for every Parisian above ground). Enter via a rectangular maintenance hole topped with a kiosk across the street from 93 quai d'Orsay, 7e.

Detour: Canal St-Martin

The shaded towpaths of the tranquil, 4.5km-long Canal St-Martin are a wonderful place for a romantic stroll or a bike ride.

Dug out in 1825, the canal was a major cargo thoroughfare by the time Marcel Carné's 1938 film *Hôtel du Nord* was set in the canalside hotel – now a **cafe/bar** (www.hoteldunord.org; 102 quai de Jemmapes, 10e; 9am-1.30am; ; M Jacques Bonsergent) – of the same name. The canal's fortunes fell in the 1960s when barge transportation declined. It was slated to be concreted over and turned into a roadway until local residents rallied to save it. When the title character of *Amélie* skipped stones here in 2001, the cheap rents and quaint setting were just starting to lure artists, designers and students, who set up artists' collectives, vintage and offbeat boutiques, and a bevy of neo-retro cafes and bars.

Today Canal St-Martin is the centre of Paris' *bobo* (bohemian bourgeois) life, but maritime legacies endure, including old swing-bridges that still pivot 90 degrees when barges pass through the canal's double-locks. Take a **canal boat cruise** (www.canauxrama.com; adult/student & senior/4-12yr €16/12/8.50) to savour the full flavour.

Tours

BICYCLE

Fat Tire Bike Tours Cycling

(Map p72; 01 56 58 10 54; www.fattirebiketours.com) Day and night bike tours of the city, both in central Paris and further afield to Versailles and Monet's garden in Giverny.

BOAT

Bateaux-Mouches Boat

(Map p72; 01 42 25 96 10; www.bateaux-mouches.com; Port de la Conférence, 8e; adult/child €13.50/5.50; Apr-Dec; M Alma Marceau) The largest river cruise company in Paris and a favourite with tour groups. Cruises (70 minutes) run regularly from 10.15am to 11pm April to September and 13 times a day between 11am and 9pm the rest of the year. Commentary is in French and English. It's located on the Right Bank, just east of the Pont de l'Alma.

Bateaux Parisiens Boat

(Map p72; www.bateauxparisiens.com; Port de la Bourdonnais, 7e; adult/child €14/6; M Bir Hakeim or RER Pont de l'Alma) This vast operation runs 1½-hour river circuits (every 30 minutes from 10am to 10.30pm April to September, hourly 10am to 10pm October to March), with recorded commentary in 13 languages and a host of themed lunch/dinner cruises. It has two locations: one by the Eiffel Tower, the other south of Notre Dame.

BUS

L'Open Tour Bus Tour

(Map p72; www.parisopentour.com; 1-day pass adult/child €31/16) Hop-on, hop-off bus tours aboard open-deck buses with four different circuits and 50 stops to jump on/off at – top for a whirlwind city tour.

WALKING

Parisien d'un jour – Paris Greeters Walking Tour

(www.parisgreeters.fr; tours by donation) See Paris through local eyes with these two- to three-hour city tours. Volunteers – knowledgeable Parisians who are passionate about their city – lead groups (maximum six people) to their favourite spots. Minimum two weeks' notice needed.

THATLou Tours

(06 86 13 32 12; www.thatlou.com; per person excluding admission fees Louvre/d'Orsay €25/35) Absolutely inspirational, THATLou headed up by bilingual Daisy Plume organises

PAWEL LIBERA/GETTY IMAGES ©

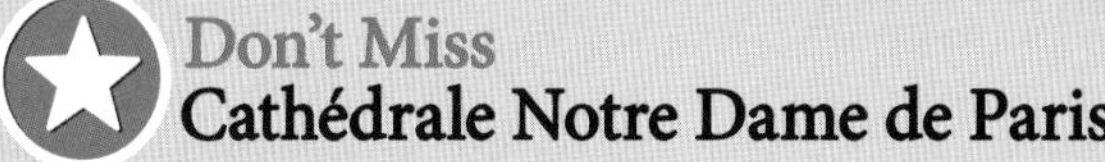

Don't Miss
Cathédrale Notre Dame de Paris

Notre Dame, Paris' most visited unticketed site with upwards of 14 million visitors a year, is a masterpiece of French Gothic architecture. It was the focus of Catholic Paris for seven centuries, its vast interior accommodating 6000-plus worshippers.

Highlights include its three spectacular **rose windows**, **treasury**, and bell **towers** which can be climbed. From the North Tower, 400-odd steps spiral to the top of the western facade, where there's a spectacular view of Paris.

Construction of Cathédrale Notre Dame was begun in 1163 according to the design of Bishop Maurice de Sully and largely completed by the early 14th century. The cathedral was badly damaged during the Revolution; architect Eugène Emmanuel Viollet-le-Duc carried out extensive renovations between 1845 and 1864.

Inside, the **central choir**, with its carved wooden stalls and statues representing the Passion of the Christ, is noteworthy. The **trésor** (treasury) in the southeastern transept contains artwork, liturgical objects and first-class relics.

Notre Dame is the heart of Paris – distances from Paris to every part of metropolitan France are measured from **place du Parvis Notre Dame**, the vast square in front of the Cathedral of Our Lady of Paris. A bronze star across the street from the cathedral's main entrance marks the exact location of **Point Zéro des Routes de France**.

One of the best views of the cathedral is from **square Jean XXIII**, the little park behind the cathedral, where you can better appreciate the forest of ornate **flying buttresses** that encircle the chancel and support its walls and roof.

NEED TO KNOW

Map p64; ☎ 01 53 10 07 00; www.cathedraledeparis.com; 6 place du Parvis Notre Dame, 4e; cathedral free, towers adult/child €8.50/free, treasury €2/1; ⏰ cathedral 7.45am-6.45pm Mon-Sat, to 7.15pm Sun, towers 10am-6.30pm, to 11pm Fri & Sat Jul & Aug; Ⓜ Cité

Notre Dame

TIMELINE

1160 Maurice de Sully becomes bishop of Paris. Mission: to grace growing Paris with a lofty new cathedral.

1182–90 The **choir with double ambulatory** ❶ is finished and work starts on the nave and side chapels.

1200–50 The **west façade** ❷, with rose window, three portals and two soaring towers, goes up. Everyone is stunned.

1345 Some 180 years after the foundation stone was laid, the Cathédrale de Notre Dame is complete. It is dedicated to notre dame (our lady), the Virgin Mary.

1789 Revolutionaries smash the original **Gallery of Kings** ❸, pillage the cathedral and melt all its bells except the great bell Emmanuel. The cathedral becomes a Temple of Reason then a warehouse.

1831 Victor Hugo's novel *The Hunchback of Notre Dame* inspires new interest in the half-ruined Gothic cathedral.

1845–50 Architect Viollet-le-Duc undertakes its restoration. Twenty-eight new kings are sculpted for the west façade. The heavily decorated **portals** ❹ and **spire** ❺ are reconstructed. The neo-Gothic **treasury** ❻ is built.

1860 The area in front of Notre Dame is cleared to create the parvis, an alfresco classroom where Parisians can learn a catechism illustrated on sculpted stone portals.

1935 A rooster bearing part of the relics of the Crown of Thorns, St Denis and St Geneviève is put on top of the cathedral spire to protect those who pray inside.

1991 The architectural masterpiece of Notre Dame and its Seine-side riverbanks become a Unesco World Heritage Site.

2013 Notre Dame celebrates 850 years since construction began with a bevy of new bells and restoration works.

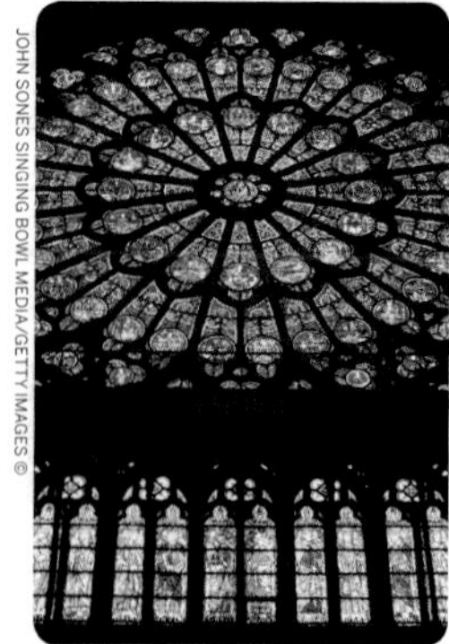

Virgin & Child

Spot all 37 artworks representing the Virgin Mary. Pilgrims have revered the pearly-cream sculpture of her in the sanctuary since the 14th century. Light a devotional candle and write some words to the *Livre de Vie* (Book of Life).

North Rose Window

See prophets, judges, kings and priests venerate Mary in vivid blue and violet glass, one of three beautiful rose blooms (1225–70), each almost 10m in diameter.

Flying Buttresses

❶

Choir Screen

No part of the cathedral weaves biblical tales more evocatively than these ornate wooden panels, carved in the 14th century after the Black Death killed half the country's population. The faintly gaudy colours were restored in the 1960s.

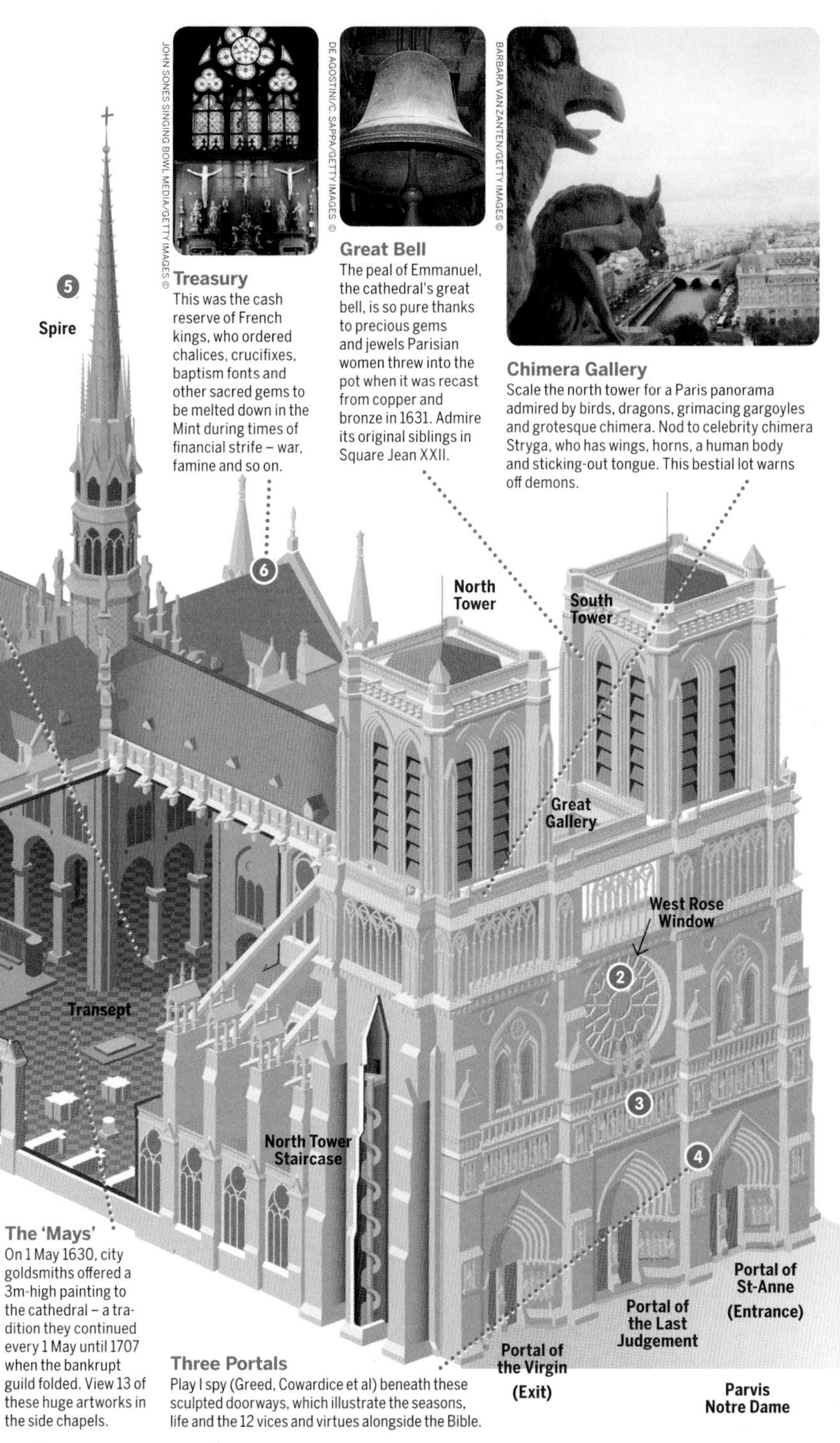

JOHN SONES SINGING BOWL MEDIA/GETTY IMAGES ©
DE AGOSTINI/C. SAPPA/GETTY IMAGES ©
BARBARA VAN ZANTEN/GETTY IMAGES ©
Treasury
This was the cash reserve of French kings, who ordered chalices, crucifixes, baptism fonts and other sacred gems to be melted down in the Mint during times of financial strife – war, famine and so on.
Great Bell
The peal of Emmanuel, the cathedral's great bell, is so pure thanks to precious gems and jewels Parisian women threw into the pot when it was recast from copper and bronze in 1631. Admire its original siblings in Square Jean XXII.
Chimera Gallery
Scale the north tower for a Paris panorama admired by birds, dragons, grimacing gargoyles and grotesque chimera. Nod to celebrity chimera Stryga, who has wings, horns, a human body and sticking-out tongue. This bestial lot warns off demons.
5
Spire
6
North Tower
South Tower
Great Gallery
West Rose Window
2
3
4
Transept
North Tower Staircase
The 'Mays'
On 1 May 1630, city goldsmiths offered a 3m-high painting to the cathedral – a tradition they continued every 1 May until 1707 when the bankrupt guild folded. View 13 of these huge artworks in the side chapels.
Three Portals
Play I spy (Greed, Cowardice et al) beneath these sculpted doorways, which illustrate the seasons, life and the 12 vices and virtues alongside the Bible.
Portal of the Virgin (Exit)
Portal of the Last Judgement
Portal of St-Anne (Entrance)
Parvis Notre Dame

treasure hunts in English or French for groups of two people or more in the Louvre, Musée d'Orsay (THATd'Or) and streets of the Latin Quarter (THATrue). Participants form teams and play alone or against another team, and have to photograph themselves in front of 20 to 30 works of art (treasure). Hunts typically last 90 minutes to two hours.

Paris Walks Walking Tour
(☎01 48 09 21 40; www.paris-walks.com; adult/child €12/8) Long established and highly rated by our readers, Paris Walks offers two-hour thematic walking tours (art, fashion, chocolate, the French Revolution etc).

Sleeping

Paris has a huge choice of accommodation, from hostels through to deluxe hotels, some of which rank among the world's finest. Yet, although the city has in excess of 1500 establishments, you'll still need to book well ahead during the warmer months (April to October) and all public and school holidays.

EIFFEL TOWER AREA & 16E

Hôtel Vic Eiffel Boutique Hotel €
(www.hotelviceiffel.com; 92 bd Garibaldi, 15e; s/d from €99/109; 📶; M Sèvres-Lecourbe) Outstanding value for money, this pristine hotel with chic orange and oyster-grey rooms (two are wheelchair accessible) is a short walk from the Eiffel Tower, with the metro on the doorstep. Budget-priced Classic rooms are small but perfectly functional; midrange Superior and Privilege rooms offer increased space. Friendly staff go out of their way to help.

Sublim Eiffel Design Hotel €€
(☎01 40 65 95 95; www.sublimeiffel.com; 94 bd Garibaldi, 15e; d from €140; ❄📶; M Sèvres-Lecourbe) There's no forgetting what city you're in with the Eiffel Tower motifs in reception and rooms (along with Parisian street-map carpets and metro-tunnel-shaped bedheads) plus glittering tower views from upper-floor windows. Edgy design elements also include cobblestone staircase carpeting (there's also a lift/elevator) and, fittingly in *la ville lumière*, technicoloured in-room fibre optic lighting. The small wellness centre/hammam offers massages.

ÉTOILE & CHAMPS-ÉLYSÉES

Hidden Hotel Boutique Hotel €€€
(Map p72; ☎01 40 55 03 57; www.hidden-hotel.com; 28 rue de l'Arc de Triomphe, 17e; d €389-454; ❄@📶; M Charles de Gaulle-Étoile) 🍃 The Hidden is one of the Champs-Élysées' best secrets. It's serene, stylish, reasonably spacious, and it even sports green credentials: the earth-coloured tones are the result of natural pigments (no paint), and all rooms feature handmade wooden furniture, stone basins, and linen curtains surrounding

Paris at night
PARIS/ALAMY ©

the beds. The queen-size Emotion rooms are among the most popular.

LOUVRE & LES HALLES

Hôtel Tiquetonne Hotel €

(Map p64; ☎01 42 36 94 58; www.hoteltiquetonne.fr; 6 rue Tiquetonne, 2e; d €65, with shared shower €50; 📶; Ⓜ Étienne Marcel) What heart-warmingly good value this 45-room cheapie is. This serious, well-tended address has been in the hotel business since the 1900s and is much-loved by a loyal clientele of all ages. Rooms range across seven floors, are spick and span, and sport an inoffensive mix of vintage decor – roughly 1930s to 1980s –with brand new bathrooms and parquet flooring in recently renovated rooms.

Hôtel Vivienne Hotel €

(Map p72; ☎01 42 33 13 26; www.hotel-vivienne.com; 40 rue Vivienne, 2e; d €108-150, tr & q €160; @📶👪; Ⓜ Grands Boulevards) This stylish two-star hotel is amazingly good value for Paris. While the 45 rooms are not huge, they have all the mod cons; some even boast little balconies. Family rooms accommodate up to two children on a sofa bed.

Hôtel de la Place du Louvre Boutique Hotel €€

(Map p64; ☎01 42 33 78 68; www.paris-hotel-place-du-louvre.com; 21 rue des Prêtres St-Germain l'Auxerrois, 1er; d €135-205; ❄📶; Ⓜ Pont Neuf) Not to be confused with the **Relais du Louvre (Map p64; ☎01 40 41 96 42; www.relaisdulouvre.com; s €135-180, d €175-263, tr €235-263; ❄📶; Ⓜ Pont Neuf)** next door, this fairly recent addition to the Parisian hotel scene is warmly welcomed. It has just 20 rooms split across five floors – a couple on each floor are lucky enough to ogle the majestic Louvre across the street.

Edgar Boutique Hotel €€

(Map p72; ☎01 40 41 05 19; www.edgarparis.com; 31 rue d'Alexandrie, 2e; d €235-295; ❄📶; Ⓜ Strasbourg St-Denis) Twelve playful rooms, each decorated by a different team of artists or designers, await the lucky few who secure a reservation at this former convent/seamstress workshop. The Milagros room conjures up all the magic of the Far West, while Dream echoes the rich imagination of childhood with surrealist installations. Breakfast is served in the popular downstairs restaurant, and the hidden tree-shaded square is a fabulous location.

Detour: Cimetière du Père Lachaise

The world's most visited cemetery, **Cimetière du Père Lachaise (☎01 43 70 70 33; www.pere-lachaise.com; 16 rue du Repos & bd de Ménilmontant, 20e; ⏰8am-6pm Mon-Fri, 8.30am-6pm Sat, 9am-6pm Sun; Ⓜ Père Lachaise or Gambetta) FREE**, opened its one-way doors in 1804. Its 69,000 ornate, even ostentatious, tombs of the rich and/or famous form a verdant, 44-hectare sculpture garden. Among those buried here are composer Chopin; playwright Molière; poet Apollinaire; writers Balzac, Proust, Gertrude Stein and Colette; actors Sarah Bernhardt and Yves Montand; painters Pissarro, Seurat, Modigliani and Delacroix; chanteuse Édith Piaf; and dancer Isadora Duncan.

Particularly visited graves are those of Oscar Wilde, interred in division 89 in 1900, and 1960s rock star Jim Morrison, who died in a flat at 17-19 rue Beautreillis (4e) in the Marais in 1971 and is buried in division 6.

Père Lachaise has five entrances, two of which are on blvd de Ménilmontant. Free maps of noteworthy graves are available from the conservation office.

Below: Cimetière du Père Lachaise (p81); Right: Canal St-Martin (p76)

OPÉRA & GRANDS BOULEVARDS

Hôtel France Albion Hotel €

(Map p72; 01 45 26 00 81; www.albion-paris-hotel.com; 11 rue Notre Dame de Lorette, 9e; s €77-103, d €97-123, f €163; ; St-Georges) For the quietest night's sleep, go for a room facing the courtyard of this neat-as-a-pin budget hotel. Its rooms all have en suite bathrooms and, for Paris, are decently sized. Staff are eager to please and the location, near Opéra, is fabulous.

Hôtel Langlois Historic Hotel €€

(Map p72; 01 48 74 78 24; www.hotel-langlois.com; 63 rue St-Lazare, 9e; s €150-160, d €180-190; @; Trinité) Built in 1870, this 27-room hotel has kept its charm, from the tiny caged elevator to sandstone fireplaces (sadly decommissioned) in many rooms as well as original bathroom fixtures and tiles. Room 64 has wonderful views of Montmartre's rooftops.

MONTMARTRE & PIGALLE

Loft Apartment €€

(Map p72; 06 14 48 47 48; www.loft-paris.fr; 7 cité Véron, 18e; apt €100-270; ; Blanche) Book months in advance to secure one of the stylish apartments in this gem, which offers an intimacy that simply cannot be replicated in a hotel. Just around the corner from the Moulin Rouge, this apartment block offers choices ranging from a two-person studio to a loft that can fit a large family or group. The owner, a culture journalist, is a great resource.

Hôtel des Arts Hotel €€

(Map p72; 01 46 06 30 52; www.arts-hotel-paris.com; 5 rue Tholozé, 18e; s/d from €145/160; ; Abbesses or Blanche) The Hôtel des Arts is a friendly, attractive 50-room hotel, convenient to both place Pigalle and Montmartre. It has comfortable midrange rooms that are excellent value; consider spending an extra €20 for the superior rooms, which have nicer views. Just up

the street is the old-style windmill Moulin de la Galette. Better rates are often available online.

Hôtel Amour Boutique Hotel **€€**
(Map p72; 01 48 78 31 80; www.hotelamourparis.fr; 8 rue Navarin, 9e; s €145, d €170-225; ; M St-Georges or Pigalle) Planning a romantic escapade to Paris? Say no more. The inimitable black-clad Amour (formerly a love hotel by the hour) features original design and artwork in each room – you won't find a more unique place to lay your head in Paris at these prices. You have to be willing to forgo television – but who needs TV when you're in love?

LE MARAIS & BASTILLE

Cosmos Hôtel Hotel **€**
(01 43 57 25 88; www.cosmos-hotel-paris.com; 35 rue Jean-Pierre Timbaud, 11e; s €62-75, d €68-75, tr/q €85/94; ; M République) Cheap, brilliant value and just footsteps from the nightlife of rue JPT, Cosmos is a shiny star with retro style on the budget-hotel scene. It has been around for 30-odd years but, unlike most other hotels in the same price bracket, Cosmos has been treated to a thoroughly modern makeover this century. Breakfast €8.

Hôtel Jeanne d'Arc Hotel **€€**
(Map p64; 01 48 87 62 11; www.hoteljeannedarc.com; 3 rue de Jarente, 4e; s €72, d €98-120, q €250; ; M St-Paul) About the only thing wrong with this gorgeous address is everyone knows about it; book well in advance. Games to play, a painted rocking chair for tots in the bijou lounge, knick-knacks everywhere and the most extraordinary mirror in the breakfast room create a real 'family home' air in this 35-room house.

Hôtel Emile Design Hotel **€€**
(Map p64; 01 42 72 76 17; www.hotelemile.com; 2 rue Malher, 4e; s €170, d €180-230, ste €350; ; M St-Paul) Prepare to be dazzled – literally. Retro B&W, geometrically patterned carpets, curtains, wallpapers and drapes dress this chic hotel, wedged between boutiques and restaurants in the

Marais. Pricier 'top floor' doubles are just that, complete with breathtaking outlook over Parisian roofs and chimney pots. Breakfast, included in the price, is on bar stools in the lobby; open the cupboard to find the 'kitchen'.

Hôtel Caron de Beaumarchais Boutique Hotel **€€**
(Map p64; ☎01 42 72 34 12; www.carondebeaumarchais.com; 12 rue Vieille du Temple, 4e; d €160-198; @ wi-fi; M St-Paul) The attention to detail at this unique themed hotel, decorated like an 18th-century private house, is impressive. From the period card table set as if time stopped halfway through a game, to the harp and well-work sheet music propped on the music stand, the decor evokes the life and times of the 18th-century playwright after whom the hotel is named.

LATIN QUARTER

Hôtel Minerve Hotel **€€**
(Map p64; ☎01 43 26 26 04; www.parishotelminerve.com; 13 rue des Écoles, 5e; s €125, d €146-202, tr €202; ❄ @ wi-fi; M Cardinal Lemoine) Oriental carpets, antique books, frescoes of French monuments and wall tapestries make this family-run hotel a lovely and reasonably priced place to stay. Room styles are a mix of traditional and modern (renovated 2014); some have small balconies with views of Notre Dame, while the 1st-floor rooms all have parquet floors.

Five Hotel Boutique Hotel **€€€**
(Map p64; ☎01 43 31 74 21; www.thefivehotel.com; 3 rue Flatters, 5e; s €255, d €285-305; ❄ wi-fi; M Les Gobelins) Choose from one of five perfumes to fragrance your (small) room at this contemporary romantic sanctum. Its private apartment, One by the Five, has a phenomenal 'levitating' bed. Rates are often discounted by up to 50% online, making it a better deal than it first appears.

ST-GERMAIN & LES INVALIDES

Hôtel Danemark Boutique Hotel **€€**
(Map p64; ☎01 43 26 93 78; www.hotel-danemark.com; 21 rue Vavin, 6e; d €185-205; ❄ @ wi-fi; M Vavin) In a peaceful location near the Jardin du Luxembourg, this stone-walled hotel has 15 scrumptious, eclectically furnished rooms. All are well soundproofed and at least 20 sq metres, which is bigger than many Parisians' apartments. Also unlike many residential apartments, all have bathtubs.

Hôtel d'Angleterre Historic Hotel **€€€**
(Map p64; ☎01 42 60 34 72; www.hotel-dangleterre.com; 44 rue Jacob, 6e; s €175, d €250-275; @ wi-fi; M St-Germain des Prés) If the walls could talk...this former garden of the British Embassy is where the Treaty of Paris ending the American Revolution was prepared in 1783. Hemingway lodged here in 1921, as did Charles Lindbergh in 1927 after completing the world's first solo nonstop flight from New York to Paris. Its 27 exquisite rooms are individually decorated. Rates include breakfast.

L'Hôtel Boutique Hotel **€€€**
(Map p64; ☎01 44 41 99 00; www.l-hotel.com; 13 rue des Beaux Arts, 6e; d €275-495; ❄ @ wi-fi pool; M St-Germain des Prés) In a quiet quayside street, this award-winning hostelry is the stuff of romance, Parisian myths and urban legends. Rock- and film-star patrons fight to sleep in room 16, where Oscar Wilde died in 1900 and which is now decorated with a peacock motif, or in the art deco room 36 (which entertainer Mistinguett once stayed in), with its huge mirrored bed.

L'Apostrophe Design Hotel **€€€**
(Map p64; ☎01 56 54 31 31; www.apostrophe-hotel.com; 3 rue de Chevreuse, 6e; d €299-353; ❄ @ wi-fi; M Vavin) A street work-of-art with its stencilled facade, this art hotel's 16 dramatically different rooms pay homage to the written word. Spray-painted graffiti tags cover one wall of room U (for *urbain*) which has a ceiling shaped like a skateboard ramp. Room P (for Paris parody) sits in the clouds overlooking Paris' rooftops. Rates tumble down to midrange territory outside of high season.

Eating

The inhabitants of some cities rally around local sports teams, but in Paris they rally around *la table* – and everything on it. Pistachio macarons, shots of tomato consommé, decadent *boeuf bourguignon*, a gooey wedge of Camembert running onto the cheese plate...food is not fuel here, it's the reason you get up in the morning.

EIFFEL TOWER AREA & 16E

Choux d'Enfer — Patisserie €

(**☎01 47 83 26 67; cnr rue Jean Rey & quai Branly, 15e; bag sweet/savoury choux €5/7, with cream filling €6-17; ⏰10am-8pm; M Bir-Hakeim or RER Champ de Mars-Tour Eiffel)** This kiosk gives street food a whole new spin. The creation of top French chefs Alain Ducasse and Christophe Michalak, it cooks up *choux* (pastry puffs). Grab a brown paper bag of nine *choux salées* (savoury cheese puffs) spiced with pepper, curry or cumin; or go sweet with almond, cocoa, coffee, lemon and vanilla *chouquettes*, with or without cream filling.

Le Casse Noix — Modern French €€

(**☎01 45 66 09 01; www.le-cassenoix.fr; 56 rue de la Fédération, 15e; 2-/3-course lunch menus €21/26, 3-course dinner menu €33; ⏰noon-2.30pm & 7-10.30pm Mon-Fri; M Bir Hakeim)** Proving that a location footsteps from the Eiffel Tower doesn't mean compromising on quality, quantity or authenticity, 'the nutcracker' is a neighbourhood gem with a cosy retro interior, affordable prices and exceptional cuisine that changes by season and by the inspiration of owner/chef Pierre Olivier Lenormand, who has honed his skills in some of Paris' most fêted kitchens. Book ahead.

Hugo Desnoyer — Butcher €€

(**☎01 46 47 83 00; www.hugodesnoyer.fr; 28 rue du Docteur Blanche, 16e; menu €50, mains €16-32; ⏰7am-8pm Tue-Fri, 7am-7.30pm Sat; M Jasmin)** Hugo Desnoyer is Paris' most famous butcher and the trip to his shop in the 16e is well worth it. Arrive by noon or reserve to snag a table and settle down to a *table d'hôte* feast of homemade terrines, quiches, foie gras and cold cuts followed by the finest meat in Paris – cooked to perfection *naturellement*. Watch out for another Desnoyer opening in 2015.

Restaurant David Toutain — Gastronomic €€€

(**Map p72; ☎01 45 51 11 10; http://davidtoutain.com; 29 rue Surcouf, 7e; lunch menus €42, lunch & dinner menus €68-98; ⏰noon-2.30pm & 8-10pm Mon-Fri; M Invalides)** Prepare to be wowed: David Toutain pushes the envelope at his eponymous new restaurant with some of the most creative high-end cooking in Paris today. Mystery

Macarons

degustation courses include unlikely combinations such as smoked eel in green-apple and black-sesame mousse, or candied celery and truffled rice pudding with artichoke praline (stunning wine pairings available).

Les Ombres Modern French **€€€**
(Map p72; ☎01 47 53 68 00; www.lesombres-restaurant.com; 27 quai Branly, 7e; 2-/3-course lunch menu €32/42, dinner menu €68, mains €32-44; ⏲noon-2.15pm & 7-10.20pm; Ⓜléna or RER Pont de l'Alma) This glass-enclosed rooftop restaurant on the 5th floor of the Musée du Quai Branly is named the 'Shadows' after the patterns cast by the Eiffel Tower's webbed ironwork. Dramatic Eiffel views are complemented by kitchen creations such as *gambas* (prawns) with black rice and fennel, or pan-seared Burgundy snails in watercress sauce. Reserve.

ÉTOILE & CHAMPS-ÉLYSÉES

Ladurée Patisserie **€**
(Map p72; www.laduree.com; 75 av des Champs-Élysées, 8e; pastries from €1.50; ⏲7.30am-11.30pm Mon-Fri, 8.30am-12.30am Sat, 8.30am-11.30pm Sun; ⓂGeorge V) One of the oldest patisseries in Paris, Ladurée has been around since 1862 and was the original creator of the lighter-than-air *macaron*. Its tearoom is the classiest spot to indulge on the Champs. Alternatively, pick up some pastries to go – from croissants to its trademark *macarons*, it's all quite heavenly.

Le Hide French **€€**
(Map p72; ☎01 45 74 15 81; www.lehide.fr; 10 rue du Général Lanrezac, 17e; 2-/3-course menus €25/34; ⏲noon-2pm Mon-Fri, 7-10pm Mon-Sat; ⓂCharles de Gaulle–Étoile) A perpetual favourite, Le Hide is a tiny neighbourhood bistro serving scrumptious traditional French fare: snails, baked shoulder of lamb with pumpkin purée or monkfish in lemon butter. Unsurprisingly, this place fills up faster than you can scamper down the steps of the nearby Arc de Triomphe. Reserve well in advance.

Philippe & Jean-Pierre Traditional French **€€**
(Map p72; ☎01 47 23 57 80; www.philippeetjeanpierre.fr; 7 rue de Boccador, 8e; 4-/5-course menu €40/50, mains €24-26; ⏲noon-2.15pm & 7.15-10.45pm Mon-Sat; ⓂAlma Marceau) Philippe graciously oversees the elegant, parquet-floored, white tableclothed dining

Ladurée

room, while co-owner Jean-Pierre helms the kitchen. Seasonal menus incorporate dishes like cauliflower cream soup with mushrooms and truffles, sautéed scallops with leek and Granny Smith sauce and melt-in-the-middle *moelleux au chocolat* cake. Given the service, quality and gilt-edged Triangle d'Or location, prices are a veritable bargain.

LOUVRE & LES HALLES

Frenchie To Go Fast Food €

(Map p72; www.frenchietogo.com; 9 rue du Nil, 2e; sandwiches €8-14; 8.30am-4.30pm Mon-Fri, 9.30am-5.30pm Sat & Sun; ; M Sentier) Despite the drawbacks – limited seating, eye-poppingly expensive donuts – the fast-food outpost of the burgeoning Frenchie (p88) empire is a wildly popular destination. Bilingual staff transform choice ingredients (eg cuts of meat from the Ginger Pig in Yorkshire) into American classics like pulled-pork and pastrami sandwiches, accompanied by cornets of fries, coleslaw and pickled veggies.

Claus Breakfast €

(Map p64; 01 42 33 55 10; www.clausparis.com; 14 rue Jean-Jacques Rousseau, 1er; breakfasts €13-18, plat du jour €13; 8am-5pm Mon-Fri, 9.30am-5pm Sat & Sun; M Étienne Marcel) Dubbed the '*haute-couture* breakfast specialist' in Parisian foodie circles, this inspired *épicerie du petit-dej* (breakfast grocery shop) has everything you could possibly desire for the ultimate gourmet breakfast and brunch – organic mueslis and cereals, fresh juices, jams, honey and so on.

Blend Burgers €

(Map p72; www.blendhamburger.com; 44 rue d'Argout, 2e; burger & fries €14; noon-11pm daily; M Sentier) A burger cannot simply be a burger in gourmet Paris, where burger buffs dissolve into raptures of ecstacy over gourmet creations at Blend. Think home-made brioche buns and ketchup, hand-cut meat and the most inventive of toppings that transforms the humble burger into something rather special. Fries cost extra.

Parisian Food Markets

Nowhere encapsulates Paris' village atmosphere more than its markets. No markets take place on Mondays.

Marché aux Enfants Rouges (Map p64; 39 rue de Bretagne, 3e; 8.30am-1pm & 4-7.30pm Tue-Fri, 4-8pm Sat, 8.30am-2pm Sun; M Filles du Calvaire) Paris' oldest covered market with communal tables for lunch.

Marché Bastille (Map p64; bd Richard Lenoir, 11e; 7am-2.30pm Thu & Sun; M Bastille or Richard Lenoir) Arguably the best open-air market in Paris.

Marché Raspail (Map p64; bd Raspail btwn rue de Rennes & rue du Cherche Midi, 6e; regular market 7am-2.30pm Tue & Fri, organic market 9am-3pm Sun; M Rennes) Especially popular on Sundays, when it's filled with organic produce.

Rue Cler (Map p72; rue Cler, 7e; most shops 8am-7pm Tue-Sat, to noon Sun; M École Militaire) Fabulous commercial street that almost feels like a party on weekends, when the whole neighbourhood seemingly shops en masse.

Rue Mouffetard (Map p64; 8am-7.30pm Tue-Sat, to noon Sun; M Censier Daubenton) Paris' most photogenic commercial street.

Pirouette Neobistro €€

(Map p64; 01 40 26 47 81; 5 rue Mondétour, 1er; lunch menu €18, 3-/6-course dinner menu €40/60; noon-2.30pm & 7.30-10.30pm Mon-Sat; M Les Halles) In one of the best restaurants in the vicinity of the old 'belly of Paris', chef Tomy Gousset's kitchen crew is working wonders at this cool loft-like space, serving up tantalising creations that range from seared duck, asparagus and Buddha's hand fruit to rum baba with chantilly and lime. Some unique ingredients and a new spin for French cuisine.

L'Ardoise Bistro €€

(Map p72; ☎01 42 96 28 18; www.lardoise-paris.com; 28 rue du Mont Thabor, 1er; menu €38; ⏰noon-2.30pm Mon-Sat, 7.30-10.30pm Mon-Sun; Ⓜ Concorde or Tuileries) This is a lovely little bistro with no menu as such (*ardoise* means 'blackboard', which is all there is), but who cares? The food – *fricassée* of corn-fed chicken with morels, pork cheeks in ginger, hare in black pepper, prepared dexterously by chef Pierre Jay (ex-Tour d'Argent) – is superb.

Frenchie Bistro €€€

(Map p72; ☎01 40 39 96 19; www.frenchie-restaurant.com; 5-6 rue du Nil, 2e; prix fixe menu €48; ⏰7-11pm Mon-Fri; Ⓜ Sentier) Tucked down an alley you wouldn't venture down otherwise, this bijou bistro with wooden tables and old stone walls is iconic. Frenchie is always packed and for good reason: excellent-value dishes are modern, market-driven (the menu changes daily with a choice of two dishes) and prepared with just the right dose of unpretentious creative flair by French chef Gregory Marchand.

Verjus Modern American €€€

(Map p72; ☎01 42 97 54 40; www.verjusparis.com; 52 rue de Richelieu, 1er; prixe-fixe menu €60; ⏰7-10pm Mon-Fri; Ⓜ Bourse or Palais Royal–Musée du Louvre) Opened by American duo Braden Perkins and Laura Adrian, Verjus was born out of a wildly successful clandestine supper club known as the Hidden Kitchen. The restaurant builds on that tradition, offering a chance to sample some excellent, creative cuisine (gnocchi with shiitake relish and parmesan, wild-boar confit with cherry compote) in a casual space. The tasting menu is a series of small plates, using ingredients sourced straight from producers.

Reservations are advised, but walk-ins sometimes end up with a table, especially if you don't mind eating late. If you're just after an apéritif or a prelude to dinner, the **Verjus Bar à Vins** (Map p72; 47 rue de Montpensier, 1er; small plates €8-14, sandwiches €10; ⏰12:30-2pm Tue-Fri, 6-11pm Mon-Fri; Ⓜ Bourse or Palais Royal-Musée du Louvre) cooks up what foodies rightfully claim to be the best buttermilk-fried chicken (€10) in the city, among other small plates. No reservations – arrive early to snag one of 10 bar stools. It also serves gourmet sandwiches at lunch.

OPÉRA & GRANDS BOULEVARDS

Chez Plume Rotisserie €

(Map p72; www.chezplume.fr; 6 rue des Martyrs, 9e; dishes €3.50-8.50; ⏰10.15am-2.45pm Mon-Fri, 5-8pm Tue-Fri, 9.30am-8.30pm Sat, 9.30am-3pm Sun; Ⓜ Notre Dame de Lorette) This rotisserie specialises in free-range chicken from southwest France, prepared in a variety of fashions: simply roasted, as a crumble, or even in a quiche or sandwich. It's wonderfully casual: add a side or two (potatoes, polenta, seasonal veggies) and pull up a counter seat.

Richer Neobistro €€

(Map p72; 2 rue Richer, 9e; mains €16-25; ⏰kitchen noon-2.30pm & 7.30-10.30pm; Ⓜ Poissonière or Bonne Nouvelle) Run by the same team as across-the-street neighbour **L'Office** (Map p72; ☎01 47 70 67 31; 3 rue Richer, 9e; 2-/3-course lunch menus €22/27, dinner menus €28/34; ⏰noon-2.30pm & 7.30-10.30pm Mon-Fri; Ⓜ Poissonière or Bonne Nouvelle), Richer's pared-back, exposed-brick decor is a smart setting for genius creations like trout tartare with cauliflower and tomato and citrus mousse, and quince and lime cheesecake for dessert. It doesn't take reservations, but if it's full, Richer posts a list of recommended local addresses outside. Fantastic value.

Floquifil Traditional French €€

(Map p72; ☎01 84 19 42 12; www.floquifil.fr; 17 rue de Montyon, 9e; mains €14-25; ⏰11am-midnight Mon-Fri, from 6.30pm Sat; Ⓜ Grands Boulevards) If you were to envision the ultimate backstreet Parisian wine bar, it would probably look a lot like Floquifil: table-strewn terrace, dark timber furniture, aquamarine-painted walls and bottles galore. But while the by-the-glass wines are superb, you're missing out if you don't dine here (on rosemary-roasted lamb with ratatouille or at the very least a chacuterie platter).

MONTMARTRE & PIGALLE

Le Petit Trianon — Cafe €

(Map p72; ☎01 44 92 78 08; 80 bd de Rochechouart, 18e; mains €7.50-13.50; ⏰8am-2pm; Ⓜ Anvers) With its large windows and a few carefully chosen antiques, this recently revived belle époque cafe at the foot of Montmartre feels about as timeless as the Butte itself. Dating back to 1894 and attached to the century-old Le Trianon theatre, it's no stretch to imagine artists like Toulouse-Lautrec and crowds of show-goers once filling the place in the evening.

Well-prepared standards (steak tartare, grilled swordfish) are served throughout the day; you can also just stop in for a drink.

Cul de Poule — Modern French €€

(Map p72; ☎01 53 16 13 07; 53 rue des Martyrs, 9e; 2-/3-course lunch menus €16/19, dinner menu €24/29; ⏰noon-2.30pm & 8-11pm Mon-Sat; Ⓜ Pigalle) With plastic, orange cafeteria seats outside, you probably wouldn't wander into the Cul de Poule by accident. But the light-hearted spirit (yes, there is a mounted chicken's derrière on the wall) is deceiving; this is one of the most affordable quality kitchens in the Pigalle neighbourhood, with excellent neobistro fare that emphasises quality ingredients from the French countryside.

Le Miroir — Bistro €€

(Map p72; ☎01 46 06 50 73; http://restaurant-miroir.com; 94 rue des Martyrs, 18e; lunch menu €19.50, dinner menus €27-34; ⏰noon-2.30pm & 7.30-11pm Tue-Sat; Ⓜ Abbesses) This unassuming modern bistro is smack in the middle of the Montmartre tourist trail, yet it remains a local favourite. There are lots of delightful pâtés and rillettes to start off with – guinea hen with dates, duck with mushrooms, haddock and lemon – followed by well-prepared standards like stuffed veal shoulder.

Le Pantruche — Bistro €€

(Map p72; ☎01 48 78 55 60; www.lepantruche.com; 3 rue Victor Massé, 9e; lunch/dinner menus €19/35; ⏰12.30-2.30pm & 7.30-10.30pm Mon-Fri; Ⓜ Pigalle) Named after a nearby 19th-century theatre, classy Pantruche has been making waves in the already crowded dining hot spot of South Pigalle. No surprise, then, that it hits all the right notes: seasonal bistro fare, reasonable prices and an intimate setting. The menu

Fresh produce market

runs from classics (steak with béarnaise sauce) to more daring creations (scallops served in a parmesan broth with cauliflower mousseline).

LE MARAIS & BASTILLE

Candelaria — Taqueria €

(Map p64; www.candelariaparis.com; 52 rue Saintonge, 3e; tacos €3.20-3.75, quesadillas & tostadas €3.50, lunch menu €11.50; ⌚noon-midnight Thu-Sat, to 11pm Sun-Wed; M Filles du Calvaire) You need to know about this terribly cool taqueria to find it. Made of pure, unadulterated hipness in that brazenly nonchalant manner Paris does so well, clandestine Candelaria serves delicious homemade tacos, quesadillas and tostadas in a laidback setting – squat at the bar in the front or lounge out back around a shared table with bar stools or at low coffee tables.

Le Clown Bar — Wine Bar €

(Map p64; ☎01 43 55 87 35; 114 rue Amelot, 11e; mains €15-20; M Filles du Calvaire) A historic monument next to the city's winter circus, the Cirque d'Hiver (1852), this unique address is practically a museum with its painted ceilings, mosaics on the wall, zinc bar and purist art deco style. A restaurant for decades, the mythical address was taken over in early 2014 by chef-sommelier duo Sven Chartier and Ewen Lemoigne.

Le 6 Paul Bert — Bistro €€

(☎01 43 79 14 32; 6 rue Paul Bert, 12e; 2-/3-course lunch menus €15/19, 4-course dinner menu €44; ⌚noon-2pm Tue, noon-2pm & 7.30-11pm Wed-Sat; M Faidherbe-Chaligny) Opened by Bertrand Auboyneau of neighbouring **Bistrot Paul Bert (☎01 43 72 24 01; 18 rue Paul Bert, 11e; 3-course lunch/dinner menus €19/38; ⌚noon-2pm & 7.30-11pm Tue-Sat; M Faidherbe-Chaligny)** and Québecois chef Louis-Philippe Riel, Le 6 serves mind-blowing multicourse menus of small(ish) plates. The exquisitely prepared and presented creations from Riel's open kitchen change daily but invariably involve unexpected flavour combinations (quail/turnip, asparagus/monkfish, artichoke/white chocolate).

Bones — Bistro €€

(☎09 80 75 32 08; www.bonesparis.com; 43 rue Godefroy Cavaignac, 11e; bar dishes €4-16, 4-/5-course menus €47/55; ⌚kitchen 7-11pm Tue-Sat; M Voltaire) Even if you don't score a first-service reservation (7pm to 7.30pm) for red-hot Australian chef James Henry's stripped-back new premises, you have a couple of back-up options. The second service (9.30pm to 10.30pm) is walk-in only. Or you can order Henry's signature small plates (smoked oyster, beef heart, sea-bass carpaccio, house-cured charcuterie) at the bar.

Le Petit Marché — Bistro €€

(Map p64; ☎01 42 72 06 67; 9 rue de Béarn, 3e; mains €18-26; ⌚noon-4pm &

Berthillon

7.30-midnight; **M** Chemin Vert) A faintly fusion cuisine is what makes this cosy bistro, footsteps from place des Vosges, stand out. Dishes such as raw tuna wrapped in sesame seeds or caramelised duck breast served with roasted bananas lend a welcome Asian kick to a menu that otherwise reassures with old French bistro favourites that have been around for centuries. Also has a summer pavement terrace.

Derrière Modern French **€€**
(Map p64; ☎ 01 44 61 91 95; www.derriere-resto.com; 69 rue des Gravilliers, 3e; lunch menus €25, mains €17-24; ⏰ noon-2.30pm & 8-11pm Mon-Sat, noon-4.30pm Sun; M Arts et Métiers) Play table tennis, sit on the side of the bed, glass of champers in hand, or lounge between book cases – such is the nature of this restaurant with courtyard seating. Chilled vibe in a trendy 'shoes-off' style aside, Derrière (literally 'behind') is deadly serious in the kitchen. Classic French bistro dishes and more inventive creations are excellent, as is Sunday brunch.

Bofinger Brasserie **€€**
(Map p64; ☎ 01 42 72 87 82; www.bofinger-paris.com; 5-7 rue de la Bastille, 4e; menus €36.50-59, mains €22.50-46; ⏰ noon-3pm & 6.30pm-midnight; M Bastille) Founded in 1864, Bofinger is reputedly Paris' oldest brasserie, though its polished art nouveau brass, glass and mirrors flag redecoration a few decades later. Specialities include Alsatian-inspired dishes such as *choucroute* (sauerkraut), oysters and seafood dishes. Ask for a seat downstairs and under the *coupole* (stained-glass dome).

Septime Modern French **€€€**
(☎ 01 43 67 38 29; 80 rue de Charonne, 11e; lunch menus €28-55, dinner menus €58; ⏰ 7-10pm Mon, 12.15-2pm & 7-10pm Tue-Fri; M Charonne) Reading the menu at newly Michelin-starred Septime won't get you far, as it looks mostly like an obscure shopping list (hanger steak/chicory/roots, chicken's egg/foie gras/*lardo*). And that's if you even get a menu – if you order the excellent five-course meal (available for both lunch and dinner), you won't even know what's being served until it arrives. Reserve in advance.

THE ISLANDS

Café Saint Régis Cafe **€**
(Map p64; http://cafesaintregisparis.com; 6 rue du Jean de Bellay, 4e; salads & mains €14.50-28; ⏰ 7am-2am; 📶; M Pont Marie) Hip and historical with an effortless dose of retro vintage thrown in, Le Saint Régis – as those in the know call it – is a deliciously Parisian hang-out any time of day. From pastries for breakfast to a mid-morning pancake, brasserie lunch or early-evening oyster platter, Café St-Regis gets it just right. Come midnight it morphs into a late-night hot spot.

Berthillon Ice Cream **€**
(Map p64; 31 rue St-Louis en l'Île, 4e; 2-/3-/4-scoop cone or tub €2.50/5.50/7; ⏰ 10am-8pm Wed-Sun; M Pont Marie) Berthillon is to ice cream what Château Lafite Rothschild is to wine and Valrhona is to chocolate. Among its 70-odd flavours, the fruit-flavoured sorbets are renowned, as are its rich chocolate, coffee, *marrons glacés* (candied chestnuts) and Agenaise (Armagnac and prunes). Watch for seasonal flavours like roasted pineapple and basil, or ginger and caramel. Eat in or take away.

LATIN QUARTER

Café de la Nouvelle Mairie Wine Bar **€€**
(Map p64; 19 rue des Fossés St-Jacques, 5e; mains €14-16; ⏰ 8am-midnight Mon-Fri; M Cardinal-Lemoine) Shhhh...just around the corner from the Panthéon but hidden away on a small, fountained square, the narrow wine bar Café de la Nouvelle is a neighbourhood secret, serving blackboard-chalked natural wines by the glass and delicious seasonal bistro fare from oysters and ribs (*à la française*) to grilled lamb sausage over lentils.

Les Pipos Wine Bar **€€**
(Map p64; ☎ 01 43 54 11 40; www.les-pipos.com; 2 rue de l'École Polytechnique, 5e; mains €13.90-26.90; ⏰ 8am-2am Mon-Sat; M Maubert-Mutualité) A veritable feast for the senses, this *bar à vins* is above all worth a visit for its food. The bistro standards (bœuf bourguignon) and *charcuteries de terroir* (regional cold meats and sausages)

are mouth-watering, as is the cheese board, which includes all the gourmet names (bleu d'Auvergne, St-Félicien, St-Marcellin). No credit cards.

L'AOC Traditional French €€

(Map p64; ☎01 43 54 22 52; www.restoaoc.com; 14 rue des Fossés St-Bernard, 5e; 2-/3-course lunch menus €21/29, mains €19-36; ⏰noon-2.30pm & 7.30-10.30pm Tue-Sat; M Cardinal Lemoine) *'Bistrot carnivore'* is the strapline of this ingenious restaurant concocted around France's most respected culinary products. The concept is Appellation d'Origine Contrôlée (AOC), meaning everything has been reared or produced according to strict guidelines. The result? Only the best! Choose between meaty favourites (steak tartare) or the rotisserie menu, ranging from roast chicken to suckling pig.

Le Coupe-Chou French €€

(Map p64; ☎01 46 33 68 69; www.lecoupechou.com; 9 & 11 rue de Lanneau, 5e; 2-/3-course menus €27/33; ⏰noon-2.30pm & 7.30-10.30pm; M Maubert-Mutualité) This maze of candlelit rooms inside a vine-clad 17th-century townhouse is overwhelmingly romantic. Ceilings are beamed, furnishings are antique, and background classical music mingles with the intimate chatter of diners. As in the days when Marlene Dietrich dined here, advance reservations are essential.

Sola Fusion €€€

(Map p64; ☎dinner 01 43 29 59 04, lunch 09 65 01 73 68; www.restaurant-sola.com; 12 rue de l'Hôtel Colbert, 5e; lunch/dinner €48/98; ⏰noon-2pm & 7-10pm Tue-Sat; M St-Michel) For serious gourmands, Sola is arguably the Latin Quarter's proverbial brass ring. Pedigreed chef Hiroki Yoshitake combines French technique with Japanese sensibility, resulting in gorgeous signature creations (such as miso-marinated foie gras on *feuille de brick* served on a slice of tree trunk). The artful presentations and attentive service make this a great choice for a romantic meal – go for the full experience and reserve a table in the Japanese dining room downstairs.

ST-GERMAIN & LES INVALIDES

JSFP Traiteur Delicatessen €

(Map p64; http://jsfp-traiteur.com; 8 rue de Buci, 6e; dishes €3.40-5.70; ⏰9.30am-8.30pm; 🌶; M Mabillon) Brimming with big bowls of salad, terrines, pâté and other prepared delicacies, this deli is a brilliant bet for quality Parisian 'fast food' such as quiches in a variety of flavour combinations (courgette and chive, mozzarella and basil, salmon and spinach...) to take to a nearby park, square or stretch of riverfront.

Au Pied de Fouet Bistro €

(Map p64; ☎01 43 54 87 83; www.aupieddefouet.com; 50 rue St-Benoît, 6e; mains €9-12.50; ⏰noon-2.30pm & 7-11pm Mon-Sat; M St-Germain des Prés) Classic bistro dishes such as *entrecôte* (steak), *confit de canard* (duck cooked slowly its own fat) and *foie de volailles sauté* (pan-fried chicken livers) at this busy bistro are astonishingly good value. Round off your meal with a *tarte Tatin*, wine-soaked prunes or bowl of *fromage blanc* (a cross between yoghurt, sour cream and cream cheese).

Bouillon Racine Brasserie €€

(Map p64; ☎01 44 32 15 60; www.bouillonracine.com; 3 rue Racine, 6e; weekday lunch menu €16, menus €31-42; ⏰noon-11pm; 👪; M Cluny–La Sorbonne) Set inconspicuously in a quiet street, this heritage-listed 1906 art-nouveau 'soup kitchen', with mirrored walls, floral motifs and ceramic tiling, was built in 1906 to feed market workers. Despite the magnificent interior, the food, inspired by age-old recipes, is by no means an afterthought.

Brasserie Lipp Brasserie €€

(Map p64; ☎01 45 48 53 91; 151 bd St-Germain, 6e; mains €22-38; ⏰11.45am-12.45am; M St-Germain des Prés) Waiters in black waistcoats, bow ties and long white aprons serve brasserie favourites like *choucroute garnie* (pickled cabbage) and *jarret de porc aux lentilles* (pork knuckle with lentils) at this illustrious wood-panelled establishment. (Arrive hungry: salads aren't allowed as meals.) Opened by Léonard Lipp in 1880, the brasserie achieved immortality when Hemingway sang its praises in *A Moveable Feast*.

Polidor Traditional French **€€**

(Map p64; ☎01 43 26 95 34; www.polidor.com; 41 rue Monsieur le Prince, 6e; menu €22-35; ⌚noon-2.30pm & 7pm-12.30am Mon-Sat, noon-2.30pm & 7-11pm Sun; 👪; Ⓜ Odéon) A meal at this quintessentially Parisian *crèmerie-restaurant* is like a trip to Victor Hugo's Paris: the restaurant and its decor date from 1845. *Menus* of tasty, family-style French cuisine ensure a stream of diners eager to sample bœuf bourguignon, *blanquette de veau à l'ancienne* (veal in white sauce) and Polidor's famous *tarte Tatin*. Expect to wait. No credit cards.

Drinking & Nightlife

St James Paris Bar

(Map p72; ☎01 44 05 81 81; www.saint-james-paris.com; 43 rue Bugeaud, 16e; drinks €15-25, Sun brunch €65; ⌚7-11pm; 📶; Ⓜ Porte Dauphine) Sure, it's a hotel bar, but a drink at St James might well be one of your most memorable in Paris. Tucked behind a stone wall, this historic mansion opens its bar each evening to non-guests – and the setting redefines extraordinary. Winter drinks are in the library, in summer they're in the impossibly romantic garden.

Angelina Teahouse

(Map p72; 226 rue de Rivoli, 1er; ⌚8am-7pm Mon-Fri, 9am-7pm Sat & Sun; Ⓜ Tuileries) Clink china with lunching ladies, their posturing poodles and half the students from Tokyo University at Angelina, a grand dame of a tearoom dating to 1903. Decadent pastries are served here, against a fresco backdrop of belle époque Nice, but it is the superthick, decadently sickening 'African' hot chocolate (€8.20), which comes with a pot of whipped cream and a carafe of water, that prompts the constant queue for a table at Angelina.

Experimental Cocktail Club Cocktail Bar

(Map p72; www.experimentalcocktailclub.com; 37 rue St-Saveur, 2e; ⌚7pm-2am; Ⓜ Réaumur-Sébastopol) Called ECC by trendies, this fabulous speakeasy with grey facade and old-beamed ceiling is effortlessly hip. Oozing spirit and soul, the cocktail bar – with retro-chic decor by American interior designer Cuoco Black and sister bars in

Brasserie Lipp

HEMIS/ALAMY ©

London and New York – is a sophisticated flashback to those *années folles* (crazy years) of Prohibition New York.

Le Baron Rouge Wine Bar

(Map p64; 1 rue Théophile Roussel, 12e; 10am-2pm & 5-10pm Tue-Fri, 10am-10pm Sat, 10am-4pm Sun; Ledru-Rollin) Just about the ultimate Parisian wine-bar experience, this place has barrels stacked against the bottle-lined walls. As unpretentious as you'll find, it's a local meeting place where everyone is welcome and it's especially busy on Sunday after the **Marché d'Aligre (Map p64; http://marchedaligre.free.fr; rue d'Aligre, 12e; 8am-1pm & 4-7.30pm Tue-Sat, 8am-1.30pm Sun; Ledru-Rollin)** wraps up. All the usual suspects – cheese, charcuterie and oysters – will keep your belly full.

Harry's New York Bar Cocktail Bar

(Map p72; www.harrysbar.fr; 5 rue Daunou, 2e; noon-2am; Opéra) One of the most popular American-style bars in the prewar years, Harry's once welcomed writers like F Scott Fitzgerald and Ernest Hemingway, who no doubt sampled the bar's unique cocktail and creation: the Bloody Mary. The Cuban mahogany interior dates from the mid-19th century and was brought over from a Manhattan bar in 1911.

Au Sauvignon Wine Bar

(Map p64; 80 rue des St-Pères, 7e; 8.30am-10pm Mon-Sat, to 9pm Sun; Sèvres-Babylone) Grab a table in the evening sun at this wonderfully authentic *bar à vin* or head to the quintessential bistro interior, with an original zinc bar, tightly packed tables and hand-painted ceiling celebrating French viticultural tradition. A plate of *casse-croûtes au pain Poilâne* – toast with ham, pâté, terrine, smoked salmon, foie gras... – is the perfect accompaniment.

Les Deux Magots Cafe

(Map p64; www.lesdeuxmagots.fr; 170 bd St-Germain, 6e; 7.30am-1am; St-Germain des Prés) If ever there were a cafe that summed up St-Germain des Prés' early-20th-century literary scene, it's this former hangout of anyone who was anyone. You will spend *beaucoup* to sip a coffee in a wicker chair on the terrace shaded by dark-green awnings and geraniums spilling from window boxes, but it's an undeniable piece of Parisian history.

Café La Palette Cafe

(Map p64; www.cafelapaletteparis.com; 43 rue de Seine, 6e; 8am-2am; ; Mabillon) In the heart of gallery land, this *fin-de-siècle* cafe and erstwhile stomping ground of Paul Cézanne and Georges Braque attracts a grown-up set of fashion-industry professionals and local art dealers. Its summer terrace is beautiful.

Le Pure Café Cafe

(www.purecafe.fr; 14 rue Jean Macé, 11e; 7am-2am Mon-Fri, 8am-2am Sat, 9am-midnight Sun; Charonne) A classic Parisian haunt, this

Moulin Rouge
SUPPLIED BY MOULIN ROUGE®/ HABAS-SMADJA ©

rustic, cherry-red corner cafe featured in the art-house film *Before Sunset*, but it's still a refreshingly unpretentious spot for a drink, cheese or charcuterie platter, fusion cuisine or Sunday brunch.

Entertainment

Paris' two premier listings guides *Pariscope* (€0.40) and *L'Officiel des Spectacles*, both in French, are available from newsstands on Wednesdays and are crammed with everything that's on in the capital.

CABARET

Whirling lines of feather boa–clad, high-kicking dancers are a quintessential fixture on Paris' entertainment scene – for everyone but Parisians. Still, the dazzling sets, costumes and routines guarantee an entertaining evening (or matinee). Tickets to major cabaret spectacles start from around €90 (from €130 with lunch, from €150 with dinner), and usually include a half-bottle of champagne. Reservations are essential; venues sell tickets online.

Moulin Rouge Cabaret

(Map p72; ☎01 53 09 82 82; www.moulinrouge.fr; 82 bd de Clichy, 18e; M Blanche) Immortalised in the posters of Toulouse-Lautrec and later on screen by Baz Luhrmann, the Moulin Rouge twinkles beneath a 1925 replica of its original red windmill. Yes, it's rife with bus-tour crowds. But from the opening bars of music to the last high kick it's a whirl of fantastical costumes, sets, choreography and Champagne. Booking advised.

OPERA & BALLET

Palais Garnier Opera

(Map p72; ☎08 92 89 90 90; www.operadeparis.fr; place de l'Opéra, 9e; M Opéra) The city's original opera house is smaller than its Bastille counterpart, but has perfect acoustics. Due to its odd shape, some seats have limited or no visibility – book carefully. Ticket prices and conditions (including last-minute discounts) are available from the **box office (Map p72; cnr rues Scribe & Auber, 9e; ⌚11am-6.30pm Mon-Sat)**.

Opéra Bastille Opera, Ballet

(Map p64; ☎08 92 89 90 90; www.operadeparis.fr; 2-6 place de la Bastille, 12e; M Bastille) This 3400-seat venue is the city's main opera hall; it also occasionally stages ballet and classical concerts. Tickets go on sale online up to two weeks before they're available by telephone or at the **box office (Map p64; ☎01 40 01 19 70; 130 rue de Lyon, 12e; ⌚2.30-6.30pm Mon-Sat; M Bastille)**. Standing-only tickets (*places débouts;* €5) are available 90 minutes before performances begin.

Shopping

Paris Rendez-Vous Concept Store

(Map p64; 29 rue de Rivoli, 4e; ⌚10am-7pm Mon-Sat; M Hôtel de Ville) Only the city of Paris could be so chic as to have its own designer line of souvenirs, sold in its own uber-cool concept store inside the Hôtel de Ville. Shop here for everything from clothing and homewares to Paris-themed books, toy sailing boats and signature Jardin du Luxembourg's Fermob chairs. *Quel style!*

Chez Hélène Confectionery

(Map p64; www.chezhelene-paris.com; 28 rue Saint-Gilles, 3e; ⌚11.30am-7.30pm Mon-Sat, 11am-1pm & 3-7pm Sun; M Rambuteau) Pure indulgence is what this irresistible *bonbon* (sweets) boutique – a child's dream come true – is about. Old-fashioned toffees and caramels, fudge, liquorice, Eiffel Tower sugar cubes, designer lollipops, artisanal marshmallows, Provencal *calissons*...the choice of quality, well-made *bonbons* and *gourmandises* (sweet treats) is outstanding.

La Manufacture de Chocolat Food, Drink

(Map p64; www.lechocolat-alainducasse.com; 40 rue de la Roquette, 11e; ⌚10.30am-7pm Tue-Sat; M Bastille) If you dine at superstar chef Alain Ducasse's restaurants, the chocolate will have been made here at Ducasse's own chocolate factory – the first in Paris to produce 'bean-to-bar' chocolate – which he set up with his former executive pastry chef Nicolas Berger. Deliberate over ganaches, pralines and truffles and no fewer than 44 flavours of chocolate bar.

You can also buy Ducasse's chocolates at his Left Bank boutique, **Le Chocolat Alain Ducasse** (Map p64; www.lechocolat-alainducasse.com; 26 rue St-Benoît, 6e; ⌚10.30am-7.30pm Tue-Sat; Ⓜ St Germain des Prés).

38 Saint Louis — Cheese

(Map p64; 38 rue St-Louis en l'Île, 4e; ⌚9am-9.30pm Tue-Sat, to 7pm Sun & Mon; Ⓜ Pont Marie) Saturday wine tastings, artisan fruit chutneys, grape juice and prepared dishes to go: there is far more to this thoroughly modern *fromagerie* than its old-fashioned facade and absolutely superb selection of first-class French *fromage* (cheese). The shop is run by a young, dynamic duo, driven by food. Buy a wooden box filled with vacuum-packed cheese to take home.

Gab & Jo — Concept Store

(Map p64; www.gabjo.fr; 28 rue Jacob, 6e; ⌚11am-7pm Mon-Sat; Ⓜ St-Germain des Prés) Forget mass-produced, imported souvenirs: for quality local gifts to take home, browse the shelves of Gab & Jo, the country's first-ever concept store stocking only made-in-France items. Designers include Marie-Jeanne de Grasse (scented candles), Marius Fabre (Marseille soaps), Germaine-des-Prés (lingerie), MILF (sunglasses) and Monsieur Marcel (T-shirts).

Guerlain — Perfume

(Map p72; ☎spa 01 45 62 11 21; www.guerlain.com; 68 av des Champs-Élysées, 8e; ⌚10.30am-8pm Mon-Sat, noon-7pm Sun; Ⓜ Franklin D Roosevelt) Guerlain is Paris' most famous parfumerie, and its shop (dating from 1912) is one of the most beautiful in the city. With its shimmering mirror and marble art-deco interior, it's a reminder of the former glory of the Champs-Élysées. For total indulgence, make an appointment at its decadent spa.

Didier Ludot — Fashion

(Map p72; www.didierludot.fr; 19-20 & 23-24 Galerie de Montpensier, 1er; ⌚10.30am-7pm Mon-Sat; Ⓜ Palais Royal–Musée du Louvre) In the rag trade since 1975, collector Didier Ludot sells the city's finest couture creations of yesteryear in his exclusive twinset of boutiques, hosts exhibitions, and has published a book portraying the evolution of the little black dress, brilliantly brought to life in his shop that sells just that, **La Petite Robe Noire** (Map p72; 125 Galerie de Valois, 1er; ⌚11am-7pm Mon-Sat; Ⓜ Palais Royal-Musée du Louvre).

Shakespeare & Company — Books

(Map p64; www.shakespeareandcompany.com; 37 rue de la Bûcherie, 5e; ⌚10am-11pm Mon-Fri, from 11am Sat & Sun; Ⓜ St-Michel) This bookshop is the stuff of legends. A kind of spell descends as you enter, weaving between nooks and crannies overflowing with new and secondhand English-language books. The original shop (12 rue l'Odéon, 6e; closed by the Nazis in 1941) was run by Sylvia Beach and became the meeting point for Hemingway's 'Lost Generation'. Readings by emerging and illustrious authors take place at 7pm most Mondays; it also hosts workshops and festivals.

Merci — Concept Store

(Map p64; www.merci-merci.com; 111 bd Beaumarchais, 3e; ⌚10am-7pm Mon-Sat; Ⓜ St-Sébastien Froissart) A Fiat Cinquecento marks the entrance to this unique concept store which donates all its profits to a children's charity in Madagascar. Shop for fashion, accessories, linens, lamps and nifty designs for the home; and complete the experience with a coffee in its hybrid used-bookshop-cafe or lunch in its stylish basement.

Galeries Lafayette — Department Store

(Map p72; http://haussmann.galerieslafayette.com; 40 bd Haussmann, 9e; ⌚9.30am-8pm Mon-Sat, to 9pm Thu; Ⓜ Auber or Chaussée d'Antin) *Grande dame* department store Galeries Lafayette is spread across the main store (whose magnificent stained-glass dome is over a century old), **men's store** (Map p72) and **homewares store** (Map p72), and includes a gourmet emporium.

Catch modern art in the **gallery** (Map p72; www.galeriedesgaleries.com; 1st fl; ⌚11am-7pm Tue-Sat) FREE; take in a **fashion show** (☎bookings 01 42 82 30 25; ⌚3pm Fri Mar-

DAISY CORLETT/ALAMY ©

Don't Miss
Flea Markets

Marché aux Puces de St-Ouen (www.marcheauxpuces-saintouen.com; rue des Rosiers, av Michelet, rue Voltaire, rue Paul Bert & rue Jean-Henri Fabre; 9am-6pm Sat, 10am-6pm Sun, 11am-5pm Mon; M Porte de Clignancourt) Founded in the late 19th century and said to be Europe's largest.

Marché aux Puces de la Porte de Vanves (http://pucesdevanves.typepad.com; av Georges Lafenestre & av Marc Sangnier, 14e; 7am-2pm Sat & Sun; M Porte de Vanves) The Porte de Vanves flea market is the smallest and one of the friendliest of the lot.

Jul & Sep-Dec by reservation); see the free, windswept rooftop panorama; or take a break at one of its 19 restaurants and cafes.

Pierre Hermé — Food

(Map p64; www.pierreherme.com; 72 rue Bonaparte, 6e; 10am-7pm Sun-Wed, to 7.30pm Thu & Fri, to 8pm Sat; M Odéon or RER Luxembourg) It's the size of a chocolate box, but once you're in, your taste buds will go wild. Pierre Hermé is one of Paris' top chocolatiers and this boutique is a veritable feast of perfectly presented petits fours, cakes, chocolates, nougats, *macarons* and jam.

Le Bon Marché — Department Store

(Map p64; www.bonmarche.fr; 24 rue de Sèvres, 7e; 10am-8pm Mon-Wed & Sat, to 9pm Thu & Fri; M Sèvres Babylone) Built by Gustave Eiffel as Paris' first department store in 1852, Le Bon Marché is the epitome of style, with a superb concentration of men's and women's fashions, beautiful homewares, stationery, books and toys as well as chic dining options.

The icing on the cake is its glorious food hall, **La Grande Épicerie de Paris** (Map p64; www.lagrandeepicerie.fr; 36 rue de Sèvres, 7e; 8.30am-9pm Mon-Sat; M Sèvres Babylone).

Information

Paris Convention & Visitors Bureau (Office du Tourisme et des Congrès de Paris; Map p72; www.parisinfo.com; 27 rue des Pyramides, 1er; ⌚9am-7pm May-Oct, 10am-7pm Nov-Apr; M Pyramides) Main branch of the Paris Convention & Visitors Bureau, about 500m northwest of the Louvre.

Getting There & Away

Air

Most international airlines fly to Aéroport de Charles de Gaulle, 28km northeast of central Paris. In French the airport is commonly called 'Roissy' after the suburb in which it is located. A €1.7 billion project to create a high-speed train link between Charles de Gaulle and Gare de l'Est in central Paris is on the table, but no track will be laid until 2017. When complete in 2023, the CDG Express will cut the current 40-odd minute journey to 20 minutes.

Aéroport de Charles de Gaulle (CDG; www.aeroportsdeparis.fr)

Aéroport d'Orly (ORY; ☎01 70 36 39 50; www.aeroportsdeparis.fr) Aéroport d'Orly is located 19km south of central Paris but, despite being closer than CDG, it is not as frequently used by international airlines and public transportation options aren't quite as straightforward. If you have heavy luggage or young kids in tow, consider a taxi.

Aéroport de Beauvais (BVA; ☎08 92 68 20 66; www.aeroportbeauvais.com) Beauvais Airport is 75km north of Paris and a few low-cost flights go through here – but before you snap up that bargain, consider if the post-arrival journey is worth it.

Train

Gare du Nord (rue de Dunkerque, 10e; M Gare du Nord) Trains to/from the UK, Belgium, northern Germany, Scandinavia, Moscow; terminus of the high-speed Thalys trains to/from Amsterdam, Brussels, Cologne and Geneva and Eurostar to London; trains to the northern suburbs of Paris and northern France, including TGV Nord trains to Lille and Calais.

Gare de l'Est (bd de Strasbourg, 10e; M Gare de l'Est) Trains to/from Luxembourg, parts of Switzerland (Basel, Lucerne, Zurich), southern Germany (Frankfurt, Munich) and points further east; regular and TGV Est trains to areas of France east of Paris (Champagne, Alsace and Lorraine).

Gare de Lyon (bd Diderot, 12e; M Gare de Lyon) Gare de Lyon is the terminus for trains from Provence, the Alps, the Riviera and Italy. Also serves Geneva. Located in eastern Paris.

Gare d'Austerlitz (bd de l'Hôpital, 13e; M Gare d'Austerlitz) Trains to/from Spain and Portugal; Loire Valley and non-TGV trains to southwestern France (eg Bordeaux and Basque Country).

Gare Montparnasse (av du Maine & bd de Vaugirard, 15e; M Montparnasse Bienvenüe) Trains to/from Brittany and places en route from Paris (eg Chartres, Angers, Nantes); TGV Atlantique Ouest and TGV Atlantique Sud-Ouest trains to Tours, Nantes, Bordeaux and other destinations in southwestern France.

Gare St-Lazare (rue St-Lazare & rue d'Amsterdam, 8e; M St-Lazare) Normandy (eg Dieppe, Le Havre, Cherbourg).

Getting Around

Getting around Paris is comparatively easy for a big city. Most visitors combine the efficient metro with walking. Buses offer a good view of the city, but can be hard to figure out and slowed by traffic. More tempting is the city's communal bike-share scheme, Vélib'.

To/From the Airports

Aéroport Roissy Charles de Gaulle

A taxi to the city centre takes 40 minutes. During the day, pay around €50; the fare increases 15% between 5pm and 10am and on Sundays. Only take taxis at a clearly marked rank. Never follow anyone who approaches you at the airport and claims to be a driver.

Bus

There are six main bus lines:

Les Cars Air France line 2 (€17, 1¼ hours, every 20 minutes, 6am to 11pm) Links the airport with the Arc de Triomphe. Children aged two to 11 pay half price.

Les Cars Air France line 4 (€17.50, every 30 minutes, 6am to 10pm from CDG, 6am to 9.30pm from Paris) Links the airport with Gare de Lyon (50 minutes) in eastern Paris and Gare Montparnasse (55 minutes) in southern Paris. Children aged two to 11 pay half price.

Roissybus (€10.50, 45 to 60 minutes, every 15 minutes, 5.30am to 11pm) Links the airport with the Opéra.

RATP bus 350 (€5.70, 50 minutes, every 30 minutes, 5.30am to 11pm) Links the airport with Gare de l'Est in northern Paris.

RATP bus 351 (€5.70, 60 minutes, every 30 minutes, 5.30am to 11pm) Links the airport with place de la Nation in eastern Paris.

Noctilien bus 140 & 143 (€7.60 or four metro tickets, hourly, 12.30am to 5.30pm) Part of the RATP night service, Noctilien has two buses that go to CDG: bus 140 from Gare de l'Est, and 143 from Gare de l'Est and Gare du Nord.

Train

CDG is served by the RER B line (€9.50, approx 50 minutes, every 10 to 15 minutes), which connects with the Gare du Nord, Châtelet–Les Halles and St-Michel–Notre Dame stations in the city centre. Trains run from 5am to 11pm; there are fewer trains on weekends.

Aéroport d'Orly

A taxi to the city centre takes roughly 30 minutes. During the day, pay between €40 and €55; the fare increases 15% between 5pm and 10am and on Sundays.

Bus

There are several bus lines and a state-of-the-art tram line that serve Orly:

Air France bus 1 (€12.50, one hour, every 20 minutes 5am to 10.20pm from Orly, 6am to 11.20pm from Invalides) This bus runs to/from the Gare Montparnasse (35 minutes) in southern Paris, Invalides in the 7e, and the Arc de Triomphe. Children aged two to 11 pay half price.

Orlybus (€7.50, 30 minutes, every 15 minutes, 6am to 11.20pm from Orly, 5.35am to 11.05pm from Paris) This bus runs to/from the metro station Denfert Rochereau in southern Paris, making several stops en route.

Tramway T7 (€1.70, every six minutes, 40 minutes, 5.30am to 12.30am Monday to Saturday, 6.30am to 12.30am Sunday) In service since the end of 2013, this tramway links Orly with Villejuif-Louis Aragon metro station in southern Paris; buy tickets from the machine at the tram stop as no tickets are sold onboard. Pick up traffic updates on Twitter @T7_RATP.

Train

There is no direct train to/from Orly; you'll need to change halfway. Note that while it is possible to take a shuttle to the RER C line, this service is quite long and not recommended.

RER B (€10.90; 35 minutes, every four to 12 minutes) This line connects Orly with the St-Michel–Notre Dame, Châtelet–Les Halles and Gare du Nord stations in the city centre. In order to get from Orly to the RER station (Antony), you must first take the Orlyval automatic train. The service runs from 6am to 11pm (fewer on weekends). You only need one ticket to take the two trains.

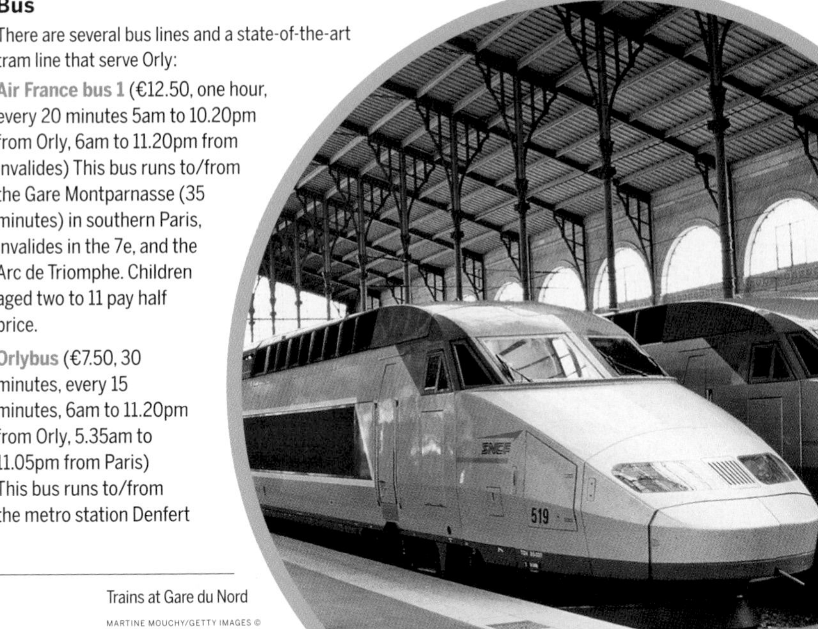

Trains at Gare du Nord

Bicycle

The **Vélib'** (**http://en.velib.paris.fr; day/week subscription €1.70/8, bike hire up to 30min/60min/90min/2hr free/€1/2/4**) bike share scheme puts 20,000-odd bikes at the disposal of Parisians and visitors to get around the city. There are some 1800 stations throughout the city, each with anywhere from 20 to 70 bike stands. The bikes are accessible around the clock.

- To get a bike, you first need to purchase a one-/seven-day subscription (€1.70/8). There are two ways to do this: either at the terminals found at docking stations or online.
- The terminals require a credit card with an embedded smartchip – this means the majority of North Americans cannot subscribe here. But fret not because you can purchase a subscription online. Just be sure to do this before you leave your hotel.
- After you authorise a deposit (€150) to pay for the bike should it go missing, you'll receive an ID number and PIN code and you're ready to go.
- Bikes are rented in 30-minute intervals: the first half-hour is free, the second is €2, the third and each additional half-hour are €4. If you return a bike before a half-hour is up and then take a new one, you will not be charged.
- If the station you want to return your bike to is full, log in to the terminal to get 15 minutes for free to find another station.
- Bikes are geared to cyclists aged 14 and over, and are fitted with gears, an antitheft lock with key, reflective strips and front/rear lights. Bring your own helmet (they are not required by law).

Public Transport

Paris' underground network is run by RATP and consists of two separate but linked systems: the metro and the Réseau Express Régional (RER) suburban train line. The metro has 14 numbered lines; the RER has five main lines (but you'll probably only need to use A, B and C). When buying tickets consider how many zones your journey will cover; there are five concentric transportation zones rippling out from Paris (5 being the furthest); if you travel from Charles de Gaulle airport to Paris, for instance, you will have to buy a zone 1–5 ticket.

- The same RATP tickets are valid on the metro, the RER (for travel within the city limits), buses, trams and the Montmartre funicular.
- A ticket – white in colour and called *Le Ticket t+* – costs €1.70 (half price for children aged four to nine years) if bought individually and €13.70 for adults for a *carnet* (book) of 10.
- Tickets are sold at all metro stations: ticket windows accept most credit cards; however, automated machines *do not* accept North American credit cards.
- One ticket lets you travel between any two metro stations (no return journeys) for a period of 1½ hours, no matter how many transfers are required. You can also use it on the RER for travel within zone 1, which encompasses all of central Paris.
- A single ticket can be used to transfer between buses, but not to transfer from the metro to bus or vice-versa. Transfers are not allowed on Noctilien buses.
- Always keep your ticket until you exit from your station; if you are stopped by

Cathédrale Notre Dame de Paris (p77)

a ticket inspector, you will have to pay a fine if you don't have a valid ticket.

Tourist Passes

The Mobilis and Paris Visite passes are valid on the metro, RER, SNCF's suburban lines, buses, night buses, trams and Montmartre funicular railway. No photo is needed, but write your card number on the ticket. Passes are sold at larger metro and RER stations, SNCF offices in Paris, and the airports.

The Mobilis card allows unlimited travel for one day and costs €6.80 (two zones) to €16.10 (five zones). Buy it at any metro, RER or SNCF station in the Paris region. Depending on how many times you plan to hop on/off the metro in a day, a *carnet* might work out cheaper.

Paris Visite allows unlimited travel as well as discounted entry to certain museums and other discounts and bonuses. The 'Paris+Suburbs+Airports' pass includes transport to/from the airports and costs €22.85/34.70/48.65/59.50 for one/two/three/five days. The cheaper 'Paris Centre' pass, valid for zones 1 to 3, costs €10.85/17.65/24.10/34.70 for one/two/three/five days. Children aged four to 11 years pay half price.

Taxi

- The *prise en charge* (flagfall) is €2.50. Within the city limits, it costs €1 per kilometre for travel between 10am and 5pm Monday to Saturday (*Tarif A;* white light on taxi roof and meter).
- At night (5pm to 10am), on Sunday from 7am to midnight, and in the inner suburbs the rate is €1.24 per km (*Tarif B;* orange light).
- Travel in the outer suburbs is at *Tarif C,* €1.50 per kilometre (blue light).
- There's a €3 surcharge for taking a fourth passenger, but drivers sometimes refuse for insurance reasons. The first piece of baggage is free; additional pieces over 5kg cost €1 extra.
- Flagging down a taxi in Paris can be difficult; it's best to find an official taxi stand.
- To order a taxi, call or reserve online with Taxis G7 (**3607; www.taxisg7.fr**), Taxis Bleus (**01 49 36 10 10; www.taxis-bleus.com**) or Alpha Taxis (**01 45 85 85 85; www.alphataxis.com**).
- Increasingly big in Paris is Uber (**www.uber.com/cities/paris**) taxi, whereby you order a taxi and pay via your smartphone.

AROUND PARIS

Disneyland Resort Paris

It took almost €4.6 billion to turn the beet fields 32km east of Paris into Europe's first Disney theme park. What started out as Euro-Disney in 1992 today comprises the traditional **Disneyland Park** theme park, the film-oriented **Walt Disney Studios Park**, and hotel-, shop- and restaurant-filled **Disney Village**.

One-day admission fees at **Disneyland Resort Paris** (**hotel bookings 01 60 30 60 30, restaurant reservations 01 60 30 40 50; www.disneylandparis.com; 1 day adult/child €64/58; hours vary; M RER Marne-la-Vallée/Chessy**) include unlimited access to attractions in *either* Disneyland Park or Walt Disney Studios Park. The latter includes entry to Disneyland Park three hours before it closes. A multitude of multiday passes, special offers and packages are available.

Sights

Disneyland Park Theme Park

(**10am-11pm May-Aug, to 10pm Sep, to 6pm Oct-Apr, hours can vary**) Disneyland Park has five themed *pays* (lands): the 1900s-styled **Main Street USA**; **Frontierland**, home of the legendary Big Thunder Mountain ride; **Adventureland**, which evokes exotic lands in rides like the Pirates of the Caribbean and Indiana Jones and the Temple of Peril; **Fantasyland**, crowned by Sleeping Beauty's castle; and the high-tech **Discoveryland**, with massive-queue rides such as Space Mountain: Mission 2, Star Wars and Buzz Lightyear Laser Blast.

Walt Disney Studios Park Theme Park

(**10am-7pm May-Sep, to 6pm Oct-Apr, hours can vary**) The sound stage, production back lot and animation studios provide an up-close illustration of how films, TV programs and cartoons are produced, with behind-the-scenes tours, larger-than-life characters and spine-tingling rides like the Twighlight Zone Tower of

Around Paris

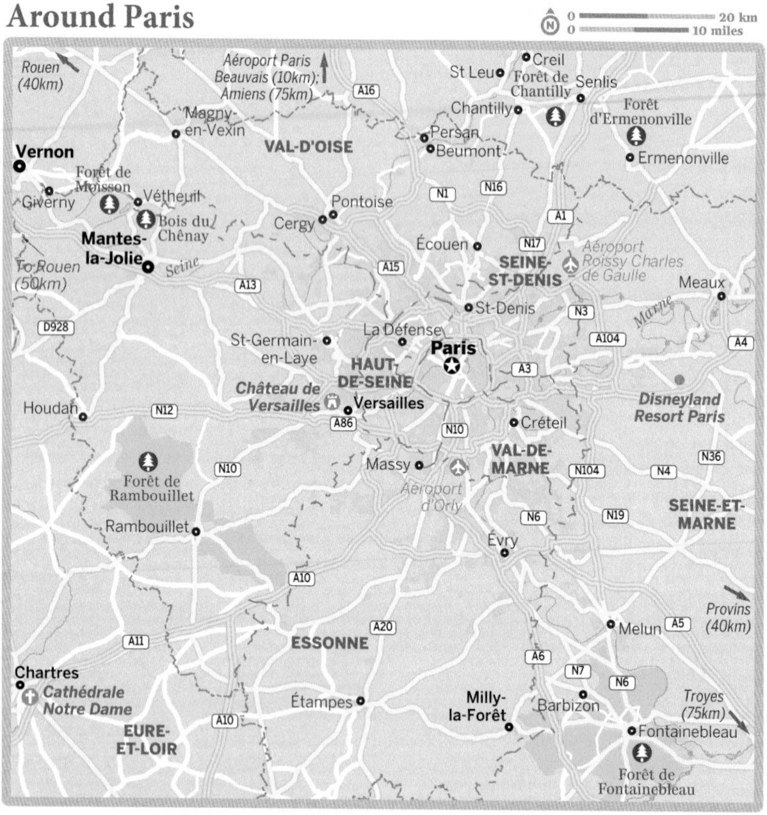

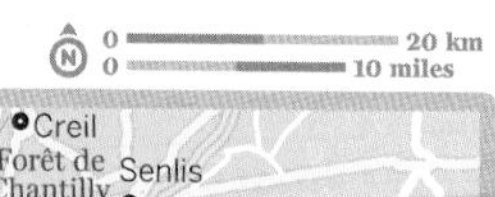

Terror. Its latest addition is the outsized Ratatouille ride, based on the winsome 2007 film about a rat who dreams of becoming a top Parisian chef and offering a multisensory rat's perspective of Paris' rooftops and restaurant kitchens aboard a trackless 'ratmobile'.

Getting There & Away

Marne-la-Vallée/Chessy, Disneyland's RER station, is served by line A4; trains run frequently from central Paris (€7.10).

By car, follow route A4 from Porte de Bercy (direction Metz-Nancy) and take exit 14.

Versailles

Louis XIV transformed his father's hunting lodge into the monumental Château de Versailles in the mid-17th century, and it remains France's most famous, grandest palace. Situated in the prosperous, leafy and bourgeois suburb of Versailles, 28km southwest of Paris, the baroque château was the kingdom's political capital and the seat of the royal court from 1682 up until the fateful events of 1789 when revolutionaries massacred the palace guard and dragged Louis XVI and Marie Antoinette back to Paris, where they were ingloriously guillotined.

By noon queues for tickets and entering the château spiral out of control: arrive early morning and avoid Tuesday and Sunday, its busiest days. Save time by pre-purchasing tickets on the château's website or at Fnac branches and head straight to Entrance A.

Try to time your visit for the Grandes Eaux Musicales or the after-dark

Grandes Eaux Nocturnes, truly magical 'dancing water' displays – set to music composed by baroque- and classical-era composers – throughout the grounds in summer.

 Sights

To access areas that are otherwise off limits and to learn more about Versailles' history, take a 90-minute guided tour of the Private Apartments of Louis XV and Louis XVI and the Opera House or Royal Chapel. Tour tickets include access to the most famous parts of the palace, such as the Hall of Mirrors and the King's and Queen's State Apartments; prebook online.

Château de Versailles Palace

(**☎01 30 83 78 00; www.chateauversailles.fr; passport ticket incl estate-wide access adult/child €18/free, with musical events €25/free, palace €15/free; ⏲9am-6.30pm Tue-Sat, to 6pm Sun Apr-Oct, to 5.30pm Tue-Sun Nov-Mar; M RER Versailles-Château–Rive Gauche**) Amid magnificently landscaped formal gardens, this splendid and enormous palace was built in the mid-17th century during the reign of Louis XIV – the Roi Soleil (Sun King) – to project the absolute power of the French monarchy, which was then at the height of its glory. The château has undergone relatively few alterations since its construction, though almost all the interior furnishings disappeared during the Revolution and many of the rooms were rebuilt by Louis-Philippe (r 1830–48).

Some 30,000 workers and soldiers toiled on the structure, the bills for which all but emptied the kingdom's coffers.

Work began in 1661 under the guidance of architect Louis Le Vau (Jules Hardouin-Mansart took over from Le Vau in the mid-1670s); painter and interior designer Charles Le Brun; and landscape artist André Le Nôtre, whose workers flattened hills, drained marshes and relocated forests as they laid out the seemingly endless gardens, ponds and fountains.

Le Brun and his hundreds of artisans decorated every moulding, cornice,

Local Knowledge

Versailles

BY SYLVAIN POSTOLLE, OFFICIAL GUIDE, CHÂTEAU DE VERSAILLES

1 **KING'S PRIVATE APARTMENT**

This is the most fascinating part of the palace as it shows the king as a man and reflects his daily life in the 18th century. Of the 10 or so rooms, the most famous is his bedroom where he not only slept but also held ceremonies. Up to 150 courtiers and people would watch him have supper here each evening! By the 1780s, the king's life had become more private – he had an official supper just once a week on Sunday.

2 **KING LOUIS VXI'S LIBRARY**

This is a lovely room – full of books, a place where you can imagine the king coming to read for hours. Louis XVI loved geography and his copy of *The Travels of James Cook* – in English – is here.

3 **HERCULES SALON**

From the Hercules Salon you can see all the rooms comprising the King's State Apartment, and to the right, through the gallery leading to the opera house. The salon served as a passageway for the king to go from his state apartment to the chapel to celebrate daily mass.

4 **THE ROYAL CHAPEL**

This is an exquisite example of the work of architect Jules Hardouin-Mansart (1646–1708). The paintings, representative of art fashions at the end of the reign of Louis XIV, are also stunning: they evoke the idea that the French king was chosen by God, and as such was God's lieutenant on earth. This is the chapel where, in 1770, the future king Louis XVI wed Marie Antoinette – the beginning of the French Revolution.

5 **ENCELADE GROVE**

Versailles' gardens are extraordinary but my favourite spot is this grove, typical of the gardens created for Louis XIV by André Le Nôtre. A gallery of trellises surround a pool with a statue of Enceladus, chief of the Titans. The fountains are also impressive.

Versailles

A DAY IN COURT

Visiting Versailles – even just the State Apartments – may seem overwhelming at first, but think of it as a house where people ate, drank, worked, slept and conspired and you'll be on the right path.

Some two decades into his long reign, Louis XIV began turning his father's hunting lodge into a palace large enough to house his entire court (to keep closer tabs on the 6000-strong army of courtiers). Sparing no expense, the Sun King employed the greatest artists and craftspeople of the day and by 1682 he'd created the most extravagant dormitory in history.

The royal schedule was as accurate and predictable as a Swiss watch. By following this itinerary of rooms you can recreate the king's day, starting with the **King's Bedchamber** 1 and the **Queen's Bedchamber** 2, where the royal couple was roused at about the same time. The royal procession then leads through the **Hall of Mirrors** 3 to the **Royal Chapel** 4 for morning Mass and returns to the **Council Chamber** 5 for late-morning meetings with ministers. After lunch the king might ride or hunt or visit the **King's Library** 6. Later he could join courtesans for an 'apartment evening' starting from the **Hercules Drawing Room** 7 or play billiards in the **Diana Drawing Room** 8 before supping at 10pm.

VERSAILLES BY NUMBERS

- **Rooms** 700 (11 hectares of roof)
- **Windows** 2153
- **Staircases** 67
- **Gardens and parks** 800 hectares
- **Trees** 200,000
- **Fountains** 50 (with 620 nozzles)
- **Paintings** 6300 (measuring 11km laid end to end)
- **Statues and sculptures** 2100
- **Objets d'art and furnishings** 5000
- **Visitors** 5.3 million per year

Queen's Bedchamber
Chambre de la Reine
The queen's life was on constant public display and even the births of her children were watched by crowds of spectators in her own bedchamber. **DETOUR »** The Guardroom, with a dozen armed men at the ready.

LUNCH BREAK

Diner-style food at Sister's Café, crêpes at Le Phare St-Louis or picnic in the park.

King's Library
Bibliothèque du Roi
The last resident, bibliophile Louis XVI, loved geography and his copy of *The Travels of James Cook* (in English, which he read fluently) is still on the shelf here.

SAVVY SIGHTSEEING

Avoid Versailles on Monday (closed), Tuesday (Paris' museums close, so visitors flock here) and Sunday, the busiest day. Also, book tickets online so you don't have to queue.

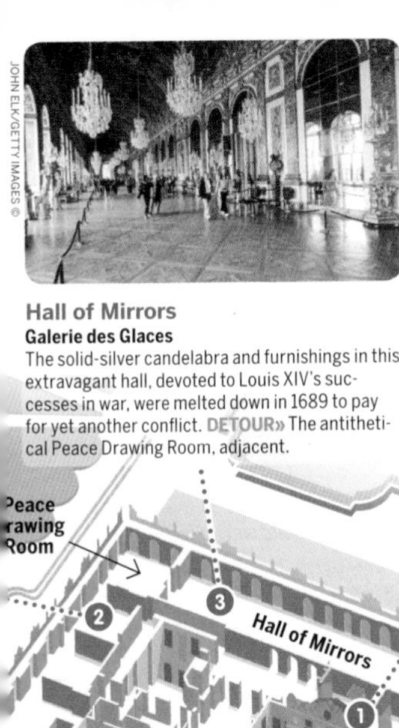

Hall of Mirrors

Galerie des Glaces

The solid-silver candelabra and furnishings in this extravagant hall, devoted to Louis XIV's successes in war, were melted down in 1689 to pay for yet another conflict. **DETOUR»** The antithetical Peace Drawing Room, adjacent.

King's Bedchamber

Chambre du Roi

The king's daily life was anything but private and even his *lever* (rising) at 8am and *coucher* (retiring) at 11.30pm would be witnessed by up to 150 sycophantic courtiers.

Council Chamber

Cabinet du Conseil

This chamber, with carved medallions evoking the king's work, is where the monarch met his various ministers (state, finance, religion etc) depending on the days of the week.

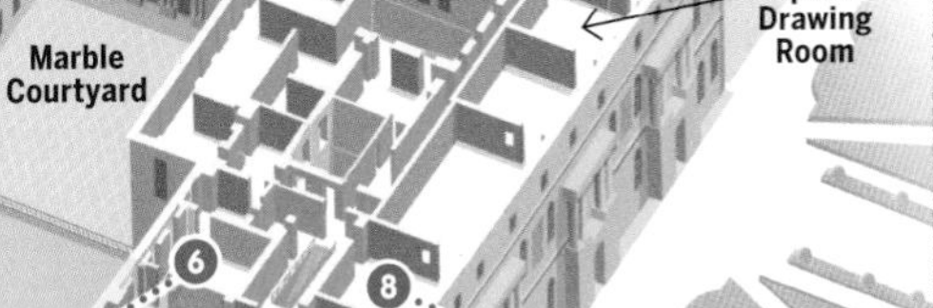

Diana Drawing Room

Salon de Diane

With walls and ceiling covered in frescos devoted to the mythical huntress, this room contained a large billiard table reserved for Louis XIV, a keen player.

Royal Chapel

Chapelle Royale

This two-storey chapel (with gallery for the royals and important courtiers, and the ground floor for the B-list) was dedicated to St Louis, patron of French monarchs. **DETOUR»** The sumptuous Royal Opera.

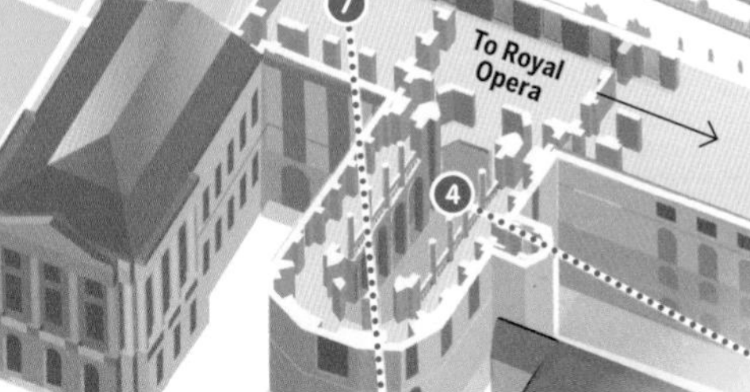

Hercules Drawing Room

Salon d'Hercule

This salon, with its stunning ceiling fresco of the strong man, gave way to the State Apartments, which were open to courtiers three nights a week. **DETOUR»** Apollo Drawing Room, used for formal audiences and as a throne room.

ceiling and door of the interior with the most luxurious and ostentatious of appointments: frescos, marble, gilt and woodcarvings, many with themes and symbols drawn from Greek and Roman mythology. The King's Suite of the Grands Appartements du Roi et de la Reine (King's and Queen's State Apartments), for example, includes rooms dedicated to Hercules, Venus, Diana, Mars and Mercury. The opulence reaches its peak in the Galerie des Glaces (Hall of Mirrors), a 75m-long ballroom with 17 huge mirrors on one side and, on the other, an equal number of windows looking out over the gardens and the setting sun.

The current €400 million restoration program is the most ambitious yet, and until it's completed in 2020, at least a part of the palace is likely to be clad in scaffolding when you visit.

Château de Versailles Gardens & Park Garden

(except during musical events admission free; ⌚gardens 9am-8.30pm Apr-Oct, 8am-6pm Nov-Mar, park 7am-8.30pm Apr-Oct, 8am-6pm Nov-Mar) The section of the vast gardens nearest the palace, laid out between 1661 and 1700 in the formal French style, is famed for its geometrically aligned terraces, flowerbeds, tree-lined paths, ponds and fountains. The 400-odd statues of marble, bronze and lead were made by the most talented sculptors of the era. The English-style Jardins du Petit Trianon are more pastoral and have meandering, sheltered paths.

Versailles Stables Stables

Today the **Petites Écuries (Little Stables)** FREE are used by Versailles' School of Architecture. The **Grandes Écuries (Big Stables)** are the stage for the prestigious **Académie du Spectacle Équestre (Academy of Equestrian Arts; ☎01 39 02 07 14; www.acadequestre.fr; 1 av Rockefeller; training session adult/child €12/6.50; ⌚45min training session 11.15am last Sat & Sun of month)**. It presents spectacular **Reprises Musicales (Musical Equestrian Shows; adult/child from €25/16; ⌚6pm Sat, 3pm Sun)**, for which tickets sell out weeks in advance; book ahead online. In the stables' main courtyard is a new *manège* where horses and their riders train. Show tickets and training sessions include a stable visit.

Gardens at Château de Versailles

CALLE MONTES/GETTY IMAGES ©

Information

Tourist Office (☎01 39 24 88 88; www.versailles-tourisme.com; 2bis av de Paris; ⏰10am-6pm Mon, 9am-7pm Tue-Sun Apr-Oct, 9am-6pm Tue-Sat, 11am-5pm Sun & Mon Nov-Mar) Sells the passport to Château de Versailles and detailed visitor's guides.

Getting There & Away

RER C5 (€3.25, 45 minutes, frequent) goes from Paris' Left Bank RER stations to Versailles-Château–Rive Gauche station.

SNCF operates trains from Paris' Gare Montparnasse to Versailles-Chantiers, and from Paris' Gare St-Lazare to Versailles-Rive Droite, 1.2km from the château.

Chartres

Step off the train in Chartres, 91km southwest of Paris, and the two very different spires – one Gothic, the other Romanesque – of its glorious 13th-century cathedral beckon. Don't miss a stroll around Chartres' carefully preserved old town. Adjacent to the cathedral, staircases and steep streets lined with half-timbered medieval houses lead downhill the narrow western channel of the Eure River, romantically spanned by footbridges.

Sights

Cathédrale Notre Dame Cathedral

(www.cathedrale-chartres.org; place de la Cathédrale; ⏰8.30am-7.30pm daily year-round, to 10pm Tue, Fri & Sun Jun-Aug) One of Western civilisation's crowning architectural achievements, the 130m-long Cathédrale Notre Dame de Chartres is renowned for its brilliant-blue stained-glass windows and sacred holy veil. Built in the Gothic style during the first quarter of the 13th century to replace a Romanesque cathedral that had been devastated by fire – along with much of the town – in 1194, effective fundraising and donated labour meant construction took only 30 years, resulting in a high degree of architectural unity.

Getting There & Away

Frequent SNCF trains link Paris' Gare Montparnasse (€15.60, 55 to 70 minutes) with Chartres, some of which stop at Versailles-Chantiers (€13.20, 45 to 60 minutes).

If you're driving from Paris, follow the A6 from Porte d'Orléans (direction Bordeaux–Nantes), then the A10 and A11 (direction Nantes) and take the 'Chartres' exit.

Normandy & Brittany

Stretching along France's northern coastline overlooking La Manche (the English Channel), Normandy has been at the centre of French history for more than 1000 years. And so it's a region awash with historical sights, from the iconic spires of Mont St-Michel and the handwoven epic of the Bayeux Tapestry to the landmark beaches of D-Day. It's also home to three of the nation's favourite 'C's – Camembert, cider and the potent apple-flavoured spirit Calvados.

Across the border is Brittany. Once an independent kingdom, it's still governed by its own culture, language and fiery Celtic spirit. This wild and windswept region boasts France's craggiest coastline, as well as a whole host of prehistoric monuments, medieval châteaux and timeless towns including the corsair city of St-Malo and its lovely half-timbered capital, Quimper.

Étretat cliff, Normandy

Normandy & Brittany

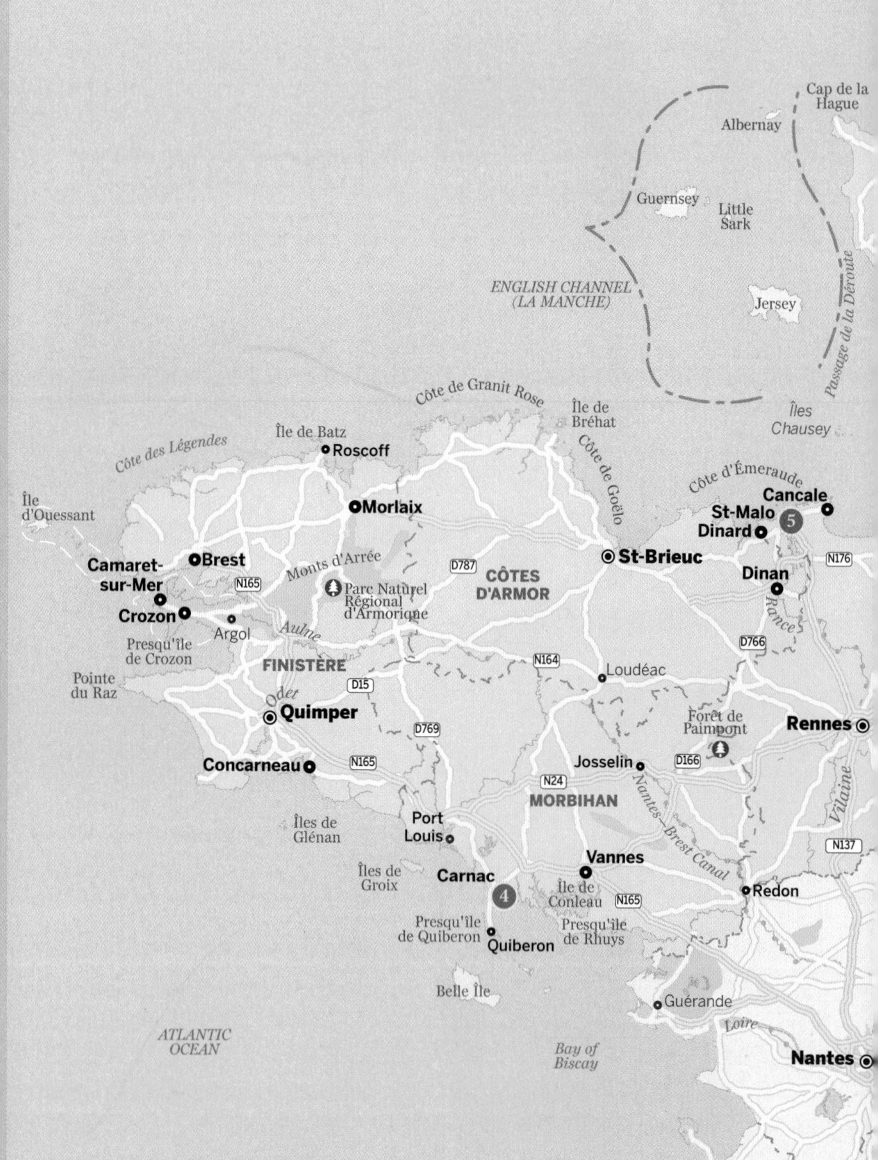

0 50 km
0 25 miles
English Channel
(La Manche)
SOMME
Côte d'Albâtre
Dieppe
A28
D915
Cherbourg
Aéroport
Étretat
Cherbourg
SEINE-MARITIME
Le Havre
Aéroport
A29
D-Day Landing Beaches
Utah
Beach
Pointe du
Hoc Ranger
Memorial
N13
N15
Abbaye de
Jumièges
A151
Pont de
Normandie
A28
Rouen
Longues-
sur-Mer
Honfleur
Le Marais
Vernier
N31
Juno
Beach
Trouville
N13
D79
Deauville
A13
Aéroport
Rouen Vallée
du Seine
OISE
Omaha Beach
Parc Naturel
Régional des
Marais du
Cotentin et
du Bessin
Bayeux
Aéroport
Caen-
Carpiquet
Caen
N175
Les Andelys
Touques
Seine
CALVADOS
A13
EURE
Giverny
A84
A28
Vire
D562
Charentonne
N13
Collines de Normandie
Falaise
Granville
Vire
D973
Orne
D836
Avranches
D977
Iton
MANCHE
Risle
Dreux
Mont St-
Michel
ORNE
Parc Naturel
Régional
Normandie-Maine
Collines du Perche
A84
Montagne-
au-Perche
Park Naturel
Régional du
Perche
Chartres
A11
Alençon
Eure
N12
EURE-ET-LOIR
N12
A84
Sarthe
A28
Vitré
MAYENNE
SARTHE
A11
A81
Laval
ILLE-ET-
VILAINE
Le Mans
LOIRET
N171
A11
1 Mont St-Michel
2 Giverny
3 Bayeux Tapestry
4 Carnac Megaliths
5 St-Malo
ANJOU
Angers
A11
Tours
MAINE-
ET-LOIRE
INDRE-
ET-LOIRE
Indre
INDRE
DEUX-
SÈVRES
VENDÉE
VIENNE

Normandy & Brittany's Highlights

Mont St-Michel

The charm of the Mont (p129) is in the *marais* (salt marshes) and the immense view – so magical, so mysterious. It evokes the crossing of the Red Sea. Pilgrims have trekked across the sand since the 8th century and it's steeped in legend.

1

2

Giverny

Discover your inner impressionist in the village of Giverny (p125), where Claude Monet lived and worked for 43 years surrounded by the gardens and lilyponds that inspired his most celebrated paintings. Also home to a museum exploring the work of impressionists in France, Giverny makes an ideal day trip from either Rouen or Paris.

FRENCH SCHOOL/GETTY IMAGES ©

3 Bayeux Tapestry

Travel back 1000 years with the world's oldest comic strip, the 68.3m Bayeux Tapestry (p122), which recounts the story of the Norman invasion of England in 1066. It is believed to have been commissioned by Bishop Odo of Bayeux, William the Conqueror's half-brother, to celebrate the opening of Bayeux cathedral in 1077, although opinion is divided on where it was actually made.

VINCENT JARY/GETTY IMAGES ©

4 Carnac Megaliths

If your imagination's fired by ancient history, you definitely shouldn't miss Carnac (p141). Comprising 3000 menhirs arranged in parallel lines measuring over 6km end to end, it's one of the world's most monumental prehistoric building projects. No one has managed to definitively explain exactly how – or why – the monument was built. Then again, the megalithic mystery is all part of the fun.

5 St-Malo

Seaside cities don't come much more spectacular than St-Malo (p133), the 'Corsaire City', which is ringed by defensive walls designed by the great military architect Vauban during the 18th century. Though badly damaged during WWII, St-Malo has been impeccably restored over the last half-century; don't miss a stroll along the ramparts and a cruise to nearby Dinard.

Normandy & Brittany's Best...

Museums

Musée des Impressionnismes Giverny Impressionism in the Norman countryside. (p125)

Bayeux Tapestry Devour the illustrated exploits of William the Conqueror. (p122)

Musée Eugène Boudin Art aplenty in lovely Honfleur. (p127)

Caen Mémorial Immerse yourself in WWII at this audiovisual extravaganza. (p127)

Musée Départemental Breton Quimper's Breton-history museum. (p140)

Dining

Le Bistro de Jean Fabulous, elbow-to-elbow bistro dining in St-Malo. (p135)

Le Coquillage Dine in serious style near Cancale courtesy of celebrity chef Olivier Roellinger. (p138)

Les Nymphéas Rouen address known for its imaginative take on Norman dishes. (p120)

Le Balafon Much-loved modern and unpretentious bistro in Dinard. (p136)

Au P'tit Mareyeur Dine on Norman-style bouillabaisse overlooking Honfleur's harbour. (p128)

Boat Trips

Île de Batz Ferries link Roscoff with this offshore escape. (p139)

Île d'Ouessant Brave the waves en route to this craggy, windswept island. (p136)

Honfleur Take a memorable cruise from Honfleur's historic harbour. (p127)

St-Malo to Dinard Catch the water taxi between these seaside neighbours. (p135)

Dinan Canal boats putter along the River Rance to St-Malo. (p143)

Culinary Must-Tries

- **Cider** Try Breton cider at Cancale's Breizh Café. (p137)
- **Oysters** Eat freshly shucked oysters on Cancale's quayside. (p137)
- **Crêpes** Quimper's Crêperie du Quartier is a favourite for Breton pancakes. (p142)
- **Calvados** Order this fiery apple brandy in any Norman bar.
- **Camembert** Sample Normandy's soft cheese at the Président Farm. (p129)

Left: Camembert cheese labels; **Above:** Ile d'Ouessant (p136)

Need to Know

ADVANCE PLANNING

- **At least a month before** Book hotels in St-Malo, Dinard, Dinan and Rouen.
- **Two or three weeks before** Reserve your table at the big restaurants.
- **One day before** Reserve ferries to offshore islands such as the Île d'Ouessant, especially in July and August.

RESOURCES

- **Brittany Tourism** (www.brittanytourism.com) Brittany's main tourist site.
- **Normandy Tourism** (www.normandie-tourisme.fr) Normandy's main tourist site.
- **Normandie Mémoire** (www.normandiememoire.com) Multimedia D-Day site.
- **Cider Route** (www.larouteducidre.fr) Site for cider lovers.
- **Bretagne Rando** (www.bretagne-rando.com) Hiking, biking, kayaking and canoeing trails in Brittany.

GETTING AROUND

- **Budget flights** Fly from the UK to Dinard, Brest and Nantes.
- **Ferries** The main ports for cross-channel ferries are Roscoff, St-Malo and Cherbourg, although some ferries sail to Le Havre, Dieppe and Ouistreham (Caen).
- **Trains & Buses** Trains serve major towns, but you'll be stuck with buses to the smaller villages.
- **Car** Gives you maximum freedom, but be prepared for summertime traffic jams and incomprehensible one-way systems in big cities.
- **Organised minibus tours** An excellent way to visit the D-Day beaches; book through Bayeux tourist office.

BE FOREWARNED

- **Mont St-Michel** The climb to the top involves lots of steps, many spiral and steep. Pay attention to tide times when walking to the mount. Arrive early or late in the day to avoid the worst crowds.
- **St-Malo** Accommodation books up fast in summer. If you decide to stay in the old city, you'll probably have to park outside, beyond the city walls.

Normandy & Brittany Itineraries

History seems to be etched into the landscape all over Normandy and Brittany, from medieval towns to ancient monuments. There's also a truly stirring coastline.

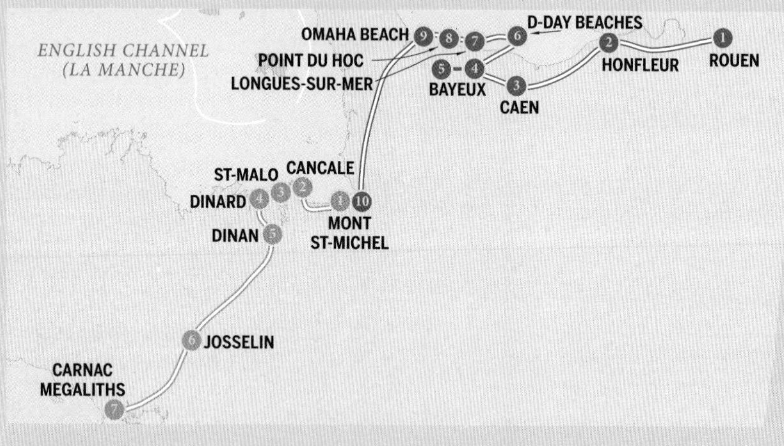

ROUEN TO MONT ST-MICHEL

NORMAN HIGHLIGHTS

Start with a day exploring the old town of ❶ **Rouen**, famous for its half-timbered architecture and Joan of Arc connections (the Maid of Orleáns was burned at the stake here in 1431). Factor in the Musée des Beaux-Arts and the Cathédrale Notre Dame, followed by a meal to remember at Les Nymphéas and an overnight at Hôtel de Bourgtheroulde.

On day two head west to ❷ **Honfleur** for lunch at one of the busy quayside bistros around the Vieux Bassin. Spend the afternoon at the ❸ **Caen Mémorial**, which documents the history of WWII in impressive fashion. In the early evening, arrive in ❹ **Bayeux** and check in to Les Logis du Rempart – don't leave without tasting the homemade *calvados* and cider.

Day three begins with a visit to the ❺ **Bayeux Tapestry**, followed by an afternoon tour around the ❻ **D-Day beaches**. Detour via the massive cannons of ❼ **Longues-sur-Mer** and the ❽ **Pointe du Hoc Ranger Memorial** before finishing up at ❾ **Omaha Beach**, where you can pay your respects at the American military cemetery, featured in the opening shots of *Saving Private Ryan*. If time allows, continue to ❿ **Mont St-Michel** for the start of our Breton tour.

MONT ST-MICHEL TO CARNAC

THE BEST OF BRITTANY

This whistle-stop tour of Brittany begins just across the Norman border at ❶ **Mont St-Michel**, France's famous island abbey. Summer crowds can be oppressive, so arrive early to dodge the crush or, better still, take a guided walk across the sands, followed by an atmospheric night-time visit.

Day two starts with a spin along the coast to sample fresh oysters in ❷ **Cancale** before arriving at the walled city of ❸ **St-Malo**, where you can take a walk around the town's ramparts and choose from plenty of excellent restaurants. On day three catch the boat across the water to the elegant resort town of ❹ **Dinard**, a favourite seaside getaway for wealthy Parisians since the days of the belle époque.

On day four visit delightfully medieval ❺ **Dinan** before cutting across Brittany's centre to visit ❻ **Château de Josselin**. Spend your last day exploring the monumental ❼ **Carnac Megaliths**, the largest prehistoric structure anywhere on earth.

Omaha beach (p124), Normandy
DENNIS MACDONALD/GETTY IMAGES ©

Discover Normandy & Brittany

At a Glance

- **Normandy** (p118) A joy to visit for its soft cheese, rolling countryside, iconic abbey of Mont St-Michel and historic D-Day beaches.
- **Brittany** (p133) Privy to its own history, heritage and language (not to mention cuisine), this spectacular coastal region is unique.

Cathédrale Notre Dame (p119), Rouen
SHAUN EGAN/GETTY IMAGES ©

NORMANDY

Ever since the armies of William the Conqueror set sail from its shores in 1066, Normandy has played a pivotal role in European history, from the Norman invasion of England to the Hundred Years War and the D-Day beach landings of 1944. This rich and often brutal past is what draws travellers to the region today, though the pastoral landscapes, small fishing ports, dramatic coastline and waistline-expanding cuisine are all equally good reasons to include this accessible and beautiful chunk of France on any trip.

Rouen

POP 119,927

With its elegant spires, beautifully restored medieval quarter and soaring Gothic cathedral, the ancient city of Rouen is one of Normandy's highlights. Rouen has had a turbulent history – it was devastated several times during the Middle Ages by fire and plague, and was occupied by the English during the Hundred Years War. The young French heroine Joan of Arc (Jeanne d'Arc) was tried for heresy and burned at the stake in the central square in 1431.

Sights

Place du Vieux Marché Square

This is where 19-year-old Joan of Arc was executed for heresy in 1431. Dedicated in 1979, thrillingly modernist **Église Jeanne d'Arc** (place du Vieux Maré; 10am-noon & 2-6pm, closed Fri & Sun mornings), with its fish-scale exterior, stands on the spot where Joan was burned at the stake. The church's soaring interior is lit by some marvellous 16th-century stained glass.

Cathédrale Notre Dame Cathedral

(place de la Cathédrale; 2-6pm Mon, 9am-7pm Tue-Sat, 8am-6pm Sun Apr-Oct, shorter hours Nov-Mar) Rouen's stunning Gothic cathedral, built between the late 12th and 16th centuries, was famously the subject of a series of canvases painted by Monet at various times of the day and year. The 75m-tall **Tour de Beurre** (Butter Tower) was financed by locals in return for being allowed to eat butter during Lent – or so the story goes.

A free **sound-and-light spectacular** is projected on the facade every night from mid-June (at 11pm) to late September (at 9.30pm).

Musée des Beaux-Arts Art Museum

(02 35 71 28 40; www.rouen-musees.com; esplanade Marcel Duchamp; adult/child €5/free, 3 museums adult €8; 10am-6pm Wed-Mon) Housed in a grand structure erected in 1870, Rouen's outstanding fine-arts museum features canvases by Caravaggio, Rubens, Modigliani, Pissarro, Renoir, Sisley (lots) and, of course, several works by Monet.

Abbatiale St-Ouen Church

(place du Général de Gaulle; 10am-noon & 2-6pm Tue-Thu, Sat & Sun) This 14th-century abbey is a marvellous example of the Rayonnant Gothic style. The entrance is through the lovely garden on the south side, facing rue des Faulx.

Aître St-Maclou Historic Quarter

(186 rue Martainville; 9am-6pm) Decorated with lurid woodcarvings of skulls, crossbones, gravediggers' tools and hourglasses (a reminder that your time, my friend, is running out), this macabre ensemble of half-timbered buildings was used for centuries as a cemetery for plague victims. Built between 1526 and 1533, it now houses Rouen's École des Beaux-Arts (fine arts school).

Sleeping

Le Vieux Carré Hotel €

(02 35 71 67 70; www.hotel-vieux-carre.com; 34 rue Ganterie; r €60-68;) Set around a little medieval courtyard, this quiet, half-timbered hotel has a delightfully old-fashioned *salon de thé* (tearoom) and 13 small, practical rooms, all of which were renovated in 2012 and '13.

Hôtel de Bourgtheroulde Luxury Hotel €€€

(02 35 14 50 50; www.hotelsparouen.com; 15 place de la Pucelle; r €265-450;) Rouen's finest hostelry serves up a sumptuous mix of early 16th-century architecture – Flamboyant Gothic, to be precise – and sleek, modern luxury. The 78 rooms are spacious and gorgeously appointed. Amenities include a pool (19m), sauna and spa in the basement, and a lobby bar with live piano music on Saturday evening.

Eating

La Rose des Vents Modern French €

(02 35 70 29 78; 37 rue St-Nicolas; mains €15; noon-about 3pm Tue-Sat) Tucked away inside a retro secondhand shop, this stylish establishment is hugely popular with foodies and hipsters. Patrons rave about the two lunch mains, which change weekly according to what's available in the market. Reservations are highly recommended.

Dame Cakes Patisserie €

(02 35 07 49 31; www.damecakes.fr; 70 rue St-Romain; lunch mains €11, menu €14.50-23.50; 10.30am-7pm Mon-Sat;) Walk through the historic, early 20th-century facade and you'll discover a delightfully civilised selection of pastries, cakes and chocolates. From noon to 3pm you can tuck into delicious quiches, *gratins* and salads in the attached *salon de thé*. Lovely.

Gill Côté Bistro Bistro €€

(02 35 89 88 72; www.gill.fr; 14 place du Vieux Marché; 2-course menu €22.50; noon-3pm & 7.30-10.30pm) Sleek contemporary design,

Rouen

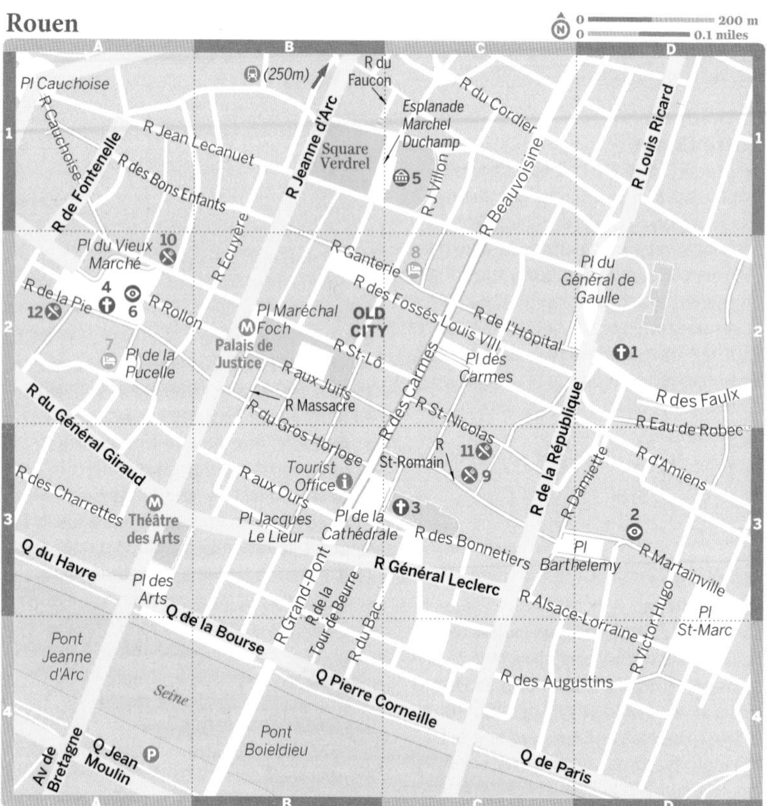

Rouen

Sights

1 Abbatiale St-Ouen ... D2
2 Aître St-Maclou ... D3
3 Cathédrale Notre Dame ... C3
4 Église Jeanne d'Arc ... A2
5 Musée des Beaux-Arts ... C1
6 Place du Vieux Marché ... A2

Sleeping

7 Hôtel de Bourgtheroulde ... A2
8 Le Vieux Carré ... C2

Eating

9 Dame Cakes ... C3
10 Gill Côté Bistro ... A2
11 La Rose des Vents ... C3
12 Les Nymphéas ... A2

traditional French and Lyonnaise cuisine, and wine by the glass (€4.20 to €5.90) are featured at this popular bistro, under the tutelage of renowned chef Gilles Tournadre.

Les Nymphéas Gastronomic **€€€**
(**02 35 89 26 69; www.lesnympheas-rouen.com; 7-9 rue de la Pie; weekday lunch menu €27, other menus €42-74; 12.15-2pm Wed-Sun, 7-9pm Tue-Sat)** With its formal tables arrayed under 16th-century beams, Les Nymphéas has long been a top address for fine dining. Young chef Alexandre Dessaux, in charge since 2013, serves up French cuisine that manages to be both traditional and creative. Reservations are a must on weekends.

Information

Tourist Office (02 32 08 32 40; www.rouentourisme.com; 25 place de la Cathédrale; 9am-7pm Mon-Sat, 9.30am-12.30pm & 2-6pm

Sun & holidays May-Sep, 9.30am-12.30pm & 1.30-6pm Mon-Sat Oct-Apr) Housed in a 1500s Renaissance building facing the cathedral. Can provide English brochures on Normandy and details on guided tours in English (July and August). Rouen's only exchange bureau is at the back.

Getting There & Away

The train station, Rouen-Rive-Droite, is 1.2km north of the cathedral. In the city centre, train tickets are available at the Boutique SNCF (cnr rue aux Juifs & rue Eugène Boudin; 12.30-7pm Mon, 10am-7pm Tue-Sat). Direct services include:

Caen €26.80, 1½ hours, five or six daily

Paris' Gare St-Lazare €23.50, 1¼ hours, 25 daily Monday to Friday, 13 to 18 Saturday and Sunday

Bayeux

POP 14,350

Bayeux has become famous throughout the English-speaking world thanks to a 68m-long piece of painstakingly embroidered cloth: the 11th-century Bayeux Tapestry, whose 58 scenes vividly tell the story of the Norman invasion of England in 1066. But there's more to Bayeux than this unparalleled piece of needlework. The first town to be liberated after D-Day (on the morning of 7 June 1944), it is one of the few in Calvados to have survived WWII practically unscathed. A great place to soak up the Norman atmosphere, Bayeux' delightful city centre is crammed with 13th- to 18th-century buildings, including lots of wood-framed Norman-style houses, and a fine Gothic cathedral. Bayeux also makes an ideal launch pad for exploring the D-Day beaches just to the north.

Sights

Cathédrale Notre Dame Cathedral

(rue du Bienvenu; 8.30am-7pm) Most of Bayeux' spectacular Norman Gothic cathedral dates from the 13th century, though the crypt (take the stairs on the north side of the choir), the arches of the nave and the lower parts of the entrance towers are 11th-century Romanesque. The central tower was added in the 15th century; the copper dome dates from the 1860s. First prize for tackiness has got to go to 'Litanies de la Sainte Vierge', a 17th-century, haut-relief retable in the first chapel on the left as you enter the cathedral.

Detour: Abbaye de Jumièges

Following the Seine valley west of Rouen, the D982 road winds through little towns, occasionally following the banks of the Seine as it climbs and descends. About 27km west of Rouen, in Jumièges, the Abbaye de Jumièges is an absolute must-see, even if you're not a history buff. With its ghostly white stone set off by a backdrop of trees, it's one of the most evocative ruins in Normandy. The church was begun in 1020, and William the Conqueror attended its consecration in 1067. It declined during the Hundred Years War and then enjoyed a renaissance under Charles VII. It continued to flourish until the 18th-century revolutionaries booted out the monks and allowed the buildings to be mined for construction materials.

Conservatoire de la Dentelle Lace Workshop

(Lace Conservatory; 02 31 92 73 80; http://dentelledebayeux.free.fr; 6 rue du Bienvenu; 9.30am-12.30pm & 2.30-5pm, closed Sun & holidays) FREE Lacemaking, brought to Bayeux by nuns in 1678, once employed 5000 people. The industry is long gone, but at the Conservatoire you can watch some of France's most celebrated lacemakers create intricate designs using dozens of bobbins and hundreds of pins; a small shop sells some of their delicate

FRENCH SCHOOL/GETTY IMAGES ©

Don't Miss
Bayeux Tapestry

The world's most celebrated embroidery depicts the conquest of England by William the Conqueror in 1066 from an unashamedly Norman perspective. Commissioned by Bishop Odo of Bayeux, William's half-brother, for the opening of Bayeux' cathedral in 1077, the 68.3m-long cartoon strip tells the dramatic, bloody tale with verve.

Fifty-eight action-packed scenes of pageantry and mayhem occupy the centre of the canvas, while religious allegories and illustrations of everyday 11th-century life, some of them naughty, adorn the borders. The final showdown at the Battle of Hastings is depicted in graphic fashion, complete with severed limbs and decapitated heads (along the bottom of scene 52). Halley's Comet, which blazed across the sky in 1066, appears in scene 32.

A 16-minute film gives the conquest historical, political and cultural context, including crucial details on the grooming habits of Norman and Saxon knights. Also worth a listen is the lucid, panel-by-panel audioguide, available in 14 languages. A special audioguide for kids aged seven to 12 is available in French and English.

NEED TO KNOW

☎ 02 31 51 25 50; www.tapestry-bayeux.com; rue de Nesmond; adult/child incl audioguide €9/4; ⏲9am-6.30pm mid-Mar–mid-Nov, to 7pm May-Aug, 9.30am-12.30pm & 2-6pm mid-Nov–mid-Mar

creations. The half-timbered building housing the workshop, decorated with carved wooden figures, dates from the 1400s.

Musée Mémorial de la Bataille de Normandie Museum

(Battle of Normandy Memorial Museum; www.bayeuxmuseum.com; bd Fabien Ware; adult/child €6/4; ⏲9.30am-6.30pm May-Sep, 10am-

12.30pm & 2-6pm Oct-Apr) Using well-chosen photos, personal accounts, dioramas and wartime objects, this first-rate museum offers an excellent introduction to the Battle of Normandy. The 25-minute film is screened in both French and English.

Sleeping

Les Logis du Rempart B&B €
(☎02 31 92 50 40; www.lecornu.fr; 4 rue Bourbesneur; d €60-100, tr €110-130;) The three rooms of this delightful *maison de famille* ooze old-fashioned cosiness. Our favourite, the Bajocasse, has parquet floor and Toile de Jouy wallpaper. The shop downstairs is the perfect place to stock up on top-quality, homemade cider and *calvados* (apple brandy).

Hôtel d'Argouges Traditional Hotel €€
(☎02 31 92 88 86; www.hotel-dargouges.com; 21 rue St-Patrice; d/tr/f €140/193/245; closed Dec & Jan;) Occupying a stately 18th-century residence with a lush little garden, this graceful hotel has 28 comfortable rooms with exposed beams, thick walls and Louis XVI–style furniture. The breakfast room, hardly changed since 1734, still has its original wood panels and parquet floors.

Eating

La Reine Mathilde Patisserie €
(47 rue St-Martin; cakes from €2.20; 9am-7.30pm Tue-Sun) This sumptuously decorated patisserie and *salon de thé* (tearoom), ideal for a sweet breakfast or a relaxing cup of afternoon tea, hasn't changed much since it was built in 1898.

Le Pommier Norman €€
(☎02 31 21 52 10; www.restaurantlepommier.com; 38-40 rue des Cuisiniers; lunch menu €15-18, other menus €21-39.50; noon-2pm & 7-9pm, closed Sun Nov-Feb;) At this romantic restaurant, delicious Norman classics include steamed pollock and Caen-style tripe. A vegetarian menu – a rarity in Normandy – is also available, with offerings such as soybean steak in Norman cream.

Information

Tourist Office (☎02 31 51 28 28; www.bayeux-bessin-tourisme.com; pont St-Jean; 9.30am-12.30pm & 2-6pm Mon-Sat) Covers both Bayeux and the surrounding Bessin region, including the D-Day beaches. Has a walking-tour map of town and bus and train schedules, and sells books on the D-Day landings in English. Charges €2 to book hotels and B&Bs.

Getting There & Away

Bayeux' train station is 1km southeast of the cathedral. Direct services include:

Caen €6.60, 20 minutes, at least hourly

Pontorson (Mont St-Michel) €23.90, 1¾ hours, three daily

D-Day Beaches

Code-named 'Operation Overlord', the D-Day landings were the largest military operation in history. On the morning of 6 June 1944, swarms of landing craft – part of an armada of over 6000 ships and boats – hit the northern Normandy beaches and tens of thousands of soldiers from the USA, the UK, Canada and elsewhere began pouring onto French soil.

The majority of the 135,000 Allied troops stormed ashore along 80km of beaches north of Bayeux code-named (from west to east) Utah, Omaha, Gold, Juno and Sword. The landings on D-Day – known as 'Jour J' in French – were followed by the 76-day Battle of Normandy, during which the Allies suffered 210,000 casualties, including 37,000 troops killed. German casualties are believed to have been around 200,000; another 200,000 German soldiers were taken prisoner. About 14,000 French civilians also died.

Caen's Mémorial (p127) and Bayeux' Musée Mémorial (p122) provide a comprehensive overview of the events of D-Day, and many of the villages near the landing beaches (eg Arromanches) have local museums with insightful exhibits.

If you've got your own wheels, you can follow the D514 along the D-Day coast or several signposted circuits around the battle sites – look for signs for 'D-Day-Le Choc' in the American sectors and 'Overlord-L'Assaut' in the British and Canadian sectors. A free booklet called *The D-Day Landings and the Battle of Normandy*, available from tourist offices, has details on the eight major visitors' routes.

 Tours

An organised minibus tour is an excellent way to get a sense of the D-Day beaches and their place in history. The Bayeux tourist office can handle reservations.

Tours by Mémorial – Un Musée pour la Paix Minibus Tour
(☎02 31 06 06 45; www.memorial-caen.fr; adult/child morning €64/64, afternoon €81/64; ⏰9am & 2pm Apr-Sep, 1pm Oct-Mar, closed 3 weeks in Jan) Excellent year-round minibus tours (four to five hours), with cheaper tours in full-size buses (€39) from June to August. Rates include entry to Le Mémorial – Un Musée pour la Paix. Book online.

Normandy Sightseeing Tours Guided Tour
(☎02 31 51 70 52; www.normandy-sightseeing-tours.com; adult/child morning €45/25, all-day €90/50) This experienced outfit offers morning tours of various beaches and cemeteries, as well as all-day excursions.

Normandy Tours Guided Tour
(☎02 31 92 10 70; www.normandy-landing-tours.com; 26 place de la Gare, Bayeux; adult/student €62/55) Offers well-regarded four- to five-hour tours of the main sites starting at 8.15am and 1.15pm on most days, as well as personally tailored trips. Based at Bayeux' Hôtel de la Gare, facing the train station.

 Getting There & Away

Bus Verts (www.busverts.fr) links Bayeux' train station and place St-Patrice with many of the villages along the D-Day beaches.

ARROMANCHES

In order to unload the vast quantities of cargo needed by the invasion forces without having to capture – intact! – one of the heavily defended Channel ports (a lesson of the 1942 Dieppe Raid), the Allies set up prefabricated marinas, code-named **Mulberry Harbour**, off two of the landing beaches.

The harbour established at Omaha was completely destroyed by a ferocious gale just two weeks after D-Day, but the remains of the second, **Port Winston** (named after Churchill), can still be seen near Arromanches, 10km northeast of Bayeux. At low tide you can walk out to one of the caissons from the beach.

Down in Arromanches itself and right on the beach, the **Musée du Débarquement** (Landing Museum; ☎02 31 22 34 31; www.musee-arromanches.fr; place du 6 Juin; adult/child €7.90/5.80; ⏰9am-12.30pm & 1.30-5pm Oct-Apr, 9am-5pm May-Sep, closed Jan), redesigned in 2004 for the 60th anniversary of D-Day, makes an informative stop before visiting the beaches.

LONGUES-SUR-MER

Part of the Nazis' Atlantic Wall, the massive casemates and 150mm German guns near Longues-sur-Mer, 6km west of Arromanches, were designed to hit targets some 20km away, including both Gold Beach (to the east) and Omaha Beach (to the west). Over six decades later, the mammoth artillery pieces are still in their colossal concrete emplacements – the only in situ large-calibre weapons in Normandy.

Parts of the classic D-Day film, *The Longest Day* (1962), were filmed both here and at Pointe du Hoc.

OMAHA BEACH

The most brutal fighting on D-Day took place on the 7km stretch of coastline around Vierville-sur-Mer, St-Laurent-sur-Mer and Colleville-sur-Mer, 15km northwest of Bayeux, known as 'Bloody Omaha' to US veterans. Sixty years on, little evidence of the carnage unleashed here on 6 June 1944 remains except for concrete German bunkers, though at very low tide you can see a few remnants of the Mulberry Harbour.

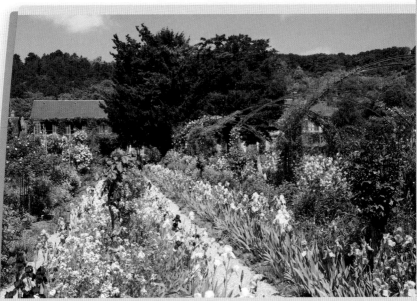

EURASIA PRESS/GETTY IMAGES ©

Don't Miss Giverny

The tiny country village of Giverny, 15km south of Les Andelys, is a place of pilgrimage for devotees of impressionism, and can feel swamped by the tour-bus crowd in the summer months. Monet lived here from 1883 until his death in 1926, in a rambling house surrounded by flower-filled gardens that's now the immensely popular **Maison et Jardins de Claude Monet.** Monet bought the Jardin d'Eau (Water Garden) in 1895 and set about creating his trademark lily pond, as well as the famous Japanese bridge (since rebuilt). Seasons have an enormous effect on Giverny. From early to late spring, daffodils, tulips, rhododendrons, wisteria and irises appear, followed by poppies and lilies. By June, nasturtiums, roses and sweet peas are in flower. Around September, there are dahlias, sunflowers and hollyhocks.

Giverny's other lure is the **Musée des Impressionnismes Giverny**, 100m down the road from the Maison de Claude Monet. Surrounded by beautiful gardens, this museum displays works by various impressionists as well as temporary exhibitions.

From Paris Gare St-Lazare there are up to 15 daily trains to Vernon (€14.30, 50 minutes), 7km to the west of Giverny. Shuttle buses (€8 return, 20 minutes, four daily April to October) meet most trains to and from Paris, or you can catch a taxi outside the station for around €15.

NEED TO KNOW

Maison et Jardins de Claude Monet (02 32 51 28 21; www.fondation-monet.com; 84 rue Claude Monet; adult/child €9.50/5, incl Musée des Impressionnismes Giverny €16.50/8; 9.30am-6pm Apr-Oct)

Musée des Impressionnismes Giverny (02 32 51 94 65; www.mdig.fr; 99 rue Claude Monet; adult/child €7/4.50, incl Maison et Jardins de Claude Monet €16.50/8; 10am-6pm Apr-Oct)

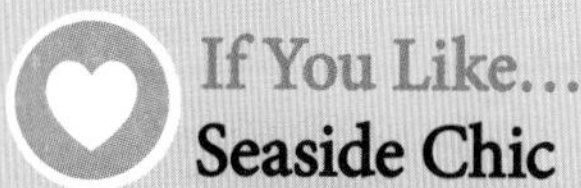

If You Like… Seaside Chic

If you love the see-and-be-seen vibe of hip Honfleur, you might just find yourself extending your catwalk strut along the boardwalks with these two enticing beach towns. Both are hugely popular with trendy Parisians who flock here at weekends year-round and all week long April to September.

1 DEAUVILLE

Chic Deauville (population 4100), 15km southwest of Honfleur, has been a playground of the wealthy ever since it was founded by Napoléon III's half-brother, the Duke of Morny, in 1861. Exclusive, expensive and brash, it's packed with designer boutiques, deluxe hotels, renowned horse-racing tracks, and public gardens of impossible neatness. The rich and beautiful strut their stuff along the beachside Promenade des Planches, a 643m-long boardwalk lined with cabins named after famous Americans (mainly film stars).

2 TROUVILLE

Trouville (population 5075), another veteran beach resort with the celebrity set, is also a working fishing port and, in many ways, a more attractive place to visit. The town was frequented by painters and writers during the 19th century, including Mozin and Flaubert, and many French celebrities have holiday homes here, lured by the 2km-long sandy beach, casino and laid-back seaside ambience. The town's history is recounted in the **Musée de Trouville** (☎02 31 88 16 26; 64 rue du Général Leclerc; adult/child €2/1.50; ⏲2-5.30pm Wed-Mon Apr–mid-Nov, opens 11am Sat, Sun & holidays), inside the fine beach-facing Villa Montebello. Trouville is linked to Deauville by Pont des Belges, just east of Deauville's train and bus stations, and by a low-tide footpath near the river's mouth.

On a bluff above the beach, the huge **Normandy American Cemetery & Memorial** (www.abmc.gov; Colleville-sur-Mer; ⏲9am-6pm mid-Apr–mid-Sep, to 5pm rest of the year), 17km northwest of Bayeux, is the largest American cemetery in Europe. Featured in the opening scenes of Steven Spielberg's *Saving Private Ryan*, it contains the graves of 9387 American soldiers, including 41 pairs of brothers, and a memorial to 1557 others whose remains were never found. White marble crosses and Stars of David stretch off in seemingly endless rows, surrounded by an immaculately tended expanse of lawn.

Opened in 2007, the **visitor center**, mostly underground so as not to detract from the site, has an excellent free multimedia presentation on the D-Day landings.

POINTE DU HOC RANGER MEMORIAL

At 7.10am on 6 June 1944, 225 US Army Rangers commanded by Lt Col James Earl Rudder scaled the 30m cliffs at Pointe du Hoc, where the Germans had a battery of huge artillery guns perfectly placed to rain shells onto the beaches of Utah and Omaha. Unbeknown to Rudder and his team, the guns had already been transferred inland, and they spent the next two days repelling fierce German counterattacks. By the time they were finally relieved on 8 June, 81 of the rangers had been killed and 58 more had been wounded.

Today the **site** (☎02 31 51 90 70; www.abmc.gov; ⏲9am-6pm mid-Apr–mid-Sep, to 5pm rest of the year) FREE, which France turned over to the US government in 1979, looks much as it did more than half a century ago. The ground is pockmarked with bomb craters, and the German command post (no longer open to the public because it's too close to the eroding cliff) and several of the concrete gun emplacements are still standing, scarred by bullet holes and blackened by flame-throwers.

As you face the sea, Utah Beach is 14km to the left.

UTAH BEACH

This beach is marked by memorials to the various divisions that landed here and the **Musée du Débarquement** (Utah Beach Landing Museum; ☎02 33 71 53 35; www.

utah-beach.com; Ste-Marie du Mont; adult/child €8/3.50; 9.30am-7pm Jun-Sep, 10am-6pm Oct-May, closed Jan).

CAEN MÉMORIAL

Situated 3km northwest of Caen city centre, the innovative **Mémorial – Un Musée pour la Paix** (Memorial – A Museum for Peace; 02 31 06 06 44; www.memorial-caen.fr; esplanade Général Eisenhower; adult/child €19/11.50; 9am-7pm daily mid-Feb–mid-Nov, 9.30am-6.30pm Tue-Sun mid-Nov–mid-Feb, closed 3 weeks in Jan) provides an insightful and vivid account of the Battle of Normandy. The visit begins with a whistle-stop overview of Europe's descent into total war, tracing events from the end of WWI and the Treaty of Versailles, through the rise of fascism in Europe and the German occupation of France, right up through the Battle of Normandy. It's a hugely impressive affair, using sound, lighting, film, animation and audio testimony, as well as a range of artefacts and exhibits, to graphically evoke the realities of war, the trials of occupation and the joy of liberation. A second section focuses on the Cold War. There's also an underground gallery dedicated to winners of the Nobel Peace Prize, located in bunkers used by the Germans in 1944. To get here by car, follow the signs marked 'Mémorial'.

Honfleur

POP 8350

Long a favourite with painters but now more popular with the Parisian jet set, Honfleur is arguably Normandy's most charming seaside town. Even though it can be overrun with tourists in the summer months, it's hard not to love its graceful beauty.

Sights

Église Ste-Catherine Church

(place Ste-Catherine; 9am-5.15pm or later) Initially intended as a temporary structure, this extraordinary wooden church was built by local shipwrights during the late 15th and early 16th centuries after its stone predecessor was destroyed during the Hundred Years War. Wood was used so money would be left over to strengthen the city's fortifications. From the inside, the remarkable twin naves and double-vaulted roof resemble two overturned ships' hulls. Situated a block southwest (up the hill) from the northern end of the Vieux Bassin.

Musée Eugène Boudin Art Museum

(02 31 89 54 00; www.musees-honfleur.fr; 50 rue de l'Homme de Bois; adult/child €5.60/4.10, late Jun-Sep €6.50/5; 10am-noon & 2-6pm Wed-Mon mid-Mar–Sep, 2.30-5.30pm Wed-Mon, 10am-noon Sat & Sun Oct–mid-Mar) Features superb 19th- and 20th-century paintings of Normandy's towns and coast, including works by Dubourg, Dufy and Monet.

Honfleur

One room is devoted to Eugène Boudin, an early impressionist painter, born here in 1824, whom Baudelaire called the 'king of skies' for his luscious skyscapes. An English audioguide costs €2. Situated five short blocks northwest of the northern end of the Vieux Bassin.

Les Maisons Satie Museum
(**02 31 89 11 11; www.musees-honfleur.fr; 67 bd Charles V & 90 rue Haute; adult/child €6.10/4.60; 10am-6pm Wed-Mon, last entry 1hr before closing)** Like no other museum you've ever seen, this complex captures the whimsical spirit of the eccentric avant-garde composer Erik Satie (1866–1925), who lived and worked in Honfleur and was born in one of the two half-timbered *maisons Satie* (Satie houses). Visitors wander through the utterly original rooms, each hiding a surreal surprise, with a headset playing Satie's strangely familiar music. Situated 350m northwest of the northern end of the Vieux Bassin.

Sleeping

À l'École Buissonnière B&B €€
(**06 16 18 43 62; www.a-lecole-buissonniere.com; 4 rue de la Foulerie; d incl breakfast €100-120;**) Occupying a former girls' school built in the 1600s, this welcoming B&B, lovingly restored, has five luxurious rooms with antique wood furnishings. For lunch, stop by the *bar à fromages* (cheese bar), or have them prepare a picnic lunch (€15). Bikes cost €15 a day. Situated three short blocks southwest of Église Ste-Catherine.

La Petite Folie B&B €€
(**06 74 39 46 46; www.lapetitefolie-honfleur.com; 44 rue Haute; d €145-160, apt €185-295;**) Penny Vincent, an American who moved to France from San Francisco, and her French husband Thierry are the gracious hosts at this elegant townhouse, built in 1830 and still graced by the original stained glass and tile floors. Hard to believe, but this was beachfront property back then! There's a two-night minimum. Situated four short blocks northwest of the northern end of the Vieux Bassin.

Eating

Au P'tit Mareyeur French €€
(**02 31 98 84 23; www.auptitmareyeur.fr; 4 rue Haute; lunch/dinner menu €28/35; noon-2pm & 7-10pm Thu-Mon, closed Jan)** Arrayed under 17th-century beams, this 'semi-gastronomique' restaurant serves up Norman-style fish and langoustine, foie gras and *bouillabaisse honfleuraise* (fish and seafood stew made with potatoes and saffron; €32); some of the side dishes feature South Indian spices. A new dining area opened upstairs in 2014. Situated two blocks northwest of the northern end of the Vieux Bassin.

L'Endroit French €€
(**02 31 88 08 43; 3 rue Charles et Paul Bréard; weekday lunch menu €21, other menus €28.50; noon-1.30pm & 7.30-9pm Thu-Mon)** Normandy-grown heritage vegetables accompany the traditional French fish and meat dishes at L'Endroit, a classy and very well-regarded bistrot whose open kitchen lets you watch the chefs as they cook. Situated three blocks block southeast of the southern end of the Vieux Bassin.

Information

Tourist Office (**02 31 89 23 30; www.ot-honfleur.fr; quai Lepaulmier; 9.30am-12.30pm & 2-6pm Mon-Sat Sep-Jun, 9.30am-6pm Jul & Aug, also open 9.30am-5pm Sun Easter-Sep;**) Has a free map detailing three enjoyable walking circuits, audioguides (€3.50) for a walking tour of the town (in English, French and German), and bus schedules. Internet access costs €1 for 15 minutes. Situated a long block southeast of the Vieux Bassin, inside the ultra-modern Médiathèque (library) building.

Getting There & Away

The **bus station** (**quai Lepaulmier**) is two blocks east of the tourist office. **Bus Verts** (**08 10 21 42 14; www.busverts.fr**) services include Deauville and Trouville (€2, 30 minutes, four to seven daily) and Caen (bus 20 €6.95, 2½ hours, seven to 13 daily; bus 39 €11.15, one hour, one or two daily).

Camembert

Some of the most enduring names in the pungent world of French *fromage* come from Normandy, including **Pont L'Évêque**, **Livarot** and, most famous of all, **Camembert**, all of which are named after towns south of Honfleur, on or near the D579.

The invention of Camembert is generally credited to Marie Harel, who was supposedly given the secret of soft cheesemaking by an abbot from Brie on the run from Revolutionary mobs in 1790. Whatever the truth of the legend, the cheese was a huge success at the local market in Vimoutiers, and production of Camembert quickly grew from a cottage industry into an international operation. The distinctive round wooden boxes, in which Camembert is wrapped, have been around since 1890; they were designed by a local engineer to protect the soft disc during long-distance travel.

To see how cheese is made, take a guided tour of the **Président Farm (☎02 33 12 10 37; www.fermepresident.com; adult/child €3.50/1.50; ⏰10am-noon & 2-5pm daily May-Sep, Wed-Sun Apr & Oct, Fri-Sun mid-Feb–Mar, closed Nov–mid-Feb)**, an early-19th-century farm restored by Président, one of the region's largest Camembert producers. It's in the centre of the town of Camembert, which is about 60km south of Honfleur.

Mont St-Michel

POP 43

It's one of France's most iconic images: the slender towers and sky-scraping turrets of the abbey of Mont St-Michel rising from stout ramparts and battlements, the whole ensemble connected to the mainland by a narrow causeway (which will be replaced by a bridge by 2014; see www.projetmontsaintmichel.fr for more information on the changes that are under way). Fortunately, although it's visited by huge numbers of tourists, both French and foreign, the Mont still manages to whisk you back to the Middle Ages, its fantastic architecture set against the backdrop of the area's extraordinary tides.

The bay around Mont St-Michel is famed for having Europe's highest tidal variations; the difference between low

Pont L'Évêque, Normandy

ROBERT ZEHETMAYER/ALAMY ©

Mont St-Michel

TIMELINE

708 Inspired by a vision of **St Michael** ❶, Bishop Aubert is inspired to 'build here and build high'.

966 Richard I, Duke of Normandy, gives the Mont to the Benedictines. The three levels of the **abbey** ❷ reflect their monastic hierarchy.

1017 Development of the abbey begins. Pilgrims arrive to honour the cult of St Michael. They walk barefoot across the mudflats and up the **Grande Rue** ❸ to be received in the almonry (now the bookshop).

1203 The monastery is burnt by the troops of Philip Augustus, who later donates money for its restoration and the Gothic 'miracle', **La Merveille** ❹, is constructed.

1434 The Mont's **ramparts** ❺ and fortifications ensure it withstands the English assault during the Hundred Years War. It is the only place in northern France not to fall.

1789 After the Revolution, Monasticism is abolished and the Mont is turned into a prison. During this period the **treadmill** ❻ is built to lift up supplies.

1878 The Mont is linked to the mainland by a **causeway** ❼.

1979 The Mont is declared a Unesco World Heritage Site.

2014 The causeway is replaced by a bridge.

TOP TIPS

➡ Pick up a picnic lunch at the supermarket in La Caserne to avoid the Mont's overpriced fast food.

➡ Allow 45 minutes to an hour to get from the new parking lot in La Caserne to the Mont.

➡ If you step off the island pay close attention to the tides - they can be dangerous.

➡ Don't forget to pick up the Abbey's excellent audioguide – it tells some great stories.

JOHN ELK III/GETTY IMAGES ©

ÎLOT DE TOMBELAINE

Occupied by the English during the Hundred Years War, this islet is now a bird reserve. From April to July it teems with exceptional birdlife.

Treadmill
The giant treadmill was powered hamsterlike by half a dozen prisoners, who, marching two abreast, raised stone and supplies up the Mont.

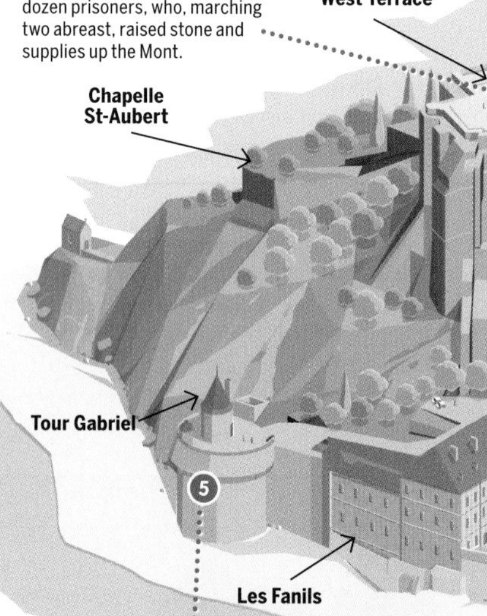

Ramparts
The Mont was also a military garrison surrounded by machicolated and turreted walls, dating from the 13th to 15th centuries. The single entrance, Porte de l'Avancée, ensured its security in the Hundred Years War. Tip: Tour du Nord (North Tower) has the best views.

ROCCO FASANO/GETTY IMAGES ©

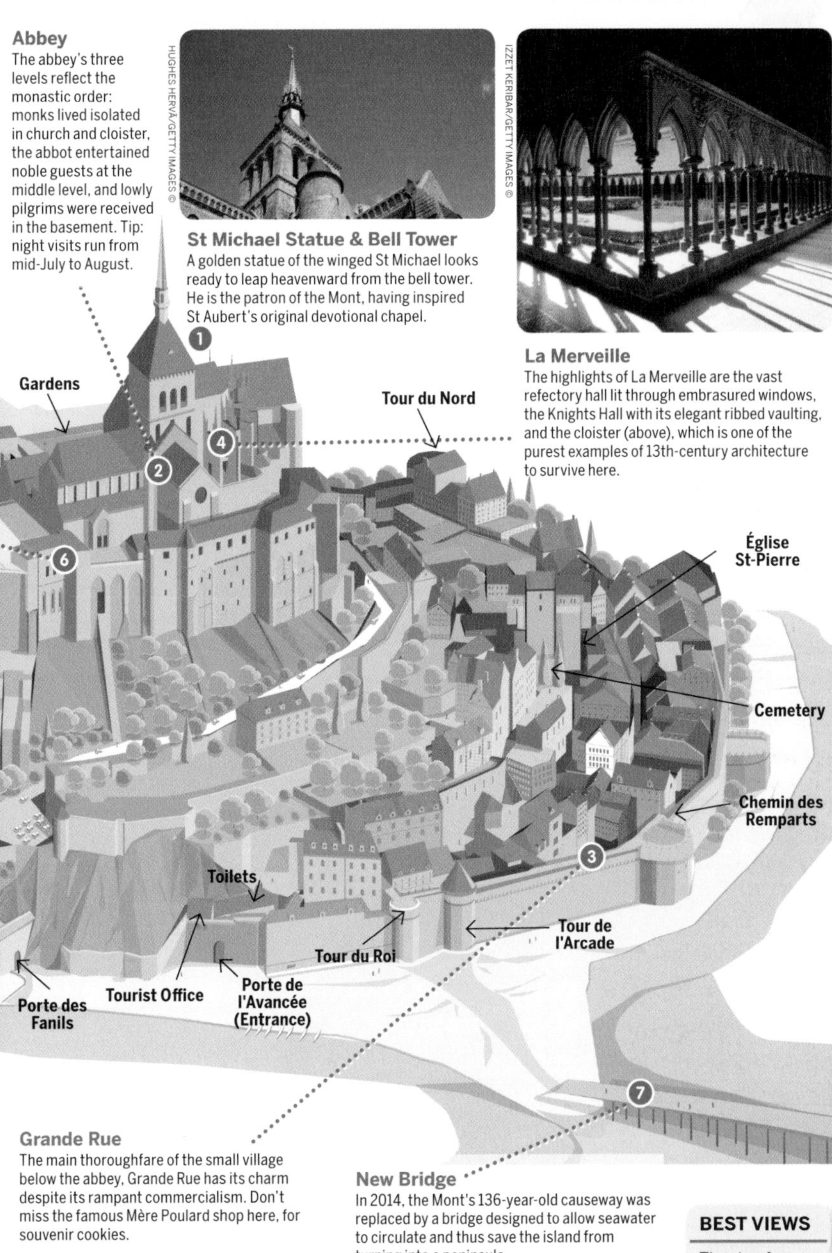

Abbey
The abbey's three levels reflect the monastic order: monks lived isolated in church and cloister, the abbot entertained noble guests at the middle level, and lowly pilgrims were received in the basement. Tip: night visits run from mid-July to August.

St Michael Statue & Bell Tower
A golden statue of the winged St Michael looks ready to leap heavenward from the bell tower. He is the patron of the Mont, having inspired St Aubert's original devotional chapel.

La Merveille
The highlights of La Merveille are the vast refectory hall lit through embrasured windows, the Knights Hall with its elegant ribbed vaulting, and the cloister (above), which is one of the purest examples of 13th-century architecture to survive here.

Grande Rue
The main thoroughfare of the small village below the abbey, Grande Rue has its charm despite its rampant commercialism. Don't miss the famous Mère Poulard shop here, for souvenir cookies.

DAVID TOMLINSON/GETTY IMAGES ©

New Bridge
In 2014, the Mont's 136-year-old causeway was replaced by a bridge designed to allow seawater to circulate and thus save the island from turning into a peninsula.

ART WIDAK/DEMOTIX/CORBIS ©

BEST VIEWS

The view from the Jardin des Plantes in nearby Avranches is unique, as are the panoramas from Pointe du Grouin du Sud near the village of St-Léonard.

and high tides can reach an astonishing 15m. At low tide the Mont is surrounded by bare sand for kilometres around, but at high tide, barely six hours later, the whole bay can be submerged.

Be prepared for lots of steps, some of them spiral – alas, the Mont is one of the least wheelchair-accessible sites in France.

Sights

Abbaye du Mont St-Michel Abbey
(02 33 89 80 00; www.monuments-nationaux.fr; adult/child incl guided tour €9/free; 9am-7pm, last entry 1hr before closing) The Mont's star attraction is the stunning architectural ensemble high up on top: the abbey. Most areas can be visited without a guide, but it's well worth taking the one-hour tour included in the ticket price; English tours (usually) begin at 11am and 3pm from October to March, with three or four daily tours in spring and summer. You can also take a 1½-hour audioguide tour (one/two people €4.50/6), available in six languages.

Église Abbatiale Church
(Abbey Church) Built on the rocky tip of the mountain cone, the transept rests on solid rock, while the nave, choir and transept arms are supported by the rooms below. This church is famous for its mix of architectural styles: the nave and south transept (11th and 12th centuries) are solid Norman Romanesque, while the choir (late 15th century) is Flamboyant Gothic.

La Merveille Historic Site
The buildings on the northern side of the Mont are known as 'The Marvel'. The famous **cloître** (cloister) is surrounded by a double row of delicately carved arches resting on granite pillars. The early-13th-century, barrel-roofed **réfectoire** (dining hall) is illuminated by a wall of recessed windows – remarkable given that the sheer drop precluded the use of flying buttresses. The Gothic **Salle des Hôtes** (Guest Hall), dating from 1213, has two enormous fireplaces.

Information

Mont St-Michel Tourist Office (02 33 60 14 30; www.ot-montsaintmichel.com; 9am-12.30pm & 2-6pm Sep-Jun, 9am-7pm Jul & Aug) Has an *horaire des marées* (tide table) posted, changes money and sells an excellent detailed map of the Mont (€3). Next door are toilets (€0.40) and an ATM. It's just inside Porte de l'Avancée, up the stairs to the left.

Getting There & Away

Bus

Inter-city buses stop next to the Mont's new car park in La Caserne, very near the shuttles to the Mont.

Bus 1 (every hour or two, more frequently in July and August), operated by Transdev, links La Caserne with the village of Beauvoir (€3, five minutes) and the train station in Pontorson

Abbaye du Mont St-Michel
LEMAIRE STEPHANE/HEMIS.FR/GETTY IMAGES ©

(€3, 18 minutes); times are coordinated with the arrival in Pontorson of some trains from Caen and Rennes.

Car

Visitors who arrive by car must leave their vehicles in one of the new car parks (two/24 hours €6/12) situated a few hundred metres east of La Caserne's hotel strip.

Train

The town of Pontorson, 7km south of the La Caserne parking area, is the area's main rail hub. Services from Pontorson include:

Bayeux €23.90, 1¾ hours, three daily

Caen €26.10, 1¾ hours, three daily

BRITTANY

Brittany is for explorers. Its wild, dramatic coastline, medieval towns and thick forests make an excursion here well worth the detour from the beaten track. This is a land of prehistoric mysticism, proud tradition and culinary wealth, where fiercely independent locals celebrate Breton culture and Paris feels a long way away indeed.

St-Malo

POP 48,800

The enthralling mast-filled port town of St-Malo has a cinematically changing landscape. With one of the world's highest tidal ranges, brewing storms under blackened skies see waves lash the top of the ramparts ringing its beautiful walled city. Hours later, the blue sky merges with the deep marine-blue sea, exposing beaches as wide and flat as the clear skies above and creating land bridges to the granite outcrop islands.

The town became a key port during the 17th and 18th centuries as a base for both merchant ships and government-sanctioned privateers (pirates, basically) against the constant threat of the English. These days English arrivals are tourists, for whom St-Malo, a short ferry hop from the Channel Islands, is a summer haven.

Local Knowledge

Mont St-Michel Don't Miss List

BY JACK LECOQ, WALKING GUIDE

1 THE BAREFOOT WALK

You can wear plastic shoes, but walking the 13km from Bec d'Andaine in Genêts to Mont St-Michel barefoot is wonderful. We walk across pitch sand, quicksand, sand flats and endless ripple marks made by the tides.

2 ÎLOT DE TOMBELAINE

After walking for about an hour (3km) this islet, occupied by the English for 35 years during the Hundred Years War, pops up. It is now a bird reserve and, from April to July, full of exceptional birdlife. November to March, once the birds have left, you can follow a tiny footpath to the top of the islet for an exceptional view of Mont St-Michel.

3 ABBAYE DU MONT ST-MICHEL

We cross the River Couesnon, the medieval border between Normandy and Brittany, and there is the Mont. The abbey is marvellous. It has beautiful works of art and rooms: the hall where pilgrims gathered is magnificent, as is the Salle des Chevaliers (Knights Hall), where monks spent hours illuminating manuscripts.

4 AVRANCHES

After visiting the abbey it's worth going to Avranches to **Le Scriptorial** (Musée des Manuscrits du Mont St-Michel; ☎ 02 33 79 57 00; place d'Estouteville; adult/child €7/3; ⏰10am-7pm daily Jul & Aug, shorter hours rest of year) where all the historical documents and manuscripts scribed at the abbey are preserved. It illuminates Mont St-Michel's many legends.

5 MEMORABLE MOUNT VIEWS

The view from the Jardin des Plantes in Avranches is unique; as are the bay panoramas from Pointe du Grouin du Sud near the fishing village of St-Léonard, 5km southwest, and the clifftops in Carolles, 20km north.

Sights & Activities

For the best views of the walled city, either stroll along the **jetty** that pokes out to sea off the southwestern tip of Intra Muros from the end of which you'll get the wide angle view or, to zoom in, clamber along the top of the **ramparts**, constructed at the end of the 17th century under military architect Vauban, and measuring 1.8km.

Cathédrale St-Vincent Cathedral

(place Jean de Châtillon; 9.30am-6pm) The city's centrepiece was constructed between the 12th and 18th centuries. During the ferocious fighting of August 1944 the cathedral was badly hit; much of its original structure (including its spire) was reduced to rubble. The cathedral was subsequently rebuilt and reconsecrated in 1971. A mosaic plaque on the floor of the nave marks the spot where Jacques Cartier received the blessing of the bishop of St-Malo before his 'voyage of discovery' to Canada in 1535.

Musée d'Histoire de St-Malo Museum

(02 99 40 71 57; www.ville-saint-malo.fr/culture/les-musees; Château; adult/child €6/3; 10am-12.30pm & 2-6pm Apr-Sep, Tue-Sun Oct-Mar) Within **Château de St-Malo**, built by the dukes of Brittany in the 15th and 16th centuries, this museum looks at the life and history of the city through nautical exhibits, model boats and marine artefacts, as well as an exhibition covering the city's cod-fishing heritage. There's also background info on the city's sons, including Cartier, Surcouf, Duguay-Trouin and the writer Chateaubriand.

Île du Grand Bé & Fort du Petit Bé Island, Castle

(06 08 27 51 20; www.petit-be.com; Fort du Petit Bé guided tours adult/child €5/3; Fort du Petit Bé by reservation, depending on tides) The walled city feels too claustrophobic for you? At low tide, cross the beach to walk out via the Porte des Bés to the rocky islet of Île du Grand Bé, where the great St-Malo-born 18th-century writer Chateaubriand is buried. Once the tide rushes in, the causeway remains impassable for about six hours; check tide times with the tourist office.

Fort National Ruin

(www.fortnational.com; adult/child €5/3; Easter, school holidays & Jun-Sep) The St-Malo ramparts' northern stretch looks across to the remains of this former prison, built by Vauban in 1689. Standing atop a rocky outcrop, the fort can only be accessed at low tide. Ask at the tourist office for times of tours.

Sleeping

Hôtel San Pedro Hotel €

(02 99 40 88 57; www.sanpedro-hotel.com; 1 rue Ste-Anne; s €65-69, d €75-83;) Tucked at the back of the old city, the San Pedro has a cool, crisp, neutral-toned decor with subtle splashes of yellow paint, friendly service, great breakfast, private parking (€10) and a few bikes available for free. It features 12 rooms on four floors served by a miniature lift (forget those big suitcases!); two rooms come with sea views.

Hôtel Quic en Groigne Hotel €€

(02 99 20 22 20; www.quic-en-groigne.com; 8 rue d'Estrées; s €69-72, d €79-112; Feb-Dec;) This exceptional hotel has 15 recently renovated rooms that are the epitome of clean, simple style; many a hotel twice the price should be envious of this place. It offers excellent service and an ideal location on a quiet, old town street just a few metres from a beach.

Eating

L'Absinthe Modern French €€

(02 99 40 26 15; www.restaurant-absinthe-cafe.fr; 1 rue de l'Orme; mains €18-24, menus €28-45; noon-2pm & 7-10pm) Hidden away in a quiet street near the covered market, this fab (and very French) eatery is housed in an imposing 17th-century building. Ingredients fresh from the nearby market are whipped into shape by the talented chef, Stéphane Brebel, and served in cosy surrounds. The wine list is another hit, with an all-French cast from white to red and rosé.

Le Bistro de Jean Bistro **€€**
(**☎02 99 40 98 68; 6 rue de la Corne de Cerf; mains €19-20, menus €14-19; ⏰noon-1.30pm Mon-Sat, 7-9.15pm Mon, Tue, Thu & Fri**) Want to know where the locals choose to eat inside the walls? Peer through the windows of this lively, authentic bistro and you'll get your answer. The place is packed at lunchtime with loyal regulars, which is a good sign. The flavourful cuisine, based on fresh ingredients, includes duck breast, lamb shanks and succulent line-caught sea bass. Excellent homemade desserts, too.

Information

Tourist Office (**☎08 25 13 52 00; www.saint-malo-tourisme.com; esplanade St-Vincent; ⏰9am-7.30pm Mon-Sat, 10am-6pm Sun**) Just outside the walls.

Getting There & Away

Brittany Ferries (**www.brittany-ferries.com**) sails between St-Malo and Portsmouth, and **Condor Ferries** (**www.condorferries.co.uk**) runs to/from Poole via Jersey or Guernsey. Car ferries leave from the Gare Maritime du Naye.

In July and August **Compagnie Corsaire** (**☎08 25 13 80 35; www.compagniecorsaire.com; adult/child return €8.10/5.30**) runs a Bus de Mer shuttle service (10 minutes, at least half-hourly) between St-Malo and Dinard. Outside the July-August peak season both frequency, and cost, falls.

Various trains run from St-Malo:

Dinan €10, one hour, six daily (requiring a change in Dol de Bretagne)

Paris Montparnasse €50 to €66, three hours, three direct TGVs daily

Rennes €14.60, one hour, roughly hourly

Dinard

POP 11,230

Visiting Dinard 'in season' is a little like stepping into one of the canvases Picasso painted here in the 1920s. Belle époque mansions built into the cliffs form a timeless backdrop to the beach dotted with blue-and-white striped bathing tents and the beachside carnival. Out of season, when holidaymakers have packed up their buckets and spades, the town is decidedly dormant, but wintry walks along the coastal paths are spectacular.

Fort National, St-Malo

If You Like... Islands

Île de Batz is just one of many idyllic islands dotted around the Breton coastline. Blessed with beautiful beaches, rich wildlife and stunning coastal walks, the islands are perfect day-trip fodder.

1 **ÎLE D'OUESSANT**

There's a real end-of-the-world air to go-slow Île d'Ouessant, a remote paradise with little to do bar hike its 45km craggy coastal path, picnic or flop in the sun. Its black-and-white-striped **Phare de Créac'h** is the world's most powerful lighthouse; discover its history inside in the **Musée des Phares et des Balises** (Lighthouse & Beacon Museum; ☎02 98 48 80 70; adult/child €4.30/3; ⏰10.30am-6pm Jul-Aug, 11am-5pm Apr-Jun & Sep). **Penn Ar Bed** (☎02 98 80 80 80; www.pennarbed.fr) ferries depart from Brest (adult/child return €34.80/27.80, 2½ hours) and the Brittany's most westerly point, Le Conquet (same prices, 1½ hours).

2 **ÎLE MOLÈNE**

Scarcely 1km wide, Île Molène is carless, virtually treeless, home to just 270 people and its electricity supply comes from a single diesel generator. The only village is Le Bourg, a huddle of white-washed fisher cottages clustered around a granite quay. Explore on foot, or hire a kayak or canoe at the port. Ferries to Ouessant stop here en-route.

3 **BELLE ÎLE**

Brittany's largest island (population 5200), with its dramatic Vauban-designed citadel and quaint Le Palais port, sees its population swell ten-fold in summer. Surfers get a kick out of **Plage de Donnant** while hikers pound the 95km coastal path; the fretted southwestern coast has spectacular rock formations and caves including Grotte de l'Apothicairerie (Cave of the Apothecary's Shop). **Compagnie Océane** (☎08 20 05 61 56; www.compagnie-oceane.fr; adult/child return from €31.65/19.60) sail here from Quiberon (45 minutes, year-round).

Sights & Activities

Beautiful seaside trails extend along the coast in both directions. Two-hour **guided walks** (adult/child €5/3) explaining the town's history, art and architecture (in English and French) depart from the tourist office.

Beaches & Swimming
Swimming

Framed by fashionable hotels, a casino and neo-Gothic villas, **Plage de l'Écluse** (Grande Plage) is the perfect place to shade yourself in style by renting one of Dinard's trademark blue-and-white striped bathing tents. Reproductions of Picasso's paintings are often planted in the sand here in high summer.

When the Plage de l'Écluse gets too crowded, savvy Dinardais take refuge at the town's smaller beaches, including **Plage du Prieuré**, 1km to the south, and **Plage de St-Énogat**, 1km to the west.

Eating

Le Balafon
Modern French **€€**

(☎02 99 46 14 81; www.lebalafon-restaurant-dinard.fr; 31 rue de la Vallée; mains €17-24, lunch menu €17, other menus €29-39; ⏰noon-2pm & 7-9.30pm Tue-Sat, noon-2pm Sun) Away from the tourist hustle and bustle of the seafront, this is a quality modern neighbourhood bistro serving freshly made meals using produce from the nearby market. The daily lunch menu consists of a couple of well-chosen and presented dishes, usually one fish and one meat. It's totally unpretentious, well priced and many locals rate it as the best place in town.

La Passerelle du Clair de Lune
Modern French **€€**

(☎02 99 16 96 37; www.la-passerelle-restaurant.com; 3 av Georges V; menus €25-38; ⏰noon-2pm & 8-9.30pm Thu-Mon) Creative, modern seafood is served up at this intimate little restaurant with stunning views over the former home of the fish now sitting on your plate.

Information

Tourist Office (**☎02 99 46 94 12; www.ot-dinard.com; 2 bd Féart; ⏰9.30am-12.15pm & 2-6pm Mon-Sat)** Staff book accommodation for free. Two-hour guided walks (adult/child €5/3) explaining the town's history, art and architecture (in English and French) depart from here. They also dole out maps and leaflets detailing self-guided walking tours taking in the best of the town's architecture.

Getting There & Away

Compagnie Corsaire (**☎08 25 13 81 00; www.compagniecorsaire.com)** runs a Bus de Mer (ferry) shuttle service (10 minutes) between St-Malo and Dinard, operating at least half-hourly.

Illenoo (**www.illenoo-services.fr)** buses connect Dinard and the train station in St-Malo (€2.30, 30 minutes, hourly).

Cancale

POP 5440

The idyllic little fishing port of Cancale, 14km east of St-Malo, is famed for its offshore *parcs à huîtres* (oyster beds).

Sights

Ferme Marine — Farm

(**☎02 99 89 69 99; www.ferme-marine.com; corniche de l'Aurore; adult/child €7/3.70; ⏰guided tours in French 11am, 3pm & 5pm Jul-mid-Sep, in English 2pm)** Learn about the art of *ostréiculture* (oyster farming) at this well-organised museum a couple of kilometres southwest of the port.

Eating

Breizh Café — Crêperie €

(**☎02 99 89 61 76; www.breizhcafe.com; 7 quai Thomas; mains €5-14; ⏰noon-3pm & 7.30-11pm Thu-Mon)** Not your average *crêperie*, the Breizh Café is renowned for its gourmet crêpes and *galettes* made from organic flours. The cappuccino-and-cream decor gives it a fresh, modern feel, and the crêpes are really first-class. Where else could you savour a *galette* stuffed with langoustines and cheese? Wash it all down with a tipple from their range of top-notch local ciders.

Breizh Café

AA WORLD TRAVEL LIBRARY/ALAMY ©

Le Coquillage Gastronomic **€€€**
(☎02 99 89 64 76; www.maisons-de-bricourt.com; D155, rte du Mont St-Michel, Le Buot; lunch menu €31, other menus €75-139; ⏰noon-2pm & 7-9pm) Super chef Olivier Roellinger's sumptuous restaurant is housed in the extremely impressive Château Richeux, 4km to the south of Cancale. Roellinger's creations have earned him three Michelin stars and you won't have trouble seeing why if you're lucky enough to get a table here. The food takes in the culinary highlights of both Brittany and Normandy, all beautifully cooked and imaginatively served.

Information

Tourist Office (☎02 99 89 63 72; www.cancale-tourisme.fr; 44 rue du Port; ⏰9.30am-1pm & 2.30-7pm) At the top of rue du Port. In July and August there's an annexe on quai Gambetta.

Getting There & Away

Keolis Emeraude (www.ksma.fr) has year-round bus services to and from St-Malo (€1.25, 30 minutes).

Roscoff

POP 3780

Unlike many of its industrial and less-than-beautiful sister Channel ports, Roscoff (Rosko in Breton) provides a captivating first glimpse of Brittany. Granite houses dating from the 16th century wreathe the pretty docks, which are surrounded by emerald-green fields producing cauliflowers, onions, tomatoes, new potatoes and artichokes.

Sights & Activities

Église Notre Dame de Kroaz-Batz Church
(place Lacaze-Duthiers; ⏰9am-noon & 2-6pm) The most obvious sight in Roscoff is this unusual church at the heart of the old town. With its Renaissance belfry rising above the flat landscape, the 16th-century Flamboyant Gothic structure is one of Brittany's most impressive churches.

Maison des Johnnies Museum
(☎02 98 61 25 48; 48 rue Brizeux; adult/child €4/free; ⏰tours 11am, 3pm & 5pm Mon-Fri) Photographs at this popular museum

Île de Batz

trace Roscoff's roaming onion farmers, known as 'Johnnies', from the early 19th century. A visit is by guided tour only. Call ahead for tour times, as they change frequently.

Centre de Découverte des Algues — Museum

(☎02 98 69 77 05; www.algopole.fr; quai d'Auxerre; ⏲10am-12.30pm & 2.30-7pm Mon-Sat) FREE You can learn about local seaweed harvesting at this enthusiastically run museum, which also organises guided walks and gives regular free lectures (often in English and German). There's also a shop.

Île de Batz — Island

(www.iledebatz.net) Bordering what is basically a 4-sq-km vegetable garden fertilised by seaweed, the beaches on the Île de Batz (pronounced 'ba, Enez Vaz' in Breton) are a peaceful place to bask. The mild island climate supports a luxuriant botanical garden, which was founded in the 19th century, with over 1500 plants from all five continents.

Ferries (adult/child return €8.50/4.50, bike €8.50, 15 minutes each way) between Roscoff and Île de Batz run every 30 minutes between 8am and 8pm in July and August, with less-frequent sailings the rest of the year.

Bicycles can be rented on the island for around €10 per day.

Sleeping & Eating

Hôtel aux Tamaris — Hotel €€

(☎02 98 61 22 99; www.hotel-aux-tamaris.com; 49 rue Edouard Corbière; d €85-115; ⏲mid-Jan–Dec; wi-fi) This smart, family-run place in an old granite building overlooking the water at the western end of town is an excellent choice, with well-equipped, light, seabreeze-filled rooms, all with a pleasant maritime aura and yacht sails for ceilings (don't worry, there's a proper ceiling as well!). Rooms with sea views cost a lot more.

Hôtel du Centre — Hotel €€

(☎02 98 61 24 25; www.chezjanie.fr; Le Port; d €104-130; ⏲mid-Feb–mid-Nov; wi-fi) You couldn't wish for a better Roscoff base than this refreshingly simple hotel perched above Chez Janie's bistro. The layouts are a bit awkward, but each room has a maritime-themed poem painted on the wall, and the bathrooms are in top nick. The sea-view rooms looking out over the postcard-pretty old port are well worth the extra cost.

L'Écume des Jours — Modern French €€€

(☎02 98 61 22 83; http://lecume-des-jours.pagesperso-orange.fr; quai d'Auxerre; menus €15-55; ⏲noon-1.45pm & 7-9.15pm Thu-Tue) Regarded as the best restaurant in town, this elegant place is housed inside a former shipowner's house and serves magnificent, inventive local dishes that marry seafood tastes with land-lubbers' delights. There's also an excellent wine list. It has stone walls, vintage hearth and hefty beams inside; and outside, a sun-trap terrace for fine weather.

Information

Tourist Office (☎02 98 61 12 13; www.roscoff-tourisme.com; quai d'Auxerre; ⏲9am-12.30pm & 1.30-7pm Mon-Sat, 10am-12.30pm & 2.30-7pm Sun Jul-Aug, 9.15am-noon & 2-6pm Mon-Sat Sep-Jun) Next to the lighthouse.

Getting There & Away

Brittany Ferries (☎reservations in France 08 25 82 88 28, reservations in UK 0871 244 0744; www.brittany-ferries.com) links Roscoff to Plymouth in England (five to nine hours, one to three daily year-round) and Cork in Ireland (14 hours, once-weekly June to September). Boats leave from Port de Bloscon, about 2km east of the town centre.

There are regular trains and SNCF buses to Morlaix (€6.20, 35 minutes), where you can make connections to Brest, Quimper and St-Brieuc.

Quimper

POP 66,911

Small enough to feel like a village, with its slanted half-timbered houses and narrow cobbled streets, and large enough to buzz as the troubadour of Breton culture and arts, Quimper (kam-pair) is Finistère's thriving capital. Derived from the Breton word *kemper*, meaning 'confluence', Quimper sits at the juncture of the small Rivers Odet and Steïr, criss-crossed by footbridges with cascading flowers. Despite being one of Brittany's most charming towns, it is often overlooked by visitors.

Sights

Cathédrale St-Corentin Church
(place St-Corentin; 8.30am-noon & 1.30-6.30pm Mon-Sat, 8.30am-noon & 2-6.30pm Sun) At the centre of the city is Quimper's cathedral with its distinctive kink, said to symbolise Christ's inclined head as he was dying on the cross. Construction began in 1239 but the cathedral's dramatic twin spires weren't added until the 19th century. High on the west facade, look out for an equestrian statue of King Gradlon, the city's mythical 5th-century founder.

Musée Départemental Breton Museum
(02 98 95 21 60; www.museedepartementalbreton.fr; 1 rue du Roi Gradlon; adult/child €5/3; 9am-12.30pm & 1-5pm Tue-Sat, 2-5pm Sun) Beside the Cathédrale St-Corentin, recessed behind a magnificent stone courtyard, this superb museum showcases Breton history, furniture, costumes, crafts and archaeology, in a former bishop's palace.

Tours

Vedettes de l'Odet Boat Trip
(02 98 57 00 58; www.vedettes-odet.com; quai Neuf; adult/child from €28/17; Jun-Sep) From June to September, Vedettes de l'Odet runs boat trips from Quimper along the serene Odet estuary to Bénodet. You can stop for a look about Bénodet and then hop on a boat back.

Sleeping

Hôtel Manoir des Indes Hotel €€
(02 98 55 48 40; www.manoir-hoteldesindes.com; 1 allée de Prad ar C'hras; s €99-125, d €158-189;) This stunning hotel conversion, located in an old manor house just a short drive from the centre of Quimper, has been restored with the globe-trotting original owner in mind. Decor is minimalist and modern, with Asian objets d'art and lots of exposed wood. It's located a five-minute drive west of Quimper, a little way north of the D100.

Best Western Hôtel Kregenn Hotel €€
(02 98 95 08 70; www.hotel-kregenn.fr; 13 rue des Réguaires; d €109-180;) A timber-decked courtyard and a guest lounge with oversized mirrors and white leather sofas give you the initial impression that Quimper's

Cathédrale St-Corentin
TONY EMMETT/GETTY IMAGES ©

PHOTOGRAPHER CHRIS ARCHINET/GETTY IMAGES ©

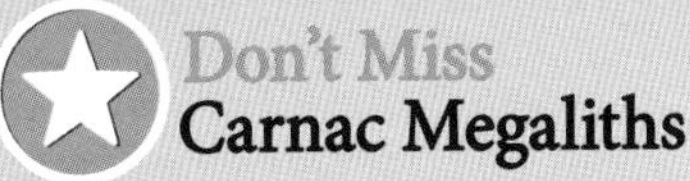

Don't Miss Carnac Megaliths

Predating Stonehenge by around 100 years, Carnac (Garnag in Breton) also tops it with the sheer number of ancient sites found in the vicinity, making this the world's greatest concentration of megalithic sites. There are no fewer than 3000 of these upright stones, most around thigh-high, erected between 5000 and 3500 BC.

Carnac, some 32km west of Vannes, comprises the old stone village Carnac-Ville and the seaside resort of Carnac-Plage, 1.5km south, bordered by the 2km-long sandy beach. Its megaliths stretch 13km north from Carnac-Ville and east as far as the village of Locmariaquer.

Sign up for a one-hour guided visit at the **Maison des Mégalithes**. Opposite, the largest menhir field – with 1099 stones – is the **Alignements du Ménec**, 1km north of Carnac-Ville; the eastern section is accessible in winter. From here, the D196 heads northeast for about 1.5km to the equally impressive **Alignements de Kermario** (which is open year-round). Climb the stone observation tower midway along the site to see the alignment from above. Another 500m further on are the **Alignements de Kerlescan**, a smaller grouping also accessible in winter.

Between Kermario and Kerlescan, 500m to the south of the D196, deposit your fee in an honour box at **Tumulus de Kercado,** dating from 3800 BC and the burial site of a Neolithic chieftain. From the parking area 300m further along the D196, a 15-minute walk brings you to the **Géant du Manio**, the highest menhir in the complex.

NEED TO KNOW

Maison des Mégalithes (☎02 97 52 29 81; www.carnac.monuments-nationaux.fr; rte des Alignements; tour adult/child €6/free; ⏰9.30am-7.30pm Jul & Aug, to 5pm Sep-Apr, to 6pm May & Jun)

coolest hotel is contemporary in style, but the plush rooms decked out in warm colours evoke a traditional feel. Some rooms have ancient stone walls. A safe bet.

Eating & Drinking

Crêperie du Quartier Crêperie €
(☎02 98 64 29 30; 16 rue du Sallé; mains €5-9; noon-2pm Mon-Sat, 7-10pm Mon, Wed, Fri & Sat) In a town where the humble crêpe is king, this cosy stone-lined place is one of the best. Its wide-ranging menu includes a *galette* of the week and, to follow up, try a crêpe stuffed with apple, caramel, icecream, almonds and chantilly.

Erwan Regional Cuisine €
(☎02 98 90 14 14; 3 rue Aristide Briand; mains €12-20, menus €17-24; noon-2pm & 7-8.30pm Mon-Sat) The contemporary Breton menu at this appealing eatery emphasises seasonal regional ingredients in dishes ranging from *kig ha farz* (buckwheat dumpling and meat stew; available daily) to a wicked Breton hamburger (served in winter only).

Information

Tourist Office (☎02 98 53 04 05; www.quimper-tourisme.com; place de la Résistance; 9am-7pm Mon-Sat, 10am-12.45pm & 3-5.45pm Sun Jul-Aug, 9.30am-12.30pm & 1.30-6.30pm Mon-Sat, 10am-12.45pm Sun Jun & Sep) Sells the Pass Quimper (€12) whereby you can access four attractions or tours of your choice from a list of participating organisations.

Getting There & Away

There are frequent train services:

Brest €17.70, 1¼ hours, up to seven daily

Paris Montparnasse €55 to €65, 4¾ hours, six direct daily

Rennes €29.50 to €37, 2½ hours, 13 direct daily

Vannes €16.50 to €20.70, 1½ hours, hourly

Château de Josselin

Guarded by its three round towers, the extraordinary town castle of **Château de Josselin** (☎02 97 22 36 45; www.chateau-josselin.com; Josselin; adult/child €8.40/5; 11am-6pm mid-Jul-Aug, 2-6pm Apr-mid-Jul, 2-5.30pm Sep) is an incredible sight that remains the home of the Rohan family today. As such, it can only be visited by guided tour: one English-language tour departs daily (2.30pm) from June to September; otherwise you can ask for a leaflet in English. The château is filled with treasures, including an ornate writing desk of which only two others exist (one in Windsor Castle), a clock that has so many gadgets it must have been considered the iPhone of its time and a magnificent library containing 3000 books, some of which date back to the 17th century.

Château de Josselin
CHRISTOPHE LEHENAFF/GETTY IMAGES ©

Rennes

POP 212,200

A crossroads since Roman times, Brittany's vibrant capital sits at the junction of highways linking northwestern France's major cities. It's a beautifully set-out city, with an elaborate and stately centre and a charming old town that's a joy to get lost in. At night, this student city has no end of lively places to pop in for a pint and its restaurants are also superb.

Sights

Cathédrale St-Pierre Cathedral

(rue de la Monnaie; 9.30am-noon & 3-6pm) Crowning Rennes' old town is the 17th-century cathedral, which has an impressive, if dark, neoclassical interior.

Palais du Parlement de Bretagne Law Courts

(place du Parlement de Bretagne; adult/child €7/free) This 17th-century former seat of the rebellious Breton parliament has in more recent times been home to the Palais de Justice. In 1994 this building was destroyed by a fire started by demonstrating fishermen. It was reopened in 2004 after a major restoration and now houses the Court of Appeal. Daily guided tours (request in advance for a tour in English) take you through the ostentatiously gilded rooms. Tour bookings must be made through the tourist office.

Musée des Beaux-Arts Museum

(02 23 62 17 45; www.mbar.org; 20 quai Émile Zola; adult/child €5/free; 10am-6pm Tue, 10am-noon & 2-6pm Wed-Sun) Rooms devoted to the Pont-Aven school are the highlight of the Musée des Beaux-Arts, which also has a 'curiosity gallery' of antiques and illustrations amassed in the 18th century. It also hosts numerous temporary exhibitions.

Champs Libres Cultural Centre

(02 23 40 66 00; www.leschampslibres.fr; 10 cours des Alliés; noon-9pm Tue, noon-7pm Wed-Fri, 2-7pm Sat & Sun) Rennes' futuristic cultural centre is home to the **Musée de Bretagne** (02 23 40 66 00; www.musee-bretagne.fr; 10 cours des Alliés; adult/child €4/3; noon-9pm Tue, noon-7pm Wed-Fri, 2-7pm Sat-Sun), with displays on Breton history and culture. Under the same roof is **Espace des Sciences** (02 23 40 66 40;

If You Like... Medieval Towns

If you've been smitten by the olde-worlde charms of Château de Josselin, you'll love exploring the region's other medieval marvels.

1 DINAN

If you're looking for Brittany's most authentic medieval town, look no further than Dinan, still encircled by its medieval battlements and watchtowers. Set high above the fast-flowing Rance River, the narrow cobblestone streets and squares lined with crooked half-timbered houses of the old town have barely changed since the days when doublet and hose were still in fashion. Get the lowdown on Dinan at the **tourist office** (02 96 87 69 76; www.dinan-tourisme.com; 9 rue du Château; 9.30am-7pm Mon-Sat, 10am-12.30pm & 2-6pm Sun).

2 VANNES

Street art, sculptures and intriguing galleries pop up unexpectedly throughout the medieval city of Vannes, a town with a distinctly quirky, creative bent overlooking the Golfe du Morbihan. Duck into the **tourist office** (08 25 13 56 10; www.tourisme-vannes.com; quai de Tabarly; 9.30am-7pm Mon-Sat, 10am-6pm Sun Jul-Aug, 9.30am-12.30pm & 1.30-6pm Mon-Sat Sep-Jun) at the newly developed marina before getting lost in the walled old town framed by a flower-filled moat.

3 VITRÉ

With its winding streets and colossal castle complete with witch-like pointy turrets, Vitré rivals Dinan as one of Brittany's prettiest medieval towns. Its **tourist office** (02 99 75 04 46; www.ot-vitre.fr; place Général de Gaulle; 9.30am-12.30pm & 2-6.30pm Mon-Sat, 10am-12.30pm & 3-6pm Sun) is right outside the train station.

Rennes

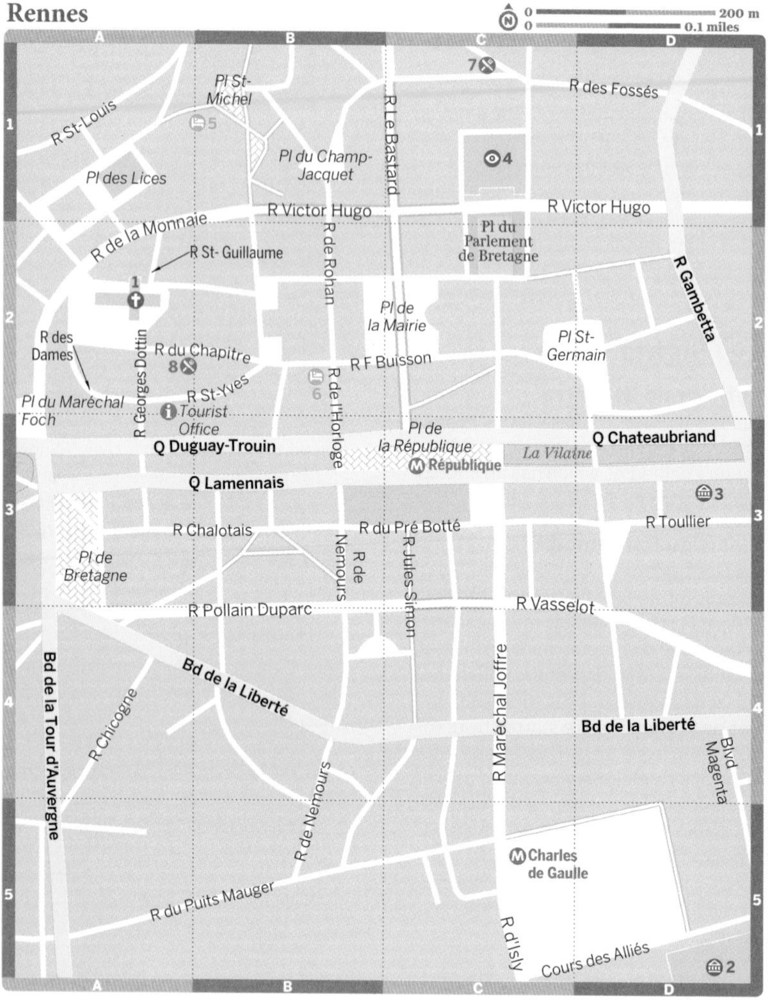

0 200 m
0 0.1 miles

A B C D
1 2 3 4 5

R St-Louis
Pl St-Michel
5
Pl du Champ-Jacquet
R Le Bastard
7
R des Fossés
4
Pl des Lices
R de la Monnaie
R Victor Hugo
R Victor Hugo
Pl du Parlement de Bretagne
R St- Guillaume
R de Rohan
R Gambetta
1
Pl de la Mairie
R des Dames
R Georges Dottin
R du Chapitre
8
R F Buisson
Pl St-Germain
6
R de l'Horloge
R St-Yves
Pl du Maréchal Foch
Tourist Office
Pl de la République
Q Duguay-Trouin
République
La Vilaine
Q Chateaubriand
Q Lamennais
3
R Chalotais
R du Pré Botté
R Toullier
R de Nemours
R Jules Simon
Pl de Bretagne
R Pollain Duparc
R Vasselot
Bd de la Tour d'Auvergne
Bd de la Liberté
R Maréchal Joffre
R Chicogne
Bd de la Liberté
Blvd Magenta
R de Nemours
Charles de Gaulle
R du Puits Mauger
R d'Isly
Cours des Alliés
2

www.espace-sciences.org; 10 cours des Alliés; adult €4.50-8, child €3-5; noon-9pm Tue, noon-7pm Wed-Fri, 2-7pm Sat-Sun), an interactive science museum, along with a planetarium, a temporary exhibition space and a library.

Sleeping

Symphonie des Sens B&B €€
(**02 99 79 30 30, 06 51 86 69 19; www.symphoniedessens.com; 3 rue du Chapitre; d incl breakfast €129;**) Bang in the heart of the historic quarter, this 1435-built house has been transformed into an incredible *maison d'hôte*. Conscientious owner Fabrice has exquisitely decorated rooms with both modern touches and charming antiques. All five rooms open onto a suntrap interior courtyard. An unexpected haven of peace in central Rennes. Good English is spoken.

Hôtel des Lices Hotel €€
(**02 99 79 14 81; www.hotel-des-lices.com; 7 place des Lices; s €85-98, d €88-103;**)

Rennes

Sights

1 Cathédrale St-Pierre A2
Champs Libres .... (see 2)
2 Espace des Sciences D5
Musée de Bretagne .... (see 2)
3 Musée des Beaux-Arts D3
4 Palais du Parlement de Bretagne C1

Sleeping

5 Hôtel des Lices B1
6 Symphonie des Sens B2

Eating

7 La Réserve C1
8 La Saint-Georges A2

You can peer down from the balconies or through the floor-to-ceiling glass doors to see the Saturday-morning market, which snakes right past the front door of this modern six-storey hotel. Inside, rooms are small but sleek, with contemporary furnishings and textured walls; most bathrooms have been recently upgraded. Rooms at the back are quieter and have views of the old ramparts.

Eating

La Saint-Georges Crêperie **€**

(**02 99 38 87 04; www.creperie-saintgeorges.com; 11 rue du Chapitre; mains €5-17, lunch menu €12; noon-2pm & 7-10.30pm Tue-Sat)** Whereas most crêperies play on the twee old-Breton style, this one takes a totally eccentric approach, despite the fact it occupies a heritage building – with its purple, green and gold furnishings, fluffy carpets and luxurious chairs, this place looks more like a glam Ibizan chill-out club.

La Réserve Bistro **€€**

(**02 99 84 02 02; www.lareserve-rennes.fr; 36 rue de la Visitation; mains €14-23, lunch menus €15-17, other menus €19-42; noon-2.15pm & 7-10.45pm Mon-Sat)** What's so suprising about this contemporary bistro is how unfazed it is by its great success: it's usually full every night, yet the 'bistro chic' cuisine never wavers, the atmosphere is congenial and the prices are good value for Rennes.

Information

Tourist Office (**02 99 67 11 11; www.tourisme-rennes.com; 11 rue St-Yves; 9am-6pm Mon-Sat, 11am-1pm & 2-6pm Sun)** This tourist office offers an audioguide to the city, which takes you on a walking tour of eight sights for €6.90 (or it can be downloaded for free from the website). Staff can book accommodation at no cost.

Getting There & Away

Destinations with frequent train services:

Dinan €12.70 to €17.90, one hour including a change

Paris Montparnasse €40 to €61, 2¼ hours

Quimper €29.50 to €41, 2½ hours

St-Malo €14.60 to €17, one hour

Vannes €17.50 to €25, one hour

Champagne & Northern France

Nowhere sums up the effervescent French spirit better than Champagne. This region has been famous for its bubbly since the 17th century, when a monk by the name of Dom Pierre Pérignon added some fizz to his otherwise humdrum wine and discovered he'd created something altogether more exciting.

A couple of centuries on, you'll find famous Champagne houses dotted throughout the region, especially around the elegant towns of Reims and Épernay: a tasting tour of their musty cellars is an absolutely unforgettable experience.

Looking west, the regions of Alsace and Lorraine crackle with a unique blend of French and Germanic cultures. And to the north, the many memorials and cemeteries dotted around Picardy and the Pas-de-Calais recall the region's tragic history as one of the key battlegrounds of WWI.

Vineyards in Champagne (p156)

Champagne & Northern France

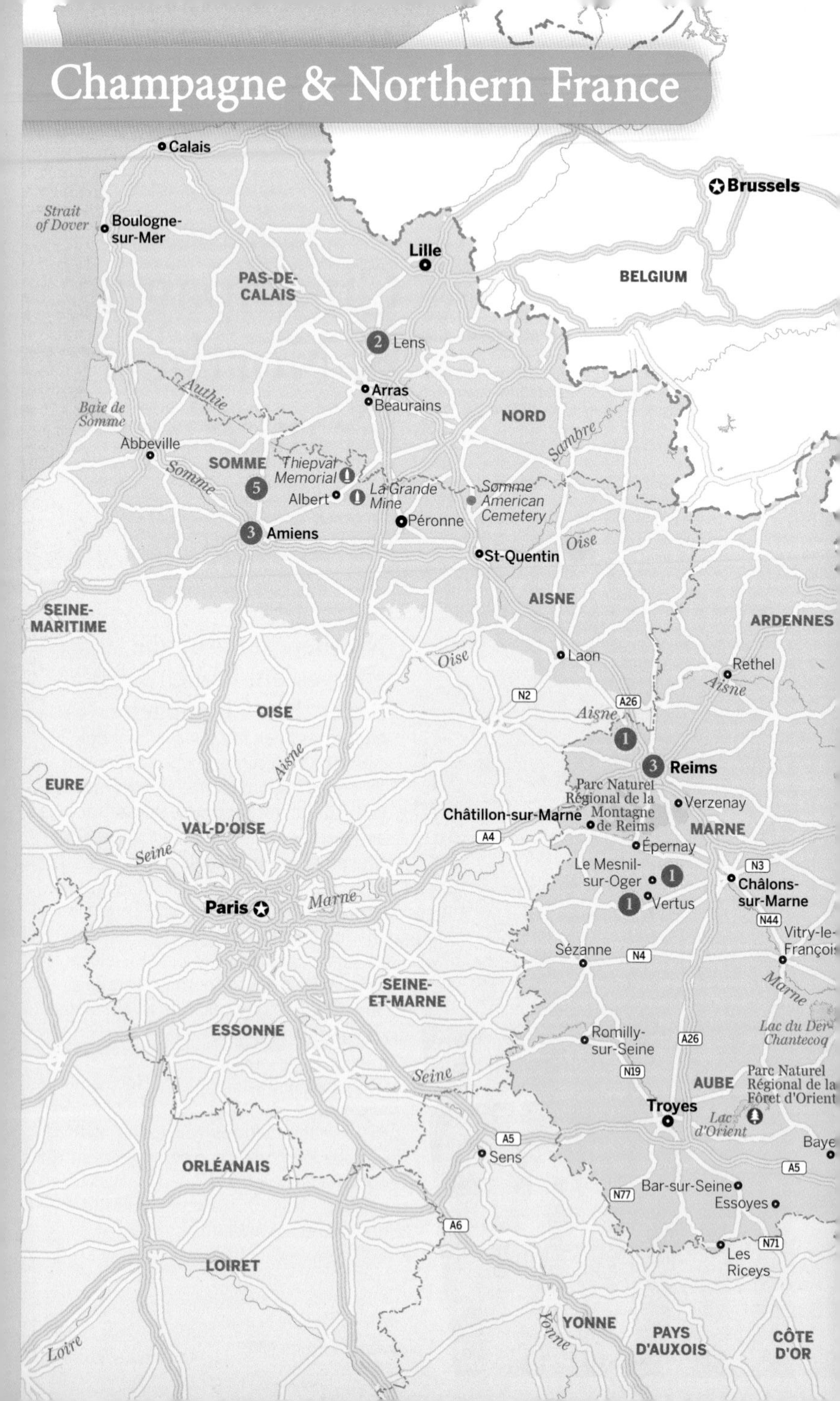

Calais
Strait of Dover
Boulogne-sur-Mer
Brussels
Lille
BELGIUM
PAS-DE-CALAIS
2 Lens
Arras
Beaurains
Authie
Baie de Somme
NORD
Sambre
Abbeville
SOMME
Somme
Thiepval Memorial
5
Albert
La Grande Mine
Somme American Cemetery
Péronne
3 Amiens
St-Quentin
Oise
AISNE
SEINE-MARITIME
ARDENNES
Oise
Laon
Rethel
Aisne
N2
A26
OISE
Aisne
1
Aisne
3 Reims
EURE
Parc Naturel Régional de la Montagne de Reims
Verzenay
Châtillon-sur-Marne
VAL-D'OISE
A4
MARNE
Épernay
Seine
Le Mesnil-sur-Oger
1
N3
Châlons-sur-Marne
1
Vertus
Paris
Marne
N44
Vitry-le-François
Sézanne
N4
SEINE-ET-MARNE
Marne
ESSONNE
Romilly-sur-Seine
A26
Lac du Der-Chantecoq
N19
Seine
AUBE
Parc Naturel Régional de la Forêt d'Orient
Troyes
Lac d'Orient
A5
Sens
ORLÉANAIS
A5
Bar-sur-Seine
N77
Essoyes
A6
N71
Les Riceys
LOIRET
YONNE
Yonne
PAYS D'AUXOIS
CÔTE D'OR
Loire

0 50 km
0 25 miles
NETHERLANDS
Maas
GERMANY
LUXEMBOURG
Luxembourg
1 Winetasting, Champagne
2 Louvre-Lens
3 Reims & Amiens Cathedrals
4 Alsace
5 WWI Sites
Romagne-sous-Montfaucon
Veckring
Saarbrücken
MOSELLE
Douaumont
Fleury
Forêt d'Argonne
Verdun
Metz
St-Avold
Rhine
A4
MEUSE
Metz-Nancy-Lorraine Airport
Lac de Madine
Butte de Montsec
Karlsruhe/Baden Baden Airport
BAS-RHIN
Bar-le-Duc
Nancy
MEURTHE-ET-MOSELLE
Strasbourg
St-Dizier
N4
Strasbourg Airport
Dambach-la-Ville
Marne
Moselle
Château du Haut Kœnigsbourg
Sélestat
Colombey-les-Deux-Églises
Ribeauvillé
VOSGES
Col du Bonhomme (949m)
Riquewihr
GERMANY
N19
Épinal
Kaysersberg
Col de la Schucht (1139m)
Colmar
Chaumont
Petit Ballon (1267m)
HAUTE-MARNE
A5
A31
Grand Ballon (1424m)
A31
Ballon d'Alsace (1247m)
HAUT-RHIN
Saône
TERRITOIRE DE BELFORT
HAUTE-SAÔNE
Basel
SWITZERLAND

Champagne & Northern France's Highlights

Wine Tasting in Champagne

There's only one place in the world where you can taste Champagne straight from the source. The world's most prestigious bottles of bubbly are aged in cellars beneath Épernay (p161) and Reims (p156), while smaller vineyards and châteaux carpet the surrounding countryside; those in Le Mesnil-sur Oger and Vertus are worth seeking out.

1

2 Louvre-Lens

As well as the Centre Pompidou-Metz (p170), northern France lures art lovers with the Louvre-Lens (p172), an offshoot of the original in Paris. Its location – an unknown, former coal mining town – is incongruous with its celebrity stature, but that is the point: art is for everyone This is reflected in the Louvre-Lens' open architecture and invitation to visitors to peek behind the scenes into its storerooms and restoration studios.

JESÃºS NICOLÃIS SÃINCHEZ/GETTY IMAGES ©

Reims & Amiens Cathedrals

3

Cathedrals don't get much grander than this Gothic duo, both Unesco World Heritage Sites. Until the Revolution, French monarchs were crowned at Reims (p160), and it remains one of France's most regal cathedrals. Further north, highlights of Amiens' cathedral (p173) include a famous 'weeping' angel and a jewel-encrusted skull rumoured to be John the Baptist's. Right: Cathédrale Notre Dame, Amiens (p173)

PETER BURNETT/GETTY IMAGES ©

4

Alsace

Sprinkled with picturesque vineyards, hilltop villages and fortified towns, this region is chock-full of rustic charm. Start out with a few days exploring stately **Strasbourg** (p164), then spin south for a couple more days on the peaceful canals of **Colmar** (p167). Finish up with a road trip along the 170km **Route des Vins d'Alsace** (p171) to sample local wines and grandstand views. Above: Strasbourg (p164)

5

WWI Sites

It's been nine decades since the guns of the Western Front fell silent, but the echoes of WWI can still be felt across much of northern France. Dozens of moving memorials and cemeteries (p175) commemorate the millions of men who laid down their lives during the course of the conflict, and you can visit many sites associated with the infamous battles of **Verdun** and the **Somme**. Above: Ossuaire de Douaumont (p175)

Champagne & Northern France's Best...

Culinary Experiences

- **Winstubs** Tuck into hearty fare at these cosy Alsatian restaurants. (p171)
- **Sweet treats** Pick up handmade chocolates and gingerbread in Strasbourg. (p164)
- **Biscuits Roses** Try these sweet pink bites with a glass of Champagne.
- **Bergamotes de Nancy** Try Nancy's unique bergamot-flavoured bonbons. (p168)
- **Alsace Wines** Sample local vintages in Ribeauvillé. (p171)

Photogenic Views

- **Reims' Cathedral** Climb the tower of Reims' Cathédrale de Notre Dame for 360-degree views. (p160)
- **Petite Venise** See the sights around Colmar's prettiest neighbourhood. (p167)
- **Château du Haut Kœnigsbourg** This fairy-tale castle offers one of Alsace's best panoramas. (p171)
- **Petite France** Gaze across the water to Strasbourg's monumental Barrage Vauban. (p164)
- **Quartier Impérial** Admire the architecture in Metz' Germanic quarter. (p170)

Art Pilgrimages

- **Centre Pompidou-Metz** & **Louvre-Lens** Satellite branches of Paris' Pompidou and Louvre. (p170; p172)
- **Musée des Beaux-Arts, Reims** Centuries of fine art in an 18th-century abbey. (p157)
- **Musée Bartholdi** Visit Colmar to see where the Statue of Liberty was created. (p168)
- **Atelier Renoir, Essoyes** A painter's paradise, much-loved by Renoir. (p162)

Soul-stirring Surprises

- **Place Notre Dame, Amiens** Most uplifting in summer when light shows illuminate the cathedral. (p173)
- **Place Stanislas, Nancy** The neoclassical square is a World Heritage Site. (p168)
- **Maison de Jules Verne, Amiens** Yes, this is the sci-fi pioneer's former home. (p173)
- **Café du Palais, Reims** Champagne by dozens of producers sipped amid art deco splendour. (p158)

Left: Quiche and grapes; **Above:** Petite Venise (p167)

Need to Know

ADVANCE PLANNING

- **A month before** Book accommodation as early as possible, especially in Reims, Strasbourg, Épernay and Metz.
- **Two weeks before** Reserve a guided tour of some Champagne cellars.
- **One week before** Research money-saving city passes. Strasbourg and Reims both have passes covering sights, museums and public transport.

RESOURCES

- **Champagne-Ardenne** (www.tourisme-champagne-ardenne.com) Walks, sights and general ideas for the Champagne region.
- **Northern France Tourist Office** (www.cdt-nord.fr) Offers several themed routes around the region.
- **Alsace** (www.tourisme-alsace.com) Travel tips in and around Alsace.
- **Lorraine** (www.tourism-lorraine.com) Main portal for the Lorraine region.
- **Somme Battlefields** (www.somme-battlefields.co.uk)

GETTING AROUND

- **Car** Useful for Champagne's more out-of-the-way spots, and pretty much essential in Alsace. Just don't overdo the bubbly.
- **Train** The big cities can be easily reached by train. Reims, Épernay and Metz all make excellent day trips from Paris.
- **Eurostar** (www.eurostar.com) The high-speed Eurostar connects London with Lille and Strasbourg.
- **Bus** Buses are limited, making bus travel something of a no-go.

BE FOREWARNED

- **Champagne** Producers around Reims and Épernay close their doors to visitors during the *vendange* (grape harvest) in September and October.
- **Hotels** Reims and Épernay are often full at weekends Easter to September and weekdays May, June and September. Hotels in Strasbourg are often booked out during the week when European parliament is in session.
- **WWI sites** Visitor centres are often closed in January, but cemeteries are open year-round.

Champagne & Northern France Itineraries

With its famous fizz houses, chic cities and elegant architecture, Champagne and Northern France encapsulates France's love affair with the finer things in life.

PARIS TO ESSOYES

CHAMPAGNE TASTER

This trip provides a perfect introduction to the Champagne region. From ❶ **Paris**, it's an easy trip by train or car to ❷ **Reims**, home to some of the world's biggest bubbly producers. Spend the first day tasting your way around Mumm, Taittinger and the other big-name Champagne houses. Lunch in style at Le Foch before tackling the 250 steps of the city's spectacular cathedral tower. Indulge in a spot of wine and Champagne shopping, before partaking in a Champagne aperitif at Café du Palais. Overnight at Les Telliers for real 'home-away-from-home' atmosphere.

On day two, catch a train on to ❸ **Épernay** and its wealth of subterranean cellars, where 200-million-plus bottles of Champers are being aged, just waiting to be popped open for some sparkling occasion. Take your pick of the city's Champagne houses before enjoying a tasty bistro lunch at La Grillade Gourmande, an afternoon's shopping and sightseeing, and an evening at C. Comme.

Spend day three on a leisurely bike ride or a guided tour of some of the region's smaller vineyards; or see what inspired Renoir in ❹ **Essoyes**.

ÉPERNAY TO COLMAR
ARCHITECTURE

This trip takes in some of northeast France's top architectural sights. Train is easiest between cities, but car is best along the Route des Vins d'Alsace. From 1 **Épernay** head to elegant 2 **Metz**. Visit its cathedral and celebrated modern landmark, the Centre Pompidou-Metz.

Next, move on to 3 **Nancy**. Its splendid 18th-century buildings are best seen around Unesco-listed place Stanislas.

Then head to stately 4 **Strasbourg**, the official home of the EU parliament. It's a suitably grand city, with elements from nearly all of the key periods of French architecture. Step back into the Middle Ages around Grande Île and Petite France, admire the Renaissance at the Palais Rohan, experience 19th-century splendour on the place de la République and marvel at the bold modern statement of the Musée d'Art Moderne et Contemporain.

Spend a couple of days exploring the wider Alsace region. Follow the 5 **Route des Vins d'Alsace** through picturesque vineyards and hilltop villages, before finishing up in atmospheric 6 **Colmar**.

Route des Vins d'Alsace (p171)

Discover Champagne & Northern France

At a Glance

- **Champagne** (p156) Famed the world over for its bubbly, this region in northeast France seduces wine-lovers with Europe's elite fizz houses and smaller vignerons aplenty.
- **Northern France** (p163) Travellers who make it this far north won't regret it – experience some of France's most fascinating cities or emotional moments at WWI battlefields.

Palais du Tau
JULIAN ELLIOTT PHOTOGRAPHY/GETTY IMAGES ©

CHAMPAGNE

Champagne arouses all of the senses: the eyes feast on vine-covered hillsides and vertical processions of tiny, sparkling bubbles; the nose is tantalised by the damp soil and the heavenly bouquet of fermentation; the ears rejoice at the clink of glasses and the barely audible fizz; and the palate tingles with every sip.

Reims

POP 184,984

No matter what you have read, nothing can prepare you for that first skyward glimpse of Reims' gargantuan Gothic **cathedral**. Rising golden and imperious above the city, the cathedral is where, over the course of a millennium (816 to 1825), some 34 sovereigns – among them two dozen kings – began their reigns. Along with Épernay, it is the most important centre of Champagne production and a fine base for exploring the Montagne de Reims Champagne Route.

Sights

Palais du Tau Museum

(http://palais-tau.monuments-nationaux.fr; 2 place du Cardinal Luçon; adult/child €7.50/free, incl cathedral tower €11/free; 9.30am-12.30pm & 2-5.30pm Tue-Sun) A Unesco World Heritage Site, this former archbishop's residence, constructed in 1690, was where French princes stayed before their coronations – and where they hosted sumptuous banquets afterwards. Now a museum, it displays truly exceptional statuary, liturgical objects and tapestries from the cathedral, some in the impressive, Gothic-style Salle de Tau (Great Hall).

Basilique St-Rémi Basilica
(place du Chanoine Ladame; admission free; 8am-7pm) This 121m-long former Benedictine abbey church, a Unesco World Heritage Site, mixes Romanesque elements from the mid-11th century (the worn but stunning nave and transept) with early Gothic features from the latter half of the 12th century (the choir, with a large triforium gallery and, way up top, tiny clerestory windows). Next door, **Musée St-Rémi (53 rue Simon; adult/child €4/free; 2-6.30pm Mon-Fri, to 7pm Sat & Sun)**, in a 17th- and 18th-century abbey, features local Gallo-Roman archaeology, tapestries and 16th- to 19th-century military history.

Musée des Beaux-Arts Art Museum
(8 rue Chanzy; adult/child €4/free; 10am-noon & 2-6pm Wed-Mon) This institution's rich collection, housed in an 18th-century abbey, boasts one of the four versions of Jacques-Louis David's world-famous *The Death of Marat* (yes, the bloody corpse in the bathtub), 27 works by Camille Corot (only the Louvre has more), 13 portraits by German Renaissance painters Cranach the Elder and the Younger, lots of Barbizon School landscapes, some art nouveau creations by Émile Gallé, and two works each by Monet, Gauguin and Pissarro.

Tours

Mumm Champagne House
(03 26 49 59 70; www.mumm.com; 34 rue du Champ de Mars; 1 hr tours incl tasting €14-25; tours 9am-5pm daily, shorter hours & closed Sun winter) Mumm (pronounced 'moom'), the only *maison* in central Reims, was founded in 1827 and is now the world's third-largest producer (almost eight million bottles a year). Engaging and edifying one-hour tours take you through cellars filled with 25 million bottles of fine bubbly. Wheelchair accessible. Phone ahead if possible.

Taittinger Champagne House
(03 26 85 45 35; www.taittinger.com; 9 place St-Niçaise; tours €16.50-45; 9.30am-5.30pm, shorter hours & closed Sun in winter) The headquarters of Taittinger are an excellent place to come for a clear, straightforward presentation on how Champagne is actually made – there's no claptrap about 'the Champagne mystique' here. Parts of the cellars occupy 4th-century Roman stone quarries; other bits were excavated by 13th-century Benedictine monks. No need to reserve. Situated 1.5km southeast of Reims centre; take the Citadine 1 or 2 bus to the St-Niçaise or Salines stops.

Sleeping

Les Telliers B&B **€€**
(09 53 79 80 74; http://telliers.fr; 18 rue des Telliers; s €67-83, d €79-114, tr €115-134, q €131-155;) Enticingly positioned down a quiet alley near the cathedral, this bijou B&B extends one of Reims' warmest *bienvenues*. The high-ceilinged rooms are big on art deco character, handsomely decorated with ornamental fireplaces, polished oak floors and the odd antique. Breakfast costs an extra €9 and is a generous spread of pastries, fruit, fresh-pressed juice and coffee.

La Parenthèse B&B **€€**
(03 26 40 39 57; www.laparenthese.fr; 83 rue Clovis; min 2-night stay d €180-220;) Tucked away in the backstreets of old Reims, this little B&B has got everything going for it. The rooms are tastefully done with wood floors and bursts of pastel colour, and all come with kitchenettes. The good-natured owner will squeeze in a cot if you ask.

Eating

L'Éveil des Sens Bistro **€€**
(03 26 35 16 95; www.eveildessens-reims.com; 8 rue Colbert; menus €30-38; 12.15-2pm & 7.15-10pm, closed Sun & Wed) The 'awakening of the senses' is a fitting name for this terrific bistro. Monochrome hues and white linen create a chic yet understated setting for market-fresh cuisine delivered with finesse. Nicolas Lefèvre's specialities appear deceptively simple on paper, but the flavours are profound – be it scallops with tangy Granny Smith apple or braised beef ravioli on white bean velouté.

Reims

0 — 200 m
0 — 0.1 miles

A B C D
1 2 3 4 5

R MCForiaux
R Franklin Roosevelt
Av de Laon
Cimetière du Nord
R du Champ de Mars
5
R Edouard Mignot
Pl de la République
Pl du Boulingrin
Bd Lundy
Les Halles
Esplanade du Colonel Bouchez
Bd Joffre
R du Temple
R de Mars
R du Général Sarrail
R des Templiers
Train Station
Bd Foch
R Linguet
R St-Hilaire
Hôtel de Ville
Pl Léon Bourgeois
Square Colbert
R Thiers
7
Bd Louis Roederer
Pl de l'Hôtel de Ville
R Jean-Jacques Rousseau
Pl Aristide Briand
R de Talleyrand
Cours JB Langlet
R Pluche
R Courmeaux
Pl Drouet d'Erlon
6
Pl du Forum
11
Bd Général Leclerc
R Cadran St-Pierre
9
8
R Condorcet
R Cérès
Pl Royale
R de l'Étape
R Carnot
10
Pl Myron-Herrick
R Guillaume de Machault
R Buirette
R Théodore Dubois
Palais de Justice
R de Thillois
Théâtre
1
2
Pl du Cardinal Luçon
Cathédrale Notre Dame
R Jeanne d'Arc
3
4
Pl Carnegie
R Voltaire
Médiathèque
R de Vesle
R des Capucins
R Libergier
R Chanzy
La Parenthèse (400m)

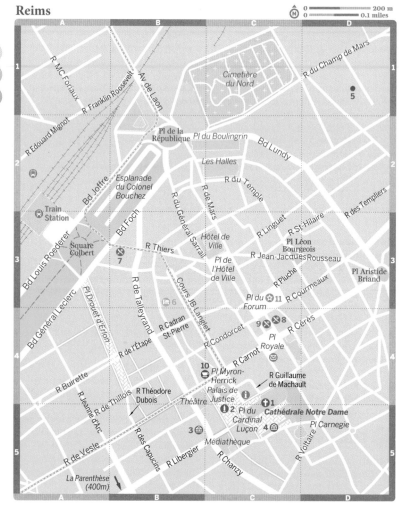

Le Millénaire Gastronomic **€€€**
(☎03 26 08 26 62; www.lemillenaire.com; 4-6 rue Bertin; menus €35-94; ⏰noon-1.45pm & 7.30-9.30pm Mon-Fri, 7.30-9.30pm Sat) Sand and claret hues and contemporary artworks create an air of intimate sophistication at this Michelin-starred haunt. Chef Laurent Laplaige keeps flavours crisp and seasonal with specialities such as wild sea bass with celery, truffle risotto and Champagne sauce.

Drinking

Café du Palais Cafe
(www.cafedupalais.fr; 14 place Myron-Herrick; ⏰9am-8.30pm Tue-Fri, 9am-9.30pm Sat) Run by the same family since 1930, this art deco cafe is *the* place to sip a glass of Champagne. Lit by a skylight is an extraordinary collection of bric-a-brac ranging from the inspired to the kitsch.

Reims

Don't Miss Sights

1 Cathédrale Notre Dame C4

Sights

2 Joan Of Arc Statue C5
3 Musée des Beaux-Arts B5
4 Palais du Tau C5

Activities, Courses & Tours

5 Mumm D1

Sleeping

6 Les Telliers B3

Eating

7 Le Foch B3
8 Le Millénaire C4
9 L'Éveil des Sens C4

Drinking & Nightlife

10 Café du Palais B4

Entertainment

11 Amphitheatre C3

Information

Tourist Office (☎03 26 77 45 00; www.reims-tourisme.com; 2 rue Guillaume de Machault; 9am-7pm Mon-Sat, 10am-6pm Sun)

Getting There & Away

Reims train station, 1km northwest of the cathedral, was renovated in 2010; the bullet marks on the facade date from both world wars. Frequent services run to Paris Gare de l'Est (€36 to €44, 46 minutes to one hour, 12 to 17 daily). Direct services also go to Épernay (€6.80, 22 to 42 minutes, 19 daily) and Laon (€10.20, 36 to 47 minutes, three to nine daily). The journey to Troyes (€55 to €79, 2½ to three hours, eight daily) involves at least one change.

Champagne Routes of the Marne

The **Champagne Routes** (www.tourisme-en-champagne.com, in French) of the Marne *département* wend their way among neat rows of hillside vines, through hilltop forests and across lowland crop fields. Along the way, they call on wine-making villages and hamlets. At almost every turn, beautiful panoramas unfold and small-scale, family-run Champagne wineries welcome travellers in search of bubbly.

MONTAGNE DE REIMS CHAMPAGNE ROUTE

Linking Reims with Épernay by skirting the Parc Natural Régional de la Montagne de Reims, a regional park covering the forested Reims Mountain plateau, this meandering, 70km route passes through vineyards planted mainly with pinot noir vines.

For the region's best introduction to the art of growing grapes and the cycles of the seasons, head to the **Phare de Verzenay** (Verzenay Lighthouse; www.lepharedeverzenay.com; D26; lighthouse adult/child €3/2, incl museum €8.50/4.50; 10am-5pm Tue-Fri, to 5.30pm Sat & Sun, closed Jan-mid-Mar), on a hilltop at the eastern edge of the village. Exactly 101 spiral stairs lead to the top of the lighthouse, constructed as a publicity stunt in 1909, which rewards visitors with unsurpassed 360-degree views of vine, field and forest – and, if you're lucky, a tiny TGV zipping by in the distance. The Sillery sugar mill, visible on the horizon, turns an astounding 16,000 tonnes of beets (a major regional crop) into 2600 tonnes of sugar each day! After brushing up on the seasonal processes involved in Champagne production in the museum, stop by the tasting room for a glass of fizz (there are 30 varieties to sample).

VALLÉE DE LA MARNE CHAMPAGNE ROUTE

A stronghold of pinot meunier vines, this 90km itinerary winds from Épernay to Dormans, heading more or less west along the hillsides north of the River Marne; it then circles back to the east along the river's south bank.

Perching above a sea of emerald vines and ablaze with forsythia and tulips in spring, **Hautvillers** (population 790), 6km north of Épernay, is where Dom Pierre Pérignon is popularly believed to have created Champagne. The good Dom's tomb is in front of the altar of the Église Abbatiale, adorned with

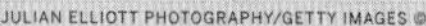

Don't Miss
Cathédrale Notre Dame

Imagine the egos and extravagance of a French royal coronation. The focal point of such bejewelled pomposity was Reims' resplendent Gothic cathedral, begun in 1211 on a site occupied by churches since the 5th century. The interior is a rainbow of stained-glass windows; the finest are the western facade's 12-petalled **great rose window**, the north transept's **rose window** and the vivid **Chagall** creations (1974) in the central axial chapel. The tourist office rents audioguides (€6) for self-paced cathedral tours.

Among the other highlights of the interior are a flamboyant **Gothic organ case** (15th and 18th centuries) topped with a figure of Christ, a 15th-century wooden **astronomical clock**, and a statue of **Joan of Arc in full body armour** (1901); there's a second **statue** of her outside on the square, to the right as you exit the cathedral.

The single most famous event to take place here was the coronation of Charles VII, with Joan of Arc at his side, on 17 July 1429. This was one of 25 coronations that took place between 1223 and 1825.

A Unesco World Heritage Site since 1991, the cathedral celebrated its 800th anniversary in 2011. To get the most impressive first view, approach the cathedral from the west, along rue Libergier. Here your gaze will be drawn to the restored architectural features of the facade, lavishly encrusted with sculptures. Among them is the 13th-century *L'Ange au Sourire* (Smiling Angel), presiding above the central portal.

Feeling as strong as Goliath? (Look for his worn figure up on the west facade, held in place with metal straps.) Then consider climbing 250 steps up the **cathedral tower** on a one-hour tour. Book at the Palais du Tau.

NEED TO KNOW

www.cathedrale-reims.culture.fr; place du Cardinal Luçon; tower adult/child €7.50/free, incl Palais du Tau €11/free; ⏲7.30am-7.30pm, tower tours hourly 11am-4pm Tue-Sun May-Sep

17th-century woodwork. The village is one of Champagne's prettiest, with ubiquitous medieval-style wrought-iron signs providing pictorial clues to the activities taking place on the other side of the wall.

Steps away from attractive main square, place de la République, is **Au 36 (www.au36.net; 36 rue Dom Pérignon; 10.30am-6pm Tue-Sun Apr-Oct, shorter hours in winter)**, a slinky wine boutique with a 'wall' of Champagne, innovatively arranged by aroma, and a laid-back upstairs tasting room. A two-/three-glass tasting costs €11/15.

Épernay

POP 25,000

Prosperous Épernay, the self-proclaimed *capitale du* Champagne and home to many of the world's most celebrated Champagne houses, is the best place for touring cellars and sampling bubbly. The town also makes an excellent base for exploring the Champagne Routes.

Beneath the streets in 110km of subterranean cellars, more than 200 million bottles of Champagne are being aged. In 1950 one such cellar – owned by the irrepressible Mercier family – hosted a car rally without the loss of a single bottle!

Épernay is 25km south of Reims and can be visited by train or car as a day trip from Reims.

Sights

Épernay's handsome and eminently strollable avenue de Champagne fizzes with maisons de Champagne (Champagne houses).

Moët & Chandon Champagne House
(03 26 51 20 20; www.moet.com; 20 av de Champagne; adult incl 1/2 glasses €21/28, 10-18yr €10; tours 9.30am-11.30am & 2-4.30pm, closed Sat & Sun late Jan–mid-Mar) Flying the Moët, French, European and Russian flags, this prestigious *maison* offers frequent one-hour tours that are among the region's most impressive, offering a peek

Local Knowledge

Wine Tasting in Champagne Don't Miss List

BY MICHAEL EDWARDS, GASTRONOMIC WRITER, RESTAURANT CRITIC & CHAMPAGNE CONNOISSEUR

1 **REIMS**
This great city centre of culture, gastronomy and wine tourism is easy to access: 45 minutes by TGV from Paris Gare de l'Est or 30 minutes from Paris Charles de Gaulle airport to TGV station Champagne Ardennes near the city. For me, the cathedral (p160) and Basilique St-Rémi (p157) uplift the spirit before a good meal. My favourite restaurants include **Le Jardin des Crayères** (www.lescrayeres.com), 1930s-styled Café du Palais (p158), **Brasserie du Boulingrin** (www.boulingrin.fr), and **Le Foch** (www.lefoch.com), one of France's finest fish restaurants.

2 **GROWERS' CHAMPAGNE**
The big change in the past five years is the greater availability of Champagne direct from the best grower-producers. For a real sense of place and individual flavour my top addresses include JL Vergnon and Clos Cazals in Le Mesnil-sur-Oger in the Côte des Blancs, Veuve Fourny in Vertus, Jacques Selosse and Pascal Agrapart in Avize, and Champagne Lilbert in Cramant.

3 **CHAMPAGNE PRODUCER**
A favourite is **Veuve Fourny & Fils (03 26 52 16 30; www.champagne-veuve-fourny.com; rue du Mesnil, Vertus)**. They are masters of the bone-dry, non-dosed Champagne; theirs is called Brut Nature and is a wonderful partner for all sorts of shellfish and those great cheese pastry balls called *gougères au fromage*.

4 **THE CHAMPENOIS**
I love the region so much, mainly because of the people. Reserved but with great inner warmth and a deliciously dry sense of humour, the Champenois are resilient and hard working. But they also know how to play: go to any dance hall and you'll see what I mean.

Detour: Renoir in Champagne

It's easy to see why Renoir loved **Essoyes** so much that he spent his last 25 summers here. The village, a two-hour drive from Épernay in the Aube *département* (www.aube-champagne.com), has neat stone houses, a riverfront that glows golden in the late afternoon sun and landscapes of vineyards and flower-flecked meadows that unfold in a gentle, almost artistic way.

Essoyes' *circuit découverte* is a marked trail that loops around the village, taking in viewpoints that inspired the artist, as well as the family home and the cemetery where he lies buried, his grave marked by a contemplative bronze bust. The trail begins at the **Espace des Renoir** (Renoir Centre; www.renoir-essoyes.fr; place de la Mairie; adult/child incl Atelier Renoir €8/4; 10.30-11.30am & 2-5pm Wed-Mon, shorter hours in winter), which also houses the **tourist office** (03 25 29 21 27; www.ot-essoyes.fr; place de la Mairie, Espace des Renoir; 9am-12.30pm & 1.30-5.30pm, closed Sat & Sun Oct-May). Opened in 2011, the centre screens a 15-minute film about Renoir and displays temporary exhibitions of mostly contemporary art. Marking the end of the tour and covered by the same ticket is the **Atelier Renoir** (Renoir's Studio; www.renoir-essoyes.fr; adult/child incl Espace des Renoir €8/4; 10am-12.30pm & 1.30-6.30pm daily, closed Tue Oct-Mar), with displays zooming in on the hallmarks of Renoir's work (the female form, the vibrant use of colour and light), alongside original pieces such as his antiquated wheelchair and the box he used to carry his paintings to Paris. Perhaps loveliest of all is the studio **garden**, particularly in spring to early summer when it bursts forth with tulips, anemones and roses.

at part of their 28km labyrinth of *caves* (cellars). At the shop you can pick up a 15L bottle of Brut Impérial for just €1500; a standard bottle will set you back €31.

Mercier Champagne House

(03 26 51 22 22; www.champagnemercier.fr; 68-70 av de Champagne; adult incl 1/2/3 glasses €13/18/21 Mon-Fri, €15/19/25 Sat & Sun, child 12-17yr €6; tours 9.30-11am & 2-4pm, closed mid-Dec–late Feb) France's most popular brand was founded in 1847 by Eugène Mercier, a trailblazer in the field of eye-catching publicity stunts and the virtual creator of the cellar tour. Everything here is flashy, including the 160,000L barrel that took two decades to build (for the Universal Exposition of 1889), the lift that transports you 30m underground and the laser-guided touring train.

De Castellane Champagne House

(03 26 51 19 11; www.castellane.com; 57 av de Verdun; adult incl 1 glass €10, child under 12yr free; tours 10-11am & 2-5pm, closed Christmas–mid-Mar) The 45-minute tours, in French and English, take in an informative bubbly museum dedicated to elucidating the *méthode champenoise* and its diverse technologies. The reward for climbing the 237 steps up the 66m-high tower (built 1905) is a fine panoramic view.

Tours

Champagne Domi Moreau Vineyard Tour

(06 30 35 51 07, after 7pm 03 26 59 45 85; www.champagne-domimoreau.com; tours €25-30; tours 9.30am & 2.30pm except Wed & 2nd half of Aug) This company runs scenic and insightful three-hour minibus tours, in French and English, of nearby vineyards. Pick-up is across the street from the tourist office. It also organises two-hour vineyard tours by bicycle (€25). Call ahead for reservations.

Eating & Drinking

La Grillade Gourmande Regional Cuisine **€€**
(☎03 26 55 44 22; www.lagrilladegourmande.com; 16 rue de Reims; menus €19-57; ⏰noon-2pm & 7.30-10pm Tue-Sat) This chic, red-walled bistro is an inviting spot to try char-grilled meats and dishes rich in texture and flavour, such as crayfish pan-fried in Champagne and lamb cooked until meltingly tender in rosemary and honey. Diners spill out onto the covered terrace in the warm months.

La Cave à Champagne Regional Cuisine **€€**
(☎03 26 55 50 70; www.la-cave-a-champagne.com; 16 rue Gambetta; menus €20-38; ⏰noon-2pm & 7-10pm Thu-Mon, noon-2pm Tue; 👪) 'The Champagne Cellar' is well regarded by locals for its *champenoise* cuisine (snail and pig's trotter casserole, filet of beef in pinot noir), served in a warm, traditional, bourgeois atmosphere. You can sample four different Champagnes for €24.

Information

Tourist Office (☎03 26 53 33 00; www.ot-epernay.fr; 7 av de Champagne; ⏰9.30am-12.30pm & 1.30-7pm Mon-Sat, 10.30am-1pm & 2-4.30pm Sun; 📶) The super-friendly team here hand out English brochures and maps with walking, cycling and driving tour options. They can make cellar visit reservations. Free wi-fi.

Getting There & Away

The **train station** (place Mendès-France) has direct services to Reims (€6.40, 20 to 90 minutes, seven to 18 daily) and Paris Gare de l'Est (€22, 1¼ hours, five to 10 daily).

NORTHERN FRANCE

When it comes to culture, cuisine, beer, shopping and dramatic views of land and sea – not to mention good old-fashioned friendliness – the Ch'tis (residents of France's northern tip) and their region compete with the best France has to offer. In Lille and French Flanders, the down-to-earth Flemish vibe mixes easily with French sophistication and savoir faire. And in the Somme, although WWI has been over for almost a century, memorials and cemeteries marking the front lines of 1916 remain places of pilgrimage and reflection.

Alsace is a one-off cultural hybrid, with its Germanic dialect and French sense of fashion, love of foie gras and *choucroute* (sauerkraut), fine wine and beer. Next door Lorraine's historic roll call of dukes and art-nouveau pioneers, blessedly underrated cities, cathedrals and art collections leave visitors spellbound, while its WWI battlefields render visitors speechless time and again with their painful beauty.

Moët & Chandon (p161)
OLIVER STREWE/GETTY IMAGES ©

Strasbourg

POP 276,136

Strasbourg is the perfect overture to all that is idiosyncratic about Alsace – walking a fine tightrope between France and Germany and between a medieval past and a progressive future, it pulls off its act in inimitable Alsatian style.

Sights

Cathédrale Notre-Dame Cathedral

(place de la Cathédrale; astronomical clock adult/child €2/1.50, platform adult/child €5/2.50; 7am-7pm, astronomical clock tickets sold 9.30am-11am, platform 9am-7.15pm; Grand'Rue) Nothing prepares you for your first glimpse of Strasbourg's Cathédrale Notre-Dame, completed in all its Gothic grandeur in 1439. The lace-fine facade lifts the gaze little by little to flying buttresses, leering gargoyles and a 142m spire. The interior is exquisitely lit by 12th- to 14th-century **stained-glass windows**, including the western portal's jewel-like rose window. The Gothic-meets-Renaissance **astronomical clock** strikes solar noon at 12.30pm with a parade of figures portraying the different stages of life, and Jesus with his apostles.

Grande Île Historic Quarter

(Grand'Rue) History seeps through the twisting lanes and cafe-rimmed plazas of Grande Île, Strasbourg's Unesco World Heritage–listed island bordered by the River Ill. These streets – with their photogenic line-up of wonky, timber-framed houses in sherbet colours – are made for aimless ambling. They cower beneath the soaring magnificence of the cathedral and its sidekick, the gingerbready 15th-century **Maison Kammerzell (rue des Hallebardes)**, with its ornate carvings and leaded windows. The alleys are at their most atmospheric when lantern-lit at night.

Petite France Historic Quarter

(Grand'Rue) Criss-crossed by narrow lanes, canals and locks, Petite France is where artisans plied their trades in the Middle Ages. The half-timbered houses, sprouting veritable thickets of scarlet geraniums in summer, and the riverside parks attract the masses, but the area still manages to retain its Alsatian charm,

Petite France

SHAUN EGAN/GETTY IMAGES ©

especially in the early morning and late evening. Drink in views of the River Ill and the **Barrage Vauban** from the much-photographed **Ponts Couverts** (Covered Bridges) and their trio of 13th-century towers.

Palais Rohan Historic Residence

(2 place du Château; adult/child per museum €6.50/free, all 3 museums €12/free; 10am-6pm Wed-Mon; Grand'Rue) Hailed a 'Versailles in miniature', this opulent 18th-century residence is replete with treasures. The basement **Musée Archéologique** takes you from the Palaeolithic period to AD 800. On the ground floor is the **Musée des Arts Décoratifs**, where rooms adorned with Hannong ceramics and gleaming silverware evoke the lavish lifestyle of the nobility in the 18th century. On the 1st floor, the **Musée des Beaux-Arts'** collection of 14th- to 19th-century art reveals El Greco, Botticelli and Flemish Primitive works.

Tours

Batorama Boat Tour

(www.batorama.fr; rue de Rohan; adult/child €12.50/7.20; tours half-hourly 9.30am-9.15pm, shorter hours in winter; Grand'Rue) This outfit runs scenic 70-minute boat trips, which glide along the storybook canals of Petite France, taking in the Vauban Dam and the glinting EU institutions. Tours depart on Rue de Rohan, the quay behind Palais Rohan.

Sleeping

Villa Novarina Design Hotel €€

(03 90 41 18 28; www.villanovarina.com; 11 rue Westercamp; s €87-157, d €117-257, ste €237-537; Droits de l'Homme) New-wave design is pitched just right at this light-flooded 1950s villa near Parc de l'Orangerie. Slick without being soulless, rooms and suites are liberally sprinkled with art and overlook gardens. Breakfast places the accent on organic, regional produce. There's a heated pool, whirlpool and spa for quiet moments. It's a 10-minute walk south of Droits de l'Homme tram stop.

Hôtel du Dragon Hotel €€

(03 88 35 79 80; www.dragon.fr; 12 rue du Dragon; s €44-159, d €92-159; Porte de l'Hôpital) Step through a tree-shaded courtyard and into the, ahhh... blissful calm of this bijou hotel. The dragon receives glowing reviews for its crisp interiors, attentive service and prime location near Petite France.

Cour du Corbeau Boutique Hotel €€€

(03 90 00 26 26; www.cour-corbeau.com; 6-8 rue des Couples; r €140-175, ste €220-260; Porte de l'Hôpital) A 16th-century inn lovingly converted into a boutique hotel, Cour du Corbeau wins you over with its half-timbered charm and location, just steps from the river. Gathered around a courtyard, rooms blend original touches like oak parquet and Louis XV furnishings with mod cons like flat-screen TVs.

Eating

Bistrot et Chocolat Cafe €

(www.bistrotetchocolat.net; 8 rue de la Râpe; snacks €7.50-11, brunch €12.50-26.50; 11am-7pm Mon-Thu, 10am-9pm Fri-Sun; Grand'Rue) Chilled bistro hailed for its solid and liquid organic chocolate (ginger is superb), day specials and weekend brunches.

La Cuiller à Pot Alsatian €€

(03 88 35 56 30; www.lacuillerapot.com; 18b rue Finkwiller; €17.50-26.50; noon-2.30pm & 7-10.30pm Tue-Fri, 7-10.30pm Sat; Musée d'Art Moderne) Run by a talented husband-wife team, this little Alsatian dream of a restaurant rustles up fresh regional cuisine. Its well-edited menu goes with the seasons, but might include such dishes as filet of beef with wild mushrooms and homemade gnocchi and escargots in parsley jus. The quality is second to none.

Le Gavroche Mediterranean €€€

(03 88 36 82 89; www.restaurant-gavroche.com; 4 rue Klein; menus €32-75; noon-1.30pm & 7.30-9.30pm Mon-Fri; Porte de l'Hôpital) Nathalie and Benoît Fuchs give food a pinch of creativity and southern

Strasbourg

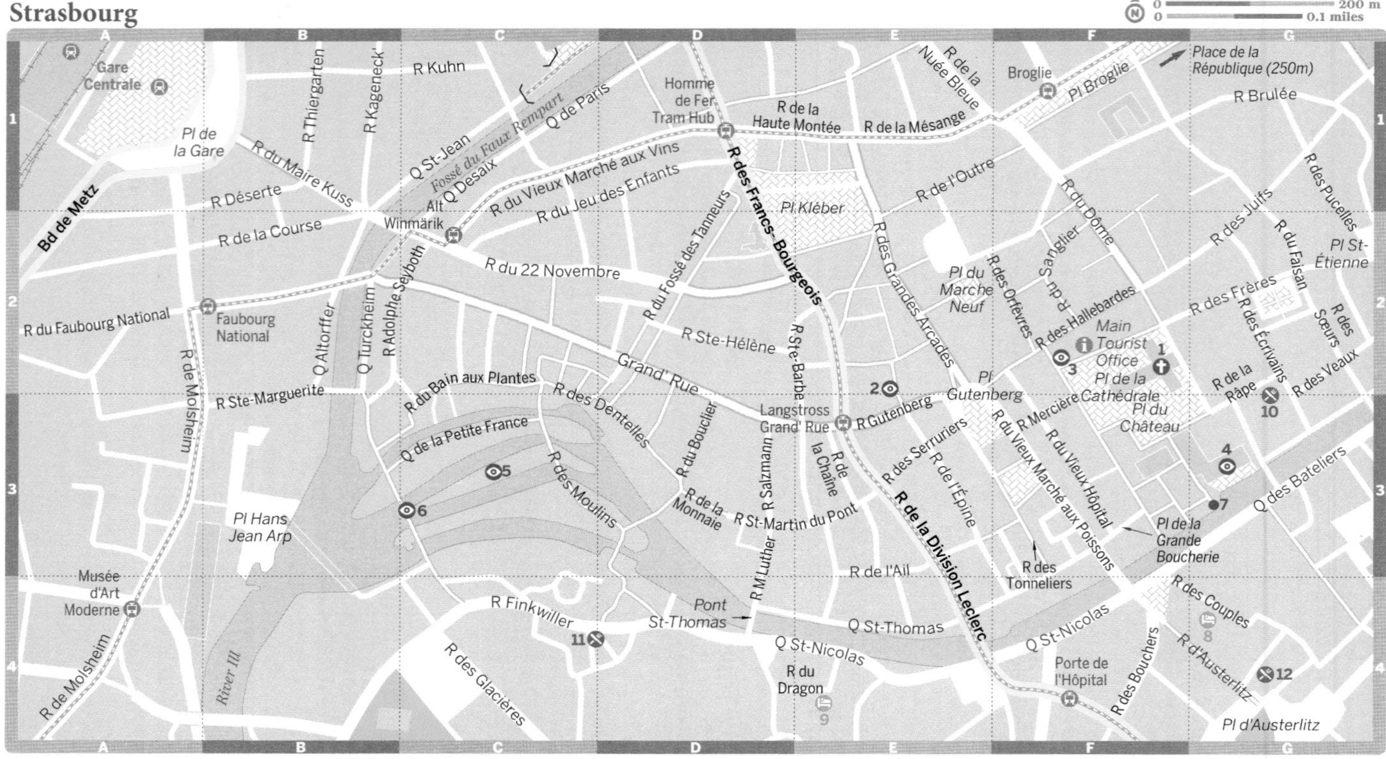
0 200 m
0 0.1 miles
Place de la République (250m)
Gare Centrale
Pl de la Gare
Bd de Metz
R Thiergarten
R Kageneck
R Kuhn
R du Maire Kuss
R Déserte
R de la Course
Q St-Jean
Fossé du Faux Rempart
Q de Paris
Q Desaix
Alt Winmärik
R du Vieux Marché aux Vins
R du Jeu des Enfants
Homme de Fer Tram Hub
R de la Haute Montée
R de la Mésange
R de la Nuée Bleue
Broglie
Pl Broglie
R Brulée
R des Francs- Bourgeois
Pl Kléber
R de l'Outre
R du Dôme
R des Juifs
R des Pucelles
Pl St-Étienne
R du Faisan
R des Sœurs
R des Frères
R des Écrivains
R des Veaux
R de la Râpe
R du 22 Novembre
R Adolphe Seyboth
R du Fossé des Tanneurs
R des Grandes Arcades
Pl du Marché Neuf
R des Orfèvres
R du Sanglier
R des Hallebardes
Main Tourist Office
Pl de la Cathédrale
Pl du Château
R du Faubourg National
Faubourg National
Q Altorffer
Q Turckheim
R Ste-Hélène
R Ste-Barbe
Grand' Rue
Langstross Grand' Rue
R Gutenberg
Pl Gutenberg
R Mercière
R de Molsheim
R Ste-Marguerite
R du Bain aux Plantes
Q de la Petite France
R des Dentelles
R du Bouclier
R Salzmann
R de la Chaîne
R des Serruriers
R de l'Épine
R du Vieux Marché aux Poissons
R du Vieux Hôpital
Pl de la Grande Boucherie
Q des Bateliers
R des Moulins
R de la Monnaie
R St-Martin du Pont
R de la Division Leclerc
R des Tonneliers
Pl Hans Jean Arp
Musée d'Art Moderne
R de Molsheim
River Ill
R Finkwiller
Pont St-Thomas
R M Luther
R de l'Ail
Q St-Thomas
Q St-Nicolas
R du Dragon
R des Glacières
Porte de l'Hôpital
R des Bouchers
R des Couples
R d'Austerlitz
Pl d'Austerlitz

Strasbourg

Sights

1 Cathédrale Notre-Dame F2
2 Grande Île E2
3 Maison Kammerzell F2
4 Palais Rohan G3
5 Petite France C3
6 Ponts Couverts C3

Activities, Courses & Tours

7 Batorama G3

Sleeping

8 Cour du Corbeau G4
9 Hôtel du Dragon E4

Eating

10 Bistrot et Chocolat G3
11 La Cuiller à Pot C4
12 Le Gavroche G4

sunshine at the intimate, softly lit Le Gavroche, which has been awarded one Michelin star. Mains such as veal in a mint crust with crispy polenta and coriander-infused artichoke tagine are followed by zingy desserts such as lime tart with lemon-thyme sorbet. There's a menu for *les petits*.

Information

Main Tourist Office (**03 88 52 28 28; www.otstrasbourg.fr; 17 place de la Cathédrale; 9am-7pm daily; Grand'Rue**) A city-centre walking map with English text costs €1; bus/tram and cycling maps are free. *Strolling in Strasbourg* (€4.50) details six architectural walking tours.

Getting There & Away

Air

Strasbourg's international **airport** (**03 88 64 67 67; www.strasbourg.aeroport.fr**) is 17km southwest of the city centre (towards Molsheim), near the village of Entzheim.

Train

Built in 1883, the Gare Centrale was given a 120m-long, 23m-high glass facade and underground galleries in order to welcome the new TGV Est Européen in grand style. On the Grande Île, tickets are available at the **SNCF Boutique** (**www.voyages-sncf.com; 5 rue des Francs-Bourgeois; Langstross**).

Destinations within France:

Lille €96 to €140, four hours, 17 daily

Lyon €75 to €145, 4½ hours, 14 daily

Marseille €125 to €185, 6¾ hours, 16 daily

Metz €26 to €42, two hours, 20 daily

Nancy €25 to €41, 1½ hours, 25 daily

Paris €75 to €134, 2¼ hours, 19 daily

Colmar

POP 68,843

Alsace wine region capital, Colmar looks for all the world as though it has been plucked from the pages of a medieval folk tale. At times the Route des Vins d'Alsace fools you into thinking it's 1454, but here, in the alley-woven heart of the old town, the illusion is complete. Half-timbered houses in chalk-box colours crowd dark, cobblestone lanes and bridge-laced canals, which have most day-trippers wandering around in a permanent daze of neck-craning, photo-snapping, gasp-eliciting wonder.

Sights

Petite Venise Historic Quarter

(rowboats per 30 min €6) If you see just one thing in Colmar, make it the Little Venice quarter. Canal connection aside, it doesn't resemble the Italian city in the slightest, but it is truly lovely in its own right, whether explored by foot or by rowboat. The winding backstreets are punctuated by impeccably restored half-timbered houses in sugared-almond shades, many ablaze with geraniums in summer. Take a medieval mosey around **rue des Tanneurs**, with its rooftop verandas for drying hides, and **quai de la Poissonnerie**, the former fishers' quarter.

Musée d'Unterlinden Art Museum

(www.musee-unterlinden.com; 1 rue d'Unterlinden; adult/child incl Église des Dominicains €8/5; 9am-6pm daily) Gathered around a Gothic-style Dominican cloister, this museum hides a prized collection of medieval stone statues, late-15th-century prints by Martin Schongauer as well as

If You Like... Art & Architecture

If you swoon over the sublimity of Reims or Amiens cathedrals, or your heart misses a beat inside Strasbourg's modern-art cube museum, there are bags more addresses to apease the art 'n architecture lover in you:

1 **LILLE**

If the seduction of its Flemish-knitted old town is not sufficient, Lille woos with a trio of first-class art museums: savour 15th- to 20th-century art in the **Palais des Beaux-Arts** (Fine Arts Museum; ☎03 20 06 78 00; www.pba-lille.fr; place de la République; adult/child €6.50/free; ⌚2-5.30pm Mon, 10am-5.30pm Wed-Sun; Ⓜ République-Beaux Arts), modern and contemporary works in the **Musée d'Art Moderne Lille-Métropole** (☎03 20 19 68 68; www.musee-lam.fr; 1 allée du Musée, Villeneuve-d'Ascq; adult/child €7/free; ⌚10am-6pm Tue-Sun), and applied arts and sculpture in **La Piscine Musée d'Art et d'Industrie** (☎03 20 69 23 60; www.roubaix-lapiscine.com; 23 rue de l'Espérance, Roubaix; adult/child €5.50/free; ⌚11am-6pm Tue-Thu, 11am-8pm Fri, 1-6pm Sat & Sun; Ⓜ Gare Jean Lebas), superbly at home in an art deco swimming pool.

2 **ARRAS**

Arras' Flemish-inspired architecture is plain to see on its market-square twinset, place des Héros and Grand'Place. For a panoramic perspective, climb the Unesco-listed belltower. For more information, head to the **tourist office** (☎03 21 51 26 95; www.explorearras.fr; place des Héros; ⌚9am-6.30pm Mon-Sat, 10am-1.30pm & 2.30-6.30pm Sun).

3 **NANCY**

Let this former capital of the Dukes of Lorraine catapult you into 18th-century splendour; Nancy's heart-soaring Unesco-listed place Stanislas was laid out in the 1750s. Pick up some info at the **tourist office** (☎03 83 35 22 41; www.nancy-tourisme.fr; place Stanislas; ⌚9am-7pm Mon-Sat, 10am-5pm Sun). Enjoy the region's bergamot-flavoured bonbons while you're here.

an ensemble of Upper Rhine Primitives. Its stellar modern art collection also contains works by Monet, Picasso and Renoir. The star attraction, however, is the late-Gothic **Rétable d'Issenheim** (Issenheim Altarpiece), which is on display until 2015 in the nearby Église des Dominicains while the museum undergoes expansion.

Musée Bartholdi Museum

(www.musee-bartholdi.com; 30 rue des Marands; adult/child €5/3; ⌚10am-noon & 2-6pm Wed-Mon Mar-Dec) In the house where Frédéric Auguste Bartholdi was born in 1834, this museum pays homage to the sculptor who captured the spirit of a nation with his Statue of Liberty. Look out for the full-size plaster model of Lady Liberty's left ear (the lobe is watermelon-sized!) and the Bartholdi family's sparklingly bourgeois apartment. A ground-floor room shows 18th- and 19th-century Jewish ritual objects.

Sleeping

Chez Leslie B&B €

(☎03 89 79 98 99; www.chezleslie.com; 31 rue de Mulhouse; s €72, d €82-87; 📶👪) Insider tips on Colmar, a high chair for your baby, afternoon tea in the garden – nothing is too much trouble for your kind host Leslie at her attractively restored 1905 townhouse. Daylight spills into uniquely decorated rooms with hardwood floors and antique beds. It's five minutes' stroll west of the train station.

Hotel Quatorze Design Hotel €€

(☎03 89 20 45 20; www.hotelquatorze.com; 14 rue des Augins; d €140-240, ste €260-420) Bringing new-wave design to the heart of the old town, Hotel Quatorze occupies a lovingly transformed pharmacy dating from 1830. The 14 rooms and suites are streamlined and open-plan, with wood floors and white walls enlivened by works by Spanish artist Alfonso Vallès. Little details like iPod docks, Aesop cosmetics and, in some suites, whirlpool tubs up the style ante.

Eating

L'Épicurien Traditional French €€
(**☎03 89 41 14 50; 11 rue Wickram; lunch menus €14.50-25, mains €21-25; ⌚noon-2pm & 7-9.30pm Tue-Sat;** 👪) Hidden away in a backstreet of Petite Venise, this is a wine bar-bistro in the classic mould, with cheek-by-jowl tables and a good buzz. Whatever is fresh at the market goes into the pot, often with a generous pinch of spice – from duck breast with sweet chilli to chunky cod fillet with lobster-basil cream and squid ink fettuccine.

JY'S Gourmet €€€
(**☎03 89 21 53 60; www.jean-yves-schillinger.com; 17 rue de la Poissonerie; lunch menu €41, dinner menus €62-82; ⌚noon-2pm & 7-10pm)** Jean-Yves Schillinger mans the stove at this Michelin-starred restaurant in Petite Venise. Behind a trompe l'oeil facade lies an urban-cool restaurant, with flattering lighting and chesterfield sofas adding to the lounge-style ambience. Every flavour shines in seasonal dishes that are cooked with imagination and care, and delivered with panache. Expect a few surprises – from olive trees to candyfloss.

Information

Tourist Office (☎03 89 20 68 92; www.ot-colmar.fr; 32 cours Sainte-Anne; ⌚9am-6pm Mon-Sat, 10am-1pm Sun Apr-Oct, shorter hours rest of the year) Can help find accommodation and supply information on hiking, cycling and bus travel (including schedules) along the Route des Vins and in the Massif des Vosges.

Getting There & Away

Colmar train connections:

Paris Gare de l'Est; €79 to €102, three hours, 17 daily

Strasbourg €12.30, 32 minutes, 30 daily

Route des Vins destinations departing from Colmar include Dambach-la-Ville (€6.40, 35 minutes) and Obernai (€9, one hour), both of which require a change of trains at Sélestat (€4.90, 10 minutes, 30 daily).

Metz

POP 124,024

Sitting astride the confluence of the Moselle and Seille rivers, Lorraine's graceful capital Metz (pronounced 'mess') is ready to be fêted. Though the city's

Metz

PIERO M. BIANCHI/GETTY IMAGES ©

Gothic marvel of a cathedral, superlative art collections and Michelin star–studded dining scene long managed to sidestep the world spotlight, all that changed with the show-stopping arrival of Centre Pompidou-Metz in 2010.

 Sights

Cathédrale St-Étienne Cathedral
(place St-Étienne; audioguide €7, combined ticket treasury & crypt adult/child €4/2; ⏲8am-6pm, treasury & crypt 9.30am-12.30pm & 1.30-5.30pm Mon-Sat, 2-6pm Sun) The lacy golden spires of this Gothic cathedral crown Metz' skyline. Exquisitely lit by kaleidoscopic curtains of 13th- to 20th-century stained glass, the cathedral is nicknamed 'God's lantern' and its sense of height is spiritually uplifting. Notice the flamboyant **Chagall windows** in startling jewel-coloured shades of ruby, gold, sapphire, topaz and amethyst in the ambulatory, which also harbours the **treasury**. The sculpture of the **Graoully** (grau-lee), a dragon said to have terrified pre-Christian Metz, lurks in the 15th-century **crypt**.

Centre Pompidou-Metz Gallery
(www.centrepompidou-metz.fr; 1 parvis des Droits de l'Homme; adult/child €7/free; ⏲11am-6pm Mon & Wed-Fri, 10am-8pm Sat, 10am-6pm Sun) Designed by Japanese architect Shigeru Ban, with a curved roof resembling a space-age Chinese hat, the architecturally innovative Centre Pompidou-Metz is the star of the city's art scene. The satellite branch of Paris' Centre Pompidou draws on Europe's largest collection of modern art to stage ambitious temporary exhibitions, such as the avant-garde works of German artist Hans Richter and the bold graphic works of American conceptual artist Sol LeWitt. The dynamic space also hosts cultural events, talks and youth projects.

Quartier Impérial Historic Quarter
The stately boulevards and bourgeois villas of the German Imperial Quarter, including rue Gambetta and av Foch, are the brainchild of Kaiser Wilhelm II. Philippe Starck lamp-posts juxtapose Teutonic sculptures, whose common theme is German imperial might, at the monumental Rhenish neo-Romanesque **train station**, completed in 1908. The massive main **post office**, built in 1911 of red Vosges sandstone, is as solid and heavy as the cathedral is light and lacy.

 Sleeping

Péniche Alclair Houseboat €
(☎06 37 67 16 18; www.chambrespenichemetz.com; allée St-Symphorien; r incl breakfast €75; 📶) What a clever idea: this old barge has been revamped into a stylish houseboat, with two cheerful wood-floored rooms and watery views. Breakfast is served in your room or on the sundeck. It's a 15-minute stroll south of the centre along the river.

Dambach-la-Ville

DOUG PEARSON/GETTY IMAGES ©

Hôtel de la Cathédrale Historic Hotel **€€**

(03 87 75 00 02; www.hotelcathedrale-metz.fr; 25 place de Chambre; d €75-120;) You can expect a friendly welcome at this classy little hotel, occupying a 17th-century townhouse in a prime spot right opposite the cathedral. Climb the wrought-iron staircase to your classically elegant room, with high ceilings, hardwood floors and antique trappings. Book well ahead for a cathedral view.

Eating

Restaurant Thierry International **€€**

(03 87 74 01 23; www.restaurant-thierry.fr; 5 rue des Piques; menus €22-40; noon-3pm & 7-11pm, closed Wed & Sun) Combining the historic backdrop of a 16th-century townhouse with the subtly spiced cuisine, lighting and bohemian flair of Morocco, this is one of Metz' most coveted tables. An aperitif in the candlelit salon works up an appetite for global flavours such as seared swordfish with red curry risotto and tagine of lamb with dried fruit.

Le Magasin aux Vivres Gastronomic **€€€**

(03 87 17 17 17; 5 av Ney; menus €47-145; noon-2pm & 7.30-10pm Tue-Fri, 7.30-10pm Sat, noon-2pm Sun) Conjurer of textures and seasonal flavours, chef Christophe Dufossé makes creative use of local produce at this sophisticated Michelin-starred restaurant. Moselle wines work well with specialities like plump scallops with fresh truffle, artichoke mousse and hazelnut oil, and Bresse chicken served three ways.

Information

Tourist Office (03 87 55 53 76; http://tourisme.mairie-metz.fr; 2 place d'Armes; 9am-7pm Mon-Sat, 10am-5pm Sun) In a one-time guardroom built in the mid-1700s. Free walking-tour and cycling maps, and free wi-fi. Can make room bookings for a €1.50 fee.

If You Like… Alsatian Villages

The 170km-long **Route des Vins d'Alsace** (Alsace Wine Route) is one of France's most evocative drives, featuring castle-topped crags and the mist-enshrouded Vosges. And every mile or so there's a roadside *cave* (wine cellar) or half-timbered village inviting you to stop, raise a glass and revel in some of France's loveliest wines.

1 **KAYSERSBERG**

Kaysersberg, 10km northwest of Colmar, is a real heart-stealer with its backdrop of gently sloping vines, hilltop castle and 16th-century fortified bridge across the River Weiss.

2 **RIQUEWIHR**

Some 14km northwest of Colmar, this might just be the most enchanting town on this driving route.

3 **RIBEAUVILLÉ**

Sample Alsatian wines at **Cave de Ribeauvillé** (03 89 73 20 35; www.vins-ribeauville.com; 2 rte de Colmar; 8am-noon & 2-6pm Mon-Fri, 10am-noon & 2-6pm Sat & Sun) FREE, France's oldest wine growers' cooperative (1895), 3km from Riquewihr.

4 **OBERNAI**

This wine-producing village features flower-bedecked alleyways and 13th-century ramparts. Feast on traditional dishes at **Winstub La Dîme** (03 88 95 54 02; 5 rue des Pélerins; menus €16-30; noon-2pm & 7-9pm Thu-Tue).

5 **DAMBACH-LA-VILLE**

Ringed by renowned Frankstein *grand cru* vineyards and sturdy pink-granite ramparts, Dambach is built from half-timbered houses painted in ice-cream colours like pistachio and raspberry.

6 **CHÂTEAU DU HAUT KŒNIGSBOURG**

Turreted red-sandstone **Château du Haut Kœnigsbourg** (www.haut-koenigsbourg.fr; adult/child €8/free; 9.15am-6pm, shorter hours in winter) is worth the detour for the wraparound panorama from its ramparts.

© SANAA, IMREY CULBERT/
HUFTON AND CROW/VIEW/CORBIS ©

Don't Miss Louvre-Lens

Opened with fanfare in 2012 in Lens, 18km north of Arras, the innovative Louvre-Lens showcases hundreds of treasures from Paris' venerable Musée du Louvre in a purpose-built, state-of-the-art exhibition space.

Unlike its Parisian cousin, there's no permanent collection here. Instead, the museum's centrepiece, a 120m-long exhibition space called the **Galerie du Temps,** displays a limited but significant, ever-rotating collection of 200-plus pieces from the original Louvre, spanning that museum's full breadth and diversity of cultures and historical periods.

A second building, the glass-walled **Pavillon de Verre,** displays temporary themed exhibits. Rounding out the museum are educational facilities, an auditorium, a restaurant and a park.

Lens is accessible by regular TGV trains from Paris' Gare du Nord (€28.50 to €51, 65 to 70 minutes), as well as regional trains from Lille (from €6.80, 40 minutes) and Arras (from €4.50, 15 minutes).

NEED TO KNOW

03 21 18 62 62; www.louvrelens.fr; 99 rue Paul Bert, Lens; 10am-6pm Wed-Mon

Getting There & Away

Metz' ornate early 20th-century **train station** (**pl du Général de Gaulle**) has a supersleek TGV linking Paris with Luxembourg.

Nancy €10.90, 37 minutes, 48 daily

Paris €60 to €75, 1½ hours, 15 daily

Strasbourg €26.40, 1½ hours, 16 daily

Verdun €15, 1½ hours, three direct daily

Amiens

POP 137,030

One of France's most awe-inspiring Gothic cathedrals is reason enough to spend time in Amiens, the comfy, if reserved, former capital of Picardy, where Jules Verne spent the last two decades of his life. The mostly pedestrianised city centre, rebuilt after the war, is complemented by lovely green spaces along the Somme river. Some 25,000 students give the town a youthful feel.

Amiens is an excellent base for visits to the Battle of the Somme Memorials.

Sights & Activities

Cathédrale Notre Dame Cathedral

(place Notre Dame; north tower adult/child €5.50/free, audioguide €4; ⌚cathedral 8.30am-6.15pm daily, north tower afternoon only Wed-Mon) The largest Gothic cathedral in France (it's 145m long) and a Unesco World Heritage Site, this magnificent structure was begun in 1220 to house the **skull of St John the Baptist**. Architecture connoisseurs rave about the soaring Gothic arches (42.3m high over the transept), unity of style and immense interior, but for locals the highlight is the 17th-century statue known as the **Ange Pleureur** (Crying Angel), in the ambulatory directly behind the over-the-top Baroque high altar.

Hortillonnages Boat Tour

(☎03 22 92 12 18; 54 bd Beauvillé; adult/child €5.90/4.10; ⌚2-5pm Apr-Oct) Amiens' market gardens – some 3 sq km in extent – have supplied the city with vegetables and flowers since the Middle Ages. Today, their peaceful *rieux* (waterways), home to seven working farms, over 1000 private gardens and countless water birds, can be visited on 12-person boats whose raised prows make them look a bit like gondolas. Available later (to 6.30pm) if weather and demand allow. A not-to-be-missed experience.

Maison de Jules Verne House Museum

(Home of Jules Verne; ☎03 22 45 45 75; www.amiens.fr/vie-quotidienne/culture/; 2 rue Charles Dubois; adult/child €7.50/4; ⌚10am-12.30pm & 2-6.30pm Mon & Wed-Fri, 2-6.30pm Tue, 11am-6.30pm Sat & Sun) Author Jules Verne (1828–1905) wrote many of his

Cathédrale Notre Dame, Amiens

HIROSHI HIGUCHI/GETTY IMAGES ©

best-known works of brain-tingling – and rather eerily prescient – science fiction under the eaves of this turreted Amiens home. The models, prints, posters and other items inspired by Verne's fecund imagination afford a fascinating opportunity to check out the future as he envisioned it over a century ago, when going around the world in 80 days sounded utterly fantastic. Signs are in French and English.

 Sleeping

Hôtel Victor Hugo Hotel €

(☎03 22 91 57 91; www.hotel-a-amiens.com; 2 rue de l'Oratoire; d €49-65; 📶) Just a block from the cathedral, this bargain-priced, family-run hotel has 10 simple but comfortable rooms. Best value, if you don't mind a long stair climb, are those on the sloped-ceilinged top floor (rooms 7 and 8) with rooftop views and lots of natural light. No parking.

Grand Hôtel de l'Univers Hotel €€

(☎03 22 91 52 51; www.hotel-univers-amiens.com; 2 rue de Noyon; d €95-125; 📶) This venerable, Best Western–affiliated hostelry has an enviable parkside location in the city's heart, only one block from the train station. Rue de Noyon is pedestrianised so you won't be bothered by noise. The 40 rooms, set around a four-storey atrium, are immaculate and very comfortable; try room 26 (€110) for its double aspect and balcony. One quibble: there's no parking.

 Eating

Le T'chiot Zinc Bistro €

(☎03 22 91 43 79; 18 rue de Noyon; menus €14-28; ⏰noon-2.30pm & 7-10pm Mon-Sat) Inviting, bistro-style decor reminiscent of the belle époque provides a fine backdrop for the tasty French and Picard cuisine, including fish dishes and *caqhuse* (pork in a cream, wine vinegar and onion sauce).

 Information

Tourist Office (☎03 22 71 60 50; www.amiens-tourisme.com; 40 place Notre Dame; ⏰9.30am-6pm Mon-Sat, 10am-noon & 2-5pm Sun) Can supply details on the Somme memorials (including minibus tours) and cultural events.

Ossuaire de Douaumont

STOCKCAM/GETTY IMAGES ©

Getting There & Away

Amiens is an important rail hub. SNCF buses (€10, 45 minutes, about seven daily) also go to the Haute Picardie TGV station, 42km east of the city.

Arras €12.70, 45 minutes, six to 13 daily

Calais-Ville €27.10, two to 2½ hours, four to five daily

Compiègne €13.90, 1¼ hours, eight to 12 daily

Lille-Flandres €21.70, 1½ hours, five to 13 daily

Paris Gare du Nord €16.50 to €22.20, 1¼ to 1¾ hours, 14 to 22 daily

Rouen €20.80, 1¼ hours, five daily

Battle of the Somme Memorials

Almost 750,000 soldiers, airmen and sailors from Great Britain, Australia, Canada, the Indian subcontinent, Ireland, New Zealand, South Africa, the West Indies and other parts of the British Empire died during WWI on the Western Front, two-thirds of them in France. They were buried where they fell, in more than 1000 military cemeteries and 2000 civilian cemeteries that dot the landscape along a wide swathe of territory – 'Flanders Fields' – running roughly from Amiens and Cambrai north via Arras and Béthune to Armentières and Ypres (Ieper) in Belgium.

Between 2014 and 2018, a number of events will commemorate the Centenary of WWI throughout the region – it's well worth timing your trip around them.

Sights

PÉRONNE

The best place to begin a visit to the Somme battlefields – especially if you're interested in WWI's historical and cultural context – is the outstanding Historial de la Grande Guerre. Tucked inside Péronne's massively fortified château, this award-winning museum tells the story of the war chronologically, with equal space

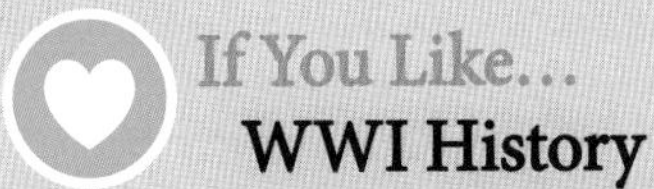

If You Like… WWI History

If you've been moved by the Somme memorials, pay your respects to those who fought in the Battle of Verdun, the longest WWI battle. By car, take the D913 and D112 and follow signs to 'Douamont', 'Vaux' or the 'Champ de Bataille 14-18'. Alternatively, **Verdun tourist office** (**☎03 29 84 55 55; www.tourisme-verdun.fr; av du Général Mangin, Pavillon Japiot; ⌚9.30am-12.30pm & 1.30-6pm Mon-Sat, 10am-noon & 2-5pm Sun;**) arranges one-hour battlefield tours (adult/child €9/7; hourly 2pm to 6pm early April to mid-November).

1 **MÉMORIAL DE VERDUN** **(www.memorial-de-verdun.fr; adult/child €7/3.50; ⌚9am-6pm, closed mid-Dec–Jan)** The village of **Fleury**, obliterated in the course of being captured and recaptured 16 times, is now the site of this memorial. It tells the story of '300 days, 300,000 dead, 400,000 wounded', with insightful displays of war artefacts and personal items.

2 **OSSUAIRE DE DOUAUMONT** **(www.verdun-douaumont.com; audiovisual presentation adult/child €6/3; ⌚9am-6pm Mon-Fri, 10am-6pm Sat & Sun)** Rising like a gigantic artillery shell above 15,000 crosses that bleed into the distance, this 137m-long ossuary is one of France's most important WWI memorials. A ticket to the 20-minute **audiovisual presentation** on the battle also lets you climb the 46m-high **bell tower.**

3 **FORT DE DOUAUMONT** **(adult/child €4/2; ⌚10am-6pm)** This is the strongest of the 38 fortresses and bastions built along a 45km front to protect Verdun. When the Battle of Verdun began, 400m-long Douaumont had only a skeleton crew. By the fourth day it had been captured easily; four months later it was retaken by colonial troops from Morocco.

4 **MEUSE-ARGONNE AMERICAN CEMETERY** The largest US military cemetery in Europe is this WWI ground, where 14,246 soldiers lie buried, in Romagne-sous-Montfaucon, 41km northwest of Verdun along the D38 and D123.

given to the German, French and British perspectives on what happened, how and why.

Excellent English brochures on the battlefields can be picked up at Péronne's tourist office, 100m from the museum entrance.

Péronne (pop 8450) is about 60km east of Amiens; from the D1029 or A29, follow the D1017 the last few kilometres into town.

LA GRANDE MINE

Just outside the hamlet of La Boisselle, this enormous crater looks like the site of a meteor impact. Some 100m across and 30m deep, the **Lochnagar Crater Memorial** (as it's officially known) was created on the morning of the first day of the First Battle of the Somme (1 July 1916) by about 25 tonnes of ammonal laid by British sappers in order to create a breach in the German lines – and is a testament to the boundless ingenuity human beings can muster when determined to kill their fellow creatures.

La Grande Mine is 4km northeast of Albert along the D929.

SOMME AMERICAN CEMETERY

In late September 1918, just six weeks before the end of WWI, American units – flanked by their British, Canadian and Australian allies – launched an assault on the Germans' heavily fortified Hindenburg Line.

Some of the fiercest fighting took place near the village of Bony, on the sloping site now occupied by the 1844 Latin Crosses and Stars of David of the Somme American Cemetery. The names of 333 men whose remains were never recovered are inscribed on the walls of the **Memorial Chapel**, reached through massive bronze doors. The small **Visitors' Building** (turn left at the flagpole) has information on the battle.

The cemetery is 24km northeast of Péronne, mostly along the D6, and 18km north of St-Quentin along the D1044. From A26, take exit 9 and follow the signs for 17km.

THIEPVAL MEMORIAL

Dedicated to 'the Missing of the Somme', this Commonwealth memorial – its distinctive outline visible for many kilometres in all directions – is the region's most visited place of pilgrimage. Situated on the site of a German stronghold that was stormed on 1 July 1916 with unimaginable casualties, it was designed by Sir Edwin Lutyens and dedicated in 1932. The columns of the arches are inscribed with the names of 73,367 British and South African soldiers whose remains were never recovered or identified. The glass-walled visitors centre is discreetly below ground level.

Vimy Ridge

Thiepval is 7.5km northeast of Albert along the D151.

VIMY RIDGE

Vimy Ridge (www.veterans.gc.ca; visitor centre 9am-5pm daily), 11km north of Arras, was the scene of some of the bloodiest and toughest trench warfare of WWI, with almost two full years of attacks. Of the 66,655 Canadians who died in WWI, 3598 lost their lives in April 1917 taking this 14km-long stretch. Its highest point – site of a heavily fortified German position – was later chosen as the site of Canada's WWI memorial.

FROMELLES (PHEASANT WOOD) MILITARY CEMETERY & MEMORIAL PARK

In Fromelles, about 20km west of Lille, this hexagonal **cemetery** (www.cwgc.org) – the first new Commonwealth cemetery in half a century – was dedicated on 19 July 2010 following the discovery of the mass graves of 250 Australian soldiers. Just 2km northwest, the Australian Memorial Park marks the spot where, on 19 and 20 July 1916, 1917 Australians and 519 British soldiers were killed during a poorly planned offensive intended to divert German forces from the Battle of the Somme.

Tours

Tourist offices (including those in Amiens, Arras and Péronne) can help book tours of battlefield sites and memorials. Respected tour companies include **The Battlefields Experience** (03 22 76 29 60; www.thebattleofthesomme.co.uk), **Western Front Tours** (www.westernfronttours.com.au; mid-Mar–mid-Nov), **Terres de Mémoire** (03 22 84 23 05; www.terresdememoire.com), **Chemins d'Histoire** (06 31 31 85 02; www.cheminsdhistoire.com) and **True Blue Digger Tours** (06 01 33 46 76; www.trueblue-digger-tours.com).

Loire Valley & Central France

In terms of architectural splendour, nowhere tops the Loire Valley. For more than 1000 years, this has been the favourite weekend retreat for the cream of French society, and it's littered with lavish châteaux left behind by generations of kings, queens and courtly nobles.

Southeast along the River Loire is Burgundy (Bourgogne in French), France's second-most-famous wine region after Bordeaux. Unsurprisingly, it makes a fantastic place to try wine and buy wine. The region's elegant capital, Dijon, is also well worth a detour for its historic art and architecture.

Further west, across the mountains of the Massif Central, lies the Dordogne (known to the French as Périgord), renowned for its rich cuisine and idyllic countryside. It was once home to France's most-ancient settlers, who left behind many stunning prehistoric artworks in the murky caves of the Vézère Valley.

Château de Chenonceau (p197)

Loire Valley & Central France

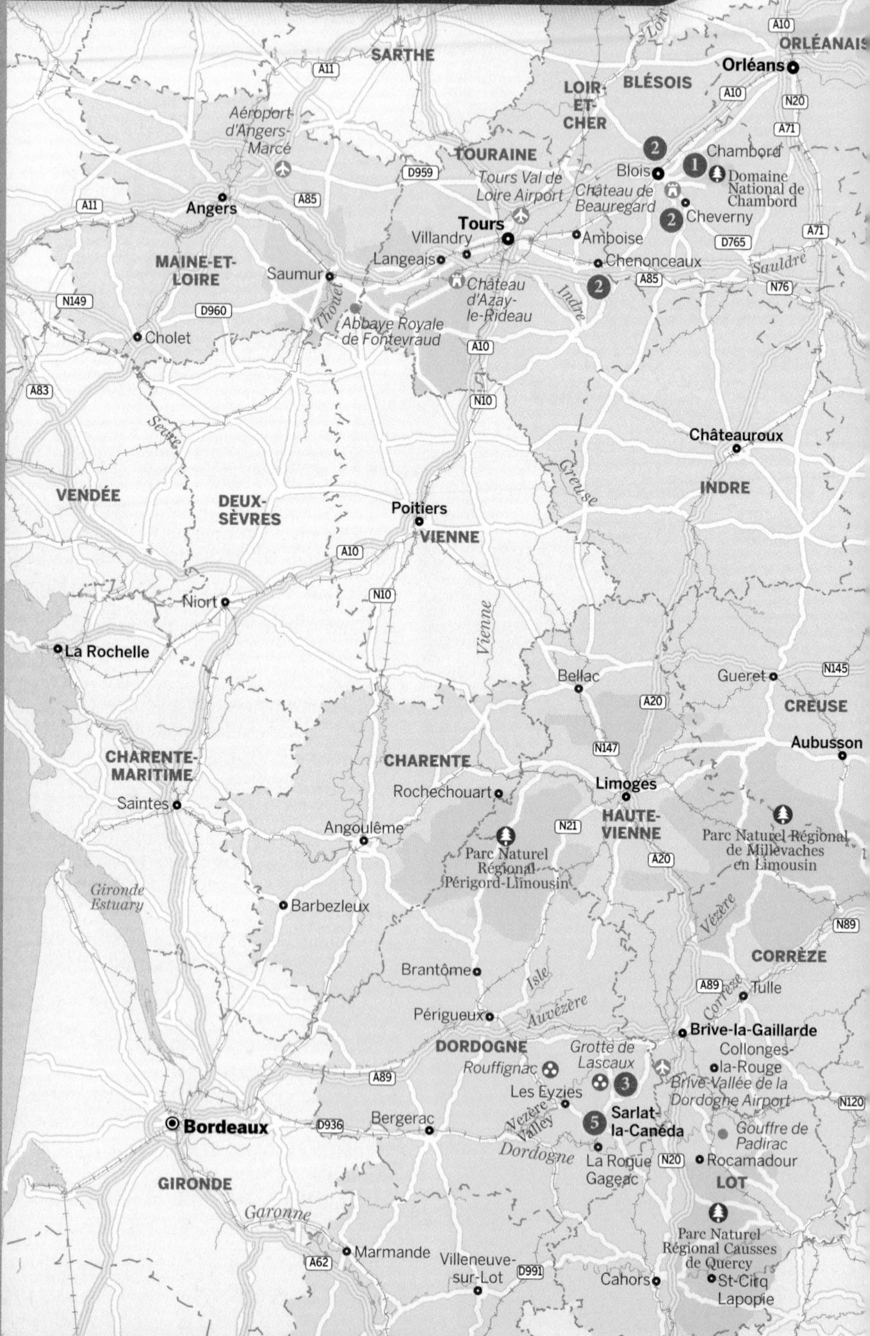

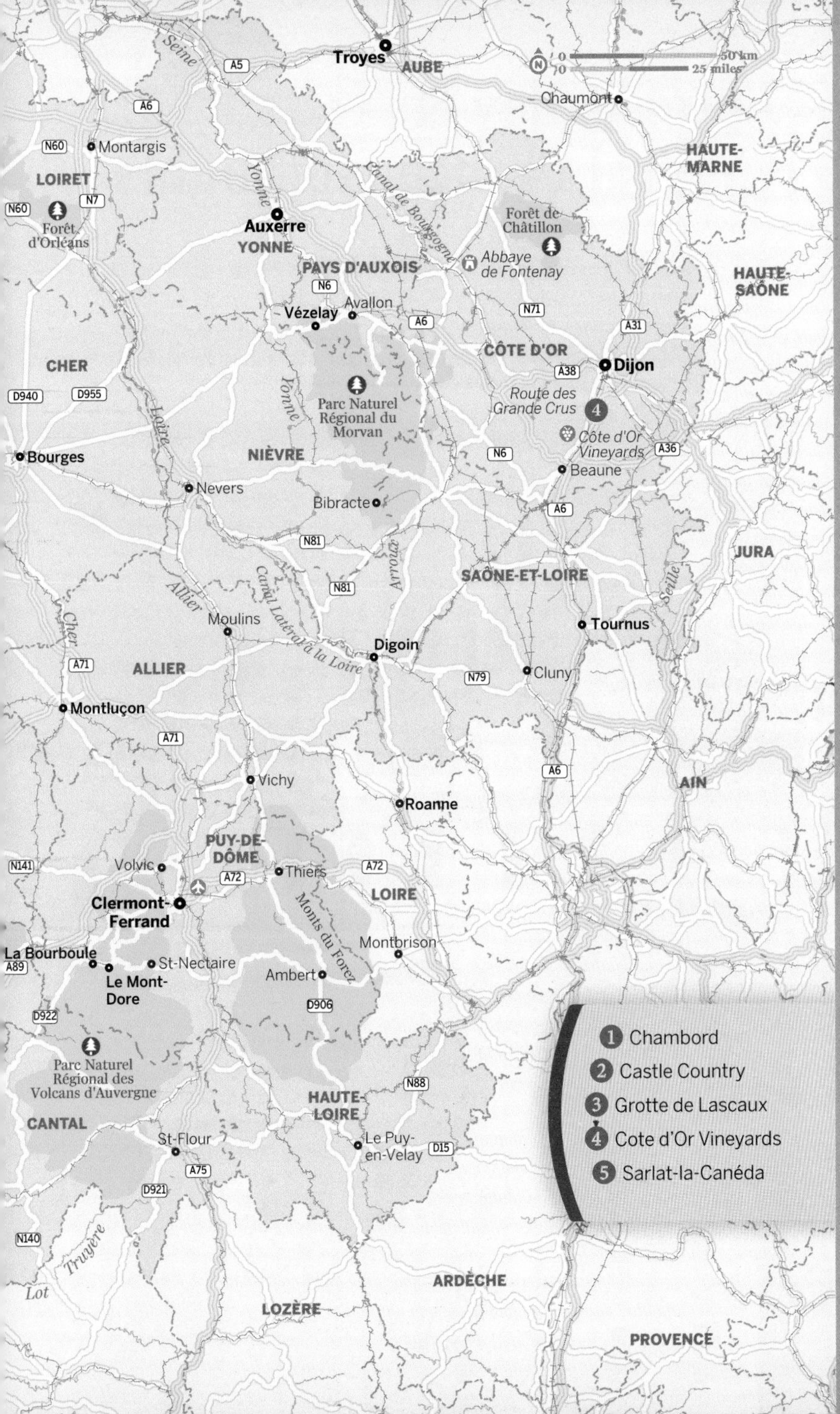

Loire Valley & Central France Highlights

Château de Chambord

If you only have time to visit one château in the Loire, it really has to be Château de Chambord (p198). Built as a hunting lodge for François 1, this really is the king of the castles – an outlandish, extravagant wonder with hundreds of rooms, architectural secrets galore and a staircase that's said to have been designed by Leonardo da Vinci.

1

2 Castle Country

For sheer architectural splendour Chambord is tough to beat, but it's not the only château worth seeing in the Loire Valley. From sturdy medieval fortresses to gran[d] Renaissance showpieces, the Loire has enough castles to fill a lifetime of visits. Top honours go to river-spanning Chenonceau (p197), graceful Cheverny (p193) and history-packed, regal Blois (p192), but there are many more to discover. Left: Château de Cheverny (p193)

SUPERSTOCK/GETTY IMAGES ©

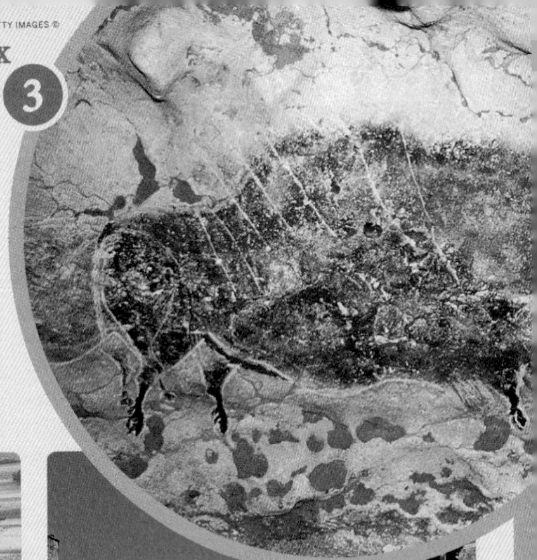

3 Grotte de Lascaux

In 1940 four teenage boys searching for their lost dog discovered the Grotte de Lascaux (p214), a vast network of subterranean chambers adorned with the most extraordinary prehistoric paintings ever found. Though the original cave is now off-limits to avoid damaging these ancient artworks, they have been meticulously recreated in another cave nearby. If you're going to visit only one cave in the prehistoric-precious Vézère Valley, make sure it's this one.

BRUNO MORANDI/CORBIS ©

4 Côte d'Or Vineyards

Cruising along peaceful country lanes laced with the vine-carpeted slopes of one of France's most prestigious wine-producing regions: this is reason enough to visit Burgundy's Côte d'Or (p208). Scenic motoring along the Route des Grands Crus, intimate cellar visits with local vignerons (wine growers), tasting, drinking and buying is all part and parcel of exploring this world-class 'Golden Hillside' wine region. Above: Burgundy vineyards

5 Sarlat-la-Canéda

Few places in France feel as convincingly medieval as quaint Sarlat (p213). With its jumble of alleyways, culs-de-sac and honey-coloured stone houses, it makes a sublime base for exploring the caves of the Vézère Valley. Don't miss the wonderful Saturday market, where local producers from all over the Dordogne set up shop on the cobbles of the main square.

Loire Valley & Central France's Best...

Historic Architecture

- **Château Royal de Blois** A whistle-stop tour through French architecture. (p192)
- **Abbaye de Fontenay** Inner peace in a Cistercian abbey. (p203)
- **Palais des Ducs et des États de Bourgogne** Dijon's ducal palace is now a superb arts museum. (p204)
- **Château Royal d'Amboise** Climb this regal château's spiralling towers. (p201)
- **Hôtel-Dieu des Hospices de Beaune** Marvel at this medieval hospital. (p209)

Gardens

- **Château de Chaumont-sur-Loire** English-style park and host to an international garden fest. (p194)
- **Château de Chenonceau** Exquisite formal gardens with yew-tree labyrinth. (p197)
- **Le Clos Lucé** Amboise gardens dotted with Leonardo da Vinci miniatures. (p201)
- **Château de Villandry** Water gardens, maze, green love and the poshest veg patch ever. (p209)

Photo Opps

- **Chambord's rooftop** Get a bird's-eye perspective of the Loire's grandest château. (p198)
- **St-Cirq Lapopie** Unparalleled Lot Valley panorama atop this tiny clifftop village. (p217)
- **Sarlat-la-Canéda** Ride a panoramic lift inside Église Ste-Marie for a 360-degree view. (p213)
- **Brantôme** Scale an 11th-century belltower to peep down on Brantôme's waterways. (p212)
- **La Roque Gageac** Snap away afloat a *gabarre* (barge). (p212)

Curiosities

- **Chantier Médiéval de Guédelon** See a 13th-century château being built. (p212)
- **Gouffre de Padirac** Sail a subterranean river through a breathtaking cave. (p217)
- **Maison de la Magie** Be befuddled by optical illusions and magic tricks in Blois. (p191)
- **Soupe des Chiens** Join the dogs' dinner at Cheverny. (p194)
- **École Nationale d'Équitation** Watch the amazing dressage displays of the Cadre Noir. (p202)

Left: Château de Chenonceau (p197); **Above:** St-Cirq Lapopie (p217)

Need to Know

ADVANCE PLANNING

- **As early as possible** Book accommodation, particularly in hotspots such as Amboise, Dijon and Sarlat-la-Canéda.
- **Two weeks before** Book tours for Saumur's École Nationale d'Équitation (p202), Grotte de Lascaux (p214) and Grotte de Font de Gaume (p216).
- **One week before** Choose your châteaux and work out the best ticket combination (p191), if you can buy online, etc.

RESOURCES

- **Châteaux Tourisme** (www.chateauxtourisme.com) General info on the Loire Valley.
- **Val de Loire** (www.valdeloire.org) Loire Valley heritage site.
- **Randonée en Val de Loire** (www.randonnee-en-val-de-loire.com) Loire Valley walks and cycling routes.
- **Burgundy Tourism** (www.burgundy-tourism.com) Burgundy tourist board.
- **Wines of Burgundy** (www.bourgogne-wines.com) Burgundy wine.

GETTING AROUND

- **Train** Regular trains travel from Paris to major cities; for regional route planners see www.mobigo-bourgogne.com and www.destineo.fr.
- **Car** Having a car means more flexibility; essential for the Vézere Valley.
- **Organised bus tours** A great way of exploring the Loire châteaux (p189) and Burgundy vineyards (p206).
- **Bicycle** See **Les Châteaux à Vélo** (www.chateauxavelo.com) and **Loire à Vélo** (www.loireavelo.fr) for routes, maps and MP3 guides. For bike rental see **Détours de Loire** (www.locationdevelos.com) or contact local tourist offices. To bike Burgundy see www.burgundy-by-bike.com.

BE FOREWARNED

- **Vézère Valley** Most caves are closed in winter; visitor numbers are limited in summer. Book ahead.
- **Grotte de Lascaux** April to October tickets can *only* be bought next to the tourist office in Montignac.
- **Crowds** Can be a problem, especially in the Loire and the Dordogne and in July and August.

Loire Valley & Central France Itineraries

With its Renaissance châteaux, tranquil rivers and renowned cave paintings, there's so much to see in this region that you might find it takes up your entire trip.

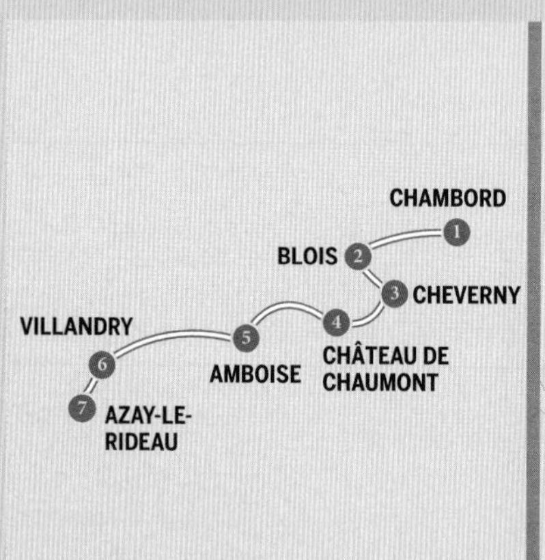

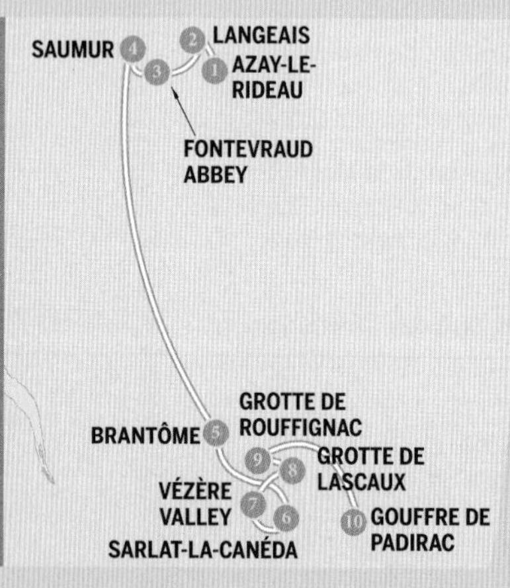

3 DAYS

CHAMBORD TO AZAY-LE-RIDEAU
CHÂTEAU CLASSICS

For maximum freedom you'll want your own car in the Loire, although organised minibus trips can be good if time is short. This tour of the Loire's top châteaux begins with the biggest, boldest and best, ❶ **Château de Chambord**. Tour the interior with an audioguide before scaling the double-helix staircase to the rooftop for sweeping views of the grounds, surrounded by a Tolkien-esque jumble of cupolas, domes, chimneys and lightning rods. Overnight in ❷ **Blois**.

You should have time to squeeze in at least two châteaux on day two, starting with Renaissance elegance at ❸ **Château de Cheverny**, followed by medieval heritage at ❹ **Château de Chaumont**. ❺ **Amboise** makes an ideal place to end the day, with lots of luxurious sleeps to choose from: one of our favourites is Le Clos d'Amboise.

On day three, visit Château Royal d'Amboise and get to know original Renaissance man Leonardo da Vinci at Le Clos Lucé. In the afternoon, head west to see the remarkable ornamental gardens of ❻ **Château de Villandry**. Wrap up with a night-time visit to the Loire's oldest and best *son-et-lumière* (sound and light show), projected directly onto the walls of moat-encircled ❼ **Château d'Azay-le-Rideau**.

AZAY-LE-RIDEAU TO SARLAT-LA-CANÉDA

CASTLES TO CAVE ART

Head west from 1 **Azay-le-Rideau** along the Loire. You'll find a quintessential medieval castle at 2 **Langeais**, ramparts, drawbridge and all. Spend the afternoon at 3 **Fontevraud Abbey** and overnight in 4 **Saumur**.

On day two, head south towards the Dordogne. You'll reach the riverside village of 5 **Brantôme** by afternoon, where you could stop for a late lunch or a canal cruise before heading on to 6 **Sarlat-la-Canéda**. Sarlat makes an ideal base for exploring the Dordogne region, but it deserves a day in its own right – don't miss its buzzy morning market and medieval architecture.

On day four, head off to view the amazing Stone Age art in the 7 **Vezère Valley**. Book guided visits to the Grotte de Font de Gaume and the Grotte des Combarelles before heading over to the famous 8 **Grotte de Lascaux** in the afternoon.

On the last day, you should be able to fit in two unforgettable underground adventures: a trip aboard the rattling train deep into the 9 **Grotte de Rouffignac** and a punt along the spooky subterranean river at the 10 **Gouffre de Padirac**.

Brantôme (p212)

Discover the Loire Valley & Central France

At a Glance

- **Loire Valley** (p189) A fairy-tale mirage of châteaux, all shapes, sizes and historical designs, lace the banks of France's most regal river.
- **Burgundy** (p204) Vineyards here produce France's finest wine.
- **The Dordogne** (p213) Medieval villages, clifftop castles and prehistoric works of art enhance this rural region in the pretty heart of France.

Cathédrale Ste-Croix
IAN DAGNALL/ALAMY ©

THE LOIRE VALLEY

In centuries past, the River Loire was a key strategic area, one step removed from the French capital and poised on the crucial frontier between northern and southern France. Kings, queens, dukes and nobles established their feudal strongholds and country seats along the Loire, and the broad, flat valley is sprinkled with many of the most extravagant castles and fortresses in France. From sky-topping turrets and glittering banquet halls to slate-crowned cupolas and crenellated towers, the hundreds of châteaux dotted around the Loire Valley – a Unesco World Heritage Site – comprise 1000 years of astonishingly rich architectural and artistic treasures.

Orléans

POP 116,830

There's a definite big-city buzz around the boulevards, flashy boutiques and elegant buildings of Orléans, 100km south of Paris. It's a city with enduring heritage: already an important settlement by the time of the Romans' arrival, Orléans sealed its place in history in 1429 when a young peasant girl by the name of Jeanne d'Arc (Joan of Arc) rallied the armies of Charles VII and staged a spectacular rout against the besieging English forces, a key turning point in the Hundred Years War.

Sights

Cathédrale Ste-Croix Cathedral

(http://orleans.catholique.fr/cathedrale; place Ste-Croix; ⌚9.15am-noon & 2.15-5.45pm) In a country of jaw-dropping churches, the

Cathédrale Ste-Croix still raises a gasp. Towering above place Ste-Croix, Orléans' Flamboyant Gothic cathedral was originally built in the 13th century and then underwent collective tinkering by successive monarchs. Joan of Arc came and prayed here on 8 May 1429, and was greeted with a procession of thanks for saving the town.

Musée des Beaux-Arts Art Museum

(**02 38 79 21 55; www.orleans.fr; 1 rue Fernand Rabier; adult/child incl audioguide €4/free, 1st Sun of the month free; 10am-6pm Tue-Sun)** Orléans' five-storeyed fine-arts museum is a treat, with an excellent selection of Italian, Flemish and Dutch paintings (including works by Correggio, Velázquez and Bruegel), as well as a huge collection by French artists such as Léon Cogniet (1794–1880) and Orléans-born Alexandre Antigna (1817–78), and Paul Gaugin, who spent some of his youth in Orléans.

Maison de Jeanne d'Arc Museum

(**02 38 68 32 63; www.jeannedarc.com.fr; 3 place du Général de Gaulle; adult/child €4/free; 10am-6pm Tue-Sun Apr-Sep, 2-6pm Tue-Sun Oct-Mar)** The best place to get an overview of Joan of Arc's life story is this reconstruction of the 15th-century house that hosted her between April and May 1429 (the original was destroyed by British bombing in 1940). Start with its main feature: a 15-minute movie (in French or English) tracing her origins, accomplishments and historical impact.

Châteaux Tours

Hard-core indie travellers might balk at the idea of a minibus tour of the châteaux, but don't dismiss it out of hand, especially if you don't have your own transport. Many private companies offer a choice of well-organised itineraries, taking in various combinations of Azay-le-Rideau, Villandry, Cheverny, Chambord and Chenonceau (plus wine-tasting tours). Half-day trips cost between €23 and €36; full-day trips range from €50 to €54. Many also offer custom-designed tours. Entry to the châteaux isn't included, though you often get slightly discounted tickets. Reserve online or via the Tours or Amboise tourist offices, from where most tours depart.

Loire Valley Tours (02 54 33 99 80; www.loire-valley-tours.com)

Quart de Tours (06 30 65 52 01; www.quartdetours.com)

St-Eloi Excursions (06 70 82 78 75; www.chateauxexcursions.com)

Touraine Evasion (06 07 39 13 31; www.tourevasion.com)

Sleeping

Hôtel de l'Abeille Historic Hotel €€

(**02 38 53 54 87; www.hoteldelabeille.com; 64 rue Alsace-Lorraine; d €98-135, q €170-195;**) Bees buzz, floorboards creak and vintage Orléans posters adorn the walls at this gorgeous turn-of-the-century house, run by the same family for four generations. It's deliciously old-fashioned, from the scuffed pine floors and wildly floral wallpapers to the hefty dressers and bee-print curtains. For breakfast (€12) there's a choice of coffees, teas, juices and exotic jams. Only downside: no lift.

Hôtel d'Arc Hotel €€

(**02 38 53 10 94; www.hoteldarc.fr; 37ter rue de la République; s €112-190, d €126-230;**) Ride the vintage-style lift to 35 slick rooms at this Best Western–affiliated hotel, conveniently located between the train station and the pedestrianised centre. Rooms vary in size, and the Prestige and Deluxe come with plush robes, but all are done up comfortably.

Eating

Les Fagots Traditional French €

(**02 38 62 22 79; 32 rue du Poirier; menus €13-17; noon-2pm & 7.30-10pm Tue-Sat)** Delightful smoky smells lure you in to

Orléans

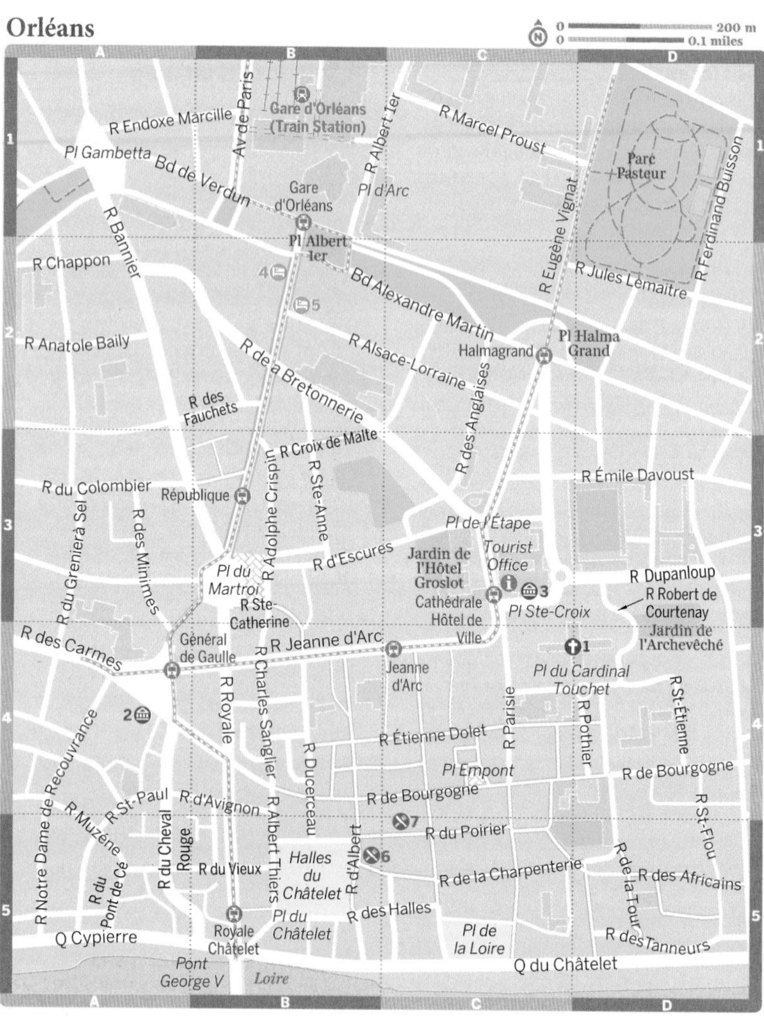

Orléans

Sights

1 Cathédrale Ste-Croix C4
2 Maison de Jeanne d'Arc A4
3 Musée des Beaux-Arts C3

Sleeping

4 Hôtel d'Arc B2
5 Hôtel de l'Abeille B2

Eating

6 La Parenthèse B5
7 Les Fagots C5

this unpretentious eatery whose menu revolves around roasted meat. The Auvergnat owner cooks everything over an open fire, including grilled tomatoes and baked potatoes slathered with crème fraiche and chives.

La Parenthèse Modern French **€€**
(**☎02 38 62 07 50; www.restaurant-la-parenthese.com; 26 place du Châtelet; menus lunch €15-17, dinner €24-28; ⏰lunch & dinner Tue-Sat)** Book ahead for this very popular restaurant, a labour of love for youthful chef

David Sterne. Produce from the Halles marketplace across the street forms the basis for ever-changing, bargain-priced *plats du jour* (€10), plus creative lunch and dinner menus. Choose from relaxed sidewalk seating or two more refined indoor dining rooms.

Information

Tourist Office (☎02 38 24 05 05; www.tourisme-orleans.com; 2 place de l'Étape; ⏲9.30am-1pm & 2-6.30pm Mon-Sat May-Jun & Sep, 9am-7pm Mon-Sat, 10am-1pm & 2-5pm Sun Jul & Aug, shorter hours rest of year) Well-stocked with guides (like the Loiret cycle guide) and event information, in many languages.

Getting There & Away

The city's two stations, Gare d'Orléans and Gare Les Aubrais-Orléans (the latter is 2km to the north), are linked by tram and frequent shuttle trains.

Blois €11.20, 35 minutes, hourly

Paris' Gare d'Austerlitz €20.80, 65 minutes, hourly

Tours €20.10, 1¼ hours, hourly

Blois

POP 48,110

Looming on a rocky escarpment on the northern bank of the Loire, Blois' historic château (formerly the feudal seat of the powerful counts of Blois) provides a whistle-stop tour through the key periods of French history and architecture.

Sights

Blois château, *son et lumière* show and/or Maison de la Magie combination tickets save some cash. Admission to any two attractions costs €15/7 per adult/child or for all three €19.50/10.50. Kids under six are free.

Old City Historic Quarter

Despite serious damage by German attacks in 1940, Blois' old city is worth exploring, especially around 17th-century

Pass Châteaux

Many of the châteaux in the Blésois are covered by Le Pass Châteaux multi-site discount tickets. For information, contact the tourist offices in Blois, Cheverny and Chambord.

- Blois-Chambord-Cheverny €28
- Blois-Chenonceau-Chambord-Cheverny €39
- Blois-Chaumont-Chambord-Cheverny €36.80
- Blois-Chambord-Amboise-Clos Lucé €42

Cathédrale St-Louis (place St-Louis; ⏲9am-6pm), with its lovely multistoreyed bell tower, dramatically floodlit after dark. Most of the stained glass inside was installed by Dutch artist Jan Dibberts in 2000.

Across the square, the facade of **Maison des Acrobates** (3bis place St-Louis) – one of the few surviving 15th-century houses – is decorated with wooden sculptures of medieval farces. Another example around the corner at No 13 rue Pierre de Blois is called **Hôtel de Villebrême**.

Maison de la Magie Museum

(www.maisondelamagie.fr; 1 place du Château; adult/child €9/5; ⏲10am-12.30pm & 2-6.30pm Apr-Aug, 2-6.30pm Mon-Fri, 10am-12.30pm & 2-6.30pm Sat & Sun Sep) Opposite the château you can't miss the former home of watchmaker, inventor and conjurer Jean Eugène Robert-Houdin (1805–71), whose name was later adopted by American magician Harry Houdini. Dragons emerge roaring from the windows on the hour, while the museum inside hosts daily **magic shows**, exhibits on the history of magic, displays of optical trickery and a short historical film about Houdini.

IAN DAGNALL/ALAMY ©

Don't Miss Château Royal de Blois

Intended more as an architectural showpiece (look at that ornately carved facade!) than a military stronghold, Blois' chateau bears the creative mark of several successive French kings. It makes an excellent introduction to the chateaux of the Loire Valley, with elements of Gothic (13th century), Flamboyant Gothic (1498–1503), early Renaissance (1515–24) and classical (1630s) architecture in its four grand wings.

The most famous feature of the Renaissance wing, the royal apartments of François I and Queen Claude, is the **loggia staircase**, decorated with salamanders and curly Fs (heraldic symbols of François I).

Highlights also include the **bedchamber** in which Catherine de Médicis (Henri II's machiavellian wife) died in 1589. According to Alexandre Dumas, the queen stashed her poisons in secret cupboards behind the elaborately panelled walls of the **studiolo**, one of the few rooms in the castle with its original decor.

The 2nd-floor **king's apartments** were the setting for one of the bloodiest episodes in the château's history: in 1588 Henri III had his arch-rival, Duke Henri I de Guise, murdered by royal bodyguards (the king hid behind a tapestry). He had the Duke's brother, the Cardinal de Guise, killed the next day. Henri III himself was murdered just eight months later by a vengeful monk. Period paintings chronicle the gruesome events.

In spring and summer, don't miss the nightly **son et lumière** (sound & light show; ☎02 54 55 26 31; adult/child €8/5; ⏰10pm Apr, May & Sep, 10.30pm Jun-Aug), which brings the château's history and architecture to life with dramatic lighting and narration.

NEED TO KNOW

☎02 54 90 33 33; www.chateaudeblois.fr; place du Château; adult/child €9.80/5, audioguide €4, English tours Jul & Aug free; ⏰9am-6.30pm Apr-Sep, to 7pm Jul & Aug, shorter hours rest of year

Sleeping

Côté Loire — Hotel €

(☎02 54 78 07 86; www.coteloire.com; 2 place de la Grève; r €59-95;) Spotless rooms come in cheery checks, bright pastels and the odd bit of exposed brick; some have Loire views. Breakfast (€10.50) is served on a quaint interior wooden deck, and the restaurant (*menus* €21–31) dishes up delicious local cuisine. Find it a block off the river, southwest of Pont Jaques Gabriel.

La Maison de Thomas — B&B €€

(☎02 54 46 12 10; www.lamaisondethomas.fr; 12 rue Beauvoir; r incl breakfast €90;) Four spacious rooms and a friendly welcome await travellers at this beautiful B&B on a pedestrianised street halfway between the château and the cathedral. There's bike storage in the interior courtyard and a wine cellar where you can sample local vintages.

Eating

Les Banquettes Rouges — French €€

(☎02 54 78 74 92; www.lesbanquettesrouges.com; 16 rue des Trois Marands; menus €17.50-32.50; ⏲noon-2pm & 7-10pm Tue-Sat) Handwritten slate menus and wholesome food distinguish the Red Benches: pork with chorizo and rosemary, duck with lentils, and *fondant au chocolat* top it off.

L'Orangerie — Gastronomic €€€

(☎02 54 78 05 36; www.orangerie-du-chateau.fr; 1 av du Dr Jean Laigret; menus €35-80; ⏲noon-1.30pm & 7-9pm Tue-Sat) This acclaimed eatery is cloud nine for connoisseurs of haute cuisine. Plates are artfully stacked (duck liver, langoustine, foie gras) and the sparkling *salon* would make Louis XIV envious. On summer nights, dine in the courtyard.

Information

Tourist Office (☎02 54 90 41 41; www.bloischambord.com; 23 place du Château; ⏲9am-7pm Apr-Sep, to 5pm Oct-Mar) Helpful, and sells joint châteaux tickets. Download the Visit' Blois smartphone app.

Getting There & Away

Bus From April through August, **TLC** (☎02 54 58 55 44; www.tlcinfo.net) runs a château shuttle (Line 18, €6) that offers as many stops as you like on a Blois–Chambord–Cheverny–Beauregard–Blois circuit.

TLC also operates regular buses from Blois' train station (tickets €2 on board): Chambord (Line 3, 25 to 40 minutes, two Monday to Saturday) and Cheverny (Line 4, 45 minutes, three Monday to Friday, one Saturday).

Train The **Blois-Chambord train station** (av Jean Laigret) is 600m uphill from Blois' château.

- **Amboise** €7, 20 minutes, 10 daily
- **Orléans** €11.20, 45 minutes, hourly
- **Paris' Gares d'Austerlitz and Montparnasse** From €28.60, 1½ to two hours, 26 daily
- **Tours** €10.90, 40 minutes, 13 daily

Château de Cheverny

Thought by many to be the most perfectly proportioned château of all, **Cheverny** (☎02 54 79 96 29; www.chateau-cheverny.fr; adult/child €9.50/6.50; ⏲9am-7pm Apr-Sep, 10am-5pm Oct-Mar) represents the zenith of French classical architecture, the perfect blend of symmetry, geometry and aesthetic order.

Built from gleaming stone from the nearby Bourré quarries and surrounded by lush parkland, Cheverny is one of the few châteaux whose original architectural vision has survived the centuries practically unscathed. Since its construction between 1625 and 1634 by Jacques Hurault, an intendant to Louis XII, the castle has hardly been altered, and its interior decoration includes some of the most sumptuous furnishings, tapestries and objets d'art anywhere in the Loire Valley. The Hurault family has owned (and inhabited) the castle for the last six centuries and its fabulous **art collection** includes a portrait of Jeanne of Aragon by Raphael's studio, an 18th-century De la Tour pastel, and a who's who of court painters.

Behind the main château, the 18th-century **Orangerie**, where many priceless

artworks, including the *Mona Lisa*, were stashed during WWII, is now a tearoom.

Near the château's gateway, the **kennels** house pedigreed French pointer/English foxhound hunting dogs still used by the owners of Cheverny: feeding time, known as the **Soupe des Chiens**, takes place daily at 5pm April to September and 3pm October to March.

Getting There & Away

Cheverny is on the D102, 16km southeast of Blois and 17km southwest of Chambord.

Château de Chaumont

Set on a defensible bluff behind the Loire, **Chaumont-sur-Loire** (**02 54 20 99 22; www.domaine-chaumont.fr; adult/child €10.50/6.50, with gardens €16/11; 10am-6.30pm Apr-Sep, to 6pm Oct-Mar**) presents a resolutely medieval face, with its cylindrical corner turrets and sturdy drawbridge, but the interior mostly dates from the 19th century.

At least two earlier fortresses occupied the site (whose name derives from Chauve Mont, 'Bald Hill'), but the main phase of construction for the present château began sometime around 1465 under Pierre d'Amboise. Originally a strictly defensive fortress, the castle became a short-lived residence for Catherine de Médicis following the death of Henry II in 1560, and later passed into the hands of Diane de Poitiers (Henry II's mistress), who was forced to swap the altogether grander surroundings of Chenonceau for Chaumont by the ruthless Catherine.

The château was thoroughly renovated by Princess de Broglie, heiress to the Say sugar fortune, who bought it in 1875 (and knocked down one entire wing to provide a better view of the river). The most impressive room is the **Council Chamber**, with its original maiolica-tiled floor, plundered from a palace in Palermo, but the château's finest architecture is arguably reserved for the **Écuries** (stables), built in 1877 to

Left: Château de Chaumont; **Below:** Château de Cheverny (p193)
(LEFT) LIONEL LOURDEL/GETTY IMAGES ©; (BELOW) DEA/G. DAGLI ORTI/GETTY IMAGES ©

house the Broglies' horses in truly sumptuous style (the thoroughbreds all had their own personal padded stalls). A collection of vintage carriages is now displayed inside.

Chaumont's English-style gardens can be visited independently or together with the château. They gardens are at their finest during the annual **Festival International des Jardins** (International Garden Festival; adult/child €12/7.50; 10am-7pm late Apr-Oct).

Getting There & Away

Chaumont-sur-Loire is 17km southwest of Blois. Onzain, a 2.5km walk from Chaumont across the Loire, has trains to Blois (€3.60, 10 minutes, 13 daily) and Tours (€8.60, 30 minutes, 10 daily). An Azalys (09 69 36 93 41; www.azalys-blois.fr; 2 place Victor Hugo; tickets €1.20; 8.30am-6.30pm Mon-Fri, 9.30am-12.30pm & 1.30-5pm Sat, closed Sat afternoon Jul & Aug) shuttle runs from Blois.

Tours

POP 138,590

Bustling Tours has a life of its own despite being one of the hubs of castle country. It's a smart, vivacious kind of place, filled with wide 18th-century boulevards, parks and imposing public buildings, as well as a busy university of some 25,000 students.

Sights

Musée des Beaux-Arts Art Museum
(02 47 05 68 82; www.mba.tours.fr; 18 place François Sicard; adult/child €5/2.50, 1st Sun of the month free; 9am-12.45pm & 2-6pm Wed-Mon) This fine-arts museum in the archbishop's gorgeous 18th-century palace encircles free gardens and Gallo-Roman ruins, and flaunts grand rooms with works spanning several centuries. Highlights include paintings by Delacroix, Degas and

Detour: Château d'Azay-le-Rideau

Romantic, moat-ringed **Azay-le-Rideau** (☎02 47 45 42 04; www.azay-le-rideau.monuments-nationaux.fr/en; adult/child €8.50/free; ⊙9.30am-6pm Apr-Sep, to 7pm Jul & Aug, 10am-5.15pm Oct-Mar) is adorned with slender turrets, geometric windows and decorative stonework, wrapped up within a shady, landscaped park. Built in the 1500s on a natural island in middle of the River Indre, the château is one of the Loire's loveliest.

Its most famous feature is its open **loggia staircase**, in the Italian style, overlooking the central courtyard and decorated with the salamanders and ermines of François I and Queen Claude. The interior is mostly 19th century, remodelled by the Marquis de Biencourt from the original 16th-century château built by Gilles Berthelot, chief treasurer for François I. In July and August, a **son et lumière** (adult/teen/child €11/8/3) is projected onto the castle walls nightly. Audioguides (adult/child €4.50/3) are available in five languages, and 45-minute guided tours in French are free.

Château d'Azay-le-Rideau is 26km southwest of Tours. The D84 and D17, on either side of the Indre, are a delight to cycle. Touraine Fil Vert's bus TF (€2.20) travels between Langeais, Azay-le-Rideau and Chinon four times daily. An SNCF bus stops near the château.

Azay-le-Rideau's station is 2.5km west of the château. Trains run eight times daily to Tours (€5.80, 25 to 30 minutes) and Chinon.

Monet, a rare Rembrandt miniature and a Rubens *Madonna and Child*.

Cathédrale St-Gatien Church
(place de la Cathédrale; ⊙9am-7pm) With its twin towers, flying buttresses, dazzling stained glass and gargoyles, this cathedral is a show-stopper. The interior dates from the 13th to 16th centuries, and signs in English explain the intricate stained glass. The domed tops of the two 70m-high towers are Renaissance. On the north side is the **Cloître de la Psalette** (adult/child €3/free; ⊙9.30am-12.30pm & 2-6pm Mon-Sat, 2-6pm Sun, closed Mon & Tue Oct-Mar), built from 1442 to 1524.

Eating

Cap Sud Bistro €€
(☎02 47 05 24 81; www.capsudrestaurant.fr; 88 rue Colbert; menus lunch €14-19, dinner €26; ⊙noon-1.30pm & 7.15-9.30pm Tue-Sat) The hot-rod red interior combines nicely with genial service and refined culinary creations made from the freshest ingredients. Expect stylishly presented dishes such as warm St-Maure cheese with a pistachio-herb crumble and baby vegetables, or mullet fillet with sweet peppers, squid risotto and a ginger-tomato emulsion. Reserve ahead.

L'Arôme Modern French €€
(☎02 47 05 99 81; larome.tours@yahoo.fr; 26 rue Colbert; menus lunch €13, 3-course dinner €24-41; ⊙noon-1.30pm & 7.30-9.30pm Tue-Sat) One of Tours' most popular new spots, L'Arôme fills with lucky locals (they've reserved ahead) who come for the vivacious modern ambience and creative dishes, smack in the centre of town. Great wine selection too.

Information

Tourist Office (☎02 47 70 37 37; www.tours-tourisme.fr; 78-82 rue Bernard Palissy; ⊙8.30am-7pm Mon-Sat, 10am-12.30pm &

2.30-5pm Sun Apr-Sep, shorter hours rest of year)** Abundant info; slightly reduced châteaux tickets.

Getting There & Away

Train Tours is the Loire Valley's main rail hub. Regular trains serve Tours Centre station and TGV trains serve St-Pierre-des-Corps, 4km east and linked to Tours by frequent shuttle trains. Some destinations, like Paris, Angers and Orléans, are served by both stations.

Tours Centre services include:

Amboise €5.60, 20 minutes, 13 daily

Blois €10.90, 40 minutes, 13 daily

Chenonceaux €6.80, 25 minutes, 10 daily

Orléans €20.10, 1¼ hours, hourly

Paris' Gare d'Austerlitz €35, two to 2¾ hours, five daily (slow trains)

Paris' Gare Montparnasse €46 to €68, 1¼ hours, eight daily (high-speed TGVs)

Saumur €12, 45 minutes, 10 daily

St-Pierre-des-Corps TGV trains include:

Bordeaux €52, 2¾ hours

Paris' Gare Montparnasse €46 to €68, one hour

Château de Chenonceau

Spanning the languid Cher River via a series of supremely graceful arches, the castle of **Chenonceau (☎02 47 23 90 07; www.chenonceau.com; adult/child €12.50/9.50, with audioguide €17/13.50; ⏲9am-7pm Apr-Sep, shorter hours rest of year; 📶)** is one of the most elegant and unusual in the Loire Valley.

This architectural fantasy land is largely the work of several remarkable women (hence its alternative name, Le Château des Dames: 'Ladies' Château'). The initial phase of construction started in 1515 for Thomas Bohier, a court minister of King Charles VIII, although much of the work and design was actually overseen by his wife, Katherine Briçonnet. The château's distinctive arches and one of the formal gardens were added by Diane de Poitiers, mistress of King Henri II. Following Henri's death, Diane was forced to exchange Chenonceau for the rather less grand château of Chaumont by the king's scheming widow, Catherine de Médicis, who completed the construction and added the huge yew-tree **labyrinth** and the western rose garden. Louise of

Château d'Azay-le-Rideau (p196)

PHILIPPE BODY/GETTY IMAGES ©

Don't Miss Château de Chambord

For full-blown château splendour, you can't top Chambord, one of the crowning examples of French Renaissance architecture, and by far the largest, grandest and most visited château in the Loire Valley.

information 02 54 50 40 00, tour & spectacle reservations 02 54 50 50 40

www.chambord.org

adult/child €11/9, parking €4, 1hr tour adult/child €5/3, 2hr tour €7/5

9am-6pm Apr-Sep, 10am-5pm Oct-Mar

History

Begun in 1519 as a weekend hunting lodge by François I, Chambord quickly snowballed into one of the most ambitious (and expensive) architectural projects ever attempted by any French monarch. Construction was repeatedly halted by financial problems, design setbacks and military commitments (not to mention the kidnapping of the king's two sons in Spain). When Chambord was finally finished 30-odd years later, François decided he found the place too draughty, and only stayed here for 42 days during his entire reign from 1515 to 1547.

Architecture

Despite its apparent architectural complexity, Chambord is laid out according to simple mathematical rules. Each section is arranged on a system of symmetrical grid squares around a Maltese cross. At the centre stands the rectangular keep, crossed by four great hallways, and at each corner stands one of the castle's four circular bastions. Through the centre winds the famous double-helix staircase, leading up to the lantern tower and the castle's rooftop. In total, the castle boasts an astonishing 440 rooms, 365 fireplaces and 84 staircases.

Guided tours

For historical background on the château (and to avoid getting lost!) it's well worth borrowing the multilingual audio or videoguide (audio adult/child version €5/2.50, videoguide €6). For a more in-depth tour, there are guided tours in English several times daily. During school holidays, there are special tours with costumed guides, perfect for kids.

Local Knowledge

Chambord Don't Miss List

BY ELSA SAUVÉ, CHÂTEAU DE CHAMBORD

1 DOUBLE-HELIX STAIRCASE & ROOFTOP

The double-helix staircase that whisks visitors from the ground floor to the rooftop keep is *the* highlight. This theatrical and majestic staircase is composed of two open parallel flights wrapped around a hollow core, the magic being that two people can see each other go up and down it without their paths ever crossing. A magnificent view of the estate unfolds from the rooftop terraces, an unforgettable place with its sculpted chimney and turrets, really a place of contemplation and daydream.

2 THE 1ST FLOOR

Take time to explore the *premier étage* (1st floor), a historical panorama of the inhabitants of Chambord from François I to Louis XIV and beyond into the 19th century. In the apartments you can really see how château lifestyle evolved over the centuries: all the furniture in Francois I was made to be dismantled and transported with him from château to château.

3 SON ET LUMIÈRE

Every evening in July and August *Chambord, Rêve de Lumières* (Chambord, Dream of Lights) is projected on the facade of the castle. The 50-minute sound-and-light show is a voyage through time. It relives the construction of the château and the arrival of the court of the king, the balls and banquets he threw. Through beautiful images, music and dance, it tugs at the audience's senses and emotions.

4 THE RUTTING SEASON

Chambord is unique in that it is a monument in the middle of a vast forested park. This gives Chambord an additional magic, a place to discover the natural environment as well as culture and history. The park is a wildlife reserve with stags and wild boars. Observatories allow visitors to observe the animals during *le brame*, the rutting or mating season that falls from mid-September to mid-October. The best time to see the animals in action is at sunrise or sunset – bring binoculars.

Lorraine's most interesting contribution was her **mourning room**, on the top floor, all in black, to which she retreated when her husband, Henri III, was assassinated.

Chenonceau had a heyday under the aristocratic Madame Dupin, who made the château a centre of fashionable 18th-century society and attracted guests including Voltaire and Rousseau (the latter tutored her son).

The château's interior is crammed with wonderful furniture and tapestries, several stunning original tiled floors and a fabulous **art collection** including works by Tintoretto, Correggio, Rubens, Murillo, Van Dyck and Ribera.

The *pièce de resistance* is the 60m-long window-lined **Grande Gallerie** spanning the Cher, scene of many a wild party hosted by Catherine de Médicis and Madame Dupin. During WWII the Cher also marked the boundary between free and occupied France; local legend has it that the Grand Gallery was used as the escape route for many refugees fleeing the Nazi occupation.

Skip the drab wax museum and instead visit the **gardens**: it seems as if there's one of every kind imaginable (maze, English, vegetable, playground, flower...). In July and August the illuminated château and grounds are open for the **Promenade Nocturne.** (adult/child €6/free; 9.30-11.30pm).

Getting There & Away

The château is 34km east of Tours, 10km southeast of Amboise and 40km southwest of Blois. From Chenonceaux, the town just outside the château grounds (spelled with an 'x', unlike the château!), seven daily trains run to Tours (€6.50, 24 minutes). Touraine Fil Vert's bus Line C (€2.20) also runs once daily from Chenonceaux to Amboise (25 minutes). **Croisières Fluivales La Bélandre** (02 47 23 98 64; www.labelandre.com; adult/child €9.50/6.50; Apr-Oct) offers 50-minute boat trips along the Cher River in summer, passing directly beneath the château's arches.

Amboise

POP 12,860

The childhood home of Charles VIII and the final resting place of the great Leonardo da Vinci, elegant Amboise is pleasantly perched on the southern bank of the Loire and overlooked by its fortified 15th-century château. With some

Château Royal d'Amboise (p201)

CHRISTOPHE LEHENAFF/GETTY IMAGES ©

seriously posh hotels and a wonderful weekend market, Amboise has become a very popular base for exploring nearby châteaux, and coach tours arrive en masse to visit da Vinci's Clos Lucé.

Sights & Activities

Château Royal d'Amboise Château

(☎02 47 57 52 23; www.chateau-amboise.com; place Michel Debré; adult/child €10.70/7.20, with audioguide €14.70/10.20; ⏲9am-7pm Jul & Aug, to 6pm Apr-Oct, shorter hours Nov-Mar) Elegantly tiered on a rocky escarpment above town, this easily defendable castle presented a formidable prospect to would-be attackers – but saw little military action. It was more often a weekend getaway from the official royal seat at Blois.

Charles VIII (r 1483–98), born and bred here, was responsible for the château's Italianate remodelling in 1492. Today just a few of the original 15th- and 16th-century structures survive, notably the Flamboyant Gothic wing and Chapelle St-Hubert, the final resting place of Leonardo da Vinci. They have thrilling views to the river, town and gardens.

Clos Lucé Historic Building

(☎02 47 57 00 73; www.vinci-closluce.com; 2 rue du Clos Lucé; adult/child €14/9, joint family tickets reduced; ⏲9am-8pm Jul & Aug, 9am-7pm Feb-Jun & Sep-Oct, 9am-6pm Nov & Dec, 10am-6pm Jan) Leonardo da Vinci took up residence at this grand manor house in 1516 on the invitation of François I. An admirer of the Italian Renaissance, François named da Vinci 'first painter, engineer and king's architect'. Already 64 by the time he arrived, da Vinci spent his time sketching, tinkering and dreaming up new contraptions, scale models of which are now displayed throughout the home and its expansive gardens. Visitors tour rooms where da Vinci worked and the bedroom where drew his last breath on 2 May 1519.

Sleeping

Le Vieux Manoir B&B €€

(☎02 47 30 41 27; www.le-vieux-manoir.com; 13 rue Rabelais; r incl breakfast €160-200; ❄📶) Set back in a lovely walled garden, this restored mansion is stuffed floor to ceiling with period charm. Rooms get lots of natural light, and owners Gloria and Bob (expat Americans who had an award-winning Boston B&B) are generous with their knowledge of the area.

Le Clos d'Amboise Historic Hotel €€€

(☎02 47 30 10 20; www.leclosamboise.com; 27 rue Rabelais; r €140-210, ste €210-295; ❄@📶🏊) Backed by a vast grassy lawn, complete with 200-year-old trees, a heated pool and parking, this posh pad offers a taste of country living in the heart of town. Stylish features abound, from luxurious fabrics to wood-panelling and antique beds. The best rooms have separate sitting areas, original fireplaces or garden-front windows.

Eating & Drinking

Chez Bruno Bistro €

(☎02 47 57 73 49; www.bistrotchezbruno.com; 38-40 place Michel Debré; mains €8-12; ⏲lunch & dinner Tue-Sat) Uncork a host of local vintages in a lively contemporary setting just beneath the towering château. Tables of chatting visitors and locals alike dig into delicious, inexpensive regional cooking. If you're after Loire Valley wine tips, this is the place.

Bigot Patisserie €

(☎02 47 57 04 46; www.bigot-amboise.com; place du Château; mains €6-11; ⏲noon-7.30pm Mon, 9am-7.30pm Tue-Fri, 8.30am-7.30pm Sat & Sun) Since 1913 this award-winning chocolaterie and patisserie has been creating some of the Loire's creamiest cakes and gooiest treats: multicoloured *macarons*, handmade chocolates and petits fours, alongside savoury omelettes, salads and quiches.

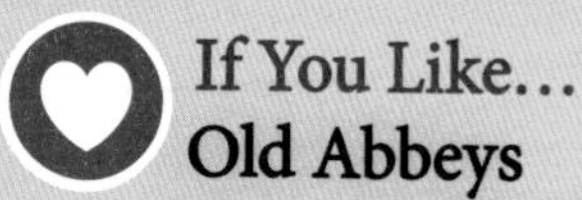

If You Like... Old Abbeys

For history buffs who've already devoured the region's châteaux collection, a trio of abbeys beautifully evokes the medieval glory of monastic life in the Middle Ages.

1 **ABBAYE DE FONTEVRAUD**
(02 41 51 73 52; www.abbayedefontevraud.com; adult/child €9.50/7, audioguide €4.50, smartphone app free; 9.30am-6.30pm Apr-mid-Nov, 10am-5.30pm Tue-Sat mid-Nov–Mar, closed Jan) Until its closure in 1793 this huge 12th-century complex was one of the largest ecclesiastical centres in Europe. The extensive grounds include a **chapter room** with murals of the Passion of Christ by Thomas Pot. And look for the multi-chimneyed, rocket-shaped **kitchen**, built entirely from stone to make it fireproof.

2 **ABBAYE DE FONTENAY**
(Fontenay Abbey; 03 80 92 15 00; www.abbayedefontenay.com; adult/child self-guided tour €10/7, guided tour €12.50/7.90; 10am-6pm mid-Apr–mid-Nov, 10am-noon & 2-5pm rest of year) Founded in 1118 and restored to its medieval glory a century ago, Abbaye de Fontenay offers a fascinating glimpse of the austere, serene surroundings in which Cistercian monks lived lives of contemplation, prayer and manual labour. The abbey, a Unesco World Heritage Site, includes a Romanesque church, a barrel-vaulted monks' dormitory and the first metallurgical factory in Europe with a forge from 1220. Guided **tours** are in French with printed information in six languages.

3 **CLUNY**
Deep in the heart of Burgundy, Cluny, 80km south of Beaune, was home to Christendom's largest church until the construction of St Peter's Basilica in the Vatican. What remains is fragmentary and scattered, but it's still possible to imagine Cluny's Benedictine abbey in the 12th century when it held sway over 1100 priories and monasteries stretching from Poland to Portugal. Buy tickets to visit the **Église Abbatiale** (Abbey Church; 03 85 59 15 93; www.cluny.monuments-nationaux.fr; adult/child €9.50/free; 9.30am-7pm Jul & Aug, to 6pm Apr-Jun & Sep, to 5pm Oct-Mar) inside the **Palais Jean de Bourbon**.

La Fourchette Traditional French **€€**
(06 11 78 16 98; 9 rue Malebranche; lunch/dinner menus €15/24; noon-1.30pm Tue-Sat, 7-9.30pm Fri & Sat) Tucked into a back alley behind the tourist office, this is Amboise's favourite address for straightforward home cooking. Chef Christine makes you feel like you've been invited to her house for lunch... It's small so reserve ahead.

Information

Tourist Office (02 47 57 09 28; www.amboise-valdeloire.com; quai du Général de Gaulle; 9.30am-6pm Mon-Sat, 10am-1pm & 2-5pm Sun, closed Sun Nov-Mar) Sells walking and cycling maps, plus discount ticket combinations for the château, Clos Lucé and the Pagode de Chanteloup, and offers walking tours. Amboise Tour is their free app. Located riverside.

Getting There & Away

The **train station** (bd Gambetta) is 1.5km north of the château on the opposite side of the Loire.

Blois €7, 20 minutes, 13 daily

Paris' Gare d'Austerlitz (express train) €15, 1¾ hours, four daily

Tours €5.60, 20 minutes, 13 daily

Saumur

POP 29,650

There's an air of Parisian sophistication around Saumur, but also a sense of laid-back contentment. The food is good, the wine is good, the spot is good – and the Saumurites know it. The town is renowned for its École Nationale d'Équitation, a national cavalry school that's been home to the crack riders of the Cadre Noir since 1828.

Sights & Activities

École Nationale d'Équitation Riding School
(National Equestrian School; 02 41 53 50 60; www.cadrenoir.fr; rte de Marson, St-Hilaire-St-Florent; tour adult/child €8/6; mornings Tue-Sat & afternoons Mon-Fri mid-Apr–mid-

Oct, shorter hours rest of year) Anchored in France's academic-military riding tradition, Saumur has been an equine centre since 1593. Its École Nationale d'Équitation is one of France's foremost riding academies, responsible for training the country's Olympic teams and members of the elite Cadre Noir. Advance reservations are required for their one-hour guided visits (enquire about English-language tours), and the semi-monthly **Cadre Noir presentations (adult/child €16/9)** are not to be missed: they are like astonishing horse ballets. Check the website for dates and reservations.

Château de Saumur Château
(☎02 41 40 24 40; www.chateau-saumur.com; adult/child €9/5; ⏰10am-6.30pm mid-Jun–mid-Sep, 10am-1pm & 2-5.30pm Tue-Sun mid-Sep–mid-Jun) Soaring above the town's rooftops, Saumur's fairy-tale château was largely built during the 13th century by Louis XI, and has variously served as a dungeon, fortress and country residence. Its defensive heritage took a knock in 2001 when a chunk of the western ramparts collapsed without warning. After a decade-long restoration, the castle's porcelain collection reopened on the 1st floor. The 2nd floor is due to reopen soon; for now its impressive collection of vintage equestrian gear is housed in the adjacent abbatiale.

Sleeping

Château Beaulieu B&B **€€**
(☎02 41 50 83 52; www.chateaudebeaulieu.fr; 98 rte de Montsoreau; d incl breakfast €95-130, ste €140-200; 📶🏊) Irish expats Mary and Conor welcome you to their sprawling home with a glass of bubbling crémant (sparkling wine), delicious home-made breakfasts and a wealth of friendly advice on surrounding attractions. Rooms are imaginatively and comfortably done up and the mood among gregarious clientele is one of extended family. Sun yourself by the pool or play billiards in the grand salon. Parking is free.

Château de Verrières Hotel **€€€**
(☎02 41 38 05 15; www.chateau-verrieres.com; 53 rue d'Alsace; r €170-260, ste €290-330; 📶🏊) Each of the 10 rooms in this impeccably wonderful 1890 château, ensconced within the woods and ponds of a 1.6-hectare English park, is different. But the feel is universally kingly: antique writing desks, original artwork, wood panelling and fantastic bathrooms. Some, like the top-of-the-line Rising Sun suite (with a dash of modish Japanese minimalism), have views of the sun rising over the Saumur château.

Statue of St Andrew, Abbaye de Fontevraud (p202)

Eating

L'Aromate Modern French €€

(☎02 41 51 31 45; www.laromate-restaurant.com; 42 rue Maréchal Leclerc; lunch menus €14, 3-course dinner €20-28; ⏲noon-1.30pm & 7.30-9pm Tue-Sat) The newest entry on Saumur's hot culinary scene, L'Aromate is buzzy and bright with changing menus that dare to mingle Asian and other influences with classic French cuisine.

Le Pot de Lapin Modern French €€

(☎02 41 67 12 86; 35 rue Rabelais; tapas €5-7, mains €14-18; ⏲noon-2pm & 7-9.45pm Tue-Sat) Jazzy music wafts from the cheery dining room through the wine bar and onto the streetside terrace as Chef Olivier works the tables, proposing perfect wine pairings and serving up tempting platefuls of ever-changing tapas and French classics. Somehow the vibe here is, simply put, happiness – happy staff, happy clients.

Le Gambetta Gastronomic €€€

(☎02 41 67 66 66; www.restaurantlegambetta.com; 12 rue Gambetta; lunch menus €25.50, dinner €32-99; ⏲noon-1.30pm Tue & Thu-Sun, 7.15-9.45pm Tue & Thu-Sat) This is one to write home about: a fantastic regional restaurant combining refined elegance and knock-your-socks-off creative food. The parade of exquisitely presented dishes ranges from rosemary-and-thyme roasted pork with an asparagus-lemon-parmesan *maki* to surprisingly delicious wasabi crème brûlée. Some menus include wine pairings, and all are punctuated by surprise treats from the kitchen.

Information

Tourist Office (☎02 41 40 20 60; www.saumur-tourisme.com; 8bis quai Carnot; ⏲9.15am-7pm Mon-Sat, 10.30am-5.30pm Sun mid-May–Sep, shorter hours rest of year; 📶) Loads of info, transport schedules, slightly reduced châteaux tickets, smartphone app.

Getting There & Away

Saumur's station is across the river, 1.2km from the tourist office.

Paris' Gare Montparnasse €72, 2½ hours (requires one transfer)

Tours €12, 30 to 50 minutes, 12 daily

BURGUNDY

Burgundy (Bourgogne in French) offers some of France's most gorgeous countryside: rolling green hills dotted with medieval villages, and mustard fields blooming in bright contrast. Two great French passions, wine and food, come together here in a particularly rich and enticing form.

Dijon

POP 250,000

Dijon is one of France's most appealing cities. Filled with elegant medieval and Renaissance buildings, the lively centre is wonderful for strolling, especially if you like to leaven your cultural enrichment with excellent food, fine wine and shopping.

Sights

Palais des Ducs et des États de Bourgogne Palace

(Palace of the Dukes & States of Burgundy; place de la Libération) Once home to Burgundy's powerful dukes, this monumental palace with a neoclassical façade overlooks place de la Libération, Old Dijon's magnificent central square dating from 1686. The palace's eastern wing houses the outstanding Musée des Beaux-Arts, whose entrance is next to the **Tour de Bar**, a squat 14th-century tower that once served as a prison.

Musée des Beaux-Arts Art Museum

(☎03 80 74 52 09; mba.dijon.fr; audioguide €4; ⏲9.30am-6pm Wed-Mon May-Oct, 10am-5pm Nov-Apr) FREE Housed in the monumental Palais des Ducs, these sprawling galleries (works of art in themselves) constitute one of France's most outstanding museums. The star attraction, reopened in September 2013 after extensive renovations, is the

Dijon

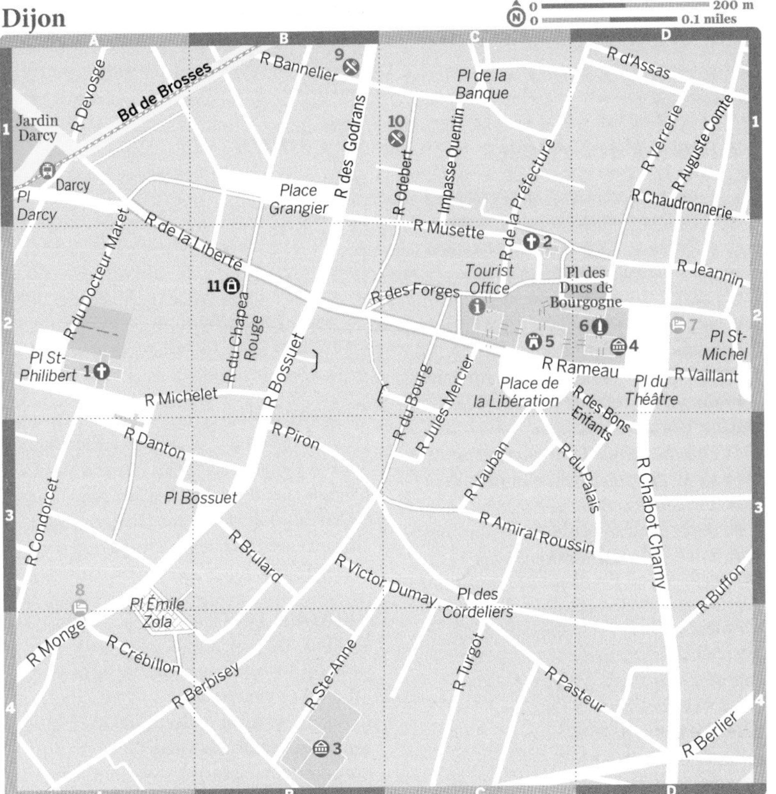

Dijon

Sights

1 Cathédrale St-Bénigne A2
2 Église Notre Dame C2
3 Musée de la Vie Bourguignonne B4
4 Musée des Beaux-Arts D2
5 Palais des Ducs et des États de Bourgogne C2
6 Tour de Bar D2

Sleeping

7 Hôtel des Ducs D2
8 Hôtel Le Sauvage A3

Eating

9 Chez Léon B1
10 DZ'Envies C1

Shopping

11 Moutarde Maille B2

wood-panelled **Salle des Gardes**, which houses the ornate, carved, late-medieval sepulchres of dukes John the Fearless and Philip the Bold. Other sections focus on Egyptian art, the Middle Ages in Burgundy and Europe, and six centuries of European painting, from the Renaissance to modern times.

Église Notre Dame Church

(place Notre-Dame) A block north of the Palais des Ducs, this church was built between 1220 and 1240. Its extraordinary facade's three tiers are lined with leering gargoyles separated by two rows of pencil-thin columns. Atop the church, the 14th-century **Horloge à Jacquemart**, transported from Flanders in 1383 by Philip the Bold who claimed it as a trophy of war, chimes every quarter-hour.

Detour: MuséoParc Alésia

Opened in 2012, the sensational **MuseoParc Alésia** (www.alesia.com; Alise-Ste-Reine; adult/child museum only €9.50/6, museum & Gallo-Roman site €11.50/7; 10am-7pm Jul & Aug, 10am-6pm Apr-Jun, Sep & Oct, 10am-5pm Nov, Feb & Mar, closed Dec & Jan), near the village of Alise-Ste-Reine in the Pays d'Auxois, is well worth the drive from Dijon (67km).

This was the site of what was once Alésia, the camp where Vercingétorix, the chief of the Gaulish coalitions, was defeated by Julius Caesar after a long siege. The defeat marked the end of the Gallic/ Celtic heritage in France.

You can visit the well-organised interpretative centre as well as the vestiges of the Gallo-Roman city that developed after the battle. The MuséoParc Alésia also offers entertaining programs and workshops for kids.

Cathédrale St-Bénigne Church
(place St-Philibert) Built over the tomb of St Benignus (believed to have brought Christianity to Burgundy in the 2nd century), Dijon's Burgundian Gothic-style cathedral was built around 1300 as an abbey church. Some of Burgundy's great figures are buried in its crypt.

Musée de la Vie Bourguignonne Museum
(03 80 48 80 90; 17 rue Ste-Anne; 9.30am-12.30pm & 2-6pm Wed-Mon) FREE Housed in a 17th-century Cistercian convent, this museum explores village and town life in Burgundy in centuries past with evocative tableaux illustrating dress, customs and traditional crafts. On the first floor, a whole street has been re-created, complete with 19th-century pharmacy and numerous antique-filled shops (grocer, furrier, hat-maker, clock-maker, toy store and more).

Tours

Walking Tours Walking Tour
(08 92 70 05 58; adult €6-15, child €1) A slew of different tours depart from the main tourist office, which distributes a handy schedule listing times and prices. Couples receive a €3 discount. Wine-tasting is included in the more expensive 'Dijon and wine' tour.

Segway Tour History Tour
(adult/child €19/8; 10.30am & 2.30pm Sun Apr-Oct, plus afternoon tours Sat Apr & May, Fri & Sat Jun, Sep & Oct, Mon-Sat Jul & Aug) Run by the tourist office, this 1½-hour tour zips around the city centre. No children under 12.

Vineyard Tours Wine Tour
Minibus tours in English introduce the Côte d'Or vineyards. Reserve by phone, internet or via the tourist office. Operators include **Alter & Go** (06 23 37 92 04; www.alterandgo.fr; tours from €70) with an emphasis on history and winemaking methods; **Authentica Tour** (06 87 01 43 78; www.authentica-tours.com; tours €55-125); and **Wine & Voyages** (03 80 61 15 15; www.wineandvoyages.com; tours from €53).

Sleeping

Hôtel Le Sauvage Hotel €
(03 80 41 31 21; www.hotellesauvage.com; 64 rue Monge; s €42-67, d €46-74, tr €85;) Set in a 15th-century *relais de poste* (coaching inn) that ranges around a cobbled, vine-shaded courtyard, this little hotel is definitely good value. Rooms 10, 12, 14 and 17, with exposed beams, are the cosiest. It's just steps from lively Place Zola, yet the rooms are pleasingly quiet. Parking €5.

Hôtel des Ducs Hotel €€
(03 80 67 31 31; www.hoteldesducs.com; 5 rue Lamonnoye; d €89-119;) This modern, three-star hotel has been recently

renovated. Rooms are fresh and airy and the contemporary design scheme is easy on the eye. Comfortable and convenient if you want to stay smack-dab in the centre of things. Parking €12.

Eating

DZ'Envies Regional Cuisine **€€**

(**☎03 80 50 09 26; www.dzenvies.com; 12 rue Odebert; mains €16-20, lunch menus €13-20, dinner menus €29-36; ⏰noon-2pm & 7-10pm Mon-Sat)** This zinging restaurant with cheery decorative touches is a good choice if you're tired of heavy Burgundian classics. The menu always involves seasonal, fresh ingredients, and dishes are imaginatively prepared and beautifully presented. At €18, the lunchtime *I love Dijon* menu is a steal.

Chez Léon Regional Cuisine **€€**

(**☎03 80 50 01 07; www.restochezleon.fr; 20 rue des Godrans; mains €17-23, lunch menus €15-19, dinner menus €25-29; ⏰noon-2pm & 7-10.30pm Tue-Sat)** From bœuf bourguignon (beef marinated in young red wine) to *andouillettes* (chitterling sausages), this is the perfect primer course in hearty regional fare celebrated in a cosy and joyful atmosphere. The dining room is cluttered but there's outdoor seating in warmer months.

Shopping

Moutarde Maille Mustard

(**☎03 80 30 41 02; www.maille.com; 32 rue de la Liberté; ⏰10am-7pm Mon-Sat)** When you enter the factory boutique of this mustard company, tangy odours assault your nostrils. There are 36 kinds of mustard, such as cassis or truffle and celery, including three on tap that you can sample.

Moutarde Maille
NATIONAL GEOGRAPHIC IMAGE COLLECTION/ALAMY ©

Information

Tourist Office (☎08 92 70 05 58; www.visitdijon.com; 11 rue des Forges; ⏰9.30am-6.30pm Mon-Sat, 10am-6pm Sun Apr-Sep, shorter hours rest of year) Helpful office offering tours and maps. Also sells the €16 Dijon Côte de Nuits Pass, which offers free admission to Dijon city tours plus museums and attractions in the nearby Côte de Nuits vineyards.

Getting There & Away

Connections from Dijon's **train station (rue du Dr Rémy)** include the following:

Lyon-Part Dieu Regional train/TGV €31/36, two/1½ hours, 25 daily

Marseille TGV €89, 3½ hours, six direct daily

Paris Gare de Lyon Regional train/TGV €45/65, three/1½ hours; 25 daily

CÔTE D'OR VINEYARDS

Burgundy's most renowned vintages come from the vine-covered Côte d'Or (literally 'Golden Hillside', but it is actually an abbreviation of Côte d'Orient or Eastern Hillside), the narrow, eastern slopes of a range of hills made of limestone, flint and clay that runs south from Dijon for about 60km.

The Côte d'Or vineyards are divided into two areas, Côte de Nuits to the north and Côte de Beaune to the south.

Noted for its powerful reds, the **Côte de Nuits** wine-growing area extends from Marsannay-la-Côte, just south of Dijon, to Corgoloin, a few kilometres north of Beaune. **Château du Clos de Vougeot** (03 80 62 86 09; www.closdevougeot.fr; Vougeot; adult/child €5/2.50; 9am-6.30pm Apr-Sep, 9-11.30am & 2-5.30pm Oct-Mar, closes 5pm Sat year-round), 20km south of Dijon in **Vougeot,** provides a wonderful introduction to Burgundy's winemaking techniques. Originally the property of the Abbaye de Cîteaux, the 16th-century country castle served as a getaway for the abbots. Almost 5km south in **Nuits St-Georges**, gleaming modern museum **L'Imaginarium** (03 80 62 61 40; www.imaginarium-bourgogne.com; av du Jura; adult incl basic/grand cru tasting €8/15, child €5; 2-7pm Mon, 10am-7pm Tue-Sun) is the place to learn about Burgundy wines and winemaking technique through movies, exhibits and interactive displays.

Known for top-quality dry whites and delicate reds, the **Côte de Beaune** area extends from Ladoix-Serrigny, just a few kilometres north of Beaune, to Santenay, about 18km south of Beaune. The delightful village of **Chassagne-Montrachet** boasts Burgundy's most fabled vineyards, while **Château de Meursault** (03 80 26 22 75; www.meursault.com; Meursault; admission incl tasting €18; 9.30am-noon & 2-6pm Oct-Apr, 9.30am-6.30pm May-Sep) – among the prettiest Côte de Beaune châteaux – has beautiful grounds and produces some of the most prestigious white wines in the world. For red wine lovers, a visit to **Château de Pommard** (03 80 22 12 59; www.chateaudepommard.com; 15 rue Marey-Monge, Pommard; guided tour incl tasting €21, children admitted free; 9.30am-6.30pm), 3km south of Beaune, is the ultimate Burgundian pilgrimage.

Marché aux Vins (p209)

Beaune

POP 22,720

Beaune (pronounced similarly to 'bone'), 44km south of Dijon, is the unofficial capital of the Côte d'Or. This thriving town's *raison d'être* and the source of its *joie de vivre* is wine: making it, tasting it, selling it, but most of all, drinking it. Consequently Beaune is one of the best places in all of France for wine tasting.

The jewel of Beaune's old city is the magnificent Hôtel-Dieu, France's most splendiferous medieval charity hospital.

Sights & Activities

Hôtel-Dieu des Hospices de Beaune Historic Building

(www.hospices-de-beaune.com; rue de l'Hôtel-Dieu; adult/child €7/3; 9am-6.30pm) Built in 1443, this magnificent Gothic hospital (until 1971) is famously topped by stunning turrets and pitched rooftops covered in multicoloured tiles. Interior highlights include the barrel-vaulted **Grande Salle** (look for the dragons and peasant heads up on the roof beams); the mural-covered **St-Hughes Room**; an 18th-century **pharmacy** lined with flasks once filled with elixirs and powders; and the multipanelled masterpiece **Polyptych of the Last Judgement** by 15th-century Flemish painter Rogier van der Weyden, depicting Judgment Day in glorious technicolour.

Marché aux Vins Wine Tasting

(www.marcheauxvins.com; 2 rue Nicolas Rolin; 10am-noon & 2-6.30pm Sep-Jun, 10am-6.30pm Jul-Aug) Sample seven wines for €11, or 10 for €15, in the candle-lit former Église des Cordeliers and its cellars. Wandering among the vintages takes about an hour. The finest wines are at the end; look for the *premier crus* and the *grand cru* (wine of exceptional quality).

Patriarche Père et Fils Wine Tasting

(www.patriarche.com; 7 rue du Collège; audioguide tour €16; 9.30-11.30am & 2-5.30pm) Spanning 2 hectares, Burgundy's largest

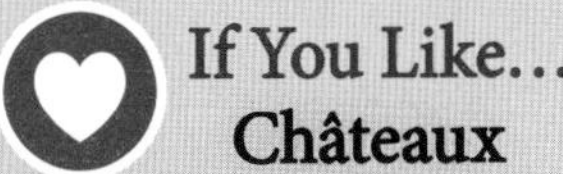

If You Like... Châteaux

Once you've done the big three – Chambord, Chenonceau and Cheverny – it's worth taking the time to discover this trio of lesser-known, equally dreamy châteaux.

1 **CHÂTEAU DE VILLANDRY**
(02 47 50 02 09; www.chateauvillandry.com; chateau & gardens adult/child €10/6.50, gardens only €6.50/4.50, audioguides €4; 9am-6pm Apr-Oct, shorter hours rest of year, closed mid-Nov–mid-Dec) Completed in 1756, one of the last major Renaissance châteaux to be built in the Loire Valley, Villandry is deservedly famous for what lies outside the château, not what lies within. Encircled by tall walls, the château's glorious **landscaped gardens** (closing 30 minutes after the château) are some of the finest in France, occupying over 6 hectares filled with painstakingly manicured lime trees, ornamental vines, cascading flowers, razor-sharp box hedges and tinkling fountains.

2 **CHÂTEAU DE BEAUREGARD**
(02 54 70 41 65; www.beauregard-loire.com; Cellettes; adult/child €12.50/5; 10.30am-6.30pm Apr-Sep, 1.30-5pm Mon-Fri, from 10.30am Sat & Sun mid-Feb–Mar & Oct–mid-Nov) Less visited than its sister châteaux, peaceful Beauregard has charms all its own. Built as yet another hunting lodge by François I, the highlight is an amazing **portrait gallery** depicting 327 notables of European royalty, clergy and intelligentsia. Spot famous faces including Christopher Columbus, Sir Francis Drake, Cardinal Richelieu, Catherine de Médicis, Anne de Bretagne, Henry VIII of England and his doomed wife Anne Boleyn, and every French king since Philippe VI. The quiet, 40-hectare grounds encompass numerous **gardens**, including the Garden of Portraits with 12 colour variations.

3 **CHÂTEAU D'USSÉ**
(02 47 95 54 05; www.chateaudusse.fr; adult/child €14/4; 10am-6pm, to 7pm Apr-Aug, closed early Nov–mid-Feb) The main claim to fame of elaborate Château d'Ussé is as the inspiration for Charles Perrault's classic fairy tale, *La Belle au Bois Dormant* (known to English-speakers as *Sleeping Beauty*).

Below: *Quenelles de sandre* (pike fish dumplings) **Right:** Noyers-sur-Serein

cellars have 5km of corridors lined with about five million bottles of wine. (The oldest is a Beaune Villages AOC from 1904!) Visitors armed with multilingual audioguides can tour the premises in 60 to 90 minutes, tasting 13 wines along the way and taking the *tastevin* home.

Moutarderie Fallot Mustard Factory
(Mustard Mill; ☎03 80 22 10 10; www.fallot.com; 31 rue du Faubourg Bretonnière; adult/child €10/8; ⏰tasting room 9.30am-6pm Mon-Sat, tours 10am & 11.30am Mon-Sat mid-Mar–mid-Nov, plus 3.30pm & 5pm Jun-Sep, by arrangement rest of year) Burgundy's last family-run stone-ground mustard company offers guided tours through its mustard museum, focusing on mustard's history, folklore and traditional production techniques, with kid-friendly opportunities for hand-milling mustard seeds. An alternate tour focuses on Fallot's modern mustard production facility. Reserve tours ahead at Beaune's tourist office. Drop-ins can sample and purchase over a dozen varieties in the brand-new *dégustation* room.

Eating

Le Comptoir des Tontons Regional Cuisine **€€**
(☎03 80 24 19 64; www.lecomptoirdestontons.com; 22 rue du Faubourg Madeleine; menus €29-42; ⏰noon-1pm & 7.30-9pm Tue-Sat) Decorated in a hip bistro style, this local treasure entices with the passionate Burgundian cooking of chef Pepita. Most ingredients are organic and locally sourced. Does the beef with paprika taste better than the fat duck in aniseed sauce? You be the judge. Service is prompt and friendly.

Loiseau des Vignes Gastronomic **€€€**
(☎03 80 24 12 06; www.bernard-loiseau.com; 31 rue Maufoux; lunch menus €20-28, dinner menus €59-95; ⏰noon-2pm & 7-10pm Tue-Sat) For that special meal with your significant other, this culinary shrine is the place to

go. Expect stunning concoctions ranging from caramelised pigeon to *quenelles de sandre* (dumplings made from pike fish), all exquisitely presented. And even the most budget-conscious can indulge – lunch menus are a bargain. In summer, the verdant garden is a plus.

Information

Tourist Office (**☎03 80 26 21 30; www.beaune-tourisme.fr; 6 bd Perpreuil; ⌚9am-6.30pm Mon-Sat, 9am-6pm Sun**) Sells Pass Beaune and has lots of brochures about the town and nearby vineyards. An **annexe** (**1 rue de l'Hôtel-Dieu; ⌚10am-1pm & 2-6pm**) opposite the Hôtel-Dieu keeps shorter hours.

Getting There & Away

Bus Transco (**☎03 80 11 29 29; www.mobigo-bourgogne.com**) bus 44 links Beaune with Dijon (€1.50, 1½ hours, two to seven daily), stopping at Côte d'Or villages such as Vougeot, Nuits-St-Georges and Aloxe-Corton. Services reduced in July and August. In Beaune, buses stop along the boulevards around the old city. Timetables at the tourist office.

Train Services connect the following places:

Dijon €7.80, 25 minutes, 40 daily

Lyon-Part Dieu €26.50, 1¾ hours, 16 daily

Mâcon €15.60, 55 minutes, 19 daily

Nuits-St-Georges €3.60, 10 minutes, eight daily

Paris Regional train (€49, 3½ hours, seven direct daily); TGV (€75, 2¼ hours, two daily)

Noyers-sur-Serein

A must-see on any Burgundy itinerary, the absolutely picturesque medieval village of Noyers (pronounced 'nwa-yair'), 30km southeast of Auxerre, is surrounded by rolling pastureland, wooded hills and a sharp bend in the River Serein. Stone ramparts and fortified battlements enclose much of the village and, between the two imposing stone gateways, cobbled streets lead past

If You Like... Picture-Perfect Villages

Swoon over Sarlat, grab the smelling salts, then swoon again over these other drop-dead gorgeous Dordogne villages.

1 LA ROQUE GAGEAC

La Roque Gageac's jumble of amber buildings crammed into the cliff-face above the Dordogne has earned it recognition as another of France's *plus beaux villages*. It's an idyllic launch pad for a canoe trip or cruise, while a trio of the region's most famous castles are within a few minutes' drive.

2 BRANTÔME

With its five medieval bridges and romantic riverfront architecture, Brantôme, 27km north of Périgueux, befits its moniker 'Venice of the Périgord'. Set along the banks of the River Dronne, it's an enchanting spot to while away an afternoon or embark on a boat ride or paddle in a kayak. For more information, visit the **tourist office** (**☎05 53 05 80 63; www.perigord-dronne-belle.fr; Abbaye de Brantôme; ⌚10am-1pm & 2-6pm Apr-Sep, shorter hours rest of year**).

3 GIMEL-LES-CASCADES

A mixture of flower-clad cottages and slate roofs, gorgeous **Gimel-les-Cascades** (tourist office **☎05 55 21 44 32; www.gimellescascades.fr; ⌚10am-noon & 2-5pm Mon-Fri, to 6pm Sat & Sun Apr-Sep**) is a place to wander the lanes, drink in the atmosphere, and stroll along the banks of the river. The three crashing **cascades**, after which the village is named, are reached via a riverside path at the foot of the village.

4 COLLONGES-LA-ROUGE

Red sandstone houses and an 11th-century church huddle in the lanes of **Collonges-la-Rouge** (tourist office **☎05 55 25 32 25; www.ot-collonges.fr; ⌚10am-12.30pm & 2.30-6pm**), one of France's official *beaux villages* (beautiful villages). Its skyline is cut from conical turrets, rickety rooftops and historic buildings built from rust-red sandstone (hence its name).

15th- and 16th-century gabled houses, wood and stone archways and several art galleries.

Noyers is a superb base for walking. Just outside the clock-topped southern gate, Chemin des Fossés leads eastwards to the River Serein and a streamside walk around the village's 13th-century fortifications, 19 of whose original 23 towers are extant. Lunch afterwards at **Les Millésimes** (**☎03 86 82 82 16; www.maison-paillot.com; 14 place de l'Hôtel de Ville; menu €27; ⌚noon-3pm Tue-Sun, 7pm-9pm Tue-Sat**), a meticulously restored medieval house complete with large fireplace and sturdy wooden tables which specialises in *terroir* creations ranging from *jambon au chablis* (ham flavoured with Chablis wine) to *tourte à l'Époisses* (Époisses cheese pie). It's also renowned for its respectable wine list.

Chantier Médiéval de Guédelon

About 45km southwest of Auxerre and 7km southwest of St-Sauveur-en-Puisaye, a team of skilled artisans, aided by archaeologists, has been hard at work building a fortified castle at the **Chantier Médiéval de Guédelon** (**☎03 86 45 66 66; www.guedelon.fr; D955 near Treigny; adult/child €12/10; ⌚10am-6pm mid-Apr–Jun, to 7pm Jul & Aug, to 5.30pm Thu-Tue mid-Mar–mid-Apr & Sep-early Nov**) since 1997 using only 13th-century techniques. No electricity or power tools here: stone is quarried on site using iron hand tools forged by a team of blacksmiths, who also produce vital items like door hinges. Clay for tiles is fired for three days using locally cut wood and the mortar, made on site with lime, is transported in freshly woven wicker baskets. A very worthwhile guided tour, sometimes in English, costs €2 per person. Wear closed shoes, as the site is often a sea of muck. Child-oriented activities include stone carving (using especially soft stone).

THE DORDOGNE

This is the heart and soul of *la belle France,* a land of dense oak forests, emerald-green fields and famously rich country cooking. It's the stuff of which French dreams are made: turreted châteaux and medieval villages line the riverbanks, wooden-hulled *gabarres* (barges) wander the waterways, and market stalls overflow with foie gras, truffles, walnuts and fine wines.

The Dordogne, known to the French as the Périgord, has long been a favourite getaway for Brits looking for a second home and French families on *les grandes vacances*. It's also famous for having some of France's finest prehistoric cave art, which litters the caverns and rock shelters of the Vézère Valley.

Sarlat-la-Canéda

POP 9943

A picturesque tangle of honey-coloured buildings, alleyways and secret squares make up the beautiful town of Sarlat-la-Canéda, which boasts some of the region's best-preserved medieval architecture and makes the perfect base for exploring the Vézère Valley.

Sights

Cathédrale St-Sacerdos Cathedral

(place du Peyrou) Once part of Sarlat's Cluniac abbey, the original abbey church was built in the 1100s, redeveloped in the early 1500s and remodelled again in the 1700s, so it's a real mix of styles. The belfry and western facade are the oldest parts of the building, while the nave, organ and interior chapels are later additions.

Chapelle St-Benoît Chapel

(Chapelle des Pénitents Bleus) Two medieval courtyards, the **Cour des Fontaines** and the **Cour des Chanoines**, can be reached via an alleyway off rue Tourny or from the Jardin des Enfeus. The passage from Cour des Chanoines leads to the Chapelle St-Benoît aka Chapelle des Pénitents Bleus, a 12th-century Romanesque chapel and the oldest remnant of Sarlat's abbey.

Place de la Liberté, Sarlat-la-Canéda

PALEOLITHIC/GETTY IMAGES ©

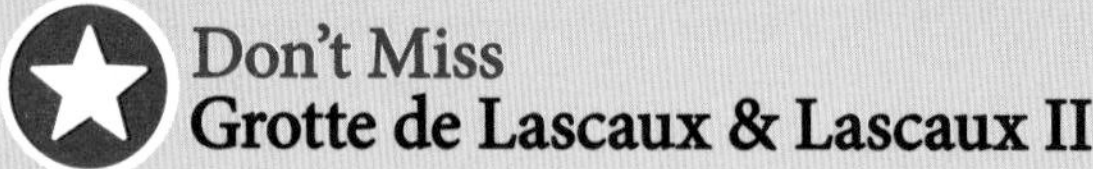

Don't Miss
Grotte de Lascaux & Lascaux II

France's most famous prehistoric cave paintings are at the Grotte de Lascaux, 2km southeast of Montignac. Completely sealed and protected for ages, it was discovered in 1940 by four teenage boys out searching for their lost dog. It contains a vast network of chambers adorned with the most complex prehistoric paintings ever found. The original cave was opened to visitors in 1948, but within a few years it became apparent that human breath, temperature changes and introduced elements were causing irreparable damage, and the cave was closed in 1963. A cm-by-cm replica of the most famous sections of the original cave was created a few hundred metres away – a massive undertaking that required the skills of 20 artists over 11 years.

From mid-April to mid-October, tickets (either same-day or for the future) are sold *only* in Montignac at a ticket office next to the tourist office; the rest of the year you can get them at the cave entrance.

Lascaux has often been referred to as the prehistoric equivalent of the Sistine Chapel, and it's a fitting comparison. Renowned for their artistry, the 600-strong menagerie of animal figures are depicted in technicolor shades of red, black, yellow and brown, ranging from reindeer, aurochs, mammoths and horses to a monumental 5.5m-long bull, the largest single cave drawing ever found. After a visit in 1940, Picasso allegedly muttered, 'We have invented nothing'.

Carbon dating has shown that the paintings are between 15,000 and 17,000 years old, but it's still a mystery why the prehistoric painters devoted so much time and effort to their creation, and why this particular site seems to have been so important.

NEED TO KNOW

☎ 05 53 51 95 03; www.semitour.com; Montignac; adult/child €9.90/6.40, joint ticket with Le Thot €13.50/9.40; 🕒 guided tours (some in English and Spanish) 9am-7pm Jul & Aug, 9.30am-6pm Apr-Jun, 9.30am-noon & 2-6pm Sep & Oct, shorter hours rest of year, closed Jan

Église Ste-Marie Church, Market

(place de la Liberté) Église Ste-Marie was ingeniously converted by acclaimed architect Jean Nouvel, whose parents still live in Sarlat, into Sarlat's touristy **Marché Couvert** (Covered Market; 8.30am-2pm daily, to 8pm Fri mid-Apr–mid-Nov, closed Mon, Thu & Sun rest of year). Its **panoramic lift** offers 360-degree views across Sarlat's countryside.

Place du Marché aux Oies Square

A life-size statue of three bronze geese stands in the centre of beautiful place du Marché aux Oies (Goose Market Sq), where live geese are still sold during the Fest'Oie. The square's architecture is exceptional.

Sleeping

Villa des Consuls B&B **€€**

(05 53 31 90 05; www.villaconsuls.fr; 3 rue Jean-Jacques Rousseau; d €95-110, apt €150-190; @) Despite its Renaissance exterior, the enormous rooms here are modern through and through, with shiny wood floors and sleek furnishings. Several delightful self-contained apartments dot the town, all offering the same mix of period plushness – some also have terraces overlooking the town's rooftops.

La Maison des Peyrat Hotel **€€**

(05 53 59 00 32; www.maisondespeyrat.com; Le Lac de la Plane; r €80-109) This beautifully renovated 17th-century house, formerly a nuns' hospital and later an aristocratic hunting lodge, is set on a hill about 1.5km from Sarlat centre. Eleven generously sized rooms are decorated in modern farmhouse style; the best have views over gardens and the countryside beyond. Good restaurant too.

Eating

Sarlat Markets Market

(place de la Liberté & rue de la République; 8.30am-1pm Wed, 8.30am-6pm Sat) For an introductory French market experience visit Sarlat's heavily touristed Saturday market, which takes over the streets around Cathédrale St-Sacerdos. Depending on the season, delicacies include local mushrooms and duck- and goose-based products such as foie gras. Get *truffe noir* (black truffle) at the winter **Marché aux Truffes** (Sat morning Dec-Feb). An atmospheric, largely organic **night market** (6-10pm) operates on Thursday. Seasoned market-goers may prefer others throughout the region.

Le Bistrot Regional Cuisine **€€**

(05 53 28 28 40; www.le-bistrot-sarlat.com; 14 place du Peyrou; menus €18-30; noon-2pm & 6.30-10pm Tue-Sun, open daily Jul & Aug) This little bistro is the best of the bunch on cafe-clad place du Peyrou. The menu's heavy on Sarlat classics, especially walnuts, duck breast and finger-lickin' *pommes sarlardaises* (potatoes cooked in duck fat).

Le Grand Bleu Gastronomic **€€€**

(05 53 31 08 48; www.legrandbleu.eu; 43 av de la Gare; menus €54-125; 12.30-2pm Thu-Sun, 7.30-9.30pm Tue-Sat) This eminent Michelin-starred restaurant run by chef Maxime Lebrun is renowned for its creative cuisine with elaborate menus making maximum use of luxury produce: truffles, lobster, turbot and scallops, with a wine list to match. Cooking courses (€40) are also available. Located 1.5km south of the centre.

Information

Tourist Office (05 53 31 45 45; www.sarlat-tourisme.com; 3 rue Tourny; 9am-7pm Mon-Sat, 10am-1pm & 2-6pm Sun May-Aug, shorter hours Sep-Apr;) Sarlat's tourist office is packed with info, but often gets overwhelmed by visitors; the website has it all.

Getting There & Away

The **train station** (av de la Gare) is 1.3km south of the old city. Many destinations require a change at Le Buisson or Libourne.

Bordeaux €27.50, 2¾ hours, six daily

Les Eyzies €9.80, one to two hours depending on connections, four daily

The Vézère Valley

Flanked by limestone cliffs, subterranean caverns and ancient woodland, the Vézère Valley is world famous for its prehistoric sites, notably its incredible collection of cave paintings – the highest concentration of Stone Age art found in Europe. The many underground caves around the Vézère provided shelter for Cro-Magnon people, and the area is littered with tangible reminders of their time here. The otherworldly atmosphere is pretty much shattered by the summer crowds and most of the valley's sites are closed in winter, so spring and autumn are definitely the best times to visit.

Sarlat-la-Canéda, between the Vézère and Dordogne valleys to the west, is a convenient base for exploring this part of the Dordogne.

Sights

Musée National de Préhistoire
Prehistory Museum

(**☎05 53 06 45 45; www.musee-prehistoire-eyzies.fr; 1 rue du Musée; adult/child €6/4.50, 1st Sun of month free; ⏰9.30am-6.30pm daily Jul & Aug, 9.30am-6pm Wed-Mon Jun & Sep, 9.30am-12.30pm & 2-5.30pm Wed-Mon Oct-May**) Inside a marvellous modern building alongside the cliffs, this museum provides a fine prehistory primer (providing your French is good) with the most comprehensive collection of prehistoric finds in France. Highlights include a huge gallery of Stone Age tools, weapons and jewellery, and skeletons of some of the animals that once roamed the Vézère (including bison, woolly rhinoceros, giant deer and cave bears). A collection of carved reliefs on the 1st floor includes a famous frieze of horses and a bison licking its flank.

Grotte de Font de Gaume
Prehistoric Site

(**☎05 53 06 86 00; http://eyzies.monuments-nationaux.fr; adult/child €7.50/free; ⏰guided tours 9.30am-5.30pm Sun-Fri mid-May–mid-Sep, 9.30am-12.30pm & 2-5.30pm Sun-Fri mid-Sep–mid-May**) This extraordinary cave contains the only original polychrome (as opposed to single colour) paintings still open to the public. About 14,000 years ago, prehistoric artists created the gallery of over 230 figures, including bison, reindeer, horses, mammoths, bears and wolves, although

The River Lot

ANN TAYLOR-HUGHES/GETTY IMAGES ©

only about 25 are included in the fantastically atmospheric tour. Look out for the famous **Chapelle des Bisons**, a scene of courting reindeer and stunningly realised horses, several caught in mid-movement. Try to reserve ahead by phone as far in advance as you can.

Grotte des Combarelles Prehistoric Site

(☎05 53 06 86 00; http://eyzies.monuments-nationaux.fr; adult/child €7.50/free; ⏲guided tours 9.30am-5.30pm Sun-Fri mid-May–mid-Sep, 9.30am-12.30pm & 2-5.30pm Sun-Fri mid-Sep–mid-May) This narrow cave 1.5km east of Font de Gaume was the first rediscovered in the valley, in 1901, and is renowned for its animal engravings, many of which cleverly use the natural contours of the rock to sculpt the animals' forms. Look out for mammoths, horses and reindeer, as well as a fantastic mountain lion that seems to leap from the rock face. Go early on the day to buy tickets at the Font de Gaume ticket office for 45-minute eight-person tours.

Grotte de Rouffignac Prehistoric Site

(☎05 53 05 41 71; www.grottederouffignac.fr; Rouffignac-St-Cernin-de-Reilhac; adult/child €7/4.60; ⏲9-11.30am & 2-6pm Jul & Aug, 10-11.30am & 2-5pm mid-Apr–Jun & Sep-Oct, closed Nov–mid-Apr) Hidden in pretty woodland 15km north of Les Eyzies, this enormous tri-level cave is one of the most complex and rewarding to see in the Dordogne. Board an **electric train** to explore a 1km maze of tunnels in the massive cavern plunging 8km into the earth.

Highlights include the frieze of 10 mammoths in procession, one of the largest cave paintings ever discovered, and the awe-inspiring Great Ceiling, with over 65 figures from ibex to aurochs. You'll also see nests of long-extinct cave bears, and 17th-century graffiti.

The Lot

Southeast of the Dordogne stretches the Lot Valley, a picturesque landscape of limestone cliffs, hilltop towns and canyons carved out by the serpentine River Lot. The main town is **Cahors**, another area that's celebrated for its vineyards.

Teetering at the crest of a sheer cliff high above the River Lot 26km east is miniscule **St-Cirq Lapopie**, a village whose terracotta-roofed houses and ramshackle streets tumble down the steep hillside, affording incredible valley views. It's one of the most magical settings in the Lot.

Sights

Gouffre de Padirac Cave

(☎05 65 33 64 56; www.gouffre-de-padirac.com; adult/child €10.30/6.90; ⏲hours vary, approx 9.30am-7pm Apr–mid-Nov) Discovered in 1889, the spectacular Gouffre de Padirac features some of France's spangliest underground caverns. The cave's navigable river, 103m below ground level, is reached through a 75m-deep, 33m-wide chasm. Boat pilots ferry visitors along 1km of subterranean waterways, visiting a series of glorious floodlit caverns, including the soaring **Salle de Grand Dôme** and the **Lac des Grands Gours**, a 27m-wide subterranean lake. You can book online. From Rocamadour, the caverns are 15km northeast.

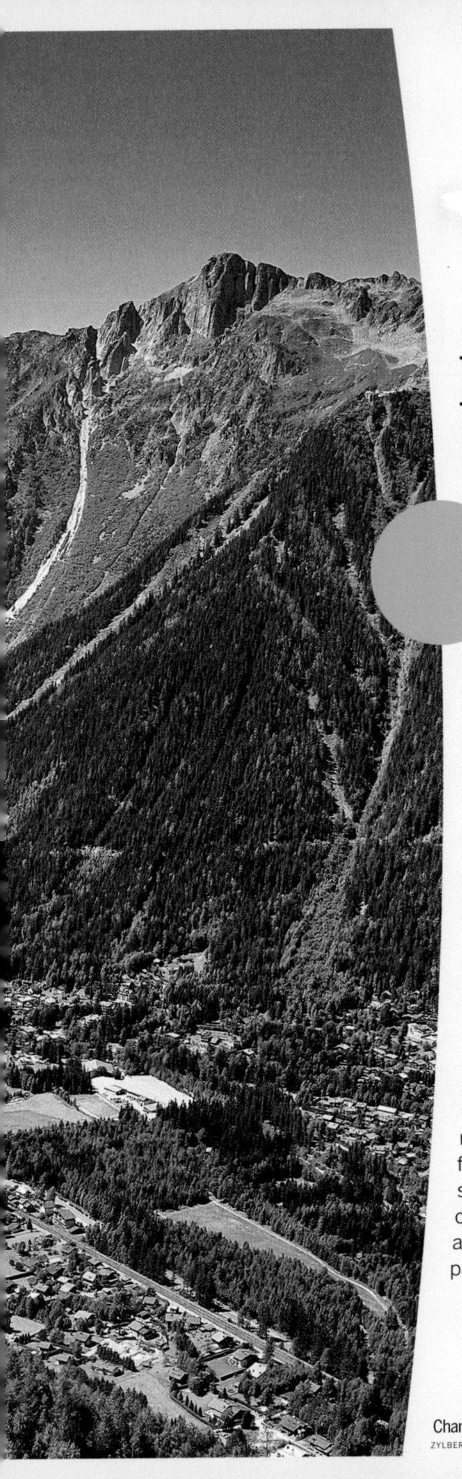

Lyon & the French Alps

The French Alps is a place of boundless natural beauty.

Whether it's virgin snow in Chamonix, the rhythm of boots on a lonely mountain pass, or the silence of a summer's morning as the first rays illuminate Mont Blanc, these colossal mountains offer a symphony of unforgettable experiences. Needless to say, the Alps are a paradise for hikers, bikers and wildlife spotters, but it's the epic pistes and après-ski that keep people coming back year after year.

At the foothills of the Alps lies grand old Lyon, France's third-largest metropolis and arguably its gastronomic capital. It's a place to savour, with Roman amphitheatres, romantic parks and a delightful old town, but for many people nothing beats tucking into some hearty Lyonnais dishes in a traditional city *bouchon* (Lyonnais bistro) – old-world atmosphere, checked tablecloths, clattering pans and all.

Chamonix (p240)

Lyon & the French Alps

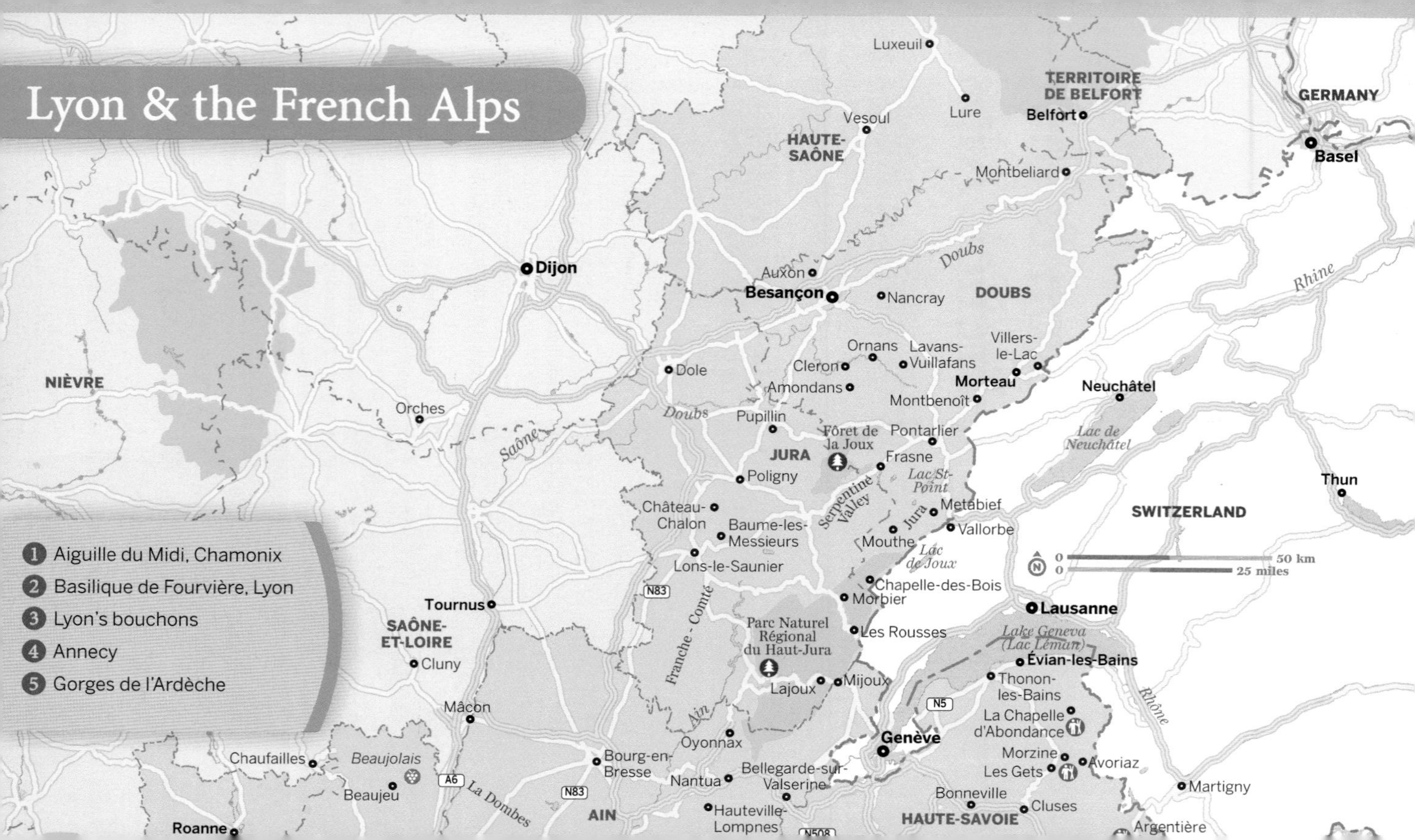

Le Grand Bornand
Chamonix
1
Aiguille du Midi (3842m)
Villefranche-sur-Saône
Villars-les-Dombes
Joyeux
N7
Perouges
Annecy
4
La Clusaz
Les Houches
Veyrier-du-Lac
Sévrier
Menthon-St-Bernard
Megève
Mont Blanc Massif
Mer de Glace
Val Ferret
VALLE D' AOSTA
A72
L'Arbresle
Lac d'Annecy
Col du Petit St-Bernard
La Tourette
2
3
Lyon
Lyon St-Exupéry
Rhône
Belley
Lac Bourget
Parc Régional du Massif des Bauges
LOIRE
N89
La Feclaz
Ecoly
Albertville
N90
Seez
Parco Nazionale del Gran Paradiso
Monts du Forez
Montbrison
A46
A43
Givors
Avressieux
A43
Chambery
Tarentaise Valley
Tarentaise
Val d'Isère
Tignes
A47
Vienne
N6
SAVOIE
Parc Naturel Régional du Livradois-Forez
A48
St-Martin de Belleville
Les Trois Vallées
Courchevel
Meribel
Espace Killy
Parc National de la Vanoise
St-Étienne
Firminy
Voiron
Parc Régional de Chartreuse
Isère
Vanoise Mountains
Maurienne Valley
Val Thorens
Col du Mont Cenis
Crêt de la Perdrix (1430m)
N82
Côte du Rhône
ISÈRE
Drac
Lac de Mont Cénis
ITALY
Annonay
A7
Grenoble
Défilé de Maupas
Vaujany
Col du Galibier (2645m)
Susa
HAUTE-LOIRE
Le Chambon-sur-Lignon
Tain l'Hermitage
Lans-en-Vercors
Villard de Lans
N532
Bourg d'Oisans
Alpe d'Huez (1860m)
La Grave
Le Monêtier-es-Bains
Sestriere
Le Puy-en-Velay
Corrençon-en-Vercors
Les Deux Alpes
Glacier du Mont du Lans (3425m)
D15
N85
Barre des Écrins (4102m)
La Berarde
Col du Montgenèvre
Briançon
PIEDMONT
Valence
Gorges de l'Allier
Parc Naturel Régional du Vercors
THE FRENCH ALPS
Parc National des Écrins
N94
Parc Naturel Regional du Queyras
ARDÈCHE
Privas
Rhône
Po
Langogne
N104
DRÔME
HAUTES-ALPES
Embrun
N102
Aubenas
Rochemaure
A7
Gap
Ardèche
N102
Montelimar
Lac de Serre-Ponçon
LOZÈRE
Vallée de la Blanche
Le Lauzet-Ubaye
Ubaye
5
Ruoms
Gorges de l'Ardèche
St-Remèze
PROVENCE
Mont Lozère
Vallon-Pont-d'Arc
Nyons
Eyguians
Pierrelatte
Parc National des Cévennes
Gorge de l'Ardèche Réserve Naturelle
D94
Val d'Allos
Durance
ALPES-MARITIMES
ALPES DE HAUTE-PROVENCE
GARD
Orange
VAUCLUSE

Lyon & the French Alps' Highlights

Aiguille du Midi, Chamonix

Ever since Mont Blanc, the highest peak in the Alps, was first climbed in 1786, Chamonix has attracted travellers worldwide. It's a mecca for mountaineers and adrenaline junkies, with dramatic mountain views on every horizon – best appreciated from the 3842m-high Aiguille du Midi (p242).

1

2 Basilique de Fourvière, Lyon

Set high on a hilltop above Lyon, this 18th-century basilica (p233) commands a panoramic position overlooking the city's rooftops. Fourvière was once the site of the Roman settlement of Lugdunum, and an intriguing museum near the basilica explores the city's Roman connections. If you don't fancy the uphill climb, catch the creaky funicular from Vieux Lyon instead.

GREG ELMS/GETTY IMAGES ©

Feasting in Lyon's Bouchons 3

Savouring lavish dishes and delicacies in timeless, checked-tableclothed *bouchons* (Lyonnais bistros, p236) or contemporary cutting-edge spaces is an essential part of the Lyon experience. Honour your feast with a respected red from a local Brouilly, Beaujolais, Côtes du Rhône or Mâcon vineyard.

Right: *Saucisson de Lyon* (beef and bacon sausage) with potatoes

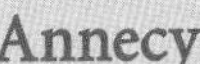

FIONLINE DIGITALE BILDAGENTUR GMBH/ALAMY ©

4 Annecy

Criss-crossed by canals and set around the shores of a sparkling Alpine lake, Annecy (p247) is blessed with one of the loveliest settings in the Alps. The town is tailor-made for unwinding: wander peaceful backstreets, picnic by the water's edge, snap your picture by the famous Lovers' Bridge or just soak up the brilliant Alpine atmosphere.

5 Gorges de l'Ardèche

These fabulous river canyons (p245) make a fantastic day trip from Lyon. The best way to explore them is by kayak or canoe – you'll find outdoors operators all along the course of the River Ardèche. The best views are from the lookout points dotted along the Haute Corniche (D290) – but be prepared for traffic jams in summer.

Lyon & the French Alps' Best...

High Altitude Thrills

- **Mer de Glace** Catch the rack-and-pinion train to Chamonix' 'sea of ice'. (p241)
- **Télécabine Panoramique Mont Blanc** Dangle above glacial crevasses in this dizzying cable-car ride from Aiguille du Midi to Pointe Helbronner. (p242)
- **La Vallée Blanche** Ski 20km of mind-blowing off-pîste with this legendary Chamonix trail. (p241)
- **Morzine** Brave a knuckle-whitening 3300m mountain-bike descent. (p246)

Hiking

- **Parc National de la Vanoise** Hit the trails in France's oldest national park between June and September. (p248)
- **Le Brévent** A multitude of routes cover this 2525m peak, offering breathtaking views of Mont Blanc. (p240)
- **Annecy** Walk or rollerblade round the shores of Lac d'Annecy. (p247)
- **Parc National des Écrins** Escape the crowds in France's second-largest national park. (p248)

Cultural Sights

- **Musée des Beaux-Arts** Lyon's art museum is a showstopper. (p229)
- **Musée Lumière** Visit the boyhood Lyonnais home of cinematic pioneers Auguste and Louis Lumière. (p233)
- **Maison des Canuts** The story of Lyon's silkweavers in a 19th-century workshop. (p232)
- **Musée des Tissus** Discover Lyon's extraordinary silk heritage. (p229)
- **Château d'Annecy** Savoyard history in a château setting. (p248)

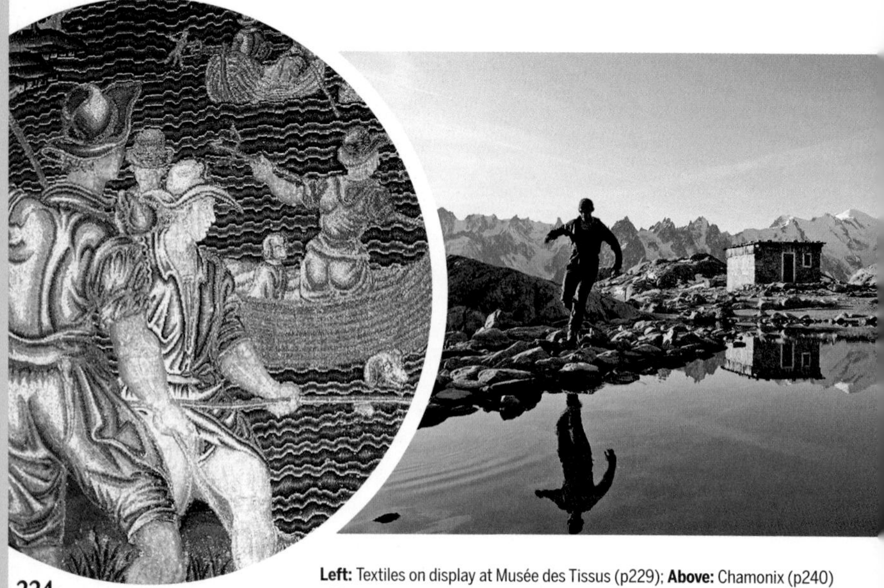

Left: Textiles on display at Musée des Tissus (p229); **Above:** Chamonix (p240)

Dining

- **Le Bouchon des Filles** Contemporary take on traditional Lyonnais *bouchon* dining. (p236)
- **La Mère Brazier** Mythical gastronomic temple in Lyon. (p237)
- **L'Esquisse** 'The' address in Annecy with just six tables. (p249)
- **Le Cap Horn** Sophisticated dining in the shadow of Mont Blanc. (p244)

Need to Know

ADVANCE PLANNING

- **As early as possible** Book accommodation and ski packages.
- **Two weeks before** Arrange hiking, cycling, skiing and activity tours with local guides.
- **One week before** Book for big-name restaurants. Buy *forfaits* (ski passes) online, ensure you have mountain-rescue insurance.

RESOURCES

- **Lyon** (www.lyon.fr) Official city website.
- **Rhône-Alpes Tourisme** (www.rhonealpes-tourisme.com) Regional tourist information.
- **France Montagnes** (www.france-montagnes.com) Guides, maps, snow reports and more.
- **Bulles de Gones** (www.bullesdegones.com) What to do with kids (up to 12 years) in and around Lyon.

GETTING AROUND

- **Airports** Major airports: **Lyon St-Exupéry** (www.lyon.aeroport.fr), **Grenoble** (www.grenoble-airport.com), **Geneva** (www.gva.ch).
- **Car & Motorcycle** Traffic on mountain roads can be hellish at weekends. Road signs indicate if mountain passes are blocked. Fit snow tyres in winter and carry snow chains.
- **Train** Lyon has excellent rail connections to anywhere in France.
- **Satobus Alpes** (http://lys.altibus.com/) Bus shuttle between Lyon St-Expéry airport and major ski resorts.
- **Aeroski-Bus** (www.alpski-bus.com) Buses to/from Geneva airport.

BE FOREWARNED

- **Opening times** *Bouchons* (Lyonnais bistros) shut on weekends; many restaurants close on Mondays.
- **High-Season Prices** Over Christmas, New Year and during French school holidays in late February/early March.
- **Ski season** Runs from mid-December to late April. Summer alpine skiing on glaciers in high-altitude resorts runs for two weeks to two months, June to August.
- **Avalanches** Ski resorts announce the daily risk through signs and coloured flags. Don't ski/hike alone.

Lyon & the French Alps Itineraries

For sheer natural drama, nowhere in France tops the Alps. Its snowy peaks attract skiers, hikers, boarders and bikers, plus those who like big, wild views.

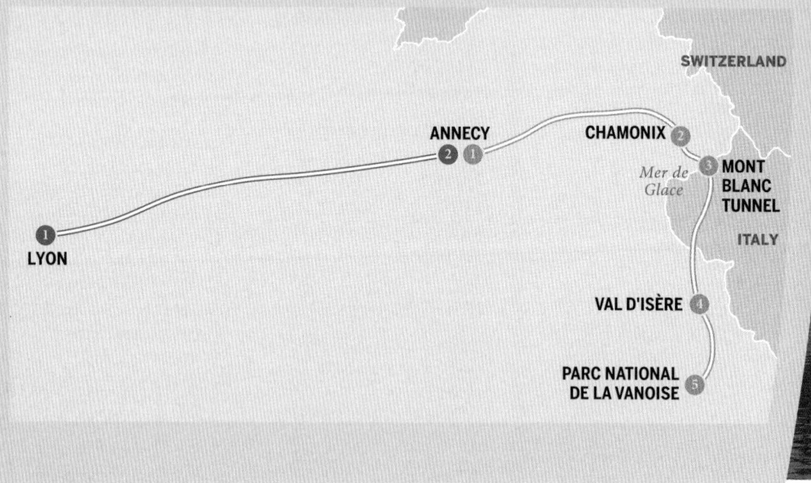

3 DAYS

LYON TO ANNECY

BIG CITY, LITTLE CITY

No city demands a weekend getaway more than ❶ **Lyon**, a place most travellers arrive in unexpectedly, are pleasantly surprised by and yearn to return to.

You'll need at least a couple of days to do it justice. Devote the first to exploring the Presqu'île and Vieux Lyon, and allow a leisurely couple of hours for that quintessential long French lunch in a homely Lyonnais *bouchon* such as Les Adrets.

With downtown Lyon under your belt, day two's for exploring further afield. Delve into the city's insider heart in Croix Rousse, with its lush morning market, mysterious maze of *traboules* (secret passages) and vibrant cafe life. In the afternoon catch the funicular to Fourvière for a peek at the Roman ruins and the basilica, before descending back to the old town for an alfresco drink on one of the city's grand squares. Reward yourself with dinner at Mère Brazier.

On day three, quit the big city for the altogether more-tranquil setting of ❷ **Annecy**, a chic lakeside town with a sparkling lake to swim in and another beautiful old town to get lost in.

ANNECY TO CHAMONIX
ALPINE ADVENTURES

❶ **Annecy** makes the ideal springboard for venturing into the spectacular peaks and valleys of the French Alps. In winter France's main playground for skiers and snowboarders, come summer it's a paradise for hikers and mountain-bikers. The following trip traverses some high Alpine passes, so it's a summer-only adventure.

From Annecy, head straight for the source – ❷ **Chamonix**, renowned as one of Europe's top spots for mountain sports. Don't miss the *télécabine* up to the Aiguille du Midi, where you can enjoy a high-altitude lunch with views over Mont Blanc. Another key sight is the Mer de Glace, the aptly named 'Sea of Ice', where you can step inside an ice cave that has to be recarved every year due to the movement of the glacier.

After a couple of days in Chamonix, head out of town via the ❸ **Mont Blanc tunnel**. Detour briefly into Italy before crossing back into France en route to ❹ **Val d'Isère**, another of the Alps' classic mountain resorts. To the south sprawls ❺ **Parc National de la Vanoise**, where you can spend the remainder of your trip strolling wildflower-laced trails and spotting wildlife.

Lyon (p228)

Lyon & the French Alps

At a Glance

- **Lyon** (p228) Grand old Roman city, France's third-largest, with Unesco-listed old town, majestic monuments and a gastronomy to die for.
- **French Alps** (p240) High in altitude and attitude, this is France's world-class outdoor playground where skiers, hikers, summer strollers and nature lovers flock like bees to a honeypot.

Place des Terreaux (p229)

LYON

POP 487,980

Commercial, industrial and banking powerhouse for the past 500 years, today Lyon is France's third-largest city.

Outstanding museums, a dynamic cultural life, busy clubbing and drinking scene, thriving university and fantastic shopping lend the city a distinctly sophisticated air, while adventurous gourmets can indulge in their wildest gastronomic fantasies.

Sights

The excellent-value **Lyon City Card** (**www.en.lyon-france.com/Lyon-City-Card; 1/2/3 days adult €22/32/42, child €13.50/18.50/23.50**) offers free admission to every Lyon museum, the roof of Basilique Notre Dame de Fourvière, guided city tours, Guignol puppet shows and river excursions (April to October), along with numerous other discounts.

The card also includes unlimited city-wide transport on buses, trams, the funicular and metro. Full-price cards are available at the tourist office and some hotels, or save 10% by booking online and presenting your confirmation number at the tourist office.

VIEUX LYON

Lyon's Unesco-listed old town, with its narrow streets and medieval and Renaissance houses, is divided into three quarters: St-Paul (north), St-Jean (middle) and St-Georges (south).

Cathédrale St-Jean Cathedral
(**place St-Jean, 5e; 8.15am-7.45pm Mon-Fri, to 7pm Sat & Sun; M Vieux Lyon**) Lyon's partly Romanesque cathedral was built between

the late 11th and early 16th centuries. The portals of its Flamboyant Gothic facade, completed in 1480, are decorated with 280 square stone medallions. Inside, the highlight is the **astronomical clock** in the north transept. It was recently off-limits due to restoration work, but is expected to resume its regular daily chiming (at noon, 2pm, 3pm and 4pm) by the time you read this.

Medieval & Renaissance Architecture Architecture
(M Vieux Lyon) Lovely old buildings line rue du Bœuf, rue St-Jean and rue des Trois Maries. Crane your neck upwards to see gargoyles and other cheeky stone characters carved on window ledges along rue Juiverie, home to Lyon's Jewish community in the Middle Ages.

Musées Gadagne Museum
(www.museegadagne.com; 1 place du Petit Collège, 5e; 1 museum adult/child €6/free, both museums €8/free; 11am-6.30pm Wed-Sun; M Vieux Lyon) Housed in a 16th-century mansion built for two rich Florentine bankers, this twin-themed exhibition space incorporates an excellent local history museum (Musée d'Histoire de Lyon) chronicling the city's layout as its silk-weaving, cinema and transportation evolved, and an international puppet museum (Musée des Marionettes du Monde) paying homage to Lyon's iconic puppet, Guignol. On the 4th floor, a cafe adjoins tranquil, terraced gardens, here since the 14th century.

PRESQU'ÎLE

Lyon's city centre lies on this 500m- to 800m-wide peninsula bounded by the rivers Rhône and Saône.

Musée des Beaux-Arts Art Museum
(www.mba-lyon.fr; 20 place des Terreaux, 1er; adult/child incl audioguide €7/free; 10am-6pm Wed, Thu & Sat-Mon, 10.30am-6pm Fri; M Hôtel de Ville) This stunning and eminently manageable museum showcases France's finest collection of sculptures and paintings outside of Paris from antiquity onwards. Highlights include works by Rodin, Rubens, Rembrandt, Monet, Matisse and Picasso. Pick up a free audioguide and be sure to stop for a drink or meal on the delightful stone terrace off its cafe-restaurant or take time out in its tranquil cloister garden.

Place des Terreaux Square
(M Hôtel de Ville) The centrepiece of the Presqu'île's beautiful central square is a 19th-century **fountain** made of 21 tonnes of lead and sculpted by Frédéric-Auguste Bartholdi (of *Statue of Liberty* fame). The four horses pulling the chariot symbolise rivers galloping seawards.

The **Hôtel de Ville** (Town Hall; Place des Terreaux; M Hôtel de Ville) fronting the square was built in 1655 but was given its present ornate facade in 1702. When Daniel Buren's polka-dot 'forest' of 69 **granite fountains** (embedded in the ground across much of the square) are on, join the kids in a mad dash as the water dances up, down, disappears for a second and gushes back again.

Opéra de Lyon Opera House
(M Hôtel de Ville) Lyon's neoclassical 1831-built opera house was modernised in 1993 by renowned French architect Jean Nouvel, who added the striking semi-cylindrical glass-domed roof. On its northern side, boarders and bladers buzz around the fountains of **place Louis Pradel**, surveyed by the **Homme de la Liberté** (Man of Freedom) on roller skates, sculpted from scrap metal by Marseille-born César.

Musée des Tissus Museum
(www.musee-des-tissus.com; 34 rue de la Charité, 2e; adult/child €10/7.50, after 4pm €8/5.50; 10am-5.30pm Tue-Sun; M Ampère) Extraordinary Lyonnais and international silks are showcased here. Ticket includes admission to the adjoining **Musée des Arts Décoratifs** (34 rue de la Charité, 2e; free with Musée des Tissus ticket; 10am-noon & 2-5.30pm Tue-Sun), which displays 18th-century furniture, tapestries, wallpaper, ceramics and silver.

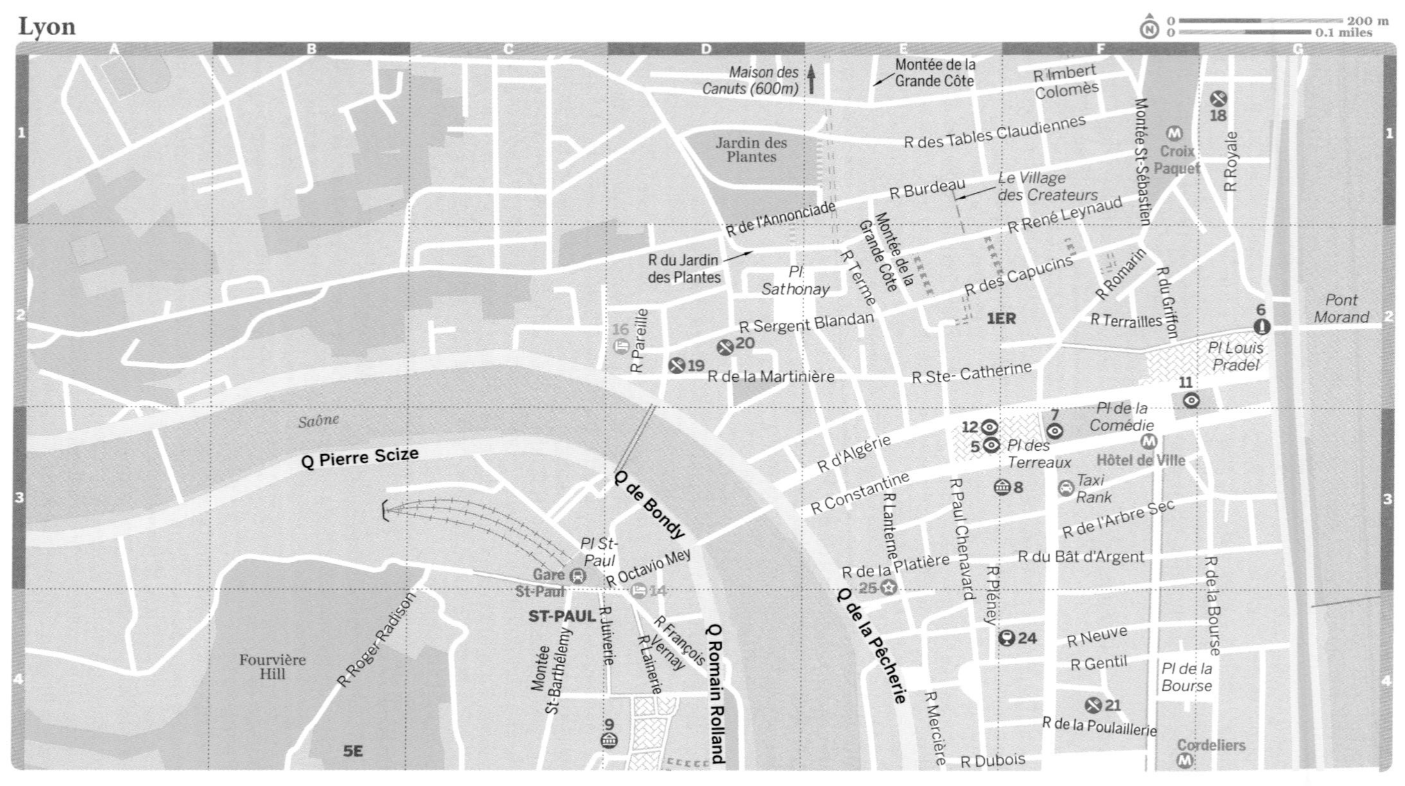
Lyon
0 200 m
0 0.1 miles
Maison des Canuts (600m)
Montée de la Grande Côte
R Imbert Colomès
R des Tables Claudiennes
Jardin des Plantes
Montée St-Sébastien
Croix Paquet
R Royale
18
R Burdeau
Le Village des Createurs
R de l'Annonciade
R René Leynaud
R du Jardin des Plantes
Pl Sathonay
R Terme
Montée de la Grande Côte
R des Capucins
R Romarin
R du Griffon
R Terrailles
1ER
6
Pont Morand
Pl Louis Pradel
16
R Pareille
20
19
R Sergent Blandan
R de la Martinière
R Ste- Catherine
11
Saône
Q Pierre Scize
12
5
7
Pl de la Comédie
Pl des Terreaux
Hôtel de Ville
R d'Algérie
R Constantine
8
Taxi Rank
R de l'Arbre Sec
Q de Bondy
Pl St-Paul
R Octavio Mey
Gare St-Paul
14
ST-PAUL
R Lanterne
R Paul Chenavard
R du Bât d'Argent
R de la Platière
25
R Pléney
R de la Bourse
Q de la Pêcherie
24
R Neuve
R Gentil
Pl de la Bourse
21
R de la Poulaillerie
Cordeliers
R Mercière
R Dubois
Q Romain Rolland
R François Vernay
R Lainerie
R Juiverie
Montée St-Barthélemy
9
R Roger-Radisson
Fourvière Hill
5E
A
B
C
D
E
F
G
1
2
3
4

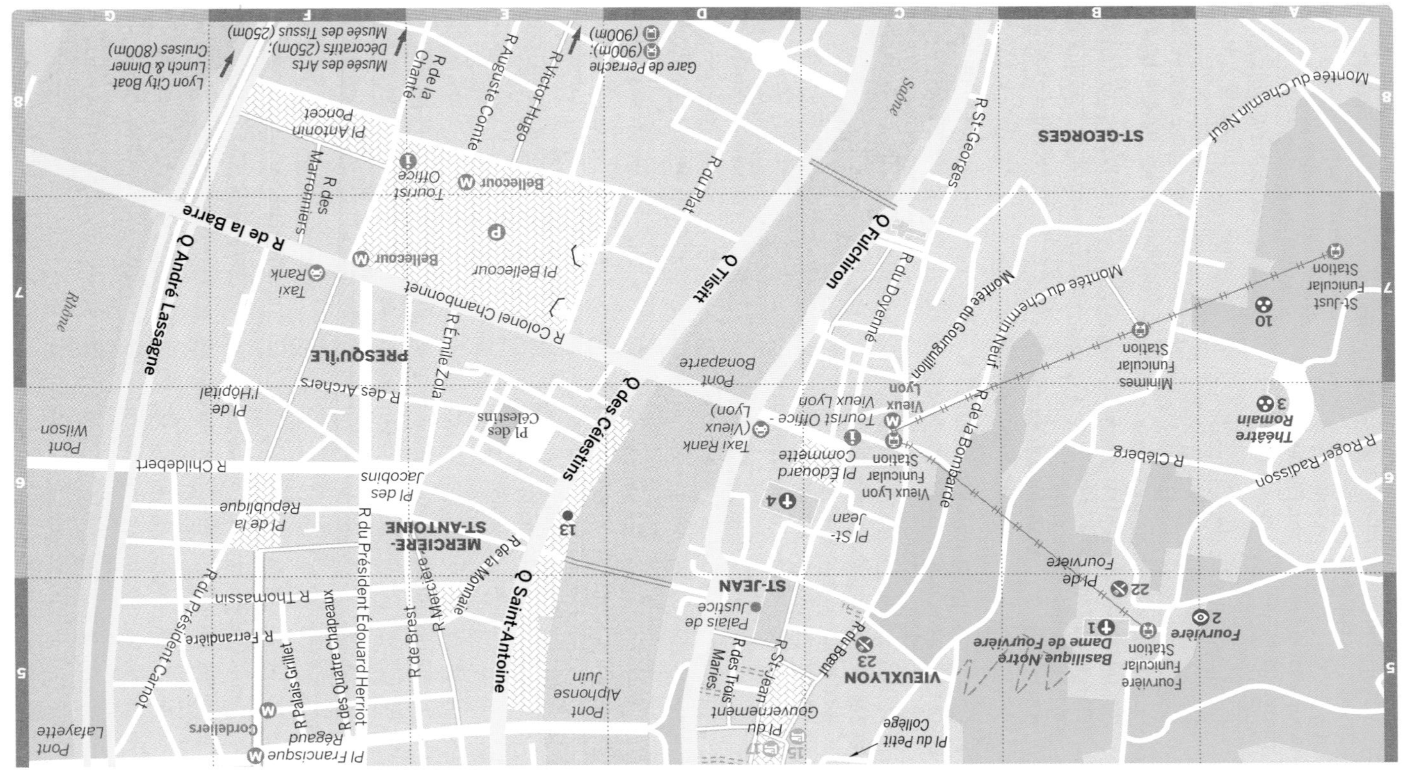
Pont Lafayette
Pont Wilson
Rhône
Saône
Lyon City Boat Lunch & Dinner Cruises (800m)
Musée des Arts Décoratifs (250m); Musée des Tissus (250m)
Gare de Perrache (900m); (900m)
Q André Lassagne
R de la Barre
R du Président Carnot
Pl Francisque Régaud
Cordeliers
R Palais Grillet
R des Quatre Chapeaux
R Ferrandière
R Thomassin
Pl de la République
R Childebert
Pl de l'Hôpital
R du Président Édouard Herriot
R de Brest
R Mercière
MERCIÈRE-ST-ANTOINE
R de la Monnaie
Q Saint-Antoine
Pl des Jacobins
R des Archers
PRESQU'ÎLE
Taxi Rank
R des Marronniers
Bellecour
Pl Antonin Poncet
Tourist Office
R de la Chanté
R Auguste Comte
R Victor Hugo
Pl Bellecour
R Colonel Chambonnet
R Émile Zola
Pl des Célestins
13
Q des Célestins
Pont Alphonse Juin
Q Tilsit
R du Plat
Pont Bonaparte
Q Fulchiron
R du Doyenné
R St-Georges
ST-GEORGES
Montée du Chemin Neuf
Montée du Gourguillon
R de la Bombarde
Taxi Rank (Vieux Lyon)
Tourist Office - Vieux Lyon
Vieux Lyon
Vieux Lyon Funicular Station
Pl Édouard Commette
Pl St-Jean
4
ST-JEAN
Palais de Justice
R des Trois Maries
R St-Jean
Pl du Gouvernement
15
17
Pl du Petit Collège
VIEUXLYON
23
R du Bœuf
Basilique Notre Dame de Fourvière
1
Pl de Fourvière
22
Fourvière Funicular Station
Fourvière
2
R Cléberg
Minimes Funicular Station
Théâtre Romain
3
10
St-Just Funicular Station
R Roger Radisson
A
B
C
D
E
F
G
5
6
7
8

Lyon

Don't Miss Sights
1 Basilique Notre Dame de Fourvière ... B5
2 Fourvière ... A5
3 Théâtre Romain ... A6

Sights
4 Cathédrale St-Jean ... D6
5 Fountain ... E3
6 Homme de la Liberté Statue ... G2
7 Hôtel de Ville ... F3
8 Musée des Beaux-Arts ... F3
9 Musées Gadagne ... D4
10 Odéon ... A7
11 Opéra de Lyon ... F2
12 Place des Terreaux ... E3

Activities, Courses & Tours
13 Lyon City Boat ... E6

Sleeping
14 Collège Hotel ... D4
15 Cour des Loges ... D5
16 Hôtel St-Vincent ... D2
17 Lyon Renaissance ... D5

Eating
18 La Mère Brazier ... G1
19 Le Bistrot du Potager ... D2
20 Le Bouchon des Filles ... D2
21 Le Musée ... F4
22 Le Restaurant de Fourvière ... B5
23 Les Adrets ... C5

Drinking & Nightlife
24 La Cave d'à Côté ... F4

Entertainment
25 Hot Club de Lyon ... E3
Opéra de Lyon ... (see 11)

LA CONFLUENCE

Meet Lyon's newest neighbourhood: the **Confluence** (www.lyon-confluence.fr), where the Rhône and the Saône meet at Presqu'île's southern tip. This former industrial wasteland has recently been brought back to life by a multimillion-euro urban renewal project, recognised for its cutting-edge, environmentally sustainable design by the French government, the European Commission and the WWF.

In Phase One of the project, focused on the Saône riverbanks, dozens of architecturally audacious, energy-efficient buildings have sprung up, including the ambitious science-and-humanities museum, **Musée des Confluences** (www.museedesconfluences.fr; 28 Boulevard des Belges, 6e), housed in a futuristic steel-and-glass crystal at the meeting of the two rivers.

Phase Two of the Confluence project, to be initiated in 2015 by Swiss architects Herzog and de Meuron (of Tate Modern and Beijing Olympic Stadium fame), will make the new neighbourhood more liveable, adding a substantial residential and market district and linking the Confluence to the rest of Lyon with three new bridges.

CROIX ROUSSE

Independent until it became part of Lyon in 1852, and retaining its own distinct character with its bohemian inhabitants and lush outdoor food market, the hilltop quarter of Croix Rousse slinks north up the steep *pentes* (slopes).

Following the introduction of the mechanical Jacquard loom in 1805, Lyonnais *canuts* (silk weavers) built tens of thousands of workshops in the area, with large windows to let in light and hefty wood-beamed ceilings more than 4m high to accommodate the huge new machines. Most workshops are chic loft apartments today.

Maison des Canuts — Silk Workshop

(www.maisondescanuts.com; 10-12 rue d'Ivry, 4e; adult/child €6.50/3.50; 10am-6.30pm Mon-Sat, tours 11am & 3.30pm Mon-Sat; M Croix Rousse) On a 50-minute guided tour, learn about weavers' labour-intensive life and the industry's evolution, see manual looms in use and browse the silk boutique.

Atelier de Passementerie — Silk Workshop

(04 78 27 17 13; www.soierie-vivante.asso.fr; 21 rue Richan, 4e; guided tour adult/child €6/4, combined ticket with Atelier de Tissage €9/5; boutique 2-6.30pm Tue, 9am-noon & 2-6.30pm Wed-Sat, guided tours & demonstrations 2pm & 4pm Tue-Sat; M Croix Rousse) Preserved for posterity by the Soierie Vivante association, this silk trimmings workshop functioned until 1979, weaving braids and intricate pictures. Browse fabrics in the attached boutique (admission free), or learn the history of the looms and see them at work on a 30-minute afternoon tour.

IMAGEBROKER/ALAMY ©

Don't Miss Fourvière

Over two millennia ago, the Romans built the city of Lugdunum on the slopes of **Fourvière**. Today, Lyon's 'hill of prayer' – topped by a basilica and the Tour Métallique – affords spectacular views of the city and its two rivers. Footpaths wind uphill but the **funicular** departing from place Édouard Commette is the least taxing way up; use a metro ticket or buy a funicular ticket (one way €1.70).

Crowning the hill, with stunning city panoramas from its terrace, the **Basilique Notre Dame de Fourvière** is a superb example of late-19th-century French ecclesiastical architecture and is lined with intricate mosaics. One-hour discovery visits take in the main features of the basilica and crypt; 75-minute rooftop tours climax on the stone-sculpted roof.

Fourvière is also home to Lyon's Théatre Romain (Roman theatre), which was built around 15 BC and enlarged in AD 120, and sat an audience of 10,000.

NEED TO KNOW

Basilique Notre Dame de Fourvière (www.fourviere.org; place de Fourvière, 5e; rooftop tour adult/child €6/3; 🕒 8am-7pm; funicular Fourvière)

Théâtre Romain (rue Cléberg, 5e; funicular Fourvière or Minimes)

RIVE GAUCHE

Musée Lumière Museum

(www.institut-lumiere.org; 25 rue du Premier Film, 8e; adult/child €6.50/5.50; 🕒 10am-6.30pm Tue-Sun; Ⓜ Monplaisir-Lumière) Cinema's glorious beginnings are showcased at the art nouveau home of Antoine Lumière, who moved to Lyon with sons Auguste and Louis in 1870. The brothers shot the first reels of the world's first motion picture, *La Sortie des Usines Lumières*

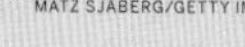

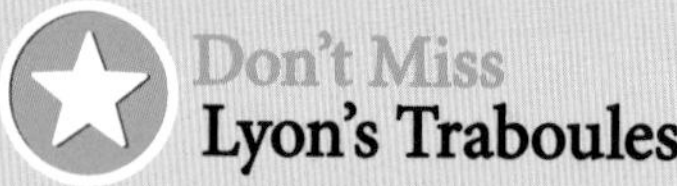

Don't Miss Lyon's Traboules

Deep within Vieux Lyon and Croix Rousse, dark, dingy *traboules* (secret passages) wind their way through apartment blocks, under streets and into courtyards. In all, 315 passages link 230 streets, with a combined length of 50km.

A couple of Vieux Lyon's *traboules* date from Roman times, but most were constructed by *canuts* (silk weavers) in the 19th century to transport silk in inclement weather. Resistance fighters found them equally handy during WWII.

Genuine *traboules* (derived from the Latin *trans ambulare,* meaning 'to pass through') cut from one street to another. Passages that fan out into a courtyard or cul-de-sac aren't *traboules* but *miraboules* (two of the finest examples are at 16 rue Boeuf and 8 rue Juiverie, both in Vieux Lyon).

Vieux Lyon's most celebrated *traboules* include those connecting 27 rue St-Jean with 6 rue des Trois Maries and 54 rue St-Jean with 27 rue du Bœuf (push the intercom button to buzz open the door).

Step into Croix Rousse's underworld at 9 place Colbert, crossing cour des Voraces – renowned for its monumental seven-storey staircase – to 14bis montée St Sébastien, and eventually emerging at 29 rue Imbert Colomès. From here a series of other *traboules* zigzags down the slope most of the way to Place des Terreaux.

For more detailed descriptions and maps of Lyon's *traboules,* visit www.lyontraboules.net or pick up a copy of the French-language guidebook *200 Cours et Traboules dans les Rues de Lyon* by Gérald Gambier (€9.95, available at Lyon's tourist office). The tourist office also includes *traboules* on many of its guided walking tours.

NEED TO KNOW

Traboules Guided Tours begin at 27 rue du Bœuf, push the intercom button to buzz open the door; adult/child/student €9/€5/ €5

(Exit of the Lumières Factories) here on 19 March 1895.

Parc de la Tête d'Or Park

(www.loisirs-parcdelatetedor.com; blvd des Belges, 6e; 6.30am-10.30pm mid-Apr–mid-Oct, to 8.30pm rest of year; C1, C5, M Masséna) Spanning 117 hectares, France's largest urban park was landscaped in the 1860s. It's graced by a lake (rent a row boat), botanic gardens with greenhouses, rose gardens, a zoo and a **puppet theatre** (Le Véritable Guignol du Parc; 04 78 93 71 75; www.theatre-guignol.com; place de Guignol). Take Bus C1 (from Part-Dieu train station) or Bus C5 (from Place Bellecour and Hôtel de Ville) to the Parc Tête d'Or-Churchill stop.

Tours

Walking Tours Walking Tour

(04 72 77 69 69; www.en.lyon-france.com/Guided-Tours-Excursions; adult/child €10/6) The tourist office organises a variety of excellent tours through Vieux Lyon and Croix Rousse with local English-speaking guides; tours of several additional city attractions, including the new Confluence neighbourhood, are available in French. Tours are free with a Lyon City Card; book in advance (online, by phone or in person at the tourist office).

Lyon City Boat Boat Tour

(Navig'inter; 04 78 42 96 81; www.lyoncity-boat.com; 2 quai des Célestins, 2e; river excursions adult/child €10/7; M Bellecour or Vieux Lyon) From April to October, river excursions depart from Lyon City Boat's dock along the Saône. One free excursion is included with the Lyon City Card. Advance bookings are essential for **lunch and dinner cruises** (23 quai Claude Bernard, 7e; 3hr lunch cruise €48-58, 6hr lunch cruise €54-63, 3hr dinner cruise €51-60; M Ampère or Guillotière, T1), which leave from a separate dock on the Rhône.

Le Grand Tour Bus Tour

(04 78 56 32 39; www.lyonlegrandtour.com; adult 1-/2-day ticket €19/22, child 1 or 2 days €8, Lyon by Night adult/child €15/8; 10am-6.15pm Apr-Oct, to 5.15pm Nov-Mar) Hop-on, hop-off double-decker bus tours. On Thursday and Saturday evenings from June to mid-September, a Lyon by Night tour is also offered at 9.30pm.

Sleeping

Hôtel St-Vincent Hotel €

(04 78 27 22 56; www.hotel-saintvincent.com; 9 rue Pareille; s/d €56/72; ; M Hôtel de Ville) High-beamed ceilings, giant-sized windows, a couple of old stone walls and original wooden floors give this three-floor, 32-room hotel atmosphere to spare. The location halfway between Hôtel de Ville and Vieux Lyon is another big plus.

Lyon Renaissance Apartment €€

(04 27 89 30 58; www.lyon-renaissance.com; 3 rue des Tourelles, 5e; apt €95-115; ; M Vieux Lyon) Friendly owners Françoise and Patrick rent these two superbly situated Vieux Lyon apartments with beamed ceilings and kitchen facilities. The smaller 3rd-floor walk-up sleeps two, with windows overlooking a pretty tree-shaded square. A second unit, opposite Vieux Lyon's most famous medieval tower, has a spacious living room with ornamental fireplace and fold-out couch, plus a mezzanine with double bed.

Collège Hotel Hotel €€

(04 72 10 05 05; www.college-hotel.com; 5 place St-Paul, 5e; d €130-160; @ ; M Vieux Lyon, Hôtel de Ville) With bright white, minimalist guestrooms and school-themed decor throughout, this four-star hotel is one of Vieux Lyon's more unique lodging options. Enjoy breakfast on your balcony, on the rooftop garden terrace, or in the *salle de classe petit dejeuner*, bedecked like a classroom of yesteryear.

Cour des Loges Hotel €€€

(04 72 77 44 44; www.courdesloges.com; 2-8 rue du Bœuf, 5e; d €190-485, junior ste €340-655; @ ; M Vieux Lyon) Four 14th- to 17th-century houses wrapped around a *traboule* (secret passage) with preserved features such as Italianate *loggias* make this an exquisite place to stay. Individually decorated rooms woo with designer

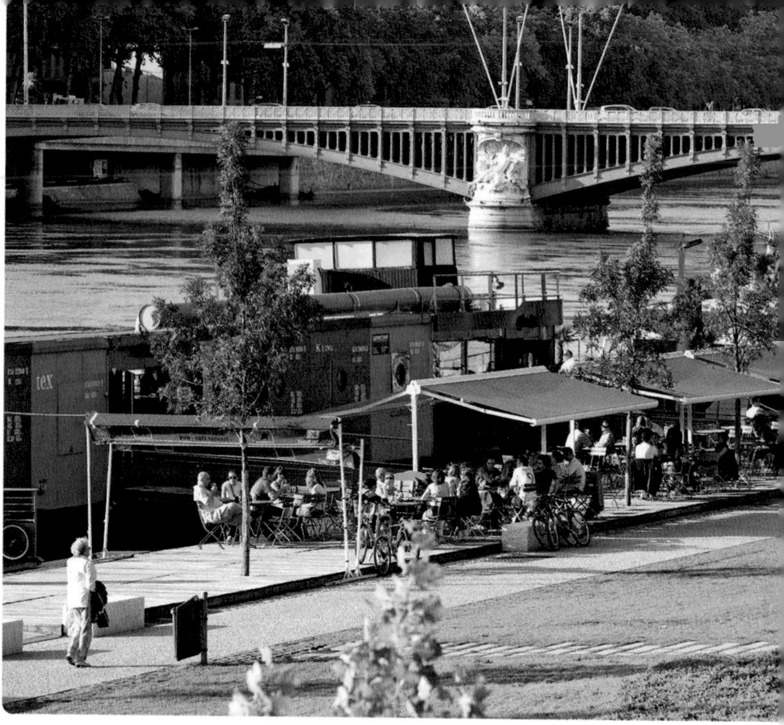

bathroom fittings and bountiful antiques, while decadent facilities include a spa, an elegant restaurant (menus €85 to €105), swish cafe (lunch menu €17.50, mains €22 to €30) and cross-vaulted bar.

 Eating

Cobbled rue Mercière, rue des Marronniers and the northern side of place Antonin Poncet – both in the 2e (M Bellecour) – are chock-a-block with eating options (of widely varying quality) overflowing with pavement terraces in summer. Near the opera house, rue Verdi (1er) is likewise table filled.

Le Musée — Bouchon €€

(**04 78 37 71 54; 2 rue des Forces; lunch/dinner menus €23/28; noon-2pm & 7.30-9.30pm Tue-Sat; M Cordeliers**) Housed in the stables of Lyon's former Hôtel de Ville, this delightful *bouchon* serves a splendid array of meat-heavy Lyonnais classics alongside veggie-centric treats such as roasted peppers with fresh goat cheese. The daily changing menu features 10 appetizers and 10 main dishes, plus five scrumptious desserts, all served on cute china plates at long family-style tables.

After dinner the gregarious owner offers history tours featuring the *traboule* out back.

Les Adrets — Lyonnais €€

(**04 78 38 24 30; 30 rue du Bœuf, 5e; lunch menu €17.50, dinner menus €27-45; noon-1.30pm & 7.45-9pm Mon-Fri; M Vieux Lyon**) This atmospheric spot serves an exceptionally good-value lunch *menu* (€17.50 including wine and coffee). The mix is half classic *bouchon* fare, half alternative choices such as Parma ham and truffle risotto, or duck breast with roasted pears.

Le Bouchon des Filles — Lyonnais €€

(**04 78 30 40 44; 20 rue Sergent Blandan, 1er; menus €25; 7-10pm Mon-Fri, noon-1.30pm & 7-10pm Sat & Sun; M Hôtel de Ville**) This contemporary ode to Lyon's legendary

Left: Quai Victor Augagneur (p238); **Below:** Opéra de Lyon (p238)

culinary *mères* (mothers) is run by an enterprising crew of young women with deep roots in the local *bouchon* scene and a flair for fine cooking. The light and fluffy *quenelles* are among the best you'll find in Lyon, and the rustic atmosphere is warm and welcoming, especially on Sundays when families flock in for lunch.

Le Bistrot du Potager Tapas **€€**

(☎ 04 78 29 61 59; www.lebistrotdupotager.com; 3 rue de la Martinière, 1er; tapas €6-15; ⏰ noon-2pm & 7.30-10pm Tue-Sat; Ⓜ Hôtel de Ville) An offshoot of the renowned Potager des Halles restaurant, this corner tapas bar is a dreamy spot to while away an evening. Happy diners throng the high-ceilinged main dining room, cozy upstairs balcony and sidewalk tables opposite the Fresque des Lyonnais, lingering over wine, Provençal-style beef tartare, grilled fish with tempura squash blossoms, or platters of cheeses and charcuterie.

Le Restaurant de Fourvière Lyonnais **€€**

(☎ 04 78 25 21 15; www.restaurant-fourviere.fr; 9 place de Fourvière, 5e; lunch menus €17, dinner menus €28-46; ⏰ noon-2.30pm & 7-10.30pm; funicular Fourvière) The views are so incredible that it'd be easy for this superbly located restaurant to be a tourist trap, so it's all the more impressive because it's not. Instead it concentrates on well-prepared local specialities including a stellar *salade lyonnaise* (lettuce, bacon, poached egg and croutons).

La Mère Brazier Gastronomic **€€€**

(☎ 04 78 23 17 20; www.lamerebrazier.fr; 12 rue Royale; lunch menus €57-70, dinner menus €70-140; ⏰ noon-1.30pm & 7.45-9.15pm Mon-Fri Sep-Jul; Ⓜ Croix Paquet) Chef Mathieu Vianney has reinvented the mythical early-20th-century restaurant that earned Mère Eugénie Brazier Lyon's first

Detour: Pérouges

French film buffs will recognise photogenic Pérouges. Situated on a hill 30km northeast of Lyon, this enchanting yellow-stone medieval village has long been used as a set for films like *Les Trois Mousquetaires* (the *Three Musketeers*). Brave the summertime crowds and stroll Pérouges' uneven cobbled alleys, admire its half-timbered stone houses and 1792-planted **liberty tree** on place de la Halle, then wolf down some *galettes de Pérouges* (warm, thin-pizza-crust-style, sugar-crusted tarts) with cider.

To appreciate Pérouges' charm after the day trippers have left, book a romantic room (try for one with a canopied bed) at the historic **Hostellerie de Pérouges** (04 74 61 00 88; www.hostelleriedeperouges.com; place du Tilleul; s €98-147, d €136-257).

Pérouges' tiny **tourist office** (04 74 46 70 84; www.perouges.org; 9 route de la Cité; 10am-5pm May-Aug, reduced hours Sep-Apr) is on the main road opposite the village entrance.

Cars Philibert (04 78 98 56 00; www.philibert-transport.fr) bus 132 (€2, one hour) runs two to eight times daily from central Lyon to the Pérouges turnoff on route D4 (a 15-minute walk from the village).

trio of Michelin stars in 1933 (a copy of the original guidebook takes pride of place). Vianney is doing admirable justice to Brazier's legacy, claiming two Michelin stars himself for his assured cuisine accompanied by an impressive wine list.

Drinking & Entertainment

Along the Rhône's left bank, a string of *péniches* (barges) with onboard bars rock until around 3am. Depending on the season you'll find upwards of a dozen moored along quai Victor Augagneur between Pont Lafayette in the north and Pont de la Guillotière in the south. Many have DJs and/or live bands.

La Cave d'à Côté Wine Bar
(04 78 28 31 46; 7 rue Pleney, 1er; 11.30am-2pm & 6.30pm-late Mon-Sat; M Cordeliers) Hidden in a tiny alleyway, this cultured bar and wine shop feels like a rustic English gentlemen's club with leather sofa seating and library.

Hot Club de Lyon Live Music
(www.hotclubdelyon.org; 26 rue Lanterne, 1er; 6.30pm-late Tue-Sat; M Hôtel de Ville) Lyon's leading jazz club, around since 1948. Main acts take the stage at 9.30pm.

Opéra de Lyon Opera House
(www.opera-lyon.com; place de la Comédie, 1er; M Hôtel de Ville) Lyon's premier venue for opera, ballet and classical music.

Information

Tourist Office (04 72 77 69 69; www.lyon-france.com; place Bellecour, 2e; 9am-6pm; M Bellecour) In the centre of Presqu'île, Lyon's exceptionally helpful, multilingual and well-staffed main tourist office offers a variety of city walking tours and sells the Lyon City Card. There's a smaller **branch** (Av du Doyenné, 5e; 10am-5.30pm; M Vieux Lyon) just outside the Vieux Lyon metro station.

Getting There & Away

Air

Lyon-St-Exupéry Airport (www.lyonaeroports.com) Located 25km east of the city, with 40 airlines (including many budget carriers) serving over 100 direct destinations across Europe and beyond.

Train

Lyon has two main-line train stations: Gare de la Part-Dieu (M Part-Dieu), 1.5km east of the Rhône, and Gare de Perrache (M Perrache). Some local trains stop at Gare St-Paul (M Vieux Lyon), and Gare Jean Macé (M Jean Mace). There's also a TGV station at Lyon-St-Exupéry Airport. Buy tickets at the stations or at the SNCF Boutique (2 place Bellecour; M Bellecour) downtown.

Destinations by direct TGV include the following:

Dijon €36, 1½ hours, at least six daily

Lille-Europe €113, three hours, at least eight daily

Marseille €52, 1¾ hours, every 30 to 60 minutes

Paris Charles de Gaulle Airport €95, two hours, at least 11 daily

Paris Gare de Lyon €73, two hours, every 30 to 60 minutes

Getting Around

To/From the Airport

The Rhônexpress (www.rhonexpress.fr; adult/youth/child €15.70/13/free) tramway links the airport with the Part-Dieu train station in under 30 minutes. It's a five- to 10-minute walk from the arrivals hall; follow the red signs with the Rhônexpress train logo. Trams depart every 15 minutes between 6am and 9pm, less frequently from 4.25am to 6am and 9pm to midnight. Online purchases and round-trip travel qualify for discounts.

By taxi, the 30- to 45-minute trip between the airport and the city centre costs around €50 during the day and €65 between 7pm and 7am.

Public Transport

Buses, trams, a four-line metro and two funiculars linking Vieux Lyon to Fourvière and St-Just are operated by TCL (www.tcl.fr). Public transport runs from around 5am to midnight.

Tickets valid for all forms of public transport cost €1.70 (€15.10 for a *carnet* of 10) and are available from bus and tram drivers as well as machines at metro entrances. Tickets allowing two consecutive hours of travel after 9am or unlimited travel after 7pm cost €2.80, and an all-day ticket costs €5.20. Bring coins as machines don't accept notes (or some international credit

Pérouges

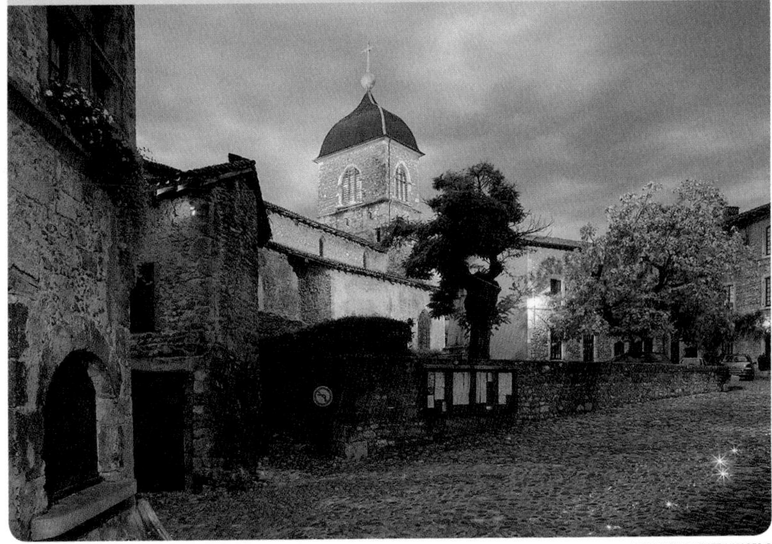

MAREMAGNUM/GETTY IMAGES ©

cards). Time-stamp tickets on all forms of public transport or risk a fine.

Holders of the Lyon City Card (p228) receive free unlimited access to Lyon's transport network for the duration of the card's validity (one, two or three days).

THE FRENCH ALPS

The French Alps are a place of boundless natural beauty. We could rhapsodise about colossal peaks, wondrous white glaciers and sapphire lakes, but seeing really is believing when it comes to Europe's Alpine heartland. Schussing down slopes with Mont Blanc hogging the horizon, driving roller coaster roads up to middle-of-nowhere Alpine passes, hiking to summits where mountain huts perch like eyries: this region will elevate you, make your heart pound and leave you crying 'encore!' like few other places on earth.

Chamonix

POP 9378 / ELEV 1037M

With the pearly white peaks of the Mont Blanc massif as its sensational backdrop, being an icon comes naturally to Chamonix. First 'discovered' by Brits William Windham and Richard Pococke in 1741, this is the mecca of mountaineering, its birthplace, its flag-bearer. It is also a wintertime playground of epic proportions that entices Olympic champions and hard-core skiers to its pistes, and party-mad boarders to its boot-stompin' bars.

Sights

Le Brévent Viewpoint

The highest peak on the western side of the Chamonix Valley, Le Brévent (2525m) has tremendous views of the Mont Blanc massif, myriad hiking trails, ledges to paraglide from and the summit restaurant **Le Panoramic**. Reach it on the **Télécabine de Planpraz** (www.compagniedu-montblanc.fr; adult/child one way €13.20/11.20, round trip €16/13.60), 400m west of the tourist office, and then the **Téléphérique du Brévent** (www.compagniedumontblanc.co.uk; 29 rte Henriette d'Angeville; adult/child one-way €22/18.70, return €29.50/25; mid-Dec–mid-Apr & mid-Jun–mid-Sep). Plenty of family-friendly trails begin at **Planpraz** (2000m).

Mer de Glace

Mer de Glace — Glacier

France's largest glacier, the glistening 200m-deep Mer de Glace (Sea of Ice) snakes 7km down on the northern side of Mont Blanc, moving up to 1cm an hour (about 90m a year). The **Train du Montenvers** (www.compagniedumontblanc.co.uk; adult/child one-way €24/20.40, return €29.50/25; closed late Sep–mid-Oct), a picturesque, 5km-long cog railway opened in 1909, links Chamonix' Gare du Montenvers with Montenvers (1913m), from where a cable car takes you down to the glacier and the **Grotte de la Mer de Glace** (closed last half of May & late Sep–mid-Oct), an ice cave whose frozen tunnels and ice sculptures change colour like mood rings.

Activities

Maison de la Montagne — Outdoor Activities

(190 place de l'Église; 8.30am-noon & 3-7pm) Get the **Mont Blanc** lowdown here, opposite the tourist office. Inside is the highly regarded **Compagnie des Guides de Chamonix** (04 50 53 00 88; www.chamonix-guides.com 8.30am-noon & 2.30-7.30pm, closed Sun & Mon late Apr–mid-Jun & mid-Sep–mid-Dec); the **École de Ski Français** (ESF; 04 50 53 22 57; www.esfchamonix.com); and the **Office de Haute Montagne** (OHM; 04 50 53 22 08; www.ohm-chamonix.com), which has information on trails, hiking conditions, weather forecasts and *refuges*, and topo-guides and maps that are free to consult.

WINTER

La Vallée Blanche — Skiing

(guided trip for group of 4 €305) This legendary descent – a jaw-dropping 2800 vertical metres – is the off-piste ride of a lifetime. Beginning at the Aiguille du Midi, zipping over the crevasse-riddled Mer de Glace glacier and returning to Chamonix through the forest, it can only be tackled with a *guide de haute montagne* (specially trained mountain guide). Skiers should be red-piste level and in reasonable physical shape; off-piste experience is a plus. Snow conditions are generally best in February and March, and sometimes into April.

Local Knowledge

Chamonix Don't Miss List

BY ERIC FAVRET, MOUNTAIN GUIDE, COMPAGNIE DES GUIDES DE CHAMONIX

1 SKIING IN GRANDS MONTET

Chamonix has six main ski areas. Grands Montet is particularly heavenly, with long off-piste glacial runs, easily accessible from lifts and offering over 6000ft of vertical drop!

2 AIGUILLE DU MIDI

The Aiguille du Midi, with one of the highest cable cars in the world, cannot be missed. Beyond the summit ridge is a world of snow and ice offering some of the greatest intermediate off-piste terrain in the Alps.

3 OFF-PISTE THRILLS

The Vallée Blanche has to be seen. But the Aiguille du Midi also has amazing off-piste runs, such as Envers du Plan, a slightly steeper and more advanced version of Vallée Blanche, offering dramatic views in the heart of the Mont-Blanc range. There is also the less-frequented run of the 'Virgin' or 'Black Needle', offering different views and a close-up look at the Giant's seracs.

4 SUMMER HIKES ON MONT BUET

Mont Buet is a favourite. It is a summit in itself and offers outstanding 360-degree panoramas over the Mont Blanc massif and its surrounding range. It requires a good level of fitness to do in a day, but there is a hut to split the trip into two days, which also takes you into a wildlife sanctuary.

5 BEST-EVER MONT BLANC VIEW

The Traverse from Col des Montets to Lac Blanc. It's as popular as the Eiffel Tower for hikers in summer. I love swimming in mountain lakes, so I stop at Lac des Chéserys, just below: what's better than a swim while looking at Mont Blanc, the Grandes Jorasses and Aiguille Verte?

WWW.TONNAJA.COM/GETTY IMAGES ©

Don't Miss

Aiguille du Midi

A jagged finger of rock soaring above glaciers, snowfields and rocky crags, 8km from the hump of Mont Blanc, the Aiguille du Midi (3842m) is one of Chamonix' most distinctive geographical features. If you can handle the altitude, the 360-degree views of the French, Swiss and Italian Alps from the summit are (quite literally) breathtaking. Year-round, you can float in a cable car from Chamonix to the Aiguille du Midi on the vertiginous Téléphérique de l'Aiguille du Midi.

From the Aiguille du Midi, between mid-June and August, you can continue for a further 30 minutes of mind-blowing scenery – think glaciers and spurs, seracs and shimmering ice fields – in the smaller bubbles of the Télécabine Panoramique Mont Blanc to Pointe Helbronner (3466m) on the French–Italian border. A new cable car from there to the Val d'Aosta ski resort of Courmayeur, on the Italian side of Monte Bianco, is set to open in 2015.

NEED TO KNOW

Téléphérique de l'Aiguille du Midi (www.compagniedumontblanc.co.uk; place de l'Aiguille du Midi; adult/child return to Aiguille du Midi €55/47, to Plan de l'Aiguille summer €29.50/25, winter €16/14; ⌚ 1st ascent btwn 7.10am & 8.30am, last ascent btwn 3.30pm & 5pm)

Télécabine Panoramique Mont Blanc (adult/child return from Chamonix €80/68; ⌚ last departure from Aiguille du Midi 2.30pm)

SUMMER

Grand Balcon Sud Trail — Walking

This easygoing trail, linking **Col des Montets** (12km northeast of Chamonix) with **Les Houches** (8km southwest of Chamonix), skirts the western side of the valley at an altitude of around 2000m, commanding terrific views across the valley to Mont Blanc. To avoid hoofing it 900m up the slope, take **Téléphérique de la Flégère** (www.compagniedumontblanc.fr; adult/child from Les Praz €13.20/11.20) from Les Praz or Télécabine de Planpraz (p240) from Chamonix; walking between the two takes about two hours. A variety of other great trails begin at the top of both these lifts.

Lac Blanc Hike — Walking

From the top of **Télésiège de l'Index** (www.compagniedumontblanc.fr; adult/child one way from Les Praz €22/18.70), a gentle 1¼- to two-hour trail leads along the valley's western flank to turquoise **Lac Blanc** (literally 'White Lake'; 2352m) and its breathtaking scenery. You can also hike from the top of Téléphérique de la Flégère but the trail, while wider, involves more of an ascent. Another option: hike up (1050 vertical metres!) from Argentière (3½ hours one way). Reserve ahead to overnight at the **Refuge du Lac Blanc** (☎04 50 53 49 14; refugedulacblanc@gmail.com; dm incl half board €50; ⏲ mid-Jun–Sep), a wooden chalet famed for its top-of-Europe Mont Blanc views.

Cycling Trails — Cycling

Lower-altitude trails such as the Petit Balcon Sud from Argentière to Servoz are perfect for biking. Most outdoor-activity specialists arrange guided mountain-biking expeditions.

Paragliding — Paragliding

Come summer, the sky above Chamonix is speckled with colourful paragliders wheeling down from the heights. Tandem flights from Planpraz (2000m) cost €100 per adult or child; from the Aiguille du Midi, count on paying €220. Paragliding schools include **Summits** (☎04 50 53 50 14; www.summits.fr; 81 rue Joseph Vallot) and **AirSports Chamonix** (☎06 76 90 03 70; www.airsportschamonix.fr; 24 ave de la Plage); contact them ahead for details on meeting points.

Sleeping

Auberge du Manoir — Hotel €€

(☎ 04 50 53 10 77; www.aubergedumanoir.com; 8 rte du Bouchet; s/d/tr €130/150/220; ⏲ closed 2 wks in late Apr & 2 wks in autumn; 📶 👪) This beautifully converted farmhouse, ablaze with geraniums in summer, offers 18 pine-panelled rooms that are quaint but never cloying, pristine mountain views, an outdoor hot tub, a sauna and a bar whose open fire keeps things cosy. Family-owned.

A paraglider near Mont Blanc

Hotel L'Oustalet Hotel €€

(04 50 55 54 99; www.hotel-oustalet.com; 330 rue du Lyret; d/q €148/190; closed mid-May–mid-Jun & mid-Oct–mid-Dec;) A block from the Aiguille du Midi cable car, this lift-equipped hotel has 15 decent rooms, snugly built of thick pine, that open onto balconies with Mont Blanc views. To unwind, you can curl up by the fire with a *chocolat chaud* or loll about in the Jacuzzi, hamam or sauna – or, in summer, take a dip in the garden pool.

Hôtel Aiguille du Midi Hotel €€

(04 50 53 00 65; www.hotel-aiguilledumidi.com; 479 chemin Napoléon, Les Bossons; d €75-160, incl half board €146-236; closed Oct–mid-Dec & early Apr–mid-May;) Run by the same family for five generations (since 1908), this welcoming hotel affords some of the valley's finest views of the Aiguille du Midi and Mont Blanc. The 39 pine-panelled rooms are comfortable and cosy. Summer amenities include an outdoor heated pool and a clay tennis court. For travel to/from Chamonix, there are bus and train stops right around the corner.

Hôtel Faucigny Boutique Hotel €€€

(04 50 53 01 17; www.hotelfaucigny-chamonix.com; 118 place de l'Église; s/d/q €200/250/350; closed 2 wks in May & 2 wks in Nov;) A delicious slice of minimalist Alpine cool, with 28 rooms, shiny and tasteful, accented by touches of crimson. Also has afternoon tea, a mini-spa and a summer terrace with Mont Blanc views.

Eating

Le Cap Horn French €€

(04 50 21 80 80; www.caphorn-chamonix.com; 78 rue des Moulins; lunch menu €20, other menus €29-39; noon-1.30pm or 2pm & 7-9pm or 10pm daily year-round) Housed in a gorgeous, two-storey chalet decorated with model sailboats – joint homage to the Alps and Cape Horn – this highly praised restaurant, opened in 2012, serves French and Asian-inflected dishes such pan-seared duck breast with honey and soy sauce, fisherman's stew and, for dessert, *soufflet au Grand Marnier*. Reserve for dinner Friday and Saturday in winter and summer.

Le Cap Horn

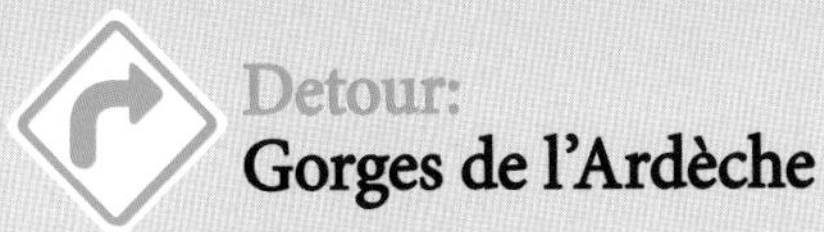

Detour: Gorges de l'Ardèche

The Ardèche River slithers between mauve, yellow and grey limestone cliffs from near **Vallon Pont d'Arc** (population 2420) to **St-Martin de l'Ardèche** (population 910), a few kilometres west of the Rhône. En route, it passes beneath the **Pont d'Arc**, a natural stone bridge created by the river's torrents. The river forms the centrepiece of the 1575-hectare **Réserve Naturelle des Gorges de l'Ardèche** (www.gorgesdelardeche.fr/reserve-naturelle.php). Eagles nest in the cliffs and there are numerous caves to explore.

Souvenir-shop-filled Vallon Pont d'Arc is the area's main hub; its **tourist office** (04 75 88 04 01; www.vallon-pont-darc.com; 1 place de l'Ancienne Gare; 9am-12.30pm & 2-6pm Mon-Fri, to 5pm Sat, 9am-1pm Sun;) is in the village centre. The scenic D579 out along the gorges is lined by campgrounds and canoeing rental outlets, including the **Base Nautique du Pont d'Arc** (04 75 37 17 79; www.canoe-ardeche.com; rte des Gorges de l'Ardèche; per adult/child half-day €17/12, full day €27/18, 2-day €40/27; Apr-Nov). A half-day descent (8km) starts from €16/11 per adult/child (minimum age is seven).

About 300m above the gorge's waters, the **Haute Corniche** (D290) has a dizzying series of *belvédères* (panoramic viewpoints). About halfway between St-Martin and Vallon Pont d'Arc, the **Maison de la Réserve** (04 75 98 77 31; www.gorgesdelardeche.fr; D290; 10am-5pm mid-Mar–mid-Nov) provides information on local flora, fauna and recreational opportunities. A further 2km west along the D290 is the trailhead for the **Sentier Aval des Gorges**, which descends 2km to the river, then follows the gorge for another 10km.

La Petite Kitchen International €€
(04 50 54 37 44; www.lapetitekitchen.fr; 80 place du Poilu; lunch/dinner menus €14/39; 11am-2.30pm & 7-11pm, closed dinner Oct, Nov & May) The little kitchen is just that: a handful of tables for the lucky few. Steaks with homemade *frites* and hot fudge will send you rolling happily out the door.

Le Bistrot Modern French €€€
(04 50 53 57 64; www.lebistrotchamonix.com; 151 av de l'Aiguille du Midi; lunch menu €20, other menus €55-85; noon-1.30pm & 7-9pm daily;) Sleek and hushed, this is a real gastronome's paradise. Michelin-starred chef Mickey experiments with textures and seasonal flavours to create taste sensations – specialities include roasted lamb with artichoke, roasted scallops with pan-fried foie gras and warm chocolate macarons with raspberry and red pepper coulis.

Drinking & Entertainment

Chambre Neuf Bar
(272 av Michel Croz; 7am-1pm daily year-round;) Chamonix' most spirited après-ski party (4pm to 8pm), fuelled by a Swedish band and dancing on the tables, spills out the front door of Chambre Neuf. Wildly popular with seasonal workers.

MBC Microbrewery
(Micro Brasserie de Chamonix; www.mbchx.com; 350 rte du Bouchet; 4pm-2am Mon-Thu, 10am-2am Fri-Sun) Run by four Canadians, this trendy microbrewery is fab. Be it with their phenomenal burgers (€10 to €15), cheesecake of the week, live music (Sunday from 9.30pm) or amazing beers, MBC delivers. Busiest from 5pm to 11pm.

If You Like... Epic Skiing

The French Alps is a land of infinite world-class pistes, of top-of-Europe elation. If you've caught the downhill bug in Chamonix, here's where else to go.

1 **TROIS VALLÉES**

Carve legendary slopes and party in the après-ski bars in the Three Valleys (elevation 1450-2300m; www.les3vallees.com), the world's largest ski area comprising **Val Thorens** (2300m), Europe's highest ski area; ever-so-British **Méribel** (1450m); and ritzy **Courchevel** (1550m to 1850m).

2 **VAL D'ISÈRE**

It's not just rollercoaster Olympic runs at Val d'Isère (1850m; www.valdisere.com). Equally known for its community spirit, this resort inspires everlasting love and loyalty. Along with nearby **Tignes** (elevation 2100m), it forms part of the **Espace Killy** skiing area.

3 **ALPE D'HUEZ**

Purpose-built Alpe d'Huez (1860m; www.alpedhuez.com) has 245km of groomed pistes, dead-easy to death-defying: 16km **La Sarenne** is Europe's longest black run.

4 **LES DEUX ALPES**

Year-round skiing on the **Glacier du Mont de Lans**, glorious powder, and a party atmosphere make Les Deux Alpes (1600m; www.les2alps.com) a resort with big air and big altitude. For the truly hardcore, there's the near-vertical **Vallons de la Meije** descent in La Grave, 21km east.

5 **LES PORTES DU SOLEIL**

'The Gates of the Sun' (1000-2466m; www.portesdusoleil.com) covers 12 villages along the French–Swiss border, including **Morzine** (1000m) with one of the most charming eat–sleep options in the Alps in the form of **The Farmhouse** (04 50 79 08 26; www.thefarmhouse.fr; Le Mas de la Coutettaz, Morzine; d incl half board €224-478; mid-Dec–mid-Apr & Jun–mid-Sep;); trendy and chic, car-free **Avoriaz** (1800m); and family-friendly, Brit-busy **Les Gets** (1172m).

Information

Tourist Office (04 50 53 00 24; www.chamonix.com; 85 place du Triangle de l'Amitié; 9am-12.30pm & 2-6pm, longer hours winter & summer) Information on accommodation, activities, the weather and cultural events.

Getting There & Away

Bus Chamonix' **bus station** (04 50 53 01 15; place de la Gare; 8-11.30am & 1.15-6.15pm in winter, shorter hours rest of year) is to the right as you exit the train station.

Geneva (airport and bus station) One-way/return €30/50, 1½ to two hours, three daily. Operated by **SAT-Mont Blanc** (04 50 78 05 33; www.sat-montblanc.com).

Courmayeur (Italy) One-way/return €14/22, 45 minutes, two to six daily. Run jointly by SAT-Mont Blanc and **Savda** (+39 01 65 36 70 32; www.savda.it), with onward connections to Aoste and Milan.

Train The scenic Mont Blanc Express glides from St-Gervais-Le Fayet, 23km west of Chamonix, to the Swiss town of Martigny (€24.70 from Chamonix). En route, it stops at stations such as Les Houches, Chamonix (€5.50 from St-Gervais, 45 minutes, hourly), Argentière and Vallorcine.

From St-Gervais-Le Fayet, there are infrequent trains to cities around France, often with a change in Bellegarde or Annecy.

Megève & St-Gervais

A Mont Blanc massif backdrop makes for fabulously scenic skiing and summertime hiking in très chic Megève (population 4076, elevation 1113m), a super-stylish ski village for beginner and cruisy intermediate skiers that was developed in the 1920s for Baroness de Rothschild (of the famous banking family). Almost too perfect to be true, the place is akin to a 3D postcard of horse-drawn sleighs and exquisitely arranged boutique windows spilling into cobbled, medieval-style streets.

Sitting snug below Mont Blanc, 24km west of Chamonix, neighbouring St-Gervais-les-Bains (population 5813, elevation 850m) is another picture-perfect Savoyard village with a baroque church and old-fashioned carousel. For spirit-soaring mountain views with zero effort, arrive here aboard the legendary **Mont Blanc Express** from Chamonix; or hop on France's highest train, the **Tramway du Mont Blanc** (www.compagniedumontblanc.fr; rue de la Gare, St-Gervais; return to Bellevue/Nid d'Aigle €29.50/35; ⌚ 4-6 departures daily mid-Dec-early Apr, hourly mid-Jun-early Sep), in St-Gervais-Le Fayet.

Information

Megève Tourist Office (☎04 50 21 27 28; www.megeve.com; 70 rue de Monseigneur Conseil; ⌚ 9am-12.30pm & 2-6.30pm Mon-Sat, also open Sun in high season)

St-Gervais-les-Bains tourist office (%04 50 47 76 08; www.saintgervais.com; 43 rue du Mont-Blanc; h 9am-noon & 2-6pm or later Mon-Sat, also open Sun in high season)

Getting There & Away

From Megève bus station, there are seven daily buses to/from St-Gervais-Le Fayet train station, the main train station for Chamonix: towns are linked by the Mont Blanc Express. Other services include several day trains to Paris (€97, 5½ hours), Lyon (€34, 3½ hours), Annecy (€14.50, 1½ hours) and Geneva (€13, 1½ hours).

Annecy

POP 52,161

Even Savoyards spoilt rotten with Alpine views every day of their lives grow wistful at the mention of Annecy. Why? Just look around you: the mountains rise steep, wooded and snow-capped above Lac d'Annecy, so startlingly turquoise it looks unreal; the Vieille Ville (Old Town) is a ludicrously pretty ensemble of pastel-daubed, geranium-strewn houses; the turreted castle – wait, even the old prison – ticks all the medieval-fantasy boxes.

Sights

Palais de l'Isle Museum

(musees.agglo-annecy.fr; 3 passage de l'Île; adult/child €3.70/1.70; ⌚ 10am-noon & 2-5pm Wed-Mon, no midday closure Jun-Sep) Sitting on a triangular islet surrounded by the Canal du Thiou, the whimsically turreted, 12th-century Palais de l'Isle has been a

Annecy

GRAHAM LAWRENCE/GETTY IMAGES ©

If You Like... Hiking in Alpine Heaven

Have those tantalising glimpses in Lyon of a snow-glittering Mont Blanc far on the horizon left you craving glaciated grandeur close up? Then dip into one of these spectacular national parks:

1 **PARC NATIONAL DE LA VANOISE**

(www.parcnational-vanoise.fr) Rugged snowcapped peaks, mirrorlike lakes and 53 sq km of glaciers characterise the 529-sq-km Parc National de la Vanoise, France's oldest national park. It's renowned for its rare wildlife, including marmots, chamois, bouquetins, bearded vultures and golden eagles.

2 **PARC NATUREL RÉGIONAL DU VERCORS**

The gently rolling pastures, plateaux and chiselled limestone peaks of this 1750-sq-km park are perfect for soft adventure, making it a real family favourite. You can cross-country ski, snowshoe, cave and hike. From **Lans-en-Vercors** (elevation 1020m), 28km southwest of Grenoble, buses shuttle downhill skiers to the **Montagnes de Lans** ski area, with 30km of pistes.

3 **PARC NATIONAL DES ÉCRINS**

(www.ecrins-parcnational.fr) France's second-largest national park (918 sq km), Parc National des Écrins stretches between the towns of Bourg d'Oisans, Briançon and Gap. Enclosed by steep, narrow valleys, the area was sculpted by the Romanche, Durance and Drac rivers and their erstwhile glaciers. Some 700km of footpaths criss-cross the park.

lordly residence, courthouse, mint and prison over the centuries. Today Annecy's most visible landmark hosts exhibits on local architecture and history.

Vieille Ville & Lakefront Historic Quarter

It's a pleasure simply to wander aimlessly around Annecy's medieval old town, a photogenic jumble of narrow pedestrian-only streets, crystal-clear canals – the reason Annecy is known as 'Venice of the Alps' – and colonnaded passageways.

On the tree-fringed lakefront, the flowery **Jardins de l'Europe** are linked to the grassy **Champ de Mars**, a popular picnic spot, by the poetic iron arch of the **Pont des Amours** (Lovers' Bridge).

Château d'Annecy Castle

(**musees.agglo-annecy.fr; rampe du Château; adult/child €5.20/2.60; 10am-noon & 2-5pm Wed-Mon Oct-May, 10.30am-6pm Jun-Sep**) Rising dramatically above the old town, this 13th- to 16th-century castle was once home to the Counts of Geneva. The exhibits inside are diverse, ranging from medieval sculpture and Savoyard furniture to Alpine landscape painting and contemporary art, with a section on the natural history of Lac d'Annecy. English signage is planned for 2015.

Tours

Compagnie des Bateaux Boat Tour

(**www.annecy-croisieres.com; 2 place aux Bois; 1hr lake cruises adult/child €14/9.50; mid-Feb–mid-Dec**) Runs boat excursions and, from mid-April to late September, cruises to villages around the lake. Also has romantic dinner cruises (€58.50).

Sleeping

Hôtel Alexandra Hotel €€

(**04 50 52 84 33; www.hotelannecy-alexandra.fr; 19 rue Vaugelas; s/d/tr/q €65/90/95/105;**) The 25 smallish rooms, each unique, are sparely furnished but they're soundproofed and spotless and the welcome here is warm. Six rooms have balconies and a couple come with canal views.

Splendid Hôtel Boutique Hotel €€

(**04 50 45 20 00; www.hotel-annecy-lac.fr; 4 quai Eustache Chappuis; s/d from €123/137;** @) This aptly named hotel, with green, breezy views of the adjacent

Champ de Mars, has 47 classy, contemporary rooms with parquet floors. It's geared up for families: whether you need an extra bed or a babysitter, the friendly staff will oblige.

Eating

L'Esquisse Gastronomic **€€**
(☎ 04 50 44 80 59; www.esquisse-annecy.fr; 21 rue Royale; lunch menu €23, other menus €31-60; ⌚ 12.15-1.15pm & 7.30-9pm, closed Wed & Sun) A talented husband-and-wife team runs the show at this intimate restaurant, with just seven tables. Their passion shines through in the service, wine list and carefully composed *menus* that sing with natural flavours, from wild mushrooms to – well, it depends on the season. Reserve ahead.

Le Denti French **€€**
(☎ 04 50 64 21 17; 25bis av de Loverchy; lunch menu €17, other menus €20-41; ⌚ noon-1.15pm & 7.30-9pm, closed Sun dinner, Tue & Wed) A few blocks off the beaten track but worth seeking out, this unassuming restaurant serves traditional French cuisine – their speciality is fish – prepared so the taste of the super-fresh ingredients shines through. The menu changes twice a month according to the seasonal produce available in the markets.

La Ciboulette Gastronomic **€€€**
(☎ 04 50 45 74 57; www.laciboulette-annecy.com; passage du Pré Carré; menus €36-70; ⌚ lunch & dinner Tue-Sat) Crisp white linen sets the scene at this elegant restaurant, where chef Georges Paccard prepares fresh seasonal specialities such as fillet of veal in a nut crust with cream of *vin jaune* (Jura wine). Reservations are highly recommended on weekends and for dinner. Situated down the alley from 8 rue Vaugelas.

Information

Tourist Office (☎ 04 50 45 00 33; www.lac-annecy.com; 1 rue Jean Jaurès, courtyard of Centre Bonlieu; ⌚ 9am-12.30pm & 1.45-6pm Mon-Sat year-round, 9am-12.30pm Sun Apr-early Oct & Dec, also open 1.45-6pm Sun mid-May–mid-Sep) Has free maps and brochures, and details on cultural activities all around the lake.

Getting There & Away

Direct services from Annecy's new **train station** (place de la Gare), opened in 2012, include:

Aix-les-Bains €8.10, 40 minutes, hourly

St-Gervais-Le-Fayet (for Chamonix) €15.30, 1½ hours, five daily Sunday to Friday, three Saturday

Lyon Part-Dieu €26 to €50, two hours, 13 daily Monday to Friday, eight daily Saturday and Sunday

Paris Gare de Lyon €80 to €101, 3¾ hours, four to seven daily

Bordeaux & French Basque Country

For wine aficionados, nowhere lights up the imagination quite like Bordeaux. For centuries this has been the undisputed heartland of French *viticulture* (winemaking), and the region is littered with some of the most illustrious names from the world of wine. But while the fruits of the vine are undoubtedly the main reason for a visit to the Bordeaux region, they're far from the only one.

South of Bordeaux, France's Atlantic Coast unfurls through a string of sandy beaches, sparkling bays and beautiful towns, all of which are worth a visit in their own right. There's Arcachon – famous for producing some of France's finest oysters – and Biarritz, a seaside getaway since the belle époque, now the centre of a thriving surf culture. And then there's the French Basque Country, a fiery and independent region that fizzes with a passion, energy and culture all of its own.

Vineyards in Bordeaux (p260)

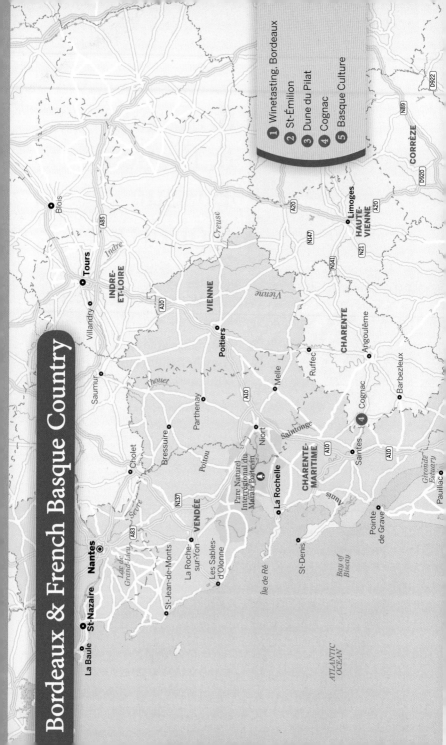

Bordeaux & French Basque Country

1 Winetasting, Bordeaux
2 St-Émilion
3 Dune du Pilat
4 Cognac
5 Basque Culture

Mouton Rothschild & Lafitte Rothschild
1
Bordeaux
1
2
St-Émilion
Perigueux
Isle
A89
DORDOGNE
Brive-la-Gaillarde
CANTAL
D940
N120
Aurillac
D936
Bergerac
Dordogne
N122
Arcachon
Cap Ferret
GIRONDE
Aquitaine
0 50 km
0 25 miles
3
Dune du Pilat
A62
N21
A20
LOT
Figeac
D921
Marmande
D991
Célé
Parc Naturel Régional Causses de Quercy
LOT-ET-GARONNE
Villeneuve-sur-Lot
Cahors
AVEYRON
Biscarro
Parc Naturel Régional des Landes de Cascogne
Rodez
Garonne
Agen
Sabres
N20
A70
D933
TARN-ET-GARONNE
N88
D964
D15
Lake de Léon
LANDES
Mont-de-Marsan
Seviac
Condom
A62
Montauban
Turn
Moliets
Leon
Tartas
Gaillac
Albi
Soustons
N21
A20
A88
TARN
N112
Hossegor
Seignosse
Adour
GERS
Aéroport Toulouse-Blagnac
Auch
Castres
Parc Naturel Régional du Haut-Languedoc
5
N124
Toulouse
Biarritz
Bayonne
A64
Armagnac
Save
N126
5
St-Jean de Luz
BAB Airport
Orthez
Ciboure
Ossau
Pau
Pau-Pyrénées Airport
Montagne Noir
San Sebastián
Espelette
Ainhoa
Pau
A64
Midi Pyrénées
A64
St-Jean Pied de Port
Arros
Carbonne
N113
Tarbes
Iparla
PYRÉNÉES-ATLANTIQUES
Aspe
Tarbes-Lourdes-Pyrénées Airport
Garonne
Lourdes
Vallée des Gaves
HAUTES-PYRÉNÉES
Montrejeau
Salat
Montagnes du Plantaurel
AUDE
Vallée d'Ossau
St-Savin
Vallée d'Azun
Pic du Midi
The Pyrénées
St-Girons
Artouste-Fabrèges
Cauterets
D117
Pamplona
Parc National des Pyrénées
St-Lary Soulan
ARIÈGE
Ussat-les-Bains
Ría Arga
SPAIN
Ariège
Perpignan

Bordeaux & French Basque Country's Highlights

Bordeaux Winetasting

Rivalled only by Burgundy, Bordeaux (p260) is home to the most prestigious names in French wine: Margaux, Lafite-Rothschild, Pauillac, Pétrus, Cheval Blanc and many more. Touring the vineyards (p267) – either on a guided tour or under your own steam – is guaranteed to be one of your most memorable French experiences. Below: L'Intendant wine shop, Bordeaux

1

2 St-Émilion

Perched on a limestone ridge 40km east of Bordeaux, the honey-hued town of St-Émilion (p268) is a must for wine connoisseurs. Surrounded by vines as far as the eye can see, it's also home to some of France's most hallowed châteaux – so it's a fantastic place to sample or buy wines. But don't forget to leave time for a tour into the murky catacombs beneath the town's cathedral.

GERARD LABRIET/GETTY IMAGES ©

3 Dune du Pilat

This colossal sand dune (p266) stretches for almost 3km to the south of Arcachon and is still spreading eastwards at up to 4.5m a year (swallowing trees, roads and even a hotel in the process). Hum the theme tune from *Lawrence of Arabia* as you scale it for a memorable panorama over the Bassin d'Arcachon – it's the closest you'll get to the Sahara without leaving Europe.

DIRECTPHOTO/GETTY IMAGES ©

4 Cognac

While Bordeaux is mainly known for its fine wines, it's not the region's only alcoholic tipple. The double-distilled spirit cognac (p269) is produced according to a strict set of rules that have remained largely unchanged for the last three centuries. You can quaff it in musty cellars all around town, but at a minimum of 40% proof, you'll definitely need to name a designated driver... Above: Cognac barrels, Otard (p270)

5 Basque Culture

A passion for bullfighting, *pelota* (ball games), peppers and spicy ham make the French Basque Country (p271) feel closer to Spain than to the rest of France. Governed by its own culture, costumes and language, it's a region in its own right. The lively towns of Bayonne and St-Jean de Luz both make great bases for further exploration, situated within easy reach of the sparkling beaches of Biarritz. Above: Men in traditional Basque outfits

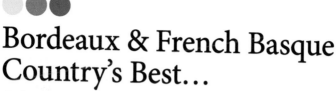

Bordeaux & French Basque Country's Best...

Culinary Shopping

- **La Winery** Groundbreaking winery with 1000 different Bordeaux wines. (p265)
- **St-Émilion** With one wine shop for every eight residents, wine shopping in St-Émilion's a breeze. (p268)
- **Bayonne** Shop for Bayonne's famous ham. (p271)
- **Cognac** Superb brandy to take home. (p269)

Cultural Highs

- **Musée des Beaux-Arts, Bordeaux** Enjoy one of France's finest fine-art museums. (p261)
- **St-Émilion rooftops** Slog up the bell tower for views of this hilltop hamlet. (p268)
- **St-Jean Pied de Port** Mingle with pilgrims following the way of St James through France to Spain. (p279)
- **Musée Basque et de l'Histoire de Bayonne** Devour Basque history and culture. (p272)
- **Lourdes** Take an icy dip in a sacred bath. (p280)

Beach Retreats

- **Biarritz** A classic beach resort since the belle époque, now the top surfer choice. (p274)
- **Arcachon** Sandy beaches pepper the beautiful Bassin d'Arcachon. (p265)
- **Île de Ré** Beautiful beaches lace the southern coast of this irresistible island. (p272)
- **St-Jean de Luz & Ciboure** Kick back on the golden sands of these twin Basque towns. (p277)

Left: Biarritz (p274); **Above:** Sanctuaires Notre Dame de Lourdes (p280)

Seafood Dining

- **Marché des Capucins** Oysters and white wine = classic Bordeaux market experience. (p269)
- **La Boîte à Huîtres** Best place in Bordeaux for fresh Arcachon oysters and sausages. (p263)
- **Le Clos Basque** Taste Basque flavours in this renowned Biarritz address. (p276)
- **Grillerie du Port** Grilled fish caught that morning in St-Jean de Luz. (p278)
- **Bistrot de Claude** Heady mix of oysters, seafood and Cognac. (p271)

Need to Know

ADVANCE PLANNING

- **As early as possible** Book accommodation, particularly for Bayonne and Biarritz in July and August.
- **Two weeks before** Ask at the Bordeaux tourist office (p264) about the Bordeaux Box package, which includes accommodation, admissions, a city tour, a vineyard tour and a bottle of wine.
- **One week before** Book visits at Cognac houses (p270), Bordeaux vineyards (p267) and big-name restaurants.

RESOURCES

- **Loire Atlantique** (www.ohlaloireatlantique.com) General traveller info for the Loire Atlantique region.
- **Bordeaux** (www.bordeaux.com) Become a wine expert.
- **Cognac World** (www.cognac-world.com) For Cognac aficionados.
- **Tourisme Gironde** (www.tourisme-gironde.fr) Bordeaux, its vineyards and elsewhere in the Gironde region.

GETTING AROUND

- **Air** The region's main airports are in Bordeaux, Nantes, Biarritz-Anglet-Bayonne and Pau, all served by low-cost operators among others.
- **Train** Speedy TGVs serve Bordeaux, Biarritz and several other cities. Most smaller towns and villages can be reached via regional trains.
- **Car** Allows maximum freedom, but be careful not to overtipple if you're tasting wine or cognac.

BE FOREWARNED

- **St-Émilion** Wear flat comfy shoes: the village's steep, uneven streets are hard going.
- **Bassin d'Arcachon** Take care swimming in this area: powerful currents swirl out to sea from the deceptively tranquil *baïnes* (little bays).
- **Bordeaux wine châteaux** Generally close their doors during October's grape harvest.
- **Finding a hotel bed** Bayonne is tough from mid-July to mid-August and near impossible during the Fêtes de Bayonne.
- **Lourdes** So quiet in winter that most hotels shut down.

Bordeaux & French Basque Country Itineraries

The southwest is one of France's most popular regions. There's lots to pack in, but don't rush – life here cruises along at its own laid-back pace.

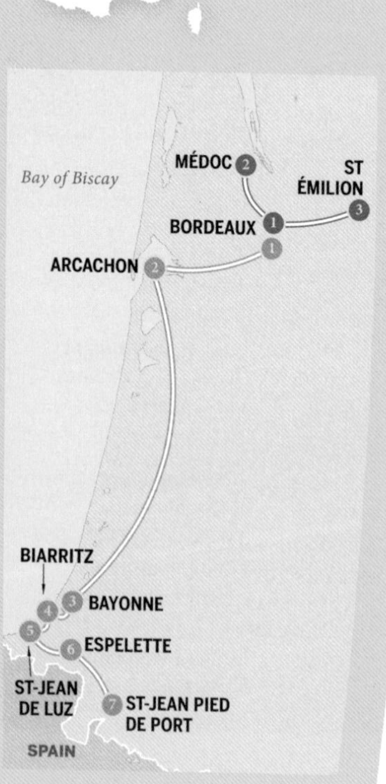

3 DAYS

BORDEAUX TO ST-ÉMILION

A VINTAGE TRIP

If you're going to get to grips with Bordeaux wine, there's only one place to start. ❶ **Bordeaux** is one of France's most impressive cities – in fact, Unesco has put most of it on the World Heritage list. Devote at least a day to sightseeing – don't miss the Cathédrale St-André and a climb up the Tour Pey-Berland, a visit to CAPC Musée d'Art Contemporain and a river cruise, followed by supper at Le Cheverus Café or La Tupina.

On day two take a guided tour of some of the region's celebrated vineyards, including the illustrious names of the ❷ **Médoc**. There will be plenty of opportunities to buy some bottles en route, or treat yourself to some serious wine and cheese over lunch at Bordeaux's Baud et Millet. Stay overnight in Bordeaux.

On day three travel east to beautiful ❸ **St-Émilion**. Perched on a limestone ridge surrounded by seemingly endless green vines, the town has umpteen wine shops and châteaux to visit. Don't miss a guided tour into the musty caverns hollowed out beneath the 11th-century Église Monolithe.

Top Left: St-Émilion (p268); **Top Right:** Bayonne (p271)

5 DAYS

BORDEAUX TO BIARRITZ

INTO THE BASQUE COUNTRY

After ❶ **Bordeaux**, it's time to head south into the fiery heartland of the French Basques. First stop is ❷ **Arcachon**, a popular seaside town that's famous for its oysters and the nearby, enormous sand dune, Dune du Pilat. If you have time, you won't regret a boat trip across the bay to the pretty peninsula of Cap Ferret.

Further south, the Basque Country begins in earnest at ❸ **Bayonne**, where you can watch a game of *pelota*, buy some delicious Basque ham, dine at a delightful riverside restaurant or gorge on *pintxo* (tapas).

On day three head to hip ❹ **Biarritz**, a quick trip from Bayonne, where you'll find fantastic beaches, a thriving surf culture and invigorating views of the coast from the Rocher de la Vierge. It's also a great place to try some classic Basque cuisine – for seafood by the water, ramshackle beach shack Casa Juan Pedro is the address.

On days four and five, make time for some beach-lounging in ❺ **St-Jean de Luz**, chilli-eating in ❻ **Espelette** and village-wandering in ❼ **St-Jean Pied de Port**. Got the Basque bug? Don't fret – the Spanish border's just 8km away...

Discover Bordeaux & French Basque Country

At a Glance

- **Atlantic Coast** (p260) From fine wine in Bordeaux to ritzy beaches in Biarritz.
- **French Basque Country** (p271) Straddling the Franco-Spanish border, this fiery region feels like another country.

Cathédrale St-André

ATLANTIC COAST

With quiet country roads winding through vine-striped hills and wild stretches of coastal sands interspersed with misty islands, the Atlantic coast is where France gets back to nature. Much more laid-back than the Med (but with almost as much sunshine), this is the place to slow the pace right down.

The one thing that unites the people of this area is a love of the finer things in life. The region's exceptional wine is famous worldwide, and to wash it down you'll find fresh-from-the-ocean seafood wherever you go and plenty of regional delicacies including crêpes in the north, snails in the centre and foie gras in the south.

Bordeaux

POP 240,500

The new millennium was a major turning point for the city long known as La Belle au Bois Dormant (Sleeping Beauty). The mayor, former Prime Minister Alain Juppé, roused Bordeaux, pedestrianising its boulevards, restoring its neoclassical architecture and implementing a high-tech public transport system. His efforts paid off: in mid-2007 half of the entire city (18 sq km, from the outer boulevards to the banks of the Garonne) was Unesco-listed, making it the largest urban World Heritage Site.

Sights & Activities

Cathédrale St-André Cathedral

(Place Jean Moulin) Lording over the city, and a Unesco World Heritage Site prior to the city's classification, the cathedral's oldest section dates from 1096; most of what you see today was built in the 13th and 14th centuries. Exceptional masonry carvings can be seen in the north portal.

Musée d'Aquitaine Museum

(www.musee-aquitaine-bordeaux.fr; 20 cours Pasteur; 11am-6pm Tue-Sun) FREE Gallo-Roman statues and relics dating back 25,000 years are among the highlights at the impressive Musée d'Aquitaine. Ask to borrow an English-language catalogue.

CAPC Musée d'Art Contemporain Gallery

(rue Ferrére, Entrepôt 7; temporary exhibitions adult/child €5/2.50; 11am-6pm Tue & Thu-Sun, to 8pm Wed) Built in 1824 as a warehouse for French colonial produce like coffee, cocoa, peanuts and vanilla, the cavernous Entrepôts Lainé creates a dramatic backdrop for cutting-edge modern art at the CAPC Musée d'Art Contemporain.

Entry to the permanent collection is free but there is a cover charge for any temporary exhibitions.

Musée des Beaux-Arts Gallery

(20 cours d'Albret; 11am-6pm daily mid-Jul–mid-Aug, closed Tue rest of year) FREE The evolution of Occidental art from the Renaissance to the mid-20th century is on view at Bordeaux's Musée des Beaux-Arts, which occupies two wings of the 1770s-built Hôtel de Ville, either side of the Jardin de la Mairie (an elegant public park).

The museum was established in 1801; highlights include 17th-century Flemish, Dutch and Italian paintings. Temporary exhibitions are regularly hosted at its nearby annexe, **Galerie des Beaux-Arts (place du Colonel Raynal; adult/child €5/2.50; 11am-6pm daily mid-Jul–mid Aug, closed Tue rest of year)**.

Musée des Arts Décoratifs Gallery

(39 rue Bouffard; 2-6pm Wed-Mon) FREE Faience pottery, porcelain, gold, iron, glasswork and furniture are displayed at the Musée des Arts Décoratifs.

Local Knowledge

Bordeaux Wine Tourism Don't Miss List

BY JANE ANSON, RESIDENT WINE WRITER & AUTHOR

1 **WINE VILLAGES**
Not to be missed: St-Émilion (p268), one of the most beautiful places on the Right Bank of the Dordogne River; and **Bages village**, just outside Pauillac (p264), on the Left Bank.

2 **BOTH SIDES OF THE RIVER**
Right Bank and Left Bank – such different personalities! Right Bank properties tend to be smaller, the type of place where the owner ends up showing you around. Wines are usually merlot-based, fruity, easy to drink. The Left Bank is more the dream châteaux you imagine: big properties with turrets and moats. Cabernet sauvignon is the main grape and wines are big, powerful.

3 **GOING OFF THE BEATEN TRACK**
Two Right Bank places: **Fronsac,** 10 minutes from St-Émilion but much quieter, is beautiful with plenty of lesser-known châteaux to visit. And the **Côtes de Bordeaux** (Castillon, Cadillac, Blaye and Francs) are beautiful with lots of young winemakers to get to know.

4 **CHÂTEAUX TASTINGS**
Château Lynch-Bages (www.lynchbages.com) has an excellent tour. Further north is the world-famous **Château Mouton Rothschild** (www.chateau-mouton-rothschild.com). South of Bordeaux, **Château Smith Haut Lafitte** (www.smith-haut-lafitte.com) has a red-wine jacuzzi.

5 **FAVOURITE PRODUCERS**
So difficult! Right now, for red it is **Château Haut Bailly** (www.chateau-haut-bailly.com) and for white, **Château Olivier** (www.chateau-olivier.com) and **Domaine de Chevalier** (www.domainedechevalier.com), all in the Pessac–Léognan wine-growing area close to the Bordeaux city centre.

Bordeaux

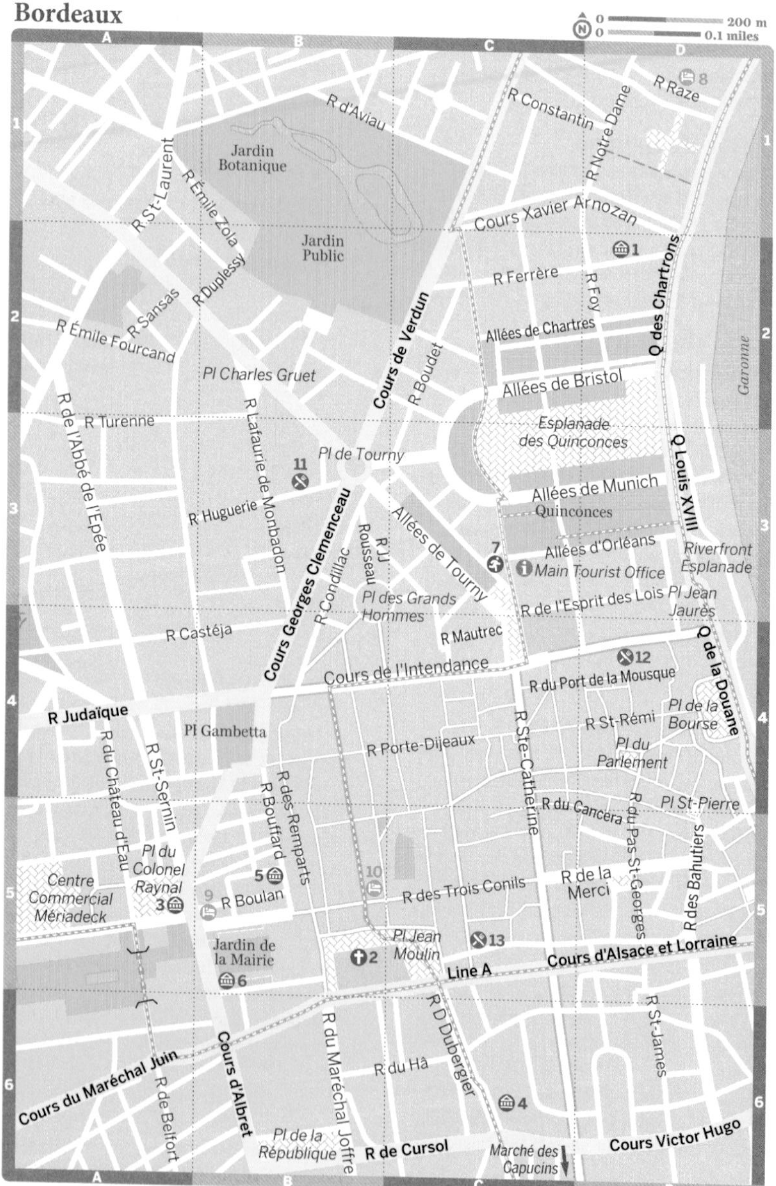

Sleeping

Les Chambres au Coeur de Bordeaux B&B **€€**
(05 56 52 43 58; www.aucoeurdebordeaux.fr; 28 rue Boulan; r €105-155;) This renovated townhouse is now a swish B&B run like a small boutique hotel. Its five charming rooms are a very Bordeaux-appropriate mix of the old and the new, and most evenings your hosts offer an *apero* and tapas tasting session (€20 to €25) at 7pm.

Bordeaux

Ecolodge des Chartrons — B&B €€

(05 56 81 49 13; www.ecolodgedeschartrons.com; 23 rue Raze; s €107-205, d €119-228;) This place is hidden away in a little side street off the quays in Bordeaux's Chartrons wine-merchant district. The owner-hosts of this *chambre d'hôte*, Veronique and Yann, have stripped back and limewashed the stone walls of an old house, scrubbed the wide floorboards and brought in recycled antique furniture to create a highly memorable place to stay.

L'Hôtel Particulier — Boutique Hotel €€€

(05 57 88 28 80; www.lhotel-particulier.com; 44 rue Vital-Carles; apt from €89, d from €203;) When you step into this fabulous boutique hotel, with its secret courtyard garden, and find 1000 eyes staring at you from the reception walls, not to mention the lampshades made only of feathers, you realise you've stumbled upon somewhere really special. The rooms don't disappoint – they are highly extravagant affairs with huge fireplaces, carved ceilings, free-standing bathtubs and quality furnishings.

Eating

Le Cheverus Café — Bistro €

(05 56 48 29 73; 81-83 rue du Loup; menus from €12.50; noon-3pm & 7-9pm Mon-Sat) In a city full of neighbourhood bistros, this one, smack in the city centre, is one of the most impressive. It's friendly, cosy and chaotically busy (be prepared to wait for a table at lunchtime). The food tastes fresh and home-cooked and it dares to veer slightly away from the bistro standards of steak and chips.

La Boîte à Huîtres — Oysters €€

(05 56 81 64 97; 36 cours du Chapeau Rouge; lunch menu €20, 6 oysters from €8; noon-2pm & 7-11pm) This rickety, wood-panelled little place feels like an Arcachon fisherman's hut. It's a sensation that's quite appropriate because this is by far the best place in Bordeaux to munch on fresh Arcachon oysters. Traditionally they're served with sausage but you can have them in a number of different forms, including with that other southwest delicacy, foie gras.

Baud et Millet — Cheese, Wine €€

(05 56 79 05 77; 19 rue Huguerie; mains €23-25; noon-2pm & 7-9.30pm Mon-Sat) If you like cheese or wine, or both of them, then this cute neighbourhood place with over 140 different cheeses served in myriad forms, alongside almost as many wines, is unmissable. Serious *fromage* fans should go for the *Tour de France* (€15) a French cheese blow out!

La Tupina — Regional Cuisine €€€

(05 56 91 56 37; www.latupina.com; 6 rue Porte de la Monnaie; menus €18-74, mains €27-45) Filled with the aroma of soup simmering inside an old *tupina* ('kettle' in Basque) over an open fire, this white-tableclothed place is feted far and wide for its seasonal southwestern French specialities such as a minicasserole of foie gras and eggs, milk-fed lamb or goose wings with potatoes and parsley.

Information

Main Tourist Office (☎05 56 00 66 00; www.bordeaux-tourisme.com; 12 cours du 30 Juillet; ⏰9am-7pm Mon-Sat, 9.30am-6pm Sun) The tourist office runs an excellent range of city and regional tours. There's also a small but helpful **branch** (☎05 56 91 64 70; ⏰9am-noon & 1-6pm Mon-Sat, 10am-noon & 1-3pm Sun) at the train station.

Getting There & Away

Train Bordeaux is one of France's major rail-transit points. The station, Gare St-Jean, is about 3km from the city centre at the southern terminus of cours de la Marne.

Bayonne (€35, two hours)

Paris Gare Montparnasse (from €77, three hours, at least 16 daily)

Toulouse (from €33, 2¼ hours)

The Médoc

Northwest of Bordeaux, along the western shore of the Gironde Estuary, lie some of Bordeaux's most celebrated vineyards. On the banks of the muddy Gironde, the port town of **Pauillac** (population 1300) is at the heart of the wine country, surrounded by the distinguished Haut-Médoc, Margaux and St-Julien appellations. The Pauillac wine appellation encompasses 18 *crus classés* including the world-renowned Mouton Rothschild, Latour and Lafite Rothschild.

The town's tourist office houses the **Maison du Tourisme et du Vin** (☎05 56 59 03 08; www.pauillac-medoc.com; ⏰9.30am-7pm Mon-Sat, 10am-1pm & 2-6pm Sun), which has information on châteaux and how to visit them.

The lack of a public-transport system to most of the châteaux means this area is best explored in your own car or on one of the tours organised by the tourist

Left: A cellar at Château Mouton Rothschild (p261); **Below:** Bassin d'Arcachon
(LEFT) LUIS DAVILLA/GETTY IMAGES ©; (BELOW) HEMIS/ALAMY ©

office in Bordeaux. There are several different types of tour, which get chopped and changed on a regular basis; at the time of research, half-day **Médoc tours** taking in two châteaux and including wine tastings left the Bordeaux tourist office at 1.45pm on Fridays and Mondays (tours run to other wine regions the rest of the week) at a cost of €87. Cheaper is the half-day **Châteaux et Terroirs** tour, which runs daily (€34; 1.15pm), but takes in different châteaux and regions each day. There are dozens of other combinations. For any of these tours, advance reservations are essential. **Bordeaux Excursions** (☎06 24 88 22 09; www.bordeaux-excursions.com) customises private wine-country tours, starting from €210 for one to four people (excluding châteaux fees) for a half-day trip.

Also, don't miss Philippe Raoux' **La Winery** (☎05 56 39 04 90; www.winery.fr; Rond-point des Vendangeurs, D1; ⏰10am-7pm). A first for France, this vast glass-and-steel wine centre mounts concerts and contemporary-art exhibits alongside various fee-based wine tastings, including innovative tastings that determine your *signe œnologique* (wine sign) costing from €16 (booking required). Impressively, it also stocks more than 1000 different wines.

Arcachon

POP 11,750

A long-time oyster-harvesting area on the southern side of the tranquil, triangular Bassin d'Arcachon (Arcachon Bay), this seaside town lured bourgeois Bordelaise at the end of the 19th century. Its four little quarters are romantically named for each of the seasons, with villas that evoke the town's golden past amid a scattering of 1950s architecture.

SILVIA OTTE/GETTY IMAGES ©

Don't Miss
Dune du Pilat

This colossal sand dune (sometimes referred to as the Dune de Pyla because of its location in the resort town of Pyla-sur-Mer), 8km south of Arcachon, stretches from the mouth of the Bassin d'Arcachon southwards for almost 3km. Already the largest in Europe, it's spreading eastwards at 4.5m a year – it has swallowed trees, a road junction and even a hotel.

The view from the top – approximately 114m above sea level – is magnificent. To the west you can see the sandy shoals at the mouth of the Bassin d'Arcachon, including the **Banc d'Arguin bird reserve** and Cap Ferret. Dense dark-green pine forests stretch from the base of the dune eastwards almost as far as the eye can see.

Take care swimming in this area: powerful currents swirl out to sea from the deceptively tranquil *baïnes* (little bays).

NEED TO KNOW

www.bassin-arcachon.com

Sights

Plage d'Arcachon Beach

In the **Ville d'Été** (Summer Quarter), Arcachon's sandy beach, Plage d'Arcachon, is flanked by two piers. Lively **Jetée Thiers** is at the western end. In front of the eastern pier, **Jetée d'Eyrac**, stands the town's turreted **Casino de la Plage**. The sheltered basin in which Arcachon sits means the water is always absolutely flat calm and ideal for families – a far cry from most Atlantic beaches.

On the Wine Trail

Thirsty? The 1000-sq-km winegrowing area around the city of Bordeaux is, along with Burgundy, France's most important producer of top-quality wines.

The Bordeaux region is divided into 57 appellations (production areas whose soil and microclimate impart distinctive characteristics to the wine produced there). The majority of the Bordeaux region's reds, rosés, sweet and dry whites and sparkling wines have earned the right to include the abbreviation AOC (Appellation d'Origine Contrôlée) on their labels, indicating that the contents have been grown, fermented and aged according to strict regulations that govern such viticultural matters as the number of vines permitted per hectare and acceptable pruning methods.

Bordeaux has more than 5000 châteaux (also known as *domaines*, *crus* or *clos*), referring not to palatial residences but rather to the properties where grapes are raised, picked, fermented and then matured as wine. The smaller châteaux sometimes accept walk-in visitors, but at many places you have to make advance reservations. Many close during the *vendange* (grape harvest) in October.

Whet your palate with the tourist office's informal introduction to wine and cheese courses (adult €25), held every Thursday (and Saturdays mid-July to mid-August).

Serious students of the grape can enrol at the **École du Vin** (Wine School; ☎05 56 00 22 66; www.bordeaux.com), within the **Maison du Vin de Bordeaux** (3 cours du 30 Juillet), across the street from the tourist office.

Tours

Les Bateliers Arcachonnais Boat Tours

(☎05 57 72 28 28; www.bateliers-arcachon.com; Île aux Oiseaux adult/child/under 5yr €16/11/5.5; Banc d'Arguin adult/child/under 3yr €26/17.50/9) Daily, year-round cruises sail around the **Île aux Oiseaux**, the uninhabited 'bird island' in the middle of the bay. It's a haven for tern, curlew and redshank, so bring your binoculars. In summer there are regular all-day excursions (11am to 5.30pm) to the **Banc d'Arguin**, the sand bank off the Dune du Pilat.

Eating

The bay's oysters (served raw and accompanied by the local small, flat sausages, *crepinettes*) appear on *menus* everywhere.

Aux Mille Saveurs Traditional French €€

(☎05 56 83 40 28; 25 bd du Général Leclerc; menus €19.50-50; closed Wed & dinner Sun &Tue) In a light-filled space of flowing white tablecloths, this genteel restaurant is renowned for its traditional French fare artistically presented on fine china.

Cafe de la Plage Seafood €€

(Chez Pierre; ☎05 56 22 52 94; www.cafedelaplage.com; 1 bd Veyrier Montagnères; menus from €30, seafood platters €25-42; noon-2.30pm & 7-9.30pm) This see-and-be-seen restaurant serves up an ocean of seafood.

Information

Tourist Office (☎05 57 52 97 97; www.arcachon.com; Esplanade Georges Pompidou; 9am-7pm Jul-Aug, 9am-6pm Mon-Sat, 10am-1pm & 2-5pm Sun Apr-Jun & Sep, shorter hours rest of year) The town's helpful tourist office is five minutes back from the beach, near the train station.

ROY PHILIPPE/HEMIS.FR/GETTY IMAGES ©

Don't Miss · St-Émilion

The medieval village of St-Émilion perches above vineyards renowned for producing full-bodied, deeply coloured red wines. Named after Émilion, a miracle-working Benedictine monk who lived in a cave here between AD 750 and 767, the village and its vineyards are now Unesco-listed. Today, despite masses of tourists descending onto the town, it's well worth venturing 40km east from Bordeaux to experience St-Émilion's magic, particularly when the sun sets over the valley and the limestone buildings glow with halo-like golden hues.

For captivating views of the hilltop hamlet, climb the church **clocher** (bell tower; admission €1.50) – collect the key from the tourist office – or the 118 steps of 13th-century **La Tour du Roi** (King's Tower). Or dig deep beneath the pretty streets into a fascinating labyrinth of catacombs with a guided tour organised by the tourist office.

Blind tastings and games (available in English) are a fun and informative introduction to wine tasting at **L'École du Vin de St-Émilion**; adjacent Maison du Vin also offers bilingual 1½-hour classes starting at 11am. Eight hiking circuits, from 4km to 14km, loop through the greater World Heritage jurisdiction; the tourist office has maps.

Hungry for lunch in the company of fine wine? Reserve in advance at double-Michelin-starred restaurant, Hostellerie de Plaisance.

NEED TO KNOW

Tourist Office ☎05 57 55 28 28; www.saint-emilion-tourisme.com; place des Créneaux; ⏰9.30am-8pm mid-Jul–mid-Aug, shorter hours rest of year

L'École du Vin de St-Émilion ☎05 57 24 61 01; www.vignobleschateaux.fr; 4 rue du Clocher; tasting courses from €75

Restaurant Hostellerie de Plaisance ☎05 57 55 07 55; www.hostellerie-plaisance.com; place du Clocher; menus €120-160; ⏰lunch only Tue-Fri, lunch & dinner Sat

Getting There & Away

Train There are frequent trains between Bordeaux and Arcachon (€11.20, 50 minutes).

Cognac

POP 19,500

On the banks of the River Charente amid vine-covered countryside, Cognac, 120km north of Bordeaux, is known worldwide for the double-distilled spirit that bears its name.

Sights & Activities

Half-timbered 15th- to 17th-century houses line the narrow streets of the **Vieille Ville** (old city), which sits snugly between the partly Romanesque **Église St-Léger** (rue Aristide Briand) and the river.

Musée d'Art et d'Histoire Museum

(☎05 45 32 07 25; www.musees-cognac.fr; 48 bd Denfert-Rochereau; adult/child €5/free, ticket also valid for the Musée des Arts du Cognac; ⊙2-5.30pm Wed-Mon) At the southern corner of the leafy **Jardin Public** is the Musée d'Art et d'Histoire, showcasing the town's history.

Musée des Arts du Cognac Museum

(☎05 45 36 21 10; place de la Salle Verte; adult/child €5/free, ticket also valid for the Musée d'Art et d'Histoire; ⊙2-5.30pm Tue-Sun) The Musée des Arts du Cognac takes you step by step through the production of Cognac – from vine to bottle.

La Dame Jeanne River Cruise

(☎05 45 82 10 71; adult/child €7/4; ⊙May-Sep) You can float with the sticklebacks down the River Charente on *La Dame Jeanne*, a re-creation of one of the flat-bottomed cargo boats known as *gabarres* that were once the lifeblood of trade along the river. The trip lasts 90 minutes; reservations should be made through the tourist office.

Local Knowledge

Bordelaise Cuisine Don't Miss List

BY JEAN-PIERRE XIRADAKI, CULINARY WRITER & CELEBRITY RESTAURANT OWNER SINCE 1968

1 MARCHÉ DES CAPUCINS

Cuisine bordelaise (Bordeaux cuisine) originates from the south, from Basque-country women who came to work in the great Bordelaise houses. And the diversity of produce is enormous. We have river and sea fish, shellfish, oysters, fowl (duck and geese), lamb, beef, vegetables, truffles ... We have everything. I buy my produce from local producers and markets: **Marché des Capucins** (⊙7am-noon) and the twice-weekly market in Blaye (Wednesday and Saturday mornings).

2 CASSOULET, MACARONADE & EELS

I love *cassoulet*, typical to the rural southwest and traditionally eaten to celebrate; it's a heart-warming haricot bean stew with a few giblets, bit of sausage and pork thrown in. Then there's *macaronade aux cèpes et au foi gras*, fresh macaroni with local *cèpes* (boletus mushrooms), foie gras and cream. It is very rich, very delicious and demands a healthy appetite! *Lamproie à la Bordelaise* (eel-like lamprey), a river fish cooked with wine and leeks, is typical of our cuisine.

3 LA SOUPE

In winter at La Tupina (p263) we always have a cauldron of soup cooking in the fireplace. We throw in cabbage, carrots, beans, a bit of duck or pork to give it taste and so on, just as peasants did centuries ago. For them it provided all the daily nutrition they needed – water, vegetables and a little meat.

4 WINE & OYSTERS

L'Essentiel (www.essentielthunevin.com) in St-Émilion is *the* place to taste wine and La Boîte à Huîtres (p263) in Bordeaux is the *dégustation* (tasting) address for oysters.

If You Like... Family Fun

When the sun fades or you start to tire of the sand and sea, try this trio of Atlantic Coast entertainers, enthralling whatever the weather.

1 **LES MACHINES DE L'ÎLE DE NANTES** (www.lesmachines-nantes.fr; Parc des Chantiers, Blvd Léon Bureau; adult/child €8/6.50; 10am-7pm Jul-Aug, hours vary rest of year) The quirkiest sight in Nantes has to be Les Machines de l'Île de Nantes. Inside this fantasy world it's perfectly possible to prance around like a maharajah on the back of a 45-tonne **mechanical elephant** with a secret lounge inside its belly, or voyage on a boat through dangerous oceans where attacks by oversized squid and giant prawns are common. We can only think that Jules Verne would be smiling in his grave if he could see this lot!

2 **AQUARIUM LA ROCHELLE** (www.aquarium-larochelle.com; quai Louis Prunier; adult/child €15/11.50, audioguide €3; 9am-11pm Jul-Aug, 9am-8pm Apr-Jun & Sep, 10am-8pm Oct-Mar) La Rochelle's number-one tourist attraction is this state-of-the-art family-friendly aquarium. A visit begins by descending in a clunky old 'submarine' to the ocean floor, where, serenaded by the sound of crashing waves and classical music, you step out to be greeted by the pouting fish of the North Atlantic. After which you swim through the oceans and seas of the world learning about all its diverse lifeforms.

3 **FUTUROSCOPE** (05 49 49 11 12; www.futuroscope.com; Avenue René Monory, Chasseneuil-du-Poitou; adult/child €42/32; 10am-dark, closed Jan–mid-Feb) Futuristic theme park Futuroscope takes you whizzing through space, diving into the deep-blue ocean depths, racing around city streets and on a close encounter with creatures of the future among many other space-age cinematic experiences. To keep things cutting edge, one-third of the attractions change annually. Many are motion-seat set-ups requiring a minimum height of 120cm, but there's a play area for littlies with miniature cars and so on.

COGNAC HOUSES

According to local lore, divine intervention plays a role in the production of Cognac. Made of grape *eaux-de-vie* (brandies) of various vintages, Cognac is aged in oak barrels and blended by an experienced *maître de chai* (cellar master). Each year some 2% of the casks' volume – *la part des anges* (the angels' share) – evaporates through the pores in the wood, nourishing the tiny black mushrooms that thrive on the walls of Cognac warehouses. That 2% might not sound like much, but it amounts to around 20 million bottles a year – if the angels really are up there knocking back 20 million bottles of Cognac a year, then all we can say is roll on our time behind the pearly gates!

The best-known **Cognac houses** are open to the public, running tours of their cellars and production facilities, and ending with a tasting session. Opening times vary annually; it's a good idea to reserve in advance.

Camus (05 45 32 72 96; www.camus.fr; 29 rue Marguerite de Navarre; adult/child from €8.50/free; 2-6pm Mon, 10.30am-12.30pm & 2-6pm Tue-Sat May-Sep) Located 250m northeast of the Jardin Public.

Hennessy (05 45 35 72 68; www.hennessy.com; 8 rue Richonne; adult/12-18yr/under 12 €11/6/free; 10am-11.30am & 1.30-5pm mid-Apr-Sep, shorter hours rest of year, closed Jan & Feb) Situated 100m uphill from quai des Flamands; tours include a film (shown in English) and a boat trip across the Charente to visit the cellars.

Martell (05 45 36 33 33; www.martell.com; place Édouard Martell; adult/child €7.50/4; 10am-5pm Mon-Fri, noon-5pm Sat & Sun Apr-Oct, closed Sun Oct) Found 250m northwest of the tourist office.

Otard (05 45 36 88 86; www.otard.com; 127 bd Denfert-Rochereau; adult/child €10/4.50; 11am-12pm & 1.30-6pm Jul-Aug, shorter hours rest of year, closed Jan-Mar) Housed in the 1494 birthplace of King François I, the Château de Cognac, 650m north of place François 1er.

Rémy Martin (☎05 45 35 76 66; www.visitesremymartin.com) Two locations: the **estate** (adult/child €18/8; ⏰by appointment only, Mon-Sat mid-Apr–Sep), 4km southwest of town towards Pons; and, in town, the **house** (adult/child €28/7; ⏰by appointment), for intimate tastings in groups of up to eight.

The tourist office has a list of smaller Cognac houses near town; most close between October and mid-March.

Sleeping & Eating

Hôtel Le Cheval Blanc Hotel €
(☎05 45 82 09 55; www.hotel-chevalblanc.fr; 6 place Bayard; d from €66; ❄📶) Miniature bottles of Cognac in the vending machine satiate midnight cravings at this hotel, where rooms are set around a courtyard. Although not vast, the rooms are immaculate, and there's good wheelchair access.

Bistrot de Claude Bistro €€
(☎05 45 82 60 32; 35 rue Grande; menus €20-32; ⏰7-9.30pm Mon-Fri) Set in a lovely old wiggly timber building in the heart of the old town, this character-infused restau-

rant specialises in oysters and both river and sea fish.

Getting There & Away

Cognac's **train station** (av du Maréchal Leclerc), 1km south of the town centre, has regular trains to/from La Rochelle (from €16, from 1¼ hours).

FRENCH BASQUE COUNTRY

Gently sloping from the foothills of the Pyrenees into the deep-sapphire-blue Bay of Biscay, the Basque Country straddles France and Spain. Yet this feisty, independent land remains profoundly different from either of the nation states that have adopted it.

Bayonne

POP 46,200

Surrounded by sturdy fortifications and splashed in red and white paint, Bayonne (Baiona in Basque), capital of the French Basque Country, is one of the most attractive towns in southwest France. Its

Charente River and Hennessy

Detour: Île de Ré

Bathed in the southern sun, drenched in a languid atmosphere and scattered with villages of green-shuttered, whitewashed buildings with red Spanish-tile roofs, Île de Ré is one of the most delightful places on the west coast of France. The island spans just 30km from its most easterly and westerly points, and just 5km at its widest section. But take note, the secret's out and in the high season it can be almost impossible to move around and even harder to find a place to stay.

On the northern coast, about 12km from the toll bridge that links the island to **La Rochelle**, is the quaint fishing port of **St-Martin-de-Ré** (population 2600), the island's main town. Surrounded by 17th-century fortifications (you can stroll along most of the ramparts), the port town is a mesh of streets filled with craft shops, art galleries and sea views. St-Martin's **tourist office** (☎05 46 09 00 05; www.iledere.com; av Victor Bouthillier; ⏰10am-6pm Mon-Sat, to noon Sun) can provide information for the entire island. For an overview of the island, climb to the **Phare des Baleines** (☎05 46 29 18 23; www.lepharedesbaleines.fr; adult/child €6/3; ⏰9.30am-9pm mid-Jun–mid-Sep, shorter hours rest of year), a lighthouse on the island's northern tip.

The island's best **beaches** are along the southern edge and around the western tip (northeast and southeast of Phare-des-Baleines).

Criss-crossed by well-maintained bicycle paths, the pancake-flat island is ideal for cycling. A biking map is available at tourist offices.

The one-way automobile toll (paid on your way to the island) is €8 (€16 from mid-June to mid-September).

perfectly preserved old town (until 1907 it was actually forbidden to build outside the town's fortifications) and shoals of riverside restaurants are an absolute delight to explore.

Sights

Musée Basque et de l'Histoire de Bayonne — Museum

(☎05 59 59 08 98; www.musee-basque.com; 37 quai des Corsaires; adult/child €6.50/free; ⏰10am-6.30pm Jul-Aug, closed Mon rest of year) The seafaring history, traditions and cultural identity of the Basque people are all explored at this superb museum, where exhibits include a reconstructed farm and the interior of a typical *etxe* (home). Labelling is in French, Spanish and Basque only but English information sheets are available.

Cathédrale Ste-Marie — Cathedral

(Place Louis Pasteur; ⏰10-11.45am & 3-6.15pm Mon-Sat, 3.30-6.15pm Sun, cloister 9am-12.30pm & 2-6pm) The twin towers of Bayonne's Gothic cathedral soar above the city. Construction began in the 13th century, and was completed in 1451; the mismatched materials in some ways resemble Lego blocks. Above the north aisle are three lovely stained-glass windows; the oldest, in the Chapelle Saint Jérôme, dates from 1531. The entrance to the stately 13th-century **cloister** is on place Louis Pasteur.

Tours

City Tours — Tour

(adult €5-45) The tourist office organises a range of different city tours (some in English), ranging from a historical tour of old Bayonne to others which focus on food, or museums. Departure times and tour type vary – contact the tourist office (p274) for details.

Sleeping

Hôtel des Arceaux Boutique Hotel €

(☎05 59 59 15 53; www.hotel-arceaux.com; 26 rue Port Neuf; r with shared bathroom €50, d €69-79; ) The rooms and communal areas at this hotel, which is located on one of the prettiest streets in the old town, are a cacophony of noisy colours and stately antiques, and it's very well run. All the rooms (some of which can accommodate families) are different, so ask to see a few first.

Péniche Djébelle Houseboat €€

(☎05 59 25 77 18; www.djebelle.com; face au 17 Quai de Lesseps; d incl breakfast €150; closed Oct-Apr;) This unique *chambre d'hôte* isn't a bricks-and-mortar hotel at all, but a houseboat floating in the River Ardour. The two vast rooms are imaginatively decorated and absolutley sublime; one has a Moroccan theme and the other, which has the boat's steering wheel built into the bathroom, is full of thoughts of tropical islands.

Hôtel Côte Basque Hotel €€

(☎05 59 55 10 21; www.hotel-cotebasque.fr; 2 rue Maubec; r from €85;) Ride the clanky, old-fashioned lift up to your modern room with low-slung (but rather small) beds and colourful art on the walls. Sitting opposite the train station, this modern place offers sizzling value for money.

Eating

Bar-Restaurant du Marché Basque €

(☎05 59 59 22 66; 39 rue des Basques; menus from €9, mains from €8; noon-2.30pm Mon-Sat) Run by a welcoming Basque-speaking family, this unpretentious place is an absolute institution where everyone knows everyone (which some people may find slightly intimidating, but don't worry, just dive right in – nobody cares!). Simple but ample home-cooked dishes full of the flavours of the neighbouring market are dished up to all comers.

La Feuillantine Gastronomic €€

(☎05 59 46 14 94; www.lafeuillantine-bayonne.com; 21 quai Amiral Dubourdieu; menus €17-39, mains €20) This riverside place might be

La Rochelle

quite small, but it's garnered an impressive reputation for its excellent Basque dishes, which are served with flair and style in its colourful dining room. The culinary skills of chef Nicolas Bertegui have received virtually universal praise in the mainstream French media.

Information

Tourist Office (08 20 42 64 64; www.bayonne-tourisme.com; place des Basques; 9am-7pm Mon-Sat, 10am-1pm Sun Jul-Aug, 9am-6.30pm Mon-Fri, 10am-1pm & 2-6pm Sat Mar-Jun & Sep-Oct, shorter hours rest of year) Efficient office providing stacks of informative brochures and bike rental, plus guided city tours.

Getting There & Away

Train TGVs run between Bayonne and Paris Gare Montparnasse (€67 to €109, five to six hours, eight daily).

There are five trains daily to St-Jean Pied de Port (€10, 1¼ hours) and fairly frequent services to St-Jean de Luz (€5, 25 minutes) via Biarritz (€3, nine minutes).

Other services:

Bordeaux from €31, two hours, at least 10 daily

Toulouse from €43, 3¾ hours, five daily

Biarritz

POP 26,067

As ritzy as its name suggests, this stylish coastal town, 8km west of Bayonne, took off as a resort in the mid-19th century when Napoléon III and his Spanish-born wife, Eugénie, visited regularly. Along its rocky coastline are architectural hallmarks of this golden age, and the belle époque and art deco eras that followed. Although it retains a high glamour quotient (and high prices to match), it's also a magnet for vanloads of surfers, with some of Europe's best waves.

Sights & Activities

Biarritz' raison d'être is its fashionable beaches, particularly the two central **Grande Plage** and **Plage Miramar**, which are lined end to end with sunbathing bodies on hot summer days. Stripy 1920s-style beach tents can be hired for €9.50 per day. The other central Biarritz beach is the tiny cove of **Plage du Port Vieux** which, thanks to its lack of swell, is the best one for young children to splash about on. North of Pointe St-Martin, the adrenaline-pumping surfing beaches of **Anglet** (the final 't' is pronounced) continue northwards for more than 4km. Take bus 10 or 13 from the bottom of av Verdun (just near av Édouard VII).

Climbing the 258 twisting steps inside the 73m-high **Phare de Biarritz**, the town's 1834 lighthouse, rewards you with sweeping views of the Basque coast.

Plage du Port Vieux

Biarritz

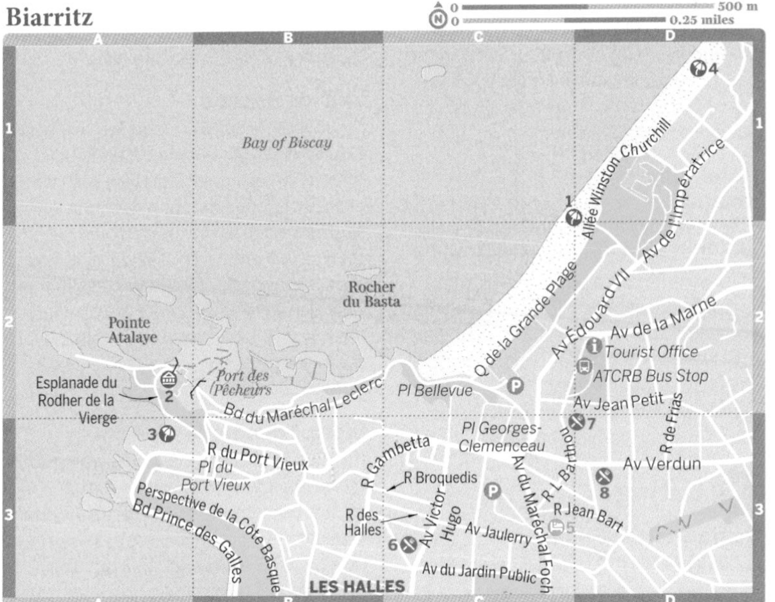

Biarritz

Sights

1 Grande Plage C1
2 Musée de la Mer A2
3 Plage du Port Vieux A3
4 Plage Miramar D1

Sleeping

5 Hôtel Villa Koegui C3

Eating

6 Bistrot des Halles C3
7 Le Clos Basque D3
8 Restaurant le Pim'pi D3

Cité de l'Océan Museum

(05 59 22 75 40; www.citedelocean.com; 1 av de la Plage; adult/child €11/7.30; 10am-10pm Jul-Aug, 10am-7pm Easter, Apr-Jun & Sep-Oct, shorter hours rest of year) We don't really know whether it's fair to call the Cité de l'Océan a mere 'museum'. At heart it's simply a museum of the ocean but this is entertainment, cutting-edge technology, theme park and science museum all rolled into one. During a visit you will learn all you ever wanted to know about the ocean and (sort-of) ride in a submarine to watch giant squid and sperm whales do battle.

Musée de la Mer Museum

(05 59 22 75 40; www.museedelamer.com; esplanade du Rocher de la Vierge; adult/child €14/10; 9.30am-midnight Jul-Aug, 9.30am-8pm Apr-Jun & Sep-Oct, shorter hours rest of year) Housed in a wonderful art deco building, Biarritz's Musée de la Mer is seething with underwater life from the Bay of Biscay and beyond, including huge aquariums of sharks and dainty tropical reef fish, as well as exhibits on fishing recalling Biarritz's whaling past. It's the seals, though, that steal the show (feeding time, always a favourite with children, is at 10.30am and 5pm). In high season it's possible to have the place almost to yourself by visiting late at night.

Sleeping

Hôtel Mirano Boutique Hotel €€

(05 59 23 11 63; www.hotelmirano.fr; 11 av Pasteur; d €72-132;) Squiggly purple, orange and black wallpaper and oversize orange

perspex light fittings are some of the rad '70s touches at this boutique retro hotel. Oh, and there's a flirty Betty Boop in the bar. The staff go above and beyond the call of duty in order to please. All up, it's one of the best deals in town.

Hôtel Villa Koegui Boutique Hotel **€€€**
(**05 59 50 07 77; www.hotel-villakoegui-biarritz.fr; 7 rue de Gascogne; r from €200;**) This fab little place has swanky, bright rooms filled with locally made furnishings and decoration and is set around a leafy courtyard garden. What really makes it stand out though is that it's run with the kind of warmth and care normally only found in small, family-run B&Bs.

Eating

Restaurant le Pim'pi French **€€**
(**05 59 24 12 62; 14 av Verdun; menus €14-28, mains €17; noon-2pm Tue, noon-2pm & 7-9.30pm Wed-Sat)** A small and resolutely old-fashioned place unfazed by all the razzmatazz around it. The daily specials are chalked up on a blackboard – most are of the classic French bistro style but are produced with such unusual skill and passion that many consider this one of the town's better places to eat.

Le Clos Basque Basque **€€**
(**05 59 24 24 96; 12 rue Louis Barthou; menus €26, mains €14.50; noon-1.30pm & 7.45-9.30pm Tue-Sat, noon-1.30pm Sun)** With its tiles and exposed stonework hung with abstract art, this tiny place could have strayed in from Spain. The cuisine, however, is emphatically Basque, traditional with a contemporary twist or two. Only the finest of local ingredients make it into the dishes. Reserve ahead to secure a terrace table.

Bistrot des Halles Basque **€€**
(**05 59 24 21 22; 1 rue du Centre; mains €17-19; noon-2pm & 7.30-10.30pm Tue-Sat)** One of a cluster of restaurants along rue du Centre that get their produce directly from the nearby covered market, this bustling place stands out from the pack for serving excellent fish and other fresh modern French market fare from the blackboard menu, in an interior adorned with old metallic advertising posters. Open daily during Easter and the summer holidays.

Bistrot des Halles

Information

Tourist Office (☎05 59 22 37 10; www.biarritz.fr; square d'Ixelles; ⏱9am-7pm Jul-Aug, shorter hours rest of year) In July and August there are tourist-office annexes at the airport, train station and at the roundabout just off the Biarritz sortie (exit) 4 from the A63.

Getting There & Away

Bus Buses run frequently between Bayonne and Biarritz; they work out much cheaper than taking the train as you'll pay the same to get from Biarritz' train station to its town centre as you will to get from Bayonne to Biarritz directly on the bus.

Ten daily **ATCRB** (www.transports-atcrb.com) buses travel down the coast to St-Jean de Luz (€2) from the stop just near the tourist office beside square d'Ixelles.

Train Biarritz-La Négresse train station is about 3km south of the town centre; walking to the centre isn't advised due to busy roads without footpaths, so catch bus A1. Times, fares and destinations are much the same as for Bayonne, a nine-minute train journey away.

St-Jean de Luz & Ciboure

POP 14,200

If you're searching for the quintessential Basque seaside town – with atmospheric narrow streets and a lively fishing port pulling in large catches of sardines and anchovies that are cooked up at authentic restaurants – you've found it. St-Jean de Luz, 24km southwest of Bayonne, sits at the mouth of the River Nivelle and is overlooked by the lush Pyrenean foothills. Its sleepy, smaller alter ego, Ciboure, is on the western curve of the bay, separated from St-Jean de Luz by the fishing harbour.

Sights

St-Jean de Luz' beautiful banana-shaped sandy **beach** sprouts stripy bathing tents from June to September. Ciboure has its own modest beach, **Plage de Socoa**, 2km west of Socoa on the corniche (the

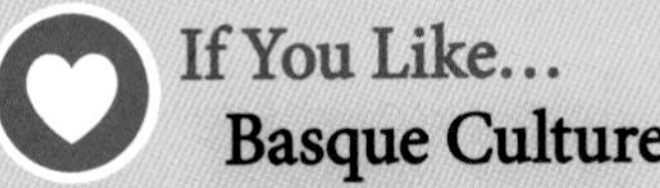

If You Like... Basque Culture

Visit Bayonne's Musée Basque, then deepen your understanding of the region's unique culture with these quintessentially Basque experiences.

1 FÊTES DE BAYONNE CULTURAL FESTIVAL
(www.fetes.bayonne.fr) A five-day extravaganza of food, drink, dance and fireworks in early August.

2 FOIRE AU JAMBON
(Ham Fair) During Easter week, the town hosts a Ham Fair, honouring *jambon de Bayonne*, the acclaimed local ham. You may think this is just a recently thought up touristy gimmick to sell ham, but no – this fair in March or April has taken place annually since 1462!

3 PINTXO
Bayonne has an increasing number of *pintxo* (tapas in Basque) bars, and two of the best are **Xurasko** (16 rue Poissonnerie; tapas from €2.50; ⏱noon-11pm) and **Ibaia** (45 quai Amiral Jauréguiberry; mains from €8; ⏱noon-2pm & 7-10pm Tue-Sat). Tapas start to decorate the bar like flowers from 7pm as everyone clocks off work and stop for a glass of wine and choice titbits.

4 PIMENTS D'ESPELETTE
This spicy red chilli pepper is an essential accompaniment to Basque meals (it even has its own AOC, just like fine wine). The village of **Espelette** (www.espelette.fr) hosts its own chilli festival on the last weekend in October, culminating in the crowning of the *chevalier du piment* (knight of the chilli).

5 PELOTA
This national Basque sport encompasses 16 different games, all played with a hard ball (the *pelote*) using bare hands and a wooden paddle or scooplike racket. Catch matches in Biarritz, Bayonne and St-Jean de Luz between June and September.

D912); it's served in high season, by boats. Both beaches are protected from the wrath of the Atlantic by breakwaters and jetties, and are among the few child-friendly beaches in the Basque Country.

Église St-Jean Baptiste Church
(rue Gambetta, St-Jean de Luz; ⌚8.30am-noon & 2-7pm) The plain facade of France's largest and finest Basque church conceals a splendid interior with a magnificent baroque altarpiece. It was in front of this very altarpiece that Louis XIV and María Teresa, daughter of King Philip IV of Spain, were married in 1660. After exchanging rings, the couple walked down the aisle and out of the south door, which was then sealed to commemorate peace between the two nations after 24 years of hostilities.

Maison Louis XIV Historic Building
(☎05 59 26 27 58; www.maison-louis-xiv.fr; 6 place Louis XIV, St-Jean de Luz; adult/child €6/3.80; ⌚10.30am-noon & 2.30-6pm Wed-Mon Jul-Aug, 11am-3pm & 4-5pm Wed-Mon Easter, Jun & Sep–mid-Oct) Sitting on a pretty, pedestrianised square is the so-called Maison Louis XIV. Built in 1643 by a wealthy shipowner and furnished in period style, this is where Louis XIV lived out his last days of bachelorhood before marrying María Teresa. Half-hour guided tours (with English text) depart several times daily in July and August.

Alongside, and rather dwarfed by its more imposing neighbour, is **Hôtel de Ville**, built in 1657.

Socoa Old Town
The heart of Socoa is about 2.5km west of Ciboure along the continuation of quai Maurice Ravel (named for the *Boléro* composer, who was born in Ciboure in 1875). Its prominent **fort** was built in 1627 and later improved by Vauban. You can walk out to the Digue de Socoa breakwater or climb to the **lighthouse** via rue du Phare, then out along rue du Sémaphore for fabulous coastal views.

Sleeping

La Devinière Boutique Hotel €€
(☎05 59 26 05 51; www.hotel-la-deviniere.com; 5 rue Loquin, St-Jean de Luz; d €120-180;) You have to love a place that forsakes TVs for antiquarian books (room 11 even has its own mini-library). Beyond the living room, with its piano and comfy armchairs, there's a delightful small patio equipped with lounges and the rooms are stuffed full of antique and replica antique furnishings.

Zazpi Design Hotel €€€
(☎05 59 26 07 77; www.zazpihotel.com; 21 bd Thiers, St-Jean de Luz; r €195-310;) Seriously hip, this wonderful old mansion-turned-designer hotel is one of the most stylish hotels in southwest France. Staying here is like living in a very glam modern art gallery. There's a rooftop terrace complete with pool and sensational views over an ocean of terracotta roof tiles to the fairy-tale green Basque hills.

Eating

Buvette des Halles Seafood €
(☎05 59 26 73 59; bd Victor Hugo, St-Jean de Luz; dishes €7-14; ⌚6am-2pm & dinner, closed Tue Sep-Jun) Tucked into a corner of the covered market, this minuscule restaurant serves goat's cheese, Bayonne ham, grilled sardines, fish soup, mussels and much more. Between June and September you can eat outside beneath the plane trees on the small square; the rest of the year you can eat tucked up inside, but go early for the best pickings.

Grillerie du Port Seafood €
(☎05 59 51 18 29; quai du Maréchal Leclerc, St-Jean de Luz; mains €7.50-9.50; ⌚noon-2.30pm & 7-10.30pm Jun-Sep) It won't take long to peruse the menu at this old port-side classic. It's essentially a choice of grilled sardines or grilled tuna – all freshly caught that morning and utterly delicious.

Information

Tourist Office (**☎05 59 26 03 16; www.saint-jean-de-luz.com; 20 bd Victor Hugo, St-Jean de Luz; ⏰9am-12.30pm & 2-7pm Mon-Sat, 10am-1pm Sun**) Runs an extensive program of French-language tours around the town and across the Spanish border; ask about English-language tours in summer.

Getting There & Away

There are frequent trains to Bayonne (€5.10, 25 minutes) via Biarritz (€3.40, 15 minutes) and to Hendaye (€3.30, 15 minutes), with connections to Spain.

St-Jean Pied de Port

POP 1700

At the foot of the Pyrenees, the walled town of St-Jean Pied de Port, 53km southeast of Bayonne, was for centuries the last stop in France for pilgrims heading south over the Spanish border, a mere 8km away, and on to Santiago de Compostela, in Galicia in western Spain. Today it remains a popular departure point for hikers attempting the pilgrim trail, but there are plenty of shorter hikes and opportunities for mountain biking in the area.

St-Jean Pied de Port makes an ideal day trip from Bayonne, particularly on Monday when the market is in full swing.

Sights

Old Town — Old Town

The walled old quarter is an attractive place of cobbled streets, geranium-covered balconies and lots of quirky boutiques.

La Citadelle — Fortress

From the top of rue de la Citadelle, a rough cobblestone path ascends to the massive citadel itself, from where there's a spectacular panorama of the town and the surrounding hills. Constructed in 1628, the fort was rebuilt around 1680 by military engineers of the Vauban school. Nowadays it serves as a secondary school and is closed to the public.

Fort Socoa

GERARD LABRIET/GETTY IMAGES ©

Eating

Chez Arrambide Gastronomic **€€**
(☎05 59 37 01 01; www.hotel-les-pyrenees.com; 19 place Charles de Gaulle; menus €42-110, mains €28-45; ⏰12.15-1.45pm & 7.45-9pm Jul-Aug, Wed-Mon Sep-Jun) This twin Michelin-starred restaurant, inside the (overpriced) Hôtel Les Pyrénées, is where chef Firmin Arrambide does wonders with seasonal market produce, such as truffle and foie-gras lasagne.

Information

Tourist Office (☎05 59 37 03 57; www.saintjeanpieddeport-paysbasque-tourisme.com; place Charles de Gaulle; ⏰9am-7pm Mon-Sat, 10am-1pm & 2-7pm Sun Jul & Aug, 9am-noon & 2-6pm Mon-Sat Sep-Jun)

Getting There & Away

Train is the only option to travel to or from Bayonne (€9.20, 1¼ hours, up to five daily).

Lourdes

If you've ever wondered what a Catholic version of Las Vegas might look like, chances are it'd turn out pretty close to Lourdes. This sprawling town, 43km southeast of Pau, has been one of the world's most important pilgrimage sites since 1858, when 14-year-old Bernadette Soubirous (1844–79) saw the Virgin Mary in a series of 18 visions in a rocky grotto. The visions were subsequently confirmed by the Vatican, and Bernadette was beatified in 1933.

Now known as the Sanctuaires Notre Dame de Lourdes, the grotto is considered to be one of the holiest sites in Christendom. Over six million people arrive in Lourdes every year, to pray, pay homage and be doused in the suposedly miraculous waters. But in contrast to its spiritual importance, the modern town of Lourdes itself is a pretty dispiriting experience, with a tatty tangle of neon-signed hotels and souvenir shops selling everything from plastic crucifixes to Madonna-shaped bottles (just add holy water at the shrine).

Sights

Sanctuaires Notre Dame de Lourdes Cave
(http://fr.lourdes-france.org; ⏰Porte St-Michel & Porte St-Joseph 5am-midnight, baths 9-11am & 2-4pm Mon-Sat, 2-4pm Sun & holy days) The spiritual centre of Lourdes is the subterranean grotto where Bernadette Soubirous experienced her visions in 1858. From the **Porte St-Joseph**, a broad boulevard sweeps towards the gilded spires of the **Basilique du Rosaire** and the **Basilique Supérieure** (Upper Basilica).

Sanctuaires Notre Dame de Lourdes

Underneath is the fabled **Grotte de Massabielle**, where people queue for hours to enter and take a blessed dip in the cave's icy-cold baths, while other pilgrims content themselves by lighting candles of remembrance outside.

Château Fort Château, Museum

(Fortified Castle; www.chateaufort-lourdes.fr; adult/child €6/3; 9am-noon & 1.30-6.30pm, open all day Jul & Aug) Lourdes' imposing castle stands on a sheer hill just behind the town. There's been a stronghold here since Roman times, but the present building combines a medieval keep with fortifications added during the 17th and 18th centuries. Since the 1920s, the castle has housed the **Musée Pyrénéen**, which displays local artefacts and folk art.

A free lift takes you up to the castle from rue Baron Duprat.

Pic du Jer Viewpoint

(www.picdujer.fr; bd d'Espagne; funicular adult/child return €10/7.50; 9.30am-6pm Mar-Nov) Panoramic views of Lourdes and the central Pyrenees are on offer from this rocky outcrop just outside town. There are two routes to the top: a punishing three-hour hike (ideal for penitents) or a speedy six-minute ride on the funicular (ideal for everyone else).

Sleeping & Eating

Bestwestern Beauséjour Hotel €€

(05 62 94 38 18; www.hotel-beausejour.com; 16 av de la Gare; s €88-98, d €105-115;) Despite the heritage facade and glossy lobby, the rooms at this Best Western are as generic as ever. Still, it's handy for the station and tidier than many places. There's a bar-brasserie downstairs.

Le Cabanon Bistro €€

(05 62 41 47 87; 37 rue de la Grotte; mains €11.50-16; noon-2.30pm & 7-9.30pm) Dining out can be decidedly hit-and-miss in Lourdes, which makes this friendly bistro a doubly good find. It offers solid, no-frills French food, mainly classics like grilled steak and duck breast.

Information

Forum Information Office **(05 62 42 78 78; www.lourdes-france.com; Esplanade des Processions; 8.30am-6.30pm)** For information on the Sanctuaires Notre Dame de Lourdes.

Tourist Office **(05 62 42 77 40; www.lourdes-infotourisme.com; place Peyramale; 9am-6.30pm)** Lourdes' main tourist office has general information on the Pyrenees and advice on accommodation, transport and activities.

Getting There & Away

Lourdes has regular train connections, including direct TGVs to Pau and Paris Montparnasse.

Bayonne €16 to €21, two hours via Pau

Paris' Montparnasse €68 to €91.50, four hours via TGV

Toulouse €25, 2¼ hours

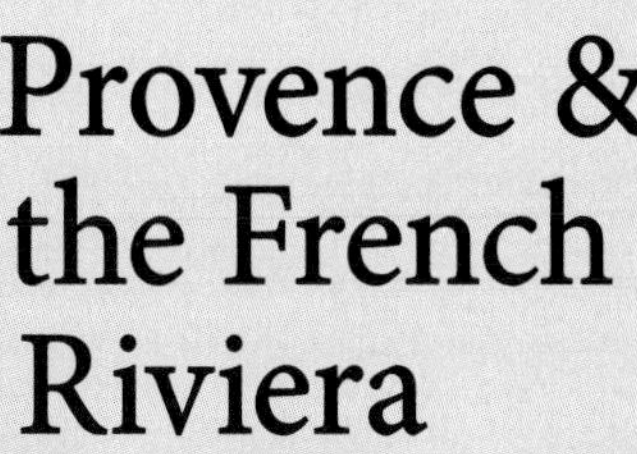

Provence & the French Riviera

There is no more sunny and celebrity-rich part of France than the south. Get set for heart and soul seduction. Travelling here means sauntering through scented lavender fields and vineyards, around vibrant morning markets groaning with fresh produce, and along paradisaical shores lapped by clear turquoise waters.

Roughly speaking, this region splits into three: east is the iconic French Riviera, wedged between glitzy star-spangled Cannes and megalomaniacal Monte Carlo in the millionaire principality of Monaco. In the middle is Provence, hinged on the coast by the wildly contrasting fishing ports of St-Tropez and Marseille, and tethered inland by a stash of Roman vestiges, hilltop villages and exceptional natural landscapes. Languedoc lies west, an upcoming region that travellers visit first and foremost for the walled city of Carcassonne and its bewitching witch's-hat turrets.

The French Riviera

Provence & the French Riviera

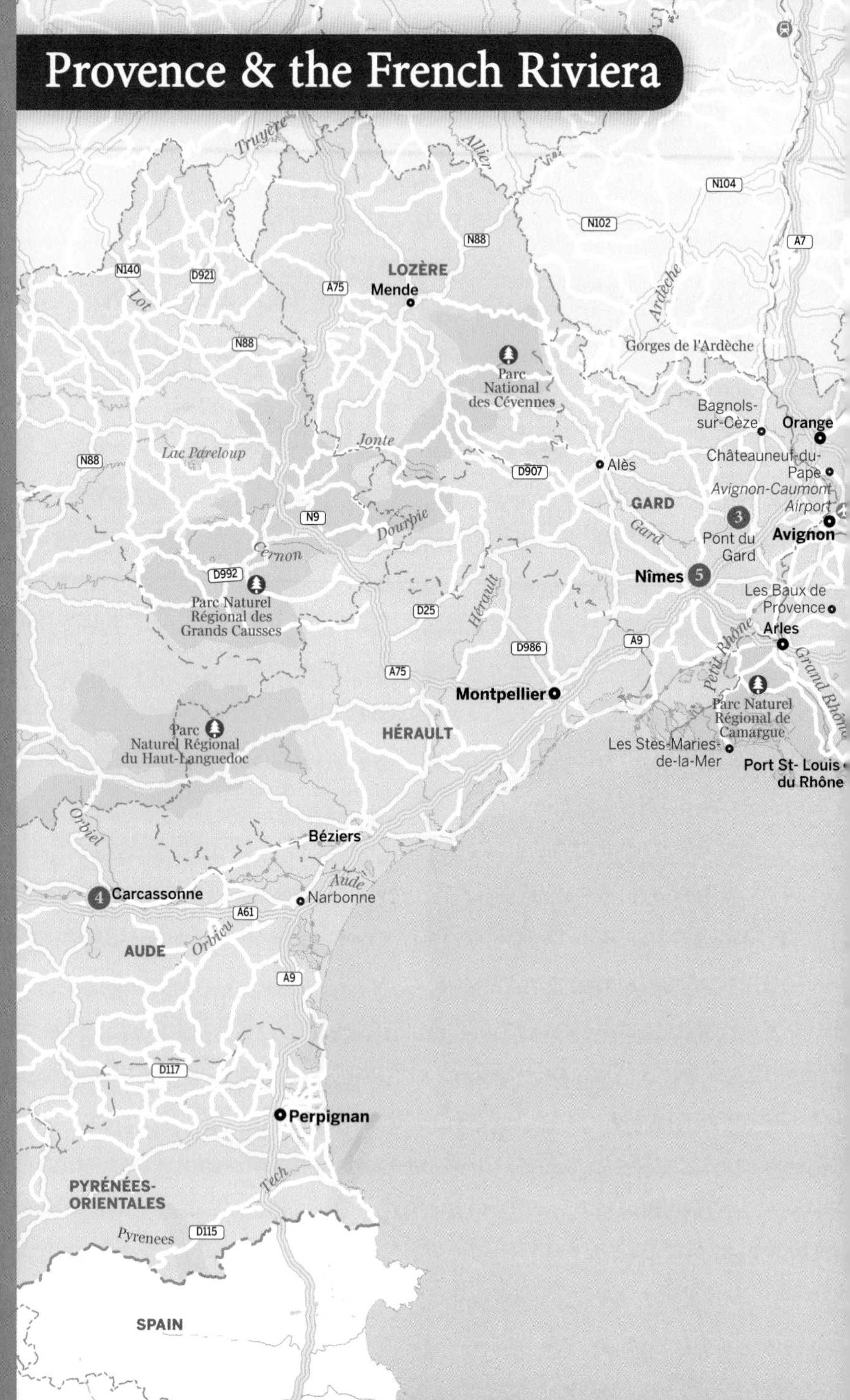

Truyère
Allier
N104
N102
N88
A7
N140
D921
Lot
LOZÈRE
A75
Mende
Ardèche
N88
Gorges de l'Ardèche
Parc National des Cévennes
Bagnols-sur-Cèze
Orange
Jonte
Lac Pareloup
N88
Alès
Châteauneuf-du-Pape
D907
Avignon-Caumont Airport
GARD
N9
Dourbie
3
Avignon
Gard
Pont du Gard
Cernon
D992
Nîmes
5
Parc Naturel Régional des Grands Causses
D25
Hérault
Les Baux de Provence
Arles
A9
Petit Rhône
D986
Grand Rhône
A75
Montpellier
Parc Naturel Régional de Camargue
Parc Naturel Régional du Haut-Languedoc
HÉRAULT
Les Stes-Maries-de-la-Mer
Port St- Louis du Rhône
Orbiel
Béziers
Aude
4
Carcassonne
Narbonne
A61
AUDE
Orbieu
A9
D117
Perpignan
Tech
PYRÉNÉES-ORIENTALES
Pyrenees
D115
SPAIN

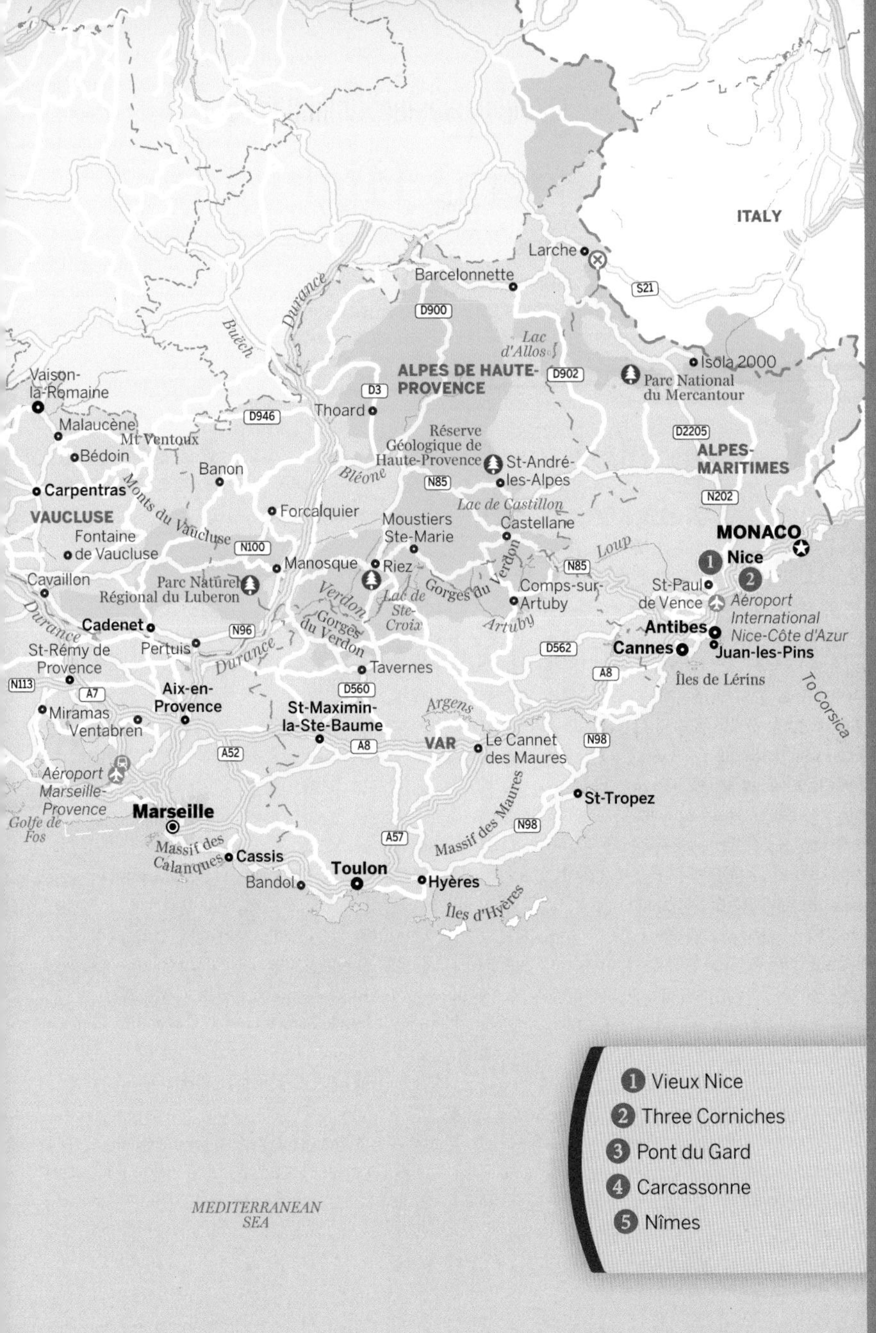
ITALY
Larche
Barcelonnette
D900
Durance
Buëch
Lac d'Allos
ALPES DE HAUTE-PROVENCE
D902
Isola 2000
Parc National du Mercantour
D3
Vaison-la-Romaine
Thoard
D946
Malaucène
Mt Ventoux
Réserve Géologique de Haute-Provence
St-André-les-Alpes
D2205
ALPES-MARITIMES
Bédoin
Banon
Bléone
N85
Carpentras
Monts du Vaucluse
Lac de Castillon
N202
VAUCLUSE
Forcalquier
Moustiers Ste-Marie
Castellane
MONACO
Fontaine de Vaucluse
N100
Loup
Nice
Manosque
Riez
N85
Cavaillon
Parc Naturel Régional du Luberon
Verdon
Lac de Ste-Croix
Gorges du Verdon
Comps-sur-Artuby
St-Paul de Vence
Aéroport International Nice-Côte d'Azur
Durance
Cadenet
N96
Gorges du Verdon
Artuby
Antibes
St-Rémy de Provence
Pertuis
Durance
D562
Cannes
Juan-les-Pins
Tavernes
A8
Îles de Lérins
N113
A7
Aix-en-Provence
D560
To Corsica
Miramas
Ventabren
St-Maximin-la-Ste-Baume
Argens
A52
A8
VAR
Le Cannet des Maures
N98
Aéroport Marseille-Provence
St-Tropez
Golfe de Fos
Marseille
Massif des Maures
N98
A57
Massif des Calanques
Cassis
Toulon
Bandol
Hyères
Îles d'Hyères
MEDITERRANEAN SEA
1 Vieux Nice
2 Three Corniches
3 Pont du Gard
4 Carcassonne
5 Nîmes
0 40 km
0 20 miles

Provence & the French Riviera's Highlights

Vieux Nice

Losing yourself well and truly in the labyrinthine lanes, church-blessed alleys and secret squares of Vieux Nice (Old Nice; p326) is an essential pilgrimage for anyone Riviera-bound. Oozing atmopshere, ambience and a healthy dose of cafes, bars and pavement terraces, Vieux Nice begs go-slow exploration. Break for a lavender or black olive ice-cream at Fenocchio (p325) and an end-of-day drink at Les Distilleries Idéales (p325).

1

2

Three Corniches

This trio of clifftop roads (p340) between Nice and Menton provides one of France's most iconic drives. Hitchcock used the corniches as a backdrop in *To Catch a Thief* (1956) starring Cary Grant and Grace Kelly (who died in a car crash on the same road in 1982). Don your shades, roll down the windows and navigate jaw-dropping hairpin bends en route to the millionaires' playground, Monaco.

Left: View of Èze (p341) on the Moyenne Corniche

COLIN MATTHIEU/HEMIS.FR/GETTY IMAGES ©

3 Pont du Gard

The scale of this Unesco World Heritage Site near Nîmes (p315) is gargantuan: the 35 arches straddling the Roman aqueduct's 275m-long upper tier contain a watercourse designed to carry 20,000 cubic metres of water per day. View it from afloat a canoe on the River Gard or pay extra to take a guided walk across its top tier.

BRUNO DE HOGUES/GETTY IMAGES ©

4 Carcassonne

The first glimpse of La Cité's sturdy stone witch's-hat turrets above Carcassonne (p317) in the Languedoc is enough to make your hair stand on end. To savour this fairy-tale walled city in its true glory, linger at dusk after the crowds have left, when the old town belongs once again to its 100-odd inhabitants and the small number of visitors staying at the few lovely hotels within its ramparts.

5 Les Arènes de Nîmes

Long before the rich and famous arrived, the Romans recognised the seductive charms of southern France. The region is studded with many well-preserved Roman monuments, including this almost-intact amphitheatre (p313) in Nîmes. Built to seat more than 10,000 spectators, it served as the stage for gladiatorial contests and bloodthirsty shows, and is – controversially – still used for bullfights to this day.

Provence & the French Riviera's Best...

Beaches

Plage de Pampelonne Play and lunch Brigitte-Bardot–style on St-Tropez's finest golden sand. (p337)

Promenade des Anglais Beach-lounge on a sky-blue chair beside Nice's mythical seaside prom. (p320)

Z Plage Glamour and creature comforts on La Croisette, Cannes. (p333)

Îles de Lérins Flee Cannes' madness for a perfect castaway cove. (p336)

Île de Port-Cros & Île de Porquerolles Catch a ferry to a bevy of beautiful island beaches. (p339)

Modern Art

Chapelle du Rosaire This bijou chapel was Matisse's pride and joy. (p330)

Fondation Maeght World-class art in St-Paul de Vence. (p329)

Musée Picasso View Picassos in Antibes in the artist's former studio turned museum. (p327)

Mamac Nice's modern-art museum is as interesting for the architecture as the art. (p320)

Aix-en-Provence Follow in the footsteps of Paul Cézanne. (p300)

Dining

L'Atelier Not a meal, but an artistic (organic) experience in Arles. (p306)

Petit Pierre Reboul Indulge yourself with the inventions of Aix' hottest chef. (p303)

Hôtel La Mirande Learn to cook in a 16th-century palace hotel in Avignon. (p311)

L'Epuisette The place to savour Marseille's famously fishy bouillabaisse. (p300)

Sea Sens French gastronomy and Asian elegance in Cannes. (p335)

Shopping

- **Aix-en-Provence** Seek out *Calissons d'Aix*, marzipan-like sweets first baked for King René's wedding banquet in 1473. (p300)
- **La Botte Camarguaise** Camargue cowboy boots cut, stitched and sold in Arles. (p308)
- **Cours Saleya Market** The place to buy silken olive oil from Provence, pressed from olives that are harvested November to January. (p326)
- **Atelier Rondini** Iconic, beach-chic sandals cobbled in St-Tropez since 1927. (p339)

Left: Cours Saleya Market (p326); **Above:** Île de Porquerolles (p339)

Need to Know

ADVANCE PLANNING

- **As early as possible** Book accommodation, especially for July, August and during the Cannes Film Festival and Monaco Grand Prix (both in May). Reserve tickets for Avignon's theatre festival (www.festival-avignon.com/en) and *férias* (bullfighting festivals) in Arles and Nîmes.
- **Two weeks before** Book tables for big-name restaurants, especially in Marseille, Nice and St-Tropez.
- **Two days before** Order bouillabaisse at Marseille's bistros (p300).

RESOURCES

- **Provence-Alpes-Côte d'Azur** (www.decouverte-paca.fr) Pan-regional information.
- **Nice Tourisme** (www.nicetourisme.com) Nice's tourist office.
- **PACA** (www.tourismepaca.fr) Umbrella site for Provence and the Riviera.
- **Côte d'Azur Tourisme** (www.cotedazur-tourisme.com) Comprehensive Riviera resource.

GETTING AROUND

- **Train** An ideal way to explore the Riviera coastline. Base yourself in Nice and take day trips to Monaco and Cannes.
- **Car** Essential in Provence. On the coast in July and August there's hellish road traffic, especially on Saturdays and pretty much all summer around St-Tropez. Take extra care when driving along the corniches.
- **Boats** Scenic cruises depart from Marseille, Cannes and St-Tropez; don't miss a trip to the Îles de Lérins (p336) or the Îles d'Hyères (p339).

BE FOREWARNED

- **Petty theft** from backpacks, pockets and bags is rife in Marseille and on the Riviera; be extra vigilant at train stations and on the beach.
- **Cannes hotel prices** soar to astronomical levels during May's film festival.
- **Dress code** Pack smart clothes for top-end Riviera restaurants, clubs and casinos.
- **Motoring in Monaco** You can't drive into Monaco Ville unless you have a Monaco or local 06 number plate.

Provence & the French Riviera Itineraries

With its swaying palm trees, hilltop towns and sparkling beaches, the French Riviera is the essence of southern France. Savour every moment.

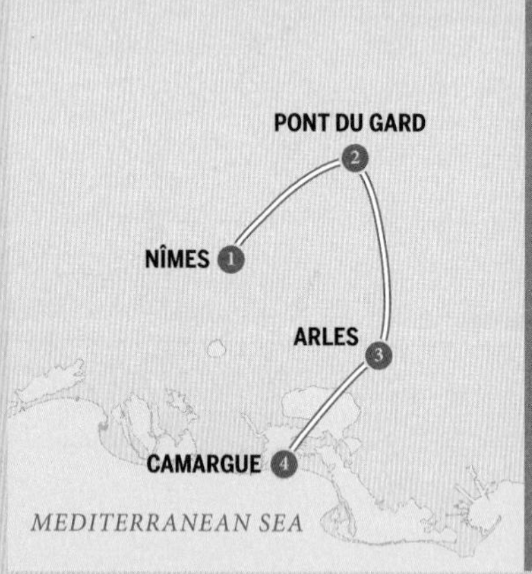

3 DAYS

NÎMES TO THE CAMARGUE
ROMAN PROVENCE

Gloriously intact amphitheatres, triumphal arches and other public buildings transport travellers back to Provence's heyday as a Gallo-Roman province.

Devote day one to ❶**Nîmes**, with its resplendent amphitheatre and theatre, still occasionally used for *férias*, concerts and bullfights. Just outside Nîmes is one of the great achievements of the Gallo-Roman world – the incredible ❷**Pont du Gard**, the world's highest aqueduct. It's particularly awe inspiring when seen up close – via either a guided walk across the top tier or a self-paddled canoe trip beneath its great arches.

Spend day two in ❸**Arles**, with its duo of impressive Roman theatres. Day three, flee the hustle and bustle of town life for the idyllic wetland of ❹**the Camargue**. Spot candy-pink flamingos, wild white horses and rare bird species (over 500 species in all) in the peaceful setting of one of France's largest natural wetlands – don't forget binoculars and a telephoto lens for your camera.

NICE TO CANNES
RIVIERA HIGHLIGHTS

This trip takes in the key sights of the Côte d'Azur. Begin in the millionaires' playground of ❶ **Monaco**, where you can ogle the yachts, have a flutter at the casino and lunch fusion-style at La Montgolfière.

On day two, tackle ❷ **the Corniches**, a trio of white-knuckle roads snaking across the clifftops west of Monaco. Stop for a wander around the clifftop gardens of ❸ **Èze**. By late afternoon you'll reach the classic Riviera city, ❹ **Nice**; check into Hôtel La Pérouse and have an authentic Niçois meal in the atmospheric old town.

Day three's for more Nice exploration: don't miss the cours Saleya street market, the Promenade des Anglais, the Musée Matisse and Musée d'Art Moderne et d'Art Contemporain (Mamac).

On day four, head inland to hilltop ❺ **St-Paul de Vence**, where everyone from Matisse to Picasso once went to paint and party. View the art collection at the Fondation Maeght, then dine and overnight at the legendary Colombe d'Or.

Your last day takes you to cinematic ❻ **Cannes**, home of France's starriest film festival. If you can spare an extra day, catch a boat to the lovely ❼ **Îles de Lérins**.

Flamingos and horses in the Camargue (p306)

Discover Provence & the French Riviera

At a Glance

- **Provence** (p292) France's hot, seductive south: sunbaked towns, lavender fields and tempting al fresco food markets.
- **Languedoc** (p313) Roman remains and rich red wines.
- **French Riviera** (p319) France's most glam coastline: mythical beaches, sparkling water and scenic but hair-raising coastal roads.

Basilique Notre Dame de la Garde
PETER PHIPP/GETTY IMAGES ©

PROVENCE

Marseille

POP 858,902

Marseillais will tell you that the city's rough-and-tumble edginess is part of its charm and that, for all its flaws, it is a very endearing place. They're right: Marseille grows on you with its history, fusion of cultures, souk-like markets, millennia-old port and corniches (coastal roads) along rocky inlets and sun-baked beaches. Their ultimate vindication came with Marseille's selection as European Capital of Culture for 2013.

The heart of central Marseille is the Vieux Port where ships have docked for more than 26 centuries. Its entrance is guarded on the southern side by **Fort St-Nicolas** (8am-7.45pm May-Aug, shorter hrs Sep-Apr) FREE, a sturdy stone fortress with benches in its terraced grounds for pondering its terrific views. Across the water, in a sister fortress, is part of MuCEM, the sparkling centrepiece of the city.

Sights

Buy a cent-saving **Marseille City Pass** (one-/two-day pass €22/29) at the tourist office (p300). It covers admission to 15 museums, a city tour, unlimited public-transport travel, boat trips and more.

Musée des Civilisations de l'Europe et de la Méditerranée Museum

(MuCEM; Museum of European & Mediterranean Civilisations; 04 84 35 13 13; www.mucem.org; 1 esplanade du J4; admission Fort St-Jean free, J4 adult/child €8/5; 9am-8pm Jul & Aug, 11am-7pm Sep-Oct & May-Jul, 11am-6pm Nov-Apr;

(M Vieux Port or Joliette) The icon of the 'new' Marseille, this stunning museum is split across two dramatically contrasting sites, linked by a vertigo-inducing foot bridge. On one side is lumbering **Fort St-Jean**, founded in the 13th century by the Knights Hospitaller of St John of Jerusalem and rebuilt by Louis XIV in the 17th century. On the other side is the contemporary **J4**, a shoebox with breathtaking 'lace' skin designed by Algerian-born, Marseille-educated architect Rudi Ricciotti.

Villa Méditerranée Museum

(www.villa-mediterranee.org; bd du Littoral, Esplanade du J4; noon-7pm Tue-Thu, noon-10pm Fri, 10am-7pm Sat & Sun; M Vieux Port or Joliette) FREE This eye-catching white structure next to MuCEM is no ordinary 'villa'. Designed by architect Stefano Boeri in 2013, the pistol-shaped edifice sports the most spectacular cantilever you are ever likely to see: it overhangs an ornamental pool of water below. Inside the building there is a viewing gallery with glass-panelled floor (look down if you dare!), and two or three temporary multimedia exhibitions evoking different aspects of the Mediterranean, be it sea life, history or transport.

Le Panier Historic Neighbourhood

(M Vieux Port) From the Vieux Port, hike north up to this fantastic history-woven quarter, dubbed Marseille's Montmartre as much for its sloping streets as its artsy ambience. In Greek Massilia it was the site of the *agora* (marketplace), hence its name, which means 'the basket'. During WWII the quarter was dynamited and afterwards rebuilt. Today it's a mishmash of lanes hiding artisan shops, *ateliers* (workshops) and terraced houses strung with drying washing.

Its centerpiece is **Centre de la Vieille Charité** (http://vieille-charite-marseille.com; 2 rue de la Charité; adult/child €5/3, with exhibitions €10/8; 10am-6pm Tue-Sun; M Joliette); nearby **Cathédrale de la Major** (10am-6.30pm Tue-Sun) stands guard between the old and 'new' ports with a 'stripy' facade made of local Cassis stone and green Florentine marble.

Basilique Notre Dame de la Garde Church

(Montée de la Bonne Mère; 7am-8pm Apr-Sep, 7am-7pm Oct-Mar) This opulent 19th-century Romano-Byzantine basilica occupies Marseille's highest point, La Garde (162m). Built between 1853 and 1864, it is ornamented with coloured marble, murals depicting the safe passage of sailing vessels and superb mosaics. The hilltop gives 360-degree panoramas of the city. The church's bell tower is crowned by a 9.7m-tall gilded statue of the Virgin Mary on a 12m-high pedestal. It's a 1km walk from the Vieux Port, or take bus 60 or the tourist train.

Château d'If Island, Castle

(www.if.monuments-nationaux.fr; adult/child €5.50/free; 10am-6pm May-Sep, shorter hrs Oct-Apr) Immortalised in Alexandre Dumas' classic 1844 novel *Le Comte de Monte Cristo* (The Count of Monte Cristo), the 16th-century fortress-turned-prison Château d'If sits on the 30-sq-km island, Île d'If, 3.5km west of the Vieux Port. Political prisoners were incarcerated here, along with hundreds of Protestants, the Revolutionary hero Mirabeau, and the Communards of 1871.

Frioul If Express (www.frioul-if-express.com; 1 quai des Belges) boats leave for Château d'If (€10.10 return, 20 minutes, around 15 daily) from the Vieux Port.

Sleeping

Hôtel Hermès Design Hotel €

(04 96 11 63 63; www.hotelmarseille.com; 2 rue Bonneterie; s €64, d €85-102; M Vieux Port) Nothing to do with the Paris design house, this excellent-value hotel has a rooftop terrace with panoramic Vieux Port views. Grab breakfast (€9) on a tray in the bright ground-floor breakfast room and ride the lift to the 5th floor for breakfast à la rooftop. Contemporary rooms have white walls and a splash of lime-green or red to complement their Scandinavian-like design.

Au Vieux Panier B&B €€

(04 91 91 23 72; www.auvieuxpanier.com; 13 rue du Panier; d €100-140; M Vieux Port)

Central Marseille

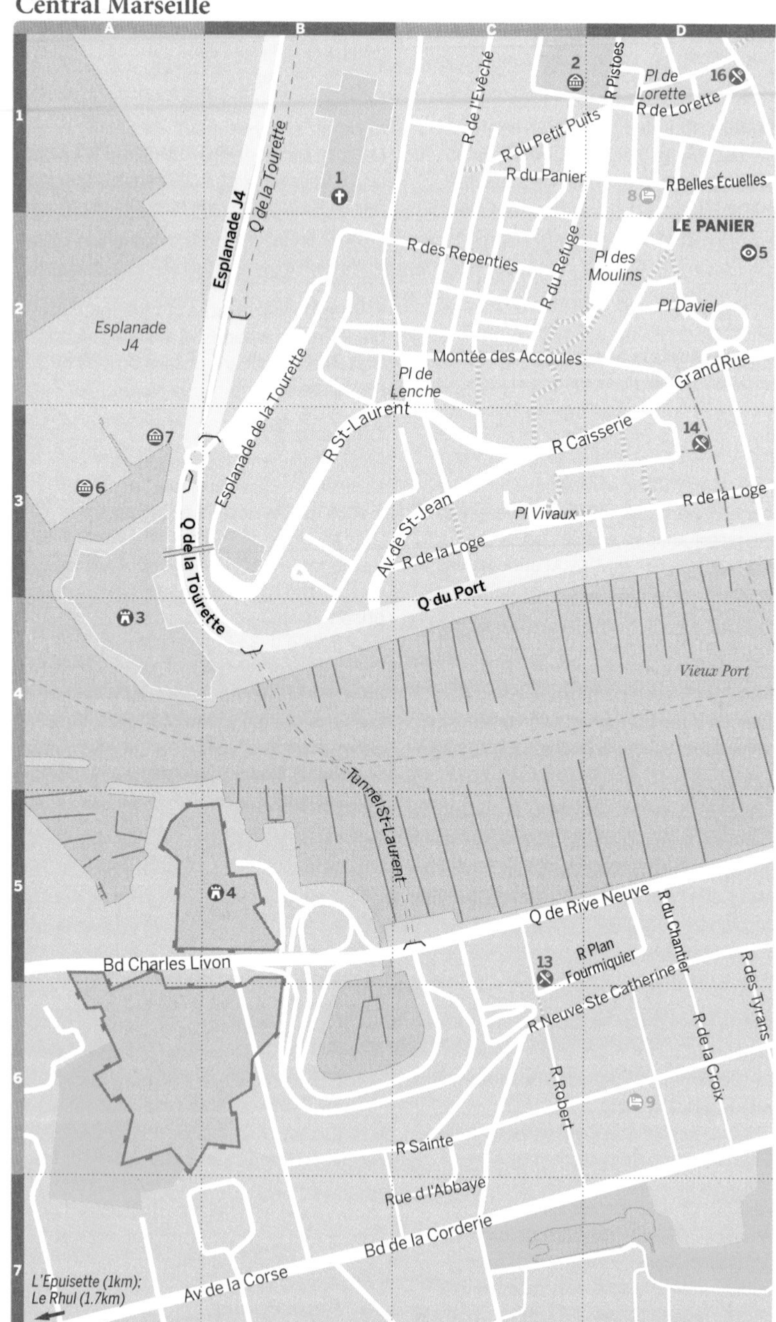

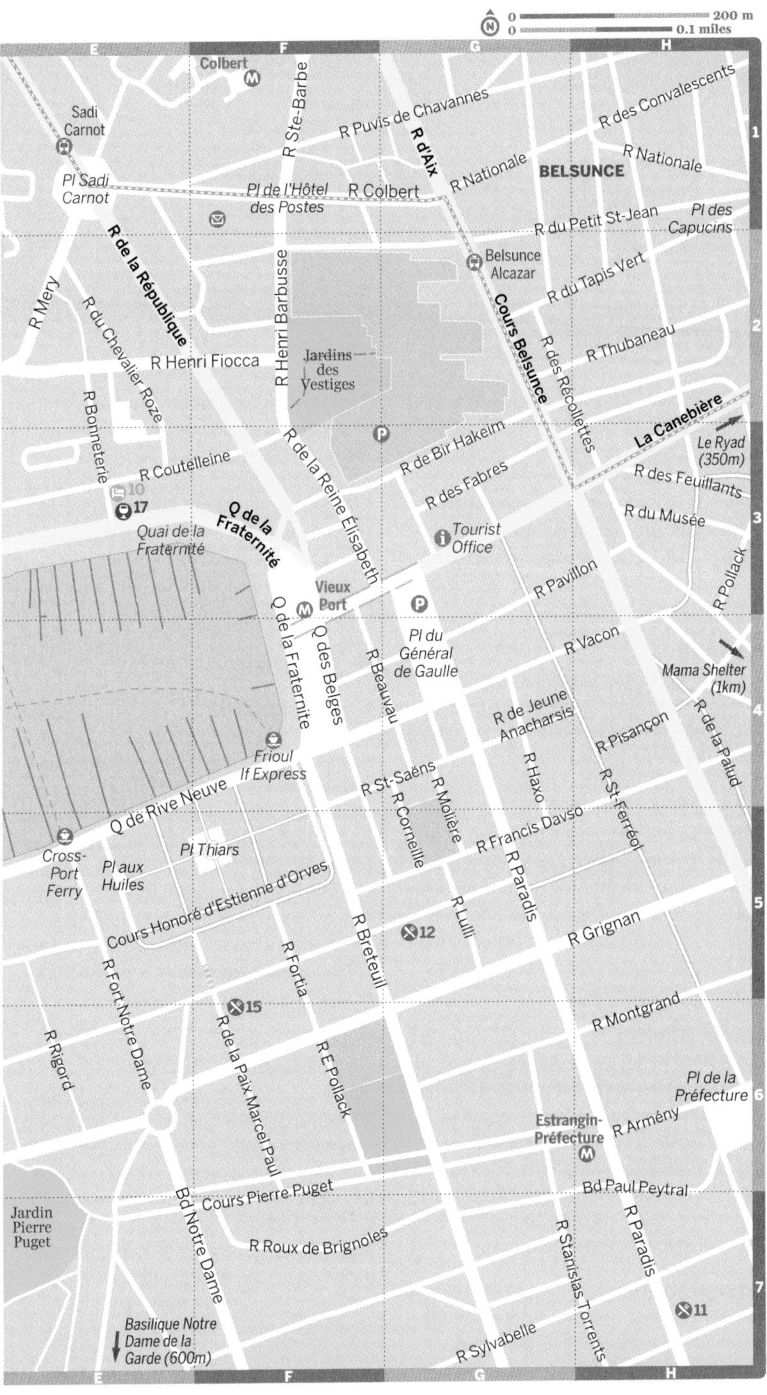

PROVENCE & THE FRENCH RIVIERA MARSEILLE

Central Marseille

Sights

1 Cathédrale de Marseille Notre Dame de Major B1
2 Centre de la Vieille Charité C1
3 Fort St-Jean A4
4 Fort St-Nicolas B5
5 Le Panier D2
6 Musée des Civilisations de l'Europe et de la Méditerranée A3
7 Villa Méditerranée A3

Sleeping

8 Au Vieux Panier D1
9 Casa Honoré D6
10 Hôtel Hermès E3

Eating

11 Café Populaire H7
12 La Part des Anges G5
13 La Passarelle C5
14 Le Café des Épices D3
15 Le Grain de Sel F6
Le Môlé Passédat .... (see 6)
16 Pizzaria Chez Étienne D1

Drinking & Nightlife

17 La Caravelle E3

The height of Le Panier shabby chic, this super-stylish *maison d'hôte* (B&Bs) woos art lovers with original works of art. Each year artists are invited to redecorate it, meaning its six rooms change annually. Staircases and corridors are like an art gallery and a drop-dead gorgeous rooftop terrace peeks across terracotta tiles to the sea on the horizon.

Le Ryad Boutique Hotel €€
(**04 91 47 74 54; www.hoteldemarseille.fr; 16 rue Sénac de Meilhan Gabriel; s €80-125, d €95-140; ; Noailles, Canebière Garibaldi)** With high ceilings, arched alcoves, warm colours and minimalist decor, super-stylish Le Ryad draws sumptuous influence from Morocco. Beautiful bathrooms, garden-view rooms and great service compensate for the sometimes-sketchy neighbourhood. Despite the four-storey walk up, it's worth booking the top-floor room for its tiny rooftop terrace. Breakfast €12.

Mama Shelter Design Hotel €€
(**01 43 48 48 48; www.mamashelter.com; 64 rue de la Loubière; d €69-149; ; Notre Dame du Monte–Cours Julien)** Sleeping in Marseille doesn't get much funkier than this. With design by Philippe Starck, nifty extras like Kiehl's bathroom products, and free in-room movies, this is the affordable-chic kid on the block.

Casa Honoré B&B €€€
(**04 96 11 01 62; www.casahonore.com; 123 rue Sainte; d €150-200; ; Vieux Port)** Los Angeles meets Marseille at this four-room *maison d'hôte*, built around a central courtyard with a lap pool shaded by banana trees. The fashion-forward style reflects the owner's love for contemporary interior design, using disparate elements like black wicker and the occasional cow skull, which come together in one sexy package.

Eating

Café Populaire Bistro €
(**04 91 02 53 96; 110 rue Paradis; tapas €8-16, mains €19-23; noon-2.30pm & 8-11pm Tue-Sat; Estrangin-Préfecture)** Vintage furniture, old books on the shelves and a fine collection of glass soda bottles lend a retro air to this trendy, 1950s-styled *jazz comptoir* (counter) – a restaurant despite its name. The crowd is chic and smiling chefs in the open kitchen mesmerise with daily specials like king prawns *à la plancha* or beetroot and coriander salad.

Pizzaria Chez Étienne Regional Cuisine €
(**43 rue de Lorette; pizza €13-15, mains €15-20; noon-2.15pm & 8-11pm Mon-Sat; Colbert)** This old Marseillais haunt has the best pizza in town, as well as succulent *pavé de boeuf* (beef steak) and scrumptious *supions frits* (pan-fried squid with garlic and parsley). Since it's a convivial meeting point for the entire neighbourhood, pop in beforehand to reserve a table (there's no phone). No credit cards.

La Passarelle Provençal €

(☎ 04 91 33 03 27; www.restaurantlapassarelle.fr; 52 rue du Plan Fourmiguier; mains €18-22; ⏲ noon-2pm Tue-Sat, 8-10.30pm Thu-Sat; Ⓜ Vieux Port) Retro tables and chairs sit on a terrace beneath a shady sail, in the middle of the leafy-green *potager* (vegetable garden) where much of the kitchen's produce is grown. Philippe and Patricia's menu is predominantly organic, with other products being strictly local, and cuisine is charmingly simple – think catch of the day with vegetables, or beef with polenta.

Le Café des Épices Modern French €€

(☎ 04 91 91 22 69; www.cafedesepices.com; 4 rue du Lacydon; 2-/3-course lunch menu €25/28, dinner menu €45; ⏲ noon-3pm & 6-11pm Tue-Fri, noon-3pm Sat; 👪; Ⓜ Vieux Port) One of Marseille's best chefs, Arnaud de Grammont, infuses his cooking with a panoply of flavours: think squid-ink spaghetti with sesame and perfectly cooked scallops, or coriander- and citrus-spiced potatoes topped by the catch of the day. Presentation is impeccable, the decor is playful, and the colourful outdoor terrace between giant potted olive trees is superb.

Le Grain de Sel Modern French €€

(☎ 04 91 54 47 30; 39 rue de la Paix Marcel Paul; 2-/3-course menu €22/26, mains €18-25; ⏲ noon-1.30pm Tue-Thu, noon-1.30pm & 8-9.30pm Fri & Sat; Ⓜ Vieux Port) The Grain of Salt is always packed, generally with locals who love their gourmet food. The short menu includes inventive dishes such as cherry gaspacho with yellow tomatoes, pistachio and *brousse* (a type of cheese) as starter, or apricot *clafoutis* with almond milk ice cream and rosemary mousse for dessert.

Le Môlé Passédat Modern French €€€

(www.passedat.fr; 1 esplanade du J4, MuCEM; menu €52; ⏲ 12.30-2.30pm & 7.30-10.30pm Mon & Wed-Sat, 12.30-2.30pm Sun) Few kitchens are so stunningly located as this. On the top floor of Marseille's iconic museum, MuCEM, Michelin-starred chef Gérald Passédat cooks up exquisite French fare and big blue views of the coastline. **La Table** is the gastronomic restaurant; **La Cuisine**, with self-service dining around shared tables (no sea view), is the cheaper choice (2-/3-course menu €21.50/35). Reserve both online.

A restaurant inside Mama Shelter

Vieux Port

AN ITINERARY

Bold, busy and open-armed in the sea, Marseille is France's oldest city. Its Vieux Port, one kilometre long either side, is guarded by the great bastions of St-Jean and St-Nicolas whose guns once trained on the rebellious population rather than out to sea.

Rise early to hear tall tales from fishers at the waterfront **fish market** ❶. Grab *un café* and balcony seat at La Caravelle – views of Basilique Notre Dame de la Garde are first-class. Then sail to **Château d'If** ❷. Back on land, hike uphill into the ancient, apricot-hued stone maze of **Le Panier** ❸. Feast on exhibits in the **Centre de la Vieille Charité** ❹ and lunch on a café terrace on the tree-shaded square opposite.

Or indulge in a late lunch with big blue sea view at Le Môle Passedat on the rooftop of MuCEM. To get here, follow rue du Panier downhill to place des 13 Cantons, beyond to **Cathédrale de la Major** ❺, then along the waterfront to architectural stunners**Villa Méditerranée** ❻ and **MuCEM** ❼. Devote the afternoon to the exhibits and views here - extraordinary in equal measure – and end with a drink in the rooftop café of 1950s sanitary station **Musée Regards de Provence** ❽.

Late afternoon walk along quai du Port and ride the cross-port ferry across the water. See martyr bones enshrined in gold at**Abbaye St-Victor** ❾, catch the sun set in the **Jardin du Pharo** ❿ and join locals for a pastis with the **Milo de Croton** ⓫.

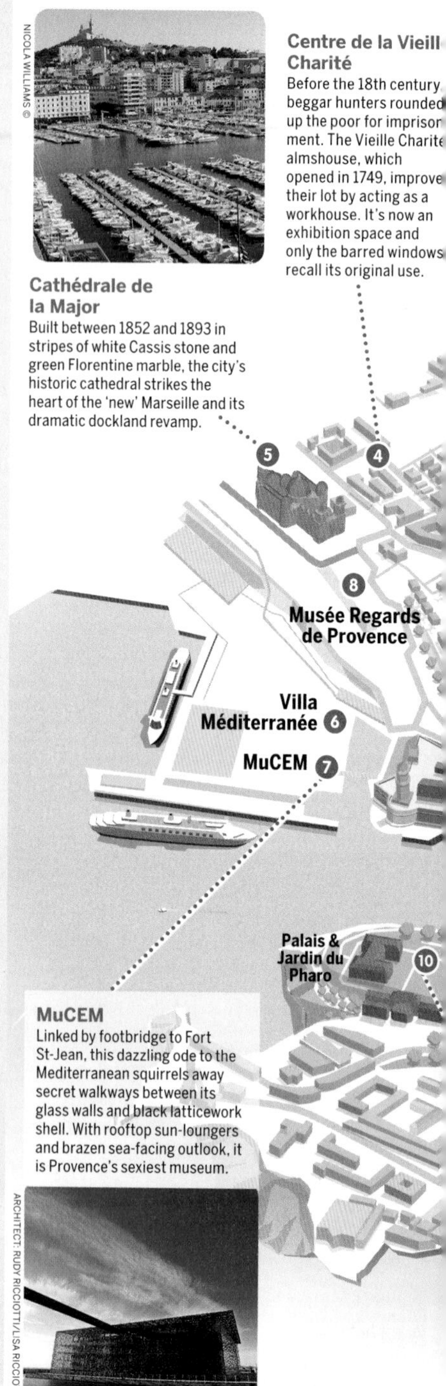

NICOLA WILLIAMS ©
Centre de la Vieill Charité
Before the 18th century, beggar hunters rounded up the poor for imprison ment. The Vieille Charité almshouse, which opened in 1749, improve their lot by acting as a workhouse. It's now an exhibition space and only the barred windows recall its original use.
Cathédrale de la Major
Built between 1852 and 1893 in stripes of white Cassis stone and green Florentine marble, the city's historic cathedral strikes the heart of the 'new' Marseille and its dramatic dockland revamp.
5
4
8
Musée Regards de Provence
Villa Méditerranée 6
MuCEM 7
Palais & Jardin du Pharo
10
MuCEM
Linked by footbridge to Fort St-Jean, this dazzling ode to the Mediterranean squirrels away secret walkways between its glass walls and black latticework shell. With rooftop sun-loungers and brazen sea-facing outlook, it is Provence's sexiest museum.
ARCHITECT: RUDY RICCIOTTI/LISA RICCIOTTI ©

GARDEL BERTRAND/GETTY IMAGES ©

Le Panier
The site of the Greek town of Massilia, Le Panier woos walkers with its sloping streets. Grand Rue follows the ancient road and opens out into place de Lenche, the location of the Greek market. It is still the place to shop for artisanal products.

Château d'If
Catch the Frioul If Express to Château d'If, France's equivalent to Alcatraz. Prisoners were housed according to class: the poorest at the bottom in windowless dungeons, the wealthiest in paid-for private cells, with windows and a fireplace.

Milo de Croton
Subversive local artist Pierre Puget carved the savage *Milo de Croton* for Louis XIV. The statue, whose original is in the Louvre, is a meditation on man's pride and shows the Greek Olympian being devoured by a lion, his Olympic cup cast down.

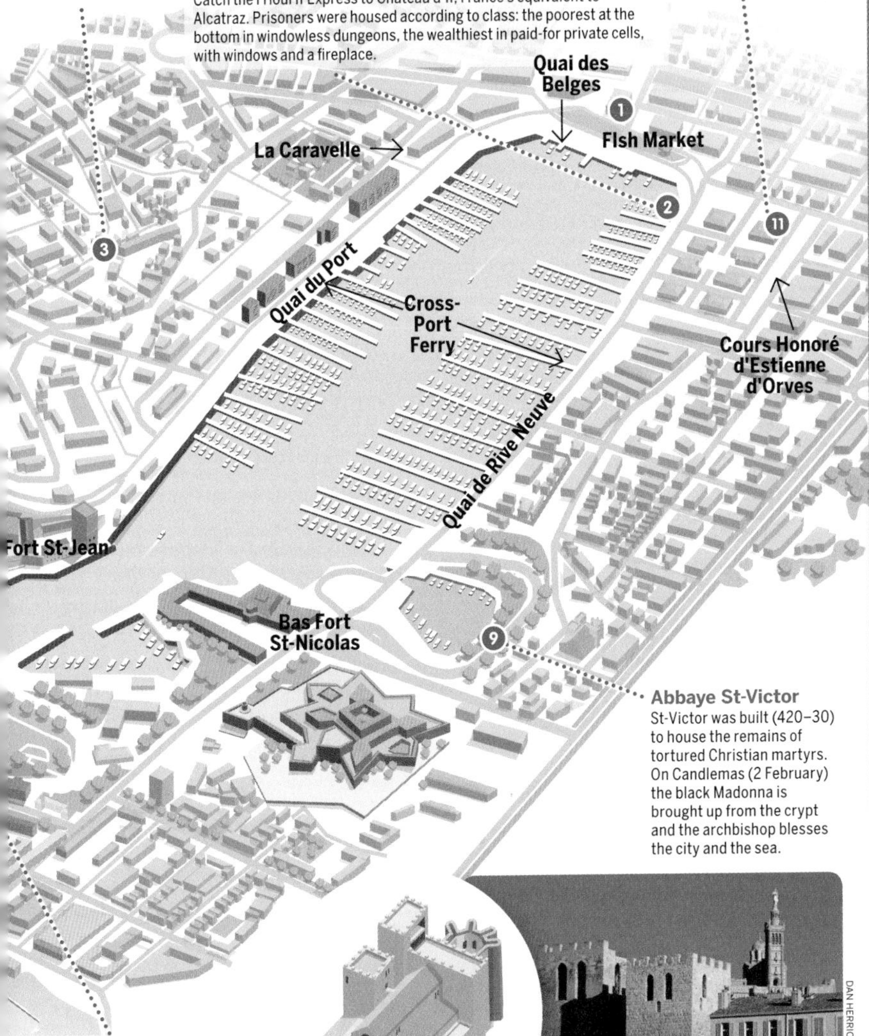

Quai des Belges
1
FIsh Market
La Caravelle
2
11
3
Quai du Port
Cross-Port Ferry
Cours Honoré d'Estienne d'Orves
Quai de Rive Neuve
Fort St-Jean
Bas Fort St-Nicolas
9

Abbaye St-Victor
St-Victor was built (420–30) to house the remains of tortured Christian martyrs. On Candlemas (2 February) the black Madonna is brought up from the crypt and the archbishop blesses the city and the sea.

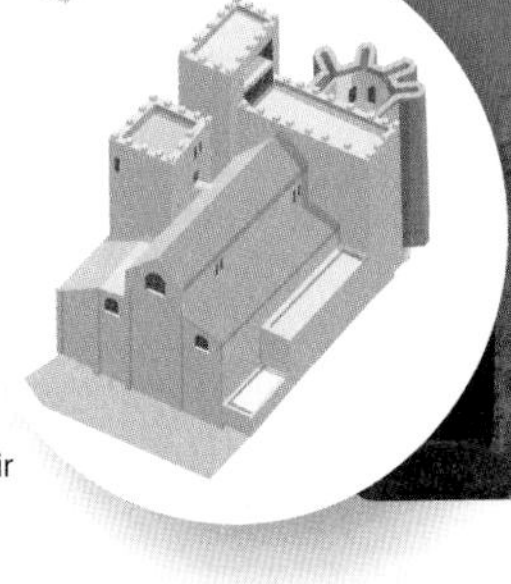

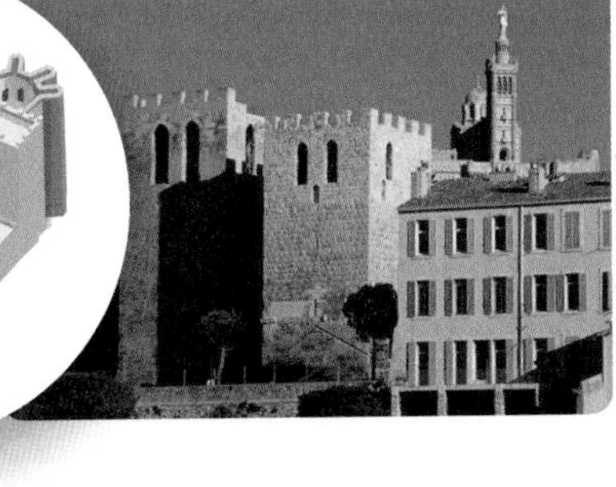

DAN HERRICK/GETTY IMAGES ©

Jardin du Pharo
Built by Napoléon for the Empress Eugénie, the Pharo Palace was designed with its 'feet in the water'. Today it is a congress centre, but the gardens with their magnificent view are open all day.

Bouillabaisse

Originally cooked by fishermen from the scraps of their catch, bouillabaisse is Marseille's classic signature dish. True bouillabaisse includes at least four different kinds of fish, sometimes shellfish. It's served in two parts: the broth *(soupe de poisson)*, rich with tomato, saffron and fennel; and the cooked fish, deboned tableside and presented on a platter. On the side are croutons and *rouille* (a bread-thickened garlic, chilli and pepper mayonnaise) and grated cheese.

The most reliably consistent spots for real bouillabaisse include the following:

Le Rhul (04 91 52 01 77; www.lerhul.fr; 269 corniche Président John F Kennedy; bouillabaisse €53; 83) This long-standing classic has atmosphere (however kitschy): a 1940s seaside hotel with Mediterranean views.

L'Epuisette (04 91 52 17 82; www.l-epuisette.com; Vallon des Auffes; bouillabaisse €90; Tue-Sat; 83) The swankest address by far with a Michelin star and knockout water-level views from an elegantly austere dining room. First courses cost €34 to €45 and desserts €20, though you'll likely not have room.

Drinking

La Caravelle Bar

(34 quai du Port; 7am-2am; M Vieux Port)
Look up or miss this standout upstairs hideaway, styled with rich wood and leather, a zinc bar and yellowing murals. If it's sunny, snag a coveted spot on the port-side terrace. On Fridays, there's live jazz from 9pm to midnight.

La Part des Anges Wine Bar

(http://lapartdesanges.com; 33 rue Sainte; 9am-2am Mon-Sat, 9am-1pm & 6pm-2am Sun)
No address buzzes with Marseille's hip, buoyant crowd more than this fabulous all-rounder wine bar, named after the amount of alcohol that evaporates through a barrel during wine or whisky fermentation: the angels' share. Take your pick of dozens of wines to try by the glass and be sure to tell the bartender if you want to eat (tables can't be reserved in advance).

Information

Tourist Office (04 91 13 89 00; www.marseille-tourisme.com; 11 La Canebière; 9am-7pm Mon-Sat, 10am-5pm Sun; M Vieux Port) Marseille's shiny modern tourist office has plenty of information on everything, including guided tours on foot, by bus, electric tourist train or boat.

Getting There & Away

Air **Aéroport Marseille-Provence** (www.marseille.aeroport.fr), also called Aéroport Marseille-Marignane, is located 25km northwest of Marseille in Marignane.

Train From Marseille, trains, including TGVs, go to destinations all over France and Europe, including the following, which all run at least half a dozen times a day:

Avignon €29.50, 35 minutes

Lyon €65, 1¾ hours

Nice €37, 2½ hours

Paris Gare de Lyon €113, three hours

Aix-en-Provence

POP 141,895

Aix-en-Provence is to Provence what the Left Bank is to Paris: an enclave of bourgeois-bohemian chic just 25km from chaotic, exotic Marseille. Some 30,000 students from the Université de Provence Aix-Marseille, many from overseas, set the mood on the street: bars, cafes and affordable restaurants. The city is rich in culture (two of Aix' most famous sons are Paul Cézanne and Émile Zola) and oh-so respectable, with plane-tree-shaded boulevards and fashionable boutiques.

Sights

The **Aix City Pass (€15)**, valid five days, includes a guided walking tour, admission to the Atelier Paul Cézanne (p307), Jas de Bouffan and Musée Granet, and a trip on the mini-tram; the **Cézanne Pass (€12)** covers his three main sights. Buy them at the tourist office, or the two Cézanne sights.

Cours Mirabeau Historic Quarter

No avenue better epitomises Provence's most graceful city than this fountain-studded street, sprinkled with Renaissance *hôtels particuliers* (private mansions) and crowned with a summertime roof of leafy plane trees. Named after the revolutionary hero Comte de Mirabeau, it was laid out in the 1640s. Cézanne and Zola hung out at **Les Deux Garçons** (53 cours Mirabeau; 7am-2am), one of a clutch of busy pavement cafes.

Musée Granet Museum

(www.museegranet-aixenprovence.fr; place St-Jean de Malte; adult/child €7/free; 11am-7pm Tue-Sun) Housed in a 17th-century priory of the Knights of Malta, this exceptional museum is named after the Provençal painter François Marius Granet (1775–1849), who donated a large number of works. Its collections include 16th- to 20th-century Italian, Flemish and French works. The modern art on show reads like a who's who: Picasso, Léger, Matisse, Monet, Klee, Van Gogh and Giacometti, among others, including the museum's pride and joy: nine Cézanne works. Excellent temporary exhibitions.

Sleeping

L'Épicerie B&B €€

(06 08 85 38 68; www.unechambreenville.eu; 12 rue du Cancel; d €100-130;) This intimate B&B is the fabulous creation of born-and-bred Aixois lad Luc. His breakfast room recreates a 1950s grocery store, and the flowery garden out back is perfect for excellent evening dining and weekend brunch (book ahead for both). Breakfast is a veritable feast. Two rooms accommodate families of four.

Hôtel des Augustins Hotel €€

(04 42 27 28 59; www.hotel-augustins.com; 3 rue de la Masse; d €109-249;) A heartbeat from the hub of Aixois life, this former 15th-century convent with magnificent stone-vaulted lobby and sweeping staircase has volumes of history: Martin Luther stayed here after his excommunication from Rome. Filled with hand-painted furniture, the largest,

Bouillabaisse

Aix-en-Provence

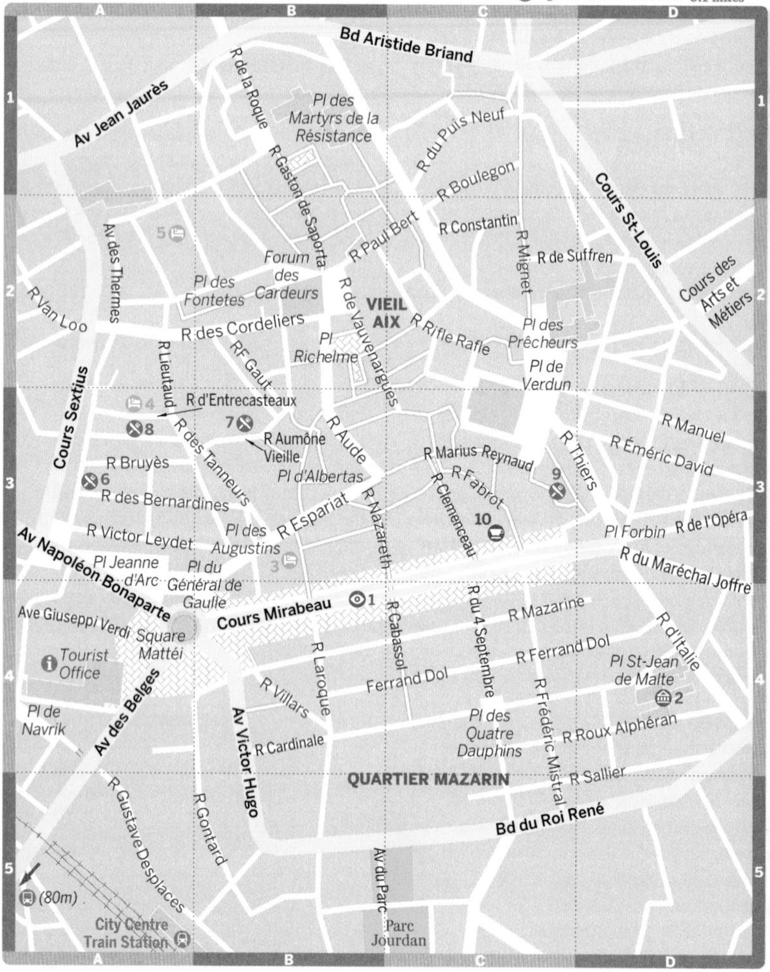

0 200 m
0 0.1 miles

Bd Aristide Briand
Av Jean Jaurès
R de la Roque
Pl des Martyrs de la Résistance
R Gaston de Saporta
R du Puits Neuf
R Boulegon
R Paul Bert
R Constantin
R Mignet
R de Suffren
Cours St-Louis
Cours des Arts et Métiers
Av des Thermes
5
Forum des Cardeurs
Pl des Fontetes
R Van Loo
R des Cordeliers
R de Vauvenargues
VIEIL AIX
R Rifle Rafle
Pl des Prêcheurs
Pl de Verdun
Pl Richelme
RF Gaut
R Lieutaud
Cours Sextius
4
R d'Entrecasteaux
7
8
R Aumône Vieille
R Aude
R des Tanneurs
R Manuel
R Émeric David
R Thiers
R Bruyès
Pl d'Albertas
R Marius Reynaud
R Fabrot
9
6
R des Bernardines
R Clemenceau
R Espariat
R Nazareth
10
R Victor Leydet
Pl des Augustins
Pl Forbin
R de l'Opéra
Av Napoléon Bonaparte
Pl Jeanne d'Arc
3
Pl du Général de Gaulle
R du Maréchal Joffre
Cours Mirabeau
1
R Cabassol
R du 4 Septembre
R Mazarine
Ave Giuseppi Verdi
Square Mattéi
R d'Italie
Tourist Office
R Ferrand Dol
Pl St-Jean de Malte
R Laroque
R Villars
Ferrand Dol
2
Pl de Navrik
Av des Belges
Av Victor Hugo
Pl des Quatre Dauphins
R Frédéric Mistral
R Roux Alphéran
R Cardinale
QUARTIER MAZARIN
R Sallier
R Gustave Desplaces
R Gontard
Bd du Roi René
Av du Parc
(80m)
City Centre Train Station
Parc Jourdan

most luxurious rooms have jacuzzis; two rooms have private terraces beneath the filigreed bell tower.

Le Manoir Hotel **€€**
(**04 42 26 27 20; www.hotelmanoir.com; 8 rue d'Entrecasteux; d €82-126, tr €114; Feb-Dec;**) Atmospherically set in a 14th-century cloister, The Manor – an easy family choice – is something of a blast from the past. Old world in spirit and location, it sits in an uncanningly quiet wedge of the old town. Rooms are clean, simple and spacious. Best up is the free parking in the gravel courtyard out front and breakfast, served alfresco in a vaulted cloister.

Eating

Jacquou Le Croquant Southwest, Provençal **€**
(**04 42 27 37 19; www.jacquoulecroquant.com; 2 rue de l'Aumône Vielle; plat du jour €10.90, menus from €14; noon-3pm & 7-11pm**) This veteran address, around since 1985,

Aix-en-Provence

Sights

1 Cours Mirabeau B4
2 Musée Granet D4

Sleeping

3 Hôtel des Augustins B3
4 Le Manoir A3
5 L'Épicerie A2

Eating

6 Charlotte A3
7 Jacquou Le Croquant B3
8 Le Petit Verdot A3
9 Petit Pierre Reboul C3

Drinking & Nightlife

10 Les Deux Garçons C3

stands out on dozens of counts: there's a buzzy jovial atmosphere, flowery patio garden and a funky interior. It has an early evening opening time, family friendly, hearty homecooking, a menu covering all price ranges, and so forth. Cuisine from southwestern France is its speciality, meaning lots of duck, but the vast menu covers all bases.

Charlotte Bistro **€**

(**04 42 26 77 56; 32 rue des Bernardines; 2-/3-course menus €16.50/20; 12.30pm-2pm & 8-10.30pm Tue-Sat;**) It's all very cosy at Charlotte, where everyone knows everyone else. French classics like veal escalope and beef steak are mainstays, and there is always a vegetarian dish and a couple of imaginative *plats du jour* (dishes of the day). In summer everything moves into the garden.

Le Petit Verdot French **€€**

(**04 42 27 30 12; www.lepetitverdot.fr; 7 rue d'Entrecasteaux; mains €15-25; 7pm-midnight Mon-Sat)** Delicious menus are designed around what's in season, and paired with excellent wines. Meats are often braised all day, and vegetables are tender, having been stewed in delicious broths. Save room for an amazing dessert. Lively dining occurs around tabletops made of wine crates (expect to talk to your neighbour), and the gregarious owner speaks multiple languages.

Petit Pierre Reboul Gastronomic **€€€**

(**04 42 52 30 42; www.restaurant-pierre-reboul.com; 11 Petite Rue St-Jean; 2-/3-course bistro menu €19-34/27-39, gastronomic menus €52 & €87; noon-2.30pm & 7.30-10.30pm Tue-Sat)** This brightly coloured address, hidden down a back alley, is the bistro arm of Pierre Reboul's gastronomic restaurant next door. The vibe is contemporary design (think acid-bright fabrics and lampshades made from pencils), and the menu throws in the odd adventurous dish alongside mainstream stalwarts like burgers, Caesar salad, grilled meats and mussels and fries.

Information

Tourist Office (**04 42 16 11 61; www.aixenprovencetourism.com; square Colonel Antoine Mattei; 8.30am-8pm Mon-Sat, 10am-1pm & 2-4pm Sun Jun-Sep, shorter hrs Oct-May)** Seriously hi-tech with no brochures, just monumental touch screens – everywhere. Sells tickets for guided tours and cultural events.

Getting There & Away

Tiny **city centre train station**, at the southern end of av Victor Hugo, serves Marseille (€8.20, 45 minutes). Aix' **TGV station**, 15km from the city centre and accessible by shuttle bus (€3.70 from the bus station), serves most of France; to Marseille it's 12 minutes (€6.20, 20 daily).

Arles

POP 54,088

Arles' poster boy is the celebrated impressionist painter Vincent van Gogh. If you're familiar with his work, you'll be familiar with Arles: the light, the colours, the landmarks and the atmosphere, all faithfully captured.

Once an important Gallo-Roman town, Arles also boasts an impressively preserved 12,000-seat Roman theatre and 20,000-seat amphitheatre, which now host lively festivals and bullfights. Arles also has a growing reputation for contemporary art, reflected in the 2014 opening of the state-of-the-art Fondation Vincent Van Gogh.

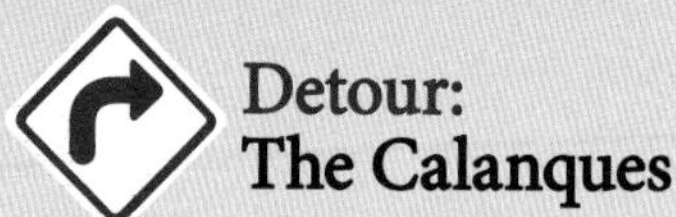

Detour: The Calanques

Marseille abuts the wild and spectacular **Parc National des Calanques** (www.parcsnationaux.fr), a 20km stretch of high, rocky promontories, rising from brilliant-turquoise Mediterranean waters. The sheer cliffs are occasionally interrupted by small idyllic beaches, some impossible to reach without a kayak.

The best way to see the Calanques, October to June, is to hike the many maquis-lined trails. During summer, trails close because of fire danger: take a boat tour either from Marseille or Cassis, but be forewarned, they don't stop to let you swim; alternatively, go sea kayaking with **Raskas Kayak** (www.raskas-kayak.com), drive or take public transport.

Calanque de Sormiou is the largest rocky inlet. Two seasonal restaurants serve lunch with fabulous views, and require reservations. **Le Château** (04 91 25 08 69; http://lechateausormiou.fr; mains €20-25; Apr–Sep) has the best food and **Le Lunch** (04 91 25 05 37; http://wp.resto.fr/lelunch; Calanque de Sormiou; mains €16-28; Apr–Oct) the better view. Diners with reservations are allowed to drive through; otherwise, the road is open to cars weekdays only, September to June.

Marseille's tourist office (p300) leads guided walks (no kids under eight) of the Calanques, and has information on walks and trail closures.

Sights & Activities

Though he painted 200-odd canvases in Arles, there are no Van Gogh artworks here today, and Van Gogh's little 'yellow house' on place Lamartine, which he painted in 1888, was destroyed during WWII. Nevertheless, there are several ways to pay homage to the master. Mapped out in a brochure (€1 or downloadable for free online) from the tourist office (p308), the evocative Van Gogh walking circuit of the city takes in scenes painted by the artist.

Les Arènes Roman Site

(Amphithéâtre; admission incl Théâtre Antique adult/child €6.50/5; 9am-7pm) Slaves, criminals and wild animals (including giraffes) met their dramatic demise before a jubilant 20,000-strong crowd during Roman gladiatorial displays at Les Arènes, built around the early 2nd century AD. During the early medieval Arab invasions the arch-laced circular structure – 136m long, 107m wide and 21m tall – was topped with four defensive towers. By the 1820s, when the amphitheatre was returned to its original use, 212 houses and two churches had to be razed on the site.

Buy tickets for bloody bullfights, bloodless *courses camarguaises*, theatre and concerts at the ticket office next to the entrance.

Fondation Vincent Van Gogh Art Museum

(04 90 49 94 04; www.fondation-vincentvangogh-arles.org; 33 ter rue du Docteur Fanton; adult/child €9/4; 11am-7pm, to 9pm Thu) This Van Gogh-themed gallery is a must-see, as much for its contemporary architecture and design, as for the art it showcases. It has no permanent art collection; rather, it hosts one or two temporary exhibitions a year, always with a Van Gogh theme and always including at least one Van Gogh masterpiece. Architectural highlights include the rooftop terrace and the kaleidescope-style bookshop 'ceiling', aka chunks of coloured glass forming a roof.

Musée Réattu Art Museum

(04 90 49 37 58; www.museereattu.arles.fr; 10 rue du Grand Prieuré; adult/child €7/free; 10am-6pm Tue-Sun, to 5pm Dec-Feb) This splendid modern-art museum is housed in the exquisitely renovated 15th-century Grand Priory of the Knights of Malta. Among its collections are works by 18th- and 19th-century Provençal artists and two paintings and 57 sketches by Picasso. It hosts wonderfully curated cutting-edge exhibitions.

Musée Départemental Arles Antique Museum

(☎04 13 31 51 03; www.arles-antique.cg13.fr; av de la Première Division Française Libre; adult/child €8/5; ⏲10am-6pm Wed-Mon) This striking, state-of-the-art cobalt-blue museum perches on the edge of what used to be the Roman chariot racing track (circus), 1.5km southwest of the tourist office. The rich collection of pagan and Christian art includes stunning mosaics and an entire wing dedicated to archeological treasures evoking Arles' commercial and navigation past.

Théâtre Antique Roman Site

(☎04 90 96 93 30; bd des Lices; adult/child €6.50/free, free with Les Arènes admission; ⏲9am-7pm May-Sep, shorter hrs Oct-Apr) Still used for summertime concerts and plays, this outdoor theatre dates to the end of the 1st century BC. For hundreds of years it was a source of construction materials, with workers chipping away at the 102m-diameter structure (the column on the right-hand side near the entrance indicates the height of the original arcade). Enter on rue de la Calade.

Sleeping

Hôtel de l'Amphithéâtre Historic Hotel €

(☎04 90 96 10 30; www.hotelamphitheatre.fr; 5-7 rue Diderot; s/d/tr/q €61/79/129/139; ❄@📶) Crimson, chocolate, terracotta and other earthy colours dress the exquisite 17th-century stone structure of this stylish hotel, with narrow staircases, a roaring fire and alfresco courtyard breakfasts. The romantic suite has a dreamy lilac-walled terrace overlooking rooftops. Breakfast €8.50.

Hôtel Arlatan Historic Hotel €€

(☎04 90 93 56 66; www.hotel-arlatan.fr; 26 rue du Sauvage; d €85-157; ⏲mid-Mar–mid-Nov; ❄@📶🏊) The heated swimming pool, pretty garden and plush rooms decorated with antique furniture are just some of

Théâtre Antique

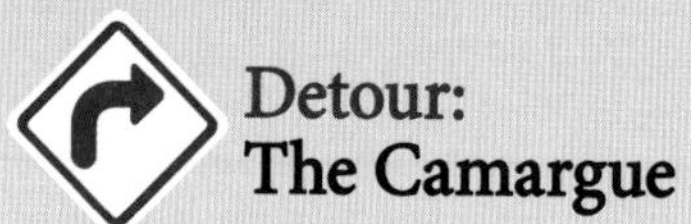

Detour: The Camargue

Just south of Arles, Provence's rolling landscapes yield to the flat, marshy wilds of the Camargue, famous for its teeming bird life, roughly 500 species. King of all is the pink flamingo, which enjoys the expansive wetlands' mild winters. Equally famous are the Camargue's small white horses; their mellow disposition makes horse riding the ideal way to explore the region's patchwork of salt pans and rice fields, and meadows dotted with grazing bulls. Bring binoculars – and mosquito repellent.

The Camargue's two largest towns are the seaside pilgrim's outpost **Stes-Maries-de-la-Mer** and, to the northwest, the walled town of **Aigues-Mortes**.

Inside an 1812-built sheep shed 10km southwest of Arles on the D570, the **Musée de la Camargue** (Musée Camarguais; ☎04 90 97 10 82; www.parc-camargue.fr; Mas du Pont de Rousty, D570; adult/child €5/free, free 1st Sun & last Wed of month; ⏰9am-12.30pm & 1-6pm Wed-Mon Apr-Oct, 10am-12.30pm & 1-5pm Nov-Mar) paints an exhaustive portrait of traditional life, its exhibitions covering local history, ecosystems, farming techniques, flora and fauna. A 3.5km trail leads to an observation tower with bird's-eye views of the *mas* (farmhouse) and its protected natural surrounds.

Pink flamingos pirouette overhead and stalk the watery landscape at **Le Parc Ornithologique du Pont de Gau** (☎04 90 97 82 62; www.parcornithologique.com; adult/child €7.50/5; ⏰9am-sunset Apr-Sep, from 10am Oct-Mar), on the D570 in Pont du Gau, 4km north of Stes-Maries-de-la-Mer.

You will need a car to visit the area, an easy day trip from Arles.

the things going for this hotel. Add to that a setting steeped in history, with Roman foundations visible through a glass floor in the lobby and 15th-century paintings on one of the lounges' ceilings. Breakfast continental/buffet €9/15.

Eating

Marché d'Arles — Food Market €

(bd des Lices; ⏰7am-1pm Sat) At Arles' enormous Saturday-morning market, Camargue salt, goats'-milk cheese and *saucisson d'Arles* (bull-meat sausage) scent the air. The scene shifts to bd Émile Combes on Wednesday morning.

Comptoir du Sud — Cafe €

(☎04 90 96 22 17; 2 rue Jean Jaurès; sandwiches €4.10-5.70; ⏰9am-6pm Tue-Fri) Gourmet sandwiches, wraps and bagels (with tasty chutneys, succulent meats, foie gras) and divine little salads are served at this stylish *épicerie fine* (gourmet grocery). Take away or eat in on bar stools and end with a sweet €3 wedge of homemade *clafoutis* (cherry pie) for dessert.

Le Gibolin — Bistro €€

(☎04 88 65 43 14; 13 rue des Porcelet; menus €27-32, glass wine €4.50-5.50; ⏰12.15-2pm & 8-10pm Tue-Sat Sep-Jul) Sup on peerless home cooking (think cod with fennel confit and crushed potatoes, and pot-au-feu), while the friendly patroness bustles between dark wood tables sharing her knowledge and passion for natural wines at Arles' most beloved *bar à vins* (wine bar). Pairings are naturally *magnifique*. No credit cards.

L'Atelier — Gastronomic €€€

(☎04 90 91 07 69; www.rabanel.com; 7 rue des Carmes; lunch menu with/without drinks €110/65, dinner menu with/without drinks €185/125; ⏰sittings begin noon-1pm & 8-9pm Wed-Sun) Consider this not a meal, but an artistic experience (with two shiny Michelin stars). Every one of the edible works of art is a wondrous composition of flavours, colours

DE AGOSTINI/C. SAPPA/GETTY IMAGES ©

Don't Miss Cézanne's Aix

The life of local lad Paul Cézanne (1839–1906) is treasured in Aix. To see where he ate, drank, studied and painted, follow the **Circuit de Cézanne** (Cézanne Trail), marked by footpath-embedded bronze plaques. The informative English-language guide to the plaques, Cézanne's Footsteps, is free at the tourist office. A mobile app, City of Cézanne in Aix-en-Provence (€2), is available online.

Cézanne's last studio, **Atelier Paul Cézanne**, 1.5km north of the tourist office, was preserved (and recreated: not all the tools and still-life models strewn around the single room were his) as it was at the time of his death. Though the studio is inspiring, none of his works hang here. Take bus 1 or 20 to the Atelier Cézanne stop, or walk 1.5km from the centre.

Visits to the other two sights must be reserved at the tourist office. In 1859 Cézanne's father bought **Le Jas de Bouffan**, a country manor west of Aix centre, where Cézanne painted 36 oils and 17 watercolours in the decades that followed depicting the house, farm and chestnut-lined alley.

In 1895 Cézanne rented a cabin at **Les Carrières de Bibernus**, where he did most of his Montagne Ste-Victoire paintings. One-hour tours of the ochre quarry take visitors on foot through the burnt-orange rocks Cézanne captured so vividly.

NEED TO KNOW

Atelier Paul Cézanne (www.atelier-cezanne.com; 9 av Paul Cézanne; adult/child €5.50/€2; 10am-noon & 2-5pm)

Le Jas de Bouffan (04 42 16 10 91; adult/child €5.50/2; guided tours 10.30am-5.30pm; 6 stop Corsy)

Les Carrières de Bibernus (Bibémus Quarries; 04 42 16 10 91; 3090 chemin de Bibémus; adult/child €5.50/2; guided tour 9.45am Jun-Sep, less frequently Oct-May)

and textures courtsey of charismatic chef Jean-Luc Rabanel. Many products are sourced from the chef's organic veggie patch and wine pairings are an adventure in themselves. Half-day cooking classes (with/without lunch €200/145).

Shopping

La Botte Camarguaise Shoes

(06 16 04 08 14; 22 rue Jean Granaud; 9am-12.30pm & 2-6.30pm Mon-Fri, 7am-noon Sat)

Buy a pair of handmade Camargue-style cowboy boots.

Information

Tourist Office (Main Office) (04 90 18 41 20; www.tourisme.ville-arles.fr; esplanade Charles de Gaulle; 9am-6.45pm Apr-Sep, to 4.45pm Mon-Fri & 12.45pm Sun Oct-Mar)

Getting There & Away

Train There are services to Nîmes (€8.60, 30 minutes), Marseille (€15.30, 45 minutes) and Avignon (€7.50, 20 minutes). The closest TGV stations are in Avignon and Nîmes.

Avignon

POP 92,454

Hooped by 4.3km of superbly preserved stone ramparts, this graceful city is the belle of Provence's ball. Its turn as the papal seat of power has bestowed Avignon with a treasury of magnificent art and architecture. Famed for its annual performing arts festival, these days Avignon is also an animated student city and an ideal spot from which to step out into the surrounding region.

Sights

The must-have discount card, *Avignon Passion*, provides discounts on museums, tours, and monuments in Avignon and Villeneuve-lès-Avignon. The first attraction visited costs full price, but each subsequent site discounts admission by 10% to 50%. The free pass covers five sites, and is valid for 15 days. Available from the tourist office (p312) and tourist sites.

Palais des Papes Palace

(Papal Palace; www.palais-des-papes.com; place du Palais; adult/child €11/9, with Pont Saint Bénezet €13.50/10.50; 9am-8pm Jul, 9am-8.30pm Aug, shorter hours Sep-Jun)

This Unesco World Heritage Site is the world's largest Gothic palace. Built when Pope Clement V abandoned Rome in 1309, it was the papal seat for 70-odd years. The immense scale testifies to the papacy's wealth; the 3m-thick walls, portcullises and watchtowers show its insecurity.

It takes imagination to picture the former luxury of these bare, cavernous stone halls, but multimedia audioguides (€2) assist. Highlights include 14th-century chapel frescos by Matteo Giovannetti, and the

Palais des Papes

HANS GEORG EIBEN/GETTY IMAGES ©

Chambre du Cerf with medieval hunting scenes. Ask at the ticket desk about guided tours.

Pont Saint Bénezet Bridge

(bd du Rhône; adult/child €5/4, with Palais des Papes €13.50/10.50; 9am-8pm Jul, 9am-8.30pm Aug, shorter hours Sep-Jun) Legend says Pastor Bénezet had three saintly visions urging him to build a bridge across the Rhône. Completed in 1185, the 900m-long bridge with 20 arches linked Avignon with Villeneuve-lès-Avignon. It was rebuilt several times before all but four of its spans were washed away in the 1600s. Don't be surprised if you spot someone dancing: in France, the bridge is known as Pont d'Avignon after the nursery rhyme: 'Sur le pont d'Avignon/L'on y danse, l'on y danse...' (On Avignon Bridge, all are dancing...)

Musée du Petit Palais Art Museum

(www.petit-palais.org; place du Palais; adult/child €6/free; 10am-1pm & 2-6pm Wed-Mon) The archbishops' palace during the 14th and 15th centuries now houses outstanding collections of primitive, pre-Rennaissance, 13th- to 16th-century Italian religious paintings by artists including Botticelli, Carpaccio and Giovanni di Paolo – the most famous is Botticelli's *La Vierge et l'Enfant* (1470).

Musée Angladon Art Museum

(www.angladon.com; 5 rue Laboureur; adult/child €6.50/4.50; 1-6pm Tue-Sun, closed Mon Apr-mid-Nov, closed Mon & Tue mid-Nov–Mar) Tiny Musée Angladon harbours Impressionist treasures, including *Railway Wagons*, the only Van Gogh in Provence (look closely and notice the 'earth' isn't paint, but bare canvas). Also displayed are a handful of early Picasso sketches and artworks by Cézanne, Sisley, Manet and Degas; upstairs are antiques and 17th-century paintings.

Sleeping

Le Limas B&B €€

(04 90 14 67 19; www.le-limas-avignon.com; 51 rue du Limas; s €125-140, d €130-200, tr €200-260; @) This chic B&B in an

Local Knowledge

Provençal Markets Don't Miss List

BY PATRICIA WELLS, COOKBOOK AUTHOR & COOKING TEACHER

1 **VAISON-LA-ROMAINE**

The Tuesday market in Vaison-la-Romaine might be 'my' market but it is truly one of Provence's greats. It has the freshest local produce, especially asparagus, strawberries, melons and heirloom tomatoes. Go to Lou Canesteou for cheese and Peyrerol for chocolate.

2 **ST-RÉMY DE PROVENCE**

My other favourite is St-Rémy on Wednesday: I love the town, the ambience. Perhaps it is more a market to buy trinkets than food, but whatever you are there for, you just always feel as though you are in the right place at the right time.

3 **UZÈS**

The third in my top three is also on Wednesday, in Uzès, west of Nîmes. The organic market on place aux Herbes, one of the prettiest little squares in all of France, is stunning – great goat's cheeses, *confitures* (jams) from the nuns and wonderful local olives and olive oil.

4 **RICHERENCHES**

My favourite speciality market is on Saturday in Richerenches, November through February. It is a fresh black truffle market – very mysterious, with lots of people selling pillow cases bulging with black truffles from the trunks of their cars. Stay until lunchtime and have a truffle omelette at one of the two cafés in the village.

5 **THE BEST PRODUCE**

Tip 1 When looking for the best meat, look for a line of elderly French women. They know how to shop! **Tip 2** Look at the vendors: if the vendor is neat, trim, clean, so will his produce be neat, trim, clean. Dirty fingernails usually mean ugly produce! **Tip 3** Tour the entire market before you buy to see what's best.

Avignon

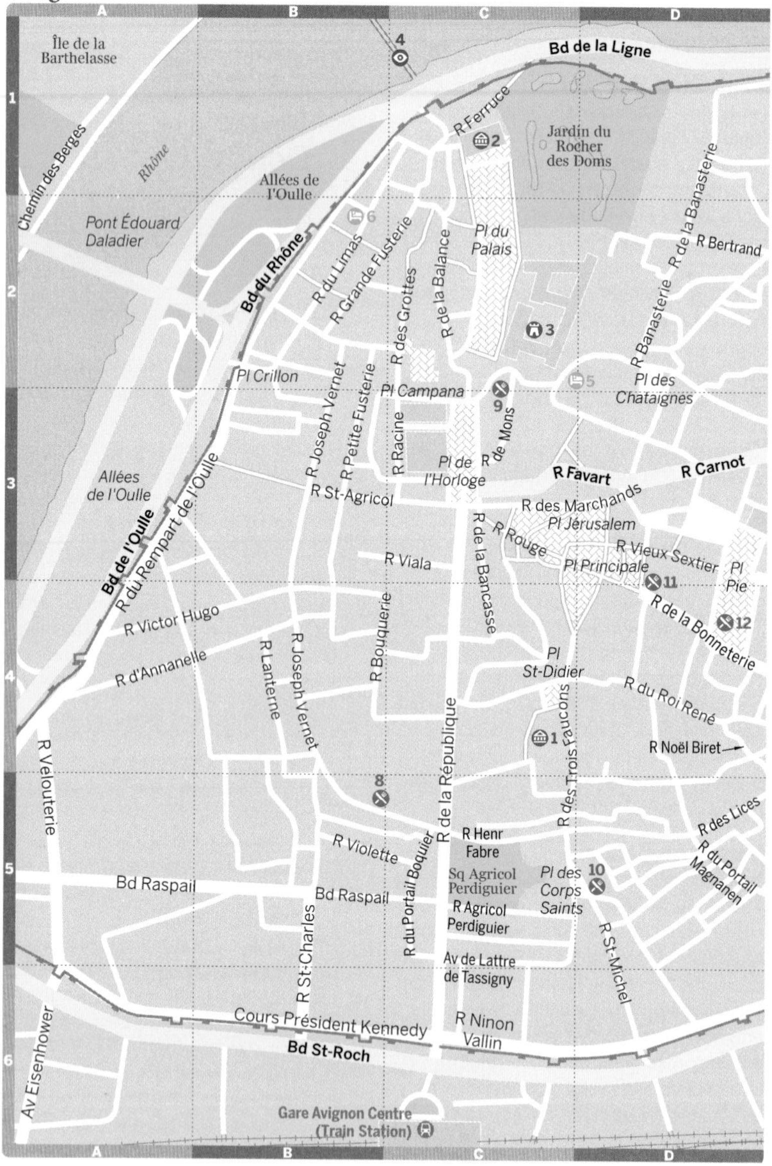

18th-century town house, like something out of *Vogue Living*, is everything designers strive for when mixing old and new: state-of-the-art kitchen and minimalist white decor complementing antique fireplaces and 18th-century spiral stairs. Breakfast on the sun-drenched terrace is divine, darling.

Lumani B&B **€€**

(**☎04 90 82 94 11; www.avignon-lumani.com; 37 rue du Rempart St-Lazare; d €110-170;** ❄📶) Art

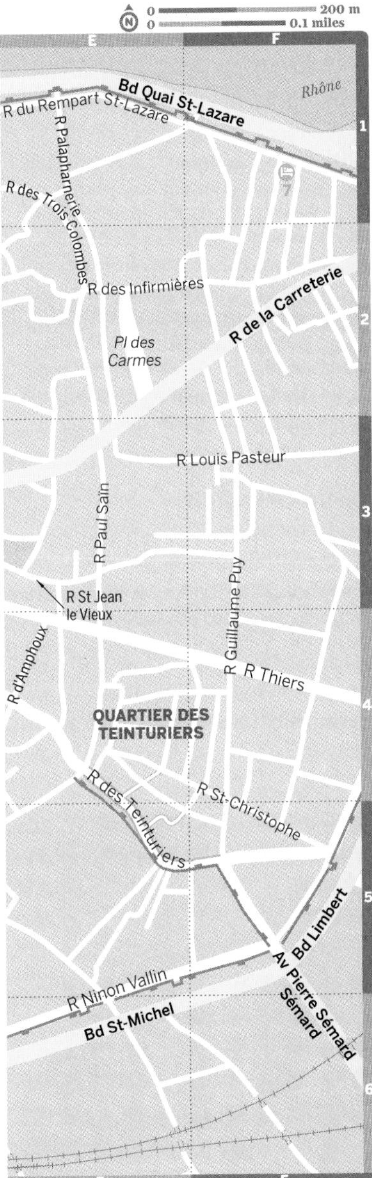

fills this fabulous *maison d'hôte*, a wealth of inspiration for painters. Rooms include two suites and there's a fountained garden.

Avignon

Sights

1 Musée Angladon C4
2 Musée du Petit Palais C1
3 Palais des Papes C2
4 Pont Saint Bénezet C1

Sleeping

5 Hôtel La Mirande C2
6 Le Limas B2
7 Lumani F1

Eating

8 83.Vernet B5
9 Christian Etienne C2
10 Ginette et Marcel D5
11 La Cuisine du Dimanche D3
12 Les Halles D4

Hôtel La Mirande Luxury Hotel **€€€**
(**04 90 14 20 20; www.la-mirande.fr; 4 place de la Mirande; d from €400;**) Avignon's top hotel occupies a converted 16th-century palace, with dramatic interiors decked in oriental rugs, gold-threaded tapestries, marble staircases and over-the-top Gallic style. Low-end rooms are small, but still conjure the feeling of staying overnight in someone's private château. Its restaurant is a slow and glittering affair that also offers cooking classes.

Eating

Les Halles Market **€**
(**www.avignon-leshalles.com; place Pie; 6am-1.30pm Tue-Fri, 6am-2pm Sat & Sun**) Over 40 food stalls showcase seasonal Provençal ingredients. Cooking demonstrations are held Saturdays at 11am. Outside on place Pie, admire Patrick Blanc's marvellous vegetal wall.

Ginette et Marcel Cafe **€**
(**27 place des Corps Saints; tartines €4-6; 11am-11pm Wed-Mon;**) With tables and chairs on one of Avignon's most happening plane-tree-shaded squares, this vintage cafe styled like a 1950s grocery is a charming spot to hang out and people-watch over a *tartine* (open-faced sandwich), tart, salad or other light dish – equally tasty for lunch or an early evening *apéro* (predinner drink). Kids adore Ginette's cherry- and violet-flavoured

cordials, and Marcel's glass jars of old-fashioned sweets.

83.Vernet — Modern French €€

(☎04 90 85 99 04; www.83vernet.com; 83 rue Joseph Vernet; lunch menu €19.50/dinner menu €24-30, mains €15; ⏰noon-3pm & 7pm-1am Mon-Sat) Forget flowery French descriptions. The menu is straightforward and to the point at this strikingly contemporary address, magnificently at home in the 18th-century cloistered courtyard of a medieval college. Expect pan-seared scallops, squid *à la plancha* and beef steak in pepper sauce on the menu, and watch for weekend events that transform the lounge-style restaurant into the hippest dance floor in town.

La Cuisine du Dimanche — Provençal €€

(☎04 90 82 99 10; www.lacuisinedudimanche.com; 31 rue de la Bonneterie; lunch menu €17, mains €18-25; ⏰noon-1.30pm & 8-9.45pm Jun-Sep, Wed-Sun Nov-Mar) Chef Marie shops every morning at Les Halles to find the freshest ingredients for her earthy flavour-packed cooking. The menu changes daily, although staples include scallops and simple roast chicken with pan gravy. The narrow stone-walled dining room mixes contemporary resin chairs with antique crystal goblets to reflect the chef's eclecticism. Evening dining is only à la carte.

Christian Etienne — Provençal €€€

(☎04 90 86 16 50; www.christian-etienne.fr; 10 rue de Mons; lunch menu €35, dinner menus €75-130; ⏰noon-2pm & 7.30-10pm Tue-Sat) One of Avignon's top tables, this much vaunted restaurant occupies a 12th-century palace, with a leafy outdoor terrace, adjacent to Palais des Papes. Interiors feel slightly dated, but the refined Provençal cuisine remains exceptional, notably the summertime-only starter-to-dessert tomato menu (€75).

ℹ Information

Tourist Office (☎04 32 74 32 74; www.avignon-tourisme.com; 41 cours Jean Jaurès; ⏰9am-6pm Mon-Sat, 10am-7pm Sun Apr-Oct, shorter hrs Nov-Mar) Organises guided walking tours of the city, and has plenty of information on other tours and activities, including boat trips and lunch cruises on the River Rhône, and wine-tasting trips to nearby Côtes du Rhône vineyards.

Les Arènes, Nîmes

GLENN BEANLAND/GETTY IMAGES ©

Getting There & Away

Avignon has two train stations: **Gare Avignon TGV**, 4km southwest in Courtine; and **Gare Avignon Centre** (42 bd St-Roch), with services to the following:

Arles €7.50, 20 minutes, half-hourly

Nîmes €9.70, 30 minutes, half-hourly

Some TGVs to Paris (€123, 3½ hours) stop at Gare Avignon Centre, but TGVs to Marseille (€25, 35 minutes) and Nice (€60, 3¼ hours) only use Gare Avignon TGV.

LANGUEDOC

Bordered to the east by sun-baked Provence, the broad, flat plains of Bas-Languedoc (lower Languedoc) boast all of the Languedoc's main towns, as well as its best beaches, richest Roman remains and (arguably) its finest wines.

Nîmes

POP 146,500

Nîmes' traffic-clogged, concrete-heavy outskirts provide an uninspiring introduction to this ancient southern city, but push on and you'll discover some of southern France's best-preserved Roman buildings – including a 2000-year-old temple and a magnificent amphitheatre, where gladiatorial battles are still staged.

Sights

Les Arènes Roman Sites

(www.arenes-nimes.com; place des Arènes; adult/child €9/7; 9am-8pm Jul & Aug, shorter hours Sep-Jun) Nîmes' twin-tiered amphitheatre is the best-preserved in France. Built around 100 BC, the arena would have seated 24,000 spectators and staged gladiatorial contests and public executions – it still provides an impressive venue for gigs, events and summer bullfights. An audioguide provides context as you explore the arena, seating areas, stairwells and corridors (rather marvellously known to Romans as *vomitora*), and afterwards you can view replicas of gladiatorial armour and original bullfighters' costumes in the museum.

Maison Carrée Roman Sites

(place de la Maison Carrée; adult/child €5.50/4; 10am-8pm Jul & Aug, shorter hours Sep-Jun) Constructed in gleaming limestone around AD 5, this temple was built to honour Emperor Augustus' two adopted sons. Despite the name, the Maison

If You Like... Wild Provence

If the Calanques and the Camargue have given you a passion for Provence's stunning landscapes, here are a few more natural wonders you won't want to miss.

1 GORGES DU VERDON

Europe's largest canyon slices a 25km swathe through Provence's limestone plateau. Hemmed in by towering cliffs ranging from 250m to 700m high, it's a wonderful place to explore on foot or by raft. The two main jumping-off points are the villages of Moustiers Ste-Marie in the west and Castellane in the east.

2 MONT VENTOUX

Visible for miles around, Mont Ventoux (1912m), nicknamed *le géant de Provence* (Provence's giant), stands like a sentinel over northern Provence. The summit is accessible and offers views all the way to the Alps and the Camargue on a clear day. It's a hikers' paradise, and in July and August, tourist offices in Bédoin and Malaucène arrange night-time expeditions up the mountain to see the sunrise.

3 PARC NATIONAL DE LA LUBÉRON

Egyptian vultures, eagle owls, wild boars, Bonelli's eagles and Etruscan honeysuckle are among the species that call the 1650-sq-km **Parc Naturel Régional du Luberon Maison du Parc** (www.parcduluberon.fr) home. Created in 1977, the park encompasses dense forests, plunging gorges and more than 60 traditional villages. The attractive town of Apt, 60km east of Avignon, is the main gateway.

Carrée (Square House) is rectangular – to the Romans, 'square' simply meant a building with right angles. The building is beautifully preserved, with stately columns and triumphal steps; it's worth paying the admission to see the interior, but probably not worth seeing the 3D film.

Carré d'Art Museum

(**www.carreartmusee.com; place de la Maison Carrée; permanent collection free, exhibitions adult/child €5/3.70; 10am-6pm Tue-Sun)** The striking glass-and-steel building facing the Maison Carrée was designed by British architect Sir Norman Foster. Inside is the **municipal library** and the **Musée d'Art Contemporain**, with permanent and temporary exhibitions covering art from the 1960s onwards. The rooftop restaurant makes a lovely spot for lunch.

Sleeping

Hôtel de l'Amphithéâtre Hotel **€€**

(**04 66 67 28 51; www.hoteldelamphitheatre.com; 4 rue des Arènes; s/d/f €72/92/130)** Down a narrow backstreet leading away from Les Arènes, this tall townhouse ticks all the boxes: smart rooms with shabby-chic furniture and balconies overlooking place du Marché; a sleek palette of greys, whites and taupes; and a great buffet breakfast. It's run by an expat Cornishman and his French wife.

Royal Hôtel Hotel **€€**

(**04 66 58 28 27; www.royalhotel-nimes.com; 3 bd Alphonse Daudet; d €82-102, f €163;**) This upmarket hotel offers grace and style. Bedrooms have a choice of street views or an outlook over the grand place d'Assas. They're split into standard and superior, all with modern-meets-heritage decor; it's worth bumping up a level for extra space and air-con. The downstairs restaurant, La Boduegita, offers solid Mediterranean dining.

Les Jardins Secrets B&B **€€€**

(**04 66 84 82 64; www.jardinssecrets.net; 3 rue Gaston Maruejols; d €195-380, ste €380-450;**) For doing Nîmes *en luxe*, nowhere tops the Secret Gardens. Decorated to resemble an 18th-century *maison bourgeoise* (mansion), it's dripping with luxury, from chaise longues and antique clawfoot baths to a wonderful Roman-style bathhouse and divine gardens. Note, however, that prices do not include breakfast or parking (an extra €25 and €20 respectively).

Eating

Le Cerf à Moustache Bistro **€€**

(**09 81 83 44 33; 38 bd Victor Hugo; mains €14-35; 11.45am-2pm & 7-11pm Tue-Sat)** Despite its weird name, the Deer with the Moustache has quickly established itself as one of Nîmes' top bistros, with quirky decor (including reclaimed

Carré d'Art

GUICHAOUA/ALAMY ©

ESPIEGLE/GETTY IMAGES ©

Don't Miss Pont du Gard

Southern France has some fine Roman sites, but nothing can top the Unesco World Heritage Site–listed Pont du Gard, 21km northeast of Nîmes. This fabulous three-tiered aqueduct was once part of a 50km-long system of water channels, built around 19 BC to transport water from Uzès to Nîmes. The scale is huge: 48.8m high, 275m long and graced with 35 precision-built arches; the bridge was sturdy enough to carry up to 20,000 cu metres of water per day.

Each block was carved by hand and transported from nearby quarries – no mean feat, considering the largest blocks weight over 5 tonnes. Amazingly, the height of the bridge descends by just 2.5cm across its length, providing just enough gradient to keep the water flowing – an amazing demonstration of the precision of Roman engineering. The **Musée de la Romanité** provides background on the bridge's construction, and the **Ludo** play area helps kids to learn in a fun, hands-on way.

You can walk across the tiers for panoramic views over the River Gard, but the best perspective on the bridge is from downstream, along the 1.4km **Mémoires de Garrigue** walking trail. Early evening is a good time to visit, as admission is cheaper and the bridge is stunningly illuminated after dark.

There are large car parks on both banks of the river, 400m walk from the bridge. Several buses stop nearby, including Edgard bus B21 (hourly Monday to Saturday, two or three on Sunday) from Nîmes to Alès.

NEED TO KNOW

☎04 66 37 50 99; www.pontdugard.fr; car & up to 5 passengers €18, after 8pm €10; ⏰visitor centre & museum 9am-8pm Jul & Aug, shorter hours Sep-Jun

Detour: Châteauneuf-du-Pape

Carpets of vineyards unfurl around the medieval village of **Châteauneuf-du-Pape**, epicentre of one of the world's great winegrowing regions. Only a ruin remains of the château – a lone wall, high on a hilltop – once the summer residence of Avignon's popes, later bombed by Germans in WWII. Now it belongs to picnickers and day hikers who ascend the hill to scout their lines with a 360-degree panorama.

Thank geology for these luscious wines: when glaciers receded, they left *galets* scattered atop the red-clay soil; these large pebbles trap the Provençal sun, releasing heat after sunset and helping grapes ripen with steady warmth. Most Châteauneuf-du-Pape wines are red; only 6% are white. Reds come from 13 different grape varieties – grenache is the biggie – and should age for at least five years. The full-bodied whites drink well young (except for all-rousanne varieties) and make an excellent, mineral aperitif wine, hard to find anywhere else.

Sample them at wine shops with free tastings *(dégustations gratuites)*, or book a two-hour wine-tasting class at **École de Dégustation** (Tasting School; ☎04 90 83 56 15; www.oenologie-mouriesse.com; 2 rue des Papes; 2hr class €40). The **tourist office** (☎04 90 83 71 08; www.pays-provence.fr; place du Portail; ⏲9.30am-6pm Mon-Sat, closed lunch & Wed Oct-May) has a brochure of estates, showing which ones allow cellar visits, have English tours, allow drop-in visitors and offer free tastings.

furniture and a wall full of old-book doodles), matched by chef Julien Salem's creative take on the classics. Go basic with burgers and risotto, or upmarket with crusted lamb and chunky steaks.

L'Imprévu Modern French **€€**
(☎04 66 38 99 59; www.l-imprevu.com; 6 place d'Assas; mains €19.50-27.50; ⏲noon-2pm & 7-10pm Thu-Mon) A fine-dining French bistro tucked away in the corner of place d'Assas, with an open-plan kitchen and a cute interior courtyard. It has a good choice of seafood and meats, from sea bass in balsamic vinaigrette to thyme-marinated lamb. Dishes are mainly à la carte, although there's a limited *menu du jour*.

Carré d'Art Gastronomic **€€**
(☎04 66 67 52 40; www.restaurant-lecarredart.fr; 2 rue Gaston Boissier; lunch/dinner menu €19.50/32; ⏲noon-3pm & 7.30-10pm Tue-Sat) Open since 1989, this gastronomic heavy-hitter is still one of Nîmes' top fine-dining places. The setting is elegant, in a 19th-century townhouse decked out with abstract art and a gorgeous shaded courtyard, and the food gives traditional French a modern spin: mackerel escabèche, or Provençal sea bass with aubergine caviar.

Information

Tourist Office (☎04 66 58 38 00; www.ot-nimes.fr; 6 rue Auguste; ⏲8.30am-8pm Mon-Fri, 9am-7pm Sat, 10am-6pm Sun Jul & Aug, shorter hours Sep-Jun) There's also a seasonal annexe (⏲usually Jul & Aug) on esplanade Charles de Gaulle.

Getting There & Away

Bus The **bus station** (☎04 66 38 59 43; rue Ste-Félicité) is next to the train station. Destinations include **Pont du Gard** (30 minutes, five to seven daily in summer).

Train TGVs run hourly to/from Paris' Gare de Lyon (€62.50 to €111, three hours) from the **train station** (bd Talabot).

Local destinations, with at least hourly departures, include:

Arles €9, 30 minutes

Avignon €8.50, 30 minutes

Montpellier €8.50, 30 minutes

Carcassonne

POP 49,100

Perched on a rocky hilltop and bristling with zig-zag battlements, stout walls and spiky turrets, from afar the fortified city of Carcassonne looks like something out of a children's storybook.

Sights & Activities

La Cité Walled City

(**Porte Narbonnaise 9am-7pm Jul & Aug, to 5pm Sep-Jun**) Carcassonne's rampart-ringed fortress is one of the Languedoc's most recognisable landmarks. Built on a steep spur of rock, it's been used as a defensive stronghold for nigh on 2000 years. The fortified town is encircled by two sets of battlements and 52 stone towers, topped by distinctive 'witch's hat' roofs (added by the architect Viollet-le-Duc during 19th-century restorations). The main gateway of **Porte Narbonnaise** leads into the citadel's interior, a maze of cobbled lanes and courtyards, now mostly lined by shops and restaurants.

Sleeping

La Maison Vieille B&B **€€**

(**04 68 25 77 24; www.la-maison-vieille.com; 8 rue Trivalle; d €85-95;**) As charming a B&B as you'll find in Carcassonne. In an old mansion, the rooms are supremely tasteful: Barbecane in blues, Cité with exposed brick, Prince Noir with an in-room bath, Dame Carcas with floaty fabrics and vintage luggage. There's a walled courtyard for breakfast, and the location is ideal for Villes Haute and Basse. Rue Trivalle lies just east of the Pont Vieux.

L'Orangerie B&B **€€**

(**04 68 77 96 84; www.bedandbreakfast-carcassonne.com; 41 av des Platanes, Montlegun; d €110-120;**) Well removed from the tourist bustle, 2.5km east of La Cité in |the suburb of Montlegun, this fine five-roomer offers a lot of elegance for your euro. It's in an 18th-century *maison du maître* (master's house), with huge rooms and heritage furniture, his-and-hers sinks and wood floors, plus a gorgeous stained-glass conservatory and garden pool.

La Cité, Carcassone

LOIC LAGARDE/GETTY IMAGES ©

Château de Palaja Hotel €€€
(☎06 63 69 88 32; www.chateau-palaja.fr; 7 rue Barri del Castel; d €120-190, f €140-210;) You don't get rampart views at this hotel 6km south of Carcassonne, but you do get serious luxury. Its six rooms and six suites would look more at home in a Parisian boutique hotel than a 1780 Languedoc château: slate tiles, neutral colours and distressed furniture set the designer tone, matched by a minimalist pool and Swedish sauna.

Hôtel du Château Hotel €€€
(☎04 68 11 38 38; www.hotelduchateau.net; 2 rue Camille St-Saëns; d €175-255;) You get the best of both worlds at this flashy hotel: knockout night-time views of La Cité's ramparts, coupled with the convenience of staying outside the walled city. The 16 rooms are snazzily finished with wood, exposed stone and boutique-style furnishings, and you can admire wonderful castle views from the heated pool and Jacuzzi.

Eating

La Marquière Gascon Cuisine €€
(☎04 68 71 52 00; www.lamarquiere.com; 13 rue St-Jean; 2-/3-course menu €30/38; noon-2.30pm & 7-10.30pm Fri-Tue) The pick of the places in the old city, a family-run bistro that serves classy, beautifully presented French cuisine in an old shuttered *auberge* (country inn), complete with beams and original hearth. It's heavy on regional dishes such as meaty *cassoulet* (rich bean, pork and duck stew), duck breast and fat fillets of Charolais beef. Ask for a table in the courtyard if it's sunny.

Au Comte Roger Modern French €€
(☎04 68 11 93 40; www.comteroger.com; 14 rue St-Louis; menus lunch €21-29, dinner €40; noon-1.30pm & 7-9.30pm Tue-Sat) This sleek restaurant looks fancy, but don't expect fireworks: it offers decent regional food, but the citadel location bumps up the prices considerably. There's a choice of

Left: Châteauneuf-du-Pape (p316); **Below:** Carcassonne

where to dine: a smart dining room with starched white tablecloths and cool grey furniture, or a pergola-covered patio beside an old well.

Bloc G Bistro **€€**
(☎04 68 47 58 20; www.bloc-g.com; 112 rue Barbacane; 3-course lunch €15, dinner mains €15-25; ⏰noon-2.30pm Tue-Sat, 7-10.30pm Wed-Sat) This modern diner offers far better food than most places in the citadel, for half the price. Its modern style is matched with modern food: white walls, white chairs, white tables, with a short menu of salads and *tarte salées* (savoury tarts) for lunch, and creative versions of southwest classics for supper. Great local wines by the glass too.

Information

La Cité Tourist Office (Porte Narbonnaise; ⏰9-6pm daily Apr-Sep, 9-6pm Sat & Sun Oct-Mar)

Getting There & Away

Carcassonne is on the main train line from Toulouse. Buses are geared around school timetables, so it's much easier and quicker to catch a train to pretty much anywhere. Destinations include:

Montpellier €22.50, 1½ hours

Toulouse €14, 50 minutes

THE FRENCH RIVIERA

With its glistening seas, idyllic beaches and fabulous weather, the Riviera (known as Côte d'Azur to the French) encapsulates many people's idea of the good life. The beauty is that there is so much more to do than just going to the beach – although the Riviera does take beach-going *very* seriously: from nudist beach to secluded cove or exclusive club, there is something for everyone.

Nice

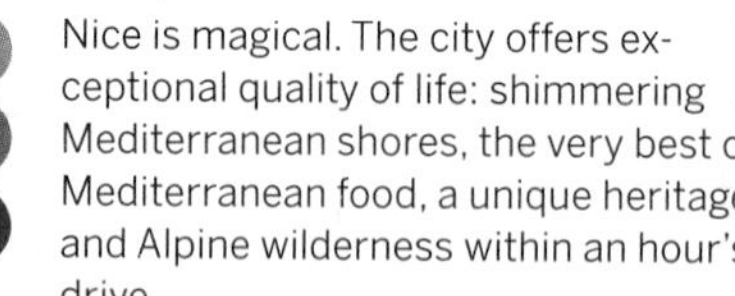

POP 344,460

Nice is magical. The city offers exceptional quality of life: shimmering Mediterranean shores, the very best of Mediterranean food, a unique heritage and Alpine wilderness within an hour's drive.

Sights & Activities

Promenade des Anglais Architecture

Palm-lined promenade des Anglais, paid for by Nice's English colony in 1822, is a fine stage for a stroll. It's particularly atmospheric in the evening, with Niçois milling about and epic sunsets. Don't miss the magnificent facade of **Hôtel Negresco**, built in 1912, or art deco **Palais de la Méditerranée**, saved from demolition in the 1980s and now part of a four-star palace. The promenade follows the whole Baie des Anges (4km) and has a cycle and skating lane.

Musée d'Art Moderne et d'Art Contemporain Art Museum

(Mamac; www.mamac-nice.org; place Yves Klein; 10am-6pm Tue-Sun) FREE European and American avant-garde works from the 1950s to the present are the focus of this museum. Highlights include many works by Nice's New Realists Christo, César, Arman, Yves Klein and Niki de Saint-Phalle. The building's rooftop also works as an exhibition space (with panoramas of Nice to boot).

Musée Matisse Art Museum

(www.musee-matisse-nice.org; 164 av des Arènes de Cimiez; 10am-6pm Wed-Mon) FREE Located about 2km north of the centre in the leafy quarter of Cimiez, the Musée Matisse houses a fascinating assortment of works by Henri Matisse documenting the artist's stylistic evolution, including oil paintings, drawings, sculptures, tapestries and Matisse's signature paper cut-outs. The permanent collection is displayed in a red-ochre 17th-century Genoese villa overlooking an olive-tree-studded park. Temporary exhibitions are hosted in the futuristic basement building. Sadly, all explanations are in French only.

Musée National Marc Chagall Art Museum

(www.musee-chagall.fr; 4 av Dr Ménard; adult/child €8/6; 10am-5pm Wed-Mon Oct-Jun, to 6pm Jul-Sep) This small museum houses the largest public collection of works by Belarusian painter Marc Chagall (1887–1985). The main hall contains 12 huge interpretations (1954–67) of stories from Genesis and Exodus. In an antechamber, an unusual mosaic of Elijah in his fiery chariot, surrounded by signs of the zodiac, is viewed through a plate-glass window and

Promenade des Anglais
SYLVAIN OLIVEIRA/ALAMY ©

reflected in a small pond. The excellent audioguide is available in English (you will need a form of ID as deposit).

Smartphone users can also download the commentary as an app. It takes about 20 minutes to walk to the museum from the centre (signposted from av de l'Olivetto).

Parc du Château Garden

(**8am-6pm in winter, to 8pm in summer**) On a rocky outcrop towering over Vieux Nice, this park offers a cinematic panorama of Nice and the Baie des Anges on one side, and the port on the other. The 12th-century castle was razed by Louis XIV in 1706; only the 16th-century **Tour Bellanda** remains. It is a fabulous place for picnics. To get here, ride the free **Château Lift** (**Ascenseur du Château; rue des Ponchettes; 9am-6pm winter, to 8pm summer**) from beneath Tour Bellanda, or hike up from the old town or the port.

Other simple attractions include **Cascade Donjon**, an 18th-century artificial waterfall crowned with a viewing platform, and kids' playgrounds.

Tours

Trans Côte d'Azur Boat Tour

(**www.trans-cote-azur.com; quai Lunel; Apr-Oct**) To escape the crowds, take a scenic cruise along the coast. Trans Côte d'Azur runs one-hour trips along the Baie des Anges and the Rade de Villefranche (adult/child €17.5/12) from April to October. From mid-June to mid-September it also runs regular excursions to Île Ste-Marguerite (€38/28, crossing one hour), St-Tropez (€63/48, crossing 2½ hours) and Monaco (€36/27.5, crossing 45 minutes). Reservations are essential.

L'OpenTour Bus Tour

(**www.nice.opentour.com; opposite 109 quai des Etats-Unis; 1-day pass adult/child €22/8**) With headphone commentary in several languages, the open-topped bus tours (1½ hours) give you a good overview of Nice. You can hop on or off at any one of 12 stops, including sights in out of the way Cimiez.

Local Knowledge

Riviera High Life Don't Miss List

BY ELIZABETH LEWIS, RADIO PRESENTER AT 106.5 RIVIERA RADIO

1 LIVE JAZZ

My favourite summer event is Juan-les-Pins Jazz Festival (p44). I do a spot of simultaneous translation work when the artists need an interpreter for media interviews, so it was such a thrill to hang out with legends like Sonny Rollins in 2012 and Marcus Miller in 2011. In Nice, there's the **Shapko** (www.shapko.com) music venue in the old town, where all the best local and visiting jazz musicians play all year round.

2 CELEBRITY SPOTTING

At Monte Carlo Sporting Club's **Salle des Étoiles** (www.sportingmontecarlo.com) I've chatted to Shirley Bassey (she lives next door to it) at a Liza Minnelli concert, stood behind Elton John (another Riviera resident) at a Grace Jones concert and spotted Julian Lennon.

3 ROOFTOP SPAS & BARS

Rooftops are prime Riviera real estate and many of the big hotels have rooftop spas and bars open to non-guests. Nice's **Hôtel Grand Aston** (www.hotel-aston.com) has a fabulous rooftop pool.

4 GLAMOUR

For pure glamour it has to be Monaco's **Monte Carlo Bay Hôtel** (www.montecarlobay.com). It's all majestic, art-deco–style colonnades and has a fantastic spa with a circular pool and a bridge that you swim under to get outside.

5 PRICELESS GEMS

Cave Romagnan (http://caveromagnan.free.fr) in Nice is a tiny, unpretentious wine bar and cellar. In Biot village, the picturesque hotel and restaurant **Les Arcades** (www.hotel-restaurant-les-arcades.com) serves good-value, proper local food and is really convivial.

Nice

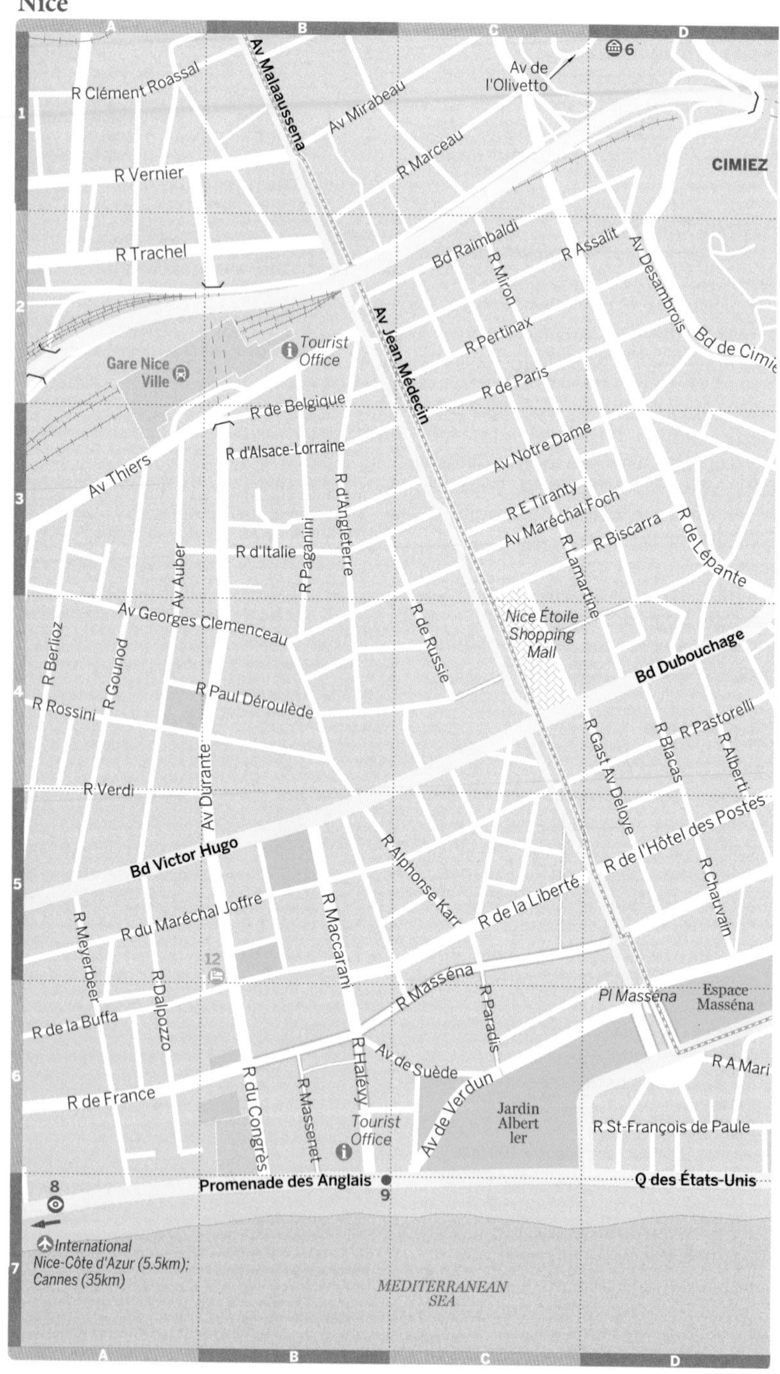

PROVENCE & THE FRENCH RIVIERA NICE

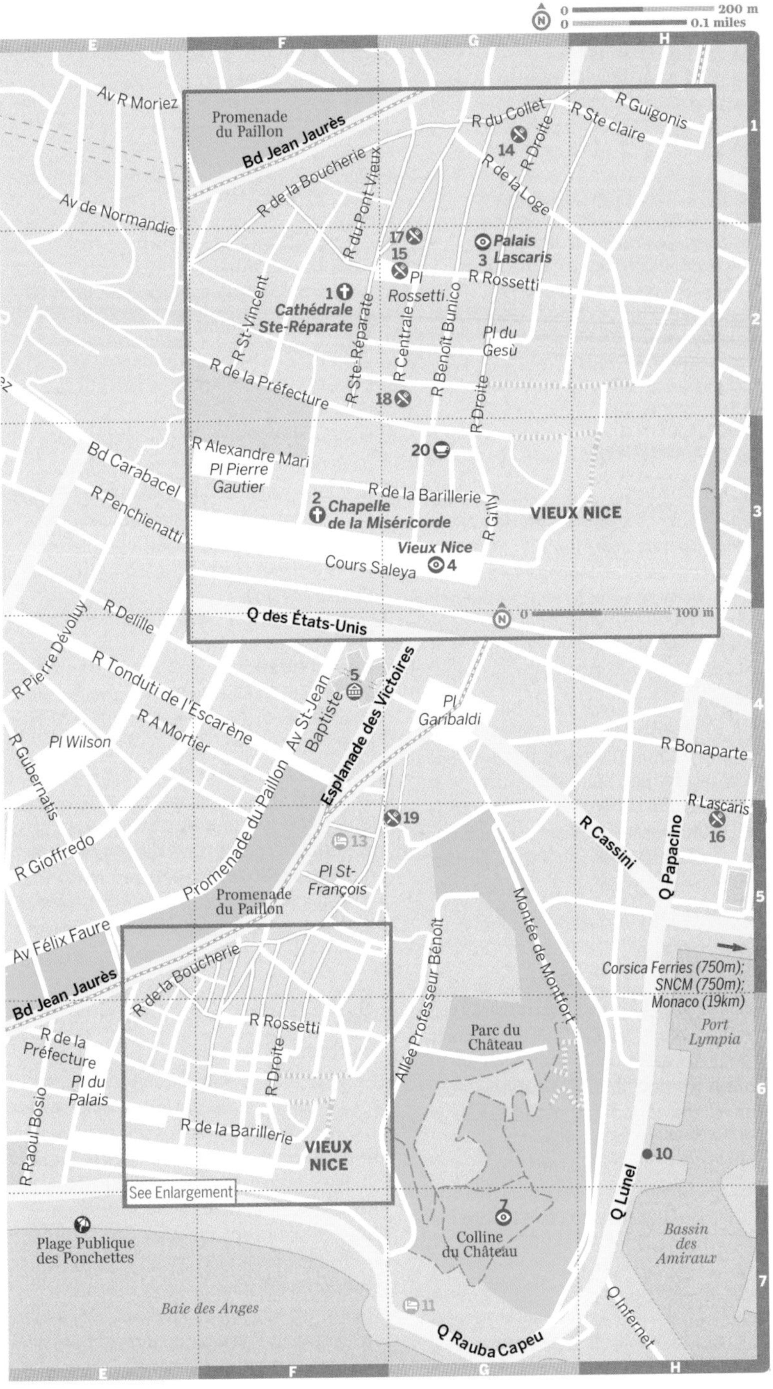

0 200 m
0 0.1 miles
Av R Moriez
Promenade du Paillon
Bd Jean Jaurès
R de la Boucherie
R du Pont Vieux
R du Collet
R Ste claire
R Guigonis
R Droite
R de la Loge
Av de Normandie
Palais Lascaris
R Rossetti
Pl Rossetti
Cathédrale Ste-Réparate
R St-Vincent
R Ste-Réparate
R Centrale
R Benoît Bunico
Pl du Gesù
R de la Préfecture
R Alexandre Mari
Pl Pierre Gautier
Bd Carabacel
R Penchienatti
R de la Barillerie
Chapelle de la Miséricorde
R Gilly
VIEUX NICE
Vieux Nice
Cours Saleya
Q des États-Unis
0 100 m
R Delille
R Pierre Dévoluy
R Tonduti de l'Escarène
R A Mortier
Av St-Jean Baptiste
Esplanade des Victoires
Pl Garibaldi
R Bonaparte
Pl Wilson
R Gubernatis
Promenade du Paillon
R Lascaris
R Cassini
Q Papacino
R Gioffredo
Pl St-François
Montée de Montfort
Allée Professeur Benoît
Av Félix Faure
Corsica Ferries (750m); SNCM (750m); Monaco (19km)
Port Lympia
Parc du Château
R de la Préfecture
Pl du Palais
R Raoul Bosio
VIEUX NICE
See Enlargement
Q Lunel
Colline du Château
Bassin des Amiraux
Plage Publique des Ponchettes
Baie des Anges
Q Rauba Capeu
Q Infernet

Nice

Don't Miss Sights
1 Cathédrale Ste-Réparate F2
2 Chapelle de la Miséricorde F3
3 Palais Lascaris G2
4 Vieux Nice G3

Sights
5 Musée d'Art Moderne et d'Art Contemporain F4
6 Musée National Marc Chagall D1
7 Parc du Château G7
8 Promenade des Anglais A7

Activities, Courses & Tours
9 L'OpenTour B7
10 Trans Côte d'Azur H6

Sleeping
11 Hôtel La Pérouse G7
12 Nice Garden Hôtel B5
13 Villa la Tour F5

Eating
14 Chez Palmyre G1
15 Fenocchio G2
16 Jan H5
17 La Rossettisserie G2
18 Le Bistrot d'Antoine G2
19 L'Escalinada G5

Drinking & Nightlife
20 Les Distilleries Idéales G3

Sleeping

Nice Pebbles Self-Contained €€

(04 97 20 27 30; www.nicepebbles.com; 1-/3-bedroom apt from €107/220;) Have you ever dreamt of feeling like a real Niçois, coming back to your designer pad in Vieux Nice, opening a bottle of ice-cold rosé and feasting on market goodies? Nice Pebbles' concept is simple: offering the quality of a 4-star boutique hotel in holiday flats. The apartments (one to three bedrooms) are gorgeous and equipped to high standards.

Guests can expect wi-fi, flat-screen TV, DVD players, fully equipped kitchens and linen bedding in most flats, and in some cases, a swimming pool, balcony or terrace.

Nice Garden Hôtel Boutique Hotel €€

(04 93 87 35 62; www.nicegardenhotel.com; 11 rue du Congrès; s/d €75/100;) Behind heavy iron gates hides this little gem of a hotel: its nine beautifully appointed rooms, the work of the exquisite Marion, are a subtle blend of old and new and overlook a delightful garden with a glorious orange tree. Amazingly, all this charm and peacefulness is just two blocks from the promenade.

Villa la Tour Boutique Hotel €€

(04 93 80 08 15; www.villa-la-tour.com; 4 rue de la Tour; d €76-183;) New owners since 2012 have injected a new lease of life into this old town favourite. Rooms have been redecorated according to painters – we loved the Nikki de St Phalle and Vaco rooms. The diminutive flower-decked roof terrace is now complemented by a street terrace ideal for watching Vieux Nice go by.

Hôtel La Pérouse Boutique Hotel €€€

(04 93 62 34 63; www.hotel-la-perouse.com; 11 quai Rauba Capeu; d from €330;) Built into the rock cliff next to Tour Bellanda, La Pérouse captures the vibe of a genteel villa. Lower-floor rooms face the lemon-tree-shaded courtyard and pool; upper-floor rooms have magnificent vistas of the promenade and sea, many with balconies or terraces to make the best of the panorama. Smart accent colours add flair to the traditional decor.

Eating

La Rossettisserie French €

(04 93 76 18 80; www.larossettisserie.com; 8 rue Mascoïnat; mains €14.50; noon-2pm & 7.30-10pm Mon-Sat) The Rossettisserie (a lovely play on word on rotisserie – roast house – and Rossetti, the name of the nearby square) only serves succulent roast meat – beef, chicken, veal, lamb or pork. It is cooked to perfection and comes with a choice of heavenly homemade mash, ratatouille or sauté potatoes and a mixed salad. The vaulted dining room in the basement is stunning.

Chez Palmyre French €

(☎04 93 85 72 32; 5 rue Droite; menu €17; ⏰noon-1.30pm & 7-9.30pm Mon-Fri) A new chef has breathed new life into this fabulously atmospheric little restaurant. The kitchen churns out Niçois standards with a light hand, service is sweet and the price fantastic; book ahead, even for lunch.

Fenocchio Ice Cream €

(www.fenocchio.fr; 2 place Rossetti; ice cream from €2; ⏰9am-midnight Feb-Oct) Dither too long over the 70-plus flavours of ice cream and sorbet at this unforgettable *glacier* (ice-cream shop) and you'll never make it to the front of the queue. Try a new taste sensation: black olive, rosemary or lavender.

Le Bistrot d'Antoine Modern French €€

(☎04 93 85 29 57; 27 rue de la Préfecture; mains €13-24; ⏰noon-2pm & 7-11pm Tue-Sat) What's so surprising about this super brasserie is how unfazed it is by its incredible success: it is full every night (booking essential), yet the 'bistro chic' cuisine never wavers, the staff are cool as a cucumber, the atmosphere is reliably jovial and the prices incredibly good value for the area.

L'Escalinada Niçois €€

(☎04 93 62 11 71; www.escalinada.fr; 22 rue Pairolière; menu €26, mains €19-25; ⏰noon-2.30pm & 7-11pm) This charming restaurant has been one of the best places in town for Niçois cuisine for the last half-century: melt-in-your-mouth homemade gnocchi with tasty *daube* (Provençal beef stew), grilled prawns with garlic and herbs, Marsala veal stew. The staff are delightful and the welcome *kir* (white wine sweetened with blackcurrant syrup) is on the house. No credit cards.

Ice cream at Fenocchio
WERNER DIETERICH/ALAMY ©

Jan Modern French €€€

(☎04 97 19 32 23; www.restaurantjan.com; 12 rue Lascaris; menu €55, mains €26-32; ⏰noon-3pm & 7.30-10pm Wed-Fri, 7.30-10pm Tue & Sat) Dining in the elegant aquamarine dining room of this gourmet restaurant is a treat – this is French gastronomy at its best, with regal service by maître d' Philippe Foucault and exquisite food by South African wonder chef Jan Hendrik van der Westhuizen. Antipodean influences are light in the menu but more pronounced in the wine list.

Drinking

Les Distilleries Idéales Cafe

(www.lesdistilleriesideales.fr; 24 rue de la Préfecture; ⏰9am-12.30am) Whether you're after an espresso on your way to the cours Saleya market or an aperitif (complete with cheese and charcuterie platters, €5.60) before trying out one of Nice's fabulous restaurants, Les Distilleries is one of the most atmospheric bars in town. Happy hour is from 6pm to 8pm.

AMANDA HALL/GETTY IMAGES ©

Don't Miss Vieux Nice

Nice's old town, a mellow rabbit warren, has scarcely changed since the 1700s. Retracing its history – and therefore that of the city – is a highlight, although you don't need to be a history buff to enjoy a stroll in this atmospheric quarter. Vieux Nice is as alive and prominent today as it ever was. Cue the **cours Saleya**: this joyous, thriving market square hosts a well-known flower market and a thriving fruit and vegetable market, a staple of local life. A flea market takes over on Mondays, and the spillover from bars and restaurants seems to be a permanent fixture.

Much of Vieux Nice has a similar atmosphere to cours Saleya, with delis, food shops, boutiques and bars crammed into tiny lanes. Rue de la Boucherie and rue Pairolière are are excellent for food shopping. There's a daily fish market at place St-François.

Much harder to spot because of the narrow lane it sits on is the baroque **Palais Lascaris**, a 17th-century mansion housing a frescoed orgy of Flemish tapestries, faience and gloomy religious paintings. On the ground floor is an 18th-century pharmacy.

Baroque aficionados shouldn't miss Nice's other architectural gems such as **Cathédrale Ste-Réparate** (place Rossetti), honouring the city's patron saint, and the exuberant **Chapelle de la Miséricorde** (cours Saleya).

NEED TO KNOW

Food markets (⏲6am-1.30pm Tue-Sun)

Palais Lascaris (15 rue Droite; guided visit €5; ⏲10am-6pm Wed-Mon, guided tour 3pm Fri)

Information

Tourist Office (☎08 92 70 74 07; www.nicetourisme.com; 5 promenade des Anglais; ⏰9am-6pm Mon-Sat) There's also a branch at the train station (av Thiers, Train Station; ⏰8am-7pm Mon-Sat, 10am-5pm Sun).

Getting There & Away

Air

Nice Côte d'Azur Airport (NCE; ☎08 20 42 33 33; www.nice.aeroport.fr; 📶) is France's second largest airport and has international flights to Europe, North Africa and even the US, with regular as well as low-cost companies.

Boat

Nice is the main port for ferries to Corsica. **SNCM** (www.sncm.fr; quai du Commerce) and **Corsica Ferries** (www.corsicaferries.com; quai du Commerce) are the two main companies.

Train

From Nice, there are services to:

Monaco (€3.30, 25 minutes, half-hourly)

Cannes (€5.80, 40 minutes, hourly)

Marseille (€37, 2½ hours, hourly)

Antibes & Juan-les-Pins

POP 76,580

With its boat-bedecked port, 16th-century ramparts and narrow cobblestone streets festooned with flowers, lovely Antibes is the quintessential Mediterranean town.

Greater Antibes embraces Cap d'Antibes, an exclusive green cape studded with luxurious mansions, and the modern beach resort of Juan-les-Pins. The latter is known for its 2km-long sandy beach and its nightlife, a legacy of the sizzling 1920s when Americans swung into town with their jazz music and oh-so-brief swimsuits.

Sights & Activities

Musée Picasso — Art Museum

(www.antibes-juanlespins.com; Château Grimaldi, 4 rue des Cordiers; adult/child €6/free; ⏰10am-noon & 2-6pm Tue-Sun)

> 'If you want to see the Picassos from Antibes, you have to see them in Antibes.'
>
> *Pablo Picasso*

The 14th-century Château Grimaldi served as Picasso's studio from July to December 1946. The museum now

Juan-les-Pins

ANGER O/GETTY IMAGES ©

houses an excellent collection of his works and fascinating photos of him.

Cap d'Antibes Walking

Cap d'Antibes' 4.8km of wooded shores are the perfect setting for a walk-swim-walk-swim afternoon. Paths are well marked. The tourist office maps show itineraries.

Eating

La Ferme au Foie Gras Delicatessen €

(www.vente-foie-gras.net; 35 rue Aubernon; sandwiches €4-7; 8am-6pm Tue-Sun) Now, this is our idea of what a good sandwich should be like: filled with foie gras or smoked duck breast, onion chutney or fig jam, truffle cheese and fresh salad. And many people seem to think the same: a queue snakes down from the tiny counter of La Ferme every lunch time.

Le Broc en Bouche Modern French €€

(04 93 34 75 60; 8 rue des Palmiers; mains €21-30; noon-2pm & 7-10pm Thu-Mon) No two chairs, tables or lights are the same at this lovely bistro: instead, every item has been lovingly sourced from antique shops and car boot sales, giving the place a sophisticated but cosy vintage feel. The charming Flo and Fred have put the same level of care into their cuisine, artfully preparing Provençal and modern French fare.

Information

Tourist Office (04 22 10 60 10; www.antibesjuanlespins.com; 55 bd Charles Guillaumont; 9am-noon & 2-6pm Mon-Sat, 10am-1pm Sun)

Getting There & Away

Antibes' train station is on the main line between Nice (€4.50, 30 minutes, five per hour) and Cannes (€2.90, 10 minutes, five per hour).

Left: Cemetery, St-Paul de Vence; **Below:** The village, St-Paul de Vence

(LEFT) HANS GEORG EIBEN/GETTY IMAGES ©; (BELOW) CARLOS ESTEVES TOP PHOTOGRAPHY/GETTY IMAGES ©

St-Paul de Vence

POP 3540

Once upon a time, St-Paul de Vence was a small medieval village atop a hill looking out to sea. Then came the likes of Chagall and Picasso in postwar years, followed by showbiz stars such as Yves Montand and Roger Moore, and St-Paul shot to fame. The village is now home to dozens of art galleries as well as the exceptional Fondation Maeght.

Sights

The Village Historic Quarter

Strolling the narrow streets is how most visitors pass time in St-Paul. The village has been beautifully preserved and the panoramas from the ramparts are stunning. The main artery, rue Grande, is lined with **art galleries**. The highest point in the village is occupied by the **Église Collégiale**; the adjoining **Chapelle des Pénitents Blancs** was redecorated by Belgian artist Folon.

Many more artists lived or passed through St-Paul de Vence, among them Soutine, Léger, Cocteau, Matisse and Chagall. The latter is buried with his wife Vava in the **cemetery** at the village's southern end (immediately to the right as you enter). The dynamic tourist office runs a series of informative, themed **guided tours** (1½ hours, adult/child €5/free).

Across from the entrance to the fortified village, the **pétanque pitch**, where many a star has had a spin, is the hub of village life. The tourist office rents out balls (€2) and can organise **pétanque lessons** (€5 per person).

Fondation Maeght Art Museum

(www.fondation-maeght.com; 623 chemin des Gardettes; adult/child €15/free; 10am-6pm)

The region's finest art museum, Fondation Maeght was created in 1964 by art collectors Aimé and Marguerite Maeght. Its collection of 20th-century works is

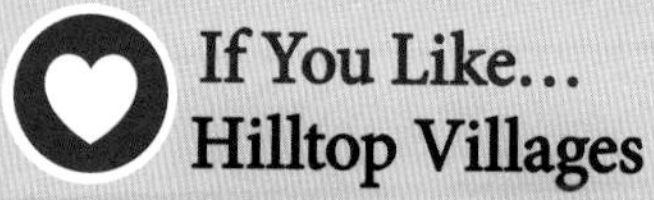

If You Like... Hilltop Villages

This iconic part of France would not be the same without its enviably photogenic hilltop villages. If you loved St-Paul de Vence, you'll simply adore these favourites:

1 LES BAUX DE PROVENCE

Clinging precariously to a limestone spur, this fortified hilltop village is among France's most visited. Cobbled lanes wend car-free up to the dramatic ruins of Château des Baux. Lunch afterwards at **L'Oustau de Baumanière** (☎04 90 54 33 07; www.oustaudebaumaniere.com; menus €166 & €199, mains €58-98; @ 📶).

2 MOUGINS

Mougins, 9km north of Cannes, looks too perfect to be real. Picasso discovered the medieval village in 1935 and lived here with his final love, Jacqueline Roque, from 1961 until his death. Highlights include the **Musée d'Art Classique de Mougins** (www.mouginsmusee.com; 32 rue Commandeur; adult/child €12/5; ⊙10am-6pm), an art museum spanning 5000 years of history, and **Les Jardins du MIP** (www.museesdegrasse.com; 979 chemin des Gourettes, Mouans-Sartoux; adult/child €3/free; ⊙10am-6pm Tue-Sun Apr-Oct), gardens featuring plants used in perfumery.

3 GORDES

The tiered village of Gordes sits spectacularly on the white rock face of the Vaucluse plateau; 4km northwest is **Abbaye Notre-Dame de Sénanque** (☎04 90 72 05 72; www.abbayedesenanque.com; adult/child €7/3; ⊙9.45-11am Mon-Sat, tours by reservation), famously framed by lavender in early summer.

4 MENERBES, LACOSTE & BONNIEUX

This mythical trio of golden-hued hilltop villages in the Luberon commands a quintessentially bucolic Provençal landscape.

5 ROUSSILLON

Famed for its distinctive red-ochre colour, this village is 11km west of the Luberon capital, Apt.

one of the largest in Europe. It is exhibited on a rotating basis, which, along with the excellent temporary exhibitions, guarantees you'll rarely see the same thing twice. Find the *fondation* 500m downhill from the village.

The building was designed by Josep Lluís Sert and is a masterpiece in itself, integrating the works of the very best: a Giacometti courtyard, Miró sculptures dotted across the terraced gardens, coloured-glass windows by Braque and mosaics by Chagall and Tal-Coat.

St Paul's tourist office runs **guided tours** (adult/child €5/free); you'll need to book ahead.

Chapelle du Rosaire — Architecture

(Rosary Chapel; www.vence.fr/the-rosaire-chapel.html; 466 av Henri Matisse; adult/child €6/3; ⊙2-5.30pm Mon, Wed & Sat, 10-11.30am & 2-5.30pm Tue & Thu) An ailing Henri Matisse moved to Vence in 1943, where he fell under the care of his former nurse and model Monique Bourgeois, who had since become a Dominican nun. She persuaded him to design this extraordinary chapel for her community, which Matisse considered his masterpiece. The artist designed everything from the decor to the altar and the priest's vestments.

From the road, all you can see are the blue-and-white ceramic roof tiles and a wrought-iron cross and bell tower. Inside, light floods through the glorious blue, green and yellow **stained-glass windows**. The colours respectively symbolise water/the sky, plants/life, the sun/God's presence; the back windows display Matisse's famous seaweed motif, while those on the side show a stylised, geometric leaf-like shape.

A line image of the **Virgin Mary and child** is painted on white ceramic tiles on the northern interior wall. The western wall is dominated by the bolder **Chemin de Croix** (Stations of the Cross). **St Dominic** overlooks the altar. Matisse also designed the chapel's stone altar, candlesticks and cross.

The beautiful priests' vestments are displayed in an adjoining hall.

Sleeping & Eating

Hostellerie Les Remparts Hotel **€€**

(**☎04 93 24 10 47; www.hostellerielesremparts.com; 72 Grande Rue; d €65-120;**) Right in the heart of the old village, in a medieval building, this family-run hotel is a charming address. The rooms are spacious and furnished in traditional French style (solid wood furniture and flowery spreads) and those overlooking the valley have fantastic views. The bathrooms are dated but functional.

Le Tilleul Modern French **€€**

(**☎04 93 32 80 36; www.restaurant-letilleul.com; place du Tilleul; menu €25, mains €20-31; 8.30am-10.30pm;**) Considering its location on the *remparts*, Le Tilleul could have easily plumbed the depths of a typical tourist trap; instead, divine and beautifully presented dishes grace your table and the all-French wine list includes a generous selection of wine by the glass. Sit under the shade of a big lime blossom tree.

The restaurant is open all day and serves breakfast and afternoon snacks outside of lunch and dinner.

La Colombe d'Or Traditional French **€€€**

(**☎04 93 32 80 02; www.la-colombe-dor.com; place de Gaulle; mains €19-55; noon-2.30pm & 7.30-10.30pm mid-Dec–Oct;**) A Léger mosaic here, a Picasso painting there: these are just some of the original modern artworks at the Golden Dove, the legendary restaurant and hotel where impoverished artists paid for meals with their creations. Dine beneath fig trees in summer or in the art-filled dining room in winter. The cuisine is surprisingly uncomplicated (terrines, grilled fish). Book well ahead.

Getting There & Away

St-Paul is served by bus 400 running between Nice (€1.50, one hour, at least hourly) and Vence (€1.50, 15 minutes).

Roussillon

PHIL HABER PHOTOGRAPHY/GETTY IMAGES ©

Cannes

POP 74,445

Most people have heard of Cannes and its eponymous film festival. The latter only lasts for two weeks in May, but the buzz and glitz are there year-round – unlike neighbouring St-Tropez, which shuts down in winter – mostly thanks to regular visits from celebrities enjoying the creature comforts of bd de la Croisette's palaces.

Sights & Activities

La Croisette Architecture

The multi-starred hotels and couture shops that line the famous bd de la Croisette (aka La Croisette) may be the preserve of the rich and famous, but anyone can enjoy the palm-shaded promenade and take in the atmosphere. In fact, it's a favourite among Cannois (natives of Cannes), particularly at night when it is lit with bright colours.

There are great views of the bay and nearby Estérel mountains, and stunning art deco architecture from the seafront palaces, such as the **Martinez** or the legendary **Carlton InterContinental**; its twin cupolas were modelled on the breasts of the courtesan La Belle Otéro, infamous for her string of lovers – Tsar Nicholas II and Britain's King Edward VII among them.

Not so elegant but imposing nonetheless is the **Palais des Festivals et des Congrès** (Festival Palace) at the western end of the prom, host of the film festival. Climb the red carpet, walk down the auditorium, tread the stage and learn about cinema's most glamorous event and its numerous anecdotes on a **Palais des Festivals guided tour** (adult/child €4/free; tours 1½hr). The tourist-office-run tours take place several times a month, except in May. Check dates on the office website (visits in English are sometimes available). Tickets can only be booked in person at the tourist office.

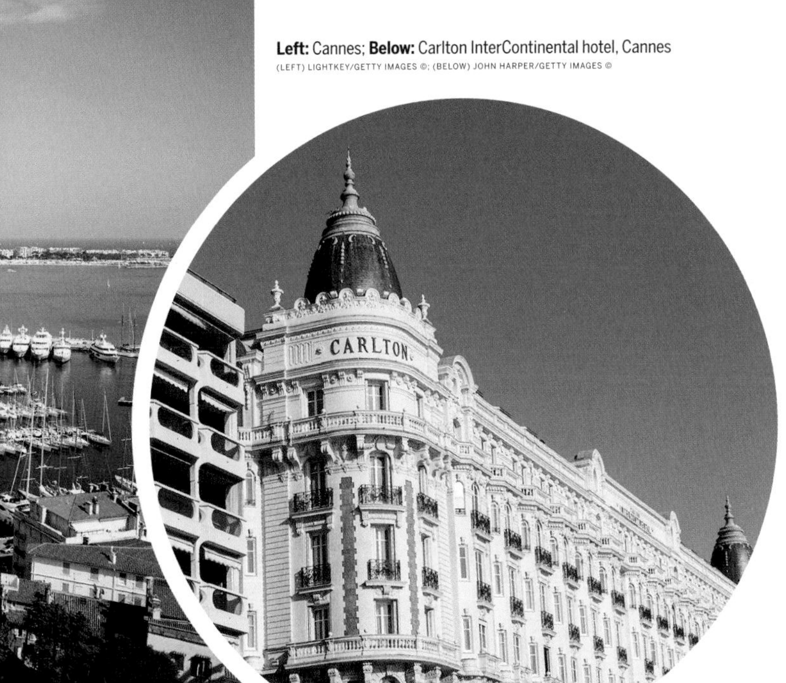

Left: Cannes; **Below:** Carlton InterContinental hotel, Cannes
(LEFT) LIGHTKEY/GETTY IMAGES ©; (BELOW) JOHN HARPER/GETTY IMAGES ©

After posing for a photograph on the 22 steps leading up to the cinema entrance, wander along allée des Étoiles du Cinéma, a path of celebrity hand imprints in the pavement.

Le Vieux Port & Le Suquet — Historic Quarter

On the western side of the Palais des Festivals lies the real Cannes. The yachts that frame the Vieux Port (Old Port) are the only reminder that this is where celebrities holiday, but they don't seem to impress the pensioners playing *pétanque* on sq Lord Brougham. Follow rue St-Antoine and snake your way up Le Suquet, Cannes's oldest district, for great views of the bay.

For local folklore, head to **Marché Forville** (rue du Marché Forville; 7am-1pm Tue-Sun), a couple of blocks back from the port. It is one of the most important markets in the region and the supplier of choice for restaurants (and for your picnic!).

Beaches — Swimming

Cannes is blessed with sandy beaches, although much of the stretch along bd de la Croisette is taken up by private beaches. This arrangement leaves only a small strip of free sand near the Palais des Festivals for the bathing hoi polloi; the much bigger **Plage du Midi** (bd Jean Hibert) and **Plage de la Bocca**, west of Vieux Port, are also free.

You can pay to access private beaches, including at the relaxed and family-friendly **Plage Vegaluna** (04 93 43 67 05; www.vegaluna.com; La Croisette; €15-25 9.30am-7pm;) which also offers water sports.

Super-stylish **Z Plage**, the beach of Hôtel Martinez, has blue loungers available for hire (front row/other row/pier €34/30/38). Book ahead.

Cannes

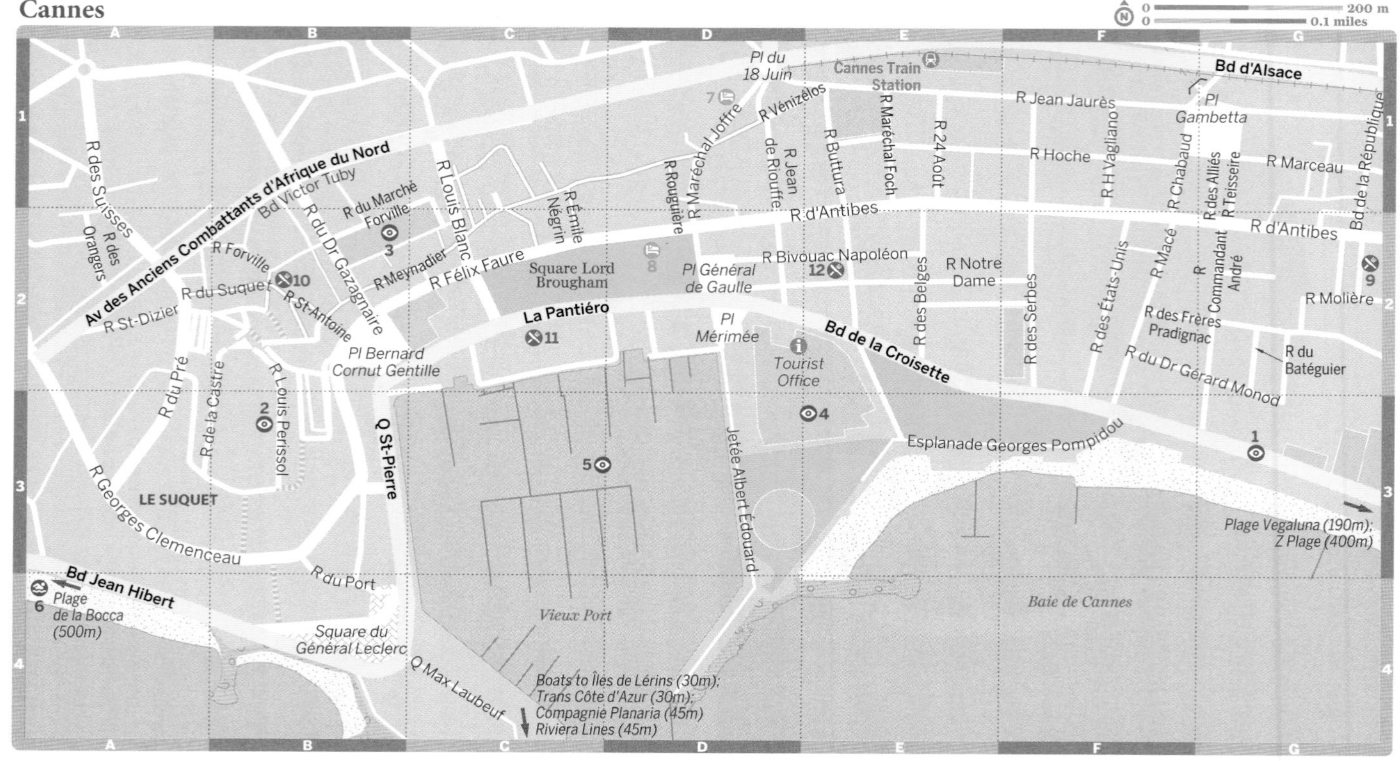
200 m
0.1 miles
Bd d'Alsace
Cannes Train Station
Pl du 18 Juin
R Jean Jaurès
Pl Gambetta
R Hoche
R Marceau
Bd de la République
R d'Antibes
R Vénizélos
R Maréchal Joffre
R Rouguière
R Jean de Riouffe
R Buttura
R Maréchal Foch
R 24 Août
R H Vagliano
R Chabaud
R des Alliés
R Teisseire
R Commandant André
R Macé
R des États-Unis
R des Serbes
R Notre Dame
R des Belges
R Bivouac Napoléon
Pl Général de Gaulle
Square Lord Brougham
R Émile Négrin
R Louis Blanc
R Félix Faure
R Meynadier
R du Marché Forville
Bd Victor Tuby
Av des Anciens Combattants d'Afrique du Nord
R des Suisses
R des Orangers
R Forville
R du Suquet
R St-Dizier
R St-Antoine
R du Dr Gazagnaire
Pl Bernard Cornut Gentille
La Pantiéro
Pl Mérimée
Tourist Office
Bd de la Croisette
R des Frères Pradignac
R Molière
R du Batéguier
R du Dr Gérard Monod
Esplanade Georges Pompidou
Jetée Albert Édouard
Q St-Pierre
R du Pré
R de la Castre
R Louis Perissol
LE SUQUET
R Georges Clemenceau
R du Port
Bd Jean Hibert
Plage de la Bocca (500m)
Square du Général Leclerc
Q Max Laubeuf
Vieux Port
Boats to Îles de Lérins (30m); Trans Côte d'Azur (30m); Compagnie Planaria (45m) Riviera Lines (45m)
Baie de Cannes
Plage Vegaluna (190m); Z Plage (400m)

Cannes

Sights
1 La Croisette G3
2 Le Suquet B3
3 Marché Forville B2
4 Palais des Festivals E3
5 Vieux Port C3

Activities, Courses & Tours
6 Plage du Midi A4

Sleeping
7 Hôtel 7e Art D1
8 Hôtel Splendid D2

Eating
9 L'Affable G2
10 Mantel B2
11 PhilCat C2
12 Sea Sens E2

Sleeping

Hôtel 7e Art Boutique Hotel **€€**

(**04 93 68 66 66; www.7arthotel.com; 23 rue Maréchal Joffre; s/d €85/106; Apr-Oct;**) Hôtel 7e Art has put boutique style within reach of budgeters. The owners schooled in Switzerland and got the basics right, with great beds, sparkling-clean baths and excellent soundproofing. The snappy design of putty-coloured walls, padded headboards and pop art, and perks like iPod docks in every room, far exceed what you'd expect at this price.

Hôtel Splendid Boutique Hotel **€€**

(**04 97 06 22 22; www.splendid-hotel-cannes.com; 4-6 rue Félix Faure; s/d from €88/122;**) This elaborate 1871 building has everything it takes to rival the nearby palaces – beautifully decorated rooms, vintage furniture, old-world feel with creature comforts, fabulous location and stunning views. A handful of rooms equipped with kitchenettes are ideal for longer stays and families.

Eating

PhilCat Delicatessen **€**

(**La Pantiéro; sandwiches & salads €4.50-6; 8.30am-5pm;**) Don't be put off by Phillipe and Catherine's unassuming prefab cabin on La Pantiéro: this is Cannes' best lunch house. Huge salads, made to order, are piled high with delicious fresh ingredients. Or if you're *really* hungry, try one of their phenomenal *pan bagna* (a moist sandwich bursting with Provençal flavours).

Mantel Modern European **€€**

(**04 93 39 13 10; www.restaurantmantel.com; 22 rue St-Antoine; menus €35-60; noon-2pm Fri-Mon, 7.30-10pm Thu-Tue**) Discover why Noël Mantel is the hotshot of the Cannois gastronomic scene at his refined old-town restaurant. Service is stellar and the seasonal cuisine divine: try the wonderfully tender glazed veal shank in balsamic vinegar or the original poached octopus *bourride*-style. Best of all though, you get not one but two desserts from the mouth-watering dessert trolley.

Sea Sens Fusion **€€€**

(**04 63 36 05 06; www.five-hotel-cannes.com; Five Hotel & Spa, 1 rue Notre Dame; menus €39-95, mains €19-48; 7-10pm Tue-Sat;**) Perched on the 5th floor of the Five Hotel, the Sea Sens is Cannes' latest food sensation, with one Michelin star to prove it. It serves divine food that blends French gastronomy and Asian elegance with panoramic views of Le Suquet and Cannes' rooftops on the side. Pastry chef De Oliveira's desserts are not to be missed.

L'Affable Modern French **€€€**

(**04 93 68 02 09; www.restaurant-laffable.fr; 5 rue Lafontaine; lunch/dinner menu €26/44, mains €36-40; noon-2.30pm & 7-10.30pm Mon-Fri, 7-10.30pm Sat**) Modern French cuisine has never tasted so good than at L'Affable. Everything from the ingredients and cooking to the presentation is done to perfection, whether it be the roasted veal with its vegetable medley, the seared sea-bream with white butter and asparagus or the house speciality, the Grand Marnier soufflé, which arrives practically ballooning at your table. Booking essential.

Information

Tourist Office (**04 92 99 84 22; www.cannes-destination.fr; Palais des Festivals, bd de la Croisette; 9am-7pm**) The place to book guided

Detour: Îles de Lérins

Although just 20 minutes away by boat, the tranquil Îles de Lérins feel far from the madding crowd.

The closest of these two tiny islands is the 3.25km by 1km **Île Ste-Marguerite**, where the mysterious Man in the Iron Mask was incarcerated during the late 17th century. Its shores are an endless succession of perfect beaches and fishing spots, and its eucalyptus and pine forest makes for a refuge from the Riviera heat.

As you get off the boat, a map indicates a handful of rustic restaurants as well as trails and paths across the island. It also directs you to **Fort Royal** (adult/child €6/3; 10.30am-1.15pm & 2.15-5.45pm Tue-Sun), built in the 17th century, and now harbouring the **Musée de la Mer**. Exhibits interpret the fort's history, with displays on shipwrecks found off the island's coast.

Smaller still, at just 1.5km long by 400m wide, **Île St-Honorat** has been a monastery since the 5th century. Its Cistercian monks welcome visitors year-round: you can visit the church and small chapels and stroll among the vineyards and forests. Camping and cycling are forbidden.

Boats for the islands leave Cannes from quai des Îles (along from quai Max Laubeuf) on the western side of the harbour. **Riviera Lines** (www.riviera-lines.com; quai Max Laubeuf) runs ferries to Île Ste-Marguerite (return adult/child €13/8.50), while **Compagnie Planaria** (www.cannes-ilesdelerins.com; quai Max Laubeuf) operates boats to Île St-Honorat (return adult/child €15.50/7.50).

tours of the city and get information on what to do and see in Cannes.

Getting There & Around

Train Cannes is well connected to Nice (€6.80, 40 minutes), Antibes (€2.90, 12 minutes), Monaco (€9.40, one hour) and St-Raphaël (€7.20, 30 minutes), with services every 20 minutes or so. There are trains to Marseille (€32, two hours) half-hourly.

St-Tropez

POP 4986

In the soft autumn or winter light, it's hard to believe that the pretty terracotta fishing village of St-Tropez is yet another stop on the Riviera celebrity circuit. It seems far removed from its glitzy siblings further up the coast, but come spring or summer, it's a different world: the town's population increases tenfold, prices triple and fun-seekers come in droves to party til dawn, strut their stuff and enjoy the creature comforts of an exclusive beach.

Sights & Activities

Place des Lices Square

St-Tropez's legendary and very charming central square is studded with plane trees, cafes and *pétanque* players. Simply sitting on a cafe terrace watching the world go by or jostling with the crowds at its extravaganza of a twice-weekly **market** (8am-1pm Tue & Sat), jam-packed with everything from fruit and veg to antique mirrors and flip-flops (thongs), is an integral part of the St-Tropez experience.

Musée de l'Annonciade Art Museum

(place Grammont; adult/child €6/4; 10am-1am & 2-6pm Wed-Mon) In a gracefully converted 16th-century chapel, this small but famous art museum showcases an impressive collection of modern art infused with that legendary Côte d'Azur light. Pointillist

Paul Signac bought a house in St-Tropez in 1892 and introduced others to the area. The museum's collection includes his *St-Tropez, Le Quai* (1899) and *St-Tropez, Coucher de Soleil au Bois de Pins* (1896).

Citadelle de St-Tropez Museum

(admission €3; 10am-6.30pm) Built in 1602 to defend the coast against Spain, the citadel dominates the hillside overlooking St-Tropez to the east. The views are fantastic. Its dungeons are home to the excellent **Musée de l'Histoire Maritime**, an all interactive museum inaugurated in July 2013 retracing the history of seafaring, from fishing, trading and exploration to travel and the navy.

Plage de Pampelonne Swimming

The golden sands of **Plage de Tahiti**, 4km southeast of St-Tropez, morph into the 5km-long, celebrity-studded **Plage de Pampelonne**, which sports a line-up of exclusive beach restaurants and clubs in summer.

Sleeping

Hôtel Lou Cagnard Hotel €€

(04 94 97 04 24; www.hotel-lou-cagnard.com; 18 av Paul Roussel; d €79-166; Mar-Oct;) Book well ahead for this great-value courtyard charmer, shaded by lemon and fig trees, and owned by schooled hoteliers. The pretty Provençal house with lavender shutters has its very own jasmine-scented garden, strung with fairy lights at night. Bright and beautifully clean rooms are decorated with painted Provençal furniture. Five have ground-floor garden terraces. The cheapest rooms have private washbasin and stand-up bathtub but share a toilet; most rooms have air-con.

Hôtel Le Colombier Hotel €€

(04 94 97 05 31; http://lecolombierhotel.free.fr; impasse des Conquettes; d/tr from €105/235; mid-Apr–mid-Nov;) An immaculately clean converted house, five minutes' walk from place des Lices, the Colombier's fresh, summery decor is feminine and uncluttered, with bedrooms in shades of white and vintage furniture.

Pastis Design Hotel €€€

(04 98 12 56 50; www.pastis-st-tropez.com; 61 av du Général Leclerc; d from €300;) This stunning townhouse-turned-hotel is the brainchild of an English couple besotted with Provence and passionate about modern art. You'll love the pop-art-inspired interior, and long for a swim in the emerald-green pool. Every room is beautiful although those overlooking av Leclerc are noisy.

Plage de Pampelonne
RUSSELL BULLEY/ALAMY ©

Eating

La Tarte Tropézienne
Cafe, bakery €

(www.latartetropezienne.fr; place des Lices; mains €13-15; ⌚6.30am-7.30pm, lunch noon-3pm) This cafe-bakery is the original creator of the eponymous cake, and therefore the best place to buy St-Tropez's delicacy. But to start, choose from delicious daily specials, salads and sandwiches which you can enjoy in the bistro inside or on the little terrace outside.

Bistro Canaille
Fusion €€

(☎04 94 97 75 85; 28 rue des Remparts; plates €8-24; ⌚7-11pm Fri & Sat Mar-May & Oct-Dec, 7-11pm Tue-Sun Jun-Sep) This fusion bistro is where locals in the know go for a night out. Jean-François and Vanessa serve imaginative, beautifully presented fusion tapas-sized dishes blending French, Spanish and Asian influences such as seared foie gras, squid-ink risotto, stir-fried scallops in soja sauce and churros. Bistro Canaille also organises regular wine tastings (and always has an excellent wine list).

Le Sporting
Brasserie €€

(place des Lices; mains €13-30; ⌚8am-1am) There's a bit of everything on the menu at always-packed Le Sporting, but the speciality is the hamburger with *foie gras* and morel cream sauce. The Brittany-born owner also serves perfect buckwheat crêpes, honest lunch deals (€13), and a simple salad and *croque monsieur* (grilled ham and cheese sandwich).

La Plage des Jumeaux
Seafood €€

(☎04 94 58 21 80; www.plagedesjumeaux.com; rte de l'Épi, Pampelonne; mains €25-40; ⌚noon-3pm; 🅿👪) The top pick of St-Tropez's beach restaurants, Les Jumeaux serves beautiful seafood (including fabulous whole fish, ideal to share) and salads on its dreamy white-and-turquoise striped beach. Families are well catered for, with playground equipment, beach toys and a kids' menu.

Au Caprice des Deux
Traditional French €€€

(☎04 94 97 76 78; www.aucapricedesdeux.com; 40 rue du Portail Neuf; menu €61, mains €35; ⌚7.30-10.30pm Thu-Sun) This traditional *mai-*

Musée Renoir

son de village (old stone terraced house) with coffee-coloured wooden shutters is an old-time favourite with locals. Its intimate interior is as traditional as its French cuisine: think beef filet with truffles or duck.

Shopping

Atelier Rondini Sandals
(www.rondini.fr; 16 rue Georges Clémenceau; 9.30am-12.30pm & 2.30-6.30pm Tue-Sat) Colette brought a pair of sandals from Greece to Atelier Rondini (open since 1927) to be replicated. They're still making the iconic sandals for about €135.

Information

Tourist Office (08 92 68 48 28; www.ot-saint-tropez.com; quai Jean Jaurès; 9.30am-12.30pm & 2-6pm) Has a kiosk in Parking du Port in July and August.

Getting There & Away

Boat **Les Bateaux Verts (04 94 49 29 39; www.bateauxverts.com; quai Jean Jaurès)** runs shuttles between St-Tropez and Ste-Maxime (one-way/return €7.50/13.50, 15 minutes), ideal to avoid St Tropez' notorious traffic.

Bus **VarLib (www.varlib.fr; tickets €3)** tickets cost €3 from the bus station (av du Général de Gaulle) for anywhere within the Var département. Four buses daily serve Toulon-Hyères airport (1½ hours).

Detour: Musée Renoir

The city of Cagnes-sur-Mer is nothing to write home about, but it's well worth a visit for the exquisite **Musée Renoir (www.cagnes-tourisme.com; Chemin des Colettes, Cagnes-sur-Mer; adult/child €6/free; 10am-noon & 2-5pm Wed-Mon)**. Le Domaine des Collettes (as the property was known) was home and studio to an arthritis-crippled Renoir (1841–1919) from 1907 until his death. He lived there with his wife and three children, and the house is wonderfully evocative. Works on display include *Les Grandes Baigneuses* (The Women Bathers; 1892), a reworking of the 1887 original, and rooms are dotted with photographs and personal possessions. The beautiful olive and citrus groves are as much an attraction as the museum itself.

The town is about 14km west of Nice and 23km east of Cannes.

Îles d'Hyères

For some inexplicable reason, these paradisiacal islands (also known as Îles d'Or – Golden Islands – for their shimmering mica rock) have remained mostly unknown to foreign crowds.

The easternmost and largest of this trio of islands is the little-visited **Île du Levant**, split into an odd combination of army land and nudist colony. **Île de Port-Cros**, the middle and smallest island, is the jewel in the islands' crown. France's first **marine national park (www.portcrosparcnational.fr)**, it boasts exceptional marine fauna and flora, which makes it a snorkelling paradise. The island is also covered with 30km of marked trails through thick forest, ragged cliff tops and deserted beaches.

The largest and westernmost island is **Île de Porquerolles (www.porquerolles.com)**. Run as a hacienda in the early 20th century, it has kept many of its sprawling plantation features. There are plenty of walking trails, but the best way to get around is by cycling. There are several bicycle-rental places, as well as a few restaurants and hotels.

Getting There & Away

Boats to the Îles d'Hyères leave from various towns along the coast. **Vedettes Îles d'Or et Le Corsaire (04 94 71 01 02; www.vedettesilesdor.fr; 15 quai Gabriel Péri)** operates boats to all three islands from Le Lavandou, and between Port-Cros and Porquerolles in summer.

The Three Corniches

Some of the Riviera's most spectacular scenery stretches between Nice and Menton. A trio of corniches (coastal roads) hugs the cliffs between Nice and Monaco, each higher up the hill than the last. The middle corniche ends in Monaco; the upper and lower continue to Menton.

CORNICHE INFÉRIEURE

Skimming the villa-lined waterfront, the Corniche Inférieure (also known as the Basse Corniche, the Lower Corniche or the N98) sticks pretty close to the train line, passing (west to east) through Villefranche-sur-Mer, Beaulieu-sur-Mer, Èze-sur-Mer and Cap d'Ail.

Villefranche-sur-Mer

This picturesque, pastel-coloured, terracotta-roofed fishing port overlooking the Cap Ferrat peninsula was a favourite with Jean Cocteau, who painted the frescos in the 17th-century **Chapelle St-Pierre** (admission €3; ⌚10am-noon & 2-6pm Wed-Mon). Steps split the steep cobblestone streets that weave through the old town, including the oldest, rue Obscure, an eerie vaulted passageway built in 1295. Looking down on the township is the 16th-century citadel. Beyond the port is a sandy beach offering picture-perfect views of the town.

St-Jean-Cap Ferrat

On the Cap Ferrat peninsula, this fishing-village turned playground for the wealthy conceals an enclave of millionaires' villas, with illustrious residents both present and past. On the narrow isthmus of the town, the extravagant **Villa Ephrussi de Rothschild** (www.villa-ephrussi.com; St-Jean-Cap Ferrat; adult/child €13/10; ⌚10am-6pm Mar-Oct, 2-6pm Nov-Feb) gives you an appreciation of the area's wealth. Housed in a 1912 Tuscan-style villa built for the Baroness de Rothschild, it's full of 18th-century furniture, paintings, tapestries and porcelain.

Beaulieu-sur-Mer

Some of the best-preserved belle époque architecture along the coast is in the seaside holiday town of Beaulieu-sur-Mer, including its elaborate 1904 **rotunda** with Corinthian columns capped by a cupola. Another belle époque beauty is the **Villa Grecque Kérylos** (www.villa-kerylos.com; Impasse Gustave Eiffel, Beaulieu-sur-Mer; adult/child €11.50/9; ⌚10am-6pm Mar-Oct, 2-6pm Nov-Feb), a reproduction of an Athenian villa built by archaeologist Théodore Reinach in 1902.

MOYENNE CORNICHE

Cut through rock in the 1920s, the Moyenne Corniche – the middle coastal road (N7) – takes drivers from Nice to Èze and Beausoleil (the French town bordering Monaco's Monte Carlo).

Villefranche-sur-Mer
VISIONS OF OUR LAND/GETTY IMAGES ©

Èze

On the pinnacle of a 427m peak is the medieval stone village of Èze (pop 2865). Once occupied by Ligurians and Phoenicians, today it's home to one-off galleries and artisan boutiques within its enclosed walls (there's only one doorway in or out of the village). The high point is the **Jardin d'Èze** **(adult/child €6/free; ⌚9am-sunset)**, a slanting cliff-side garden of exotic cacti with views of the Med all the way to Corsica (on a good day).

You can walk down from the village to Èze-sur-Mer on the coast via the steep **chemin de Nietzsche** (45 minutes); the German philosopher started writing *Thus Spoke Zarathustra* while staying in Èze and enjoyed this path.

GRANDE CORNICHE

The Grande Corniche, whose panoramas are the most dramatic of all, leaves Nice as the D2564. Stop at **Fort de la Revère** in the **Parc Natural Départemental de la Grande Corniche** for a picnic with stupendous views or a walk in the *garrigue* (Mediterranean scrub).

Further on, the town of **La Turbie**, which sits on a promontory directly above Monaco, offers vertigo-inducing views of the principality. The best views are from the town's **Trophée des Alpes** **(http://la-turbie.monuments-nationaux.fr; 18 av Albert Ier, La Turbie; adult/child €5.50/free; ⌚10am-1.30pm & 2.30-5pm Tue-Sun)**, one of only two Roman trophy monuments in the world (the other's in Romania), built by Augustus in 6 BC.

MONACO (PRINCIPAUTÉ DE MONACO)

☎377 / POP 32,350

Squeezed into just 200ha, this principality might be the world's second-smallest country (the Vatican is smaller), but what it lacks in size it makes up for in attitude. Glitzy, glam and screaming hedonism, Monaco is truly beguiling.

Although a sovereign state, the principality's status is unusual. It is not a member of the European Union, yet it participates in the EU customs territory (meaning no border formalities crossing from France into Monaco) and uses the euro as its currency.

Sights & Activities

Musée Océanographique de Monaco Aquarium

(www.oceano.mc; av St-Martin; adult/child €14/7; ⌚10am-6pm) Stuck dramatically to the edge of a cliff since 1910, the world-renowned Musée Océanographique de Monaco, founded by Prince Albert I (1848–1922), is a stunner. Its centrepiece is its aquarium, with a 6m-deep lagoon where sharks and marine predators are separated from colourful tropical fishes by a coral reef. Upstairs, two huge colonnaded rooms retrace the history of oceanography and marine biology (and Prince Albert's contribution to the field) through photographs, old equipment, numerous specimens and interactive displays.

Palais du Prince Palace

(www.palais.mc; adult/child €8/4; ⌚10am-6pm Apr-Oct) For a glimpse into royal life, you can tour the state apartments with an 11-language audioguide. The palace is what you would expect of any aristocratic abode: lavish furnishings and expensive 18th- and 19th-century art.

Cathédrale de Monaco Cathedral

(4 rue Colonel) An adoring crowd continually shuffles past Prince Rainier's and Princess Grace's graves, located inside the cathedral choir of the 1875 Romanesque–Byzantine Cathédrale de Monaco. The Monaco boys' choir, **Les Petits Chanteurs de Monaco**, sings Sunday Mass at 10.30am between September and June.

Jardin Exotique Garden

(www.jardin-exotique.mc; 62 bd du Jardin Exotique; adult/child €7.20/3.80; ⌚9am-dusk) Home to the world's largest succulent and cactus collection, from small echinocereus to 10m-tall African candelabras,

Monaco

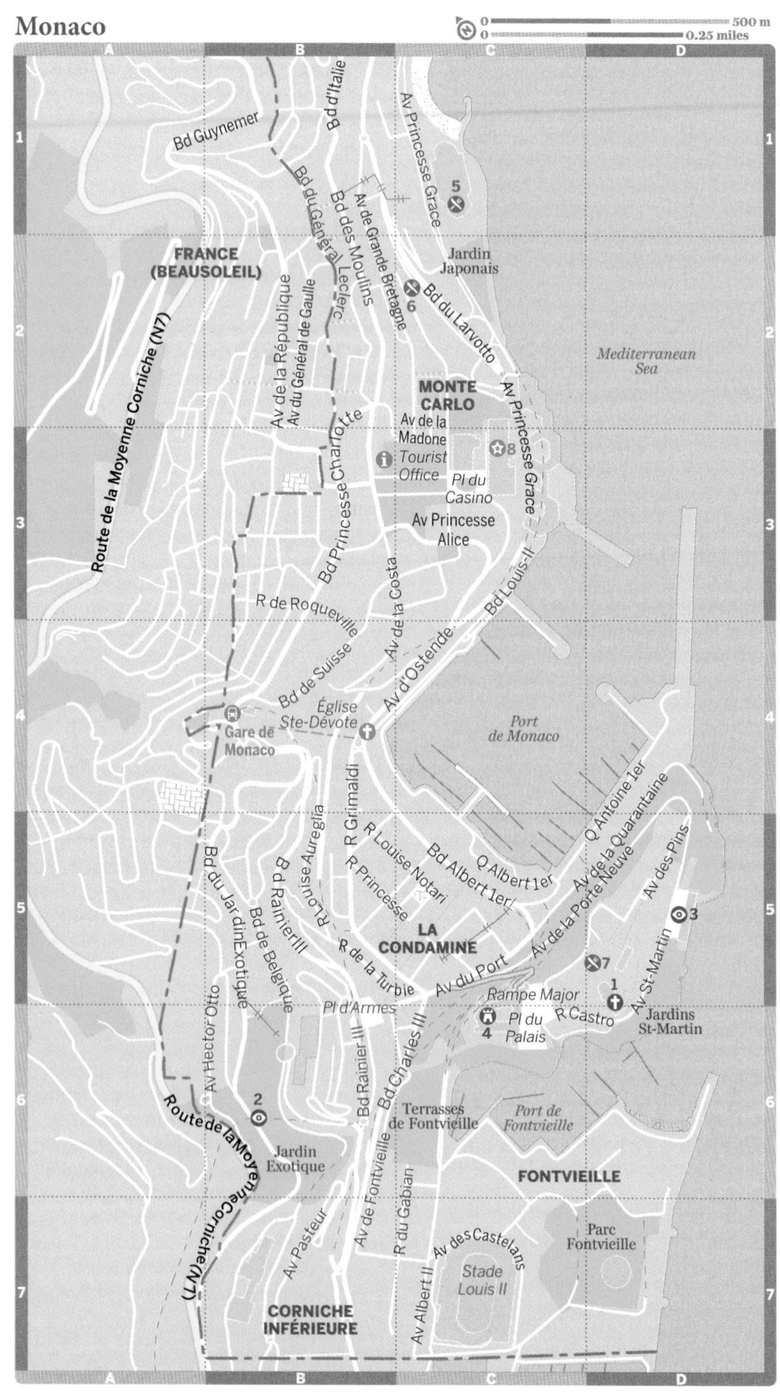
0 500 m
0 0.25 miles
Bd Guynemer
Bd d'Italie
Av Princesse Grace
5
FRANCE (BEAUSOLEIL)
Bd du Général Leclerc
Bd des Moulins
Av de Grande Bretagne
Jardin Japonais
6
Bd du Larvotto
Mediterranean Sea
Route de la Moyenne Corniche (N7)
Av de la République
Av du Général de Gaulle
MONTE CARLO
Av de la Madone
Tourist Office
8
Bd Princesse Charlotte
Pl du Casino
Av Princesse Alice
R de Roqueville
Av de la Costa
Bd Louis-II
Bd de Suisse
Av d'Ostende
Église Ste-Dévote
Gare de Monaco
Port de Monaco
R Grimaldi
Q Antoine 1er
Av de la Quarantaine
R Louise Notari
Bd Albert 1er
Q Albert 1er
Av de la Porte Neuve
Av des Pins
Bd du Jardin Exotique
Bd Rainier III
R Louise Aureglia
R Princesse
LA CONDAMINE
3
Bd de Belgique
R de la Turbie
Av du Port
7
Av St-Martin
1
Rampe Major
Pl d'Armes
Pl du Palais
R Castro
4
Jardins St-Martin
Av Hector Otto
Bd Rainier III
Bd Charles III
2
Terrasses de Fontvieille
Port de Fontvieille
Route de la Moyenne Corniche (N7)
Jardin Exotique
FONTVIEILLE
Av Pasteur
Av de Fontvieille
R du Gabian
Av des Castelans
Parc Fontvieille
Stade Louis II
Av Albert II
CORNICHE INFÉRIEURE

Monaco

Sights
1 Cathédrale de Monaco........D5
2 Jardin Exotique........B6
3 Musée Océanographique de Monaco........D5
4 Palais du Prince........C6

Eating
5 Café Llorca........C1
6 Cosmopolitan........C2
7 La Montgolfière........D5

Entertainment
8 Casino de Monte Carlo........C3

the gardens tumble down the slopes of Moneghetti through a maze of paths, stairs and bridges. Views of the principality are spectacular and the gardens are delightful. Your ticket also gets you a 35-minute **guided tour** round the Grottes de l'Observatoire.

Eating

La Montgolfière Fusion **€€**
(☎97 98 61 59; www.lamontgolfiere.mc; 16 rue Basse; mains €14-27; ⏰noon-2pm & 7.30-9.30pm Mon, Tue & Thu-Sat) This tiny fusion wonder is an unlikely find amid the touristy jumble of Monaco's historic quarter. But what a great idea Henri and Fabienne Geraci had to breathe new life into the Rocher. The couple have spent a lot of time in Malaysia, and Henri's fusion cuisine is outstanding, as is Fabienne's welcome in their pocket-sized dining room.

In winter, Henri cooks *bourride* every day, a salted cod stew typical of Monaco and Nice.

Café Llorca Modern French **€€**
(☎99 99 29 29; www.cafellorca.mc; 10 av Princesse Grace, Grimaldi Forum; menu €22, mains €15-19; ⏰noon-3pm Mon-Fri) This is Michelin-starred chef Alain Llorca's gift to lunch-goers: fabulous modern French cuisine with a fusion twist at affordable prices. The two-course lunch menu including a glass of wine is a steal. In spring/summer, make a beeline (and book) for the tables on the terrace overlooking the sea.

Cosmopolitan International **€€**
(www.cosmopolitan.mc; 7 rue du Portier; lunch menu €16-22, mains €17-31; ⏰12.30-2.30pm & 7.30-11pm; 📶) The menu at this hip restaurant features timeless classics from all corners of the world such as fish and chips, three-cheese gnocchi or veal cutlets in Béarnaise sauce, all revisited by Cosmo's talented chefs. Wash it down with one of the *many* wines on offer.

Entertainment

Casino de Monte Carlo Casino
(www.montecarlocasinos.com; place du Casino; admission Salon Europe/Salons Privés €10/20; ⏰Salon Europe 2pm-late daily, Salons Privés from 4pm Thu-Sun) Gambling – or simply watching the poker-faced gamble – in Monte Carlo's grand marble-and-gold casino is part and parcel of the Monaco experience. The building and atmosphere are attractions in their own right and you need not play huge sums. To enter the casino, you must be at least 18.

The **Salon Europe** has English and European roulette and 30/40; the **Salons Privés** offer European roulette, black jack and *chemin de fer*. A jacket and tie are required for men to enter the Salons Privés and the Salon Ordinaire in the evening.

Information

Tourist Office (www.visitmonaco.com; 2a bd des Moulins; ⏰9am-7pm Mon-Sat, 11am-1pm Sun) Smartphone users should download the tourist office's excellent app called Monaco Travel Guide.

Getting There & Away

Train Services run about every 20 minutes east to Menton (€2.10, 15 minutes) and west to Nice (€3.80, 25 minutes). Access to the station is through pedestrian tunnels and escalators from 6 av Prince Pierre de Monaco, pont Ste-Dévote, place Ste-Dévote and bd de la Belgique. The last trains leave around 11pm.

Monte Carlo Casino

TIMELINE

1863 Charles III inaugurates the first Casino on the Plateau des Spélugues. The **atrium** ❶ is a room with a wooden platform from which an orchestra 'enlivens' the gambling.

1864 Hôtel de Paris opens and the area becomes known as the 'Golden Square'.

1865 Construction of **Salon Europe** ❷. Cathedral-like, it is lined with onyx columns and lit by eight Bohemian crystal chandeliers weighing 150kg each.

1868 The steam train arrives in Monaco and **Café de Paris** ❸ is completed.

1878–79 Gambling moves to Hôtel de Paris while Charles Garnier is charged with building a new casino with a miniature replica of the Paris Opera House, **Salle Garnier** ❹.

1890 The advent of electricity casts a glow on architect Jules Touzet's newly added **gaming rooms** ❺ for high rollers.

1903 Inspired by female gamblers, Henri Schmit decorates **Salle Blanche** ❻ with caryatids and the painting *Les Grâces Florentines*.

1904 Smoking is banned in the gaming rooms and **Salon Rose** ❼, a new smoking room, is added.

1910 **Salle Médecin** ❽, immense and grand, hosts the high-spending Private Circle.

1966 Celebrations mark 100 years of uninterrupted gambling despite two world wars.

TOP TIPS

- ➡ Bring photo ID.
- ➡ Jackets are required in the private gaming rooms, and after 8pm.
- ➡ The cashier will exchange any currency.
- ➡ In the main room, the minimum bet is €5, the maximum €2000.
- ➡ In the Salons Privés, the minimum bet is €10, with no maximum.

JOHN VLAHIDES ©

Salle Blanche
Transformed into a superb bar-lounge in 2012, the Salle Blanche opens onto an outdoor gaming terrace, a must on balmy evenings. The caryatids on the ceiling were modelled on fashionable courtesans such as La Belle Otero, who placed her first bet here aged 18.

Salon Rose
Smoking was banned in the gaming rooms after a fraud involving a croupier letting his ash fall on the floor. The gaze of Gallelli's famous cigarillo-smoking nudes are said to follow you around the room, now a restaurant.

HÔTEL DE PARIS

Notice the horse's shiny leg (and testicles) on the lobby's statue of Louis XIV on horseback? Legend has it that rubbing them brings good luck in the casino.

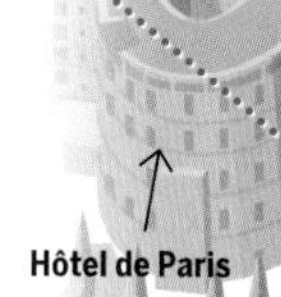

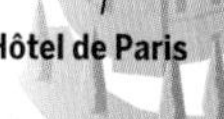

Salle Garnier
Taking eight months to build and two years to restore (2004–2006), the opera's original statuary is rehabilitated using original moulds saved by the creator's grandson. Individual air-con and heating vents are installed beneath each of the 525 seats.

JOHN VLAHIDES ©

Atrium

The casino's 'lobby', so to speak, is paved in marble and lined with 28 Ionic columns, which support a balustraded gallery canopied with an engraved glass ceiling.

Salon Europe

The oldest part of the casino, where they continue to play *trente-et-quarante* and European roulette, which have been played here since 1863. Tip: the bull's-eye windows around the room originally served as security observation points.

Café de Paris

With the arrival of Diaghilev as director of the Monte Carlo Opera in 1911, Café de Paris becomes the go-to address for artists and gamblers. It retains the same high-glamour ambience today. Tip: snag a seat on the terrace and people-watch.

Jardins et Terrasses du Casino

Place du Casino

1 2 3 4 5 6 7 8

Terraces, gardens & walkways

Hexagrace mosaic

Fairmont Monte Carlo

Salles Touzet

This vast partitioned hall, 21m by 24m, is decorated in the most lavish style: oak, Tonkin mahogany and oriental jasper panelling are offset by vast canvases, Marseille bronzes, Italian mosaics, sculptural reliefs and stained-glass windows.

Salle Médecin

Also known as Salle Empire because of its extravagant Empire-style decor, Monégasque architect François Médecin's gaming room was originally intended for the casino's biggest gamblers. Part of it still remains hidden from prying eyes as a Super Privé room.

BEST VIEWS

Wander behind the casino through manicured gardens and gaze across Victor Vasarely's vibrant op-art mosaic, *Hexagrace*, to views of the harbour and the sea.

France In Focus

Chateau d'Aiguines, Provence

France Today

A street scene in Paris (p51)

> *The future map of France could be very different*

France has by no means escaped the global economic crisis and unexpected rise of the far-right in Europe. But this ancient country of timeless Gallic pride and tradition has weathered greater storms – and the French are not sitting on their laurels. It's all hands on deck: economists are rethinking austerity, politicians redrawing the local-government map, and Parisians bringing in the city's first woman mayor. Times are a changing in *la belle France.*

A Political Earthquake

Political elections in 2014 threw up interesting results in France. April's municipal elections saw the vast majority of the country swing decisively to the right – a powerful commentary on the 'success' of socialist president François Hollande (b 1954), who assumed office in early 2012. European elections a month later packed a punch: the far-right National Front won a quarter of votes, leaving the governing left-wing Socialists in third place.

belief systems
(% of population)

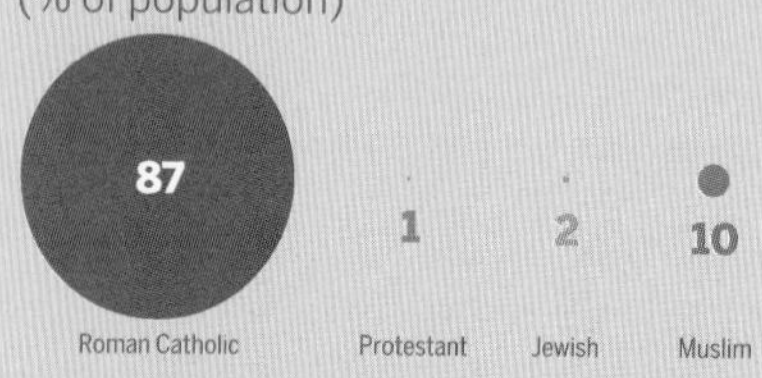

if France were 100 people

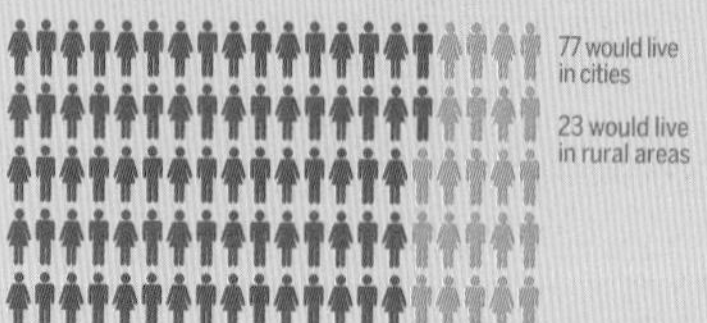

population per sq km

BRUNO DE HOGUES/GETTY IMAGES ©

French prime minister Manuel Valls was reported in the press as describing the victory of the far-right party, known for its fervent anti-immigrant stance, as 'a political earthquake in France'.

Economic Woes

Hollande has yet to fulfill his electoral promise of reducing unemployment and faces a gargantuan amount of work if he is to clear the country's debts by 2017 as pledged. Unemployment reached a record high in early 2014 and there was zero growth in the economy in the first three months of the year. The government increased corporation tax, VAT and income tax – most controversially to 75% for salaries over €1 million a year – to raise an extra €16 billion in 2013 for state coffers. Unfortunately the revenue was not quite the amount the government had forecast – it was, in fact, €14 billion short.

Shifting Borders

The future map of France could be very different. Prime Minister Manuel Valls unveiled a new administrative map of metropolitan France (the mainland and Corsica) in June 2014 – in which the country's current 22 *régions* (regions) – grouping 96 *départements*, each ruled by a Paris-appointed *préfet* (prefect) – were reduced to 14. This so-called *redécoupage territorial* (territorial redistribution) sparked a flurry of regionalist sentiment and emotion among the French, most notably in Brittany where Bretons would find themselves with Pays de la Loire; in northeastern France where Germanic Alsace and dramatically different Lorraine next door would become one *région;* and in Languedoc-Roussillon which would be fused with the Midi-Pyrénées.

Growth & Renewal

Champagne vineyards will become Unesco-protected if the region's bid to become a World Heritage Site in 2015 is successful. Meantime, such is the growing global demand for bubbly that Champagne has been given the go ahead to expand its production area for the first time since 1927. The first new vines will be planted in 40 new Champagne-producing villages in 2017.

Urban growth and renewal is just as exciting: Paris is mad about the riverside-renaissance project Les Berges de Seine; in Marseille the redevelopment of the seafaring Joliette *quartier* is breathtaking; and in Lyon the development of the Confluence *quartier* – with a roof-top dance club atop a 1930s sugar factory – continues with energy-efficient contemporary architecture and three bridges to link the rejuvenated riverside wasteland with the rest of the city.

History

MuséoParc Alésia (p206)

ARCHITECT BERNARD TSCHUMI/HEMIS/ALA

Few nations have a history as rich and rewarding as France. With everything from ancient artworks to Gothic cathedrals and regal châteaux, France often feels like one long history textbook. Even the tiniest towns and villages are littered with reminders of the nation's often turbulent past. Encompassing everything from courtly intrigue to intellectual enlightenment, artistic endeavour and bloody revolution, one thing's for sure – French history certainly isn't dull.

Prehistory

The first people to settle in France in significant numbers were small tribes of hunter-gatherers, who arrived around 35,000 to 50,000 years ago. These nomadic tribes lived seasonally from the land while pursuing game such as mammoth, aurochs, bison and deer. They often used natural caves as temporary shelters, leaving behind many sophisticated artworks, such as those in the Vézère Valley.

c 30,000 BC

Cro-Magnon people arrive in the Vézère Valley and create many cave paintings.

The next great wave of settlers arrived after the end of the last Ice Age, from around 7500 BC to 2500 BC. These Neolithic people were responsible for the construction of France's many megalithic monuments, including dolmens, burial tombs, stone circles and the massive stone alignments of Carnac. During this era, warmer weather allowed the development of farming and animal domestication, and humans increasingly established themselves in settled communities, often protected by defensive forts.

Gauls & Romans

Many of these communities were further developed from around 1500 BC to 500 BC by the Gauls, a Celtic people who migrated westwards from present-day Germany and Eastern Europe. But the Gauls' reign was shortlived; over the next few centuries their territories were gradually conquered or subjugated by the Romans. After decades of sporadic warfare, the Gauls were finally defeated in 52 BC when Caesar's legions crushed a revolt led by the Celtic chief Vercingetorix.

France flourished under Roman rule. With typical industriousness, the Romans set about constructing roads, temples, forts and other civic infrastructure, laying the foundations for many modern French cities (including Paris) and (more importantly in the opinion of many) planting the country's first vineyards, notably around Burgundy and Bordeaux.

The Rise of the Kings

Following the collapse of the Roman Empire, control of France passed to the Frankish dynasties, who ruled from the 5th to the 10th century, and effectively founded France's first royal dynasty. Charlemagne (742–814) was crowned Holy Roman Emperor in 800, around the same time that Scandinavian Vikings (also called Norsemen, thus Normans) began to raid France's western and northern coasts. Having plundered and pillaged to their hearts' content, the Normans eventually formed the independent duchy of Normandy in the early 11th century.

In 1066, the Normans launched a successful invasion of England, making William the Conqueror both Duke of Normandy and King of England. The tale of the invasion is graphically recounted in the embroidered cloth known as the Bayeux Tapestry.

During this time, Normandy was one of several independent duchies or provinces (including Brittany, Aquitaine, Burgundy, Anjou and Savoy) within the wider French kingdom. While each province superficially paid allegiance to the French crown, they were effectively self-governing and ruled by their own courts.

Intrigue and infighting were widespread. Matters came to a head in 1122 when Eleanor, Queen of Aquitaine, wed Henry, Duke of Anjou (who was also Duke of Normandy and, as William the Conqueror's great-grandson, heir to the English crown).

1500–500 BC
The Celtic Parisii tribe settle on what is now the Île de la Cité, Paris.

c AD 100–300
The heyday of Gallo-Roman France results in the construction of many splendid Roman buildings.

987
The Capetian dynasty comes to power and remains the French royal family for 800 years.

The Best... Roman Sites

1 Pont du Gard (p315)

2 Les Arènes (p304) & Théâtre Antique (p305)

3 Theâtre Romain (p233)

4 MuséoParc Alésia (p206)

5 Trophée des Alpes (p341)

Henry's ascension to the English throne in 1124 effectively brought a third of France under England's control, with battles that collectively became known as the Hundred Years' War (1337–1453), sowing the seeds for several centuries of conflict.

Following particularly heavy defeats for the French at Crécy and Agincourt, John Plantagenet was made regent of France on behalf of Henry VI in 1422, and less than a decade later he was crowned king of France. The tide of the war seemed to have taken a decisive turn, but luckily for the French, a 17-year-old warrior by the name of Jeanne d'Arc (Joan of Arc) rallied the French forces and inspired the French king Charles VII to a series of victories, culminating in the recapture of Paris in 1437.

Unfortunately things didn't turn out well for Joan – she was subsequently betrayed to the English, accused of heresy and witchcraft, and burnt at the stake in Rouen in 1431.

Renaissance to Revolution

During the reign of François I (r 1515–47), the Renaissance arrived from Italy, and prompted a great flowering of culture, art and architecture across France. Many lavish royal châteaux were built along the Loire Valley, showcasing the skills of French architects and artisans and projecting the might and majesty of the French monarchy. This great era of castle-building reached its zenith under the reign of Louis XIV (1643–1715), known as the Sun King, who emphasised the supposedly divine status of the French monarchy and constructed the ultimate playground palace at Versailles.

The pomp and profligacy of the ruling elite didn't go down well with everyone, however. Following a series of social and economic crises that rocked the country during the 18th century, and incensed by the corruption and bourgeois extravagance of the aristocracy, a Parisian mob took to the streets in 1789, storming the prison at Bastille and kickstarting the French Revolution.

Inspired by the lofty ideals of *liberté, fraternité, égalité* (freedom, brotherhood, equality), the Revolutionaries initially found favour with the French people. France was declared a constitutional monarchy, but order broke down when the hard-line Jacobins seized power. The monarchy was abolished and the nation was declared a republic on 21 September 1792. Three months later Louis XVI was publicly guillotined, as an example to the people, on Paris' place de la Concorde. His ill-fated queen, Marie-Antoinette, suffered the same fate a few months later.

1066
William the Conqueror invades England, making Normandy and England rivals of the kingdom of France.

1337–1453
The French and English battle for control of France during the Hundred Years' War.

1530s
The Reformation embraces France, leading to Protestant-Catholic conflict during the Wars of Religion (1562–98).

As the pillars of French society crumbled, chaos ensued. Violent retribution broke out across France. During the Reign of Terror (September 1793 to July 1794) churches were closed, religious monuments were desecrated, riots were suppressed and thousands of aristocrats were imprisoned or beheaded. The high ideals of the Revolution had turned to vicious bloodshed, and the nation was rapidly descending into anarchy. France desperately needed someone to re-establish order, give it new direction and rebuild its shattered sense of self. From amidst the smoke and thunder, a dashing (if diminutive) young Corsican general stepped out from the shadows – Napoléon Bonaparte.

The Napoléonic Era

Napoléon's military prowess quickly turned him into a powerful political force. In 1804 he was crowned emperor at Notre Dame Cathedral, and subsequently led the French armies to conquer much of Europe. His ill-fated campaign to invade Russia ended in disaster, however; in 1812, his armies were stopped outside Moscow and decimated by the brutal Russian winter. Two years later, Allied armies entered Paris and exiled Napoléon to Elba.

Off with His Head

Prior to the Revolution, public executions in France depended on rank: the nobility were generally beheaded with a sword or axe (with predictably messy consequences), while commoners were usually hanged (particularly nasty prisoners were also drawn and quartered, which involved being eviscerated while still alive and then pulled to pieces by four oxen).

In an effort to provide a more civilised end for the condemned, in the early 1790s a group of French physicians, scientists and engineers set about designing a clinical new execution machine involving a razor-sharp weighted blade, guaranteed to behead people with a minimum of fuss or mess. Named after one of its inventors, the anatomy professor Ignace Guillotin, the machine was first used on 25 April 1792, when the highwayman Nicolas Jacques Pelletie went down in history as the first man to lose his head to the guillotine.

During the Reign of Terror, at least 17,000 met their death beneath the machine's plunging blade. By the time the last was given the chop in 1977 (behind closed doors – the last public execution was in 1939), the contraption could slice off a head in 2/100 of a second.

1643–1715

Louis XIV assumes the French throne and shifts his royal court from Paris to Versailles.

1789–94

Revolutionaries storm the Bastille. Louis XVI and Marie-Antoinette are guillotined. Louis XVI threatened by revolutionaries, Tuileries, Paris

The Best... Historic Pilgrimages

1 Château de Versailles (p103)

2 Alignements de Carnac (p141)

3 Mont St-Michel (p129)

4 Grotte de Lascaux (p214)

5 Sanctuaires Notre Dame de Lourdes (p280)

But that wasn't the last of the Little General. In 1815 Napoléon escaped, re-entering Paris on 20 May. His glorious 'Hundred Days' ended with defeat by the English at the Battle of Waterloo. He was exiled again, this time to St Helena in the South Atlantic, where he died in 1821. His body was later reburied under the Hôtel des Invalides in Paris.

New Republics

Post-Napoléon, France was dogged by a string of ineffectual rulers until Napoléon's nephew, Louis Napoléon Bonaparte, came to power. He was initially elected president, but declared himself Emperor (Napoléon III) in 1851.

While the so-called Second Empire ran roughshod over many of the ideals set down during the Revolution, it actually proved to be a relatively prosperous time. France enjoyed significant economic growth and Paris was transformed by urban planner Baron Haussmann, who created the famous 12 boulevards radiating from the Arc de Triomphe (including the celebrated Champs-Élysées).

But like his uncle, Napoléon III's ambition was his undoing. A series of costly conflicts, including the Crimean War (1854–56), culminated in humiliating defeat by the Prussian forces in 1870. France was once again declared a republic – for the third time in less than a century.

The Belle Époque

The Third Republic got off to a shaky start: another war with the Prussians resulted in a huge war bill and the surrender of Alsace and Lorraine. But the period also ushered in a new era of culture and creativity that left an enduring mark on France's national character.

The belle époque ('beautiful age'), as it came to be known, was an era of unprecedented innovation. Architects built a host of exciting new buildings and transformed the faces of many French cities. Engineers laid the tracks of France's first railways and tunnelled out the metro system still used by millions of Parisians today. Designers experimented with new styles and materials, while young artists invented a host of new 'isms' (including impressionism, which took its title from one of Claude Monet's seminal early paintings, *Impression, Soleil Levant*).

1851
Louis Napoléon proclaims himself Emperor Napoléon III of the Second Empire (1851–70).

1914–18
WWI: 1.3 million French soldiers are killed and many historic cities destroyed.

1939–44
WWII: Nazi Germany divides France into a German-occupied zone and a puppet Vichy state.

The era culminated in a lavish Exposition Universelle (World Fair) in Paris in 1889, an event that seemed to sum up the excitement and dynamism of the age, and also inspired the construction of one of the nation's most iconic landmarks – the Eiffel Tower.

The Great War

Sadly, the *joie de vivre* of the belle époque wasn't to last. Within months of the outbreak of WWI in 1914, the fields of northern France had been transformed into a sea of trenches and shell craters; by the time the armistice had been signed in November 1918, some 1.3 million French soldiers had been killed and almost one million crippled. A trip to the battlefields of the Somme or Verdun provides a chilling reminder of the unimaginable human cost of WWI.

Desperate to forget the ravages of the war, Paris sparkled as the centre of the avant-garde in the 1920s and '30s. The liberal atmosphere (not to mention the cheap booze and saucy nightlife) attracted a stream of foreign artists and writers to the city, and helped establish Paris' enduring reputation for creativity and experimentation.

Château de Versailles (p103)

1949
France joins North America and Western Europe in a mutual defence alliance (NATO).

1981
The high-speed TGV smashes speed records. Journey time from Paris to Lyon falls to under two hours.

1994
The 50km-long Channel Tunnel links mainland France with Britain.

The French Resistance

Despite the myth of '*la France résistante*' (the French Resistance), the underground movement never actually included more than 5% of the population. The other 95% either collaborated or did nothing. Resistance members engaged in railway sabotage, collected intelligence for the Allies, helped Allied airmen who had been shot down and published anti-German leaflets, among other activities. Though the impact of their actions was relatively slight, the Resistance served as an enormous boost to French morale - not to mention the inspiration for numerous literary and cinematic endeavours.

WWII

Unfortunately, the interwar party was short-lived. Two days after Germany invaded Poland in 1939, France joined Britain in declaring war on Germany. Within a year, Hitler's *blitzkrieg* had swept across Europe, and France was forced into humiliating capitulation in June the same year. Following the seaborne retreat of the British Expeditionary Force at Dunkirk, France – like much of Europe – found itself under Nazi occupation.

The Germans divided France into two zones: the west and north (including Paris), which was under direct German rule; and a puppet-state in the south based around the spa town of Vichy. The anti-semitic Vichy regime proved very helpful to the Nazis in rounding up Jews and other undesirables for deportation to the death camps.

After four years of occupation, on 6 June 1944 Allied forces returned to French soil during the D-Day landings. Over 100,000 Allied troops stormed the Normandy coastline and, after several months of fighting, liberated Paris on 25 August. But the cost of the war had been devastating for France: half a million buildings had been destroyed, many cities had been razed to the ground and millions of French people had lost their lives.

Poverty to Prosperity

Broken and battered from the war, France was forced to turn to the USA for loans as part of the Marshall Plan to rebuild Europe. Slowly, under the government of French war hero Charles de Gaulle, the economy began to recover and France began to rebuild its shattered infrastructure. The debilitating Algerian War of Independence (1954–62) and the subsequent loss of its colonies seriously weakened de Gaulle's government, however, and following widespread student protests in 1968 and a general strike by 10 million workers, de Gaulle was forced to resign from office in 1969. He died the following year.

2002

The French franc, first minted in 1360, is dumped when France adopts the euro. €1 coins

NICK WRIGHT/GETTY IMAGES ©

2004

National Assembly bans religious symbols such as the Islamic headscarf in state schools.

Subsequent French presidents Georges Pompidou (in power from 1969 to 1974) and Giscard d'Estaing (1974–81) were instrumental in the increasing political and economic integration of Europe, a process that had begun with the formation of the EEC (European Economic Community) in 1957, and continued under François Mitterrand with the enlarged EU (European Union) in 1991. During Mitterrand's time in office, France abolished the death penalty, legalised homosexuality, gave workers five weeks' holiday and annually guaranteed the right to retire at 60.

In 1995 Mitterrand was succeeded by the maverick Jacques Chirac, who was re-elected in 2002. Chirac's attempts at reform led to widespread strikes and social unrest, while his opposition to the Iraq war alienated the US administration (and famously led to the rebranding of French fries as Freedom fries).

The Best... History Museums

1 Musée National du Moyen Âge (p67)

2 Bayeux Tapestry (p122)

3 Musée National de Préhistoire (p216)

4 Mémorial – Un Musée pour la Paix (p127)

5 Musée des Civilisations de l'Europe et de la Méditerranée (p292)

Recent Politics

Following Chirac's retirement, the media-savvy Nicolas Sarkozy was elected president in 2007, bringing a more personality-driven, American-style approach to French politics. Despite initial popularity, Sarkozy's time in office was ultimately marred by France's fallout from the 2008 financial crisis, as well as controversy about his personal affairs – particularly his marriage to Italian supermodel and singer Carla Bruni.

Presidential elections in 2012 ushered in France's first socialist president since 1995, François Hollande (b 1954). His firmly left-wing policies (including increases in corporation tax, the minimum wage and income tax for high-earners) initially proved popular, but Hollande has had a rocky ride since coming to power. France's economy has remained stubbornly in the doldrums, while his own personal affairs have come under uncomfortable scrutiny – in 2014 his alleged affair with actress Julie Gayet hit the tabloids, and led to the end of his relationship with France's First Lady, Valérie Trierweiler. With his popularity at an all-time low, it remains to be seen whether Hollande can turn things around – both politically and personally.

2007
Pro-American pragmatist Nicolas Sarkozy beats Socialist candidate Ségolène Royal to become French president.

2011
French parliamentary ban on burkas in public comes into effect; Muslim women publicly wearing the face-covering veil are fined.

2012
Amid economic crisis, elections usher in France's first socialist president in 17 years.

Family Travel

Pont du Gard (p315)

BRUNO DE HOGUES/GETTY IMAGES

Dining, celebrating or travelling, the French are great believers in doing it en famille (as a family), making France a great place to travel with kids. Be it the kid-friendly extraordinaire capital of Paris, or the rural hinterland, this country spoils families with its rich mix of cultural sights, activities and entertainment – some paid for, many free. To get the most out of travelling en famille, plan ahead.

Trip Planning

Consider the season: teen travel is a year-round affair (always something to entertain, regardless of the weather), but parents travelling with younger kids will definitely find spring the easiest: the warmer, dry weather means more relaxed and casual dining alfresco; queues are shorter so less hanging around with impatient little ones; and museum gardens suddenly open up (for quick run-arounds between galleries).

With a little planning and creativity, kid appeal can be found in almost every sight in France, top sights included. Skip the formal guided tour of Mont St-Michel, for example, and hook up with a walking guide to take you and the kids barefoot across the sand to the abbey; trade the daytime queues at the Eiffel Tower for a tour all-a-twinkle after dark; don't dismiss wine tasting in

Provence or Burgundy outright – rent bicycles and turn it into a family bike ride instead.

Paris history and art museums can be a challenge but the Louvre, Musée d'Orsay and many others offer *ateliers* (workshops) for children and/or families. Outside the capital, consider which area is best suited to your children and their interests: the fairy-tale châteaux of the Loire Valley and the high-octane activities of the French Alps are always popular, while the Atlantic Coast and French Riviera guarantee endless seaside frolics. Older kids fascinated by history might enjoy the Dordogne (prehistory), Burgundy (Roman), the Loire Valley (Renaissance), northern France (WWI) and Normandy (WWII).

The Best... Family Days Out

1 Aiguille du Midi (p242) by gondola and across glaciers into Italy (for kids aged over four years)

2 Chantier Médiéval de Guédelon (p212)

3 Les Machines de l'Île de Nantes (p270)

4 Gouffre de Padirac (p217)

5 Musée Océanographique de Monaco (p341)

6 Canoeing beneath Pont du Gard (p315) (kids over seven years)

À table!

Make eating out in France a trip highlight. Classic French mains adored by most children include gratin *dauphinois* (sliced potatoes oven-baked in cream), *escalope de veau* (breaded pan-fried veal) and bœuf bourguignon (beef stew). Alpine cheese fondue and *raclette* (melted cheese served with potatoes and cold meats) and *moules frites* (mussels and fries) are favourites with local children.

Most French restaurants are accommodating of younger diners. Many offer a *menu enfant* (set children's menu) – usually *saucisse* (sausage) or *steak haché* (beef burger) and *frites* (fries) followed by ice cream – but don't be shy in asking for a half-portion of an adult main instead.

A basket of bread, specifically crusty chunks of baguette, is brought to the table before or immediately after you've ordered. This is to the glee of children, who wolf it down while they wait. Watch for the fight to ensue over who gets the *quignon* (the knobbly end bit, an equal hit with teething babies!).

Dining *en famille* after dark is perfectly acceptable providing the kids don't run wild. Few restaurants open their doors, however, before 7.30pm or 8pm. This means that brasseries and cafes – many of which serve food continuously from 7am or 8am until midnight – are more appealing for families with younger children.

Snack Attack

France is fabulous snack-attack terrain. Parisian pavements are rife with crêpe stands and wintertime stalls selling hot chestnuts. Savoury *galettes* (pancakes) make for an easy light lunch, as does France's signature *croque monsieur* (toasted cheese and ham sandwich) served by most cafes and brasseries. *Goûter* (afternoon snack), devoured after school around 4.30pm, is golden for every French child and *salons de thé* (tea rooms) serve a mouth-watering array of cakes, pastries and biscuits. Or go local: buy a baguette, rip off a chunk and pop a slab of chocolate inside. Really!

Need to Know

- **Changing facilities** Generally only in women's toilets (dads, don't be shy...).
- **Cots** Most midrange and top-end hotels have them.
- **Health** No special inoculations required.
- **Highchairs** Hit or miss whether a place has one.
- **Kids' menus** Offered in most restaurants.
- **Nappies (diapers)** Purchase in supermarkets and pharmacies.
- **Strollers (pushchairs)** Steps and cobbles make pushchairs a challenge; bring a baby sling.
- **Transport** Reduced fares for kids on trains, buses and metros.

Accommodation

Parents with just one child and/or a baby in tow will have no problem finding hotel accommodation – most midrange hotels have baby cots/extra beds and will happily pop one in your room for minimal or no charge. Countrywide, hotels with family or four-person rooms are harder to find.

In rural France, B&Bs and farmstays, some of which cook up tasty evening meals, are the way to go. Or what about a hip baby-and-toddler house party in a Burgundy château or a chalet retreat in the French Alps? For older children, treehouses decked out with bunk beds and Mongolian yurts create a real family adventure.

Camping is wildly popular with families and for good reason: check into a self-catering mobile home, chalet or family tent; sit back on the verandah with wine in hand and watch as your kids – wonderfully oblivious to any barriers language might pose – run around with new-found friends.

Architecture

Maison Carrée (p313)

SHAUN EGAN/GETTY IMAGES ©

Love it or hate it, French architecture nearly always makes a statement. From the illustrious châteaux of the Loire Valley to modern icons such as Paris' Centre Pompidou and Pyramide du Louvre, French architecture is always on a grand scale. French leaders have long recognised the importance of an iconic building or two to their own political legacy.

Ancient & Roman Architecture

France's oldest architecture can be found in Brittany, where megalithic builders left behind many impressive stone monuments, including the 3000-odd menhirs of the Alignements de Carnac. In contrast, the nation's Gallo-Roman legacy is mainly concentrated in the south, including the impressive amphitheatres in Nîmes and Arles, and the huge Pont du Gard aqueduct near Nîmes.

Gothic Architecture

During the Gothic period, France's architects really aimed for scale, as demonstrated by monumental Gothic buildings such as Avignon's pontifical palace and the massive cathedrals of Chartres, Reims, Metz and Paris' Notre Dame. Telltale signs of French Gothic buildings include flying buttresses, ribbed vaults, pointed arches and plenty of luminous stained glass.

The Best... Contemporary Creations

1 Musée du Quai Branly (p60)

2 Centre Pompidou-Metz (p170)

3 Louvre-Lens (p172)

4 Fondation Maeght (p329)

5 Fondation Louis Vuitton (p75)

The Renaissance

During the 15th and 16th centuries architects developed a taste for extravagance, epitomised by the lavish châteaux of the Loire Valley. Embellished with sweeping staircases, gabled windows, lacy turrets and decorative motifs, these castles were built to impress rather than to defend against attack. The era of architectural showiness reached its peak with the royal palace of Versailles near Paris.

Neoclassicism & the Belle Époque

The 18th and 19th centuries were about order and elegance. This was the era of the grand boulevard and the great public square, exemplified by Arras' Place des Héros, Nancy's Place Stanislas, Strasbourg's Place de la République, and Paris' most famous street, the Champs-Élysées. The era also inspired many of Paris' best-known buildings, including the Arc de Triomphe.

The late 19th century in France was a time of artistic experimentation and industrial innovation. Belle époque architects combined iron, brick, glass and ceramics in exciting new ways, and even mundane structures – from covered markets and town halls to swimming pools and metro stations – acquired a dash of class.

Modern Architecture

After the ravages of WWII, French architects were given free reign to reinvent the nation's shattered cities. Some favoured a brutally functional style of architecture, while others adopted a more playful approach. France's most celebrated architect, Le Corbusier (1887–1965), rewrote the architectural textbook during the 1950s with his sweeping lines and sinuous forms.

The French tendency for experimentation has continued throughout the modern era. The 1970s and 1980s witnessed the construction of many exciting buildings, including the Grande Arche in the Parisian skyscraper district of La Défense, the world's first ever 'inside-out' building aka Paris' Centre Pompidou, and IM Pei's glass pyramid at the hitherto sacrosanct Louvre – an architectural cause célébre that paved the way for Mario Bellini and Rudy Ricciotti's magnificent 'flying carpet' roof atop the Louvre's Cour Visconti in 2012.

France continues to be an exciting showroom and playground for the world's most renowned contemporary architects: Frank Gehry, Norman Foster and Jean Nouvel.

The Arts & Literature

Water Lilies by Claude Monet

DEA/A. DAGLI ORTI/GETTY IMAGES ©

In a country where style and panache count for so much, it comes as no surprise that culture still matters deeply to French people. France has a long and distinguished legacy in literature, painting, sculpture and cinema, and the arts continue to play a crucial role in the nation's collective culture.

Painting

From the dreamy landscapes of the impressionists to the radical experiments of cubism, France has been the crucible for a host of artistic movements.

Classical & Romantic

According to Voltaire, French painting began with Nicolas Poussin (1594–1665), whose dramatic paintings based on mythological and biblical scenes set the benchmark for classical French art. Later, romantic painters such as David (1748–1825), Géricault (1791–1824) and Délacroix (1798–1863) drew their inspiration from French history and political events, creating lifelike canvases packed with power and emotion. Key works by all these artists can be seen in the Louvre in Paris.

Other artists moved out of their studios in search of subjects from everyday life.

The Best... Iconic Art Museums

1 Musée d'Orsay (p73)

2 Musée du Louvre (p68)

3 Louvre-Lens (p172)

4 Centre Pompidou-Metz (p170)

5 Monet's garden (p125) and Musée des Impressionismes Giverny (p125)

Jean-François Millet (1814–75), the son of a Norman farmer, depicted peasant life in France's rural villages: his *L'Angélus* (The Angelus; 1857) is the best-known French painting after the *Mona Lisa* (the original *L'Angélus* is in Paris' Musée d'Orsay).

Impressionism & Post-Impressionism

During the late 19th century, artists experimented with capturing an 'impression' of a scene, emphasising colour, light and atmosphere above strictly realistic representation. This movement (dubbed 'impressionism' after an early painting by Claude Monet, 1840–1926) included artists such as Claude Pissarro, Alfred Sisley, Eugène Boudin, Edgar Degas and Auguste Renoir, but it's Monet's work that encapsulates the spirit of impressionism for many people – particularly his series of *Nymphéas* (Water Lilies) paintings, which he composed in the grounds of his own garden in Giverny, near Paris.

During the post-impressionist period, artists continued to push the boundaries of acceptability, both in terms of subject and technique. The intense light and lush landscapes of Provence and the Riviera attracted many artists, including Paul Cézanne (1839–1906) and the Dutch artist Vincent van Gogh (1853–90), while the hustle and bustle of *fin-de-siècle* (end of the century) Paris attracted others, such as Henri de Toulouse-Lautrec (1864–1901), best known for his paintings of Parisian brothels. Other artists travelled further afield: Paul Gauguin (1848–1903) emigrated to Tahiti, where he produced rich, sensual paintings inspired by his adopted tropical home.

Meanwhile in St-Tropez, pointillist painters applied paint in small dots to produce a colourful mosaic-like effect: the works of Georges Seurat (1859–91) and his pupil Paul Signac (1863–1935) are on display at St-Tropez's Musée de l'Annonciade.

Fauvism, Cubism & Surrealism

The dawn of the 20th century inspired a bewildering diversity of artistic movements, many of which inspired considerable controversy. Fauvist artists such as Henri Matisse (1869–1954) and André Dérain (1880–1954) moved even further from the confines of representational art, often using bold, brash colours that bore little relation to reality; the movement famously got its name from a shocked art critic who compared the artists with *fauves* (wild animals) after an exhibition in 1905.

Fauvism marked the start of an experimental century. Cubism completely threw out the artistic rule book, breaking subjects into component shapes and ignoring long-established rules of perspective and composition: among its key figures were the Spanish-born artist Pablo Picasso (1881–1973) and the French artist Georges Braque (1882–1963).

Meanwhile, surrealist artists delved into their subconscious in search of hidden dreams and desires, inspired by the theories of the psychoanalyst Sigmund Freud. Dadaism, an offshoot of surrealism, was shot through with a rebellious spirit and an anarchic sense of humour – one of its most famous exponents, Marcel Duchamp (1887–1968), famously made a sculpture from a men's urinal and painted a goatee on the *Mona Lisa*.

Modern Art

After WWII, the focus shifted from Paris to southern France in the 1960s with new realists such as Arman (1928–2005) and Yves Klein (1928–62), both from Nice. In 1960 Klein famously produced *Anthropométrie de l'Époque Bleue,* a series of imprints made by naked women covered from head to toe in blue paint rolling around on a white canvas.

More recent artists have increasingly moved towards conceptual art, using practically every medium other than paint to express their concerns. Among the best known are Daniel Buren (b 1938), the *enfant terrible* of 1980s French art, and Sophie Calle (b 1953), who brazenly exposes her private life with her eye-catching installations.

The Best... Unexpected Art Museums

1 Musée Picasso (p327) and Musée Rodin (p63)

2 La Piscine Musée d'Art et d'Industrie (p168)

3 Musée des Beaux Arts, Dijon (p204)

4 Mamac (p320)

5 Fondation Maeght (p329)

Cinema

France is the nation that invented cinema, so it's hardly surprising that film continues to be one of its most enduring art forms. The *septième art*, as cinema is often known, is a quintessential French passion, celebrated every May during the annual Cannes Film Festival. The festival attracts big-name stars to the French Riviera and hands out one of the world's most coveted film prizes, the Palme d'Or.

Early Cinema

The Lumière brothers (Auguste and Louis) shot the world's first motion picture, *La Sortie des Usines Lumières* (Exit of the Lumières Factories) in one of their family factories in Lyon on 19 March 1895. Today, the Lyonnais factory houses the Musée Lumière, a museum exploring cinema's beginnings and screening classic films.

Despite several early classics, French cinema only really hit its stride in the 1930s. The classic *La Grande Illusion* (The Great Illusion; 1937) is a devastating portrayal of the folly of war, based on the trench warfare experience of director Jean Renoir (1894–1979). Hot on its heels came Renoir's seminal *Les Règle du Jeu* (The Rules of the Game; 1939), a biting satire of the French upper classes, set in the years before WWII. French cinema's reputation for stylish photography, sharp dialogue and intellectual subject matter was confirmed.

A decade later, surrealist artist-writer-philosopher Jean Cocteau made two back-to-back masterpieces, *La Belle et la Bête* (Beauty and the Beast; 1945) and *Orphée* (Orpheus; 1950). But it was the directors of the *nouvelle vague* (new wave) who arguably made the greatest contribution to French cinema as an art form. With small budgets, no complex sets and no big stars, these young French directors made highly personal films, pioneering the use of fractured narratives, documentary-style camerawork and new editing techniques.

Key directors of the new wave include Claude Chabrol, Alain Resnais and François Truffaut, but the quintessential new wave director is Jean-Luc Godard (b 1930), who captured the essence of Parisian cool in *À Bout de Souffle* (Breathless; 1960) before later branching out into experimental films such as the apocalyptic black comedy *Le Weekend* (1969).

The Best... Art Trails

1 Cézanne in Aix-en-Provence (p307)

2 Van Gogh in Arles (p303)

3 Matisse in Nice (p320)

4 Picasso in Paris (p63) and Antibes (p327)

5 Artists galore in Montmartre (p58) and St-Tropez (p336)

1970s to 1990s

After the fireworks of the new wave, French cinema lost its experimental edge. Lesser-known directors such as Éric Rohmer (b 1920) made beautiful but uneventful films in which the characters endlessly analyse their feelings. Other directors retreated into nostalgia, characterised by Jacques Demy's *Les Parapluies de Cherbourg* (The Umbrellas of Cherbourg; 1964), a bittersweet love story set in Normandy.

The trend continued into the 1970s and '80s, as filmmakers switched to costume dramas and commercial comedies in an attempt to compete with growing competition from the USA. Claude Berri's sentimental portraits of pre-war Provence in *Jean de Florette* (1986) and *Manon des Sources* (1986) found big audiences both at home and abroad, as did Jean-Paul Rappeneau's glossy version of the classic French fable *Cyrano de Bergerac* (1990); all three films starred France's best-known actor, Gérard Depardieu. Other directors such as Luc Besson gave a Gallic spin to American genres.

The 1990s also saw French cinema acquire a grittier edge, epitomised by Mathieu Kassovitz's hard-hitting *La Haine* (1995), which explored the bleak lives of French youth in Parisian housing estates.

Contemporary Cinema

French cinema has produced some significant hits over the last decade, most notably big-budget versions of the Astérix comics. *La Môme* (known overseas as *La Vie en Rose*), a biopic of Édith Piaf, scooped the Best Actress Oscar for French actress Marion Cotillard at the 2008 Academy Awards and the same year a French film won the Palme d'Or at Cannes for the first time since 1987: Laurent Cantet's *Entre Les Murs* (The Class) used real pupils and teachers to portray a year in the life of a school in a rough Parisian neighbourhood.

French Cinema in 10 Films

- *La Règle du Jeu* (The Rules of the Game, 1939)
- *Les Enfants du Paradis* (Children of Paradise, 1945)
- *Et Dieu Créa la Femme* (And God Created Woman, 1956)
- *Les Quatre Cents Coups* (The 400 Blows, 1959)
- *À Bout de Souffle* (Breathless, 1960)
- *37.2°C du Matin* (Betty Blue, 1986)
- *Delicatessen* (1991)
- *Jeanne d'Arc* (Joan of Arc, 1999)
- *Le Fabuleux Destin d'Amélie Poulain* (Amélie, 2001)
- *Bienvenue chez les Ch'tis* (Welcome to the Sticks, 2008)

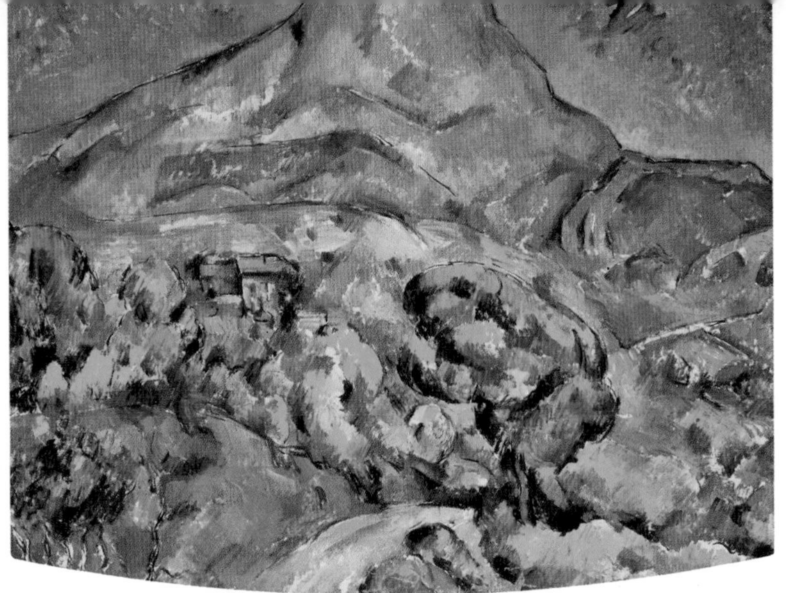

Some contemporary directors find an audience by employing shock tactics. *Enfant terrible* Gaspar Noé ruffled feathers with his violent films *Irréversible* (2002) and *Into the Void* (2009), while Jacque Audiard's tough 2009 prison drama, *Un Prophète*, narrowly missed out on an Oscar for Best Foreign Film at the 2010 Academy Awards. 'New French Extremity' is the tag given to the unforgivingly realistic, socially conscious, transgressive films of talented Paris-born, Africa-raised filmmaker Claire Denis. Watch her *Matériel Blanc* (White Material; 2009), scripted by Parisian novelist Marie NDiaye, to explore the legacy of French colonialism.

The true renaissance of French cinema came with *The Artist* (2011), a silent B&W, French-made romantic comedy set in 1920s Hollywood and starring the ever charismatic French actor Jean Dujardin. It scooped five Oscars at the 2012 ceremony, making it the most awarded French film in history.

Literature

Early Literature

The earliest surviving examples of French literature are the epic lyrical poems written during the early medieval period, most of which were based around allegorical tales and mythological legends (courtly love and King Arthur were particularly popular subjects in early French literature). Chrétien de Troyes (12th century), Pierre de Ronsard (1524–85) and the mischievous François Rabelais (1494–1553) were among the most important writers of the period, while the influential prose writer Michel de Montaigne (1533–92) penned essays on topics ranging from cannibals to public drunkenness.

The 18th century was dominated by one of France's greatest writers and philosophers, Voltaire (1694–1778), a key figure of the European Enlightenment.

Mont Saint Victoire by Paul Cézanne
PAUL CEZANNE/GETTY IMAGES

The Best... Books Set in France

1 *A Moveable Feast* (Ernest Hemingway)

2 *Birdsong* and *Charlotte Gray* (Sebastian Faulks)

3 *Perfume* (Patrick Suskind)

4 *A Year in Provence* (Peter Mayle)

5 *Chocolat* (Joanne Harris)

Through a prodigious output of novels, plays, poems, essays and political pamphlets, Voltaire tirelessly championed the values of freedom, equality and civil liberties for everyone, not solely for the ruling elite. His writings subsequently played an important role in the development of the fundamental principles of the French Revolution a century later.

The Age of the Novel

The 19th century was the great era of the novel in France. French writers took to the form with gusto. Victor Hugo (1802–85) penned historical epics such as *Les Misérables* and *Notre-Dame de Paris* (The Hunchback of Notre Dame), while Alexandre Dumas (1802–70) wrote swashbuckling tales of derring-do, such as *The Three Musketeers* and *The Count of Monte Cristo*, and Jules Verne (1828–1905) pioneered the sci-fi genre with his fanciful tales of moon rockets, submarines and round-the-world balloon flights.

Perhaps the greatest French novel writer of the period, however, was Gustave Flaubert (1821–80), whose 1857 tome *Madame Bovary* caused a storm of controversy due to its frank treatment of sex, adultery and the plight of women in French society.

The 19th century also saw the emergence of several important French poets, including Charles Baudelaire (known for his seminal collection *Les Fleurs du Mal*, 1857) and the symbolist poets Paul Verlaine (1844–96) and Arthur Rimbaud (1854–91).

Modern Literature

The early 20th century produced two great French writers: Colette (1873–1954), whose picaresque novels and short stories explored the amorous exploits of gutsy heroines such as Claudine and Gigi against the backdrop of bourgeois French society; and Marcel Proust (1871–1922), whose *À la recherche du temps perdu* (Remembrance of Things Past), published in seven volumes over 14 years, is the longest novel ever written.

After WWII, Paris' Left Bank became the centre for existentialist writers, who pondered cheery topics such as the meaningless of human existence: key figures include Jean-Paul Sartre (1905–80), Simone de Beauvoir (1908–86) and Albert Camus (1913–60), known for troubling novels including *The Outsider* and *The Plague*.

Marc Levy is France's best-selling writer. The film rights of his first novel were snapped up for the Stephen Spielberg box-office hit, *Just Like Heaven* (2005), and his novels have been translated into 42 languages. *L'étrange voyage de Monsieur Daldry* (The Strange Journey of Mr Daldry, 2011) is his latest.

No French writer better delves into the mind of France's ethnic population than Faïza Guène (b 1985), the French literary sensation who writes in a notable 'urban slang' style. She stunned critics with her debut novel, *Kiffe Kiffe Demain* (2004) and, like her first, her second novel, *Du Rêve pour les Oeufs* (2006), published in English as *Dreams from the Endz* (2008), was set on the ghetto housing estate outside Paris where she grew up.

Another French writer to address ethnic issues so engagingly is JMG Le Clézio. In 2008 he was the Nobel Prize in Literature winner, confirming France's ranking as the country with the most literary Nobel Prize winners.

French Cuisine

Macarons

MATT MUNRO/LONELY PLANET ©

If there's one thing the French are famous for, it's food. In many ways this is the nation that taught the rest of the world how to dine, and if you approach food and wine here with half the zest les français do, you'll be welcomed, encouraged and exceedingly well fed indeed.

Food

Eating well is of prime importance to most French people, who spend an inordinate amount of time thinking about, discussing and enjoying food and wine. While there are many classic national dishes, each region has its own distinctive flavours, ingredients and cooking styles.

Two natural factors determine what you eat on your French travels. Season and geography see the hot south favour olive oil, garlic and tomatoes; the cooler, pastoral regions of northern France turn to cream and butter; and coastal areas are awash with mussels, oysters, saltwater fish and other seafood.

Meals in France

The classic French breakfast *(petit déjeuner)* consists of baguette, jam, coffee, and fruit juice (croissants and pastries are traditionally reserved as treats for the weekend,

French Cheese Etiquette

- Cut small, circular cheeses into pie wedges.
- Larger cheeses already sliced into a wedge must be cut tip to rind – don't slice off the tip.
- Chop semihard cheeses horizontally.
- Only serve cheese with fresh baguette, never crackers or butter.
- Bring out the cheese board *before* dessert, not after.

although they're normally always included in hotel breakfasts).

Lunch *(déjeuner)* is served from noon to around 2pm, and is often the main meal of the day for French people. There is usually a good value two- or three-course *menu du jour* (daily menu) consisting of a *plat du jour* (daily special) with an entrée (starter) and/or a dessert. Most restaurants only offer the *menu du jour* at lunchtime, which is why it's often easier to find a free table for dinner than for lunch.

Dinner *(diner)* usually starts around 6.30pm and continues till around 10pm. Two or three courses are the norm; fixed menus generally offer better value than *à la carte*, but you'll have fewer dishes to choose from.

Cheese

France is cheese land and the *fromagerie* (cheese shop) is the pongiest shop in town. With more than 500 varieties, buying cheese can be an overwhelming affair. Any self-respecting *fromager* (cheese merchant) will let you taste before you buy.

To treat your taste buds to the perfect balance of cheese, take at least one of each type from the cheeseboard:

Goat's cheese *(fromage de chèvre)* French goat's cheese is creamy, sweet and faintly salty when fresh, but hardens and gets saltier as it matures. Key varieties include Ste-Maure de Touraine, Crottin de Chavignol and St-Marcellin, a runny white cheese.

Blue cheese Everyone knows Roquefort, a powerful, veined, marbled, mature cheese with a strong flavour and fragrance.

Soft cheese *(fromage à pâté molle)* The classic variety of French cheese, served soft, smelly and runny. Common types include Camembert and Brie (both from Normandy) and Munster (from Alsace).

Semihard cheese *(fromage à pâté demi-dure)* These cheeses, especially common in the Alps, have a squishy, semi-firm texture, a thick rind and a fairly mild flavour. Try Tomme de Savoie or Cantal.

Hard cheese *(fromage à pâté dure)* The hardest type of French cheese, typified by Beaufort, Comté, Emmental and Mimolette, an Edam-like bright-orange cheese from Lille.

Bread

Buying bread is a French daily ritual, it being served – *sans beurre* (without butter) – at breakfast, lunch and dinner. Plain old *pain* (bread) is a 400g, traditional-shaped loaf, soft inside and crusty out. The iconic classic is the baguette, a long thin crusty loaf weighing 250g and best eaten within four hours of baking (it is truly astonishing just how rock-hard a baguette becomes after 12 hours).

Meat & Charcuterie

Meat in France isn't simply a matter of steaks, chops and cutlets – French chefs make use of practically every part of the animal, including tongue, trotters and pretty much every type of offal you can imagine.

Charcuterie traditionally denotes meat products made from pork, but encompasses other things such as cold cuts, pâtés and terrines. The classic charcuterie is the *saucisson* (a cured sausage similar to salami). *Saucisse* denotes a fresh, uncooked sausage that's boiled, grilled or fried before eating.

When ordering steak, know how you like it cooked: *bleu* (almost raw), *saignant* (rare), *à point* (medium rare), *bien cuit* (with just a hint of pinkness) or *très bien cuit* (very well done).

Fish & Seafood

The coast is the obvious place to eat *poisson* (fish). In Brittany, Normandy and along the Mediterranean coastline, *moules-frites* (mussels and chips) is a menu staple alongside each region's own seafood specialities: Brittany and the Atlantic Coast are known for their shellfish and oysters; Provence and the Riviera are the best places to try *bouillabaisse* (a rich seafood stew) and *soupe de poissons* (fish soup), both traditionally accompanied by *rouille* (a spicy mayonnaise of oil, chillis and garlic).

The Best... Signature Dishes

1 Bouillabaisse, Marseille

2 Camembert, Normandy

3 Cheese fondue, French Alps

4 Oysters and shellfish, Brittany

5 Black truffles, Dordogne

Truffles

The Dordogne's most celebrated delicacy is the *diamant noir* (black diamond or black truffle), a subterranean fungus that grows in chalky soils (often around the roots of oak and hazelnut trees) and is notoriously difficult to find; a good spot one year can be inexplicably bare the next, which has made farming them practically impossible. Serious truffle hunters use specially trained dogs (and sometimes pigs) to help them search. A vintage crop of truffles can fetch as much as €850 a kilo.

The truffle season runs December to March.

Poultry

When it comes to birds, the French don't just limit themselves to chicken and turkey – they eat other types of poultry with equal gusto, including *canard* (duck), *oie* (goose), *perdrix* (partridge), *faisan* (pheasant), pigeon and *caille* (quail).

Pâté de foie gras (a rich, smooth pâté of fattened duck or goose livers, sometimes flavoured with Cognac and truffles) is a particular delicacy, especially in southwest France. *Confit de canard* and *confit d'oie* are duck or goose joints cooked very slowly in their own fat, making them very tender and packed with flavour.

Price Ranges

Price indicators refer to the average cost of a two-course meal, be it an entrée (starter) and *plat* (main course) or main and dessert, or a *menu* (pre-set meal at a fixed price). Lunch menus can often yield a better deal.

€ budget < €20
€€ midrange €20–40
€€€ top end > €40

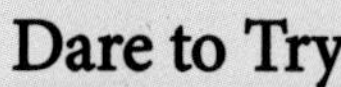

- **Andouillette** Sausage made from pig intestine; try it in Lyon.
- **Oursins** (sea urchins) Caught and eaten west of Marseille.
- **Epoisses de Bourgogne** France's smelliest cheese.
- **Escargots de Bourgogne** (snails) Oven-baked shells stuffed with garlic and parsley butter.
- **Cuisses de grenouilles** (frogs' legs) Frog farming is outlawed in France, but frogs' legs are imported from Southeast Asia, ensuring this tradition remains alive and kicking.
- **Foie gras** Fattened duck or goose liver, raw and chilled, enjoyed with Monbazillac wine.
- **Pieds de cochon** (pig trotters) Or go for *mouton* (sheep) or *veau* (calf) trotters.
- **Tête de veau** (calf's head) Just that.

Cakes & Sweets

Enter any *boulangerie* (bakery) or patisserie and face an irresistible assortment of pastries, cakes and sweet treats, including the classics: the croissant (butter pastry), *pain au chocolat* (butter pastry with dark chocolate inside), meringues, *sablés* (shortbread biscuits), *tartes aux fruits* (fruit tarts) and colourful macarons.

Indulgent desserts include *tarte tatin* (upside-down apple cake), *tarte aux pommes* (apple tart) and various types of gateaux (cakes) and crêpes (thin pancakes served with a sweet filling of jam, chocolate, Nutella, or simply butter and sugar).

French Wine

Winemaking is an ancient art that has been a part of French culture since before Roman times, and *dégustation* (tasting) is an essential part of the French travel experience.

The quality of French wine is governed by four factors: the grape type, the climate, the soil and the vigneron's skill.

Quality wines are designated Appellation d'Origine Contrôlée (AOC, label of inspected origin), equivalent to the European-wide Appellation d'Origine Protegée (AOP). French AOC can cover a wide region (eg Bordeaux), a sub-region (eg Haut-Médoc), or a commune or village (eg Pomerol). Some regions have a single AOC (eg Alsace), while Burgundy has dozens.

French wines are also divided by a complex grading system; the best are awarded the label of *grand cru* (great growth), and command a premium price.

Seven key areas produce the vast majority of French wine: Alsace, Bordeaux, Burgundy, Champagne, Languedoc, the Loire and the Rhône. Organic and biodynamic wines are increasingly popular.

Burgundy

During the reign of Charlemagne, monks began making the wine that gave Burgundy (Bourgogne in French) its sterling reputation for viticulture. Burgundy vineyards are small (rarely more than 10 hectares), hence produce small quantities of wine – reds with pinot noir grapes and whites with chardonnay. The most famed winegrowing areas are Côte d'Or, Chablis, Châtillon and Mâcon. Lesser-known Irancy is a charming, local wine-tasting favourite.

Bordeaux

Bordeaux has the perfect climate for producing wine; as a result its 1100 sq km of vineyards produce more fine wine than any other region in the world. Bordeaux reds are often described as well balanced, a quality achieved by blending several grape varieties. The grapes predominantly used are merlot, cabernet sauvignon and cabernet franc. The foremost winegrowing areas of Bordeaux are the Médoc, Pomerol, St Émilion and Graves. The nectar-like sweet whites of the Sauternes area are the world's finest dessert wines.

Côtes du Rhône

Dramatically different soil, climate, topography and grapes in the Rhône Valley region means very different wines in this vast appellation – France's second largest – covering 771 sq km. The most renowned is Châteauneuf du Pape, a full-bodied wine bequeathed to Provence by the Avignon popes who planted the distinctive stone-covered vineyards, 10km south of Orange.

Champagne

Champagne has been the centre for bubbly production since the 17th century, when the monk Dom Pierre Pérignon perfected a technique for making sparkling wine. It is made from the red pinot noir, black pinot meunier or white chardonnay grape; and is labelled *brut* (extra dry), *extra-sec* (dry, but not as dry as *brut*), *sec* (dry), *demi-sec* (slightly sweet) or *doux* (sweet). Famous Champagne houses include Dom Pérignon, Moët & Chandon, Veuve Clicquot, Mercier, Mumm, Krug, Laurent-Perrier, Piper-Heidsieck, Taittinger, De Castellane and Pommery.

Swaths of fresh-green vineyards in the Champagne region could be graced with Unesco protection if its 2013 bid to become a World Heritage Site proves successful. Meantime, such is the global demand for the 320 million bottles of fizz it sells each year that the body regulating where Champagne can be made has agreed to enlarge the production area for the first time since 1927. In 2017 the first new vines will be planted in 40 new Champagne-producing villages. *Santé*!

Picnic Perfect

- **Baguettes** from the *boulangerie* (bakery), stuffed with Camembert, pâté and *cornichons* (miniature gherkins), or *rosette de Lyon* (salami). *Voilà*, picnic perfection!
- **Macarons** from Ladurée (p86) in Paris. No sweeter way to end a picnic.
- **Kouign amann**, the world's most buttery, syrupy cake, aka Breton butter cake.
- Big juicy **black Apt cherries**, **peaches**, **apricots** and **tomatoes** from the Rhône Valley, Provence and the Riviera.
- **Provençal olives or peppers**, marinated and stuffed with edible sins from market stands.
- **Champagne** from Reims and *biscuits roses* (sweet, pink biscuit).
- Country **pâté**, **walnuts** and **foie gras** from the Dordogne.

The Best... Wine-Tasting Experiences

1 Champagne houses in Reims (p157) and Épernay (p161)

2 L'Imaginarium (p208)

3 Château de Pommard (p208)

4 Châteaux in and around Bordeaux (p260) and the Médoc (p264)

5 Self-drive Alsatian wine route, Route des Vins d'Alsace (p171)

6 Cognac houses (p270)

The Loire

The Loire's 700 sq km of vineyards rank it as France's third-largest area for the production of quality wines. The most common grapes are the muscadet, cabernet franc and chenin blanc varieties. Wines tend to be light and delicate. Be sure to sample wines from Pouilly-Fumé, Vouvray, Sancerre, Bourgueil, Chinon and Saumur.

Provence

Côtes de Provence is the region's largest appellation and France's sixth largest, producing 75% of Provençal wine. Few other appellations support such a variety of grapes – at least a dozen. Drunk young and served at 8°C to 10°C, its wines are among the world's oldest. Vines were planted by the Greeks in Massilia (Marseille) around 600 BC.

The star of Provence is deep-flavoured red Bandol, with its own AOC since 1941. West along the same coast is Cassis, known for its crisp whites.

Alsace

Alsace produces almost exclusively white wines – mostly varieties not produced elsewhere in France – that are known for their clean, fresh taste and compatibility with the often heavy local cuisine. Unusually, some of the fruity Alsatian whites also go well with red meat. Alsace's four most important varietal wines are riesling (known for its subtlety), gewürztraminer (pungent and highly regarded), pinot gris (robust and high in alcohol) and muscat d'Alsace (not as sweet as muscats from southern France).

Aperitifs & Digestifs

A meal in France is not a meal without an aperitif to kick-start it. *Kir* (white wine sweetened with a fruit syrup such as blackcurrant or chestnut) and *kir royale* (Champagne with blackcurrant syrup) are classics countrywide, while *pineau* (Cognac and grape juice) is popular in and around Bordeaux, and a glass of sweet, white, local Coteaux du Layon is favoured in the Loire Valley. In the hot south, aniseed-flavoured pastis (clear in the bottle, cloudy when mixed with water) is the aperitif to drink alfresco.

After-dinner drinks accompany coffee. France's most famous brandies are Cognac and Armagnac, both made from grapes in the regions of those names. *Eaux de vie*, literally 'waters of life', can be made with grape skins and the pulp left over after being pressed for wine (Marc de Champagne, Marc de Bourgogne), apples (*calvados*) and pears (Poire William). In the Loire Valley a shot of orange (aka a glass of local Cointreau liqueur) ends the meal well.

When in Normandy, do as the festive Normans do: refresh the palate between courses with a *trou normand* (literally 'Norman hole') – traditionally a shot of *calva* (calvados) or a contemporary scoop of apple sorbet doused in the local apple brandy.

The People

A café in Paris

ROBERTO FRANKENBERG/LONELY PLANET ©

Arrogant, bureaucratic, chauvinistic and stylish... France is a country whose people has attracted more myths and stereotypes than any other in Europe, and over the centuries dozens of tags have been pinned on the garlic-eating, beret-wearing, sacre-bleu-swearing French. (The French, by the way, hardly ever wear berets or use old chestnuts such as 'sacre bleu' anymore.)

Being French

Most people are extremely proud to be French and are staunchly nationalistic, a result of the country's republican stance, which places nationality (rather than religion, for example) at the top of the self-identity list. This has created an overwhelmingly self-confident nation, both culturally and intellectually, that often comes across as one with a superiority complex.

Contrary to popular belief, many French speak a foreign language fairly well, travel and are happy to use their language skills if necessary. French men, incidentally, deem an English gal's heavily accented French as sexy as she might find a Frenchman speaking English.

Lifestyle

The French are full of contradictions: they drink and smoke more than anyone else, yet

Faux Pas

- **Forget the school-textbook French** *'S'il vous plaît'* – never *'garçon'* (meaning 'boy') – is the *only* way to summon a waiter.
- **Don't split the restaurant bill** The person who invites pays, although close friends often go Dutch.
- **Don't fondle fruit, veg, flowers or clothing in shops** Ask if you want to touch.
- **Get the name right** 'Monsieur' for men, 'Madame' for 'Mrs' and 'Mademoiselle' for unmarried women.
- **Take Champagne or flowers** Gifts are an important gesture when invited to someone's home. But don't take chrysanthemums, only for cemeteries.

live longer; they eat like kings, but have a lower rate of obesity than most European nations. But if there were such a thing as Monsieur et Madame Tout le Monde (Mr and Mrs Everyone), what might they be like?

They'd most likely work in one of France's big cities, and rent their apartment from a private landlord (home ownership in France is low, with only 57% of households owning their own home). They'd dunk croissants in bowls (yes, bowls) of fresh coffee for breakfast, buy a baguette every day from the bakery and recycle little bar a few glass bottles.

Madame would buy a stack of weekly gossip magazines, while Monsieur would regularly pop out to meet his mates for a game of boules and a glass of *eau de vie* (brandy). They'd put everything on the *carte bleue* (credit or debit card) when shopping, and only ever holiday in August.

They'd go to the flicks once a month, work precisely 35 hours a week, and have two kids who would have both been through university (France's state-run universities are free to anyone who passes the baccalaureat).

French Kissing

Kissing is still the traditional way for French people to greet each other (although the expression 'French kissing', as in with tongues, actually doesn't exist in French).

In Paris it is definitely two kisses: anything more is deemed affected, although trendy 20-somethings and teenagers often swap three or four cheek-skimming kisses just to be different. Travel south and the *bisous* (kisses) multiply, three being the norm in Provence, and four in the Loire Valley.

To avoid any embarrassing moments, do as the French do and always start with the right cheek.

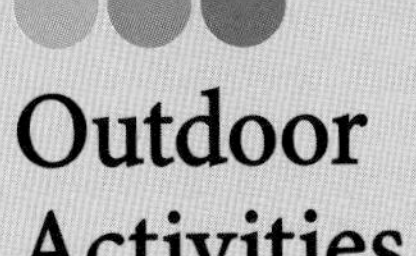

Outdoor Activities

Gorges du Verdon (p313)

From the peaks, rivers and canyons of the French Alps to the sparkling beaches and craggy cliffs of the Riviera, France offers plenty of opportunity for exhilarating outdoor adventure. Match your interests with the best bit of France in which to do it: for surfing it is Biarritz on the Atlantic Coast; the French Alps are No 1 for snow sports; and Mont Ventoux in Provence is the cyclist's ultimate idyll.

Cycling

If there's one sport the French take seriously, it's cycling. Cycling is one of the country's most popular outdoor activities, and every year swaths of the country grind to a halt during the Tour de France. The country is criss-crossed by a network of *voies vertes* (literally, 'green ways') that have been developed specifically for cycling, often along the course of old bridleways or disused railway tracks.

Road-cycling is the most popular form in France, although VTT (*vélo tout-terrain*, or mountain-biking) is rapidly catching up, especially in the Alps, Pyrenees and Massif Central. Bikes are a great (and green) way of exploring flat regions such as the Dordogne, Burgundy, the Loire Valley and much of Provence. Tourist offices can supply route suggestions and information on bike rental.

The Best... Natural Wonders

1 Dune du Pilat (p266)

2 Mont St-Michel (p129)

3 Mont Blanc, Chamonix (p240)

4 Gouffre de Padirac (p217)

5 Gorges du Verdon (p313)

Skiing & Snowboarding

France has about 400 ski resorts, all of which offer a range of groomed runs suitable for both novice and experienced skiers and boarders; some also have snowparks where adventurous types can practise jumps and tricks. The ski season in France lasts from mid-December to late March or April. The slopes get very crowded at Christmas and during the February school holidays.

The biggest (and busiest) resorts are located in the Alps. Smaller resorts in the Pyrenees tend to be quieter, cheaper and substantially less glitzy – forget posing on piste or hobnobbing over an après-ski aperitif. The Jura is the centre for *ski de fond* (cross-country skiing). Usually, the cheapest way to ski is to travel on a package deal that includes flights, lift passes and accommodation.

Hiking

The French countryside is criss-crossed by a staggering 120,000km of *sentiers balisés* (marked walking paths), which pass through every imaginable terrain in every region of the country. No permit is needed to hike. Probably the best-known walking trails are the sentiers de Grande Randonnée (GR), long-distance paths marked by red-and-white-striped track indicators.

Water Sports

France's coastline is fantastic for all types of water sports. The best surfing is on France's west coast, especially around Biarritz. Windsurfing is especially popular in Brittany, Normandy and along the Atlantic Coast.

White-water rafting, canoeing and kayaking are practised on many French rivers, especially in the Alps, but also in the deep canyons of the Gorges de l'Ardèche, Gorges du Tarn and Gorges du Verdon, and along the Dordogne and Lot Rivers.

Web Resources

France Montagnes (www.france-montagnes.com) Comprehensive information on skiing, snowboarding and other mountain pastimes.

Fédération Française de la Randonnée Pédestre (www.ffrandonnee.fr) Hiking tips from the French Ramblers' Association.

Rando Velo (http://randovelo.fr) Multilingual site offering cycling routes across France.

Voies Vertes (www.voiesvertes.com) Map of and guide to France's green trails.

Club Alpin Français (www.ffcam.fr) Mountain-activity advice from France's oldest alpine club.

ESF (www.esf.net) Ski, hike and revel in mountain fun with the largest ski school in the world, aka France's École du Ski Français.

Survival Guide

Champs-Élysées (p60), Paris
PAWEL LIBERA/GETTY IMAGES ©

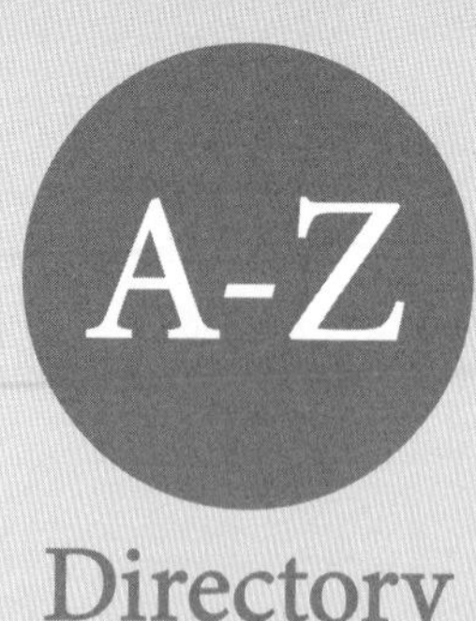

A-Z Directory

Accommodation

Be it a fairy-tale château, a boutique hideaway or floating pod on a lake, France has accommodation to suit every taste, mood and pocket.

Categories

As a rule of thumb, budget covers everything from basic hostels to small family-run places; midrange means a few extra creature comforts such as elevator and free wi-fi; while top-end places stretch from luxury five-star palaces with air conditioning, swimming pools and restaurants to boutique-chic alpine chalets.

Costs

Accommodation costs vary wildly between seasons and regions: what will buy you a night in a romantic *chambre d'hôte* (B&B) in the countryside may get a dorm bed in a major city or high-profile ski resort.

Seasons

- Rates listed are for high season.
- In ski resorts, high season is Christmas, New Year and the February–March school holidays.
- On the coast, high season is summer, particularly August.
- Hotels in inland cities often charge low-season rates in summer.
- Rates often drop outside the high season – in some cases by as much as 50%.
- In business-oriented hotels in cities, rooms are most expensive from Monday to Thursday and cheaper over the weekend.
- In the Alps, hotels usually close between seasons, from around May to mid-June and from mid-September to early December; many addresses in Corsica only open Easter to October.

Hotels

We have tried to feature well-situated, independent hotels that offer good value, a warm welcome, at least a bit of charm and a palpable sense of place.

Hotels in France are rated with one to five stars, although the ratings are based on highly objective criteria (eg the size of the entry hall), not the quality of the service, the decor or cleanliness.

- French hotels almost never include breakfast in their rates. Unless specified otherwise, prices quoted don't include breakfast, which costs around €8/12/25 in a budget/midrange/top-end hotel.
- When you book, hotels usually ask for a credit card number; some require a deposit.
- A double room generally has one double bed (sometimes two singles pushed together!); a room with twin beds *(deux lits)* is usually more expensive, as is a room with a bathtub instead of a shower.
- Feather pillows are practically nonexistent in France, even in top-end hotels.
- All hotel restaurant terraces allow smoking; if you are sensitive to smoke, you may need to sit inside.

Sleeping Price Ranges

The price indicators refer to the cost of a double room, including private bathroom (any combination of toilet, bathtub, shower and washbasin) and excluding breakfast unless otherwise noted. Breakfast is assumed to be included at a B&B. Where half board (breakfast and dinner) and full board (breakfast, lunch and dinner) is included, this is mentioned in the price.

- **€** less than €90 (less than €130 in Paris)
- **€€** from €90 to €190 (from €130 to €200 in Paris)
- **€€€** more than €190 (more than €200 in Paris)

The Fine Art of Sleeping

A château, a country manor, Parisian opulence in the shade of the Eiffel Tower – whether you want to live like a lord, sleep like a log or blow the budget, there's a room with your name on it.

Alistair Sawday's (www.sawdays.co.uk) Boutique retreats and *chambres d'hôte,* placing the accent on originality and authentic hospitality.

Châteaux & Hôtels Collection (www.chateauxhotels.com) Châteaux and other historic properties, now boutique hotels, with a thousand tales to tell.

Grandes Étapes Françaises (www.grandesetapes.fr) Beautiful châteaux-hotels and multistar residences.

iGuide (www.iguide-hotels.com) Abbeys, manors, châteaux – a real mixed bag of charming hotels.

Logis de France (www.logis-de-france.fr) Small, often family-run hotels with charm and a warm welcome.

Relais & Châteaux (www.relaischateaux.com) Seductive selection of top-end villas, châteaux and historic hotels.

Relais du Silence (www.relaisdusilence.com) Fall asleep to complete silence in a gorgeous château, spa-clad *auberge* (country inn), or vineyard hotel...

Small Luxury Hotels of the World (www.slh.com) Super-luxurious boutique hotels, chalets and resorts.

Customs Regulations

Goods brought in and out of countries within the EU incur no additional taxes provided duty has been paid somewhere within the EU and the goods are for personal consumption. Duty-free shopping is available only if you are leaving the EU.

Duty-free allowances (for adults) coming from non-EU countries (including the Channel Islands):

- 200 cigarettes
- 50 cigars
- 1L spirits
- 2L wine
- 50ml perfume
- 250ml eau de toilette
- other goods up to the value of €175 (€90 for under 15 year olds)

Higher limits apply if you are coming from Andorra; anything over these limits must be declared. For further details, see www.douane.gouv.fr (partly in English).

Discount Cards

Discount cards yield fantastic benefits and easily pay for themselves. As well as the card fee, you'll often need a passport-sized photo and some form of ID with proof of age (eg passport or birth certificate).

People over 60 or 65 are entitled to discounts on things like public transport, museum admission fees and theatres.

Discount card options:

European Youth Card (Euro<26 card; www.euro26.org; €14) Wide range of discounts for under 26 year olds. Available online.

International Student Identity Card (ISIC; www.isic.org; €13) Discounts on travel, shopping, attractions and entertainment for full-time students. Available at ISIC points listed online.

International Teacher Identity Card (ITIC; www.isic.org; €13) Travel, shopping, entertainment and sightseeing discounts for full-time teachers.

International Youth Travel Card (IYTC; www.isic.org; €13) Discounts on travel, tickets and so forth for under 26 year olds.

Electricity

230V/50Hz

Embassies & Consulates

All foreign embassies are in Paris. Many countries – including Canada, Japan, the UK, USA and most European countries – also have consulates in other major cities such as Bordeaux, Lyon, Nice, Marseille and Strasbourg.

To find a consulate or an embassy, visit www.embassiesabroad.com or look up '*ambassade*' in the **Pages Jaunes** (Yellow Pages; www.pagesjaunes.fr).

Food

For an overview of French food, see the French Cuisine chapter (p369).

Price Ranges

Price indicators refer to the average cost of a two-course meal, be it an *entrée* (starter) and *plat* (main course) or main and dessert, or a two- or three-course *menu* (pre-set meal at a fixed price). Lunch *menus* almost always yield a far better deal.

- **€** less than €20
- **€€** from €20 to €40
- **€€€** more than €40

Gay & Lesbian Travellers

The rainbow flag flies high in France, a country that left its closet long before many of its European neighbours. *Laissez-faire* perfectly sums up France's liberal attitude towards homosexuality and people's private lives in general.

- Paris has been a thriving gay and lesbian centre since the late 1970s, and most major organisations are based there.
- Bordeaux, Lille, Lyon, Montpellier, Toulouse and many other towns also have an active queer scene.
- Attitudes towards homosexuality tend to be more conservative in the countryside and villages.
- France's lesbian scene is less public than its gay male scene and is centred mainly on women's cafes and bars.
- Same-sex marriage has been legal in France since 2013.
- Gay Pride marches are held in major French cities mid-May to early July.
- **France Queer Resources Directory** (www.france.qrd.org) is a useful gay and lesbian directory.

Health

France is a healthy place, so your main risks are likely to be sunburn, foot blisters, insect bites and mild stomach problems from eating and drinking with too much gusto.

Before You Go

- Bring your medications in their original, clearly labelled, containers.
- A signed and dated letter from your physician describing your medical conditions and medications, including generic names (French medicine names are often completely different to those in other countries), is also a good idea.
- Dental care in France is usually good; however, it is sensible to have a dental check-up before a long trip.

Book Your Stay Online

For more accommodation reviews by Lonely Planet authors, check out http://hotels.lonelyplanet.com. You'll find independent reviews, as well as recommendations on the best places to stay. Best of all, you can book online.

- No vaccinations are required to travel to France but the World Health Organization (WHO) recommends that all travellers be covered for diphtheria, tetanus, measles, mumps, rubella and polio, regardless of their destination.

Availability & Cost of Health Care

- Visitors to France can get excellent health care from *hôpital* (hospital) *salles des urgences* (emergency rooms) and casualty wards and at a *cabinet médical* (doctors' office).
- For minor illnesses, trained staff in pharmacies – in every village and town with a green-cross sign outside that flashes when open – give valuable advice, sell medications, can tell you when more specialised help is needed and will point you in the right direction.
- You will need to pay upfront for any health care you receive, be it at a doctor's surgery, pharmacy or hospital, unless your insurance plan makes payments directly to providers.
- The standard rate for a consultation with a GP/specialist is €30 to €40.
- Emergency contraception is available with a doctor's prescription. *Les préservatifs* (condoms) are readily available.

Climate

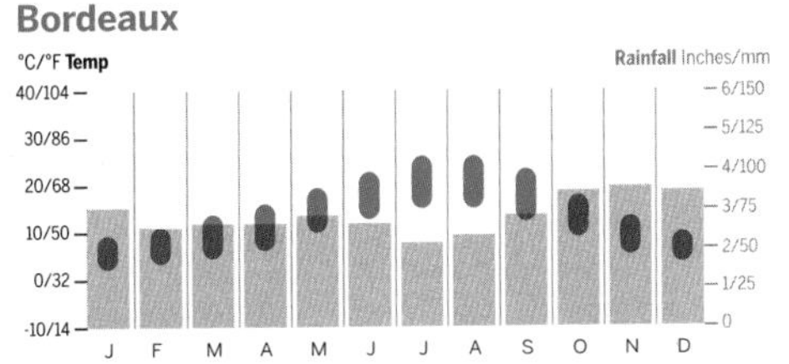

Monaco

°C/°F Temp — Rainfall Inches/mm

40/104 – 30/86 – 20/68 – 10/50 – 0/32 – -10/14

6/150 – 5/125 – 4/100 – 3/75 – 2/50 – 1/25 – 0

J F M A M J J A S O N D

Paris

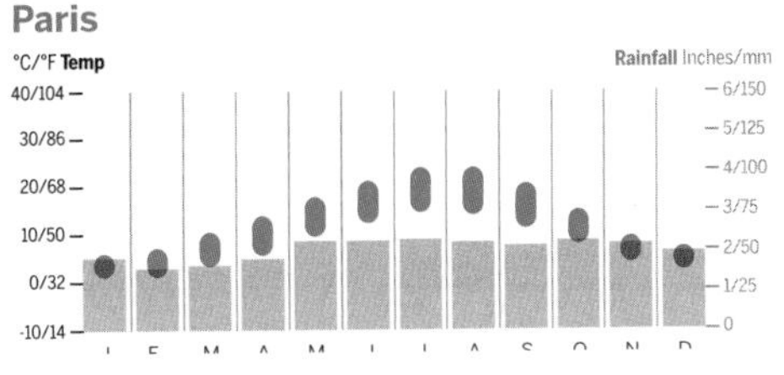

European Health Insurance Card

Citizens of the EU, Switzerland, Iceland, Norway or Liechtenstein receive free or reduced-cost, state-provided health-care cover with the European Health Insurance Card (EHIC) for medical treatment that becomes necessary while in France. Each family member will need a separate card.

UK residents can get application forms from post offices, or download them from the Department of Health website (www.dh.gov.uk), which has comprehensive information about the card's coverage.

The EHIC does not cover private health care, so make sure that you are treated by a state *conventionné* (health-care provider). You will need to pay directly and fill in a *feuille de soins* (treatment form); keep the form to claim any refunds. In general, you can claim back around 70% of the standard treatment cost.

Citizens of other countries need to check if there is a reciprocal arrangement for free medical care between their country and France.

Insurance

- Comprehensive travel insurance to cover theft, loss and medical problems is highly recommended.
- Some policies specifically exclude dangerous activities such as scuba diving, motorcycling, skiing and even trekking: read the fine print.
- Check that the policy covers ambulances or an emergency flight home.

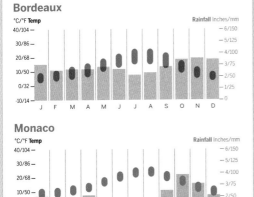

- Find out in advance if your insurance plan will make payments directly to providers or reimburse you later for overseas health expenditures.
- If you have to claim later, make sure you keep all documentation.
- Paying for your airline ticket with a credit card often provides limited travel accident insurance – ask your credit card company what it is prepared to cover.
- Worldwide travel insurance is available at www.lonelyplanet.com/travel-insurance. You can buy, extend and claim online anytime – even if you're already on the road.

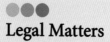

Internet Access

- Wi-fi (pronounced 'wee-fee' in French) is available at major airports, in most hotels, and at some cafes, restaurants, museums and tourist offices.
- Free public wi-fi hotspots are available in cities and many towns: Paris alone has 260 public hotspots (www.paris.fr/wifi), including parks, libraries and municipal buildings (in parks look for a purple 'Zone Wi-Fi' sign near the entrance and select the 'PARIS_WI-FI_' network to connect).
- To search for free wi-fi hot spots in France, visit www.hotspot-gratuit.com or www.hotspot-locations.co.uk.
- Internet cafes are less rife, but at least one can still be found in most large towns and cities. Prices range from €2 to €6 per hour.

> ### What the Icon Means
> In this book, only accommodation providers that have an actual computer that guests can use to access the internet are flagged with a computer icon (@). The wi-fi icon (wi-fi) indicates anywhere with wi-fi access. Where this icon appears, assume the wi-fi is free unless otherwise specified.

Legal Matters

Police

- French police have wide powers of search and seizure and can ask you to prove your identity at any time – whether or not there is 'probable cause'.
- Foreigners must be able to prove their legal status in France (eg passport, visa, residency permit) without delay.
- If the police stop you for any reason, be polite and remain calm. Verbally (and of course physically) abusing a police officer can lead to a hefty fine, and even imprisonment.
- You may refuse to sign a police statement, and have the right to ask for a copy.
- People who are arrested are considered innocent until proven guilty, but can be held in custody until trial.
- Because of the threat of terrorism, French police are very strict about security. Do not leave baggage unattended, especially at airports or train stations: suspicious objects may be summarily blown up.

Drugs & Alcohol

- French law does not distinguish between 'hard' and 'soft' drugs.
- The penalty for any personal use of *stupéfiants* (including cannabis, amphetamines, ecstasy and heroin) can be a one-year jail sentence and a €3750 fine but, depending on the circumstances, it might be anything from a stern word to a compulsory rehab program.
- Importing, possessing, selling or buying drugs can get you up to 10 years in prison and a fine of up to €500,000.
- Police have been known to search chartered coaches, cars and train passengers for drugs just because they're coming from Amsterdam.
- *Ivresse* (drunkenness) in public is punishable by a fine.

Money

ATMs

Automated Teller Machines (ATMs) – known as *distributeurs automatiques de billets* (DAB) or *points d'argent* in French – are the cheapest and most convenient way to get money. ATMs connected to international networks are situated in all cities and towns and usually offer an excellent exchange rate.

Americans, Take Note

Travellers with credit cards issued in the US, be aware that you might well find yourself occasionally stuck when it comes to paying with your card: certain places in France – notably, Vélib' in Paris and bike-share schemes in other cities, self-service toll booths on the *autoroute* (highway), and garages with self-service petrol (gas) pumps – only accept credit cards with chips and PINs. There is no solution to this bar ensuring you always have an emergency stash of cash on you.

Cash

You always get a better exchange rate in-country but it is a good idea to arrive in France with enough euros to take a taxi to a hotel if you have to.

Credit & Debit Cards

- Credit and debit cards, accepted almost everywhere in France, are convenient, relatively secure and usually offer a better exchange rate than travellers cheques or cash exchanges.
- Credit cards issued in France have embedded chips, so you have to type in a PIN to make a purchase.
- Visa, MasterCard and Amex can be used in shops and supermarkets and for train travel, car hire and motorway tolls.
- Don't assume that you can pay for a meal or a budget hotel with a credit card – enquire first.
- Cash advances are a supremely convenient way to stay stocked up with euros but getting cash with a credit card involves both fees (sometimes US$10 or more) and interest; ask your credit card issuer for details. Debit-card fees are usually much less.

Lost Cards

For lost cards, these numbers operate 24 hours:

Amex (☎ 01 47 77 70 00)

Diners Club (☎ 08 10 31 41 59)

MasterCard (☎ 08 00 90 13 87)

Visa (Carte Bleue; ☎ 08 00 90 11 79)

Moneychangers

- Commercial banks charge up to €5 per foreign-currency transaction – if they even bother to offer exchange services any more.
- In Paris and major cities, *bureaux de change* (exchange bureaux) are faster and easier, open longer hours and often give better rates than banks.
- Some post-office branches exchange travellers cheques and banknotes in a variety of currencies but charge a commission for cash; most won't take US$100 bills.

Tipping

By law, restaurant and bar prices are *service compris* (include a 15% service charge), so there is no need to leave a *pourboire* (tip). If you were extremely satisfied with the service, however, you can – as many locals do – show your appreciation by leaving a small 'extra' tip for your waiter or waitress.

WHERE/ WHO	CUSTOMARY TIP
bar	round to nearest euro
hotel cleaning staff	€1-1.50 per day
hotel porter	€1-1.50 per bag
restaurant	5-10%
taxi	10-15%
toilet attendant	€0.20-0.50
tour guide	€1-2 per person

Travellers Cheques

Travellers cheques, a 20th-century relic, cannot be used to pay French merchants directly – change them into euro banknotes at banks, exchange bureaux or post offices.

Opening Hours

French business hours are regulated by a maze of government regulations, including the 35-hour working week.

- The midday break is uncommon in Paris but common elsewhere; in general, the break gets longer the further south you go.

- French law requires that most businesses close on Sunday; exceptions include grocery stores, *boulangeries* (bakeries), florists and businesses catering to the tourist trade.
- In many places shops close on Monday.
- Many service stations open 24 hours a day and stock basic groceries.
- Restaurants generally close one or two days of the week, chosen according to the owner's whim. Opening days/hours are only specified if the restaurant isn't open for both lunch and dinner daily.
- Most (but not all) national museums are closed on Tuesday; most local museums are closed on Monday, though in summer some open daily. Many museums close at lunchtime.
- We give high-season hours for sights and attractions; hours are almost always shorter during the low season.

Standard Opening Hours

BUSINESS	OPENING HOURS
Bank	9am-noon & 2-5pm Mon-Fri or Tue-Sat
Bar	7pm-1am Mon-Sat
Cafe	7am or 8am-10pm or 11pm Mon-Sat
Nightclub	10pm-3am, 4am or 5am Thu-Sat
Post office	8.30am or 9am-5pm or 6pm Mon-Fri, 8am-noon Sat
Restaurant	noon-2.30pm (or 3pm in Paris) & 7-11pm (or 10pm–midnight in Paris)
Shop	9am or 10am-7pm Mon-Sat (often closed noon-1.30pm)
Supermarket	8.30am-7pm Mon-Sat, 8.30am-12.30pm Sun

Public Holidays

The following *jours fériés* (public holidays) are observed in France:

New Year's Day (Jour de l'An) 1 January – parties in larger cities; fireworks are subdued by international standards

Easter Sunday & Monday (Pâques & Lundi de Pâques) Late March/April

May Day (Fête du Travail) 1 May – traditional parades

Victoire 1945 8 May – commemorates the Allied victory in Europe that ended WWII

Ascension Thursday (Ascension) May – celebrated on the 40th day after Easter

Pentecost/Whit Sunday & Whit Monday (Pentecôte & Lundi de Pentecôte) Mid-May to mid-June – celebrated on the seventh Sunday after Easter

Bastille Day/National Day (Fête Nationale) 14 July – *the* national holiday

Assumption Day (Assomption) 15 August

All Saints' Day (Toussaint) 1 November

Remembrance Day (L'onze Novembre) 11 November – marks the WWI armistice

Christmas (Noël) 25 December

The following are *not* public holidays in France: Shrove Tuesday (Mardi Gras; the first day of Lent); Maundy (or Holy) Thursday and Good Friday, just before Easter; and Boxing Day (26 December).

Note: Good Friday and Boxing Day *are* public holidays in Alsace.

Safe Travel

France is generally a safe place in which to live and travel but crime has risen dramatically in the last few years. Although property crime is a major problem, it is extremely unlikely that you will be physically assaulted while walking down the street. Always check your government's travel advisory warnings.

France's hunting season runs from September to February. If you see signs reading *'chasseurs'* or *'chasse gardée'* strung up or tacked to trees, think twice about wandering into the area. As well as millions of wild animals, some 25 French hunters die each year after being shot by other hunters. Hunting is traditional and commonplace in all rural areas in France, especially the Vosges, the Sologne, the southwest and the Baie de Somme.

Natural Dangers

- There are powerful tides and strong undertows at many places along the Atlantic Coast, from the Spanish border north to Brittany and Normandy.
- Only swim in *zones de baignade surveillée* (beaches monitored by life guards).
- Be aware of tide times and the high-tide mark if walking or sleeping on a beach.
- Thunderstorms in the mountains and the hot southern plains can be extremely sudden and violent.
- Check the weather report before setting out on a long walk and be prepared for sudden storms and temperature drops if you are heading into the high country of the Alps or Pyrenees.
- Avalanches pose a significant danger in the French Alps.

Theft

Pickpocketing and bag/phone-snatching (eg in dense crowds and public places) are prevalent in big cities, particularly Paris, Marseille and Nice. There's no need whatsoever to travel in fear. A few simple precautions will minimise your chances of being ripped off.

- On trains, avoid leaving smartphones and tablets lying casually on the table in front of you and keep bags as close to you as possible: luggage racks at the ends of carriages are easy prey for thieves; in sleeping compartments, lock the door carefully at night.
- Be especially vigilant for bag/phone snatchers at train stations, airports, fast-food outlets, outdoor cafes, beaches and on public transport.
- Break-ins to parked cars are a widespread problem. Never, ever leave anything valuable – or not valuable – inside your car, even in the boot (trunk).
- Aggressive theft from cars stopped at red lights is occasionally a problem, especially in Marseille and Nice. As a precaution, lock your car doors and roll up the windows.

Telephone

Important Numbers

France country code	☎ 33
International access code	☎ 00
Europe-wide emergency	☎ 112
Ambulance (SAMU)	☎ 15
Police	☎ 17
Fire	☎ 18

Mobile Phones

- French mobile phone numbers begin with 06 or 07.
- France uses GSM 900/1800, which is compatible with the rest of Europe and Australia but not with the North American GSM 1900 or the totally different system in Japan (though some North Americans have tri-band phones that work here).
- Check with your service provider about roaming charges – dialling a mobile phone from a fixed-line phone or another mobile can be incredibly expensive.
- It is usually cheaper to buy a local SIM card from a French provider such as Orange, SFR, Bouygues and Free Mobile which gives you a local phone number. To do this, ensure your phone is 'unlocked'.
- If you already have a compatible phone, you can slip in a SIM card (€1.90 to €5) and rev it up with prepaid credit, though this is likely to run out fast as domestic prepaid calls cost about €0.50 per minute.
- Recharge cards are sold at most *tabacs* (tobacconist-newsagents) and supermarkets.

Which Floor?

In France, as elsewhere in Europe, 'ground floor' refers to the floor at street level; the 1st floor – what would be called the 2nd floor in the US – is the floor above that.

Phone Codes

Calling France from abroad Dial your country's international access code, then ☎ 33 (France's country

Practicalities

- **Travel Conditions** In many areas, Autoroute Info (107.7MHz; www.autorouteinfo.fr) has round-the-clock traffic information.
- **Classifieds** Surf FUSAC (www.fusac.fr) for classified ads about housing, babysitting, jobs and language exchanges in and around Paris.
- **Laundry** Virtually all French cities and towns have at least one *laverie libre-service* (self-service laundrette). Machines run on coins.
- **Newspapers & Magazines** Locals read their news in centre-left **Le Monde** (www.lemonde.fr), right-leaning **Le Figaro** (www.lefigaro.fr) or left-leaning **Libération** (www.liberation.fr).
- **Radio** For news, tune in to the French-language France Info (105.5MHz; www.franceinfo.fr), multilanguage RFI (738kHz or 89MHz in Paris; www.rfi.fr) or, in northern France, the BBC World Service (648kHz) and BBC Radio 4 (198kHz). Popular national FM music stations include **NRJ** (www.nrj.fr), **Skyrock** (www.skyrock.radio.fr) and **Nostalgie** (www.nostalgie.fr).
- **Smoking** Smoking is illegal in all indoor public spaces, including restaurants and pubs (though, of course, smokers still light up on the terraces outside).
- **TV & Video** TV is Secam; videos work on the PAL system.
- **Weights & Measures** France uses the metric system.

code), then the 10-digit local number *without* the initial zero.

Calling internationally from France Dial ☎00 (the international access code), the *indicatif* (country code), the area code (without the initial zero if there is one) and the local number. Some country codes are posted in public telephones.

Directory inquiries For national *service des renseignements* (directory inquiries) dial ☎11 87 12 or use the service for free online at www.118712.fr.

Emergency numbers Can be dialled from public phones without a phonecard.

Hotel calls Hotels, *gîtes*, hostels and *chambres d'hôte* are free to meter their calls as they like. The surcharge is usually around €0.30 per minute but can be higher.

International directory inquiries For numbers outside France, dial ☎11 87 00.

Phonecards

- Although mobile phones and Skype may have killed off the need for public phones, they do still exist. In France they are all *télécarte*-(phonecard) operated, but in an emergency you can use your credit card to call.
- All public phones can receive domestic and international calls. If you want someone to call you back, give them France's country code (☎33) and the 10-digit number, usually written after the words 'Ici le...' or 'No d'appel' on the tariff sheet or on a sign inside the phone box. Remind them to drop the initial '0' of the number. When there's an incoming call, the words '*décrochez – appel arrive*' (pick up receiver – incoming call) will appear in the LCD window.
- Public phones require a credit card or *télécarte* (€7.50/15 for 50/120 calling units), sold at post offices, *tabacs*, supermarkets, SNCF ticket windows, Paris metro stations and anywhere you see a blue sticker reading '*télécarte en vente ici*' (phonecard for sale here).
- Prepaid *télécartes* with codes such as Allomundo (www.allomundo.com) can be up to 60% cheaper for calling abroad than a standard *télécarte*.
- The shop you buy a *télécarte* from should be able to tell you which type is best for the country you want to call. Using *télécartes* from a home phone is much cheaper than using them from public phones or mobile phones.

Time

France uses the 24-hour clock and is on Central European Time, which is one hour ahead of GMT/UTC. During daylight saving time, which runs from the last Sunday in March to the last Sunday in October, France is two hours ahead of GMT/UTC.

The following times do not take daylight saving into account:

CITY	NOON IN PARIS
Auckland	11pm
Berlin	noon
Cape Town	noon
London	11am
New York	6am
San Francisco	3am
Sydney	9pm
Tokyo	8pm

Toilets

Public toilets, signposted WC or *toilettes*, are not always plentiful in France, especially outside the big cities.

Love them (as a sci-fi geek) or loathe them (as a claustrophobe), France's 24-hour self-cleaning toilets are here to stay. Outside Paris these mechanical WCs are free, but in Paris they cost around €0.50 a go. Don't even think about nipping in after someone else to avoid paying unless you fancy a *douche* (shower) with disinfectant. There is no time for dawdling either: you have precisely 15 minutes before being exposed to passers-by. Green means *libre* (vacant) and red means *occupé* (occupied).

Some older establishments and motorway stops still have the hole-in-the-floor *toilettes à la turque* (squat toilets). Provided you hover, these are very hygienic, but take care not to get soaked by the flush.

Keep some loose change handy for tipping toilet attendants, who keep a hawk-like eye on many of France's public toilets.

The French are more blasé about unisex toilets than elsewhere, so don't blush when tiptoeing past the urinals to reach the ladies' loo.

Tourist Information

Almost every city, town and village has an *office de tourisme* (a tourist office run by some unit of local government) or *syndicat d'initiative* (a tourist office run by an organisation of local merchants). Both are excellent resources and can supply you with local maps as well as details on accommodation, restaurants and activities. If you have a special interest such as walking, cycling, architecture or wine sampling, ask about it.

Tourist office details appear under Information at the end of each city, town or area listing.

- Many tourist offices make local hotel and B&B reservations, sometimes for a nominal fee.
- *Comités régionaux de tourisme* (CRTs; regional tourist boards), their *départemental* analogues (CDTs) and their websites are a superb source of information and hyperlinks.
- French government tourist offices (usually called Maisons de la France) provide every imaginable sort of tourist information on France.

Useful websites include:

French Government Tourist Office (http://int.rendezvousenfrance.com) The low-down on sights, activities, transport and special-interest holidays in all of France's regions.

Réseau National des Destinations Départementales (www.rn2d.net) Listing of CRT (regional tourist board) websites.

Travellers with Disabilities

While France presents evident challenges for *visiteurs handicapés* (disabled visitors) – cobblestone, cafe-lined streets that are a nightmare to navigate in a *fauteuil roulant* (wheelchair), a lack of kerb ramps, older public facilities and many budget hotels without lifts – don't let that stop you from visiting. Efforts are being made to improve the situation and with a little careful planning, a hassle-free accessible stay is possible.

- Paris tourist office runs the excellent 'Tourisme et Handicap' initiative whereby museums, cultural attractions, hotels and restaurants that provide access or special assistance or facilities for those with physical, mental, visual and/or hearing disabilities display a special logo at their entrances. For a list of qualifying places, go to www.parisinfo.com and click on 'Practical Paris'.

- Paris metro, most of it built decades ago, is hopeless. Line 14 of the metro was built to be wheelchair-accessible, although in reality it remains extremely challenging to navigate in a wheechair – unlike Paris buses which are 100% accessible.
- Parisian taxi company Horizon, part of Taxis G7, has cars especially adapted to carry wheelchairs and drivers trained in helping passengers with disabilities.
- Countrywide, many SNCF train carriages are accessible to people with disabilities. A traveller in a wheelchair can travel in both the TGV and in the 1st-class carriage with a 2nd-class ticket on mainline trains provided they make a reservation by phone or at a train station at least a few hours before departure. Details are available in the SNCF booklet Le Mémento du Voyageur Handicapé (Handicapped Traveller Summary) available at all train stations.

Accès Plus (☎ 08 90 64 06 50; www.accessibilite.sncf.com) The SNCF assistance service for rail travellers with disabilities. Can advise on station accessibility and arrange a *fauteuil roulant* (wheelchair) or help getting on or off a train.

Infomobi.com (☎ 08 10 64 64 64; www.infomobi.com) Has comprehensive information on accessible travel in Paris and surrounding Île de France area.

Access Travel (☎ in UK 01942-888 844; www.access-travel.co.uk) Specialised UK-based agency for accessible travel.

Mobile en Ville (☎ 09 52 29 60 51; www.mobile-en-ville.asso.fr; 8 rue des Mariniers, 14e, Paris) Association that works hard to make independent travel within the city easier for people in wheelchairs. Among other things it organises some great family *randonnées* (walks) in and around Paris.

Tourisme et Handicaps (☎ 01 44 11 10 41; www.tourisme-handicaps.org; 43 rue Marx Dormoy, 18e, Paris) Issues the 'Tourisme et Handicap' label to tourist sites, restaurants and hotels that comply with strict accessibility and usability standards. Different symbols indicate the sort of access afforded to people with physical, mental, hearing and/or visual disabilities.

Visas

For up-to-date details on visa requirements, see the website of the **Ministère des Affaires Étrangères** (Ministry of Foreign Affairs; www.diplomatie.gouv.fr; 37 quai d'Orsay, 7e) and click 'Coming to France'. Tourist visas *cannot* be extended except in emergencies (such as medical problems). When your visa expires you'll need to leave and reapply from outside France.

Visa Requirements

- EU nationals and citizens of Iceland, Norway and Switzerland need only a passport or a national identity card in order to enter France and stay in the country, even for stays of over 90 days. However, citizens of new EU member states may be subject to various limitations on living and working in France.
- Citizens of Australia, the USA, Canada, Hong Kong, Israel, Japan, Malaysia, New Zealand, Singapore, South Korea and many Latin American countries do not need visas to visit France as tourists for up to 90 days. For long stays of over 90 days, contact your nearest French embassy or consulate and begin your application well in advance, as it can take months.
- Other people wishing to come to France as tourists have to apply for a Schengen Visa, named after the agreements that have abolished passport controls between 26 European countries. It allows unlimited travel throughout the entire zone for a 90-day period. Apply to the consulate of the country you are entering first, or your main destination. Among other things, you need travel and repatriation insurance and to be able to show that you have sufficient funds to support yourself.
- Tourist visas cannot be changed into student visas after arrival. However, short-term visas are available for students sitting university-entrance exams in France.

Transport

Getting There & Away

Flights, cars and tours can be booked online at www.lonelyplanet.com/bookings.

 Air

Smaller provincial airports with international flights, mainly to/from the UK, continental Europe and North Africa, include Paris-Beauvais, Bergerac, Biarritz, Brest, Brive (Vallée de la Dordogne), Caen, Carcassonne, Clermont-Ferrand, Deauville, Dinard, Grenoble, La Rochelle, Le Touquet (Côte d'Opale), Limoges, Montpellier, Nîmes, Pau, Perpignan, Poitiers, Rennes, Rodez, St-Étienne, Toulon and Tours.

International Airports

Aéroport de Charles de Gaulle (CDG; www.aeroportsdeparis.fr)

Paris Orly (www.aeroportsdeparis.fr)

Aéroport de Bordeaux (www.bordeaux.aeroport.fr)

Aéroport de Lille (www.lille.aeroport.fr)

Aéroport International Strasbourg (www.strasbourg.aeroport.fr)

Aéroport Lyon-Saint Exupéry (www.lyonaeroports.com)

Aéroport Marseille-Provence (www.marseille.aeroport.fr)

Aéroport Nantes Atlantique (www.nantes.aeroport.fr)

Aéroport Nice Côte d'Azur (http://societe.nice.aeroport.fr)

Aéroport Toulouse-Blagnac (www.toulouse.aeroport.fr)

EuroAirport (Basel-Mulhouse-Freiburg; www.euroairport.com)

> ### Strikes
>
> France is the only European country in which public workers enjoy an unlimited right to strike. Aggrieved truck drivers block motorways from time to time, farmers agitating for more government support have been known to dump tonnes of produce on major arteries, and train strikes sometimes disrupt travel.
>
> Getting caught in one of the 'social dialogues' that characterise labour relations in France can put a serious crimp in your travel plans. It is best to leave some wriggle room in your schedule, particularly around departure times.

Land

Car & Motorcycle

A right-hand-drive vehicle brought to France from the UK or Ireland must have deflectors affixed to the headlights to avoid dazzling oncoming traffic. In the UK, information on driving in France is available from the **RAC** (www.rac.co.uk/driving-abroad/france) and the **AA** (www.theaa.com).

A foreign motor vehicle entering France must display a sticker or licence plate identifying its country of registration.

Eurotunnel

The Channel Tunnel (Chunnel), inaugurated in 1994, is the first dry-land link between England and France since the last ice age.

High-speed **Eurotunnel Le Shuttle** (☎ in France 08 10 63 03 04, in UK 08443-35 35 35; www.eurotunnel.com) trains whisk bicycles, motorcycles, cars and coaches in 35 minutes from Folkestone through the Channel Tunnel to Coquelles, 5km southwest of Calais. Shuttles run 24 hours a day, with up to three departures an hour during peak periods. LPG and CNG tanks are not permitted, meaning gas-powered cars and many campers and caravans have to travel by ferry.

Eurotunnel sets its fares the way budget airlines

Climate Change & Travel

Every form of transport that relies on carbon-based fuel generates CO_2, the main cause of human-induced climate change. Modern travel is dependent on aeroplanes, which might use less fuel per kilometre per person than most cars but travel much greater distances. The altitude at which aircraft emit gases (including CO_2) and particles also contributes to their climate change impact. Many websites offer 'carbon calculators' that allow people to estimate the carbon emissions generated by their journey and, for those who wish to do so, to offset the impact of the greenhouse gases emitted with contributions to portfolios of climate-friendly initiatives throughout the world. Lonely Planet offsets the carbon footprint of all staff and author travel.

do: the further in advance you book and the lower the demand for a particular crossing, the less you pay; same-day fares can cost a small fortune. Fares for a car, including up to nine passengers, start at UK£23/€30.

Train

Rail services link France with virtually every country in Europe. For details on train travel within France, see **Getting Around**.

- Book tickets and get train information from **Rail Europe** (www.raileurope.com). In the UK contact **Railteam** (www.railteam.co.uk). In France ticketing is handled by **SNCF** (**from abroad +33 8 92 35 35 35, in France 36 35; http://en.voyages-sncf.com**); internet bookings are possible but they won't post tickets outside France.
- For details on Europe's 200,000km rail network, surf **RailPassenger Info** (www.railpassenger.info).
- A very useful train-travel resource is the information-packed website **The Man in Seat 61** (www.seat61.com).

Certain rail services between France and its continental neighbours are marketed under a number of unique brand names:

Eurostar

The **Eurostar** (**in France 08 92 35 35 39, in UK 08432 186 186; www.eurostar.com**) whisks you from London to Paris in 2¼ hours.

Except late at night, trains link London (St Pancras International) with Paris (Gare du Nord; hourly), Calais (Calais-Fréthun; one hour, three daily), Lille (Gare Lille-Europe; 1½ hours, eight daily) and Disneyland Resort Paris (2½ hours, one direct daily), with less frequent services departing from Ebbsfleet and Ashford, both in Kent. Weekend ski trains connect England with the French Alps late December to mid-April.

Eurostar offers a bewildering array of fares. A semi-flexible, 2nd-class, one-way ticket from Paris to London costs €172; super-discount fares start at €44.

For the best deals buy a return ticket, stay over a Saturday night, book up to 120 days in advance and don't mind non-exchangeability and non-refundability. Discount fares are available for those aged under 26 or over 60.

Sea

Some ferry companies have started setting fares the way budget airlines do: the longer in advance you book and the lower the demand for a particular sailing, the less you pay. Seasonal demand is a crucial factor (Christmas, Easter, UK and French school holidays, July and August are especially busy), as is the time of day (an early evening ferry can cost much more than one at 4am). People under 25 and over 60 may qualify for discounts.

To get the best fares, check **Ferry Savers** (**in UK 0844-371 8021; www.ferrysavers.com**).

Foot passengers are not allowed on Dover–Boulogne, Dover–Dunkirk or Dover–Calais car ferries except for daytime (and, from Calais to Dover, evening) crossings run by P&O Ferries. On ferries that do allow foot passengers, taking a bicycle is usually free.

Several ferry companies ply the waters between Corsica and Italy.

Getting Around

Driving is the simplest way to get around France but a car is a liability in traffic-plagued, parking-starved city centres, and petrol bills and *autoroute* (dual carriageway/divided highway) tolls add up.

France is famous for its excellent public-transport network, which serves everywhere bar some very rural areas. The state-owned Société Nationale des Chemins de Fer Français (SNCF) takes care of almost all land transport between *départements*. Transport within *départements* is handled by a combination of short-haul trains, SNCF buses and local bus companies.

Air

France's high-speed train network renders rail travel between some cities (eg from Paris to Lyon and Marseille) faster and easier than flying.

Airlines in France

Air France (www.airfrance.com) and its subsidiaries **Hop!** (www.hop.com) and **Transavia** (www.transavia.com) control the lion's share of France's domestic airline industry.

Budget carriers offering flights within France include **EasyJet** (www.easyjet.com), **Twin Jet** (www.twinjet.net) and **Air Corsica** (www.aircorsica.com).

Bicycle

France is great for cycling. Much of the countryside is drop-dead gorgeous and the country has a growing number of urban and rural *pistes cyclables* (bike paths and lanes, see **Voies Vertes** (www.voievertes.com) for details) and an extensive network of secondary and tertiary roads with relatively light traffic.

French law requires that bicycles must have two functioning brakes, a bell, a red reflector on the back and yellow reflectors on the pedals. After sunset and when visibility is poor, cyclists must turn on a white headlamp and a red tail lamp. When being overtaken by a vehicle, cyclists must ride in single file. Towing children in a bike trailer is permitted.

Never leave your bicycle locked up outside overnight if you want to see it – or at least most of its parts – again. Some hotels offer enclosed bicycle parking.

The SNCF does its best to make travelling with a bicycle easy; see www.velo.sncf.com for full details.

Bike Rental

Most French cities and towns have at least one bike shop that rents out *vélos tout terrains* (mountain bikes; around €15 a day), known as VTTs, as well as more road-oriented *vélos tout chemin* (VTCs), or cheaper city bikes. You usually have to leave ID and/or a deposit (often a credit-card slip) that you forfeit if the bike is damaged or stolen.

A growing number of cities – most famously Paris and Lyon, but also Aix-en-Provence, Amiens, Bordeaux, Caen, Clermont-Ferrand, Dijon, La Rochelle, Lille, Marseille, Montpellier, Mulhouse, Nancy, Nantes, Nice, Orléans, Rennes, Rouen, Toulouse, Strasbourg and Vannes – have automatic bike-rental systems, intended to encourage cycling as a form of urban transport, with computerised pick-up and drop-off sites all over town. In general, you have to sign up either short term or long term, providing credit-card details, and can then use the bikes for no charge for the first half-hour; after that, hourly charges rise quickly.

Bus

Buses are widely used for short-distance travel within *départements*, especially in rural areas with relatively few train lines (eg Brittany and Normandy). Unfortunately, services in some regions are infrequent and slow, in part because they were designed to get children to their schools in the towns rather than transport visitors around the countryside.

Over the years, certain uneconomical train lines have been replaced by SNCF buses, which, unlike regional buses, are free if you've got a rail pass.

Car & Motorcycle

Having your own wheels gives you exceptional freedom and makes it easy to visit more remote parts of France. Depending on the number of passengers, it can also work out cheaper than train. For example, by autoroute, the 925km drive from Paris to Nice (nine hours of driving) in a small car costs about €100 for petrol and €75 in tolls – by comparison, a one-way, 2nd-class TGV ticket for the 5½-hour Paris to Nice run costs €95 to €140 per person.

In the cities, traffic and finding a place to park can be a major headache. During holiday periods and bank-holiday weekends, roads throughout France also get backed up with *bouchons* (traffic jams).

Motorcyclists will find France great for touring, with good-quality winding roads and stunning scenery. Just make sure your wet-weather

Trains & Ferries

gear is up to scratch.

France (along with Belgium) has the densest highway network in Europe. There are four types of intercity roads:

Autoroutes (highway names beginning with A) Multilane divided highways, usually (except near Calais and Lille) with *péages* (tolls). Generously outfitted with rest stops.

Routes Nationales (N, RN) National highways. Some sections have divider strips.

Routes Départementales (D) Local highways and roads.

Routes Communales (C, V) Minor rural roads.

For information on autoroute tolls, rest areas, traffic and weather, go to the **Sociétés d'Autoroutes** (www.autoroutes.fr) website.

Bison Futé (www.bison-fute.equipement.gouv.fr) is also a good source of information about traffic conditions. Plot itineraries between your departure and arrival points, and calculate toll costs with an on-line mapper such as **Via Michelin** (www.viamichelin.com) or **Mappy** (www.mappy.fr).

Theft from cars is a major problem in France, especially in the south.

Car Hire

To hire a car in France, you'll generally need to be over 21 years old, have had a driving licence for at least a year, and have an international credit card. Drivers under 25 usually have to pay a *frais jeune conducteur* (surcharge) of €25 to €35 per day.

Car-hire companies provide mandatory third-party liability insurance but things such as collision-damage waivers (CDW, or *assurance tous risques*) vary greatly from company to company. When comparing rates and conditions (ie the fine print), the most important thing to check is the *franchise* (deductible/excess), which for a small car is usually around €600 for damage and €800 for theft. With many companies, you can reduce the excess by half, or perhaps to zero, by paying a daily insurance supplement of up to €20. Your credit card may cover CDW if you use it to pay for the rental but the car-hire company won't know anything about this – verify conditions and details with your credit-card issuer to be sure.

Arranging your car hire or fly/drive package before you leave home is usually cheaper than a walk-in rental, but beware of website offers that don't include a CDW or you may be liable for up to 100% of the car's value.

International car-hire companies:

Avis (☎ from abroad +33 1 70 99 47 35 08 21 23 07 60; www.avis.com)

Budget (☎ 08 25 00 35 64; www.budget.fr)

International Ferry Companies

COMPANY	CONNECTION	WEBSITE
Brittany Ferries	England–Normandy, England–Brittany, Ireland–Brittany	www.brittany-ferries.co.uk; www.brittanyferries.ie
Condor Ferries	England–Normandy, England–Brittany, Channel Islands–Brittany	www.condorferries.co.uk
CTN	Tunisia–France	www.ctn.com.tn
DFDS Seaways	England–Normandy	www.dfdsseaways.co.uk
Irish Ferries	Ireland–Normandy, Ireland–Brittany	www.irishferries.com
LD Lines	England–Channel Ports, England–Normandy	www.ldlines.co.uk
Manche Îles Express	Channel Islands–Normandy	www.manche-iles-express.com
My Ferry Link	Dover–Calais	www.myferrylink.fr
Norfolk Line (DFDS Seaways)	England–Channel Ports	www.norfolkline.com
P&O Ferries	England–Channel Ports	www.poferries.com
Stena Line Ferries	Ireland–Normandy	www.stenaline.ie
SNCM	Algeria–France, Sardinia–France, Tunisia–France	www.sncm.fr
Transmanche Ferries	England-Normandy	www.transmancheferries.co.uk

Easycar (☎ in France 08 26 10 73 23, in the UK 08710 500 444; www.easycar.com)

Europcar (☎ 08 25 35 83 58; www.europcar.com)

Hertz (☎ 08 25 86 18 61; www.hertz.com)

Sixt (☎ 0 820 007 498; www.sixt.fr)

French car-hire companies:

ADA (www.ada.fr)

DLM (☎ 03 20 06 18 80; www.dlm.fr)

France Cars (www.francecars.fr)

Locauto (☎ 04 93 07 72 62; www.locauto.fr)

Renault Rent (☎ 08 25 10 11 12; www.renault-rent.com)

Rent a Car Système (☎ 08 91 70 02 00; www.rentacar.fr)

Deals can be found online and through companies such as the following:

Auto Europe (☎ in USA 1-888-223-5555; www.autoeurope.com)

DriveAway Holidays (☎ in Australia 1300 723 972; www.driveaway.com.au)

Holiday Autos (☎ 0871 472 5229; www.holidayautos.co.uk)

Rental cars with automatic transmission are very much the exception in France; they usually need to be ordered well in advance and are more expensive than manual cars.

For insurance reasons, it is usually forbidden to take rental cars on ferries, eg to Corsica.

All rental cars registered in France have a distinctive number on the licence plate, making them easily identifiable – including to thieves. *Never* leave anything of value in a parked car, even in the boot (trunk).

Driving Licence & Documents

An International Driving Permit (IDP), valid only if accompanied by your original licence, is good for a year and can be issued by your local automobile association before you leave home.

Drivers must carry the following at all times:

- passport or an EU national ID card
- valid driving licence (*permis de conduire*; most foreign licences can be used in France for up to a year)
- car-ownership papers, known as a *carte grise* (grey card)
- proof of third-party liability *assurance* (insurance)

Fuel

Essence (petrol), also known as *carburant* (fuel), costs between €1.40 and €1.70 per litre for 95 unleaded (Sans Plomb 95 or SP95, usually available from a green pump) and €1.30 to €1.50 for diesel (*diesel*, *gazole* or *gasoil*, usually available from a yellow pump). Check and compare current prices countrywide with www.prix-carburants.gouv.fr.

Faire le plein (filling up) is most expensive at autoroute rest stops, and usually cheapest at hypermarkets.

Many small petrol stations close on Sunday afternoons and, even in cities, it can be hard to find a staffed station open late at night. In general, after-hours purchases (eg at hypermarkets' fully automatic, 24-hour stations) can only be made with a credit card that has an embedded PIN chip, so if all you've got is cash or a magnetic-strip credit card, you could be stuck.

Insurance

Assurance au tiers (third-party liability insurance) is compulsory for all vehicles in France, including cars brought in from abroad. Normally, cars registered and insured in other European countries can circulate freely in France, but it's a good idea to contact your insurance company before you leave home to make sure you have coverage – and to check whom to contact in case of a breakdown or accident.

If you get into a minor accident with no injuries, the easiest way for drivers to sort things out with their insurance companies is to fill out a Constat Aimable d'Accident Automobile (European Accident Statement), a standardised way of recording important details about what happened. In rental cars it's usually in the packet of documents in the glove compartment. Make sure the report includes any information that will help you prove that the accident was not your fault. Remember, if it *was* your fault you may be liable for a hefty insurance deductible/excess. Don't sign anything you don't fully understand. If problems crop up, call the police (☎17).

Road Distances (Km)

	Bayonne	Bordeaux	Brest	Caen	Cahors	Calais	Chambéry	Cherbourg	Clermont-Ferrand	Dijon	Grenoble	Lille	Lyon	Marseille	Nantes	Nice	Paris	Perpignan	Strasbourg	Toulouse
Bordeaux	184																			
Brest	811	623																		
Caen	764	568	376																	
Cahors	307	218	788	661																
Calais	164	876	710	339	875															
Chambéry	860	651	120	800	523	834														
Cherbourg	835	647	399	124	743	461	923													
Clermont-Ferrand	564	358	805	566	269	717	295	689												
Dijon	807	619	867	548	378	572	273	671	279											
Grenoble	827	657	1126	806	501	863	56	929	300	302										
Lille	997	809	725	353	808	112	767	476	650	505	798									
Lyon	831	528	1018	698	439	755	103	820	171	194	110	687								
Marseille	700	651	1271	1010	521	1067	344	1132	477	506	273	999	314							
Nantes	513	326	298	292	491	593	780	317	462	656	787	609	618	975						
Nice	858	810	1429	1168	679	1225	410	1291	636	664	337	1157	473	190	1131					
Paris	771	583	596	232	582	289	565	355	424	313	571	222	462	775	384	932				
Perpignan	499	451	1070	998	320	1149	478	1094	441	640	445	1081	448	319	773	476	857			
Strasbourg	1254	1066	1079	730	847	621	496	853	584	335	551	522	488	803	867	804	490	935		
Toulouse	300	247	866	865	116	991	565	890	890	727	533	923	536	407	568	564	699	205	1022	
Tours	536	348	490	246	413	531	611	369	369	418	618	463	449	795	197	952	238	795	721	593

French-registered cars have details of their insurance company printed on a little green square affixed to the windscreen.

Parking

In city centres, most on-the-street parking places are *payant* (metered) from about 9am to 7pm (sometimes with a break from noon to 2pm) Monday to Saturday, except bank holidays.

Road Rules

Enforcement of French traffic laws (see www.securiteroutiere.gouv.fr, in French) has been stepped up considerably in recent years. Speed cameras are common, as are radar traps and unmarked police vehicles. Fines for many infractions are given on the spot, and serious violations can lead to the confiscation of your driving licence and car.

Speed limits outside built-up areas (except where signposted otherwise):

Undivided N & D highways 90km/h (80km/h when raining)

Non-autoroute divided highways 110km/h (100km/h when raining)

Autoroutes 130km/h (110km/h when raining, 60km/h in icy conditions)

To reduce carbon emissions, autoroute speed limits have recently been reduced to 110km/h in some areas.

Unless otherwise signposted, a limit of 50km/h applies in *all* areas designated as built up, no matter how rural they may appear. You must slow to 50km/h the moment you come to a white sign with a red border and a place name written on it; the speed limit applies until you pass an identical sign with a horizontal bar through it.

Other important driving rules:

- Blood-alcohol limit is 0.05% (0.5g per litre of blood) – the equivalent of two glasses of wine for a 75kg adult. Police often conduct random breathalyser tests

Priority to the Right

Under the *priorité à droite* (priority to the right) rule, any car entering an intersection (including a T-junction) from a road (including a tiny village backstreet) on your right has the right of way. Locals assume every driver knows this, so don't be surprised if they courteously cede the right of way when you're about to turn from an alley onto a highway – and boldly assert their rights when you're the one zipping down a main road.

Priorité à droite is suspended (eg on arterial roads) when you pass a sign showing an upended yellow square with a black square in the middle. The same sign with a horizontal bar through the square lozenge reinstates the *priorité à droite* rule.

When you arrive at a roundabout at which you do not have the right of way (ie the cars already in the roundabout do), you'll often see signs reading *vous n'avez pas la priorité* (you do not have right of way) or *cédez le passage* (give way).

and penalties can be severe, including imprisonment.

- All passengers, including those in the back seat, must wear seat belts.
- Mobile phones may be used only if they are equipped with a hands-free kit or speakerphone.
- Turning right on a red light is illegal.
- Cars from the UK and Ireland must have deflectors affixed to their headlights to avoid dazzling oncoming motorists.
- Radar detectors, even if they're switched off, are illegal; fines are hefty.
- Children under 10 are not permitted to ride in the front seat (unless the back is already occupied by other children under 10).
- A child under 13kg must travel in a backward-facing child seat (permitted in the front seat only for babies under 9kg and if the airbag is deactivated).
- Up to age 10 and/or a minimum height of 140cm, children must use a size-appropriate type of front-facing child seat or booster.
- All vehicles driven in France must carry a high-visibility reflective safety vest (stored inside the vehicle, not in the trunk/boot), a reflective triangle, and a portable, single-use breathalyser kit. The fine for not carrying any of these items is €90.
- If you'll be driving on snowy roads, make sure you have *chaînes neige* (snow chains), required by law whenever and wherever the police post signs.
- Riders of any type of two-wheeled vehicle with a motor (except motor-assisted bicycles) must wear a helmet. No special licence is required to ride a motorbike whose engine is smaller than 50cc, which is why rental scooters are often rated at 49.9cc.

Local Transport

France's cities and larger towns have world-class public-transport systems. There are *métros* (underground subway systems) in Paris, Lyon, Marseille, Lille and Toulouse and ultramodern *tramways* (light-rail lines) in cities such as Bordeaux, Lille, Lyon, Nancy, Nantes, Nice, Reims, Rouen and Strasbourg, as well as parts of greater Paris.

In addition to a *billet à l'unité* (single ticket), you can purchase a *carnet* (booklet or bunch) of 10 tickets or a *pass journée* (all-day pass).

Taxi

All medium and large train stations – and many small ones – have a taxi stand out front. In small cities and towns, where taxi drivers are unlikely to find another fare anywhere near where they let you off, one-way and return trips often cost the same. Tariffs are about 30% higher at night and on Sundays and holidays. A surcharge is usually charged to get picked up at a train station or airport, and there's a small additional fee for a fourth passenger and/or for suitcases.

Train

Travelling by train in France is a comfortable and environmentally sustainable way to see the country. Since many train stations have car-hire agencies, it's easy to combine rail travel with rural exploration by car.

The jewel in the crown of France's public-transport system – alongside the Paris *métro* – is its extensive rail network, almost all of it run by SNCF. Although it employs the most advanced rail technology, the network's layout reflects the country's centuries-old Paris-centric nature: most of the principal rail lines radiate out from Paris like the spokes of a wheel, the result being that services between provincial towns situated on different spokes can be infrequent and slow.

Up-to-the-minute information on *perturbations* (service disruptions) can be found on www.infolignes.com (in French).

Since its inauguration in the 1980s, the pride and joy of SNCF is the **TGV** (Train à Grande Vitesse; www.tgv.com), pronounced 'teh zheh veh', which zips passengers along at speeds of up to 320km/h (198mph).

The main TGV lines (or LGVs, short for *lignes à grande vitesse*, ie high-speed rail lines) head north, east, southeast and southwest from Paris (trains use slower local tracks to get to destinations off the main line):

TGV Nord, Thalys & Eurostar Link Paris Gare du Nord with Arras, Lille, Calais, Brussels (Bruxelles-Midi), Amsterdam, Cologne and, via the Channel Tunnel, Ashford, Ebbsfleet and London St Pancras.

TGV Est Européen Connects Paris Gare de l'Est with Reims, Nancy, Metz, Strasbourg, Zurich and Germany, including Frankfurt and Stuttgart. At present, the super-high-speed track stretches only as far east as Lorraine but it's supposed to reach Strasbourg in 2016.

TGV Sud-Est & TGV Midi-Méditerranée Link Paris Gare de Lyon with the southeast, including Dijon, Lyon, Geneva, the Alps, Avignon, Marseille, Nice and Montpellier.

TGV Atlantique Sud-Ouest & TGV Atlantique Ouest Link Paris Gare Montparnasse with western and southwestern France, including Brittany (Rennes, Brest, Quimper), Tours, Nantes, Poitiers, La Rochelle, Bordeaux, Biarritz and Toulouse.

LGV Rhin-Rhône France's newest high-speed rail route bypasses Paris altogether in its bid to better link the provinces. Six services a day speed between Strasbourg and Lyon, with most continuing south to Marseille or Montpellier on the Mediterranean.

TGV tracks are interconnected, making it possible to go directly from, say, Lyon to Nantes or Bordeaux to Lille without having to switch trains in Paris or transfer from one of Paris' six main train stations to another. Stops on the link-up, which runs east and south of Paris, include Charles de Gaulle airport and Disneyland Resort Paris.

Long-distance trains sometimes split up at a station – that is, each half of the train heads off for a different destination. Check the destination panel on your car as you board or you could wind up very far from where you intended to go.

Other types of train include:

Téoz (www.corailteoz.com) Especially comfortable trains that run southward from Paris Gare d'Austerlitz to Clermont-Ferrand, Limoges, Cahors, Toulouse, Montpellier, Perpignan, Marseille and Nice.

TER (Train Express Régional; www.ter-sncf.com) A train that is not a TGV is often referred to as a *corail*, a *classique*or, for intraregional services, a TER.

Transilien (www.transilien.com) SNCF services in the Île de France area in and around Paris.

SNCF Fares & Discounts

Full-fare tickets can be quite expensive. Fortunately, a dizzying array of discounts are available and station staff are very good about helping travellers find the very best fare. But first, the basics:

- 1st-class travel, where available, costs 20% to 30% extra.
- Ticket prices for some trains, including most TGVs, are pricier during peak periods.
- The further in advance you reserve, the lower the fares.
- Children under four travel for free (€9 with a 'forfait bambin' to any destination if they need a seat).
- Children aged four to 11 travel for half price.

Discount Tickets

The SNCF's most heavily discounted tickets are called Prem's, available online, at

Left-Luggage Facilities

Because of security concerns, few French train stations have *consignes automatiques* (left-luggage lockers). In larger stations you can leave your bags in a *consigne manuelle* (staffed left-luggage facility) where items are handed over in person and X-rayed before being stowed. Charges are €5 for up to 10 hours and €8 for 24 hours; payment must be made in cash. To find out which stations let you leave your bags and when their *consignes* are open, go to www.gares-en-mouvement.com, select a station, click 'Practical Information' (Services en gare) and then the 'Services' tab.

ticket windows and from ticket machines a maximum of 90 days and a minimum of 14 days before departure. Prem's are nonrefundable and nonchangeable.

Bons Plans fares, a grab bag of really cheap options, are advertised on the SNCF website under 'Dernière Minute' (last minute).

On regional trains, discount fares requiring neither a discount card nor advance purchase include:

Loisir Week-End rates Good for return travel that includes a Saturday night at your destination or involves travel on a Saturday or Sunday.

Découverte fares Available for low-demand 'blue-period' trains to people aged 12 to 25, seniors and the adult travel companions of children under 12.

Mini-Groupe tickets In some regions, these bring big savings for three to six people travelling together, provided you spend a Saturday night at your destination.

Discount Cards

Reductions of at least 25% (for last-minute bookings), and of 40%, 50% or even 60% (if you reserve well ahead or travel during low-volume 'blue' periods), are available with several discount cards (valid for one year):

Carte Jeune (€50) Available to travellers aged 12 to 27.

Carte Enfant+ (€75) For one to four adults travelling with a child aged four to 11.

Carte Weekend (€75) For people aged 26 to 59. Discounts on return journeys of at least 200km that either include a Saturday night away or only involve travel on a Saturday or Sunday.

Carte Sénior+ (€50) For travellers over 60.

Rail Passes

Residents of Europe (who do not live in France) can purchase an **InterRail One Country Pass** (www.interrailnet.com; 3/4/6/8 days €216/237/302/344, 12–25yr €147/157/199/222), which entitles its bearer to unlimited travel on SNCF trains for three to eight days over the course of a month.

For non-European residents, Rail Europe (p392) offers the **France Rail Pass** (www.francerailpass.com; 3/6/9 days over 1 month €211/301/388).

You need to really rack up the kilometres to make these passes worthwhile.

Tickets & Reservations

Large stations often have separate ticket windows for *international*, *grandes lignes* (long-haul) and *banlieue* (suburban) lines, and for people whose train is about to leave (*départ immédiat*or *départ dans l'heure*). Nearly every SNCF station has at least one *borne libre-service* (self-service terminal) or *billeterie automatique* (automatic ticket machine) that accepts both cash and PIN-chip credit cards. Select the Union Jack for instructions in English.

Using a credit card, you can buy a ticket by phone or via the SNCF internet booking website, **Voyages SNCF** (www.voyages-sncf.com), and either have it sent to you by post (if you have an address in France) or collect it from any SNCF ticket office or from train-station ticket machines.

Before boarding the train, *composter* (validate) your ticket by time-stamping it in a *composteur*, a yellow post located on the way to the platform. If you forget (or don't have a ticket), find a conductor on the train before they find you – otherwise you can be fined.

Language

The sounds used in spoken French can almost all be found in English. There are a couple of exceptions: nasal vowels (represented in our pronunciation guides by 'o' or 'u' followed by an almost inaudible nasal consonant sound 'm', 'n' or 'ng'), the 'funny' *u* sound ('ew' in our guides) and the deep-in-the-throat *r*. Bearing these few points in mind and reading our pronunciation guides below as if they were English, you'll be understood just fine.

To enhance your trip with a phrasebook, visit **lonelyplanet.com**. Lonely Planet iPhone phrasebooks are available through the Apple App store.

BASICS

Hello./Goodbye.

Bonjour./Au revoir.	bon·zhoor/o·rer·vwa

How are you?

Comment allez-vous?	ko·mon ta·lay·voo

I'm fine, thanks.

Bien, merci.	byun mair·see

Excuse me./Sorry.

Excusez-moi./Pardon.	ek·skew·zay·mwa/par·don

Yes./No.

Oui./Non.	wee/non

Please.

S'il vous plaît.	seel voo play

Thank you.

Merci.	mair·see

That's fine./You're welcome.

De rien.	der ree·en

Do you speak English?

Parlez-vous anglais?	par·lay·voo ong·glay

I don't understand.

Je ne comprends pas.	zher ner kom·pron pa

How much is this?

C'est combien?	say kom·byun

ACCOMMODATION

I'd like to book a room.

Je voudrais réserver une chambre.	zher voo·dray ray·zair·vay ewn shom·brer

How much is it per night?

Quel est le prix par nuit?	kel ay ler pree par nwee

EATING & DRINKING

I'd like ..., please.

Je voudrais ..., s'il vous plaît.	zher voo·dray ... seel voo play

That was delicious!

C'était délicieux!	say·tay day·lee·syer

Bring the bill/check, please.

Apportez-moi l'addition, s'il vous plaît.	a·por·tay·mwa la·dee·syon seel voo play

I'm allergic (to peanuts).

Je suis allergique (aux cacahuètes).	zher swee a·lair·zheek (o ka·ka·wet)

I don't eat ...

Je ne mange pas de ...		zher ner monzh pa de ...
fish	*poisson*	pwa·son
(red) meat	*viande (rouge)*	vyond (roozh)
poultry	*volaille*	vo·lai

EMERGENCIES

I'm ill.

Je suis malade.	zher swee ma·lad

Help!

Au secours!	o skoor

Call a doctor!

Appelez un médecin!	a·play un mayd·sun

Call the police!

Appelez la police!	a·play la po·lees

DIRECTIONS

I'm looking for (a/the) ...

Je cherche ...	zher shairsh ...
bank	
une banque	ewn bongk
... embassy	
l'ambassade de ...	lam·ba·sahd der ...
market	
le marché	ler mar·shay
museum	
le musée	ler mew·zay
restaurant	
un restaurant	un res·to·ron
toilet	
les toilettes	lay twa·let
tourist office	
l'office de tourisme	lo·fees der too·rees·mer

Behind the Scenes

Author Thanks

OLIVER BERRY

Special thanks to all the authors on the France guides, to Susie & Gracie Berry, to Nicola Williams for steering the ship, to Kate Morgan for answering all my questions, and all the folks at LP for guidance and sage advice.

Acknowledgments

Climate map data adapted from Peel MC, Finlayson BL & McMahon TA (2007) 'Updated World Map of the Köppen-Geiger Climate Classification', *Hydrology and Earth System Sciences*, 11, 163344.

Illustrations p70-1, p78-9, p104-5, p130-1, p298-99, p344-5 by Javier Zarracina

Cover photographs: Front: Château de Chenonceau, Hiroshi Higuchi/Getty Images; Back: Lavender fields in Provence, Brian Jannsen/Alamy

This Book

This 4th edition of Lonely Planet's *Discover France* guidebook was coordinated by Oliver Berry, and researched and written by Alexis Averbuck, Stuart Butler, Jean-Bernard Carillet, Kerry Christiani, Gregor Clark, Emilie Filou, Catherine Le Nevez, Daniel Robinson and Nicola Williams. This guidebook was commissioned in Lonely Planet's London office and produced by the following:

Destination Editor Kate Morgan
Product Editor Luna Soo
Senior Cartographers Jennifer Johnston, Valentina Kremenchutskaya
Book Designer Mazzy Prinsep
Assisting Editors Melanie Dankel, Kate Mathews
Assisting Cartographers Hunor Csutoros, James Leversha
Cover Researcher Naomi Parker
Thanks to Sasha Baskett, Kate Chapman, Penny Cordner, Ryan Evans, Larissa Frost, Jouve India, Katherine Marsh, Anne Mason, Wayne Murphy, Jessica Rose, Wibowo Rusli, Nancy Sturgeon, Samantha Tyson, Amanda Williamson, Juan Winata

SEND US YOUR FEEDBACK

We love to hear from travellers – your comments keep us on our toes and help make our books better. Our well-travelled team reads every word on what you loved or loathed about this book. Although we cannot reply individually to postal submissions, we always guarantee that your feedback goes straight to the appropriate authors, in time for the next edition. Each person who sends us information is thanked in the next edition, and the most useful submissions are rewarded with a free book.

Visit **lonelyplanet.com/contact** to submit your updates and suggestions or to ask for help. Our award-winning website also features inspirational travel stories, news and discussions.

Note: We may edit, reproduce and incorporate your comments in Lonely Planet products such as guidebooks, websites and digital products, so let us know if you don't want your comments reproduced or your name acknowledged. For a copy of our privacy policy visit lonelyplanet.com/privacy.

Index

000 Map pages

C

000 Map pages

D

E

000 Map pages

I

J

K

L

M

N

O

P

000 Map pages

Q

R

S

T

U

V

W

How to Use This Book

These symbols will help you find the listings you want:

- Sights
- Beaches
- Activities
- Courses
- Tours
- Festivals & Events
- Sleeping
- Eating
- Drinking
- Entertainment
- Shopping
- Information/ Transport

These symbols give you the vital information for each listing:

- Telephone Numbers
- Opening Hours
- Parking
- Nonsmoking
- Air-Conditioning
- Internet Access
- Wi-Fi Access
- Swimming Pool
- Vegetarian Selection
- English-Language Menu
- Family-Friendly
- Pet-Friendly
- Bus
- Ferry
- Metro
- Tram
- Train

Reviews are organised by author preference.

Look out for these icons:

FREE No payment required

A green or sustainable option

Our authors have nominated these places as demonstrating a strong commitment to sustainability – for example by supporting local communities and producers, operating in an environmentally friendly way, or supporting conservation projects.

Map Legend

Sights
- Beach
- Buddhist
- Castle
- Christian
- Hindu
- Islamic
- Jewish
- Monument
- Museum/Gallery
- Ruin
- Winery/Vineyard
- Zoo
- Other Sight

Activities, Courses & Tours
- Diving/Snorkelling
- Canoeing/Kayaking
- Skiing
- Surfing
- Swimming/Pool
- Walking
- Windsurfing
- Other Activity/ Course/Tour

Sleeping
- Sleeping
- Camping

Eating
- Eating

Drinking
- Drinking
- Cafe

Entertainment
- Entertainment

Shopping
- Shopping

Information
- Post Office
- Tourist Information

Transport
- Airport
- Border Crossing
- Bus
- Cable Car/ Funicular
- Cycling
- Ferry
- Metro
- Monorail
- Parking
- S-Bahn
- Taxi
- Train/Railway
- Tram
- Tube Station
- U-Bahn
- Other Transport

Routes
- Tollway
- Freeway
- Primary
- Secondary
- Tertiary
- Lane
- Unsealed Road
- Plaza/Mall
- Steps
- Tunnel
- Pedestrian Overpass
- Walking Tour
- Walking Tour Detour
- Path

Boundaries
- International
- State/Province
- Disputed
- Regional/Suburb
- Marine Park
- Cliff
- Wall

Population
- Capital (National)
- Capital (State/Province)
- City/Large Town
- Town/Village

Geographic
- Hut/Shelter
- Lighthouse
- Lookout
- Mountain/Volcano
- Oasis
- Park
- Pass
- Picnic Area
- Waterfall

Hydrography
- River/Creek
- Intermittent River
- Swamp/Mangrove
- Reef
- Canal
- Water
- Dry/Salt/ Intermittent Lake
- Glacier

Areas
- Beach/Desert
- Cemetery (Christian)
- Cemetery (Other)
- Park/Forest
- Sportsground
- Sight (Building)
- Top Sight (Building)

JEAN-BERNARD CARILLET

Normandy & Brittany, Champagne & Northern France Paris-based (and Metz-born) journalist and photographer, Jean-Bernard has clocked up innumerable trips to all French regions and is a passionate ambassador of his own country. Just before researching this edition, he presented a five-episode series on French TV, named 'France's Most Beautiful Region', for which he criss-crossed France for five months with a TV crew, searching for the best travel experiences in the country.

KERRY CHRISTIANI

Champagne & Northern France Kerry has been travelling to France since her school days to brush up her Français, which she studied to MA level. Seeing Alsace's picture-book Route des Vins in spring bloom, tasting Champagne's finest in caves in Reims and Épernay, and hiking to the quietest corners of the hilly Vosges were memorable moments while researching this edition. An award-winning travel writer, Kerry has authored and co-authored some 20 guidebooks. She lists her latest work at www.kerrychristiani.com.

GREGOR CLARK

Loire Valley & Central France, Lyon & the French Alps Gregor's love affair with France started on the midnight streets of Paris at age 14, when, jetlagged and culture-shocked, he successfully ordered a crêpe using his never-before-tested high school French. He's been feeding his France obsession ever since and writing for Lonely Planet since 2000. Highlights of this research trip include bouchon-crawling in Lyon, returning to Vézelay, Salers and Gorges de l'Ardèche (three of his all-time favourites) and seeing a dog exit a boulangerie in Auxerre, baguette firmly held in mouth.

EMILIE FILOU

Provence & the French Riviera Emilie was born in Paris but spent most of her childhood holidays roaming the south of France. She now lives in London, where she works as a freelance journalist specialising in development issues in Africa. She still goes to the Côte d'Azur every summer. For this book, she loved rekindling with her Corsican heritage and finding more about her late grandmother's homeland. See more of Emilie's work on www.emiliefilou.com; she tweets at @emiliefilou.

Read more about Emilie at:
lonelyplanet.com/members/emiliefilou

CATHERINE LE NEVEZ

Paris & Around Catherine first lived in Paris aged four and she's been returning here at every opportunity since, completing her Doctorate of Creative Arts in Writing, Masters in Professional Writing, and post-grad qualifications in Editing and Publishing along the way. Catherine's writing includes scores of Lonely Planet guides to Paris, France and far beyond. Revisiting her favourite Parisian haunts and uncovering new ones remains a highlight of this and every assignment here and, wanderlust aside, Paris remains her favourite city on earth.

DANIEL ROBINSON

Normandy & Brittany, Lyon & the French Alps Daniel has been writing guidebooks and articles about France since shortly after the end of the Jurassic period. His favourite leisure activities range from walking the Grand Balcon Sud trail above Chamonix to trying to interpret the Bayeux Tapestry's naughty margin vignettes. Brought up in the United States and Israel, he holds degrees from Princeton and Tel Aviv University. His travel writing has appeared in various newspapers and magazines, including the *New York Times*, and has been translated into 10 languages.

Read more about Daniel at:
lonelyplanet.com/members/daniel_robinson

NICOLA WILLIAMS

Provence & the French Riviera British writer Nicola Williams has lived in France and written about it for more than a decade. From her hillside house on the southern shore of Lake Geneva, it's an easy hop to Provence and the south of France where she has spent endless years revelling in its extraordinary art, architecture and cuisine. Nicola has worked on numerous titles for Lonely Planet, including *France* and *Discover Paris*. Find her on Twitter at @Tripalong.

Read more about Nicola at:
lonelyplanet.com/members/nicolawilliams

Our Story

A beat-up old car, a few dollars in the pocket and a sense of adventure. In 1972 that's all Tony and Maureen Wheeler needed for the trip of a lifetime – across Europe and Asia overland to Australia. It took several months, and at the end – broke but inspired – they sat at their kitchen table writing and stapling together their first travel guide, *Across Asia on the Cheap*. Within a week they'd sold 1500 copies. Lonely Planet was born.

Today, Lonely Planet has offices in Melbourne, London and Oakland, with more than 600 staff and writers. We share Tony's belief that 'a great guidebook should do three things: inform, educate and amuse'.

Our Writers

OLIVER BERRY

Coordinating Author, Provence & the French Riviera A professional writer and photographer based in Cornwall and Bristol, Oliver has been travelling to France since the tender age of two. He has worked on several editions of Lonely Planet's *France* guides, and spends several months a year travelling around the Pyrenees and Provence. You can see his latest work at www.oliverberry.com.

ALEXIS AVERBUCK

Loire Valley & Central France Alexis first came to France when she was four and now visits every chance she gets. Whether browsing markets in the Dordogne, château-hopping in the Loire or careening through hill-top villages in Provence (she also contributes to the *Provence & Côte d'Azur* book), she immerses herself in all things French. A travel writer for two decades, Alexis has lived in Antarctica for a year, crossed the Pacific by sailboat, and is also a painter – see her work at www.alexisaverbuck.com.

Read more about Alexis at:
lonelyplanet.com/members/alexisaverbuck

STUART BUTLER

Bordeaux & French Basque Country Stuart's first encounters with southwest France came on family holidays. When he was older he spent every summer surfing off the beaches of the southwest, until one day he found himself so hooked on the region he was unable to leave – he has been there ever since. His travels for Lonely Planet, and a wide variety of magazines, have taken him beyond France to the shores of the Arctic, the deserts of Asia and the forests of Africa. His website is www.stuartbutlerjournalist.com.

Read more about Stuart at:
lonelyplanet.com/members/stuartbutler

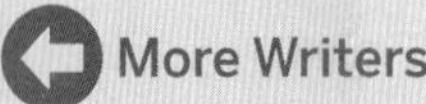

Published by Lonely Planet Publications Pty Ltd
ABN 36 005 607 983
4th edition – Mar 2015
ISBN 978 1 74321 406 0

10 9 8 7 6 5 4 3 2 1
Printed in China